Criminal Law and Practice of Papua New Guinea

Criminal Law and Practice of Papua New Guinea

by

DONALD R C CHALMERS LLB (Hons), LLM

Dean of the Faculty of Law, University of Tasmania
Barrister and Solicitor of the National Court of Papua New Guinea
Formerly, Lecturer in Law and Sub-Dean of the Faculty of Law, University of Papua New Guinea

DAVID WEISBROT BA (Hons), JD

President of the Australian Law Reform Commission
Formerly Dean of the Faculty of Law, University of Papua New Guinea
Barrister of the Supreme Court of New South Wales
Attorney and Counselor at Law, State Bar of California

SALAMO INJIA LLB, LLM

Judge of the Supreme Court and National Court of Papua New Guinea

WARWICK JOHN ANDREW CBE, LLM

Formerly Judge of the Supreme Court and National Court of Papua New Guinea
Formerly Public Solicitor of Papua New Guinea

Chapter 6 by

DIANNE NICOL BSc (Hons), LLB (Hons), LLM, PhD

Barrister and Solicitor of the Supreme Court of Tasmania
Lecturer, University of Tasmania

with a Foreword by

THE HONOURABLE SIR ARNOLD AMET KB, CBE, LLD

Chief Justice of Papua New Guinea

UPNG PRESS AND BOOKSHOP, 2009

Criminal Law and Practice of Papua New Guinea

Originally published in Sydney by Lawbook Co.
100 Harris St, Pyrmont NSW 2009

2009 - This reprint by the University of Papua New Guinea Press and Bookshop is by kind permission of the original publisher and of the Copyright Holder (**Copyright Advice Request Number—13201**)

It is produced from final proofs provided by Professor Kwa and these have been checked against a copy of the Lawbook text.

ISBN 9980-939-54-0

Copies available from:

UPNG Press and Bookshop
Box 413
University Post Office
NCD 134
Papua New Guinea

Foreword to the Third Edition

This is one of a series prepared under the auspices of the Access to Laws in Papua New Guinea Project funded by the Australian Government through the Australian Agency for International Development (AusAID). The Access to Laws Project comprised three components aimed at improving access to the laws of Papua New Guinea. The project involved updating and authenticating all the current legislation of this country and the extensive case law developed by the courts. The legislation and judicial decisions have been produced in the modern electronic CD-ROM format. Equally importantly, the project included the production of a number of legal textbooks to record the distinctive developments in the laws of Papua New Guinea.

The book publishing component of the Access to Laws Project was under the direction of the Publications Committee, which I had the pleasure of chairing. The other members of the Publications Committee were: the Commissioning Editor, Professor Don Chalmers; the Chief Magistrate, Mr George Manuhu; the Deputy Chief Magistrate, Mr John Numapo; the Hon the Attorney-General, Mr Francis Damen (previously Mr Sao Gabi and Mr Michael Gene); the Access to Laws Project Manager, Mr Bruce Fulton; the Project Team Leader, Mr Eric Kwa (previously Dr Val Haynes); representatives of AusAID (Mr Stuart Schaefer, Ms Pauline Doonar, Ms Debbie Bowman, Mr John Prescott and Ms Katherine Ruiz-Avila); a representative of the PNG Law Society, Ms Catherine Davani; and the Dean of the Law School, Mr Eric Kwa (previously Mr Gerry Linge). The Publications Committee was responsible for choosing authors, settling the contents, assessing the quality and appointing referees for each of the texts. At an early meeting of the Publications Committee it was decided that it was appropriate that Papua New Guinean authors or authors with considerable experience in Papua New Guinea should be chosen.

I am delighted that Donald Chalmers, David Weisbrot, Warwick Andrew, Salamo Injia and Dianne Nicol agreed to accept the invitation of the Commissioning Editor to agree to write this text. On behalf of the Publications Committee I commend the learned authors for their work and scholarship. I am confident that this text, together with the others in this series, will be of great value to judges, magistrates, legal practitioners, academics, students and the citizens of Papua New Guinea. If the underlying law is to be developed according to the precepts and principles embodied in our Constitution and the *Underlying Law Act* 2000, it is essential that the community of Papua New Guinea has access to texts which can state the Papua New Guinea law concisely, authoritatively and accurately. On behalf of the Publications Committee I commend the authors for their contribution to this important endeavour.

The Hon Sir Arnold Amet, Kt, CBE, LLD
Chief Justice of Papua New Guinea,
Chair of the Publications Committee,
Access to Law in Papua New Guinea
Port Moresby 2001

Foreword to the Second Edition

The first edition of this book was of great value to legal practitioners, law teachers, law students, magistrates and judges. There is absolutely no doubt at all that this timely second edition will be of the same value and will be received with much enthusiasm.

I should point out here that the Criminal Code is at present under review by a Criminal Code Review Committee chaired by Mr Justice William Kaputin. It is hoped that this Committee will make recommendations to effect some changes in the Criminal Code, which are long overdue. For instance, there is need to consider whether customary law should be given a greater role in the substantive criminal law and in criminal procedures. At present, the only part the customary law plays in the criminal justice system is in the sentencing process, that is, in mitigation of sentences.

I congratulate Messrs Chalmers, Weisbrot and Andrew for their hard work in updating their book, which once again reveals their learning and their knowledge of the criminal law. The Papua New Guinea legal world, particularly those who are involved in the criminal justice system, will always be indebted to them.

B W KIDU
Chief Justice
Papua New Guinea
August 1985

Foreword to the First Edition

The *Criminal Code Act* (No 78 1974) passed by the House of Assembly of then self-governing Papua New Guinea came into effect in 1975 – replacing the previously adopted Queensland Criminal Code. At Independence in 1975, it was adopted as an Act of the Parliament by virtue of Schedule 2.6 of the Constitution. It has been amended since in some particulars. In its present form it is quite significantly different in a number of respects from its parent Code. It has to be read in close association with many provisions of the Constitution. Its interpretation and application is worked in trials on circuit in all the provinces, far and near, of the country; and in appeals in the Supreme Court. In the past, both Bench and Bar carried with them Judge Carter's annotation of the Queensland Code as an essential tool of trade. The PNG Law Reports in their annual volumes starting from 1963 were available in most of the Court centres. And Counsel augmented their references by arming themselves with photostat copies of the "unreported" judgments (those circulated in roneoed form and numbered "N" and "S.C.") of the National and Supreme Courts.

Prior to Self-Government, an appellate court within Papua New Guinea itself had been instituted in 1969, and many decisions upon the Queensland Code as it was being applied to Papua New Guinean conditions, had been given by it. For some years advocates wishing to be sure they were in touch with all relevant cases in a given field, faced a formidable task when aided only by such indices as had been built.

In short, the time had long since come when practising lawyers and law teachers in Papua New Guinea, sorely needed their own annotated Code for the efficient practice of their professions. Such is now available to them in the shape of this work. I welcome it warmly. I commend the learned authors for their industry and scholarship. I predict a great utility in their book. I hope it will prove possible to keep it up to date by supplements until such time as the present Code may be replaced by something perhaps thought more suitable to the people's needs.

W T PRENTICE
Chief Justice
Papua New Guinea
February 1979

Preface to the Third Edition

It has been over 15 years since the second edition of this book was published. Judged by the number of times the text has been cited in National and Supreme Court decisions since 1985, it seems that the text has fulfilled its aim of assisting the courts, petitioners and students of criminal law.

The criminal law of Papua New Guinea dominates the work of the court system. Indeed, criminal cases account for some 50-70 per cent of the case workload of the courts. The courts, in particular, the Supreme Court and the National Court, have consistently guarded against infringement of the basic rights enshrined in s 37 of the *Constitution*. Due regard has been accorded to the right of an accused person to be lawfully arrested, properly charged and fairly tried for an offence that is strictly defined by written law and the right of an accused person to be presumed innocent until proven guilty according to law by the State (*Constitution* s 37(2) and (4)(b)). These and other basic rights found in s 37 have shaped the development of criminal law in the courts, particularly since the last edition of this book in 1985.

However, there are some criticisms levelled at the current system of criminal justice. The increasing criminal activity since Independence in relation to serious crimes of violence has prompted debate over the appropriateness of these basic rights. There are those who argue that the criminal law is too protective of criminals. They attribute the chronic law and order problems in PNG to the state of the criminal law. They argue that the criminal law is essentially adopted law and that the courts are not doing enough to develop a truly national criminal law based on PNG customary laws and practices. They also argue that the Parliament is not doing enough to develop the country's laws to deal with offenders. The mainstream view is that the criminal law should be maintained with minimal change because radical change would offend long-established and internationally accepted principles on the rule of law in democratic societies.

The need to make the criminal law more appropriate and more responsive to the circumstances of this country is a major challenge for the legal system. The question is how PNG should go about developing its own criminal jurisprudence. The Parliament's approach so far has been reactive to public criticism and piecemeal. The court's ability has been limited by the statutory framework in which it operates. There has, however, been some action by the Parliament and the courts in selected areas of the criminal law towards developing a more appropriate criminal law, in the following examples:

Rape in marriage

It is an element of the offence of rape that the victim must not be the accused's wife (s 347 of the *Criminal Code*). This element has been the subject of criticism over the years. In 1990, in *Jaina v The State* [1990] PNGLR 202, the Supreme Court recommended that Parliament abolish the requirement consistent with changes in Australia and other Commonwealth jurisdictions. The Supreme Court said that the "amendment to s 347 to afford married women in the circumstances of this case, greater protection under the law is long overdue". To date, Parliament has not enacted any such law. In recent years there has been much public debate over the subject. There were moves in Parliament to sponsor a Private Member's Bill to amend s 347 in line with the Supreme Court's suggestion. The amendments have not yet been enacted.

Customary compensation

In *Acting Public Prosecutor v Uname Aumane* [1980] PNGLR 510, the Supreme Court decided that the law did not authorise the courts to order customary compensation as a form of punishment for a criminal offence; customary compensation was only taken into account as a mitigating factor on sentence: *Acting Public v Nitak Mangilonde Taganis* [1982] PNGLR 299. In *Uname Aumane*, Kapi J said (at 543):

> "… the view I have taken in the present state of the law. However, I do appreciate the weight of the learned trial judge's view on the place of customary punishment to be imposed as a punishment. This is dealing with what the law should be. These are matters, not for this Court, but for legislative amendment. Such proposals for amendment of the Code have been put forward by the Law Reform Commission but so far the Parliament has not enacted them."

Twelve years later, the Parliament responded by enacting the *Criminal Law (Compensation) Act* 1992 which provided a scheme for incorporating "customary" compensation as a form of punishment. The maximum amount of compensation which the court can order is K5,000 or, in default, a term of imprisonment not exceeding six (6) months (ss 5(3)(b), 6(b) and the Schedule). In some parts of the country, such as in the Highlands region, customary compensation for all types of wrong is widely practised. However, it is evident that some demands for compensation far exceed the statutory limit. The Act has proved to be of limited use: See *The State v Lucy Moro* (1985) N1328; *The State v Angun Kakas* [1994] PNGLR 20; *The State v Billy Kawa* [1994] PNGLR 511.

Minimum penalties and Parliament

Prior to the enactment of the *Criminal Code (Minimum Penalties) Amendment Act* 1983 (No 10 of 1983), various crimes, such as break, enter and stealing as well as robbery, included prescribed maximum penalties under the Code. Due to an upsurge in crimes of violence committed by young persons, and in response to a public outcry for tougher penalties, these amendments were enacted in 1983. The amendments repealed the maximum penalty provisions for some offences and replaced them with prescribed minimum penalties. In *The State v Danny Sunu, Namarai Walter, Iku Garogo and Philip Haro* [1983] PNGLR 396, the Supreme Court decided that, though the court had no power to impose a sentence less than the minimum penalty prescribed under s 398, the court retained its discretionary powers under s 19 of the Code. The Supreme Court held that if Parliament intended to deal exhaustively with punishment, then it had to enact further amendments to remove the court's general sentencing discretion under s 19. The Parliament responded by enacting s 12 in relation to offences for which there was prescribed minimum penalty. Since then there have been ongoing discussions about minimum penalties. These discussions culminated in the challenge on the constitutionality of three minimum penalty Acts in the Supreme Court in the case of *SCR No 1 of 1984* [1984] PNGLR 314. The Supreme Court ruled that the amendments were constitutional. Criticisms of the minimum penalties continued. In 1986, the

Parliament enacted the *Criminal Code (Amendment) No 2 Act* 1986 (No 17 of 1986) which repealed all the minimum penalty provisions in the Code, including s 19(8). This Act restored maximum penalty provisions.

In 1993, Parliament reintroduced a minimum penalty of five years imprisonment for one offence, that of escape under s 139 of the *Code Criminal Code (Amendment) Act* 1983 (No 12 of 1993). Subsequently, in *The State v Aruve Waiba; SCR No 1 of 1994 (unreported, Supt Ct,* 4 April 1996), the Supreme Court confirmed the validity of this amendment and that the National Court still retained the discretion conferred by s 19 of the *Criminal Code*. Section 139 of the *Criminal Code* exists side by side with s 22 of the *Summary Offences Act*, which creates essentially the same offence but prescribes a maximum punishment of a fine of up to K200 or up to six months imprisonment. Arguments as to disparity of sentence of co-accused charged under the two statutes are common in appeals to the Supreme Court.

The adopted common law

The common law and equity of England, as at Independence Day, unaffected by statutory modification, is adopted as part of the underlying law (see ss 20-21 *Constitution*, Sch 2.2-2.3 and *The Ship "Fedeal Huron" v Ok Tedi Mining Ltd* [1986] PNGLR 5). Both the National Court and the Supreme Court have recourse to common law principles. There are three problems faced when examining those principles to ensure their applicability and appropriateness to the circumstances of the country. First, there is the problem of the courts in keeping in tune with the development of the principles of common law and equity over time as modified by statute (see *David Kofewei v PNG* [1983] PNGLR 449).

Secondly, there is a problem of lawyers and, to some extent, the courts slavishly citing or following not only English cases but also cases from other Commonwealth States, such as Australia and New Zealand, without considering their appropriateness to the circumstances of the country (see comments to this effect by Amet J in *Kekedo v Burns Philp* [1988-89] PNGLR 122 at 127-128).

Thirdly, there is the problem of how the courts determine whether a particular principle of the common law and equity is applicable or appropriate to the circumstances of the country from time to time as required by the *Constitution*. The following questions apply: What are the relevant circumstances of the country? How do the courts apply them to determine if a principle of common law is appropriate to the circumstances of the country? Should the courts require strict adherence to the rules of pleading and evidence to prove those relevant circumstances?

Custom

Custom is recognised and adopted as part of the underlying law subject to the conditions set out in Sch 2.1 of the *Constitution*. There are two types of custom. First, there are customs which apply amongst the 700-800 different linguistic and customary societies in this country. Secondly, there are customs which transcend territorial boundaries between individual clans and groups. The first category poses fewer difficulties when ascertaining a custom on a particular subject, the second category poses greater difficulties when ascertaining a *common* custom on a particular subject.

Custom of small groups or societies (Category 1). In the last 25 years, the courts have considered customs of groups and societies and either approved or rejected those customs. Examples of rejected customs include the custom of pay-back killing because it is repugnant to the general principle of humanity: *Public Prosecutor v Apava Keru* [1985] PNGLR 85; *Acting Public Prosecutor v Aia Moroi* [1985] PNGLR 78; the custom of mutilating adulterous spouses because it is repugnant to the general principles of humanity: *Public Prosecutor v Sidney Kerowa* [1985] PNGLR 85; handing over a child in reparation for a death because it is contrary to law: *The State v Joseph Kure* [1991] PNGLR 404; and the custom of giving away young single girls as part of compensation for the death of a rival clansman: In *Re Mirriam Willingal* (1997) N1506; *The State v Paulus Non Pable* (1999), N1873.

Some customs have been given statutory recognition by the legislature. For example, the *Criminal Law (Compensation) Act* 1991 recognised customary compensation and the *Sorcery Act* acknowledged the practice or custom or belief in sorcery. There are other customs which are widely practised, recognised and regulated by the courts, such as bride price payment and polygamous marriages.

National custom: onus and standard of proof (Category 2). In *Somare* [1981] PNGLR 265, the Supreme Court said that in order for a particular custom to be universally applicable throughout the country, that custom must apply at least to the majority of the provinces or it must be a custom which applies to the whole of the country. This is a question of fact which should be decided after considering relevant evidence. However, proof of, and finding the existence of, such custom may prove to be a difficult task.

Customs and the adopted common law and equity. By virtue of Sch 2.2 *Constitution*, custom is superior to the common law and equity: *Re Somare* per Kapi DCJ at 287; *Madaha Resena v PNG: Re Fisherman Island* [1991] PNGLR 174. To the extent that a rule of the common law and equity conflicts, or is inconsistent with, custom, then local custom will prevail. The task then is for the court and the lawyers to consider custom first before proceeding to examine common law. However, custom is still underdeveloped whereas the principles of common law and equity are well developed over many centuries. The tendency of the courts and lawyers is to resort to the common law and equity instead of searching for the relevant customary law.

The question then arises as to whether there should be a dual system of jurisprudence developed; one which would apply to the majority of our people who are still governed by customary norms and traditional values and another to apply to the modern elite citizens and non-citizens and modern institutions who might consider themselves not bound by the customary norms and values of this country. This question remains unresolved today. For its part, the Supreme Court has not satisfactorily resolved the issue either (see different views expressed by Kapi DCJ and Amet J in *Madaha Resena v PNG*).

Developing the underlying law "rule". Schedule 2.3 of the *Constitution* imposes the duty on the courts, in particular the National and Supreme Courts, to develop the underlying law (that is, customary law and the common law and equity of England adopted under ss 20-21 of the *Constitution* and also the new *Underlying Law Act* 2000) where there is no rule of law on a particular matter. The court is required to have regard to the various relevant statutory provisions, including the *Constitution*, decisions of the courts of PNG as well as those countries which have similar legal systems to that of PNG, and the National Goals and Directive Principles in the *Constitution*. The court is also required to have regard to the circumstances of the country from time to time. From reading Sch 2.3, the court is given a wide discretion to have regard to all relevant laws and the prevailing political, social and economic circumstances of the country (see the approach adopted in the Supreme Court in *Re Somare*).

The development of a truly Papua New Guinean criminal law needs a concerted and meaningful effort by all individuals and institutions concerned. It is hoped that this text will continue to be of assistance to the judiciary in assisting them to develop the law in this country. The lead, of course, must come from the policy makers, the legislature and the executive. The courts have a constitutional role to develop the underlying law. However, these policy questions are beyond the constitutional role of adjudication by the courts.

The authors wish to acknowledge and thank a number of people who were involved in this third edition. The authors wish to thank the Publications Committee of the Access to Laws Project in PNG, which is funded by AusAID, for the decision to select this title for publication. The bulk of the work for this edition was completed in Hobart and research assistance was given by Jo Connolly, Alison Kingston, Alia Lum and Kate Spencer. Our thanks to them and to Phillip Ingham and Fiona Dixon of Lawbook Co. for proofreading, including finding some reference errors which had survived untouched from the first edition. We would also like to give special thanks to the Supreme Court Library at Waigani for patiently collecting the paper copies of the unreported judgments; Val and Mienecke Haynes of Niumedia Pacific for invaluable assistance in referencing and for advice about the CD-Rom produced as part of the Access to Laws Project; Dr Dianne Nicol for agreeing at short notice to prepare the chapter of Evidence and finally, Gayle McElwee, who typed the manuscript for the second edition and, after a period of absence from the Law School at the University of Tasmania, returned to be confronted with a third edition, which she prepared with the same devotion and calmness.

We have endeavoured to state the law, including case law and statutory amendments, as at the end of October 2000.

D R C CHALMERS
S INJIA
D WEISBROT
W J ANDREW
Hobart, Sydney and Lae
February 2001

Preface to the Second Edition

The very warm reaction to the first edition of this book by members of the bench, practitioners, teachers and students, and our own knowledge that we could improve upon that effort encouraged us to undertake this second edition. The continually changing face of the criminal law was another factor — in the five years since the first edition there have been a number of statutory changes, the establishment of the *Revised Laws of Papua New Guinea,* and many more reported and unreported superior court judgments.

The case law contained in this edition is current to the end of July 1983; some last minute updating makes the statute law current to January 1, 1984.

In this edition we have substantially increased the textual material, especially in the addition of introductions to each set of statutes. We hope that this material — which is meant to provide, in varying degrees, background, analysis, and commentary on the legislation and the related case law — will be of value to readers in a way that bare annotations cannot be.

We have also added a new chapter on Developing a Papua New Guinean Criminal Law (Ch 1) which looks at the *Customs Recognition Act*, Schedule 2 of the Constitution (the underlying law), and other material which might assist in the development of the law in a fashion appropriate to the country. Further, we have tried to provide more information on the Village Courts, and have added a section on the *Inter-Group Fighting Act* to remedy what we regarded as unfortunate omissions in the earlier edition.

We have, after some consideration, opted to continue our policy of not citing overseas cases except where they are essential to an understanding of the decision made by the court in PNG, or are synonymous with a particular statement of the law, or have been continuously relied upon by the PNG courts.

We are aware that this may require the reader to consult other texts on occasion where, say, a section of a Papua New Guinean Act has not previously been dealt with by a Papua New Guinea court, or where there is a split of authority on a point of law. We are also aware of the packing problems we are causing courts and counsel on circuit who may need additional reference books in anticipation of the unexpected.

However, in the end we decided that our role was to make the criminal law of *Papua New Guinea* accessible to Papua New Guineans; that it would be presumptuous and inappropriate for us to select a few favoured overseas cases and present them as "the law" in a given area, particularly in view of the requirements of Schedule 2 of the Constitution; and finally that limitations of space and our own personal energy crises prohibited the extensive annotation and referencing of overseas cases which are, after all, available elsewhere. We hope that this policy does not unduly inconvenience anyone.

In this second edition we have also taken more care to provide cross-references to secondary sources, especially articles in the *Melanesian Law Journal* and publications of the PNG Law Reform Commission. We hope that this will encourage use of this growing body of worthwhile literature by those involved in the day-to-day administration of the criminal law, and reduce the gulf between academic and practitioner.

In the event that there is to be another edition of this book, we encourage readers to pass on to us any comments, questions, criticisms, or suggestions engendered by use of this edition, so as to make the third edition suit your requirements even further.

The authors wish to acknowledge and express their sincerest thanks to the many people who made this project possible, and often bearable: the Council of Law Reporting for Papua New Guinea for their substantial financial assistance; the Chief Justice, Sir Buri Kidu, for his continued strong support of the need for this book, and for the kind words in his Foreword to this edition; their Honours Justices, Amet, Bredmeyer, Narokobi and Pratt, Stipendiary Magistrates Simon Lupalrea and Geoff Lapthorne, Bob Mellor of Magisterial Services and Christine Bourke of the Public Prosecutor's Office, for their helpful comments and suggestions; Jacqui Elliott of the UPNG Law Library, and Emmanuel Giyomatala and James Fraser of the Legislative Counsel's Office, for their vital help in tracking down all the necessary legislation; the UNSW Law Library for allowing us adverse possession of all the Revised Laws and PNGLRs for many months; and Shirley Hong and Doreen Cinque in Sydney and Gayle McElwee in Hobart, for typing the manuscript with devotion beyond the call of duty.

Special thanks to our research assistant in Sydney, Julia Hall, for her active, uncomplaining and invaluable assistance in the preparation of the manuscript, and to Sandra Berns in Hobart for the monumental and painstaking preparation of the table of cases and the index.

Permission for use of the National Emblem was obtained from the Office of the Prime Minister, under s 20 of Ch No 9, *National Identity Act*.

In this edition, David Weisbrot and Don Chalmers wrote the introductory text in each chapter which precedes the annotated legislation, and Chapter 8. As was the case with the earlier edition, the preparation of the manuscript and all editorial work was undertaken by Messrs Chalmers and Weisbrot, who thank Barbara and Faith for all the soft and warm reasons.

D R C CHALMERS
D WEISBROT
W J ANDREW
Sydney
February 1984

Preface to the First Edition

This book is designed to bring together the legislation and the increasing volume of case law relating to criminal law and practice in Papua New Guinea, for the assistance of the Courts, practitioners, and students of the law.

In the early stages of the project two policy decisions were made by the authors collectively which affected the form and substance of what was to emerge: first, we decided to organise our research in the manner of an annotated reference work, rather than as an expository text. What is sacrificed in general readability, we hope, is more than made up for in utility as a working text.

Secondly, we have chosen not to cite cases from overseas jurisdictions except in a few instances where the ratio decidendi of Papua New Guinean judgments consisted almost entirely of an extensive quote from a foreign case. Thus, the raw material for our annotations is found in the unreported and reported judgments of the superior courts of Papua New Guinea, which commenced semi-regular reportage in 1953.

Until we began, no comprehensive subject index of the criminal case law of Papua New Guinea had been prepared or published, and the preparation of criminal pleadings has invariably begun in a vacuum. Most judgments, particularly those prior to the mid-1960s, have only appeared in cyclostyled form, and even published judgments are not always accessible outside the major urban centres.

After 25 years of local judgments, and perhaps even more important, after three years of independence, the great majority of cases referred to by counsel and cited by the Courts are from overseas — particularly England and Australia. We hope that this book will be a small first step in reversing that trend, and encouraging the development of a uniquely Papua New Guinean jurisprudence. We are mindful that the Chief Justice, Sir William Prentice, has already gone on record discouraging the citation of English cases and those from the non-Code Australian States except where they relate to matters on which the Code is silent (*The State v Laiarn Kiala & Meiri Gomosi* [1977] PNGLR 470).

Because we felt that a tiptoe through the annotations might not properly convey the dynamism that characterises the contemporary legal scene in Papua New Guinea, we have included an introductory chapter which briefly recounts how the criminal justice system got to where it is, and where it is likely to go in the foreseeable future.

We wish to acknowledge the substantial financial assistance provided by the Council of Law Reporting for Papua New Guinea, and the Research Committee of the University of Papua New Guinea.

Our special thanks go to the Chief Justice of Papua New Guinea, Sir William Prentice, who initiated the project and has given it his continued support, and the previous Chief Justice, Sir Sydney Frost, who also lent his support and enthusiasm during the initial stages. We thank Sir William anew for his Foreword.

We also wish to express our gratitude to many others who contributed to the final product: in Port Moresby, to Faith Wieland, for her support and patience; Bernard

Narokobi and Heather McRae for their insight; and Stephanie Cooper for her production of a readable draft manuscript out of a morass of cuttings, index cards, scribbled notes and late insertions. In Hobart, to Bill White, research assistant to the Faculty of Law 1978, who prepared draft annotations of about 100 cases, and to Leanne Topfer for preparation of the index, and to Elaine Adams.

While the manuscript was prepared in equal parts by the authors, the editorial work was completed by Messrs Chalmers and Weisbrot.

Finally, we should like to thank the editorial staff of The Law Book Company for their assistance in the publication of this book.

As with all books jointly authored, the final text reflects in varying degrees the need for compromise, consensus and resignation. There is one statement, however, on which we can all agree, and that is, "The parts I wrote are the best".

W J ANDREW
D R C CHALMERS
D WEISBROT
Port Moresby
February 1979

Table of Contents

[References are to page numbers]

Method of Citation

CASES

Most of the annotations in this volume have been prepared from the mimeographed numbered judgment initially issued in each case. If the case is subsequently reported, the PNGLR citation is given. Readers should be aware that some of the PNGLR case reports are substantially edited down. This may explain the occasion where an annotation appears to contain material not dealt with in the PNGLR case report. In such instances, the original unreported number judgment should be read as well.

After Independence, indictments have been drawn in the name of the State, rather than the Crown (R). Appeals against insufficiency of sentence will generally appear as the Public Prosecutor v the defendant. References to the Supreme Court on points of law may be made by a number of officers under the *Supreme Court Act*, and may appear as a Supreme Court Reference, Constitutional Reference, Prosecutor's Request, or PLAR (Principal Legal Advisor's Reference).

The citation of overseas cases follows the standard form.

Reported Judgments

PNGLR: The Papua New Guinea Law Reports started in 1963. The volumes from 1963 until 1973 were entitled Papua and New Guinea Law Reports but the practice is now to refer to such reports without the word "and". At the time of publication of this edition, the PNGLR were current to 1996.

Unreported Judgments

Many important cases and cases prior to 1963 are not found in the Papua New Guinea Law Reports. Unreported judgments are mimeographed and issued by the Judges of the Court for limited circulation. These unreported judgments are commonly referred to as the numbered judgments. The following are examples of citations of unreported judgments:

Supreme Court decisions until Independence, September 1975, “(1965) No346”. These unreported judgments began in 1953 and ended on Independence with case number (1975) No856.

Full Court decisions until Independence, September 1975, “(1974) FC35”. These unreported decisions began with the establishment of this Court in 1969 and ended on Independence with case number (1975) FC84.

National Court decisions following Independence, “(1975) N1”. These unreported decisions began with the establishment of the Court at Independence as successor to the old Supreme Court.

Supreme Court decisions following Independence, “(1975) SC85”. These unreported decisions began with the establishment of the Court at Independence.

The number has run on consecutively from former Full Court numbered judgments.

This edition contains annotations of National and Supreme Court cases up to July 2000.

STATUTES

This volume uses the Revised Laws of Papua New Guinea.

Statutes contained in the Revised Laws are now cited by their title and Chapter number — for example, the *Evidence Act* (Ch48) or the *Criminal Code* (Ch262). Other statutes are cited by their title and year — for example, the *Criminal Compensation Act* 1997.

After each statute annotated, a cross-reference table is provided which indicates the section number in the Revised Laws and corresponding section in the previous legislation. In the case of the Criminal Code there is also a cross-reference to the *Queensland Criminal Code (Adopted)* 1902, which applied in PNG until the enactment of the Papua New Guinea *Criminal Code* in 1974. For example, the definition of wilful murder was contained in s 301 of the Queensland Code, s 304 of the PNG Code 1974, and s 299 of the Revised Laws (Ch262), the Criminal Code.

For convenience and consistency, an editorial decision was made to convert all previous section references in the annotations of cases to the section number in the current version of the legislation.

The statutes in this edition have been updated to December 2000.

JOURNALS

"MLJ" refers to the *Melanesian Law Journal,* published by the Law Faculty, UPNG. Other journals are cited in the standard form.

JUDGES

All judges are styled as at the time of the particular judgment. This avoids the cumbersome repetition of the phrase "as he then was" or the like. We hope this causes no inconvenience to the judges concerned.

Table of Cases

[References are to page numbers]

Chapter 1

THE CONSTITUTION OF THE INDEPENDENT STATE OF PAPUA NEW GUINEA

The *Constitution* of the independent state of Papua New Guinea has special legal sanctity. The *Constitution* stands pre-eminent over all laws. All other laws must conform to the *Constitution*. Specifically, s 11(l) of the *Constitution* of the independent state of Papua New Guinea provides:

> "This Constitution and the Organic Laws are the Supreme Law of Papua New Guinea ... all acts ... that are inconsistent with them are, to the extent of the inconsistency, invalid and ineffective."

The provisions of the *Constitution*, in so far as they relate to criminal law and procedure, are the point of departure to any consideration of criminal law and procedure.

Basic rights

The most important provisions relating to criminal law and procedure are the constitutional guarantees of basic rights in Div 3 of Pt III of the *Constitution*. The basic rights provisions have a twofold effect. First, the basic rights provisions have restricted administrative competence in favour of individual liberty. Basic rights are effective for defence lawyers. Apart from this active role, the basic rights provisions have a secondary importance which may be described as their passive role. The provisions serve as a guide to legislative competence. Acts, such as the *Arrest Act*, *Search Act* and *Bail Act* conform to the framework of the basic rights provisions.

The *Constitution* lays down four basic rights enjoyed by all people in the country, irrespective of citizenship:

(a) the right to freedom (s 32);

(b) the right to life (s 35);

(c) the right to freedom from inhuman treatment (s 36); and

(d) the right to protection of the law (s 37).

The second category of rights applies to all people and covers the liberty of the person (s 42), and specifically:

(a) freedom from forced labour (s 43);

(b) freedom from arbitrary search or entry (s 44);

(c) freedom of assembly and association (s 47);

(d) freedom of employment;

(e) the right to privacy (s 49); and

(f) freedom of conscience, thought, religion and expression (ss 45 and 46).

The third category of basic rights only applies to citizens of Papua New Guinea. These are:

(a) the right to vote and stand for public office (s 50);

(b) the right to freedom of information (s 51);

(c) the right to freedom of movement (s 52);

(d) protection from unjust deprivation of property (s 53); and

(e) equality of citizens (s 55).

Importantly, the second and third categories of basic rights are covered by a qualification that their operation may be restricted by any law passed which, although in conflict with these rights, is "reasonably justifiable in a democratic society": *Constitution*, ss 38-39. This phrase traces its ancestry to the Indian and later African Constitutions. Sections 38-39 represent the extent to which wider public interests may be permitted to restrict the inviolability of private basic rights by judicial fiat. To ensure that this legislative authority is not used as a back-door method to erode basic rights, the *Constitution* provides procedural protection. Any proposed Act which qualifies a basic right must follow a special procedure which equates with the procedure for constitutional amendment. By s 38(2), the Act must:

(a) be expressly stated as a law which qualifies a basic right;

(b) specify the basic right which is to be qualified; and

(c) be certified as passed by an absolute majority in the Parliament.

This general qualification on basic rights has been considered on occasions by the superior courts. In *Stan Cory v John Blyth* [1976] PNGLR 274, an action for defamation was met by a defence that by s 46 of the *Constitution* (freedom of speech) no action could lie. It was held that s 46 did not license the making of defamatory statements. It was also held that the effect of the *Defamation Act* 1962 (now Ch 293) was to put reasonable limitations under s 38 of the *Constitution* on the right to freedom of speech.

From the point of view of criminal law and procedure, the most important of these basic rights is contained in s 37, which provides for the fundamental right of protection of the law for all individuals. Section 37 essentially states the established common law principles of the fair and impartial administration of justice in open court. As regards criminal procedure, elaborate safeguards are set out in s 37. It is provided that an accused person, unless the charge is withdrawn:

(a) shall be entitled to a fair hearing within a reasonable time by an independent and impartial court (s 37(3));

(b) is presumed innocent until proven guilty according to law (s 37(4)(a));

(c) is entitled to be informed promptly in a language which the accused understands and in detail of the nature of the offence charged (s 37(4)(b));

(d) must be given adequate time and facilities to prepare a defence (s 37(4)(c));

(e) has the right to have the free assistance of an interpreter if the language used in the court cannot be understood or spoken by the accused (s 37(4)(d));

(f) has the right to put forward a defence in person before any independent and impartial court by persons of the accused's own choice who are legal practitioners (s 37(4)(e)); and

(g) has a right to examine or have examined witnesses for and against the accused (s 37(4)(f)).

It is also provided that:

(a) it is unlawful for anyone to be held guilty of any criminal offence on account of any act or omission which did not constitute an offence at the time it was committed (s 37(7));

(b) in such a case, a heavier penalty than the one which was applicable at the time the offence was committed may not be imposed (s 37(7));

(c) no-one may be tried for an offence for which he or she has previously been convicted or acquitted unless it is by the order of a superior court (s 37(8));

(d) an accused is not compellable in a trial for an offence to be a witness against themselves (s 37(10));

(e) an accused is entitled to ensure a speedy trial. Section 37(14) provides that in the event that the trial of a person is not commenced within four months of the date on which the accused was committed for trial, a detailed report concerning the case is to be made by the Chief Justice to the Minister responsible for the National Legal Administration; and

(f) every person convicted of an offence is entitled to have the conviction and sentence reviewed by a higher court or tribunal according to law (s 37(15)).

The enforcement of basic rights

The rights and freedoms provided for in ss 32-37 and 42-56 of the *Constitution* may be enforced in the Supreme Court, the National Court or any other court. An infringement of any right or freedom may be enforced by the person concerned on her or his own initiative or upon the application by any person who has an interest in the protection and enforcement of the infringed right or freedom. Under s 57(1) of the *Constitution* the court may also entertain an action by any person who has an interest in the protection of an infringed right when that person acts on behalf of a person who is unable fully and freely to exercise his or her rights under s 57. This applies whether or not the person whose rights have been infringed had actually authorised the interested person. Furthermore, under s 57(2) the law officers of Papua New Guinea, who are the Principal Legal Advisors to the National Executive, the Public Prosecutor and the Public Solicitor (*Constitution*, s 156), have an automatic interest in the protection and enforcement of an infringed right. A court, under s 57(5), is not limited to cases of actual or imminent infringement of the guaranteed rights or freedoms under the *Constitution* but the court may, if it thinks proper to do so, make orders and declarations where there is a reasonable probability of infringement. By s 58, a court may also award damages against any person, government body or person who was responsible to a government body responsible for committing an infringement of any of the basic rights and freedoms contained in the *Constitution*.

In practice, the basic rights provisions have fallen for consideration by the judges of the National and Supreme Courts more in their breach rather than their threatened breach. Specifically, basic rights arguments are often employed as defences in criminal cases (and to a lesser degree in civil cases). Therefore, there is now a fairly well established body of leading cases that indicate the breadth of orders which the court will make when basic rights are breached. There is no equivalent established body of cases dealing with the nature of orders for threatened breaches of these rights. For example, in *The State v Peter Painke* [1976] PNGLR 210; *The State v*

Peter Painke (No 2) [1977] PNGLR 141, the accused was discharged after a delay of 11 months before he was brought to trial as not being a "fair hearing within a reasonable time" under s 37(3) of the *Constitution*. In *Constitutional Reference No 2 of 1978* [1978] PNGLR 405, prison inmates had their privileges extended after s 30 of the *Corrective Institutions Act* 1957 was declared invalid as infringing s 37(15) of the *Constitution*. Similarly, in *Constitutional Reference No 3 of 1978* [1978] PNGLR 421, s 11(3) of the *Inter-Group Fighting Act* 1977 was declared invalid as depriving the accused of the presumption of innocence (*Constitution*, s 37(4)(a)), and as a consequence there was a discontinuance of police prosecutions. In *The State v John Kosi* (1981) N306, ss 61 and 62 of the *Criminal Code* on punishment for unlawful assembly were interpreted as not infringing the rights to freedom of conscience, expression and assembly established in ss 45-57 of the *Constitution*.

Two other general sections should be noted in respect of enforcement. The *Constitution* provides an overriding enforcement section. By s 22, the provisions of the *Constitution* shall not be left without effect because of the lack of supporting machinery or procedural laws. Of more significance is the power to impose sanctions under s 23. The National Court, unless the constitutional law provides for enforcement, may impose imprisonment, fines, other "equally effective remedy" or any order that it thinks proper for preventing or remedying the breach. In *Constitutional Reference No 1 of 1977* [1977] PNGLR 295, the apparent overlap between the general ss 22 and 23 and the specific ss 57 and 58 was discussed, if not resolved. The overlap has not, however, proved troublesome as the wide ambit of s 57(3) provides a plenary and discretionary power to make "all such declarations as are necessary or appropriate". The question of the relationship between ss 22 and 23 and ss 57 and 58 still remains, in the words of Prentice DCJ, "for the future".

Constitutional interpretation and advisory opinions: ss 18, 19

The judges of the Supreme Court have the responsibility for constitutional interpretation. By s 18(l) of the *Constitution*, the Supreme Court has jurisdiction on "any question relating to the interpretation or application of any provision of a Constitutional Law". By s 18(2) questions of interpretation of the *Constitution* go directly to the Supreme Court as a matter of original jurisdiction. Other courts are obliged to refer questions relating to the interpretation of a constitutional law to the Supreme Court.

On issues of constitutional interpretation, the Supreme Court has power to decide on its own initiative subject to the terms of the *Constitution*. Bayne suggests there are four elements to such a purposive mode of interpretation:

> "In the first place, autochthony – cutting the legal tie – should render irrelevant any pre-Independence statute law that had not been adopted, and allows the courts to take a close look at the English common law or outside decisions. Secondly, s 24 enables reference to the CPC Report and the Constituent Assembly proceedings to resolve ambiguities or to give content to general expressions in the *Constitution*. Thirdly, the Preamble in general and the National Goals in particular provide statements of social goals and values which are relevant in any case before the courts. Finally, English common law or outside decisions would not be received as part of the underlying law for the purposes of interpretation except after a strict application of the tests for

applicability; a strict view in constitutional cases could be based on a recognition that the CPC was concerned that interpretation of the *Constitution* should be faithful to the principles inherent in it, and also from an awareness that it is more difficult for the Parliament to change the effect of a rule of Constitutional interpretation of the underlying law than other rules of underlying law".[1]

The most authoritative statement on the Supreme Court's adoption of the purposive approach is to be found in *Chris Haiveta v Paias Wingti (No 3)* [1984] PNGLR 197.

By s 19 (as amended by *Constitutional Amendment No 3 – Provincial Government (Consequential Amendments)*), the Supreme Court is empowered to give opinions on any question relating to the interpretation or application of any provision of a constitutional law including a proposed law. Any such opinion has the same binding effect as any other Supreme Court decision: s 19(2). Such advisory opinions may be sought by a specific list of authorities alone under s 19(3) and they are as follows:

(a) the Parliament;

(b) the Head of The State, acting with, and in accordance with, the advice of the National Executive Council;

(c) the Law Officers;

(d) the Law Reform Commission;

(e) the Ombudsman Commission;

(ea) a provincial assembly or a local-level government;

(eb) a provincial executive;

(ec) a body established for the settlement of inter-government disputes;

(f) the Speaker of Parliament (in cases where, before certification of an Act there is a doubt as to the validity of that Act: *Constitution*, s 137(3)).

The procedure is an effective method for resolving constitutional issues pending or during a trial by removing them to the Supreme Court. This avoids the problem of having to await verdict and then appeal the constitutional issue. The original interpretive and advisory constitutional jurisdiction has been and will remain of importance to the development of criminal law and procedure.

[1] Bayne, "The Constitution in the Courts 1975-1980" in Weisbrot, Paliwala and Sawyerr (eds), *Law and Social Change in Papua New Guinea* (1982), p 222.

CONSTITUTION OF THE INDEPENDENT STATE OF PAPUA NEW GUINEA

[Selected Sections Relating to Criminal Law]

18. Original interpretative jurisdiction of the Supreme Court.

(1) Subject to this *Constitution*, the Supreme Court has original jurisdiction, to the exclusion of other courts, as to any question relating to the interpretation or application of any provision of a Constitutional Law.

(2) Subject to this *Constitution*, where any question relating to the interpretation or application of any provision of a Constitutional Law arises in any court or tribunal, other than the Supreme Court, the court or tribunal shall, unless the question is trivial, vexatious or irrelevant, refer the matter to the Supreme Court, and take whatever other action (including the adjournment of proceedings) is appropriate.

When any question relating to the interpretation of the *Constitution* or a constitutional law arises in any court under s 18(2) and is referred to the Supreme Court, it must arise out of a factual situation established by the lower court, and all findings of fact necessary for the interpretation must be made by the court or tribunal before making the reference. Until this is done no question relating to interpretation arises.[2]

See *SCR No 4 of 1980; Re Petition of Michael Thomas Somare* [1981] PNGLR 265 on the question of whether the Leader of the Opposition had standing under this section.

In *Tohian v Geita and Mugugia* [1990] PNGLR 353 Los J held that in considering whether grounds exist for referring a question relating to the interpretation or application of a provision of a constitutional law to the Supreme Court, the court or tribunal must decide:

(a) whether the proposed question related to an interpretation or application of any constitutional law: *SCR No 12A of 1984; Joe Parakas v The State* [1985] PNGLR 224;

(b) whether the question was "trivial, vexatious or irrelevant"; and

(c) whether there are sufficient findings of fact upon which the Supreme Court could deliberate in order to determine the proper interpretation or application of the constitutional law: *SCR No 3 of 1982; Re ss 57 and 155(4) of the Constitution* [1982] PNGLR 405.

A magistrate hearing committal proceedings under the *District Courts Act* (Ch 40) is not exempt from the obligation imposed on "any court or tribunal" to consider whether grounds exist for referring a question allegedly relating to the interpretation or application of a provision of a constitutional law to the Supreme Court pursuant to s 18(2).[3]

---

[2] *In the Matter of an Application by the Public Solicitor SCR No 3 of 1982* [1982] PNGLR 405.
[3] *Tohian v Geita and Mugugia* [1990] PNGLR 353.

19. Special references to the Supreme Court.

(1) Subject to Subsection (4), the Supreme Court shall, on application by an authority referred to in Subsection (3), give its opinion on any question relating to the interpretation or application of any provision of a Constitutional Law, including (but without limiting the generality of that expression) any question as to the validity of a law or proposed law.

(2) An opinion given under Subsection (1) has the same binding effect as any other decision of the Supreme Court.

(3) The following authorities only are entitled to make application under Subsection (1)—

(a) the Parliament; and

(b) the Head of The State, acting with, and in accordance with, the advice of the National Executive Council; and

(c) the Law Officers of Papua New Guinea; and

(d) the Law Reform Commission; and

(e) the Ombudsman Commission; and

(ea) a Provincial Assembly or a Local-level Government; and

(eb) a provincial executive; and

(ec) a body established by a Constitutional Law or an Act of the Parliament specifically for the settlement of disputes between the National Government and Provincial Governments or Local-level governments, or between Provincial Governments, or between Provincial Governments and Local-level Governments, or Local-level governments; and

(f) the Speaker, in accordance with Section 137(3) (Acts of Indemnity).

[Subs (3)(ea) insrt *Constitutional Amendment No 3 - Provincial Government (Consequential Amendments)*; subst *Constitutional Amendment No 16 - Provincial Governments and Local-level Governments*; Subs (3)(eb) insrt *Constitutional Amendment No 3 – Provincial Government (Consequential Amendments)*; Subs (3)(ec) insrt *Constitutional Amendment No 3 – Provincial Government (Consequential Amendments)*]

(4) Subject to any Act of the Parliament, the Rules of Court of the Supreme Court may make provision in respect of matters relating to the jurisdiction of the Supreme Court under this section, and in particular as to—

(a) the form and contents of questions to be decided by the Court; and

(b) the provision of counsel adequate to enable full argument before the Court of any question; and

(c) cases and circumstances in which the Court may decline to give an opinion.

(5) In this section, "proposed law" means a law that has been formally placed before the relevant law-making body.

Kapi J held in *SCR No 4 of 1980; Re Petition of Michael Thomas Somare* [1981] PNGLR 265 that a rule be formulated under Sch 2.3 on standing, and the rule should be that an applicant must have **sufficient** interest in the matter to which the application relates. This test of sufficient interest is objective. Accordingly, this section does not cover the field in relation to those having standing to apply to the court on matters of public interest.

Kearney DCJ and Greville-Smith J dissented in *SCR No 4 of 1980; Re Petition of Michael Thomas Somare* [1981] PNGLR 265 and held that the Leader of the Opposition was not included in this section, and as this section exhaustively covered the field of those having standing to challenge the validity of a law, there is no scope or need to use the judicial initiatives of jurisdictions with different constitutional structures.

In *SCR No 4 of 1980; Re Petition of Michael Thomas Somare* [1981] PNGLR 265 at 269 the Chief Justice expressed the view that while s 19 enumerated the authorities who could protect the public interest, in practice these authorities only intervened in matters involving their own area of operation.

22. Enforcement of the Constitution.

The provisions of this Constitution that recognize rights of individuals (including corporations and associations) as well as those that confer powers or impose duties on public authorities, shall not be left without effect because of the lack of supporting, machinery or procedural laws, but the lack shall, as far as practicable, be supplied by the National Court in the light of the National Goals and Directive Principles, and by way of analogy from other laws, general principles of justice and generally-accepted doctrine.

23. Sanctions.

(1) Where any provision of a Constitutional Law prohibits or restricts an act, or imposes a duty, then unless a Constitutional Law or an Act of the Parliament provides for the enforcement of that provision the National Court may-

(a) impose a sentence of imprisonment for a period not exceeding 10 years or a fine not exceeding K10000.00; or

(b) in the absence of any other equally effective remedy under the laws of Papua New Guinea, order the making of compensation by a person (including a governmental body) who is in default, or both, for a breach of the prohibition, restriction or duty, and may make such further order in the circumstances as it thinks proper.

(2) Where a provision of a Constitutional Law prohibits or restricts an act or imposes a duty, the National Court may, if it thinks it proper to do so, make any order that it thinks proper for preventing or remedying a breach of the prohibition, restriction or duty, and Subsection (1) applies to a failure to comply with the order as if it were a breach of a provision of this *Constitution*.

(3) Where the National Court considers it proper to do so, it may include in an order under Subsection (2) an anticipatory order under Subsection (1).

See *Constitutional Reference No 1 of 1977* [1977] PNGLR 362, annotated under s 57 and, also, *The State v Peter Painke* [1976] PNGLR 210; *The State v Peter Painke (No2)* [1977] PNGLR 141.

Standing to apply under this section is not governed by s 19 but by reference to laws adopted or formulated under Sch 2.[4]

[4] *Supreme Court Reference No 4 of 1980; Re Petition of Michael Thomas Somare* [1981] PNGLR 265 (Kapi J).

Division 3 - Basic Rights
Subdivision A - Introductory

For a general discussion of human rights in Papua New Guinea, see Brunton, "*Human Rights in PNG and the Prospects for International Supervision*" (1980) 8 MLJ 143.

32. Right to freedom.

(1) Freedom based on law consists in the least amount of restriction on the activities of individuals that is consistent with the maintenance and development of Papua New Guinea and of society in accordance with this *Constitution* and, in particular, with the National Goals and Directive Principles and the Basic Social Obligations.

(2) Every person has the right to freedom based on law, and accordingly has a legal right to do anything that -

(a) does not injure or interfere with the rights and freedoms of others; and

(b) is not prohibited by law, and no person -

(c) is obliged to do anything that is not required by law; and

(d) may be prevented from doing anything that complies with the provisions of paragraphs (a) and (b).

(3) This section is not intended to reflect on the extra-legal existence, nature or effect of social, civic, family or religious obligations, or other obligations of an extra-legal nature, or to prevent such obligations being given effect to by law.

Subdivision B - Fundamental Rights

35. Right to life.

(1) No person shall be deprived of his life intentionally except-

(a) in execution of a sentence of a court following his conviction of an offence for which the penalty of death is prescribed by law; or

(b) as the result of the use of force to such an extent as is reasonable in the circumstances of the case and is permitted by any other law-

(i) for the defence of any person from violence; or

(ii) in order to effect a lawful arrest or to prevent the escape of a person lawfully detained; or

(iii) for the purpose of suppressing a riot, an insurrection or a mutiny; or

(iv) in order to prevent him from committing an offence; or

(v) for the purpose of suppressing piracy or terrorism or similar acts; or

(c) as the result of a lawful act of war.

(2) Nothing in Subsection (1) (b) relieves any person from any liability at law in respect of the killing of another.

See ss 289 *et seq* regarding homicides and related offences and see s 209 of the *Criminal Code*.

36. Freedom from inhuman treatment.

(1) No person shall be submitted to torture (whether physical or mental), or to treatment or punishment that is cruel or otherwise inhuman, or is inconsistent with respect for the inherent dignity of the human person.

(2) The killing of a person in circumstances in which Section 35(1)(a) (right to life) does not, of itself, contravene Subsection (1), although the manner or the circumstances of the killing may contravene it.

Sections 36(1), 37(17) and 41(1) of the *Constitution* require that treatment in prison shall not be harsh, oppressive, cruel or inhuman. If there is a prison law which is harsh or oppressive, a prisoner can have the law declared unconstitutional under these sections as an infringement of fundamental rights. Similarly, if a particular treatment which a prisoner receives in prison is harsh or oppressive then, even though it is not covered by a prison law, that treatment or practice can be stopped as an infringement of the prisoner's fundamental rights.[5]

In *Tom Amaiu v Commissioner of Corrective Institutions and the State* [1983] PNGLR 87 it was found that the prison regime in "B" Division (maximum security) of Bomana Gaol involved inhuman treatment in violation of constitutional guarantees. The prisoner petitioner was awarded damages (both compensatory and exemplary), and orders were made closing "B" Division, requiring the Corrective Institutions Department to draw up new regulations and introduce a new regime, and to barring warders who served in the old "B" Division from being assigned to the new "B" Divisions for two years.[6]

See *Heni Pauta and Kenneth Susuve v Commissioner of Corrective Institutions and his Servants and Agents* [1982] PNGLR 7, annotated under s 57(3) below.

See ss 57-58 regarding remedies for breaches of fundamental rights.

In *Special Constitutional Reference No 1 of 1984* [1984] PNGLR 314 one of the questions was whether provisions of the *Criminal Code (Minimum Penalties) (Amendment) Act* 1983, and related amendments were contrary to s 36(1) of the *Constitution*. The court held that such provisions do not offend s 36(1) of the *Constitution*. Kidu CJ reasoned (at 318) that:

> "[S]ection 36(1) was meant to prohibit cruel, degrading and inhumane punishment and treatment and nothing else. Minimum penalties were far from the minds of those who constituted the Constituent Assembly when s 36(1) was sanctioned and the Constitutional Planning Committee (CPC) did not, quite clearly from its recommendation, have them in mind either."

37. Protection of the law.

(1) Every person has the right to the full protection of the law, and the succeeding provisions of this section are intended to ensure that that right is fully available, especially to persons in custody or charged with offences.

---

[5] *Tom Amaiu v Commissioner of Corrective Institutions and the State* [1983] PNGLR 87.

[6] *Tom Amaiu v Commissioner of Corrective Institutions and the State* [1983] PNGLR 87 (Bredmeyer J).

Section 37(1) means that no aspect, or at least no major aspect, of a prisoner's treatment should be at the whim of the officer-in-charge or of any warder; the warders must treat a prisoner in accordance with the laws. If they fail to do so the prisoner can seek redress under ss 57 and 58 of the *Constitution*. Redress may be in the form of damages or an order compelling the warders to do something or ordering them not to do something.[7]

In *Tom Amaiu v Commissioner of Corrective Institutions and the State* [1983] PNGLR 87 it was held that there must be a law providing for the periodic review of each prisoner's confinement in "B" Division. Medical evidence indicated that confinement in "B" Division under its present regime could lead to serious mental illnesses. For the law regulating how a detainee gets out of "B" Division to be humane and not cruel, harsh or oppressive, the medical officer should have some say in the release of the person.

For the officer-in-charge of a prison division to impose his own form of special punishment (here, "special confinement") for misconduct in the division, or for detainees who come to the division with bad reputations as troublemakers elsewhere, is ultra vires the *Corrective Institutions Act* and *Corrective Institutions Regulations* which specify the forms of punishment allowed: *Tom Amaiu v Commissioner of Corrective Institutions and the State* [1983] PNGLR 87.

See *The State v Turi* [1986] PNGLR 221 for a discussion on "the right to the full protection of the law".

(2) Except, subject to any Act of the Parliament to the contrary, in the case of the offence commonly known as contempt of court, nobody may be convicted of an offence that is not defined by, and the penalty for which is not prescribed by, a written law.

Under s 19 of the *Criminal Code*, a judge may impose any of the lesser punishments prescribed (upon a conviction for wilful murder under s 299 where there is a maximum sentence of life imprisonment). The crime of wilful murder is a statutory offence and the only punishment that can be posed is set out under the Code. A judge has no power to impose any other punishment. Under s 7(e) of the *Native Customs Recognition Act*, custom shall be taken into account in determining the penalty (if any) to be imposed on a guilty party. This means that a particular custom (defined by s 4 of that Act, and recognised and enforced under s 6 of that Act and Sch 2.1 of the *Constitution*) may be taken into account to explain the offender's behaviour; for example, the offence may have been committed under customary pressure. Custom used in this sense becomes a mitigating factor (see *R v Asis* (1970) N559 (Clarkson J); *R v Iu Ketapi* [1971-1972] PNGLR 44; *R v Lakalyo Neak* (1971) N632), providing a cultural justification of the offender's behaviour, which reduces their culpability or blameworthiness. In some instances, the custom may increase the seriousness of the offender's behaviour. For instance, in incest cases, custom may regard it as immoral and may call for severe punishment. A court may also take into account customary punishment in the same way, for example, whether the offender is liable to pay compensation whatever the court's decision might be: *R v Kaupa* (1973) N765. All of this means that a judge may increase or decrease the sentence depending on whether custom mitigates or aggravates the offence and may impose the appropriate sentence within the range given by law. Section 7(e) of the *Native Customs Recognition Act* does not enlarge the power of the court under ss 19 and 209 of the Code; it may only operate within the range

[7] *Tom Amaiu v Commissioner of Corrective Institutions and the State* [1983] PNGLR 87.

provided by those sections: *Acting Public Prosecutor v Uname Aumane* [1980] PNGLR 510 (Kapi J, with Kearney DCJ agreeing).

A person may not be punished until found guilty of an offence according to law. Under s 37(2) of the *Constitution* "nobody may be convicted of an offence that is not defined by, and the penalty for which is not prescribed by, a written law". A "written law" refers to an Act of Parliament (including any law made under the Act), organic laws and the *Constitution*. The term has been used to distinguish it from what may be called the unwritten laws, custom as adopted under Sch 2.1 of the *Constitution*, common law as adopted under Sch 2.2 and the underlying law as developed under Schs 2.3 and 2.4: *Acting Public Prosecutor v Uname Aumane* [1980] PNGLR 510.

As a matter of law, a court can only impose the penalty provided by statute (in this case the *Criminal Code*). This court has no power to impose any customary punishment. The adoption, application and enforcement of customary law under Sch 2.1 of the *Constitution* is subject to, amongst other things, an Act of Parliament which regulates the use of customary law (Sch 2.1(3)(b)), such as the *Native Customs (Recognition) Act*. Under s 7(e) of this Act, custom **may be taken into account** in punishment, to mitigate or aggravate the sentence to be imposed. However, ultimately, the penalty to be imposed is as provided for under the *Criminal Code* (in this case of wilful murder) and there is no power in the court to impose customary punishment. Further, there is no room for developing the underlying law in this case. The development of an underlying law under Sch 2.3 arises only when there appears to be no rule of law that is applicable. In this case the *Criminal Code* is applicable. As to what the role of customary law should be in such cases, these are matters for the legislature rather than for the court: *Acting Public Prosecutor v Uname Aumane* [1980] PNGLR 510 (Kapi J, with Kearney DCJ agreeing).

The *Constitution* of Papua New Guinea (unlike that of Vanuatu) does not give courts power to punish breaches of customary law not defined by a written law: *Rebeka Ambi v Mary Rabi* (1980) N279 (Narokobi AJ).

See the *Customs (Recognition) Act* regarding the circumstances in which custom may be recognised, applied and enforced by the courts.

Under s 223 of the *Criminal Code*, see *Sangumu Wautu v The State* [1978] PNGLR 326 and see s 42(l)(b) of the *Constitution*.

(3) A person charged with an offence shall, unless the charge is withdrawn, be afforded a fair hearing within a reasonable time, by an independent and impartial court.

This section has no application to disciplinary proceedings: *Public Employees Association of PNG v Public Services Commission* [1983] PNGLR 206.

Though the words of s 37(3) do not cover the case of an appeal, this subsection is just as applicable to someone who is appealing against conviction as to someone awaiting trial, especially when read in conjunction with s 37(16) and (17). The words of the *Constitution* are not hollow. They are there and until they are changed the administrators and finance officials must take them into account and ensure that appeals against conviction may be heard within a reasonable time. The *Constitution* forms the very backbone of our country's laws and no judge or magistrate should tolerate a situation which prevents the requirements of that law being carried into effect: *Waraniya Wariko v Luke Pangou* (1981) N290(L).

In *The State v Peter Painke* [1976] PNGLR 210 the section was held to have been contravened where it was some 14-16 months since the alleged offence was committed, 11 months since the accused was committed for trial and six months since the case first came before the court for trial. The section was also held to have been contravened when there was a 10 month delay in bringing the proceedings on: *The State v Peter Kakam Borarae* [1984] PNGLR 99 (Woods J).

An amendment to an indictment does not necessarily amount to a refusal to afford "a fair hearing within a reasonable time": *The State v Tanedo* [1975] PNGLR 395.

If a fair hearing requires upon the evidence a determination of the merits of the case in favour of the accused, that right cannot be defeated by permitting the state to withdraw the charge, particularly if the nature of the withdrawal does not preclude further proceedings. For the state to enter a *nolle prosequi* at a stage of a trial when the state had called all the evidence available, and it was insufficient to sustain the charge, was to deny the accused a fair hearing: *R v Abia Tambule* [1974] PNGLR 250 at 253 (Frost SPJ and Minogue CJ).

> "The authorities indicate that, when a person is charged with a criminal offence, he is entitled to a fair trial within a reasonable time. I do not, however, think it follows that, he is entitled to immediate discharge as a matter of right. If the delay is without reasonable explanation, the Court may enforce the accused's right by compelling the trial to commence or dismiss the case in its discretion. However, in all cases, s 552 of the *Criminal Code* should be used as a procedure for the enforcement of *Constitution* s 37(3) breaches. Section 37(3) without question, provides a safeguard for accuseds against undue delays of their trials. That right to a speedy trial is itself a substantive ground for an application to be brought to trial under s 552 of the *Criminal Code* per Los J in *Jeffrey Balakau v The State* (OS 401/95)."[8]

See ss 521-552 of the *Criminal Code*, ss 155 and 163-166 of the *Constitution*, and the *National Court Act* 1975. See s 539 of the *Criminal Code* regarding *nolle prosequis*.

Where the trial of an accused has been interrupted and delayed by the National Court's reservation of questions of law pursuant to [old] s 20 of the *Supreme Court Act*, the Supreme Court may protect an accused's right to a speedy trial under s 37(3) of the *Constitution* by directing the National Court (under s 57 of the *Constitution*) to have the trial completed forthwith. The accused is entitled to have his or her name cleared, just as the prosecution is entitled to know whether its charge has been sustained: *Supreme Court Reference No 3 of 1979: The State v John Rumet Kaputin* [1979] PNGLR 532 at 535.

In *The State v Tom Watinga* [1994] PNGLR 255, an information was withdrawn under s 37(3) due to an unreasonable delay in prosecution. The court held that charging the defendant with the same offence five months later was an abuse of process:

> "In my view, there is no question that the Court has an inherent jurisdiction to strike out a subsequent information ... founded on the same facts as those on which a previous information is based or forming or being part of a series of offences based on the one information. There is also no question that this Court has the jurisdiction to prevent any abuse of its process, where a litigant uses the court process in an improper way".[9]

---

[8] *The State v Jeffrey Balakau* (1996) N1528 (Batari AJ).
[9] *The State v Tom Watinga* [1994] PNGLR 255 at 260-261 (Sawong AJ).

(4) A person charged with an offence-

(a) shall be presumed innocent until proved guilty according to law, but a law may place upon a person charged with an offence the burden of proving particular facts which are, or would be, peculiarly within his knowledge; and

(b) shall be informed promptly in a language which he understands, and in detail, of the nature of the offence with which he is charged; and

(c) shall be given adequate time and facilities for the preparation of his defence; and

(d) shall be permitted to have without payment the assistance of an interpreter if he cannot understand or speak the language used at the trial of the charge; and

(e) shall be permitted to defend himself before the court in person or, at his own expense, by a legal representative of his own choice, or if he is a person entitled to legal aid, by the Public Solicitor or another legal representative assigned to him in accordance with law; and

(f) shall be afforded facilities to examine in person or by his legal representative the witnesses called before the court by the prosecution, and to obtain the attendance and carry out the examination of witnesses and to testify before the court on his own behalf, on the same conditions as those applying to witnesses called by the prosecution.

[Subs (4)(a) am *Constitutional Amendment No 13 – Protection of the Law*. Note that some copies of the amendment mistakenly refer to "Section 73" of the *Constitution*.]

The words "according to law" in s 37(4)(a) encompass all the laws of Papua New Guinea as set out in s 9 of the *Constitution*, including the underlying law. It is a principle of the underlying law that the presumption of innocence continues until a court is satisfied beyond reasonable doubt of the guilt of the accused: *The State v John Koe* [1976] PNGLR 562. The proviso to s 37(4)(a) is taken to apply only to the essential ingredients or elements of the offence as they are defined and required to be proved according to law. Where the defence provided for introduces new matter altogether unrelated to the elements of the offence, proof of which will enable the defendant to avoid a finding of guilt, the provision of such a defence does not affect the presumption of innocence having regard to what the prosecution is required to prove in order to establish the offence as defined. Here the offence of passing valueless cheques under s 22A of the *Police Offences Act* (Papua) 1912 (now repealed) contains a number of elements, but an intent to defraud is not among them. The defence provided for, namely establishing a lack of intention to defraud, introduces a new ingredient which is not in contravention of the *Constitution*: *Supreme Court Reference No 1 of 1980; Re s 22A(b) Police Offences Act; Biyang v Liri Haro* [1981] PNGLR 28 (Miles J, with Andrew J concurring).

The history of s 37(4)(a) was traced (through the *Human Rights Act* 1971, s 16(3)(a) and the Final Report of the Constitutional Planning Committee Pt I at p 5/1/24) by Saldanha J in *Constitutional Reference No 3 of 1978* [1978] PNGLR 421 at 428.

As a result of s 37(4)(a), the law in Papua New Guinea relating to the proof of guilt in criminal cases is that the onus is on the prosecution to prove each element of the offence charged beyond reasonable doubt, subject to the following exceptions:

(a) in the case of a defence of insanity, where there is a presumption of sound mind until the contrary is proved;

(b) where an enactment prohibits the doing of an act save in specified circumstances, or by persons of specified classes, or with special qualification or with the licence or persuasion of specified authorities, then once the prosecutor has proved beyond reasonable doubt the doing of the act, the burden is on the persons charged to bring themselves within the exception or proviso, that is, to prove that they were entitled to do the prohibited act, independently of whether the facts they must prove to do so are, or would with the exercise of reasonable care be, peculiarly within their knowledge; and

(c) in the case of an enactment which places upon the persons charged the burden of proving particular facts which are, or would with the exercise of reasonable care be, peculiarly within their knowledge: *Supreme Court Reference No 1 of 1980; Re s 22A(b) Police Offences Act; Biyang v Liri Haro* [1981] PNGLR 28.

The intention of the framers of the *Constitution* must have been, subject to the proviso contained in this section, to adopt the concept of the so-called presumption of innocence as it stood in the common law of England at the time of the coming into force of the *Constitution*. The general rule is that in criminal cases it is for the prosecution to prove, and to prove beyond reasonable doubt, every element of the alleged offence: see *Woolmington v DPP* [1935] AC 462 at 483. The rule applies equally to negative elements as well (for example, absence of consent in rape cases), but is subject to exceptions in the case of the insanity defence, any statutory exception, and exceptions relating to matters peculiarly within the knowledge of the accused: *R v Edwards* [1974] 2 All ER 1085. Section 37(4)(a) was thus designed implicitly to accommodate and also expressly to accommodate certain shifts in the onus of proof of factual ingredients of offences, or putting it somewhat differently, in the persuasive proof of ultimate facts. It was not the intention or effect of the proviso to cut down the law or radically alter the law then being adopted, except that the general rule as expressed in *Woolmington v DPP* is no longer subject to "any statutory exception", but only to such statutory exceptions as the *Constitution* allows: *Supreme Court Reference No 1 of 1980; Re s 22A(b) Police Offences Act; Biyang v Liri Haro* [1981] PNGLR 28 (Greville-Smith J).

Refusing to make admissions to the police is not an aggravating circumstance for the purposes of sentencing. It amounts to no more than an accused standing on rights: *The State v Minambkali Asu, Lakap Erapae and John Koipui* (1980) N236.

For a discussion on the international recognition of the presumption of innocence, see the judgment of Miles J in *Supreme Court Reference No 1 of 1980* [1981] PNGLR 28.

Re s 37(4)(a) and (10), see *The State v Lasebose Kuriday* (1981) N300.

The section places on the prosecution the burden of proving the guilt of the person charged "according to law". The phrase "according to law" must be interpreted to mean existing relevant laws. The provisions must therefore be read along with Ch 5 of the *Criminal Code*, the operation of which excludes s 14(2) of the *Summary Offences Act*. Therefore, s 14(2) of the *Summary Offences Act* is not inconsistent with s 37(4)(a) of the *Constitution*. In any case, s 14(2) is not a law which creates an offence of which a person charged is presumed innocent until proved guilty according to law: *Supreme Court Reference No 2 of 1980* [1981] PNGLR 50.

Trial on separate indictments of itself is not necessarily a material irregularity that infringes constitutional rights under s 37(4): *The State v Leo Nimo* [1980] PNGLR 129.

Section 37(4)(d) makes it mandatory that every person charged shall have the assistance of an interpreter if that person cannot understand or speak the language used at the trial of the charge. Although the trial does not begin until the accused pleads to the charge, the jeopardy begins from the day of arrest: *The State v Lakio Tambai* (1980) N235.

The right of an accused to choose counsel under s 37(4)(e) cannot be an absolute right. For example, the right cannot extend to a right to have counsel who is employed as a the State Prosecutor to defend the accused, or the Public Solicitor's Office if the accused is not entitled to legal aid, or a particular officer of the Public Solicitor's Office, or a counsel who has by acceptance of a prior brief become engaged so as to be unavailable at the time of the trial, or who, as in this case, is disqualified on ethical grounds. These exceptions are not exhaustive. The accused's choice is subject to all proper exceptions. One thing that the right conferred by s 37(4)(e) does is to prevent accused persons being assigned, against their will by the State, a defence counsel whom they did not want: *Supreme Court Reference No 3 of 1980; Re Joseph Mavuk* [1980] PNGLR 507.

The word "peculiarly" does not mean "solely" or "exclusively". It has connotations of "especially" or "in the ordinary course of things likely to be". In this sense, although a person may be confused about their own psychological processes and may on a mistaken view of the law believe that they are acting honestly, ultimately the question of fact whether they have an intent to defraud is something about which they above all others have a special knowledge. In this sense, the presence or absence of a lack of intent to defraud as a question of fact is one which is peculiarly within the knowledge of the person charged: *Supreme Court Reference No 1 of 1980* [1981] PNGLR 28 (Miles J, with Andrew J agreeing).

In *Supreme Court Reference No 3 of 1978; Inter-Group Fighting Act 1977* [1978] PNGLR 421, it was held that s 11 of the *Inter-Group Fighting Act* is unconstitutional as s 11(3) provides that a person charged with an offence against the section is guilty of that offence unless they prove, to the satisfaction of the court, that they did not take part in the actual fighting. The section was contrary to the presumption of innocence.

See ss 521, 523, 552, 556, 560, 563 and 566-573 of the *Criminal Code* and ss 102, 107, 128 and 129 of the *District Courts Act*.

(5) Except with his own consent, the trial shall not take place in his absence unless he so conducts himself as to render the continuance of the proceedings in his presence impracticable and the court orders him to be removed and the trial to proceed in his absence, but provision may be made by law for a charge that a person has committed an offence the maximum penalty for which does not include imprisonment, (except in default of payment of a fine), to be heard summarily in his absence if it is established that he has been duly served with a summons in respect of the alleged offence.

To the extent that s 125 of the *District Courts Act* [prior to amendment, s 131 of the *District Courts Act*] enables an information of a simple offence punishable by imprisonment to be heard in the absence of the defendant, it is therefore a provision which goes beyond s 37(5) of the *Constitution*, and is inconsistent with it. However, the severability clause found in s 10 of the *Constitution* does save the section in a reduced form, allowing its continued application to simple offences (any offence punishable on summary conviction) punishable otherwise than by imprisonment (except in default of payment of a fine): *Supreme Court Reference No 1 of 1976(P); Peter Rakatani v South Pacific Brewery Ltd* [1976] PNGLR 537 (Frost CJ and Kearney J).

Section 37(5) should be read together with s 37(14) which adopts a standard of trials being heard within four months of committal. It was stated in *The State v Peter Painke (No2)* [1977] PNGLR 141:

> "It seems to me manifestly clear that it is desirable not only in order to achieve the National Goals and Directives, but also to secure the basic rights to individuals, that certain classes of charges involving possible imprisonment, should be capable of being heard summarily in the absence of the defendant if he consents – thus avoiding his arrest and compulsory attendances in court – even though potentially [although unlikely] imprisonment could result ... [the Supreme] Court should be prepared and is empowered to not only eliminate a phrase from an Act if by so doing constitutional validity could be secured with what it construed as Parliament's intention; but also to add or change a phrase with the intent of construing (translating) an Act so that it is valid and still expressing the clear Parliamentary intent – 'legislating' though Constitutional experts of other lands might consider this process to be."

Thus, this section should be read so as to allow ex parte proceedings, even where there is a possibility of imprisonment, upon the consent of the defendant: *Supreme Court Reference No 1 of 1976(P); Peter Rakatani v South Pacific Brewery Ltd* [1976] PNGLR 537 (Prentice DCJ, dissenting).

In *Thomas Kavali v Thomas Hoihoi* [1986] PNGLR 329, on the issue of whether the right of a person charged to be present at their trial can be waived, Kidu CJ, Woods and Barnett JJ held as follows:

- Section 37(5) of the *Constitution* entrenches the right of the person charged with an offence to be present at his trial. As it is the duty of the courts zealously to guard the rights entrenched in the *Constitution*, the courts must ensure, before such a right is denied, that the circumstances of the particular person come within the exceptions (if any) specifically outlined in the *Constitution*.
- The right guaranteed by s 37(5) of the *Constitution* applies in respect of all offences subject only to the exceptions provided for in the section itself.
- For the right guaranteed by s 37(5) of the *Constitution* to be waived by the person charged requires special circumstances from which the court must be satisfied that the person charged elects to be absent, and absents himself through caprice, malice or for the purposes of embarrassing the trial: *R v Jones (No 2)* (1972) 56 Cr App R 413 at 428 and 433 followed.

In *The State v Arey Watu* [1992] PNGLR 475, Doherty J (at 478-479) interpreted s 37(5) as follows:

> "[Section] 37(5) envisages 2 situations where a trial may proceed in the absence of a defendant:
>
> (1) where he consents to the proceeding in his absence and;
>
> (2) where his conduct within the court is such that the Court proceedings become impracticable and, as a result, the Court orders that proceedings continue without him.... Woods J in *Thomas Kavali v Thomas Hoihoi* [1986] PNGLR 329 at 337 said, 'I am satisfied that

> consent can be implied by actions as well as by express consent, however such actions must be capable of unambiguous interpretation.' Thus, one must look at the circumstances surrounding the failure to appear and only if those circumstances show deliberate intention not to appear in Court can consent be implied. Woods J gives the example of the person who walks out of the hearing with no explanation, effectively saying, 'I do not care if you carry on'. The Supreme Court suggested a person who has absconded shows an intention not to appear and may, thereby, imply consent to the hearing proceeding in his absence.... I consider escaping shows a definite decision to be absent voluntarily."

(6) Nothing in Subsection (4)(f) invalidates a law which imposes reasonable conditions that must be satisfied if witnesses called to testify on behalf of a person charged with an offence are to be paid their expenses out of public funds.

(7) No person shall be convicted of an offence on account of any act that did not, at the time when it took place, constitute an offence, and no penalty shall be imposed for an offence that is more severe in degree or description than the maximum penalty that might have been imposed for the offence at the time when it was committed.

See ss 2 and 11 of the *Criminal Code* and s 20 of the *District Courts Act*.

(8) No person who shows that he has been tried by a competent court for an offence and has been convicted or acquitted shall again be tried for that offence or for any other offence of which he could have been convicted at the trial for that offence, except upon the order of a superior court made in the course of appeal or review proceedings relating to the conviction or acquittal.

> "[Section] 560(2)(e) and s 564 of the *Criminal Code* and s162(2) of the *District Courts Act* recognize and re-enforce the accused's right under s 37(8) of the *Constitution*."[10]

See ss 16, 17, 557 and 560 of the *Criminal Code*.

(9) No person shall be tried for an offence for which he has been pardoned.

See s 560(f) of the *Criminal Code*.

(10) No person shall be compelled in the trial of an offence to be a witness against himself.

It is the privilege of a witness to decline to answer questions because those answers might tend to incriminate her or him. This privilege must be claimed by the witness, although the judge will often warn a witness of their rights. It must be a bona fide claim by the witness for self-protection and not to assist others, and it appears the claim will not be accepted as bona fide if the witness has already by other admissions been made liable to prosecution for the offence: *R v B* (1969) N561.

See also *R v Wendo* [1963] PNGLR 217 at 320-321 and *R v Simbene Dandemb* [1969-1970] PNGLR 207.

---

[10] *The State v John Nugints* [1994] PNGLR 493 at 497 (Injia AJ).

The court may not impute guilt from silence. However, if an accused person decides to remain silent and not call witnesses, the court is entitled to proceed to verdict on the basis of prosecution evidence: *Tabo Sipo v Mukara Meli* (1980) N240.

For a discussion of the practical application of an assertion of the right to remain silent, see *Paulus Pawa v The State* [1981] PNGLR 498.

For a discussion of the effect of the failure of a judge or magistrate to advise a defendant of the right to remain silent during the proceedings, see *Koi Konom v Nelson Watai* (1981) N297(M) under s 572 of the *Criminal Code*.

See s 572 of the *Criminal Code* regarding evidence in defence. See s 562 regarding standing mute upon being called to plead.

(11) A determination of the existence or extent of a civil right or obligation shall not be made except by an independent and impartial court or other authority prescribed by law or agreed upon by the parties, and proceedings for such a determination shall be fairly heard within a reasonable time.

(12) Except with the agreement of the parties, or by order of the court in the interests of national security, proceedings in any jurisdiction of a court and proceedings for the determination of the existence or extent of any civil right or obligation before any other authority, including the announcement of the decision of the court or other authority, shall be held in public.

(13) Nothing in Subsection (12) prevents a court or other authority from excluding from the hearing of the proceedings before it persons, other than the parties and their legal representatives, to such an extent as the court or other authority-

(a) is by law empowered to do and considers necessary or expedient in the interests of public welfare or in circumstances where publicity would prejudice the interests of justice, the welfare of persons under voting age or the protection of the private lives of persons concerned in the proceedings; or

(b) is by law empowered or required to do in the interests of defence, public safety or public order.

See s 566 of the *Criminal Code*.

(14) In the event that the trial of a person is not commenced within four months of the date on which he was committed for trial, a detailed report concerning the case shall be made by the Chief Justice to the Minister responsible for the National Legal Administration.

See note on *The State v Peter Painke (No2)* [1977] PNGLR 141 under s 37(3).

(15) Every person convicted of an offence is entitled to have his conviction and sentence reviewed by a higher court or tribunal according to law.

Section 27 of the *Supreme Court Act* does not prohibit appeals; it merely regulates the right of appeal. Section 37(15) of the *Constitution* subjects this right to a requirement that it be according to law; therefore a law imposing a time limit on appeals is not unconstitutional but is a "law" within the phrase "according to law": *Avia Aihi v The State (No 1)* [1981] PNGLR 81.

There is no distinction between the words "review" in this subsection and "appeal" in s 37(16): *Avia Aihi v The State (No 1)* [1981] PNGLR 81.

(16) No person shall be deprived by law of a right of appeal against his conviction or sentence by any court that existed at the time of the conviction or sentence, as the case may be.

Section 30 of the *Corrective Institutions Act* was unconstitutional where it provided that there was no appeal from a finding or extension of sentence from a visiting justice or magistrate in relation to corrective institution and police lock-up offences: *In the Matter of a Special Reference under s 19 of the Constitution* [1978] PNGLR 404.

See ss 225-226 of the *District Courts Act* and s 4 of the *Supreme Court Act*.

(17) All persons deprived of their liberty shall be treated with humanity and with respect for the inherent dignity of the human person.

Sections 36(1), 37(17) and 41(1) of the *Constitution* require that treatment in prison shall not be harsh, oppressive, cruel or inhuman. If there is a prison law which is harsh or oppressive, a prisoner can have the law declared unconstitutional under these sections as an infringement of fundamental rights. Similarly, if a particular treatment which a prisoner receives in prison is harsh or oppressive then, even though it is not covered by a prison law, that treatment or practice can be stopped as an infringement of fundamental rights: *Tom Amaiu v Commissioner of Corrective Institutions and the State* [1983] PNGLR 87.

See *Heni Pauta and Kenneth Susuve v Commissioner for Corrective Institutions and his Servants and Agents* [1982] PNGLR 7, annotated under s 57(3) below.

See ss 57-58 of the *Constitution* regarding remedies for breaches of fundamental rights.

(18) Accused persons shall be segregated from convicted persons and shall be subject to separate treatment appropriate to their status as unconvicted persons.

See *Corrective Institution Regulations*, regs 104-108.

(19) Persons under voting age who are in custody in connection with an offence or alleged offence shall be separated from other persons in custody and be accorded treatment appropriate to their age.

For sentencing considerations relevant to youthful offenders, see cases discussed under s 596 of the *Criminal Code*, especially *Acting Public Prosecutor v Clement Maki & Tom Kasen* (1981) SC205.

See *Heni Pauta and Kenneth Susuve v Commissioner for Corrective Institutions and his Servants and Agents* [1982] PNGLR 7, annotated under s 57(3) below.

See *Corrective Institution Regulations*, regs 104-108.

(20) An offender shall not be transferred to an area away from that in which his relatives reside except for reasons of security or other good cause and, if such a transfer is made, the reason for so doing shall be endorsed on the file of the offender.

(21) Nothing in this section-

(a) derogates Division IIIA (principles of natural justice); or

(b) affects the powers and procedures of village courts.

(22) Notwithstanding Subsection 21(b) the powers and procedures of village courts shall be exercised in accordance with the principles of natural justice.

Subdivision C – Qualified Rights

General

38. General qualifications on qualified rights.

(1) For the purposes of this Subdivision, a law that complies with the requirements of this section is a law that is made and certified in accordance with Subsection (2), and that-

(a) regulates or restricts the exercise of a right or freedom referred to in this Subdivision to the extent that the regulation or restriction is necessary-

(i) taking account of the National Goals and Directive Principles and the Basic Social Obligations, for the purpose of giving effect to the public interest in-

(A) defence; or

(B) public safety; or

(C) public order; or

(D) public welfare; or

(E) public health (including animal and plant health); or

(F) the protection of children and persons under disability (whether legal or practical); or

(G) the development of under-privileged or less advanced groups or areas; or

(ii) in order to protect the exercise of the rights and freedoms of others; or

(b) makes reasonable provision for cases where the exercise of one such right may conflict with the exercise of another, to the extent that the law reasonably justifiable in a democratic society having a proper respect for the rights and dignity of mankind.

(2) For the purposes of Subsection (1), a law must-

(a) be expressed to be a law that is made for that purpose; and

(b) specify the right or freedom that it regulates or restricts; and

(c) be made, and certified by the Speaker in his certificate under Section 110 (*certification as to making of laws*) to have been made, by an absolute majority.

(3) The burden of showing that a law is a law that complies with the requirements of Subsection (1) is on the party relying on its validity.

In *Supreme Court Reference No 2 of 1982 (No1); Re the Organic Law on National Elections (Amendment) Act 1981* [1982] PNGLR 214, the issue before the court was whether an amendment to the *Organic Law National Elections Act*, which required a candidate for election to Parliament to validate a nomination with a K1,000 deposit, was constitutional. It was argued, inter alia, that the law was not "reasonably justifiable for the purpose in a democratic society". Kapi J (at 235-236) considered the meaning of this phrase:

"It is extremely difficult to give any proper interpretation of the phrase. The *Constitution* itself avoided any definition of it. The only assistance the *Constitution* can offer is s 39(3) of the *Constitution*, which sets out some of the materials to which the court may have regard in deciding whether a law or thing is reasonably justifiable in a democratic society ... What is the standard of the reasonableness to be applied? The courts in India have considered this question. The *Constitution of India* used the words 'reasonable restrictions'. In the case of *The State of Madras v VG Row AIR* (1952) SC196 at 200, Patanjali Sastri CJ said:

> 'It is important in this context to bear in mind the test of reasonableness, wherever prescribed, should be applied to each individual statute impugned and no abstract standard, or general pattern, or reasonableness, can be laid down as applicable to all cases. The nature of the right alleged to have been infringed, the underlying purpose of the restrictions imposed, the extent and urgency of the evil sought to be remedied thereby, the disproportion of the imposition, the prevailing conditions at the time, should all enter into the judicial verdict. In evaluating such elusive factors and forming their own conception of what is reasonable in all circumstances of a given case, it is inevitable that the social philosophy and the scale of values of the judges participating in the decisions should play an important part, and the limit to their interference to the legislative judgment in such cases can only be dictated by their sense of responsibility and self restraint and the sobering reflection that the *Constitution* is meant not only for people of their way of thinking but for all, and that the majority of the elected representatives of the people have in authorisation the imposition of the restrictions considered by them to be reasonable.'

I would with respect adopt this. I note that this course has also been suggested by Donald Chalmers '*Human Rights and What is Reasonably Justifiable in a Democratic Society*' (1975) MLJ. (Vol 3, No 1) at 92. I find this approach is consistent with the approach given by the High Court of Uganda in *Uganda v Commissioner of Prisons; Ex parte Marobu* (1966) EALR 514."[11]

On the onus of proof under this section, Kapi J (at 238-239) held that:

"It would be sufficient for the party who alleges that a law is unconstitutional merely to prove that his right is infringed. He is only required to show a prima facie case. Where this is shown, then the onus is on the party who relies on the validity of the law to prove that it is within the limitation provided by the *Constitution* ... The onus is on the State to prove that the amendment Act is a law that is 'reasonably justifiable for the purpose in a democratic society that has regard for the rights and dignity of mankind'. In this regard, absolutely no materials have been put up by the State or the Parliament for the imposition of K1,000. I am left with the impression that the imposition of K1,000 has no regard for the level of income by the citizens of this country."[12]

See also *James Koimo v The State* [1995] PNGLR 535 on the formulation of ad hoc rules under the *Constitution* and the onus and standard of proof for violation of constitutional rights by policemen.

---

[11] *Supreme Court Reference No 2 of 1982* [1982] PNGLR 214.

[12] *Supreme Court Reference No 2 of 1982* [1982] PNGLR 214.

39. "Reasonably justifiable in a democratic society", etc.

(1) The question, whether a law or act is reasonably justifiable in a democratic society having a proper regard for the rights and dignity of mankind, is to be determined in the light of the circumstances obtaining at the time when the decision on the question is made.

(2) A law shall not be declared not to be reasonably justifiable in a society having a proper regard for the rights and dignity of mankind except by the Supreme Court or the National Court, or any other court prescribed for the purpose by or under an Act of the Parliament, and unless the court is satisfied that the law was never so justifiable such a declaration operates as a repeal of the law as at the date of the declaration.

(3) For the purposes of determining 'whether or not any law, matter or things is reasonably justified in a democratic society that has a proper regard for the rights and dignity of mankind', a court may have regard to

(a) the provisions of this Constitution generally, and especially the National Goals and Directive Principles and the Basic Social Obligations; and

(b) the Charter of the United Nations; and

(c) the Universal Declaration of Human Rights and any other declaration, recommendation or decision of the General Assembly of the United Nations concerning human rights and fundamental freedoms; and

(d) the European Convention for the Protection of Human Rights and Fundamental Freedoms and the Protocols thereto, and any other international conventions, agreements or declarations concerning human rights and fundamental freedoms; and

(e) judgements, reports and opinions of the International Court of Justice, the European Commission of Human Rights, the European Court of Human Rights and other international courts and tribunals dealing with human rights and fundamental freedoms; and

(f) previous laws, practices and judicial decisions and opinions in the country; and

(g) laws, practices and judicial decisions and opinions in other countries; and

(h) the Final Reports of the pre-Independence Constitutional Planning Committee dated 13 August 1974 and presented to the pre-Independence House of Assembly on 16 August 1974, as affected by decisions of the House on the report and by decisions of the Constituent Assembly on the draft of this Constitution; and

(i) declarations by the International Commission of Jurists and other similar organizations; and

(j) any other material that the court considers relevant.

See Chalmers, "*Human Rights and What is Reasonably Justifiable in a Democratic Society*" (1975) 2 MLJ 1 at 92-102.

The "proper regard" which characterises such a society is to be found by an examination of the *Constitution*. The other matters listed in s 39(3), however, may also be regarded: *Supreme Court Reference No 2 of 1982, The Organic Law* [1982] PNGLR 214 at 230 (Kearney DCJ).

40. Validity of emergency laws.

Nothing in this Part invalidates an emergency law as defined in Part X (emergency powers), but nevertheless so far as is consistent with their purposes and terms all such laws shall be interpreted and applied so as not to affect or derogate a right or freedom referred to in this Division to an extent that is more than is reasonably necessary to deal with the emergency concerned and matters arising out of it, but only so far as is reasonably justifiable in a democratic society having a proper regard for the rights and dignity of mankind.

41. Proscribed acts.

(1) Notwithstanding anything to the contrary in any other provision of any law, any act that is done under a valid law but in the particular case-

(a) is harsh or oppressive; or

(b) is not warranted by, or is disproportionate to, the requirements of the particular circumstances or of the particular case; or

(c) is otherwise not, in the particular circumstances, reasonably justifiable in a democratic society having a proper regard for the rights and dignity of mankind, is an unlawful act.

(2) The burden of showing that Subsection (1)(a), (b) or (c) applies in respect of an act is on the party alleging it, and may be discharged on the balance of probabilities.

(3) Nothing in this section affects the operation of any other law under which an act may be held to be unlawful or invalid.

Sections 36(1), 37(17) and 41(1) of the *Constitution* require that treatment in prison shall not be harsh, oppressive, cruel or inhuman. If there is a prison law which is harsh or oppressive, a prisoner can have the law declared unconstitutional under these sections as an infringement of fundamental rights. Similarly, if a particular treatment which a prisoner receives in prison is harsh or oppressive then, even though it is not covered by a prison law, that treatment or practice can be stopped as an infringement of fundamental rights: *Tom Amaiu v Commissioner of Corrective Institutions and the State* [1983] PNGLR 87.

See *Heni Pauta and Kenneth Susuve v Commissioner for Corrective Institutions and his Servants and Agents* [1982] PNGLR 7, annotated under s 57(3) below.

See ss 57-58 below, regarding remedies for breaches of fundamental rights.

Rights of All Persons

42. Liberty of the person

(1) No person shall be deprived of his personal liberty except-

(a) in consequence of his unfitness to plead to a criminal charge; or

Even if cautions were administered, unless they were gone over very carefully and the accused were invited to say in their own words what they understood by the cautions, it would be a mumble of words to most Papua New Guinean accused: *The State v Lakio Tambai* (1980) N235.

See s 557 of the *Criminal Code*.

> (b) in the execution of the sentence or order of a court in respect of an offence of which he has been found guilty, or in the execution of the order of a court of record punishing him for contempt of itself or another court or tribunal; or

See s 37(2) of the *Constitution*.

> (c) by reason of his failure to comply with the order of a court made to secure the fulfilment of an obligation (other than a contractual obligation) imposed upon him by law; or

In *Agua Bepi v Aiya Simon* [1986] PNGLR 233, orders for imprisonment due to the failure of the appellant's relatives to repay the bride price to her husband were unconstitutional as they deprived the appellant of her liberty in order to secure fulfilment of a contractual obligation in contravention of s 42(1)(c) of the *Constitution*.

> (d) upon reasonable suspicion of his having committed, or being about to commit, an offence; or

Under s 42 there are exceptions where the liberty of a person may be deprived. Where an accused is arrested upon reasonable suspicion of having committed an offence, and is held in custody for trial, the accused has been held in accordance with the exception set out under s 42(l)(d). Therefore, subsequent acquittal does not entitle the accused to compensation under s 58, for there was no unconstitutional infringement of a right or freedom: *The State v Wic Kor* [1983] PNGLR 24.

> (e) for the purpose of bringing him before a court in execution of the order of a court; or
>
> (f) for the purpose of preventing the introduction or spread of a disease or suspected disease, whether of humans, animals or plants, or for normal purposes of quarantine; or
>
> (g) for the purpose of preventing the unlawful entry of a person into Papua New Guinea, or for the purpose of effecting the expulsion, extradition or other lawful removal of a person from Papua New Guinea, or the taking of proceedings for any of those purposes; or

The *Constitution* makes distinction between the imposition of a sentence and other forms of deprivation of liberty. Detention for the purposes of deportation under s 14 of the *Migration Act* 1978 is not an imposition of penalty or imprisonment which must be imposed by a body within the National Judicial System: s 159(3)(a). Section 159, therefore, has no application and a Minister's detention is lawful: *Virgil Dewitt Perryman and Victoria F Perryman v Minister for Foreign Affairs and Trade* [1982] PNGLR 339.

(h) in the case of a person who is, or is reasonably suspected of being of unsound mind or addicted to drugs or alcohol, or a vagrant, for the purposes of-

(i) his care or treatment or the protection of the community, under an order of a court; or

(ii) taking prompt legal proceedings to obtain an order of a court of a type referred to in subparagraph (i).

(i) in the case of a person who has not attained the age of 18 years, for the purpose of his education or welfare under the order of a court or with the consent of his guardian.

[Subs (1)(h) subst *Constitutional Amendment No 11 – Liberty of the Person*; subs (1)(i) insrt *Constitutional Amendment No 11 – Liberty of the Person*.]

"The intention of this section is to allow imprisonment in an attempt to ensure the fulfilment of obligations, the occasion for which might or might not arise at some future time, and where fulfilment might occur in any event ... the words 'secure the fulfilment of an obligation' refer to an obligation where the occasion for fulfilment has arisen and where fulfilment in relation to that occasion is still possible, but has not yet occurred."[13]

"It is highly essential to emphasise the constitutional dictate contained in s 42(1) – that a person's personal liberty is guaranteed and may not be taken away unless one of the exceptions therein allows it. The exceptions enumerated under s 42(1) all relate to total deprivation of a person's liberty as distinct from temporary restriction of a person's freedom of movement. The word 'deprive' is defined in the *Shorter Oxford Dictionary* as meaning 'to divest, bereave, to dispossess, to take away, to remove' – ie in my view total denial or loss. So s 42(1) guarantees the right not to be denied totally of ones personal liberty unless such denial or loss is allowed by one of the exceptions."[14]

As to the remedies available for suppressing evidence obtained in violation of these provisions, see *John Alex v Martin Golu* [1983] PNGLR 117, discussed under s 57 of the *Constitution* below.

See *Criminal Code*, s 596; *Local Courts Act* 1963, s 19; and *District Courts Act* 1963, s 28.

(2) A person who is arrested or detained-

(a) shall be informed promptly, in a language that he understands, of the reasons for his arrest or detention and of any charge against him; and

(b) shall be permitted whenever practicable to communicate without delay and in private with a member of his family or a personal friend, and with a lawyer of his choice (including the Public Solicitor if he is entitled to legal aid); and

(c) shall be given adequate opportunity to give instructions to a lawyer of his choice in the place in which he is detained,

[13] *Supreme Court Reference No 1 of 1981; Re Inter-Group Fighting Act 1977* [1981] PNGLR 151 (Kidu CJ, Greville-Smith and Andrew JJ).

[14] *The State v Songke Mai and Gai Avi* [1988] PNGLR 56 at 59 (Kidu CJ).

and shall be informed immediately on his arrest of his rights under this subsection.

[Subs (2) am *Constitutional Amendment No 11 – Liberty of the Person*]

The section confers rights only on persons arrested or detained. It does not deal with the situation in which a person not under restraint volunteers a statement to a police officer. However, if on a trial the admissibility is raised of an admission obtained in breach of s 42(2), the court, upon its own initiative or on the application of the accused, has the power in the usual way or under s 57(3) to determine the question whether a protective order is required to be made that the admission be excluded: *Constitutional Reference No 1 of 1977* [1977] PNGLR 362.

In *The State v Konts Kot* [1987] N623 King AJ stated that "[s]ection 42 is a beneficial provision and should be construed liberally in favour of the citizen". In that case, the accused was brought to the police station the day before interview and kept overnight in the cells. He was not advised of his constitutional rights until the end of the interview. King AJ held that this was a clear breach of s 42(2) and rejected the record of interview.

The accused carries the onus of showing a constitutional violation on the balance of probabilities: *The State v Kevin Evertius and Thomas Kindi* [1985] PNGLR 109 (Pratt J).

In *The State v Karara Peter* (1983) N438(M) the accused made admissions and then was formally cautioned. Kidu CJ held:

> "The whole process makes a mockery of s 42 of the *Constitution* and the Judges' Rules (become) meaningless and if I allow the record of interview into evidence I would be condoning the flouting of these well-established Rules and the guarantee of rights by the *Constitution* of Papua New Guinea."

A person charged, in addition to being told of the right to see a lawyer, should be given a proper chance to decide whether to exercise this right and a real opportunity to exercise it in practice. If such an opportunity is not extended the confessional material may be regarded as unfairly obtained, depending on the circumstances, and may be excluded: *Maxwell Arthur Schliebs v H Singh* [1981] PNGLR 364, cited with approval by Brunton AJ in *The State v John Koga Ivoro* (1989) N722.

Objection to a confession on the grounds that only some of the questions and answers were recorded nor some of them asked does not go to the question of voluntariness or admissibility. The admissibility of a confession is on the balance of probabilities. Section 42(2) of the *Constitution* envisages that something more practical and useful than a mere statement of rights may be called for to give effect to the section. In *The State v Joseph Maino* [1977] PNGLR 216 the record of interview was rejected on the lack of adequate provision of constitutional rights and the failure to caution in the exercise of discretion.

In the case of *The State v Allan Woila* [1978] PNGLR 99 Kearney J took the view that the test for admissibility of a confession is proof beyond reasonable doubt.

Section 42(2) of the *Constitution* confers rights but it does not make any provision in relation to the consequences which follow if those rights were not wholly or partly afforded to a person to whom the section applies. Section 23(3) of the *Constitution* would permit the National Court to make an order where there has been a breach of s 42(2). If it were shown that there had been a serious or significant breach of the rights conferred by s 42(2), or if it were not shown that those rights had been afforded and explained, then apart from any other order the judge might make, the judge would be entitled in the exercise of their discretion to exclude a confession obtained after such breaches or until it is shown that those rights were afforded and explained: *The State v Kwambol Embogol* (1977) N91.

In *The State v Paro Wampa* [1987] PNGLR 120, Kapi DCJ held that there had been a breach of s 42(2) where a person was not informed of his rights under s 42(2) until three weeks after he was detained when a record of interview was about to be made, and at that point he was informed that he had the right to see a relative or friend "now or later". Kapi DCJ set out principles to be followed in the application of s 42(2):

1. A person is "arrested" when charged with an offence and taken into custody.
2. A person is "detained" when taken into police custody in connection with an offence but has not yet been charged with an offence.
3. A person loses "liberty" when either arrested or detained.
4. The need to inform persons arrested or detained of their rights under the section arises at the point when they lose their liberty: it is not related to the making of a record of interview.
5. The right to "communicate without delay" must be given at the same time as the persons arrested or detained are informed of their rights under the section.
6. The right of persons arrested or detained to "communicate" may be exercised or waived but only at the time it is to be given: an offer to so communicate at a later time misstates the nature of the right.
7. It is the duty of the police to permit the persons arrested or detained who exercises their right to communicate, to do so, "wherever practicable".

The principle that police detention short of arrest is illegal should not be confused with those cases where the record of interview is conducted at the same time as the arrest is made, or more accurately a person writes or makes a statement and as a result the police decide to make an arrest: *The State v John Koga Ivoro* (1989) N772 (Brunton AJ).

Where at the time of the alleged offence the accused was an escapee from lawful custody, it was the obligation of the police, upon his recapture, to have a record of interview with him promptly about the alleged fresh offence. As such, a delay of six weeks before a record of interview was taken in relation to the fresh offence amounted to a breach of s 42(2). The fact that the accused was going to be in custody in any case for two reasons; serving his original sentence and serving a further sentence for escaping, did not abolish or even suspend indefinitely his rights under s 42(2). Section 42(2) is a beneficial provision for the protection of the individual and it must apply to a person already in custody. Although this restriction does not emerge in plain terms from the words of s 42(2), the provision must have practical effect: "people are detained for particular reasons, and I think the rights given under s 42(2) must relate to particular detentions or arrests for particular reasons": *The State v Peter Moripi and Gaela Wagisa* [1987] PNGLR 376 (King AJ).

> "It is apparent ... that s 42(2) allows the police to detain a person without arresting him if the police suspect that he has committed an offence or is about to do so. The condition on this right to detain without arrest is that an Act of Parliament (as in the cases of health, quarantine, immigration, etc) must provide

for it. If such an Act is promulgated it would be sanctioned by s 42(1)(d) of the *Constitution*.

> The view that exceptions to the right guaranteed by s 42(1) must be implemented by Acts of Parliament finds support in the *Constitution*, s 52 and the Constitutional Planning Report."[15]

"[A]n arrested person must be informed promptly of all the rights guaranteed by s 42(2) but a detained person needs only to be informed of his right under s 42(2)(a). There is no obligation the part of the person who detains him to inform him of his rights under s 42(2)(b) and (c) unless he makes the request. If he does the person who detains him must allow him to exercise his rights under s 42(2)(b) and (c). This is, of course, if a law allows detention short of arrest."[16]

"Any person deprived of his liberty in breach of s 14 [of the] *Arrest Act* is not arrested – he is illegally detained and must be released."[17]

"The point to be once again emphasised is that the right to communicate with a lawyer etc must be exercised in a genuine way. There should not be any attempt, veiled or otherwise, to prevent a person from exercising this right, subject to the practicalities of a given situation."[18]

"Section 42(1) simply sets out the circumstances under which a person may be deprived of his liberty but the full extent of how this is done is to be found in other laws. One has to go to the appropriate law to determine when a person's liberty may be deprived. Support for this interpretation may be found in s 52 of the *Constitution*. This section provides for the right to freedom of movement and the exception reads 'except in consequence of a law that provides for deprivation of personal liberty in accordance with s 42 (liberty of the person)'. The reference here is to the exceptions set out under s 42(1) of the *Constitution*. This provision indicates that the exceptions set out under s 42(1) are to be provided by law. Section 42(2) is to be read together with s 42(1) of the *Constitution*. As an example, a person may be deprived of his personal liberty if he is suspected of having committed or been about to commit an offence: s 42(1)(d)."[19]

"It is clear from [the Arrest] Act that that 'arrest' is the initial step of depriving a person of his liberty and 'detention' is the means by which his liberty is continually deprived for a period. To put the matter differently, 'arrest' and 'detention' are two distinct procedures under the law and deprivation of liberty, which is common to both, commences upon 'arrest' and continues during 'detention'. The moment a person is 'arrested', he is 'detained' from that point on. 'Arrest' is very closely followed in point of time by 'detention'. That is the law relating to 'arrest' and 'detention' in relation to persons who are suspected of committing a crime. ... Can a person be detained without arrest? It has been suggested that the police may detain a person as an alternative to arrest under s 42(3)(b) of the *Constitution*. ... I would reject this submission for the following reasons. First, s 42(3) is not dealing with the law of arrest or detention, it is concerned with those who are arrested or detained in accordance with the law 'to be brought without delay before a court or a judicial officer', the police cannot detain a person without arrest in accordance with the *Arrest Act*. Secondly, to interpret the *Constitution* in this way is to grant the police a power of detention

---

[15] *The State v Songke Mai and Gai Avi* [1988] PNGLR 56 at 61 (Kidu CJ). See *Constitution*, s 52.
[16] *The State v Songke Mai and Gai Avi* [1988] PNGLR 56 at 65 (Kidu CJ).
[17] *The State v Songke Mai and Gai Avi* [1988] PNGLR 56 at 66 (Kidu CJ).
[18] *The State v Songke Mai and Gai Avi* [1988] PNGLR 56 at 67 (Kidu CJ).
[19] *The State v Songke Mai and Gai Avi* [1988] PNGLR 56 at 68 (Kapi DCJ).

without arrest which has not been provided for under the *Arrest Act*. That interpretation is not consistent s 42(1)."[20]

"When a person is arrested or detained requests to see a lawyer under s 42(2)(b) of the *Constitution*, it is not permissible for the police to follow up with a question "Do you wish to see the lawyer now or after the record of interview?"[21]

"I consider that there can be two broad situations of arrest. The first is the technical arrest effected in the manner prescribed by s 14 of the *Arrest Act*. It does not define the legal term 'arrest'. It can be suggested that when the provisions of s 14 are complied with then, and only then, can someone be under 'arrest' or 'arrested'. And therefore any other circumstance or condition of physical restraint or deprivation of personal liberty will amount to 'unlawful arrest'. If the argument is extended that 'arrest' referred to in s 42(2) is the technical arrest effected in compliance with s 14 and none other, then until that technical arrest is effected the officer holding the person is not obliged to administer s 42(2) rights. Such a construction would be to ignore the practical realities of the situations of 'arrest' lawful. This is the broad second category of 'arrest', one might term 'de facto arrest'. In my view the term 'arrest' as used in s 42(2) refers to the physical fact of a deprivation of liberty in either situation ...

I do not think that the legislature would have intended that the term 'arrest' should be strictly and narrowly construed to apply only to an arrest as prescribed by the *Arrest Act* to the point of denying the person his s 42(2) rights who is being deprived of his personal liberty, and who is for all practical purposes under arrest, but not yet so formally informed under s 14 of the Act. Such an argument would mean that the s 42(2) rights of an 'arrested' person and the obligations of the person effecting the 'arrest' could only be enforced after the technical formal arrest is effected under s 14. It would seem odd ... that a person unlawfully imprisoned/arrested should be worse off than if he had been lawfully arrested."[22]

"The particular circumstances of an 'after hours' interview, will in all likelihood, direct attention to the words 'whenever practicable' in s 42(2)(b). Those words import a question of fact to be determined by the trial judge having regard to the circumstances of the case at hand."[23]

The only potential limitation on the rights which s 42(2)(b) provides to persons arrested or detained is to be found in the inclusion of the words "whenever practicable". In case investigating officers and their corroborators even contemplate seeking undue refuge in those words, I can think of no better warning than that provided by the joint remarks of Mason J (as he then was) and Brennan J in *Williams v The Queen* (1986) 161 CLR 278 at 400, as noted with approval by Los J in *The State v Songke Mai and Gai Avi* [1988] PNGLR 56 at 89:

"Practicability is not assessed by reference to the exigencies of criminal investigation; the right to personal liberty is not what is left over after the police investigation is finished."[24]

"If a person is arrested in 'office hours' and the interview is commenced 'after hours' then it is difficult to see why that interview should not be suspended if the person arrested wishes to speak with one of the class of persons contemplated by

[20] *The State v Songke Mai and Gai Avi* [1988] PNGLR 56 at 69-70 (Kapi DCJ).
[21] *The State v Songke Mai and Gai Avi* [1988] PNGLR 56 at 72 (Kapi DCJ).
[22] *The State v Songke Mai and Gai Avi* [1988] PNGLR 56 at 76-77 (Amet J).
[23] *The State v Paro Wampa* [1987] PNGLR 120 at 123.
[24] *The State v Anis* [1990] PNGLR 239 at 247 (Ellis J).

s 42(2)(b). To merely ask what is practicable at that 'after hours' time limits the accused person's constitutional rights: consideration should also be given to what was practicable at the time of arrest when the opportunity to communicate should have been given. Any attempt to delay or defer informing an accused person of his constitutional rights so as to limit his opportunities to exercise them cannot be condoned."[25]

See *Arrest Act* and s 57 of the *Constitution*.

(3) A person who is arrested or detained-

(a) for the purpose of being brought before a court in the execution of an order of a court; or

(b) upon reasonable suspicion of his having committed, or being about to commit, an offence,

shall unless he is released, be brought without delay before a court or a judicial officer and, in a case referred to in paragraph (b), shall not be further held in custody in connection with the offence except by order of a court or judicial officer.

See *Arrest Act*; *Evidence Act*, s 28; and *Constitution*, s 57.

In *The State v Mana Turi* [1986] PNGLR 221, it was held that both s 37(1) and s 42 of the *Constitution* form the basis of any consideration of police impropriety with persons detained. In this case, McDermott AJ considered that the accused's detention for five days, the giving of two full confessional statements by the accused, his continued detention without charge or judicial remand and his subsequent subjection to a full question and answer record of interview, amounted to impropriety.

(4) The necessity or desirability of interrogating the person concerned or other persons, or any administrative requirement or convenience, is not a good ground for failing to comply with Subsection (3), but exigencies of travel which in the circumstances are reasonable may, without derogating any other protection available to the person concerned, be such a ground.

See s 28 of the *Evidence Act*.

(5) Where complaint is made to the National Court or a Judge that a person is unlawfully or unreasonably detained-

(a) the National Court or a Judge shall inquire into the complaint and order the person concerned to be brought before it or him; and

(b) unless the Court or Judge is satisfied that the detention is lawful, and in the case of a person being detained on remand pending his trial does not constitute an unreasonable detention having regard, in particular, to its length, the Court or a Judge shall order his release either unconditionally or subject to such conditions as the Court or Judge thinks fit.

This paragraph only applies to persons arrested and detained and has, therefore, no application to persons to be deported: *Virgil Dewitt Perryman and Victoria F Perryman v Minister for Foreign Affairs and Trade* [1982] PNGLR 339.

If an unreasonable delay in the proceedings has occurred, amounting to a denial of the right of the accused to a fair trial under s 37(2) of the *Constitution*, the court

[25] *The State v Anis* [1990] PNGLR 239 at 248-249 (Ellis J).

should exercise its power under s 42(5) on condition that the accused person/s attend court when requested: *The State v Peter Kakam Borarae* [1984] PNGLR 99 (Woods J). This was despite the fact that the accused persons in that case had been charged with wilful murder.

See *Re Ricky Yanepa* [1988-1989] PNGLR 166 for an example of the court exercising jurisdiction under this section and ordering release of person held in custody for 17 months after committal without any further proceeding being taken.

See also *Re Yamson Vamble and Section 42(5) of the Constitution* (1989) N743. The court ordered the release of a person held in custody for eight months who was charged with unlawful carnal knowledge, where the committal papers were lost and a substantial defence to the charge was raised.

In *Re Kopa Kaipia* (1989) N709(M), the court declared that the imprisonment of a person for failing to obey a Village Court Order to pay compensation was unlawful. Section 31 of the *Village Courts Act* must be read subject to the *Constitution*, and as such, failure to pay a civil debt or obligation does not permit a person to be deprived of their liberty as allowed by s 42 of the *Constitution*.

(6) A person arrested or detained for an offence (other than treason or wilful murder as defined by a Act of the Parliament) is entitled to bail at all times from arrest or detention to acquittal or conviction unless the interests of justice otherwise require.

> "[T]he terms 'arrested' and 'detained' (or 'arrest' and 'detain') in s 42(2), (3), (5) and (6) mean total deprivation of personal liberty – they are two different forms of deprivation of personal liberty. And the deprivation must be legal. There cannot be any legal deprivation of personal liberty outside s 42(1)."[26]

See *Re Bail Act 1977; Application by Herman Kagl Diawo* [1980] PNGLR 148 discussed under s 9 of the *Bail Act*.

(7) Where a person to whom Subsection (6) applies is refused bail-

(a) the court or person refusing bail shall, on request by the person concerned or his representative, state in writing the reason for the refusal; and

(b) the person or his representative may apply to the Supreme Court or the National Court in a summary manner for his release.

See the *Bail Act* annotated in Ch 4 below.

(8) Subject to any other law, nothing in this section applies in respect of any reasonable act of the parent or guardian of a child, or a person into whose care a child has been committed, in the course of the education, discipline or upbringing of the child.

(9) Subject to any Constitutional Law or Act of the Parliament, nothing in this section applies in respect of a person who is in custody under the law of another country-

(a) while in transit through the country; or

(b) as permitted by or under an Act of the Parliament made for the purposes of Section 206 (visiting forces).

---

[26] *The State v Songke Mai and Gai Avi* [1988] PNGLR 56 at 60-61 (Kidu CJ).

44. Freedom from arbitrary search and entry.

(1) No person shall be subjected to the search of his person or property or to entry of his premises, except to the extent that the exercise of that right is regulated or restricted by a law-

(a) that makes reasonable provision for a search or entry-

(i) under an order made by a court; or

(ii) under a warrant for a search issued by a court or judicial officer on reasonable grounds, supported by oath or affirmation, particularly describing the purpose of the search; or

(iii) that authorizes a public officer or government agent of Papua New Guinea or an officer of a body corporate established by law for a public purpose to enter, where necessary, on the premises of a person in order to inspect those premises or anything in or on them in relation to any rate or tax or in order to carry out work connected with any property that is lawfully in or on those premises and belongs to the Government or any such body corporate; or

(iv) that authorizes the inspection of goods, premises, vehicles, ships or aircraft to ensure compliance with lawful requirements as to the entry of persons or importation of goods into Papua New Guinea or departure of persons or exportation of goods from Papua New Guinea or as to standards of safe construction, public safety, public health, permitted use or similar matters, or to secure compliance with the terms of a licence to engage in manufacture or trade; or

(v) for the purpose of inspecting or taking copies of documents relating to-

(A) the conduct of a business, trade, profession or industry in accordance with regulating the conduct of that business, trade, profession or industry; or

(B) the affairs of a company in accordance with a law relating to companies; or

(vi) for the purpose of inspecting goods or inspecting or taking copies of documents, in connection with the collection, or the enforcement of payment of taxes or under a law prohibiting or restricting the importation of goods into Papua New Guinea or the exportation of, goods from Papua New Guinea; or

(b) that complies with Section 38 (general qualifications on qualified rights).

The police have no right to enter into a house and seize property. This is the very reason for the right under this section. They can only enter a house under the exceptions provided for under this section, and the *Search Act* 1977 investigations may proceed properly and effectively within the exceptions provided: *John Alex v Martin Golu* [1983] PNGLR 117.

A remedy for seizure of evidence in contravention of the rights guaranteed under this section may be granted under the general common law discretion to reject evidence obtained illegally, or under a separate and independent power conveyed by s 57 of the *Constitution*. As to the former, see s 28 of the *Evidence Act* and cases relating to general evidentiary matters in Ch 6. As to the latter, see *John Alex v Martin Golu* [1983] PNGLR 117, discussed under s 57 of the *Constitution*. See *Search Act* provisions.

49. Right to privacy.

Every person has the right to reasonable privacy in respect of his private and family life, his communications with other persons and his personal papers and effects, except to the extent that the exercise of that right is regulated or restricted by a law that complies with Section 38 (general qualifications on qualified rights).

See *Search Act* provisions.

55. Equality of citizens.

(1) Subject to this Constitution, all citizens have the same rights, privileges, obligations and duties irrespective of race, tribe, place of origin, political opinion, colour, creed, religion or sex.

(2) Subsection (1) does not prevent the making of laws for the special benefit, welfare, protection or advancement of females, children and young persons, members of under-privileged or less advanced groups or residents of less advanced areas.

(3) Subsection (1) does not affect the operation of a pre-Independence law.

See Johnson, "Equal Rights for Women in PNG: Fact or Fiction", in Weisbrot, Paliwala and Sawyerr (eds), *Law and Social Change in Papua New Guinea* (1982), p 149.

Where the police exercise discretion and charge one accused with summary offences, the law should not be used to give different treatment by charging another accused with indictable offences on the same set of facts. Moreover, punishments on one convicted accused should reflect punishment imposed on the other: *The State v Yombe Gende* (1980) N247.

Subdivision D - Enforcement

57. Enforcement of guaranteed rights and freedoms.

(1) A right or freedom referred to in this Division shall be protected by, and is enforceable in, the Supreme Court or the National Court or any other court prescribed for the purpose by an Act of the Parliament, either on its own initiative or on application by any person who has an interest in its protection and enforcement, or in the case of a person who is, in the opinion of the court, unable fully and freely to exercise his rights under this section by a person acting on his behalf, whether or not by his authority.

By force and effect of s 57(1) of the *Constitution*, the National Court may on its own initiative protect and enforce the rights or freedoms of persons whose liberties have been denied them, by, for example, ordering compensation for wrongful imprisonment: *Rebeka Ambi v Mary Rabi* (1980) N279 (Narokobi AJ).

An incorporated association, for example ICRAF (Individual Rights Advocacy Forum Inc), whose charter provides for its purposes to assist in the advancement, protection and enforcement of human rights, has standing under this section: *Re Miriam Willingal* (1997) N1506.

(2) For the purposes of this section-

(a) the Law Officers of Papua New Guinea; and

(b) any other persons prescribed for the purpose by an Act of the Parliament; and

(c) any other persons with an interest (whether personal or not) in the maintenance of the principles commonly known as the Rule of Law such that, in the opinion of the court concerned, they ought to be allowed to appear and be heard on the matter in question, have an interest in the protection and enforcement of the rights and freedoms referred to in this Division, but this subsection does not limit the persons or classes of persons who have such an interest.

(3) A court that has jurisdiction under Subsection (1) may make all such orders and declarations as are necessary or appropriate for the purposes of this section, and may make an order or declaration in relation to a statute at any time after it is made (whether or not it is in force).

(4) Any court, tribunal or authority may, on its own initiative or at the request of a person referred to in Subsection (1), adjourn, or otherwise delay a decision in, any proceedings before it in order to allow a question concerning the effect or application of this Division to be determined in accordance with Subsection (1).

(5) Relief under this section is not limited to cases of actual or imminent infringement of the guaranteed rights and freedoms, but may, if the court thinks it proper to do so, be given in cases in which there is a reasonable probability of infringement, or in which an action that a person reasonably desires to take is inhibited by the likelihood of, or a reasonable fear of, an infringement.

(6) The jurisdiction and powers of the courts under this section are in addition to, and not in derogation of, their jurisdiction and powers under any other provision of this Constitution.

Sections 23 and 57 of the *Constitution* appear to overlap. However, it emerges plainly from them that both the Supreme and National Courts are given wide discretionary powers to deal with a situation in which a right guaranteed under the provisions of Pt III, Div 3 of the *Constitution* has been denied. Amongst other things, compensation may be ordered, a traditional way in Papua New Guinea of redressing wrongs: *Constitutional Reference No 1 of 1977* [1977] PNGLR 362.

Section 18(l) of the *Constitution* confers exclusive jurisdiction on the Supreme Court as to any question relating to the interpretation or application of any constitutional law. That section is expressed to be subject to the *Constitution*, however, and under ss 57(l) and (3) and 22 it was envisaged that an order seeking enforcement of an accused's constitutional right fell within the jurisdiction of both the National and Supreme Courts. It is not possible for the National Court to exercise its jurisdiction under s 57(l) and (3) to make an order which is necessary for the protection of a constitutional right or freedom unless that court both interprets and applies the relevant constitutional provision: *The State v Peter Painke (No2)* [1977] PNGLR 141.

See Chalmers, "*Human Rights and What is Reasonably Justifiable a Democratic Society*" (1975) 2 MLJ 1 at 92-102.

Having regard to the views expressed in *Reference No 1 of 1977* [1977] PNGLR 362, it is concluded that:

- a remedy under s 57 (for exclusion of evidence obtained in contravention of rights guaranteed under s 44 of the *Constitution* regarding freedom from arbitrary search and entry) is quite separate and independent from the common law discretion to reject evidence which is obtained illegally;
- the power given under s 57 is discretionary and may be exercised in appropriate cases;
- the power given under s 57 is wide enough to extend to prohibiting of evidence which may be obtained in breach of a fundamental right or freedom;
- the power given under this provision extends further than the discretion to reject evidence on the trial; and
- orders can be made at any time after breach of a fundamental right.[27]

On the role of the *Constitution* in protecting the fundamental rights of prisoners to be treated in a way which is not cruel, inhuman, harsh or oppressive, and which reflects the inherent dignity of the human person, see *Tom Amaiu v Commissioner of Corrective Services and the State* [1983] PNGLR 87 (discussed under ss 36(1), 37(1), 37(17) and 41(1)).

Under the *Constitution*, courts other than the National and Supreme Court have no power to make orders under this section. This means that in a trial in a Magistrate's Court where issues under this section arise, such a court must adjourn its hearing and allow the defendant to make the appropriate application to either the National or Supreme Court. Such a course may disrupt the trial and cause delays. The Parliament should therefore seriously consider the possibility of allowing some of the lower courts to make orders under this section. In some provinces it is difficult to have access to the superior courts and it would be difficult to dispose of trials where the defendant has to make an application to the National or the Supreme Court: *John Alex v Martin Golu* [1983] PNGLR 117 (Kapi DCJ).

See also *Supreme Court Reference No 1 of 1982* [1982] PNGLR 178 on the application of this section to breaches of ss 36(1) and 7(17), (18) and (19) of the *Constitution*.

The common law discretion to reject evidence which was obtained in contravention of s 44 is a separate remedy from s 57 This section, therefore, extends further than a power to reject evidence at the trial. Consequently, orders under this section can be made at any time after the breach of the fundamental right: *John Alex v Martin Golu* [1983] PNGLR 117.

The Supreme Court ordered the National Court to proceed with a trial forthwith, in order to protect an accused's right under s 37(3) to a fair hearing within a reasonable time: *Supreme Court Reference No 3 of 1979; The State v John Rumet Kaputin* [1979] PNGLR 532 at 535.

58. Compensation.

(1) This section is in addition to, and not in derogation of, Section 57 (enforcement of guaranteed rights and freedoms).

---

[27] *John Alex v Martin Golu* [1983] PNGLR 117.

(2) A person whose rights or freedoms declared or protected by this Division are infringed (including any infringement caused by a derogation of the restrictions specified in Part X.5 (internment)) on the use of emergency powers in relation to internment is entitled to reasonable damages and, if the court thinks it proper, exemplary damages in respect of the infringement.

(3) Subject to Subsections (4) and (5), damages may be awarded against any person who committed, or was responsible for, the infringement.

(4) Where the infringement was committed by a governmental body, damages may be awarded either-

(a) subject to Subsection (5), against a person referred to in Subsection (3); or

(b) against the governmental body to which any such person was responsible, or against both, in which last case the court may apportion the damages between them.

(5) Damages shall not be awarded against a person who was responsible to a governmental body in respect of the action giving rise to the infringement if-

(a) the action was an action made unlawful only by Section 41(1) (proscribed acts); and

(b) the action taken was genuinely believed by that person to be required by law, but the burden of proof of the belief referred to in paragraph (b) is on the party alleging it.

Entitlement to compensation is based on infringement of a right or a freedom under s 42 of the *Constitution*. There are exceptions where the liberty of a person may be deprived (in this case s 42(1)(d)) which states that "upon reasonable suspicion" of the person having committed an offence, the person has no right to compensation under s 58: *The State v Wic Kor* [1983] PNGLR 24.

In *Heni Pauta and Kenneth Susuve v Commissioner for Corrective Institutions and his Servants and Agents* [1982] PNGLR 7, orders were made by Kidu CJ restraining the Commissioner of Corrective Institutions and his servants and agents from inflicting any cruel or inhuman treatment on detainees (see ss 36(1) and 37(17)) and transferring a juvenile detainee from "B" to "C" Division of Bomana gaol: s 37(19).

On the role of the *Constitution* in protecting the fundamental rights of prisoners to be treated in a way which is not cruel, inhuman, harsh or oppressive, and which reflects the inherent dignity of the human person, see *Tom Amaiu v Commissioner of Corrective Services and the State* [1983] PNGLR 87, discussed under ss 36(1), 37(1), 37(17) and 41(1).

Section 58 permits the award of exemplary damages. They are appropriate where there has been deliberate or flagrant misconduct by officials: *Tom Amaiu v Commissioner of Corrective Institutions and the State* [1983] PNGLR 87. See also *Heni Pauta and Kenneth Susuve v Commissioner for Corrective Institutions and his Servants and Agents* [1982] PNGLR 7.

Under s 42 there are exceptions where the liberty of a person may be deprived. Where an accused is arrested upon reasonable suspicion of having committed an offence and is held in custody for trial, he or she has been held in accordance with the exception set out under s 42(1)(d). Therefore, subsequent acquittal does not entitle the accused to compensation under s 58, for there was no unconstitutional infringement of a right or freedom: *The State v Wic Kor* [1983] PNGLR 24.

Division 4 - Principles of Natural Justice

59. Principles of natural justice.

(1) Subject to this Constitution and to any statute, the principles of natural justice are the rules of the underlying law known by that name developed for control of judicial and administrative proceedings.

(2) The minimum requirement of natural justice is the duty to act fairly and, in principle, to be seen to act fairly.

The principles of natural justice are fundamentally of common law origins. Their consistency with the requirements of Sch 2 is therefore paramount. Kapi J has noted that:

> "In discovering and applying the common law to the circumstances of this country regard should be given Sch 2.2 of the *Constitution*. The court should only consider English cases as Sch 2.2 of the *Constitution* is only concerned with the common law of England. If there are cases from other common law countries such as Australia or Canada every precaution must be taken in referring to the decisions from these jurisdictions because the courts there might give their own interpretation or application of the common law principles. If the cases from other common law countries differ from the English cases then no regard should be given to them unless this Court has found itself in a situation where the common law of England is either inconsistent or is inappropriate or contrary to the *Constitution* or any statute or the customs of the people, then the court shall have regard to these cases in formulating its own underlying law under Sch 2.3 of the *Constitution*."[28]

In *Okuk v Fallscheer* [1980] PNGLR 274, Kapi J (at 284), emphasised that "the House of Lords has established that a person who is occupying an office or status cannot be dismissed without complying with the principles of natural justice". This adopted Lord Wilberforce in *Ridge v Baldwin* [1964] AC 40, who said that "if there are relationships in which all requirements or rules of natural justice are excluded ... these must be confined to what have been called pure master and servant cases."[29]

Okuk v Fallscheer also approved the holding in *Duravappah v Fernado* [1967] 2 AC 337; [1967] 2 All ER 152. Kapi J stated the following:

> "In their Lordships' opinion there are three matters which must always be borne in mind when considering whether the principle should be applied or not: first what is the nature of the property, the office held, status enjoyed or services to be performed by the complainant of injustice. Secondly, in what circumstances or on what occasions is the person claiming to be entitled to exercise the measure or control entitled to intervene. Thirdly, when a right to intervene is proved, what sanctions in fact is the latter entitled to impose on the other. It is only on a consideration of all these matters that the question of the application of the principle can properly be determined."

How appropriate are the common law principles of natural justice to the administrative law specifically designed for Papua New Guinea, and how consistent are they with the provisions of Sch 2 of the *Constitution*? Kapi J addressed these issues when he observed:

---

[28] *Okuk v Fallscheer* [1980] PNGLR 274 at 280.
[29] *Okuk v Fallscheer* [1980] PNGLR 274.

"I am not aware of any constitutional law or statute which is inconsistent with these principles and there are no customs which may be said to be inconsistent with these principles."[30]

On an appeal against a refusal of a writ of certiorari absolute to quash a decision of the Police Appeal Tribunal for failing to give reasons for a disciplinary decision, Bredmeyer J, with whom both Greville-Smith and Kapi JJ agreed, held that the tribunal must observe the standards of natural justice under this section as there is nothing in the *Police Force (Interim Arrangements) Act* 1973 to exclude the principle: *Lawrence Allen Sausau v The Police Commissioner and The State* [1981] PNGLR 327.

60. Development of principles.

In the development of the rules of the underlying law in accordance with Sch 21 (adoption, etc, of certain laws) particular attention shall be given to the development of a system of principles of natural justice and of administrative law specifically designed for Papua New Guinea, taking special account of the National Goals and Directive Principles and of the Basic Social Obligations, and also of typically Papua New Guinean procedures and forms of organization.

Section 60 of the *Constitution* imposes a duty to develop a system of principles of natural justice which, by s 59, includes the duty to act fairly (and to be seen to act fairly). The test of bias is whether in all the circumstances a party or the public might reasonably suspect that the magistrate might not decide the questions before him or her with a fair and unprejudiced mind: *R v Watson; Ex parte Armstrong* (1976) 136 CLR 248; and *Holmes v Neilson* [1979] Tas R 89. In the circumstances where the complainant worked for the magistrate as a clerk, bias was not found where the defendant admitted the claim and the magistrate had acknowledged that he would step down if it was not admitted: *Balus Tara v Rachel Gugu* (1982) N374(M) (Bredmeyer J).

On the issue of whether the Police Appeal Tribunal ought to give reasons for its decision, Bredmeyer J observed that nothing in the relevant Act required reasons to be given. *Padfield v Minister for Agriculture* [1968] 1 All ER 694 held that the Minister was not required to give reasons. Mandamus will lie against him, whether he gave reasons or not, if it appears that his decision was designed to frustrate the policy and objects of the Act. If he does not give any reasons why he rejects what appears to be a genuine complaint, the court may infer that he had no good reason for his decision and order mandamus against him. Nevertheless, the cases of *R v Gaming Board; Ex parte Benaim* [1970] 2 QB 417 and *Taylor v Public Service Board* [1975] 2 NSWLR 278 led to the conclusion that it is not part of the English common law that administrative tribunals in general, or that disciplinary tribunals in particular, should give reasons. Whether it is part of natural justice that administrative tribunals should give reasons is a new area of law. In England, s 12 of the *Tribunal and Inquiries Act* 1958 (UK) required certain tribunals (and Ministers) to give reasons for their decisions, and that provision is not contained in s 12 of the *Tribunals and Inquiries Act* 1971. The latter section requires the tribunal or Minister to furnish a statement, either written or oral, of the reasons for decision, **if requested**, on or before the giving or notification of the decision. I agree with the learned Deputy Chief Justice that the common law principles of natural justice adopted into this country do not require reasons to be given by a tribunal such as the

[30] *Okuk v Fallscheer* [1980] PNGLR 274 at 285.

Police Appeal Tribunal: *Lawrence Sausau v The Commissioner for Police and The State* [1981] PNGLR 327 at 330. However, see *Kelly Yawip v Commissioner of Police* [1995] PNGLR 93, where Injia J held that a Commissioner of Police must give reasons for a decision to dismiss a policeman on disciplinary grounds.

On an appeal from a magistrate's decision the issue of the likelihood of bias was raised. Bredmeyer J held that:

> "the judge or magistrate must be free of bias. The test is whether in all the circumstances a party or the public might reasonably suspect that the magistrate might not decide the questions before him with a fair and unprejudiced mind *The Queen v Watson; Ex parte Armstrong* (1976) 136 CLR 248 at 262."[31]

Subdivision D - The Power of Mercy

151. Grant of pardon, etc.

(1) Subject to this Subdivision, the Head of The State, acting with, and in accordance with, the advice of the National Executive Council, may grant to a person convicted of an offence or held in penal detention under a law of Papua New Guinea-

(a) a pardon, either free or conditional; or

(b) a remission or commutation of sentence; or

(c) a respite of the execution of sentence; or

(d) a less severe form of punishment for that imposed by any sentence, and may remit or refund, in whole or in part, any fine, penalty or forfeiture paid or payable to a governmental body.

(2) Where an offence has been committed, the Head of The State, acting with, and in accordance with, the advice of the National Executive Council, may grant a pardon, either free or conditional, to an accomplice who gives evidence that leads to the conviction of a principal offender.

See s 19 of the *Criminal Code* on punishment, and s 615 of the *Criminal Code* regarding release on licence.

152. Advisory Committee on the Power of Mercy.

(1) An Organic Law shall make provision for and in respect of an Advisory Committee on the Power of Mercy, and for and in respect of its appointment, constitution, powers and procedures.

(2) Before giving any advice to the Head of State under Section 151(1) (grant of pardon, etc), the National Executive Council shall consider a report from the Advisory Committee.

---

[31] *Balus Tara v Rachel Gugu* (1982) N374 at 3.

Chapter 2

THE COURT SYSTEM

Supreme Court of Papua New Guinea

The Supreme Court of Papua New Guinea is the highest court in the national judicial system and is the country's final court of appeal under s 155(2) of the *Constitution*. With respect to criminal jurisdiction, the Supreme Court has appellate criminal jurisdiction and original constitutional jurisdiction.

Original jurisdiction

The original jurisdiction of the Supreme Court in constitutional issues has been mentioned in Ch 1 above. The Supreme Court has also an original jurisdiction in constitutional matters by virtue of ss 18 and 19 of the *Constitution*. The Supreme Court has an original jurisdiction to the exclusion of all other courts on any question relating to the interpretation or application of any provision of the *Constitution* or any other constitutional law. In addition, under s 19, special reference may be made to the Supreme Court by specified authorities, and in such cases the Supreme Court may give its opinion on any question relating to the interpretation or application of any constitutional law, or any question as to the validity of a law or proposed law. Such an opinion is as binding as any other decision of the Supreme Court: s 19(2).

Appellate jurisdiction

In criminal matters, the Supreme Court generally only exercises its appellate jurisdiction: see *Public Prosecutor v Nahau Rooney (No 2)* [1979] PNGLR 448, for a case where the Supreme Court exercised original jurisdiction in contempt proceedings.

The Supreme Court hears appeals from the National Court in criminal matters and these appeals are governed by the *Supreme Court Act* 1975. Appeal to the Supreme Court is by way of rehearing and the court has a right to hear fresh evidence: *Supreme Court Act* 1975, s 6. The court may also grant a re-trial in a criminal case if the court feels there has been a miscarriage of justice.

When hearing an appeal from the National Court, the Supreme Court is constituted by not fewer than three judges (*Constitution*, s 161(2)) and at its sitting the court is presided over by the Chief Justice or, in the absence of the Chief Justice, by the next most senior judge: *Constitution*, s 161(3). Appeal from the National Court lies to the Supreme Court as of right on a question of law or mixed fact and law, and with leave of the Supreme Court on a question of fact: *Supreme Court Act*

1975, s 4; see also ss 11, 14 and 22. A judge of the National Court may reserve a case or any point in a case for the consideration of the Supreme Court: *Supreme Court Act* 1975, s 5. Also, a judge of the National Court may refer any matter relating to the interpretation or application of a constitutional law to the Supreme Court to take appropriate action: *Constitution*, s 18(2).

Under the *Supreme Court Act* 1975, the state has no right of appeal against an acquittal. However, by s 26(1) of the *Supreme Court Act* 1975, the principal legal adviser to the National Executive may, within 40 days of an acquittal, refer any matter or question of law to the Supreme Court. The Supreme Court may then consider the point and give its opinion on a matter arising in the case. The object of s 26 is to allow the prosecution to inquire into or challenge a ruling or interpretation which was unfavourable to the prosecution. Any such ruling in no way disturbs the acquittal of the accused. It should be noted that s 26 (and also s 21 dealing with the reservation of points of law for the consideration of the Supreme Court) has been interpreted as extending only to decisions of the Supreme Court where some specific question of law is raised in the trial. Generally, the Supreme Court will not answer academic or theoretic questions: see *R v PM* [1971-1972] PNGLR 222; *R v BP* [1973] PNGLR 53; and *Prosecutor's Request No 1 of 1974* (1974) FC67.

National Court of Justice

The National Court of Justice of Papua New Guinea is established by s 163(l) of the *Constitution*. The National Court consists of the same judges as sit in the Supreme Court. The National Court in its appellate and original jurisdiction is held before a single judge.

The National Court has an unlimited original jurisdiction under s 166 of the *Constitution*. In particular, this section specifies the National Court's jurisdiction in enforcing the *Constitution*, enforcing the rights and freedoms guaranteed by the *Constitution* and reviewing any exercise of judicial authority: s 155(3)(a). The court has its principal seat at the Supreme Court Building at Waigani in the National Capital District. During the last 10 years National Court judges have been based in some of the major regional centres in the provinces: *National Court Act*, s 5.

Criminal jurisdiction

The National Court of Justice has an unlimited criminal jurisdiction. In practice, however, the National Court exercises jurisdiction over indictable offences only. Proceedings for indictable offences which are heard before the National Court are instituted by the usual common law procedure of indictment. An indictment which sets out the charges against the accused is laid by a State Prosecutor: see s 525 of the *Criminal Code*; see also Ch LVIII generally on indictments. On a trial by indictment, the "hand-up brief" proceeding takes place, or a committal proceeding takes place in a District Court to review the sufficiency of the evidence before putting the accused upon trial in the National Court.

Appellate jurisdiction

The National Court has an appellate jurisdiction hearing appeals from District Courts and from some administrative tribunals. Appellate jurisdiction is also exercised by a single judge.

Appeals from a decision of a District Court lie, as of right, to a judge of the National Court: *District Courts Act*, ss 219 and 220. Where the matter of the appeal is one of public importance, the Minister for Justice may intervene: s 219 (3). The Public Prosecutor has a right to appeal against a sentence in the case of indictable offences triable summarily. The District Court can also refer constitutional matters to the Supreme Court: *Constitution*, s 18(2). However, the government or a state prosecutor may not appeal against a complaint brought by them which has been dismissed: s 43(2). Following the *Local Courts (Repeal) Act* 2000, Local Courts were abolished and some of their special functions were transferred to the District Court by the *District Courts (Amendment) Act* 2000.

THE CONSTITUTION

[Sections Relevant to the Administration of Justice and Criminal Appeals]

Division 5 – The Administration of Justice

Subdivision A – General Structure and Principles of the National Justice Administration

154. The National Justice Administration.

The National Justice Administration consists of-

(a) the National Judicial System; and

(b) the Minister responsible for the National Justice Administration; and

(c) the Law Officers of Papua New Guinea.

155. The National Judicial System.

(1) The National Judicial System consists of-

(a) the Supreme Court; and

(b) the National Court; and

(c) such other courts as are established under Section 172 (establishment of other courts).

(2) The Supreme Court-

(a) is the final court of appeal; and

(b) has an inherent power to review all judicial acts of the National Court; and

(c) has such other jurisdiction and powers as are conferred on it by this *Constitution* or any other law.

(3) The National Court-

(a) has an inherent power to review any exercise of judicial authority; and

(b) has such other jurisdiction and powers as are conferred on it by this *Constitution* or any law, except where-

(c) jurisdiction is conferred upon the Supreme Court to the exclusion of the National Court; or

(d) the Supreme Court assumes jurisdiction under Subsection (4); or

(e) the power of review is removed or restricted by a Constitutional Law or an Act of the Parliament.

(4) Both the Supreme Court and the National Court have an inherent power to make, in such circumstances as seem to them proper, orders in the nature of prerogative writs and such other orders as are necessary to do justice in the circumstances of a particular case.

(5) In a case referred to in Subsection (3)(e), the National Court has nevertheless an inherent power of review where, in its opinion, there are over-riding considerations of public policy in the special circumstances of a particular case.

(6) Subject to any right of appeal or power of review of a decision, it is the duty of all persons (including the Law Officers of Papua New Guinea and other public officers in their respective official capacities), and of all bodies and institutions, to comply with and, so far as is within their respective lawful powers, to put into effect all decisions of the National Judicial System.

The power vested in the Supreme Court by this section will not be exercised as a matter of course. Where statutory appeal provisions are not complied with convincing reasons must be shown why this court should exercise its constitutional power. An example of this is *Avia Aihi v The State (No 2)* [1982] PNGLR 44, where there was no right of appeal under s 27 of the *Supreme Court Act* as the appeal was out of time.

The principles in *Secretary for Law v Tisunkac Nawok Domstock also known as Bisanoga* [1974] PNGLR 246; *Varney v R* [1964] VR 143; and *Queen v Tyrrel* (unreported CA, NSW, February 1980, Aust Curr Law), relating to unfettered discretion to grant leave to extend time to appeal should apply when there is an application under this paragraph. An applicant must show legal grounds exist to which the appeal relates, and an appeal against sentence will generally involve questions of excessiveness: *Avia Aihi v The State (No 2)* [1982] PNGLR 44.

For a consideration of the meaning of the words "inherent power" see the decision of Andrew J in *Avia Aihi v The State (No 1)* [1981] PNGLR 81. His Honour stated (at 101) that "it is clear enough that in general an inherent power must give way to any statutory provision with which it is in conflict", though not in the case of s 27 of the *Supreme Court Act*.

Section 155(2)(b) and (c) create distinct heads of power and jurisdiction and, accordingly para (b) invests the Supreme Court with an unfettered discretionary jurisdiction to hear an application for leave to appeal and an appeal from the National Court, even though the applicant has barred his or her statutory right to appeal by not complying with s 27 of the *Supreme Court Act*. It depends on the circumstances of the case whether this power would be exercised, but as it is wholly discretionary it would be exercised only in exceptional circumstances where some substantial injustice is manifest or the case is of special gravity: *Avia Aihi v The State (No 1)* [1981] PNGLR 81.

"I consider that this court's discretionary and reserve power under ... s 155(2)(b) is additional to the power and jurisdiction vested in the court under s 155(2)(c); this appears clearly from the language used. The latter is dependent in part on the exercise of legislative power by Parliament; the former is not. The latter is subject to limits imposed by Acts; the former is not. It is to be expected that the final court of appeal ... would be expressly vested with a discretionary jurisdiction of the type in s 155(2)(b), so as to ensure the dispensation of justice; it is a common feature of many judicial systems."[32]

The National Court has the power to review any exercise of judicial authority under s 155(3)(a). By virtue of this provision, the court has appellate jurisdiction over appeals involving sentences imposed by a Visiting Justice under the *Corrective Institutions Act*. However, this does not include appeals at first instance. Such appeals should go to the nearest senior magistrate of the region: *Joseph Marben v Francis Gesa* (1981) N314(M).

The supervisory function of the courts, which extends to every "exercise of judicial authority", covers the appeal by a prisoner against a conviction by a visiting Justice pursuant to s 30 of the *Corrective Institutions Act* (refusing to obey a lawful order): *Joseph Marben v Francis Gesa* (1981) N314(M) (Quinlivan AJ).

Where an accused is found guilty of an offence under the *Criminal Code*, the provisions of s 155(4) of the *Constitution* do not empower the National Court to make a disposition of the offender other than as provided in the Code - by proceeding to a conviction or dismissing the charge. The *Constitution* does not vest a dispositive power in the court: *Supreme Court Reference No 2 of 1981; Re s19(1)(f) Criminal Code (Ch 262)* [1982] PNGLR 150.

The provisions of s 155(4) of the *Constitution* cannot be interpreted "so far as to enable a court to make a final decision upon the circumstances of a particular case without regard to the principles of law or equity applicable for its determination." In any case "where a case for interlocutory relief falls within the well established principles of equity, there is no need for the claimant to have recourse" to the provision: *Mauga Logging Company Pty Ltd v South Pacific Oil Palm Development Pty Ltd* [1977] PNGLR 80 (Sir Sydney Frost CJ).

The section "exists only to ensure that persons' rights or interests as determined by law are properly enforced or protected, if existing laws are deficient in that respect": *Supreme Court Reference No 2 of 1981; Re s 19(1)(f) Criminal Code (Ch 262)* [1982] PNGLR 150 (Kidu CJ).

Section 155(4) was not intended to give the Supreme Court a power to override the clear provisions of s 37(15) of the *Constitution* and s 27 of the *Supreme Court Act*. The subsection cannot affect the primary rights of parties which are determined by law. In *Avia Aihi v The State (No 1)* [1981] PNGLR 81 this was an appeal regulated by Sch 2.27 of the *Constitution*.

The Supreme Court has inherent power to review all judicial acts of the National Court under s 155(2)(b) of the *Constitution* and may exercise this power under s 155(4). In *Saki v The State* [1980] PNGLR 33, the Supreme Court chose to determine a prisoner's date of discharge where there was a conflict between the Warrant of Commitment and the requirements of s 20 of the *Criminal Code*,

[32] *Avia Aihi v The State (No 1)* [1981] PNGLR 81 (Kearney DCJ).

notwithstanding that the appeal against sentence was abandoned and that the issue of date of discharge was not raised by the prisoner.

On an appeal against a decision of a single judge of the National Court for discharging an order nisi for certiorari, in reference to s 155(4), it was held that the common law principles of natural justice adopted from England do not require administrative tribunals in general, or disciplinary tribunals in particular, to give reasons for decision. Accordingly, the Police Appeal Tribunal was not required to give reasons and the appeal on that basis failed: *Lawrence Allen Sausau v The Police Commissioner and the State* [1981] PNGLR 327.

It appears that if the court were to formulate a rule under Sch 2.3 of the *Constitution* in relation to administrative tribunals giving reasons for a decision, it would be that reasons should be given if requested: *Lawrence Allen Sausau v The Police Commissioner and the State* [1981] PNGLR 327 (Bredmeyer J).

Order 81, rule 2 provides that order to show cause shall be to show cause before the Supreme Court, unless the matter appears to be one of urgency, in which case the court or judge may make the order returnable before a single judge in court or chambers. However, even if a judge of the National Court decides the matter is not one of urgency upon being apprised of the issues, he may determine the matter under s 155(4): *Sudi Yaku v Commissioner of Police; Ex parte The State* [1980] PNGLR 27. See *The State v Yaulipa Bulaim* (1980) N234, discussed under s 560 of the *Criminal Code* below, regarding the effect of this action on the courts' power to decline to accept a plea of guilty.

For a discussion of the history of relator proceedings and the prerogative writs, see the decision of Kapi J annotated under Sch 2.4 in Ch 1, above, in *Supreme Court Reference No 4 of 1980; Re Petition of Michael Thomas Somare* [1981] PNGLR 265.

Subdivision B – The Judicial Power

158. Exercise of the judicial power.

(1) Subject to this *Constitution*, the judicial authority of the People is vested in the National Judicial System.

(2) In interpreting the law the court shall give paramount consideration to the dispensation of justice.

Where the strict interpretation of the *Criminal Code* would give rise to an anomalous and unjust situation, the Supreme Court can and should, on the authority of the *Constitution* itself, and this section in particular, remedy it so as to do what Parliament would have done had they had the situation in mind: *Principle Legal Advisors Request No 1 of 1980* [1980] PNGLR 326 (Wilson J). This was applied in *Supreme Court Reference No 6 of 1994; Re Provocation* [1985] PNGLR 31.

See *The State v Yaulipa Bulaim* (1980) N234 discussed under the *Criminal Code*, s 560, regarding the effect of this section on the court's power to decline to accept a plea of guilty.

159. Tribunals, etc, outside the National Judicial System.

(1) Subject to Subsection (3), nothing in this *Constitution* prevents an Organic Law or a statute from conferring judicial authority on a person or body outside the National Judicial System, or the establishment by or in accordance with law, or by consent of the parties, of arbitral or conciliatory tribunals, whether ad hoc or other, outside the National Judicial System.

(2) Nothing in, or done in accordance with, Subsection (1) affects the operation of Section 155(4) or (5) (the National Judicial System).

(3) No person or body outside the National Judicial System, has, or may be given, power to impose a sentence of death or imprisonment, or to impose any other penalty as for a criminal offence, but nothing in this subsection prevents-

(a) the imposition, in accordance with law, of disciplinary detention or any other disciplinary punishment (other than death) by a disciplinary authority of a disciplined force on persons subject to the disciplinary law of the force; or

(b) the imposition, in accordance with law, of disciplinary punishments (other than death or detention) on members of other State or provincial services; or

(c) the imposition of reasonable penalties (other than death or detention) by an association on its members for breaches of its rules.

(4) In Subsection (3)(a), "disciplined force" has the same meaning as in Section 207 (definition of "disciplined force").

For a reference to the relevance of this section to the enforcement of the *Corrective Institutions Regulations* by visiting Justices, see *Tom Amaiu v Commissioner of Corrective Services and the State* [1983] PNGLR 87.

185. Lack of procedural provision.

If in the circumstances of a particular case before a court no provision, or no adequate provision, is made in respect of a matter of practice or procedure, the court shall give ad hoc directions to remedy the lack or inadequacy.

Ad hoc directions have been formulated in some cases. See *Nombri Ambre v The State* [1995] PNGLR 453 in relation to contempt of court and *Jamer Komio v The State* [1995] PNGLR 453.

Pending legislation, the Supreme Court held that appeals from decisions under ss 26 and 27 of the *Corrective Institutions Act* 1957 could lie to the National Court, and that such appeals be brought in accordance with the *Local Courts Act*: *Constitutional Reference No 2 of 1978* [1978] PNGLR 405.

In *Supreme Court Reference No 4 of 1980; Re Petition of Michael Thomas Somare* [1981] PNGLR 265 at 274, Kidu CJ held that this section empowered the court, in the absence of specific rules, in the situation of an application by the leader of the opposition to challenge the constitutionality of an Act of Parliament, to give directions to remedy the matter.

SUPREME COURT ACT

Chapter No 37

Being an Act to implement Subdivision VI.5.C (the *Supreme Court of Justice*) of the *Constitution* by making further provision in relation to the Supreme Court of Justice.

[Sections Relevant to Criminal Appeals]

Part III – Appeals to the Supreme Court

Division 1 – General

4. Right of appeal from National Court.

(1) An appeal in accordance with this Act lies to the Supreme Court from a judgement of the National Court.

(2) An appeal lies in any civil or criminal proceedings, to the Supreme Court for a Judge of the National Court sitting on appeal -

(a) on a question of law; or

(b) on a question of mixed fact and law; or

(c) with the leave of the Supreme Court, on a question of fact.

See s 37(15)-(16) of the *Constitution* on rights of appeal. See also ss 155 and 166 of the *Constitution* on the jurisdiction of the courts in the national judicial system.

5. Incidental directions and interim orders.

(1) Where an appeal is pending before the Supreme Court-

(a) a direction not involving the decision on the appeal; or

(b) an interim order to prevent prejudice to the claims of the parties; or

(c) an order in any proceedings (other than criminal proceedings) for security for costs; or

(d) an order dismissing an appeal in any proceedings (other than criminal proceedings) for default in furnishing security; or

(e) an order admitting an appellant to bail, may be made by a judge.

(2) A direction or order made under Subsection (1) shall be deemed to be a direction or order of the Supreme Court.

(3) A direction or order made under Subsection (1) may be discharged or varied by the Supreme Court.

6. Appeal to the Supreme Court by way of rehearing.

(1) An appeal to the Supreme Court shall be by way of rehearing on the evidence given in the court the decision of which is appealed against, subject to the right of the Supreme Court-

(a) to allow fresh evidence to be adduced where it is satisfied that the justice of the case warrants it; and

(b) to draw inferences of fact.

(2) For the purposes of hearing and determining an appeal, the Supreme Court has all the powers, authority and jurisdiction of a Judge exercising the jurisdiction of the National Court.

Where there is an appeal from a trial judge sitting without a jury, on conflicting evidence, an appellate court should allow great weight to the trial judge's advantage in seeing and hearing witnesses first hand, and could not form a different view of the evidence unless satisfied that this advantage of the trial judge is not sufficient to explain or justify the conclusion: *R v Holland* (1969) N2.

In a criminal appeal the appellate court is able to receive new material which was not before the sentencing judge: *R v Clemence Mandoma Kausigor; R v Piki Piliu* (1969) FC3.

Section 6 was first brought into existence with the enactment of the *Supreme Court Act* on Independence. It did not have a counterpart under the old *Supreme Court (Full Court) Act*. Its purpose apparently gives wide powers to the Supreme Court on the matter of fresh evidence. It would appear that s 8 now occupies the role of a machinery provision for the purpose, inter alia, of implementing the powers granted under s 6: *John Peng v The State* [1982] PNGLR 331.

The proper approach to what inferences may be drawn by a court of appeal was succinctly summarised by Lord Reid in *Benmax v Austin Motor Co Ltd* [1955] AC 370 at 376:

> "But in many cases where there is no question of the credibility or reliability of any witness, and in cases where the point in dispute is the proper inference to be drawn from proved facts, an appeal court is generally in as good a position to evaluate the evidence as the trial judge, and ought not to shrink from that task, though ought, of course, to give weight to his opinion."

This situation must be distinguished from that where the appeal is from an exercise of judicial discretion. In *Whitehorse v Jordan* [1981] 1 All ER 267 at 276, the House of Lords reaffirmed:

> "It has long been settled law that, when the decision of a trial judge is based substantially on his assessment of the quality and credibility of witnesses, an appellate court 'must, in order to reverse, not merely entertain doubts whether the decision below is right, but be convinced that it is wrong' ... And that is so irrespective of whether or not the trial judge made any observation with regard to credibility."[33]

In dealing with an appeal from a criminal case, the basic presumption of innocence must be observed that where on the evidence two opposing inferences may be drawn, one in favour and one adverse to the accused, it is a duty of the trial judge to select that which is the more favourable. In such circumstances, it would clearly be an error on the part of the trial judge to select the adverse inference: *Karo Gamoga v The State* [1981] PNGLR 443 (Pratt J).

In *Parkes* (1962) 46 Cr App R 29 at 32, the Court of Appeal expressed principles regarding the admission of fresh evidence which have been accepted as part of the law in Papua New Guinea since Independence: see *Government of Papua New Guinea and Davis v Barker* [1977] PNGLR 386; *Raphael Warakau v The State* (1980) SC 184; and *James Neap v The State* (1982) SC 228. These principles are:

> "First, the evidence that it is sought to call must be evidence which was not available at trial. Secondly, it must be evidence relevant to the issues. Thirdly, it must be evidence which is credible; it is not for this court to decide whether it is to be believed or not, but evidence which is capable of belief. Fourthly, the court

[33] *Karo Gamoga v The State* [1981] PNGLR 443 (Pratt J).

will consider whether there might have been a reasonable doubt in the minds of the jury as to the guilt of the appellant if that evidence had been given together with the other evidence at the trial."[34]

The principles governing the reception of fresh evidence on appeal are covered in *Government of Papua New Guinea and Davis v Barker* [1977] PNGLR 386 and *Raphael Warakau v The State* (1980) SC 184, and essentially follow *Orr v Holmes* (1948) 76 CLR 632 and *Ladd v Marshall* [1954] 3 All ER 745. In this last case, Lord Denning held at 478:

"In order to justify the reception of fresh evidence or a new trial, three conditions must be fulfilled: first, it must be shown that the evidence could not have been obtained with reasonable diligence for use at the trial; second, the evidence must be such that, if given, it would probably have an important influence on the result of the case, although it need not be decisive; third, the evidence must be such as is presumably to be believed, or in other words, it must be apparently creditable, although it need not be incontrovertible."

It is clear that all the criteria must be met and not one or two only: *James Neap v The State* (1981) SC 228.See note on *Wanosa v The Queen* [1971-1972] PNGLR 90, under s 22.

"An examination of the *Government of Papua New Guinea and Davis v Barker*, *Raphael Warakau v The State*, and *James Neap v PNG* reveal that they adopted principles of the common law. These cases fell into error in this regard. The discretion of the Court in admitting fresh evidence is now governed by s 6(1)(a) of the *Supreme Court Act* (Ch 37) and not the common law."[35]

"Any evidence which comes within the meaning of 'fresh evidence' in accordance with s 6(1)(a) ... does not automatically become admissible on appeal. Whether or not such evidence may be adduced on appeal is governed by the words 'where it is satisfied that the justice of the case warrants it' under s 6(1)(a)... In *John Peng v The State* (at 337) the Supreme Court concluded that, in exercising its discretion with regard to any 'fresh evidence', such evidence must be 'relevant, credible, admissible according to the rules of evidence and by it a reasonable man would be given cause to doubt', then a proper case exists where the court can exercise its discretion to admit it."[36]

"'Fresh evidence' means something that has happened since the hearing or trial, or it must be evidence which has come to the knowledge of the party applying since that hearing or trial and which could not by reasonable means have come to his knowledge before that time."[37]

"Fresh evidence pursuant to s 6(1)(a) of the *Supreme Court Act* Ch 37 means evidence which has come to light since the hearing or trial, or evidence which has come to the knowledge of the party applying since that hearing or trial and which could not by reasonable means have come to his knowledge before that time. Such evidence may be admitted on appeal if the court considers that 'it is satisfies that the justice of the case warrants it'. See *John Peng v The State* [1982] PNGLR 331 and *Abiari v The State* [1990] PNGLR 250."[38]

"[E]vidence which is sought to be tendered in the Supreme Court by a witness who has changed his or her story from the one given at the trial is fresh evidence

[34] *John Peng v The State* [1982] PNGLR 331.
[35] *Abiari v The State* [1990] PNGLR 250 at 252 (Kapi DCJ).
[36] *Abiari v The State* [1990] PNGLR 250 at 255 (Kapi DCJ).
[37] *Abiari v The State* [1990] PNGLR 250 at 255 (Kapi DCJ).
[38] *James Pari and Tine Bomai Kaupa v The State* [1993] PNGLR 173 at 176 (Kapi DCJ).

> and is subject to the same tests. I also agree with King J [in *R v Poulter* (1978) 19 SASR 370 at 385] that: 'before evidence is heard, the contents of the affidavit, including the explanation for having given false evidence should carry some degree of conviction and should give rise to a substantial apprehension of a miscarriage of justice'"[39]

Where one of three judges who heard the appeal is unavailable to continue to deliver judgment, the remaining judges should continue with the appeal unless a party objects before judgment is delivered: *John Nilkare v Ombudsman Commission* [1996] PNGLR 413.

8. Supplemental powers of Supreme Court.

(1) For the purposes of this Act, the Supreme Court may, if it thinks it necessary or expedient in the interests of justice to do so-

(a) order the production of any document, exhibit or other thing connected with the proceedings the production of which appears to it necessary for the determination of the case; and

(b) order any persons who would have been compellable witnesses at the trial to attend and be examined before the Court, whether or not they were called at the trial, or order any such person to be examined on oath before-

(i) a Judge of the National Court; or

(ii) an officer of the Supreme Court; or

(iii) a magistrate of a court of summary jurisdiction; or

(iv) any other person appointed by the Court for the purpose, and may admit as evidence and deposition so taken; and

(c) receive the evidence, if tendered, of any witness (including the appellant) who is a competent but not compellable witness, and, if the appellant consents, of the husband or wife of the appellant in cases where the evidence of the husband or wife could not have been given at the trial except with that consent; and

(d) where any question arising on the appeal involves prolonged examination of documents or accounts or any scientific or local investigation that cannot, in the opinion of the Court, conveniently be conducted before the Court-order the reference of the question for inquiry and report, in accordance with Part IV, by a referee appointed by the Court and act on the report of the referee so far as it thinks fit to adopt it; and

(e) exercise in relation to the proceedings of the Court any other powers that may for the time being be exercised by the National Court on appeals or applications; and

(f) issue any warrants necessary for enforcing the orders or sentences of the Court.

(g) The Supreme Court shall not increase a sentence in a criminal proceeding by reason of, or in consideration of, any evidence given under Subsection (1).

---

[39] *James Pari and Tine Bomai Kaupa v The State* [1993] PNGLR 173 at 177 (Kapi DCJ).

Whatever the role of its antecedent (s 15 of the old *Supreme Court (Full Court) Act*), it would appear that this section now occupies the role of a machinery provision for the purpose, inter alia, of implementing the powers granted under s 6: *John Peng v The State* [1982] PNGLR 331.

Where leave is granted to admit additional evidence on appeal to the Supreme Court pursuant to s 8(1) ... where the court "thinks it necessary or expedient in the interests of justice to do so", there is a right to call further evidence in rebuttal of that additional evidence: *Abiari v The State (No 2)* [1990] PNGLR 432.

> "It is clear ... that the nature of the power granted under s 8 goes far beyond the limited scope of s 6(1)(a) ... The evidence referred to in s 8 need not be confined to fresh evidence as defined in s 6(1)(a). There is nothing in s 8 which would so confine it. I would adopt the interpretation given by the English Court of Appeal in relation to the equivalent of s 8 in England ... The manner in which the power under s 8 of the Act may be exercised is to be governed by the words 'the Supreme Court may, if it thinks it necessary or expedient in the interests of justice'. It is clear to me that 'the interests of justice' will override all other considerations. What is necessary or expedient in the interests of justice must be determined within the facts of each particular case."[40]

Where the trial judge's judgment on matters of verdict or sentence is not available to the Supreme Court on an appeal, the Supreme Court may consider evidence from the record and draw inferences from that evidence: *Pake Kik v The State* (1996) SC 511; applied in *Mark Ninas v The State* (1998) SC 598.

As a result of the decision in *Mai Kuri v The State (No 2)* [1991] PNGLR 311, a unanimous five-member Supreme Court decision, "it is now clear beyond argument that s 8 ... is not a separate basis for fresh evidence but is merely a machinery provision which is supplemental to s 6 ... Any submission or judgment to the contrary effect is wrong in law."[41]

The court in *Mai Kuri v The State (No 2)* [1991] PNGLR 311 approved Amet J's dissenting reasons in *Abiari v The State* [1990] PNGLR 250:

> "Section 8 is, in my view, notwithstanding all the common law precedents that relate to similar or equivalent English and Australian provisions, quite simply a supplemental provision, for the purposes of the Act generally. It is a general provision 'for the purposes of this Act'. It cannot supersede a specific procedural head of power such as s 6. Section 6 is not made 'subject to s 8' or 'subject to this Act' or 'subject to other provisions of this Act'. It is not drafted in the form one might expect a superior overriding provision to be, such as 'notwithstanding this Act' or 'notwithstanding s 6' or similar expression.
>
> To construe s 8 as a separate grant of power exceeding the limitations of s 6 would render it incongruous with the s 6 limitations. The two provisions would be quite incompatible; they would not be complimentary. They would be inconsistent with one another ... I cannot conceive it to have been the legislature's intention that, while s 6 was intentionally and for good reasons limited, an all-inclusive separate head of power quite inconsistent with it should also be enacted. ... If any evidence can be called, whether it be fresh or not fresh, provided that the Court thinks it necessary or expedient in the interests of justice to do so, then s 6 becomes redundant ...

---

[40] *Abiari v The State* [1990] PNGLR 250 at 260 (Kapi DCJ disapproved of *John Peng v The State* [1982] PNGLR 331).

[41] *Mai Kuri v The State (No 2)* [1991] PNGLR 311 at 187 (Ellis J).

I am of the opinion that s 8 is a machinery provision, for the purpose, inter alia, of implementing the powers granted under s 6. It is not a separate overriding grant of power in derogation of s 6."[42]

Division 3 – Additional Provisions Relating to Appeals in Criminal Cases

20. Application of Division 3.

This Division applies to and in relation to criminal proceedings.

21. Reservation of points of law.

(1) When any person is indicted, the National Court shall, on the application of counsel for the accused person made before verdict, and may in its discretion, before or after verdict without such application, reserve any question of law, that arises on the trial for the consideration of the Supreme Court.

(2) If the accused person is convicted, and a question of law has been reserved under Subsection (1) before judgement, the National Court may -

(a) pronounce judgement on the conviction and respite execution of the judgement; or

(b) postpone the judgement until the question has been considered and decided, and may -

(c) commit the person convicted to prison; or

(d) admit him to bail on recognizance, with or without sureties, and in such sum as the Court thinks proper, conditioned to appear at such time and place as the Judge directs, and to render himself in execution, or to receive judgement, as the case may be.

(3) The National Court shall state, in the case signed by the Judge or Judges exercising the jurisdiction of the Court, the question of law reserved under Subsection (1), with the special circumstances on which it arose, and the case shall be transmitted to the Supreme Court.

(4) Any question reserved under Subsection (1) shall be heard and determined by the Supreme Court.

(5) Any question reserved under Subsection (1) shall be heard and determined after argument by and on behalf of the prosecution, and of the accused or convicted person or persons, if they desire that the question shall be argued, and the Supreme Court may -

(a) affirm the judgement given at the trial; or

(b) set aside the verdict and judgement and order a verdict of not guilty or other appropriate verdict to be entered; or

(c) arrest the judgement; or

(d) amend the judgement; or

---

[42] *Abiari v The State* [1990] PNGLR 250 at 265-267 (Amet J); approved and followed in *Mai Kuri v The State (No 2)* [1991] PNGLR 311 (Kidu CJ, Hinchliffe, Sheehan, Brown and Jalina JJ).

(e) order a new trial; or

(f) make such other order as justice requires,

or the Court may send the case back to be amended or restated.

It has always been the view of the judges in Papua New Guinea that the trial judge should decide the facts and issues involved in the case prior to making a reference to the Supreme Court under s 20. The reasons are obvious. The Supreme Court can be assembled only at monthly intervals. Accused persons cannot readily be transported across the country's great distances. In many cases bail cannot be granted. Witnesses can be lost with the passage of time; and in Papua New Guinea frequently are. And of course, there is the principle that applies in all countries, that it is highly undesirable that a court of appeal (especially a final court of appeal such as the Supreme Court) should unnecessarily become seized of a matter before it had been argued in front of a judge of first instance and that judge's study thereof (with the assistance of counsel) and conclusions thereon become available for its assistance. It must be emphasised that this section does not exist to shield the National Court from its plain duty of receiving the due assistance of counsel, and coming to decisions on the issues presented to it as quickly as is fairly and justly possible: *Supreme Court Reference No 3 of 1979: The State v John Rumet Kaputin* [1979] PNGLR 532 at 534.

> "It is not necessary in order that there may be a reference under this section for the accused to have been completely acquitted on the indictment; the section may be invoked in a case where the accused have been acquitted of the charges even though convicted on a lesser charge."[43]

The Supreme Court should generally avoid academic questions and decline to answer questions unless they are specific questions of criminal law raised at the trial: *R v PM* [1971-1972] PNGLR 222.

22. Criminal appeals.

A person convicted by the National Court may appeal to the Supreme Court -

(a) against his conviction, on any ground that involves a question of law alone; and

(b) against his conviction, on a question of mixed fact and law; and

(c) with the leave of the Supreme Court, or on the certificate of the National Court that is a fit case for appeal, against his conviction on any ground of appeal -

(d) that involves a question of fact alone; or

(e) that appears to the Supreme Court to be a sufficient ground of appeal; and

(f) with the leave of the Supreme Court, against the sentence passed on his conviction, unless the sentence is one fixed by law.

Upon the hearing of an application for leave to appeal against sentence, the Supreme Court may admit fresh evidence and consider it along with the materials

---

[43] *R v KL* [1973] PNGLR 93 at 96 (Minogue CJ and Kelly J).

available to the trial judge and determine whether the sentence imposed was wrong: *Wanosa v The Queen* [1971-1972] PNGLR 90.

On an appeal against sentence the Supreme Court does not have to consider whether a miscarriage of justice has actually occurred: *Tremellan v R* [1973] PNGLR 116.

The appeal court is limited to what was said at the time of sentence and any omitted factors which the appeal court considers to be important to the sentence. The sentencing judge is not required to refer to every possible element of crime indicating the weight given to it. Where conclusions of fact turn upon witness credibility, in an appeal, "an applicant must show that the rejection of testimony favourable to him, and the drawing of inferences adverse to him, flowed from some fundamental misconception of the evidence by the trial judge, or from his failure to take proper account (of) the evidence as a whole": *Ura Francis Miriva v The State* (1981) SC 197 (Kearney DCJ).

For an appellant to succeed in an appeal against sentence, the court must be persuaded that a more lenient sentence is warranted. The appellant must show some error on the part of the judge in imposing that sentence: see *William Norris v The State* [1979] PNGLR 605. Where the leniency is sought for a murderer on the ground that the person murdered is believed to have practised sorcery, the sentencing judge ought to know on some proper evidentiary basis about the grounds for such belief and the extent of such belief and the extent of such belief in the community to which the offender belongs: *Agoara Kebo and Karunai Uraki v The State* (1981) SC 198 (Miles J).

The Supreme Court in *Jim Kas v The State* (1999) SCRA 89/98 invalidated the requirement for leave to appeal against sentence on the grounds that this infringed an accused's right to appeal under s 37(15) of the *Constitution*. This decision was applied in *William Dot v The State* (1999) SC 621. On the prior law regarding necessity of obtaining leave to appeal to the Supreme Court in appropriate cases, see *Arthur Gilbert Smedley v The State* [1980] PNGLR 379 and *Porewa Wani v The State* [1979] PNGLR 593. In *Smedley*, the majority of the Supreme Court declined to follow the dicta on this point in *Mathias Peter Joseph Evertz v The State* [1979] PNGLR 174.

See numerous annotations of *Avia Aihi v The State (No 1)* [1981] PNGLR 81, at s 155 of the *Constitution*, for consideration of this section.

23. Determination of appeals in ordinary cases.

(1) Subject to Subsection (2), on an appeal against a conviction the Supreme Court shall allow the appeal if it thinks that -

(a) the verdict should be set aside on the ground that under all the circumstances of the case it is unsafe or unsatisfactory; or

(b) the judgement of the Court before which the appellant was convicted should be set aside on the ground of a wrong decision on any question of law; or

(c) there was a material irregularity in the course of the trial, and in any other case shall dismiss the appeal.

(2) Notwithstanding that the Supreme Court is of the opinion that the point raised in the appeal might be decided in favour of the appellant, it may dismiss the appeal if it considers that no miscarriage of justice has actually occurred.

(3) If the Supreme Court allows an appeal against conviction, it shall, subject to this Act, quash the conviction and direct a verdict of not guilty be entered.

(4) On an appeal against sentence, if the Supreme Court is of opinion that some other sentence, whether more or less severe, is warranted in law and should have been passed, it shall quash the sentence and pass the other sentence in substitution for it, and in any other case shall dismiss the appeal.

With regard to the principles to be applied by an appellate court when reviewing the findings of a lower court in Papua New Guinea, the aspect which strikes one immediately is that there is not, and never has been, trial by jury in this country. The traditional reluctance to interfere with the decisions of juries therefore has no place in Papua New Guinea. Secondly, the High Court of Australia said in *Webb v Bloch* (1928) 41 CLR 331 at 360, that the court had a constitutional duty to form its independent opinion as to the proper inferences from facts in evidence. So too in *Livingstone v Halvorsen* (referred to in *Warren v Coombes* (1979) 53 ALJR 293 at 300), where Murphy J said that the parties have a constitutional right to the decision of the court on the merits of the case. In deciding the merits of the case on appeal however, one new matter arises, and that is the decision of the trial judge. That decision, with all the findings contained in it, has to be given proper weight. A Supreme Court judge is not free to substitute his or her own findings of fact unless consideration has been given to the whole of the decision of the National Court: *John Anis Pok v The State* (1983) SC 254.

Unless the trial judge has fundamentally misconceived the evidence, an appeal court will not disturb the trial judge's findings of fact and findings as to credibility: *Mathias Peter Joseph Evertz v The State* [1979] PNGLR 174.

The court's duty should be to scrutinise only the evidence of the case under appeal, together with any other fresh evidence, which it might allow to be admissible. The time-honoured rules whereby an appeal court gives full faith and credit to the superior position of the trial tribunal as to the atmosphere of the trial, the demeanour of, and assessment of witnesses, are of the greatest importance in the administration of justice and the harmonious working of the court: *R v Erico Aufe* [1974] PNGLR 331 at 347 (Prentice J).

On appeal from a case decided on the basis of eyewitness identification, the Supreme Court may not re-try the case: *John Beng v The State* [1977] PNGLR 115.

> "On matters of credibility [the] Court will only interfere in three circumstances: first, if the jury has been misdirected as to how to assess the evidence; secondly, if there has been no direction at all when there should have been one; and thirdly, if on the whole of the evidence the jury must have taken a perverse view of a witness, but this is rare."[44]

Minogue ACJ and Frost J thought that a verdict would be unsafe or unsatisfactory under s 23(1)(a) where the Supreme Court has a lurking doubt which makes it wonder whether an injustice has been done: *R v Kampangio* [1969-1970] PNGLR 218.

> "The doubt must be of a reasonable character, as my brothers say; a more unsubstantial or fanciful doubt will not suffice."[45]

The court should not substitute "entertaining a lurking doubt" or "the general feel

[44] *R v Raymond Turnbull* (1976) Cr App R 132 at 139-140.
[45] *John Beng v The State* [1977] PNGLR 115 (Kearney J).

of the case" or "reacting unhappily" for the plain words of the section. Such a test would seem to replace proof beyond a reasonable doubt on the evidence with a new test: "beyond lurking doubt at large". The approach of the Chief Justice of Australia, in *Hayes v R* (1973) 47 ALJR 603, may be more suitable to the needs and responsive to the wishes of the people: *R v Erico Aufe* [1974] PNGLR 331 at 346 and 347 (Prentice J).

Various considerations "will no doubt from time to time give rise to doubt of a reasonable character as to the safeness or satisfactoriness of a verdict such as calls for it to be set aside. To hold that the starting up of any sort of doubt or uneasy feeling could so justify would be to give an inapt construction": *John Beng v The State* [1977] PNGLR 115 (Prentice DCJ and Williams J).

It is improper for the appellant to raise questions of fact nevertheless on the basis that an appeal is to be allowed if the verdict below is considered "unsafe or unsatisfactory" and that this in itself permits questions of fact to be raised: *John Kasaipwalova v The State* [1977] PNGLR 257 (Kearney J dissenting).

Where the appellant alleges several matters which tend to show that the verdict of the lower court was unsafe or unsatisfactory, whilst none of the matters taken individually may lead to that conclusion, the court should take into account the aggregate effect: *John Beng v The State* [1977] PNGLR 115.

It was held that a verdict was unsafe and unsatisfactory in that trial judge, when considering the evidence, had failed to expressly advert to the accused's amnesia as to the relevant events and the effect that this may have had on the prosecution's onus of proof: *Himson Mulas v R* [1969-170] PNGLR 82.

The Supreme Court may, of its own volition, increase a sentence where there is an appeal by a convicted appellant: *Lawrence Hindemba v The State* (1998) SC 593.

The sentence imposed by the trial judges should not be disturbed under s 23(4) unless it is shown to be manifestly inadequate or manifestly excessive because, for instance, the trial judge has acted on a wrong principle, or has clearly overlooked, undervalued, overestimated or misunderstood some salient features of the evidence: *Wanosa v The Queen* [1971-1972] PNGLR 90.

> "That on appeal on sentence by the prosecution, the question of adequacy of sentence was completely open – an Appeal Court should allow the appeal only where the sentence was seen to be manifestly excessive."[46]

The crime of breaking and entering, for which severe penalties are prescribed by Parliament, seems to be on the increase throughout the country. A plea of youth may no longer be a satisfactory answer to crime. Few alternatives are available to Papua New Guinea courts in dealing with youths and younger men other than to impose sentences of imprisonment. Where a particular crime becomes prevalent, deterrence is thought to be of importance at least equivalent to that of rehabilitation: *Paulus Mandatitip v The State* [1978] PNGLR 128.

> "It is not enough that members of the court would themselves have imposed a less or different sentence, or that they think the sentence over-severe. There must be some occasion for regarding the discretion confided to the court of first instance as improperly exercised. This may include some considerations which ought not to have affected the discretion, or may exclude others which ought to

[46] See *Public Prosecutor v John Aia and Peter Pino* [1978] PNGLR 224 (Sentences of 19 months and 23 months on youths aged approximately 20 were upheld).

have done so. The court may have mistaken or been misled as to the facts, or an error of law may have been made. Effect may have been given to views or opinions which are extreme or misguided. But it is not necessary that some definite or specific error should be assigned. The nature of the sentence itself, when considered in relation to the offence and the circumstances of the case, may be such as to afford convincing evidence that in some way the exercise of the discretion has been unsound."[47]

In practice, in order to persuade the Supreme Court that a sentence was manifestly excessive, an appellant will usually be required to show some error on the part of the trial judge going to sentence: see *House v The King* (1936) 55 CLR 499 at 504-505; *R v Taylor and O'Meally* [1958] VR 285 at 289-290 and 299; and *Wanosa v The Queen* [1971-1972] PNGLR 90 at 97-105 (Clarkson J).

The sentencing power is a discretionary judicial power. If no such error is shown, this court is unlikely to interfere with the sentence because a trial judge is usually in a much better position to assess the proper sentence than is a court of appeal: *William Norris v The State* [1979] PNGLR 605 (Kearney J).

It is now a well-established principle of law that an appellate court does not interfere with the sentence imposed by the court below because it is of the view that the sentence is either inadequate or excessive. It interferes only if it is apparent that the sentencing judge has fallen into error in acting on a wrong principle or has misunderstood or wrongly assessed the facts of the case. This principle is well settled in Australia (see *Skinner v The King* (1913) 16 CLR 336; *Whittaker v The King* (1928) 41 CLR 230; and *Griffiths v The Queen* (1977) 51 ALJR 749) and can now be regarded as part of the underlying law of Papua New Guinea: *Acting Public Prosecutor v Uname Aumane* [1980] PNGLR 510 (Kapi J).

Upon an appeal against sentence by the convicted person, the sentence imposed by the trial judge should not be disturbed unless it is shown, following *Wanosa v The Queen* [1971-1972] PNGLR 90, to be manifestly inadequate or manifestly excessive because, for instance, the trial judge has acted on a wrong principle, or has clearly overlooked, undervalued, overestimated or misunderstood some salient feature of the evidence: *Kali Mari v The State* (1980) SC 175.

An application to adduce fresh evidence on appeal against severity of sentence was not granted where it had not been shown that the evidence sought to be given was not available at the trial, nor that it was undiscoverable by use of ordinary diligence – the usual basic prerequisites: *John Rumet Kaputin v The State* [1979] PNGLR 559 at 560, distinguishing *R v Peter Ivoro* [1971-1972] PNGLR 374.

An appellant must always bear in mind the risk that the sentence may be increased on appeal, under s 22(4): *Saki v The State* [1980] PNGLR 33.

In accordance with the conventional principles applied to appeals against an exercise of judicial discretion, it is necessary for the appellant to show identifiable error of law on the part of the judge at first instance, or if error of law cannot be identified, that there has been manifest miscarriage of justice: *Gabriel Laku v The State* [1981] PNGLR 350.

Where there is a long delay in setting down the appeal for hearing, application may be made to the court to strike out the appeal. When such an application is not successful, the question of delay cannot be argued again. The court may, however, have regard to the question of delay if it decides to increase the sentence after

[47] *R v Harris* (1954) 90 CLR 652 at 655 and 656 (Dixon CJ, Fullagar, Kitto and Taylor JJ).

considering the merits of the case: *Acting Public Prosecutor v Andrew Lalaiva of Honi and Angelo Ume of Kivori* [1981] PNGLR 148.

Regarding trial on separate indictments or a material or mere irregularity per s 23(1)(c), see *The State v Lea Nimo* [1980] PNGLR 129, annotated at s 532 of the *Criminal Code*.

In a case where it was questioned whether there had been undue participation by judge (where the trial judge had asked some 186 questions to the prosecutor's 123), it was found that there had not been a miscarriage of justice. In the circumstances of the country, including the difficulty of eliciting answers from reticent young girls in cases of a sexual nature, and where there may be somewhat inexperienced prosecutors, it may become necessary for a judge to hold the balance between the interest of the state in enforcing the law and that of the accused defending himself against a charge, by intervention of a rather more detailed and prolonged nature than would be called for or proper in other more sophisticated settings. Another vital difference between the Papua New Guinea experience and that of other jurisdictions is that there is at present no jury which can be misled in a variety of ways by judicial intervention: *Birch v The State* [1979] PNGLR 75 (Prentice CJ, following generally the principles in *R v Butler* (1953) 70 WN 222).

See ss 19 and 596 of the *Criminal Code* regarding sentencing generally.

24. Appeal by Public Prosecutor against sentence.

(1) In this section "sentence" includes any order made on conviction with reference to the person convicted or his property.

(2) The Public Prosecutor may appeal to the Supreme Court against any decision of the National Court, whether on appeal or sitting as a court of first instance, as to sentence, and the Supreme Court may in its discretion vary the sentence and impose such sentence as it thinks proper.

The effect of this section is to confer an unfettered discretion on the Supreme Court to vary the sentence of the National Court. The Supreme Court should not, however, interfere with a sentence pronounced by a trial judge unless it is clearly satisfied that the sentence should be altered: *Public Prosecutor v Terrence Kaveku* [1977] PNGLR 110.

On this point also see *R v Mary Josephine Harley* [1971-1972] PNGLR 399 and *Public Prosecutor v Yapuna Kaso* [1977] PNGLR 209.

Despite the fact that the trial judge had the benefit of hearing the witnesses, where the objective circumstances of the crime are set out in the depositions, the trial judge's advantage should not prevail over the views of an appellate court where it is clearly satisfied that the sentence is inadequate and should be altered: *R v Harley* [1971-1972] PNGLR 399.

Where co-accused are equally responsible for a crime, there should not be too great a disparity in sentences awarded to actual participants and those who encouraged and approved the crime: *Secretary for Law v Kaibug Jimbun* [1976] PNGLR 288.

In *Wanosa v The Queen* [1971-1972] PNGLR 90, Clarkson J considered the nature of the rights and duties of the appellate court on an appeal against sentence under this section.

For an example of an appeal under this section, see *R v Bulda Melin* [1973] PNGLR 278.

The Supreme Court has an unfettered discretion on an appeal to substitute what it considers the appropriate sentence if an appeal against inadequacy of sentence is allowed: *Public Prosecutor v Willy Moke Soki* [1977] PNGLR 165.

As to the exercise of the unfettered discretion of the Supreme Court to vary the sentence imposed, see also *R v Pia-Afu* [1971-1972] PNGLR 893 and *Public Prosecutor v Wiwi Gok* [1977] PNGLR 161.

On an appeal by the Public Prosecutor, the former Full Court decision in *R v Pia-Afu* [1971-1972] PNGLR 393 is doubted in view of Barwick CJ in *Griffiths v The Queen* (1977) 51 ALJR 749 and *Kovac v The Queen* (1977) 15 ALR 637. Previously, it was laid down that on an appeal on sentence by the prosecution the question of adequacy of sentence was completely open, and in an appeal by a convicted person an appeal court should allow the appeal only where the sentence was seen to be manifestly excessive. Now the court of appeal does not have an unfettered discretion on appeal against inadequacy. The principles to be applied are the same as those applicable when the question arises of whether it is excessive: *Public Prosecutor v John Aia and Peter Pino* [1978] PNGLR 224.

On an appeal against sentence, the Supreme Court does not have to consider whether a miscarriage of justice has actually occurred: *Tremellan v R* [1973] PNGLR 116.

In an appeal against a sentence by the state, the court does not have an unfettered discretion to vary the sentence appealed against, and will only do so where it is clearly shown that the trial judge has fallen in error in the exercise of discretion: *Acting Public Prosecutor v Konis Haha* [1981] PNGLR 205 (Kidu CJ).

In an appeal against an inadequate sentence, the court may substitute the trial sentence with a heavier sentence. The fact that the co-accused persons have not been apprehended, or the case against such persons has not been considered, is immaterial and not considered as a mitigating factor: *Public Prosecutor v Michael Wunap Ngudomp* [1982] PNGLR 357.

The sentence imposed by a trial court may be set aside and substituted with a longer sentence by an appellate court, even in a case where the accused is nearing the end of the sentence. Once the appellate court has come to the conclusion that a sentence appealed against is inadequate, particularly in relation to a serious offence, a submission that the accused has almost completed the sentence would only be admitted as relevant in exceptional circumstances. It is immaterial that the accused has been on bail. Despite the potential advantages of aiming at rehabilitation in sentencing the accused, the court may impose a heavier substituted sentence in the case of robbery. In *Acting Public Prosecutor v Andrew Lalaiva of Honi and Angelo Ume* [1981] PNGLR 148 Greville-Smith J said that a "stern sentence is more likely to deter from future criminality, and to that extent make the person concerned a better person."

As to the issue of the proper function of counsel for the state in assisting the court on sentence, see *R v Tait and Bartley* (1979) 24 ALR 473 at 477, adopted by Kapi J in *Acting Public Prosecutor v Uname Aumane* [1980] PNGLR 510, and discussed under the *Criminal Code*, s 596 below.

Having regard to the time limits imposed by the Act on all other types of appeals (see ss 17 and 29), the omission by the Act to set down any time limit in which the Public Prosecutor may appeal is a clear intention that the time in which the Public Prosecutor may appeal should not be restricted by the same time limit. That being the intention of the legislation, any judge's rules that may be made under s 184 of the *Constitution* which are inconsistent with this intention, are invalid to that extent.

Rule 32 of the *Supreme Court Rules* 1977 is a clear limitation of the time in which the Public Prosecutor may appeal, which is contrary to the intention of the whole of the Act and is therefore invalid: *Acting Public Prosecutor v Uname Aumane* [1980] PNGLR 510 (Kapi J).

The lack of a time limit on appeals by the Public Prosecutor under this section occasions no difficulty or injustice. See, for example, the approach to State appeals in *R v Porter* (1953) 53 SR (NSW) 97.

For a review of the law in other common law jurisdictions with regard to the right of the prosecutor to appeal against sentence, see Greville-Smith J in *Acting Public Prosecutor v Uname Aumane* [1980] PNGLR 510.

There is no room for the suggestion that the Public Prosecutor's right of appeal under this section is subject to r 32 of the *Supreme Court Rules* 1977. Section 184 of the *Constitution*, under which the *Supreme Court Rules* were made, is quite clear; a rule of court must not be inconsistent with a constitutional law or an Act of Parliament. Rule 32, in applying a time limitation on the right of the Public Prosecutor to appeal, is inconsistent with s 24 of the *Supreme Court Act* and therefore is invalid. Section 22, governing the convicted persons right of appeal, is restricted by s 29, whilst s 24 contains no restriction nor is it restricted by any other provision of the Act: *Acting Public Prosecutor v Uname Aumane* [1980] PNGLR 510 (Kidu CJ, with whom the rest of the court agrees).

Section 12 of the *Interpretation (Interim Provisions) Act* 1975 provides that:

> "Where no time is prescribed or allowed within which an act is required or permitted by a provision to be done, the act shall or may be done, as the case may be, with all convenient speed and as often as the occasion arises."

The fair and liberal meaning of this, and that which would best dispense justice, is that once the actor embarks upon the act permitted to be done, it should be carried it out with all convenient speed. Applying this view to s 24, the "act" in question is the whole process of the appeal. The Public Prosecutor's right to institute an appeal at any time against sentence remains unaffected, but once having initiated such an appeal, he or she is bound to pursue it with all convenient speed: *Acting Public Prosecutor v Uname Aumane* [1980] PNGLR 510 (Kearney DCJ, with Kidu CJ and Andrew and Greville-Smith JJ agreeing).

Section 12 of the *Interpretation (Interim Provisions) Act* is applicable when there is no time limit imposed for the doing of an act. Where the Public Prosecutor uses discretion to file or to institute a Notice of Appeal, that act is to be done with all convenient speed. As to what is a convenient speed depends on the circumstances of the particular case. Furthermore, it is only reasonable for the prisoner to assume that after some time in prison the proper sentence is the one given by the trial judge. An appeal against sentence after a long delay must be seen to be unfair to the prisoner. In resolving what is to be regarded as a convenient time within which the Public Prosecutor must file a Notice of Appeal, regard must not only be given to the convenience of the Public Prosecutor, but also to the interests of the prisoner and the proper and speedy determination of the appeal by the Supreme Court: *Acting Public Prosecutor v Uname Aumane* [1980] PNGLR 510 (Kapi J dissenting).

See s 596 of the *Criminal Code* regarding sentencing generally.

25. Appeal against quashing of conviction.

Where the National Court has given a judgement quashing a conviction, or any count or part of a charge, the Public Prosecutor may appeal to the Supreme Court against the judgement, and the Supreme Court may -

(a) determine the appeal; and

(b) if the appeal is sustained make such order for the prosecution of the trial as it thinks necessary or desirable.

26. Reference of point of law following acquittal on indictment.

(1) Where a person tried on indictment has been acquitted whether in respect of the whole or part of the indictment and the Principal Legal Adviser desires the opinion of the Supreme Court on a point of law that has arisen in the case -

(a) the Principal Legal Adviser may, within 40 days after the acquittal, refer the point to the Supreme Court; and

(b) the Court shall, in accordance with this section, consider the point and give its opinion on it.

(2) For the purpose of its consideration of a point referred to it under this section, the Supreme Court shall hear argument -

(a) by, or by counsel on behalf of, the Principal Legal Adviser; and

(b) if the acquitted person desires to present any argument to the Court, by counsel on his behalf or, with the leave of the Court, by the acquitted person himself; and

(c) by, or by counsel on behalf of -

(i) the Public Prosecutor; and

(ii) the State Solicitor,

or either of them, if they desire to present any argument to the Court.

(3) No report of proceedings under this section shall be published that discloses the name or identity of any person charged at the trial or affected by the decision given at the trial.

(4) Any publication in contravention of Subsection (3) is punishable as contempt of the Supreme Court.

(5) A reference under this section does not affect the trial in relation to which the reference is made or any acquittal in that trial.

See *Principal Legal Advisors Request No 1 of 1980* [1980] PNGLR 326 and *Supreme Court Reference No 1 of 1976* [1976] PNGLR 377.

27. Powers of Supreme Court in special cases.

(1) If it appears to the Supreme Court that an appellant, though not properly convicted on some charge, or on some count or part of the charge, has been properly convicted on some other charge, or on some other count or part of the charge, the Court may -

(a) affirm the sentence passed on the appellant; or

(b) pass such sentence in substitution for it as it thinks proper and is warranted in law by the verdict on the charge or on the count or part of the charge, on which the Court considers that the appellant has been properly convicted.

(2) Where an appellant has been convicted of an offence and he could on the charge have been found guilty of some other offence, and the Supreme Court is satisfied as to facts that proved him guilty of the other offence, instead of allowing or dismissing the appeal the Court may -

(a) substitute for the verdict a verdict of guilty of the other offence; and

(b) pass such sentence in substitution for the sentence passed at the trial as is proper and as is warranted in law for that other offence, not being a sentence of greater severity.

(3) If on appeal it appears to the Supreme Court that although the appellant committed the act or made the omission charged against him he was not of sound mind at the time when the act or omission alleged to constitute the offence occurred, so as not to be responsible for it according to law, the Court may -

(a) quash the judgement given at the trial; and

(b) order the appellant to be kept in strict custody in the same manner as if that fact had been found under Section 592 of the *Criminal Code*.

It was held in *Simili Kara v The State* [1984] PNGLR 254 that s 27 does not invest the Supreme Court with the power to amend an indictment.

28. New trial.

(1) If on an appeal against conviction, the Supreme Court thinks that-

(a) a miscarriage of justice has occurred; and

(b) having regard to all the circumstances, the miscarriage of justice can be more adequately remedied by an order for a new trial rather than by any other order that the Court has power to make,

the Court may, of its own motion or on the application of the appellant, order a new trial in such manner as it thinks proper.

(2) Where a new trial is ordered, the Supreme Court may make such order as it thinks proper for the safe custody of the appellant or for admitting him to bail.

In determining whether or not a retrial should be ordered, the following may be relevant:

(a) the public interest in bringing to justice those guilty of serious crimes and ensuring that they do not escape because of technical blunders by the trial judge in the conduct of the trial;

(b) the expense and inconvenience to witnesses who would be involved in a new trial, when weighed against the strength of the evidence;

(c) the seriousness and prevalence of the particular offence;

(d) the consideration that a criminal trial is an ordeal which the defendant ought not be condemned to undergo for a second time through no fault of their own;

(e) the length of time elapsing between the offence and the new trial if ordered; and

(f) the strength and availability of the evidence.[48]

These matters were endorsed and adopted by Amet CJ, Kapi DCJ and Los, Injia and Sawong JJ in *Charles Bougapa Ombusu v The State* (1996) SC 502.

The Supreme Court can order a new trial should there exist one of the circumstances referred to under s 28 of the *Supreme Court Act*. In *Gibson Gunure Ohizave v The State* (1998) SC 595 it was held that excessive intervention by the trial judge in the identification evidence amounted to a miscarriage of justice, and that this miscarriage of justice could be more adequately remedied by ordering a new trial.

29. Time for appealing under Division 3.

(1) Subject to Subsection (2), where a person convicted desires to appeal or to obtain leave to appeal to the Supreme Court, he shall give notice of appeal, or notice of his application for leave to appeal, as the case may be, in the manner prescribed by the Rules of Court within 40 days after the date of conviction.

(2) The time within which notice of appeal, or notice of an application for leave to appeal, may be given may be extended at any time by the Supreme Court on application made within 40 days after the date of conviction.

(3) In the case of a conviction involving a sentence of death or of corporal punishment-

(a) the sentence shall not be carried out until after the expiration of 40 days, or such further time as is allowed under this section, after the date of conviction; and

(b) if notice is given in accordance with Subsection (1), the sentence shall not be carried out until after the determination of the appeal, or where an application for leave to appeal is finally refused, of the application.

The Supreme Court has power to dismiss appeals for want of prosecution. It has further inherent jurisdiction quite apart from the rules of the court to control its proceedings such as abuse of process. It has the power to dismiss appeals where there is undue or unwarranted delay in prosecuting an appeal. The onus is on the applicant to establish a prima facie case, after which the appellant is required to give a satisfactory explanation of the delays. What constitutes undue delays depends on the circumstances of each case. However, the court may regard 28 days as a determining guide: *Tenge Kai v Acting Public Prosecutor* [1981] PNGLR 148.

An extension of time will not be granted as a matter of course, but the court will in every case require substantial reasons to be advanced before granting such a concession:

> "When the time prescribed by the Act has expired the party convicted has lost his right to appeal, and it is for the Court to say whether, taking all the circumstances into account, it is in the interests of justice that he should be permitted to substitute and pursue his appeal ... in the exercise of our discretion,

---

[48] *Oscar Tuguine v Michael Gotaha* [1984] PNGLR 137 (Bredmeyer J).

> we ought not to do unless we are satisfied that there is, at the least grave reason to apprehend that justice has actually miscarried that is to say that the conviction was contrary to the truth and justice of the case."[49]
>
> "[T]he Supreme Court has now by a majority held that under s 155(2)(b) of the *Constitution* this Court has power to grant to the applicant the right to make application to extend time or to apply for leave to appeal out of time contrary to the provisions of s 37(15) of the *Constitution* and s 29 of the *Supreme Court Act*."[50]

The Public Prosecutor's discretionary right to appeal is absolute, unlike a convicted person's right, which is restricted by this section: see discussion of *Acting Public Prosecutor v Uname Aumane* [1980] PNGLR 510, under s 23 of this Act.

Whether r 23(1) of the *Supreme Court Rules* regarding objection to competency of appeal is mandatory or merely regulatory, a respondent is not debarred from objecting to the competency of an application for leave to appeal out of time, because questions of competency, like questions of jurisdiction, may be raised at any time. The sanction for a respondent who objects to the competency of an application for leave to appeal out of time is to be found in r 23(4), under which the respondent may in certain circumstances be deprived of costs: *Arthur Gilbert Smedley v The State* [1980] PNGLR 379 (Wilson J).

In relation to r 18 of the *Supreme Court Rules*, Kearney J in *Arthur Gilbert Smedley v The State* [1980] PNGLR 379 observed that "the Rules are not geared, in practice, to ... persons [who are unrepresented and in custody]".

For a case in which the appellant failed to give notice of his application for leave to appeal within 40 days (nor was an extension sought under s 29(2)), and thus was refused the opportunity to appeal against severity of sentence, see *Porewa Wani v The State* [1979] PNGLR 593.

See s 22 of this Act regarding those circumstances in which leave of the court is necessary in an appeal from a criminal conviction.

In *Rolf Schubert v The State* [1979] PNGLR 66, amendment was allowed in the special circumstances of a late change of the accused's counsel and the broad merits of the new ground of appeal, namely, that the evidence of a prosecutrix aged under 12 years on a charge of unlawful and indecent dealing may not have been in accordance with the provisions of s 6 of the *Oaths Affirmations and Statutory Declarations Act*. This section lays down the manner in which evidence is to be taken where it appears that a child is incapable of comprehending the nature of an oath. In this case, there was no miscarriage of justice where a judge, having observed the youth of the prosecutrix, inquired of the prosecutor as to her age, asked the prosecutor whether she could be sworn and whether she would understand the nature of an oath. Having been told she could not be sworn or understand the nature of the oath, the witness was then affirmed and gave evidence in pidgin after she had been told the importance of telling the truth. Accordingly, the trial judge acted within the "good sense" of the court as in *R v Campbell* [1956] 2 QB 432.

It is undesirable to add new grounds of appeal at the eleventh hour. A fresh ground of appeal may well be regarded as being more than an amendment, and amount to a new notice of appeal which will be struck down by s 29. It is in the

---

[49] *Secretary for Law v Tisunkac Nawok Domstock also known as Bisanoga* [1974] PNGLR 246.

[50] *Avia Aihi v The State (No 2)* [1982] PNGLR 44 (Kapi J).

court's discretion to allow new grounds to be added, and this ought only to occur in special circumstances: *Rolf Schubert v The State* [1979] PNGLR 66.

> "The tendency for counsel to seek to add further grounds of appeal on the day of hearing or shortly before now threatens the efficiency of the work of this court."[51]

DISTRICT COURTS ACT 1963

No 19 of 1964

[Selected Sections Relating to Criminal Law]

The *District Courts Act* 1963 may continue to be referred to as such irrespective of the fact that it was technically repealed by s 3 of the *Laws Repeal Act* 1975 and adopted as an Act of the National Parliament as from 16 September 1975 by Sch 2.6(2) of the *Constitution*: *Supreme Court Reference No 1 of 1976(P); Peter Rakatani v South Pacific Brewery Ltd* [1976] PNGLR 537 (Prentice DCJ).

Part III – District Courts

Division 2 – Jurisdiction of District Courts

20. Jurisdiction of Courts.

(1) Where, by law-

(a) an offence is punishable on summary conviction or a person is made liable to a penalty or punishment or to pay a sum of money for an offence, act or omission and the offence, act or omission is not an indictable offence; or

(b) subject to Subsection (1A), an indictable offence is punishable on summary conviction, being an offence specified in Schedule 2 to the *Criminal Code*,

the matter may be heard and determined by a District Court in a summary manner under this Act.

(1A) Subject to Subsections (1B) and (1C), proceedings for an offence under Subsection (1)(b) shall be heard and determined by a District Court constituted by one or more Magistrates Grade V.

(1B) The National Court has concurrent jurisdiction to hear and determine matters to which Subsection (1)(b) applies.

(1C) Where proceedings are brought in respect of two indictable offences of which-

(a) one offence is an indictable offence to which Subsection (1)(b) applies; and

---

[51] *Birch v The State* [1979] PNGLR 75 at 77-78 (Prentice CJ).

(b) the other offence is an indictable offence to which Subsection (1)(b) does not apply,

both offences shall proceed on indictment to be heard and determined together by the National Court.

(1D) Where a person is charged before a court with an indictable offence to which Subsection (1C)(b) applies, and it appears that a period of time will elapse before the matter is heard and determined by the National Court, the court before which the accused person is brought shall-

(c) by its warrant commit the person to a corrective institution, police lock-up or other place of security to be kept there safely until the time appointed for the hearing by the National Court; or

(d) admit the person to bail in accordance with Division VI.2.

(2) Where, by law, jurisdiction is conferred on one or more Magistrates to hear and determine proceedings in respect of an offence or to do an act or to exercise a power, that jurisdiction may be exercised by a Court.

[Subs (1) rep and subss (1)-(1D) insrt Act No 32, 1980 (*District Courts (Hearing of Indictable Offences) Act* 1980), s 6; subs (1)(b) am Act No 34, 1983 (*District Courts (Amendment) Act* 1983), s 1.]

District Courts have only the powers vested in them by statute and are not courts of record. Accordingly, the sentencing power of a magistrate of the District Courts is exhausted once sentence has been pronounced. The magistrate is then functus officio and has, subject to the court's power to correct a slip, no power to make any alteration which amounts to a fresh adjudication: *The State v The Senior Stipendiary Magistrate, Ex Parte The Acting Public Prosecutor* [1976] PNGLR 344.

By the *Public Prosecutor (Office and Functions) (Amendment) Act* 1980 (Act No 44 of 1980), s 4 of the *Public Prosecutor (Office and Functions) Act* 1977 was amended so that "the Public Prosecutor shall control and exercise the prosecution function of the State". The section does not give any control by the Public Prosecutor over police prosecution functions as covered by s 197 of the *Constitution*.

Section 432 (not s 420) offences are patently matters of police concern, but s 4 does not attempt to cut down s 197(2) of the *Constitution*. However, clearly it is no longer a police function to prosecute a s 432 offence where the Public Prosecutor elects that it shall proceed in a different manner.

The purpose of s 4 is to vest a discretion in the Public Prosecutor to decide whether or not he or she shall have the matters dealt with in a summary way or permit them to proceed by way of committal. In exercising a discretion, the prosecutor is electing either to proceed under the new way or to allow the matter to proceed in the ordinary way. If no election is made, the matter will proceed as always under the *District Courts Act*. It is the Public Prosecutor alone in whom the discretion vests. It is a committal matter which must proceed on that basis until the Public Prosecutor elects for it to be dealt with as a summary one: *The State v The Principal Magistrate District Court, Port Moresby Ex Parte Public Prosecutor* (1983) SC 243.

For a discussion of the principles relating to the jurisdiction of District Courts, see the judgment of Mann CJ in *Robin Kumaina v Barrington Gerald Reade* (1967) N433.

See ss 37(7) and 42(1) of the *Constitution*.

By virtue of this section the District Court is invested with jurisdiction to deal with offences under the *Native Administration Regulations* (New Guinea): *Joseph Kembu v Eko Mason* [1971-1972] PNGLR 407 at 410 and 411.

24. Transfer of proceedings.

(1) Where proceedings have been commenced in a Court, the Court may, at any time before judgement, with or without an application from an interested person for that purpose, for reasons that shall be recorded, make an order staying the proceedings and, on such terms as to it seem just transferring the proceedings for hearing and determination by some other District Court or, if the proceedings are such that they could have been instituted before the National Court in the first instance, by the National Court.

(2) The National Court may at any time before verdict or judgement, with or without an application from an interested person in that behalf, make an order staying proceedings before a District Court and ordering that the proceedings be taken before the National Court, if the proceedings are such that they could have been instituted before the National Court in the first instance.

The phrase "at any time before judgement" applies to the transfer of committal proceedings. Thus where partially heard committal proceedings were transferred from Rabaul to Port Moresby and heard by the same District Court Magistrate, the court had jurisdiction to commit for trial: *R v McEachern* [1967-1968] PNGLR 48.

25. Ex parte order may be set aside.

A conviction or order made when one party does not appear may be set aside on application to the Court on such terms as to costs or otherwise as the Court thinks just, and the Court, on service on the other party of such reasonable notice as the Court directs, may-

(a) proceed to hear and determine the information or complaint in respect of which the conviction or order was made; or

(b) adjourn the hearing and determination of the hearing to such time and place as it thinks fit and direct such notice of the adjourned hearing as it thinks fit to be given to a party.

In relation to applications for re-hearing, the magistrate's power under this section is discretionary and the discretion must be exercised according to law or in a reasonable manner. The court's discretion is to be exercised having regard to all the circumstances of the case. In *Danvers v Adamson* [1967-1968] PNGLR 357, whether the defendant had a reasonable explanation for his failure to attend was one relevant consideration, but so also was the consideration whether the defendant had a good defence and also the serious nature of the charge.

On ex parte hearings, see the general provision in s 37(5) of the *Constitution*.

Part IV – Commencement of Proceedings

Division 1 – General

28. Information and complaints.

Proceedings before a Court shall be commenced-

(a) by an information or a complaint, which may be laid by the complainant in person, or by his legal representative or other person authorized for the purpose; or

(b) by a Traffic Infringement Summons.

Section 28(c) is inoperative, because *Supreme Court Reference No 1A of 1981* [1982] PNGLR 122 ruled that amendments made are constitutionally invalid as they infringe upon a defendant's rights under s 37(4)(a) and (5) of the *Constitution*.

Division 2 – Informations

29. Information to be for one matter only.

An information shall be for one matter only, except that-

(a) in the case of indictable offences, if the matters of the information are such that they may be charged in one indictment; and

(b) in other cases, if the matters of the information are substantially of the same act or omission on the part of the defendant,

those matters may be joined in the same information.

In the case of a defective committal, the magistrate should explain the situation to the prosecutor and call upon the prosecutor to elect which alleged defence is to be proceeded on. However, if the defect is found to be one which cannot be cured by the proper exercise of any power to amend, then the proceedings are bad and should be struck out and a fresh complaint or information laid. If the prosecutor appeared not to understand the position, or if he or she refused to elect, then the magistrate should dismiss the information, treating it as a nullity: *R v Buresep* (1963) N308.

It is not duplicity when the charge is "drive a motor vehicle whilst under the influence of intoxicating liquor or a drug".[52]

The hearing of three informations together without the consent of the accused amounts to a mis-trial: *Kereku v Dodd* [1969-1970] PNGLR 176 followed. In *R v Sarea Aravapo* (1973) N775, informations without particularisation alleging various acts of sorcery – "on various days of various months in 1973 did pretend to be a sorcerer" – were held, on appeal, to be bad for uncertainty.

In *Sie v Kellaart* (1954) N62, on appeal an information alleging stealing "money or money's worth to the value of GBP 14.18.3" was held to be bad as it lacked the particularity necessary to inform an accused of what he was being charged.

In *Sebulon Wat v Peter Kari* (1975) N839, variance of dates in the information was allowed as it was not a substitution of a new offence. Prentice ACJ stated that "[i]t is not part of the duty of the Breach to regard the matter as a sporting contest; it must use its powers in the proper way to uphold the law".

Where the accused unlawfully and contemporaneously used violence against three persons it was proper to list these matters on one indictment, under s 29(b). Further, s 29(b) necessarily allows of more than one conviction: *Wama Ul v Jansen* (1975) N834.

[52] *Paul Maniwokin v Akuila Toburua* [1973] PNGLR 710, following *Thompson v Knights* [1947] 1 All ER 112.

There is nothing in the *Criminal Code* or in the *District Courts Act* to authorise a magistrate to investigate, in the same proceedings and under the same complaint, several separate and distinct criminal offences which could not be comprised in one indictment: *R v Buresep* (1963) N308. It is important to recognise that s 29(b) may cut down considerably the general provision, and it is clearly the law in Papua New Guinea that an information may be in respect of more than "one matter" if "the matters are substantially of the same act or omission on the part of the defendant". This may mean no more than that an information like an indictment may contain more than one "count" in respect of related offences, provided that the several offences are the subject of "separate statements" and subject to the court's power to require the prosecutor to confine the case to one matter or to direct separate trials in order to avoid prejudice to the accused. See *DPP v Merriman* [1973] AC 584 at 593; and *Petersen v Ford* [1975] 1 NSWLR 455, for example; *Acting Public Prosecutor v Barry Blythe Holloway* (1981) N298(M).

30. Description of persons, property and offences.

(1) Such description of persons or things as would be sufficient in an indictment is sufficient in an information.

(2) The description of an offence in the words of that Act, order or instrument creating the offence, or in similar words, is sufficient in law.

In *Jacob Hendrich Prai and Otto Ondawame v The Officer of the Government of Papua New Guinea (No 2)* [1979] PNGLR 247, an information charged the accused:

> "That on the 25th day of September 1978, you were a West Irian [sic] becoming a prohibited immigrant that you were not a holder of an entry permit to enter Papua New Guinea then in force under s 6 of the *Immigration Act*, thereby contravening s 24(l)(a) of the *Immigration Act*."

This case was appealed on the basis that the information did not allege an entry into Papua New Guinea and that the *Migration Act* was wrongly described. It was held that there had been a sufficient description of the offence in words similar to the Act.

31. Particulars.

A Court or a Magistrate may, if it or he thinks fit, direct particulars to be delivered to the defendant of a matter alleged in an information and may adjourn the hearing for that purpose.

32. Want of form or variance in information, etc.

No objection shall be taken or allowed to an information, or to a summons or warrant to apprehend a defendant issued on an information, for an alleged defect in the information in substance or in form, or for a variance between it and the evidence in support of the information, and any such variance may be amended by order of the Court at the hearing.

See the remarks of Saldanha J on defective informations in *Jacob Prai and Otto Ondawame v An Officer of the Government of Papua New Guinea* [1979] PNGLR 1, annotated under Sch 2.2.

In *Sebulon Wat v Peter Kari* (1975) N839, variance of dates in the information was allowed as it was not a substitution of a new offence.[53]

---

[53] This case on appeal is *Sebulon Wat v Peter Kari (No 2)* [1975] PNGLR 339.

The power of each court over its own process includes power to substitute amended grounds of appeal: *Sebulon Wat v Peter Kari* (1975) N839.

This section cannot be used to amend where a defendant has pleaded guilty to something that was not an offence: *Korua Kerua v Constable Koloma Vanua* (1972) N714.

This section permits amendment which may result in the charging of a cognate offence or an offence constituted by facts which would themselves be part and parcel of the offence originally charged, or where the amended charge could in the first place have been stated in the alternative. It does not permit an amendment which would result in a charge of some new offence of a different nature: *Utula Samana v Demas Waki* [1984] PNGLR 8.

33. Amendment.

If a variance specified in Section 32 appears to the Court to be such that the defendant has been deceived or misled by it, the Court may, and at the request of the defendant shall, adjourn the hearing of the case, on such terms as it thinks just, to some future day, and in the meantime may commit the defendant or discharge him on bail on recognizance for his appearance at the time and place to which the hearing is adjourned.

See the case of *Sebulon Wat v Peter Kari* (1975) N839; on appeal *Sebulon Wat v Peter Kari (No 2)* [1975] PNGLR 339.

34. Minute of amendment.

An order for the amendment of a variance shall be entered on the proceedings of the Court, and a minute of the amendment, if required, shall be given to the party against whom it was made.

35. Form of information.

(1) Where it is intended to issue a warrant in the first instance against the party charged, the information shall be in writing and on oath either by the informant or some other person.

(2) Where it is intended to issue a summons instead of a warrant in the first instance, the information need not be in writing or on oath, but may be verbal only and without oath, whether the law under which the information is laid requires it to be in writing or not.

36. Limitation of proceedings.

(1) Subject to Subsection (2), in the case of a simple offence, unless some other time is limited for laying an information by the law relating to the particular case, the information may only be laid within six months after the time when the matter of the information arose.

(2) The time limit of six months referred to in Subsection (1) does not apply to an information laid for an offence specified in Schedule 2 to the *Criminal Code Act* (Chapter 262).

[S 36 subst Act No 45, 1986 (*District Court (Amendment No 2) Act* 1986), s 1].

The section does not deprive a court of jurisdiction but provides a defendant with a defence against an information which is out of time: *Madum Towel v Kepas Tundual* (1972) N719.

Part VI – Proceedings in Case of Indictable Offences

Division 1 – General

93. Disobedience to summons.

Where a person-

(a) is charged with-

(i) an indictable offence that shall not be tried summarily; or

(ii) an offence against Section 420 of the *Criminal Code* where the offence is not to be tried summarily; and

(b) fails to appear in answer to a summons issued against him before the Court at the time and place specified in the summons, and it is made to appear to the Court on oath that the summons was duly served on him a reasonable time before the time appointed for appearing to it,

the Court may, on oath being made before it, substantiating the matter of the information to its satisfaction, issue its warrant for the arrest of the defendant to bring him before a Court to answer to the information and to be further dealt with according to the law.

[S 93 subst Act No 31, 1980 (*District Courts (Committal Proceedings in Cases of Indictable Offences) Act* 1980), s 1].

94. Copy of information, etc, to be served.

(1) Subject to Subsection (6), where a person is charged with-

(a) an indictable offence that shall not be tried summarily; or

(b) an offence against Section 420 of the *Criminal Code* where the offence is not to be tried summarily,

the informant shall serve or caused to be served, in accordance with Subsection (3), on the defendant or his legal representative-

(c) a copy of the information; and

(d) a copy of each statement that the informant intends to tender at the committal hearing; and

(e) a list of documents and exhibits referred to in a statement referred to in Paragraph (d) that the informant intends to tender at the committal hearing; and

(f) a copy of each document referred to in Paragraph (e).

(1A) A statement referred to in Subsection (1)(d) shall contain the following warning to the maker of the statement and shall be signed by the maker of the statement:-

> 'I ... certify that this statement is true to the best of my knowledge and belief. I make it knowing that if it is tendered in evidence I will be liable to prosecution if I have knowingly stated anything that is false or misleading in any particular.

Signed'.

[Subs (1A) insrt Act No 45, 1986 (*District Court (Amendment) Act* 1986), s 2(b)]

(1B) A statement referred to in Subsection (1)(d) shall, for the purposes of Division III.2 of the *Evidence Act* (Chapter 48), be treated as an affidavit.

[Subs (1B) insrt Act No 45, 1986 (*District Court (Amendment) Act* 1986), s 2(b)]

(2) Where an exhibit referred to in Subsection (1)(e) cannot be copied or adequately described, the defendant shall be notified of the place nominated by the informant where the exhibit may be inspected.

(3) Service of the documents and photographs (if any) under Subsection (1) shall be effected-

- (a) in the case of a natural person - on the person to whom they are directed by delivering them to him personally; or
- (b) in the case of a company incorporated under the *Companies Act* - on the company in accordance with that Act; and
- (c) in the case of any other corporation-
  - (i) on the secretary or public officer or other chief officer of the corporation in the country; or
  - (ii) by sending them by post to the secretary, public officer or chief officer at the last known address of the corporation in the country,

or in any other manner provided by law, at least 14 days before the date fixed for the hearing.

[Subs (3) am Act No 31, 1981 (*District Courts (Miscellaneous Provisions) Act* 1981), s 1]

(4) A person who carries out the service under Subsection (3) shall-

- (a) within seven days after service - make an affidavit stating the day and place of service; and
- (b) at least 72 hours before the date fixed for hearing - transmit the affidavit to the Clerk for production at the time and place and before the Court before which the hearing is to take place.

(5) A document purporting to be an affidavit of service under Subsection (4) is prima facie evidence of service under this section.

(6) Where a Court considers it expedient to do so, it may-

- (a) waive the requirements for service of documents or exhibits under this section; and
- (b) allow the informant or defendant to call oral evidence and tender exhibits at a committal hearing.

[S 94 subst Act No 27, 1981 (*District Courts (Amendment) Act* 1981)]

In proceedings where a person has been charged with an indictable offence that cannot be tried summarily, and documents have not been served within the time limit specified in s 101 [now s 94] of the *District Courts Act*, an order in the nature of certiorari should go to quash the committal: *The State v Rush; Ex parte Rush* [1984] PNGLR 124.

94A. Penalty for false declaration.

A person who, in relation to a statement or document referred to in Section 94(1), knowingly makes a statement that is false or misleading in any particular is guilty of an offence.

Penalty: Imprisonment for a term not exceeding three years.

[S 94A insrt Act No 31, 1980 (*District Courts (Committal Proceedings in Cases of Indictable Offences) Act* 1980), s 3]

94B. Committal for trial without consideration of the evidence.

(1) Subject to Subsection (2), a Court inquiring into an offence may, if it is satisfied that all the evidence, whether for the prosecution or the defence, consists of written statements, with or without exhibits, tendered to the Court after service in accordance with Section 94, commit the defendant for trial for the offence without consideration of the contents of the statements.

(2) Committal for trial in accordance with Subsection (1) shall not occur where-

(a) the defendant or one of the defendants does not have legal representation; or

(b) the legal representative of the defendant or one of the defendants, as the case may be, requests the Court to consider a submission that the statements referred to in Subsection (1) do not disclose sufficient evidence to put the defendant on trial for the offence.

[S 94B insrt Act No 31, 1980 (*District Courts (Committal Proceedings in Cases of Indictable Offences) Act* 1980), s 3]

94C. Regard to evidence, etc.

(1) When conducting a committal hearing under this Part, the Court may, subject to Subsection (2), have regard to-

(a) the evidence contained in a written statement; and

(b) documents and exhibits,

of which a copy has been served on the defendant under Section 94(1) or made available for inspection under Section 94(2).

(2) Before admitting a written statement, the Court shall be satisfied that the person who made the statement had read and understood it, or if unable to read, had had it read to him in a language that he understood.

[S 94C insrt Act No 31, 1980 (*District Courts (Committal Proceedings in Cases of Indictable Offences) Act* 1980), s 3]

The combined effect of ss 94(1A) and 94C(2) is that the committal court must conduct an inquiry to ensure that the statement was made by the maker of the statement whose signature appears on the statement. It must be ensured that the maker of the statement had full knowledge of not only the contents of the written statement, but also the correctness and truth of the written statement. The requirement under s 94C(2) is mandatory and requires strict compliance. This inquiry is an independent one which the court must conduct in the exercise of its judicial function. After having conducted the inquiry, the court then has a discretion to admit or reject the written statement depending on the court's conclusion. The court must then record the nature and extent of the inquiry conducted and record its findings. Failure to conduct such inquiry and record its findings may result in voiding the committal: *The State v Kai Wabu* [1994] PNGLR 94 (Injia AJ).

The combined effect of ss 94(1A) and 94C(2) also places a duty on the police informant, or any other person who obtains the statement and records it in writing, to ensure that the maker of the statement reads the statement before signing it. If the person cannot read, then the statement must be read back to him or her. If the statement is recorded in a language different from the one used by the maker of the statement, then it must be read and translated in the same language in which the statement was given. In many situations the assistance of an interpreter may be required. Where the written statement is not in a language understood by the maker of the statement and it is read back in a language that he or she understands, with or without the use of an interpreter, as the case may be, evidence of this must be produced at the committal hearing. There are various methods by which such evidence may be produced at the committal hearing. The person obtaining the written statement and/or interpreting the statement can make an endorsement on the written statement certifying that that person has read or interpreted the document to the maker of the statement before signing it. Alternatively, a separate certificate may be filed to that effect. If the person does not produce a certificate in writing, he or she must be called to give oral evidence: *The State v Kai Wabu* [1994] PNGLR 94 (Injia AJ).

95. Court to consider whether prima facie case.

(1) Where all the evidence offered on the part of the prosecution has been heard or received, the Court shall consider whether it is sufficient to put the defendant on trial.

[Subs (1) am Act No 31, 1980 (*District Courts (Committal Proceedings in Cases of Indictable Offences) Act* 1980), s 4]

(2) If the Court if of the opinion that the evidence is not sufficient to put the defendant on trial for an indictable offence, it shall immediately order the defendant, if in custody, to be discharged as to the information then under inquiry.

(3) If the court is of opinion that the evidence is sufficient to put the defendant upon his trial for an indictable offence, it shall proceed with the examination in accordance with this Division.

A magistrate may consider the demeanour and creditability of a witness, and if the magistrate, when forming an opinion under this section, considers that the prosecution evidence before the court is clearly tainted or worthless, the defendant should be discharged forthwith: *R v Wewak Resident Magistrate; Ex parte Dyer* [1967-1968] PNGLR 511.

To decide that the evidence offered by the prosecution in committal proceedings before the District Court "is sufficient to put the defendant upon his trial", the court has only to form a bona fide opinion that there is a sufficient prima facie case against the defendant: *R v McEachern* [1967-1968] PNGLR 48.

96. Accused to be asked whether he desires to give evidence.

(1) Where a court proceeds with the examination of a defendant in accordance with this Division, the court or the chairman of the Court shall read the charge to the accused and explain its nature in ordinary language and shall say to him these words, or words to the same effect -

> "Having heard the evidence for the prosecution do you wish to be sworn and give evidence on your behalf, or do you desire to say anything in answer to the charge? You are not obliged to be sworn and give evidence, nor are you required to say anything, unless you desire to do so; but whatever evidence you may give upon oath, or anything you may say, will be taken down in writing, and may be given in evidence upon your trial. You are clearly to understand that you have nothing to hope from any promise of favour, and nothing to fear from any threat, which may have been held out to you to induce you to make any admission or confession of your guilt; but whatever you now say may be given in evidence upon your trial, notwithstanding any such promise or threat."

(2) Anything which the defendant says in answer to a statement made in accordance with Subsection (1) shall be

(a) taken down in writing in the English Language and read to him; and

(b) shall be signed by the Magistrates constituting the Court and by the defendant if he so desires; and

(c) be kept with the depositions of the witnesses and transmitted with them to the Public Prosecutor.

(3) In any examination of the defendant in accordance with this Division neither the defendant nor his legal representative shall be permitted to subject any witness to cross-examination.

[S 96 am *District Courts (Amendments) Act* 2000, s 10]

In *Prosecutor's Request No 1 of 1974* (1974) N67, the prosecutor was not under a duty to tender the accused's statement. For duties of prosecutors, see generally *Richardson v R* (1974) 3 ALR 115.

Self-serving statements by an accused person, contained in a record of interview or in a statement, may be evidence in favour of an accused: *R v Joseph Haiai Sarufa* [1974] PNGLR 173.

> "Facts, including self-serving statements related by an accused in a signed statement to the police put in evidence by the Crown, and in a statement ... and subjected to cross-examination, are evidence in favour of the accused but must be considered along with all the other evidence in the trial, and the weight to be attached is a jury matter."[54]

The warning required by this section may not be very effective when an accused is unrepresented, at least in capital cases: *R v Tiendeli Pakale* (1970) N565. Cross-examination of a defendant after giving a statement on oath should not be admitted as evidence: *R v PM* [1971-1972] PNGLR 222 (Frost SPJ).

---

[54] *The State v Gaius Malaia* (1978) N78 (Raine DCJ).

Where an accused chooses to give sworn evidence, such evidence is subject to other provisions of the *District Courts Act*: see Div 2, especially s 62. Accordingly, such sworn evidence is subject to cross-examination by the police prosecutor and any questions by the magistrate, and answers to such cross-examination are available as evidence at the trial: *The State v Nagiri Topoma* [1980] PNGLR 18.

It will only do justice to defendants who are either uneducated or who are not represented by legal counsel, for the presiding magistrate to explain to the defendant the legal consequences of whether or not the defendant should say anything at all at this point or, if choosing to say anything, whether the defendant should make a sworn statement or an unsworn statement, and make specific mention of the right of the police prosecutor to cross examine if the choice is made to give sworn evidence. If the defendant is not advised of the legal consequences of the options, the National Court may, in its discretionary power, reject such statements if it feels that, in all the circumstances, it was unfair to admit answers in response to cross-examination: *The State v Nagiri Topoma* [1980] PNGLR 18 (Kapi J).

Compare this section with the provisions of s 572 of the *Criminal Code*.

97. Statement may be put in evidence at trial.

On the trial of a defendant for an offence for which he has been committed for trial or for any other offence arising out of the same transaction or set of circumstances as that offence, a statement made by him under Section 96 may be given in evidence without further proof, notwithstanding that the statement may be exculpatory or self-serving, if the statement purports to be signed by the Magistrates by or before whom it purports to have been taken, unless it be proved that it was not in fact signed by those Magistrates.

[S 97 am Act No 31, 1980 (*District Courts (Committal Proceedings in Cases of Indictable Offences) Act* 1980), s 5]

Compare this section with the provisions of s 572 of the *Criminal Code*.

98. Saving.

This Act does not prevent the prosecutor from giving in evidence an admission or confession or other statement of the defendant, which by law would be admissible as evidence against that person.

99. Defendant may call witnesses.

[Repealed]

100. Discharge or committal of defendant.

(1) When an examination under this Division is completed, the court shall consider whether the evidence is sufficient to put the defendant on trial.

(2) If, in the opinion of the Court, the evidence is not sufficient to put the defendant on trial, it shall immediately order the defendant, if in custody, to be discharged as to the information then under inquiry.

(3) Where -

(a) in the opinion of the court, the evidence is sufficient to put the defendant on trial; or

(b) the court commits the defendant for trial under Section 94B(1) –

the court shall –

(c) by warrant commit the defendant to a corrective institution, police lock-up or other place of security or other such safe custody to be kept there safely until the sitting of the National Court before which he is to be tried, or until he is delivered by due course of law; or

(d) admit him to bail in accordance with Division 2.

[S 100 subst Act No 31, 1981 (*District Courts (Miscellaneous Provisions) Act* 1981), s 2]

The test to decide whether the evidence offered by the prosecution "is sufficient to put the defendant upon his trial" for this section is the same as for s 100(1). However, the magistrate need not put the opinion formed for the purposes of s 100(1) from his or her mind if the accused then goes into evidence or witnesses are called. To form an opinion for s 107(1), the magistrate may modify an opinion formed for s 102(1) according to the sum of the evidence heard: *R v McEachern* [1967-1968] PNGLR 48.

Strutt v Haram (1963) N276 dealt with the refusal of the magistrate to hear proceedings because the matter was said to be trivial. It was held that the magistrate was dealing with committal proceedings and not summary jurisdiction.

See also *R v Akundagru* (1963) N282 and *Prosecutor's Request No 1 of 1974* (1974) N67.

At the conclusion of committal proceedings, if a magistrate has no more than a reasonable doubt whether the evidence is "sufficient", for the purposes of s 107(3), the magistrate must commit. The magistrate is concerned with whether a defendant could reasonably be convicted: (Kearney DCJ).

See *R v Wewak Resident Magistrate* (Minogue J), discussed in Griffin, *Criminal Procedure in Papua New Guinea*, p 105; *Arthur Gilbert Smedley v The State* [1980] PNGLR 379.

101. Magistrates need not be present during the whole examination.

[Repealed]

102. Statements of witnesses dead, etc.

Where a person has been committed for trial or sentence for an offence all statements tendered in evidence to the Magistrate constituting the Court may, with the consent of the National Court, be taken without further proof as evidence on the trial, whether for that offence or for any other offence arising out of the transaction or set of circumstances as that offence on proof -

(a) that the witness who made a statement is -

(i) dead or insane; or

(ii) so ill as not to be able to travel; or

(iii) kept out of the way by means of the procurement of the accused or on his behalf; or

(iv) a person registered under the *Medical Registration Act* (Chapter 398); or

(b) either by a certificate purporting to be signed by the Court or by one of the Magistrates to whom the statement was tendered, or by the oath of a credible witness that the statement was served on the accused or his legal representative.

[S 102 subst Act No 31, 1980 (*District Courts (Committal Proceedings in Cases of Indictable Offences) Act* 1980), s 8]

The section is an exclusive and complete statement of the circumstances in which a deposition can be used in a trial on indictment, and thus it takes priority over more general provisions: *R v Amdjuonye Petisakuna* (1970) N10.

103. If defendant admits guilt, etc., he may be committed for sentence.

(1) If a defendant, on being asked in accordance with Section 96 whether he wishes to say anything in answer to the charge, says that he is guilty of the charge, the Court shall further say to him these words, or words to the same effect –

"You will now be committed for sentence instead of being committed for trial."

(2) Statement by the defendant in accordance with Subsection (1) shall be–

(a) taken down in writing and read to him; and

(b) signed by the Magistrate constituting the Court and by the Defendant if he so desires; and

(c) held with the statements of witnesses and transmitted with them to the Public Prosecutor.

(3) In a case referred to in Subsection (1), the Court, instead of committing the defendant for trial, shall order him to be committed for sentence before the National Court and, in the meantime shall–

(a) by warrant commit him to a corrective institution, police lock-up or other place of security to be kept safely until the sittings of the National Court, or until he is delivered by due course of law; or

(b) admit him to bail to appear for sentence in accordance with Division 2.

[S 103 subst Act No 31, 1980 (*District Courts (Committal Proceedings Cases of Indictable Offences) Act* 1980), s 9]

Part VII – Proceedings in Case of Simple Offences and Indictable Offences Triable Summarily

[Pt heading am Act No 32, 1980 (*District Courts (Hearing of Indictable Offences) Act* 1980), s 8]

Division 1 – Venue

122. Venue of summary cases.

(1) Subject to this Part, informations of simple offences shall be heard and determined at a place appointed for holding court within the province in which the offence or breach of duty was committed or in which the defendant usually resides or is at the time when the information is laid.

(2) If the offence was committed outside a province, but within 33 km of the boundary of the province, the information may be heard and determined, subject to Subsection (6), at a place appointed for holding Court within that province or within the province in which the offence was committed.

(3) If the offence was committed on a vessel within the territorial sea, or in any case with the consent of the defendant, the information may be heard and determined at any place in the country appointed for holding court.

(4) An information of a simple offence or an indictable offence triable summarily against a law relating to companies may be heard and determined, subject to Subsection (6), in the province in which the registered office of the company is situated, or at Port Moresby.

(5) An indictable offence triable summarily under Section 420 of the *Criminal Code* shall be heard and determined in a District Court constituted by a Magistrate Grade V.

(6) For the purposes of Subsection (5), the sittings of the District Court for the hearing and determination of indictable offences triable summarily may be held at such time and place as determined by the Court.

[S 122 am Act No 32, 1980 (*District Courts (Hearing of Indictable Offences) Act* 1980), s 9; am Act No 31, 1981 (*District Courts (Miscellaneous Provisions) Act* 1981), s 3]

This provision is mandatory, and contravention of it constitutes a substantial miscarriage of justice. It is well known that jurisdiction cannot be given to magistrates to sit extra-territorially, even by consent: *R v Rumints Woie* (1972) N728.

In a case where the police arrested Central Province villagers for riotous behaviour and drove them many hours to the National Capital District, without any advance warning to their families, to be held in custody, this amounted to a breach of this section as well as s 37(17) of the *Constitution*, which provides that persons deprived of their liberty should be treated with humanity: *Yamore Memera v Matthew Bisang* [1976] PNGLR 419.

See *Constitution*, s 37(17) and s 37 generally.

123. Adjournment to different place.

Where an information of a simple offence or an indictable offence triable summarily may lawfully be heard and determined at any one of two or more places, if, on the hearing of the information at one of those places, it appears to the Court that the hearing would more conveniently take place at another of those places, the court may –

(a) adjourn the matter to that other place; and

(b) commit the defendant in the meantime or discharge him on bail on recognizance, oral or in writing, conditioned for his appearance at the time and place to which the hearing is so adjourned;

and the defendant and every witness summoned to give evidence is bound to attend at that time and place.

[S 123 am Act No 32, 1980 (*District Courts (Hearing of Indictable Offences) Act 1980*), s 10]

Division 2 – Hearing

124. Absence of complainant.

If, on the day and at the place appointed by a summons for hearing and determining an information of a simple offence or an indictable offence triable summarily –

(a) the defendant attends voluntarily in obedience to the summons, or is brought before the Court by virtue of a warrant; and

(b) the complainant, having had notice of the day and place, does not appear by himself or by his legal representative,

the Court shall dismiss the information unless for some reason it thinks proper to adjourn the hearing to some other day.

[S 124 am Act No 32, 1980 (*District Courts (Hearing of Indictable Offences) Act 1980*), s 10]

125. Absence of defendant.

If, at the time and place appointed by a summons for hearing and determining an information of a simple offence or an indictable offence triable summarily, the defendant does not appear when called, and proof is made to the Court on oath or in accordance with Section 47, of due service of the summons on the defendant a reasonable time before the time appointed for his appearance, the court may –

(a) in the case of a simple offence the maximum penalty for which does not include imprisonment (other than for default in payment of a fine) – proceed ex parte to hear and determine the case in the absence of the defendant; or

(b) in the case of an information of a simple offence or an indictable offence triable summarily – on oath being made before it, substantiating the matter to its satisfaction, issue its warrant for the arrest of the defendant to bring him before a court to answer to the information and to be further dealt with according to law.

[S 125 subst Act No 32, 1980 (*District Courts (Hearing of Indictable Offences) Act 1980*), s 12; am Act No 31, 1981 (*District Courts (Miscellaneous Provisions) Act 1981*), s 4]

To the extent that this section enables an information of a simple offence punishable by imprisonment to be heard in the absence of the defendant, it is therefore a provision which goes beyond s 37(5) of the *Constitution*, and is inconsistent with it. However, the severability clause found in s 10 of the *Constitution* does save the operation of the section in a reduced form, allowing its continued application to simple offences (any offence punishable on summary conviction) punishable otherwise than by imprisonment (except in default of payment of a fine): *Rakatani Peter v South Pacific Brewery Ltd (Reference No 1 of 1976)* [1976] PNGLR 537 (Frost CJ and Kearney J).

"It seems to me manifestly clear that it is desirable not only in order to achieve the National Goals and Directives, but also to secure the basic rights to

> individuals, that certain classes of charges involving possible imprisonment, should be capable of being heard summarily in the absence of the defendant if he so consents – thus avoiding his arrest and compulsory attendances in court – even though potentially (although unlikely) imprisonment could result. Thus, this section should be read so as to allow ex parte proceedings, even where there is a possibility of imprisonment, upon the consent of the defendant."[55]

Where it is shown that a summons in due form has been duly served, and there is no appearance of the accused, the accused's consent to the hearing taking place in his or her absence should be inferred until the reverse is shown: *R v Mitchell and Ijahuio; Ex parte Wafing* [1973] PNGLR 461 (Prentice J). Note that this case was decided prior to the *Constitution*, based on the now repealed *Human Rights Act*. See *Rakatani Peter v South Pacific Brewery Ltd (Reference No 1 of 1976)* [1976] PNGLR 537, for the post-*Constitution* law.

See s 37 of the *Constitution*, which provides for protection of the individual under law, and s 37(5) on ex parte hearings.

126. Adjournment of case.

Where a court issues its warrant under Section 125(b) of the last preceding section, it shall adjourn the hearing of the information until the defendant is arrested, and if the defendant is afterwards arrested under the warrant he shall be detained in safe custody until he can be brought before the Court at a convenient time and place, of which the complainant shall be given due notice.

127. Both parties appearing.

If both parties appear at the hearing of an information personally or by their legal representatives the Court shall proceed to hear and determine the information.

128. Proceedings at the hearing on defendant's admission.

(1) At the time appointed for the hearing of an information of a simple offence or an indictable offence triable summarily, the defendant shall be informed in open court of the offence with which he is charged as set out in the information, and shall be called on to say if he is guilty or not guilty of the charge.

[Subs (1) am Act No 31, 1981 (*District Courts (Miscellaneous Provisions) Act 1981*), s 5]

(2) When the defendant is called on under Subsection (1), the hearing is deemed to commence.

[S 128 subst Act No 32, 1980 (*District Courts (Hearing of Indictable Offences) Act 1980*), s 13].

A plea of not guilty should be entered where the accused makes a statement to the magistrate which does not clearly indicate that:

(a) the accused admits the truth of the complaint; and

(b) the accused has no cause to show why he or she should not be convicted.

A magistrate is not entitled to interrogate an accused for the purposes of obtaining admissions, but in accordance with the well-established practice of the courts of Papua New Guinea and the conditions of the country, a judicial officer may, in ascertaining whether or not the accused admits the truth of the information, put questions to the defendant as to each of the matters charged in an information. The

[55] *Rakatani Peter v South Pacific Brewery Ltd (Reference No 1 of 1976)* [1976] PNGLR 537 (Prentice DCJ dissenting).

questions should be put in the form: "Do you admit or deny the truth of the particular matter?" The object of the legislation is merely to discover whether the defendant puts the truth of the information or complaint in issue: *Kakore v Sing* [1975] PNGLR 104.

See also *Laeka Ivarabou v Nanau* [1967-1968] PNGLR 12; *Pukari-Flabu v Hambakon Sma* [1965-1966] PNGLR 348; *Aikaba v Tami* [1971-1972] PNGLR 155; and *Balu Mau'u v Pare* [1973] PNGLR 64.

Neither s 134 nor s 135 specifies the word "plea". However, in practice the defendant is asked how he or she pleads to the charge.

See ss 557, 560 and 563-565 of the *Criminal Code*. See also s 37 of the *Constitution*.

See *Monika Jon v Dominik Kuman* (1980) N253.

This section is in unusual terms as it does not provide for any plea of guilty or not guilty to be taken. However, it is clear that if the defendant has any cause to show why he or she should not be convicted, or why an order should not be made against him or her, the court is to proceed to hear and determine the case under s 135 of the *District Courts Act*. The accused must admit the truth of an information before being convicted without the magistrate proceeding to hear and determine the case. The defendant must admit every element of the charge: *Jacob Hendrich Prai and Otto Ondawame v An Officer of the Government of Papua New Guinea (No 2)* [1979] PNGLR 247 following *Towarli Tokoi v Harold Bryant* (1972) N674.

On appeal against a conviction, under the *Migration Act*, of a West Irian citizen as a prohibited immigrant, *Jacob Hendrich Prai and Otto Ondawame v An Officer of the Government of Papua New Guinea (No 2)* [1979] PNGLR 247 followed *Towarli Tokoi v Harold Bryant* (1972) N674 in holding that under this section, the substance of a charge must be put to the accused for the accused to admit every element of the charge before being convicted.

129. Where defendant does not admit the case.

(1) Where the defendant pleads not guilty of the charge contained in the information the Court shall proceed to hear the complainant and his witnesses and the defendant and his witnesses and also such witnesses as the complainant examines in reply, if the defendant has given evidence other than as to his general character.

(2) The Court, having heard what each party has to say and the evidence adduced, shall consider and determine the whole matter, and shall convict or make an order on the defendant, or dismiss the information, as justice requires.

[S 129 am Act No 32, 1980 (*District Courts (Hearing of Indictable Offences) Act 1980*), s 14]

Neither s 134 nor s 135 of the *District Courts Act* includes the word "plea", but in practice the defendant is asked by the court how he or she pleads: *Jacob Hendrich Prai and Otto Ondawame v An Officer of the v of Papua New Guinea (No 2)* [1979] PNGLR 247.

See ss 557, 560 and 563-565 of the *Criminal Code*. See also s 37 of the *Constitution*.

130. Hearing in the absence of both or either of the parties.

If, at the time and place to which a hearing or further hearing of an information for a simple offence is adjourned, either or both of the parties does not or do not appear personally or by his or their legal representative or representatives, as the case may be, the Court may proceed to the hearing or further hearing as if the party or parties were present or, if the complainant does not appear, the Court may dismiss the information with or without costs.

131. Conduct of summary proceedings.

In respect of the examination and cross-examination of witnesses and the right of addressing the Court on the case in reply, or otherwise, the practice before a Court on the hearing of an information of a simple offence or an indictable offence triable summarily shall be in accordance, as nearly as practicable, with the practice for the time being in the National Court on the trial of an issue of fact in an action at law.

[S 131 am Act No 32, 1980 (*District Courts (Hearing of Indictable Offences) Act* 1980), s 15]

See ss 522, 523, 537, 552, 561, 566 and 574 of the *Criminal Code*, and the cases dealing with those sections.

See ss 37 and 42 of the *Constitution*.

132. Conditional release, etc.

(1) Where a person is charged before a court with a simple offence or an offence triable summarily, and the Court thinks that the charge is proved but is of opinion that, having regard to –

(a) the character, antecedents, age, health or mental condition of the person charged; or

(b) the trivial nature of the offence; or

(c) the extenuating circumstances under which the offence was committed,

it is expedient to inflict punishment, or other than a nominal punishment, or that it is expedient to release the offender on probation, the Court may, without proceeding to conviction, make an order either –

(d) dismissing the charge; or

(e) discharging the offender conditionally on his entering into a recognizance, with or without sureties, to be of good behaviour and to appear for conviction and sentence when called on at any time during such period, not exceeding three years, as is specified in the order.

(2) An order made under the Subsection (1) shall, for the purpose of –

(a) revesting or restoring stolen property; and

(b) enabling the Court to make orders as to the restitution or delivery of property to the owner;

(c) the payment of money upon or in connection with that restitution or delivery; and

(d) an appeal against conviction,

have the same effect as a conviction.

[S 132 am Act No 32, 1980 (*District Courts (Hearing of Indictable Offences) Act* 1980), s 16]

The mere provision of a minimum penalty of imprisonment, as for a conviction under s 7(1)(d) of the *Dangerous Drugs (Possession) Act* 1970 for unlawful possession of marijuana, does not exclude the power of the court to give an offender, in an appropriate case, a conditional release under this section: *Henderson v Blackwell* [1973] PNGLR 223 at 225.

In *Ito Memairi and William Jiwaiba v Nelson Gua* [1984] PNGLR 66, Pratt J set out the requirements that must be satisfied before a magistrate can apply s 138 [now s 132]:

- that the charge is proved;
- that one of the three matters stated in s 138(1) [now s 132(1)] (ie, character, nature of the offence or extenuating circumstances) is applicable; and
- that there are special features about the matter which cause the magistrate to believe that it would not be proper or expedient to inflict punishment or more than nominal punishment, or that the offender should be released on probation.

One or more of the factors mentioned in s 138 [now s 132] must be established before the court may impose the punishment: *Freda Nup v Chris Hambuga* [1984] PNGLR 206.

1. "Character" refers to positively good character, as shown by, for example, voluntary work in the church or community. It means more than simply the absence of prior convictions.
2. "Antecedents" refers to prior convictions, if any, the existence of which would preclude application of the section and the absence of which does not automatically lead to the application of the section.
3. The "trivial nature of the offence" is to be ascertained separately from the place which the criminal conduct might occupy in the seriousness of crimes of that type.
4. The "extenuating circumstances under which the offence was committed" are circumstances which lessen the seeming magnitude of guilt by a partial excuse, and may include:
   (a) provocation which is not sufficient to constitute the defence of provocation; and/or
   (b) domestic or emotional stress.

As the word "complainant", where twice used in s 260(1)(a) of the *District Courts Act*, means complainant in a civil suit, the court has no power to make an order for costs when a dispositive order is made under s 138 [now s 132]. In *Harangu v Wangiwa* Bredmeyer J stated that:

> "The extended definition of complainant to include informant by s 5 only applies so far as there is no contrary intention. If that extended definition was intended, it would only have been necessary to mention the word complainant on the second occasion. I believe a contrary intention is shown in s 267(1)(a) and that 'complainant' twice used there means complainant in a civil suit."[56]

202. Reduction of imprisonment on part payment.

(1) Where a conviction adjudges the payment of a fine or costs and a term of imprisonment is imposed on the defendant in default of payment the term of imprisonment imposed on payment or satisfaction of part of the fine or costs, shall be reduced by a number of days bearing, as nearly as possible, the same proportion to the total number of days in the term as the sum paid bears to the sum adjudged to be paid.

---

[56] *Harangu v Wangiwa* [1984] PNGLR 244 at 246 (Bredmeyer J).

(2) Payment under this section may be made to –

(a) the Clerk; or

(b) the officer-in-charge of the corrective institution or police lock-up in which the defendant is detained.

(3) Where a warrant of commitment has been issued against a defendant in respect of the non-payment of a fine or costs and payment is made of part of the fine or costs to the Clerk, the Clerk shall give to the person making the payment a certificate of the payment under his hand.

(4) On receipt of a certificate under Subsection (3), or of a sum paid under this section, the officer-in-charge of the corrective institution or police lock-up in which the defendant is detained under the warrant of commitment shall endorse a memorandum of the payment and of the reduction effected by the payment on the warrant, which shall then be deemed to have been amended accordingly.

203. Discharge on payment in full.

(1) Subject to Section 204, where a defendant is detained under a warrant of commitment for non-payment of a fine or other sum, he may pay or cause to be paid to the officer-in-charge of the corrective institution or police lock-up in which he is detained the sum specified in the warrant of commitment, and the officer shall receive the sum and discharge the defendant if he is in his custody for no other matter.

(2) All sums received by the officer-in-charge of a corrective institution or police lock-up under a warrant of commitment shall be paid immediately to the Clerk of the nearest or most convenient Court, who shall immediately notify the Clerk of the Court by which the conviction was made.

204. Reduction of amount due.

Where a defendant is detained under a warrant of commitment for non-payment of a fine or other sum, and the fine or other sum is subsequently paid or levied by due process of law, the amount of the fine or other sum shall be deemed to have been reduced in proportion to the amount of imprisonment served.

205B. Restriction of movement.

(1) Notwithstanding that restriction of movement is not specified as a punishment for an offence, a District Court may, in addition to any other punishment or punishments imposed, also impose restriction of movement in accordance with this section.

(2) When a District Court is considering the punishment or punishments to be imposed in any case it shall also consider whether, in the circumstances of the case, restriction of movement is an appropriate punishment.

(3) Where a person is convicted of an offence, the District Court that convicts him may, in addition to or instead of any other punishment that may be imposed, order him-

(a) not to come or be within such part of the country as the District Court specifies; or

(b) to be returned to his home, as specified by the District Court,

during such period, not exceeding five years, as is specified by the court.

(4) An order under Subsection (3)-

(a) may be made subject to such exceptions and conditions as to the District Court seem proper, including a condition requiring the person to report his presence at regular intervals to a District Officer or Probation Officer or member of the Police Force; and

(b) remains in force for such period as is specified.

(5) An order made under Subsection (3)(b) does not operate so as to hinder or prevent a person from leaving the country.

(6) A person who, without reasonable excuse (proof of which is on him), contravenes or fails to comply with an order made under Subsection (3) is guilty of an offence.

Penalty: Imprisonment for a term not exceeding six months.

(7) A person who is convicted of an offence against Subsection (6) is liable to be again removed from the part of the country specified in the order, or to be removed to the part of the country specified by the District Court, as the case may be, or a new order under this section may be made against him.

(8) For the purposes of this section-

"home", in relation to a person, means-

(a) the place (if any) where he has resided continuously during the period of five years immediately preceding the date of the offence giving rise to the conviction in respect of which a punishment under this section is being imposed; or

(b) an area of customary land on which he may by custom build or occupy a house or garden, whether in his own right or in right of his spouse or some other relation; or

(c) an area of customary land owned by a linguistic or cultural group with which he or his spouse has customary affiliations involving usage rights in land; or

(d) an area of land leased for a term of not less than 12 months or held in freehold by him or his spouse under a law in force in the country; or

(e) In a particular case where the provisions of Paragraph (a), (b), (c) or (d) are inapplicable—any other place with which he or his spouse has connections such that it should, in the opinion of the court, be reasonably regarded as his home;

"Probation Officer" means a probation officer appointed under the *Probation Act* (Chapter 381).

[S 205B insrt Act No 20, 1986 (*District Courts (Restriction of Movement) Act 1986*)]

Part XI – Appeals from Decisions of District Courts

219. Appeal to National Court.

(1) Subject to Subsections (2) and (3), a person aggrieved by a conviction, order or adjudication of a Court, including an adjudication or order dismissing an information or complaint, may appeal to the National Court from the conviction, order or adjudication, in accordance with this Part.

(2) Except as provided in Subsection (3), Subsection (1) shall be deemed to authorize an appeal by the State against the dismissal of an information.

(3) Where, in the opinion of the National Court, the matter is one of such public importance that leave should be granted, the Secretary for justice may –

(a) appeal against a decision of a District Court on behalf of a party; or

(b) intervene in an appeal to the National Court.

In *R v Waisopo; Ex parte Secretary for Law* [1974] PNGLR 41 the Secretary for Justice applied for leave to appeal on behalf of the informant, a police officer, who was not a "person aggrieved", arguing insufficiency of sentence (six weeks' imprisonment with light labour for indecent assault) based on the alleged consideration of extraneous information and the failure to give proper weight to circumstances of aggravation, and where the prisoner had already completed his sentence. This did not amount to a matter of such public importance as to warrant the granting of leave to appeal.

(4) The Public Prosecutor may appeal to the National Court against any decision of the District Court as to sentence in respect of any indictable offence triable summarily under Section 420 of the *Criminal Code*.

[Subs (4) insrt Act No 32, 1980 (*District Courts (Hearing of Indictable Offences) Act* 1980), s 7]

In so far as there is a contest as to what took place in the court below, the general rule is that the appellate court should accept the statement of the magistrate: *Leonard Eliza v Mandina* [1971-1972] PNGLR 422 at 424.

It is not the function of the National Court to interfere with findings of fact by the trial court magistrate which are reasonably open on the evidence: *Paul Carroll v Thomas Gabriel* [1976] PNGLR 415.

Where the lower court did not really deliver a judgment, but addressed the defendant directly, as is common, this may be treated as being in the nature of a judgment rather than as a mere expostulation by the magistrate directed at the convicted defendant, unless the magistrate's words are so terse as to indicate that it would be unfair to both magistrate and accused to suggest that a reasoned judgment was being delivered: *John Kemai v Symonds* [1975] PNGLR 81 at 83.

Where a judgment is given by a magistrate or judge, and fairly full reasons are given, and the magistrate or judge sets out strong considerations one way or the other and leaves out other competing considerations, then the judgment is at risk: *John Kemai v Symonds* [1975] PNGLR 81.

It is a general principle to be applied on appeals to a superior court against sentence, that the superior court should not interfere unless it can find either that the sentence is manifestly excessive or that there are some circumstances which show that the magistrate, in awarding the sentence, acted under a misapprehension of fact or on some wrong principle: *Wilkeson, Stephens and Michalov v Grant* [1967-1968] PNGLR 112 at 114 and 115.

A recommendation of dismissal from the police force by the convicting court is not a conviction order or adjudication within the meaning of the Act, so that an appeal does not lie against the recommendation to the National Court: *Paul Maniwokin v Akuila Toburua* [1973] PNGLR 710.

The *District Courts Act* has no provision making an appeal to the National Court under Pt XI an appeal by way of re-hearing: *Aikaba v Tami* [1971-1972] PNGLR 155.

The court has power to control its own proceedings unless some competent authority restricts that power. It has power to adjourn and refuse to adjourn. The power is discretionary and will only be disturbed on serious grounds: *Buaki v Francis Mugugai* (1974) No789.

On an appeal on a driving charge see *Aruru Antar v Pius S Nime* [1975] PNGLR 296. On a defective committal by reason of duplicity see *R v Burusep* (1963) N308. On appeals on the ground of uncertainty see the cases of *Sie v Kellaart* (1954) N62 and *R v Sarea Aravapo* (1973) N775, under s 37; and see s 37(9), 37(14), 37(15) and 37(16) of the *Constitution*.

Where what is involved is a challenge to the jurisdiction of the court below, it does not matter whether the National Court deals with the issue as an appeal or as an application for certiorari to quash: *James Otto v Jack Pewa* (1981) N299 (M).

There should be no feeling of personal reflection on the magistrate, provided he or she has performed the functions assiduously and conscientiously, and any challenge to that decision is not a challenge to the integrity or ability of the particular judicial officer or to respect for law and order: *Wui Wapi v Ludwick Kembu* [1980] PNGLR 7.

As noted by Williams J in *R v Waisopo, Ex parte Secretary for Law* [1974] PNGLR 41, it is surprising that there is a dearth of authority on the meaning of the phrase "such public importance that leave should be granted". Something of "public importance" should not be confused with the notion of something being of interest to the public in the sense of being newsworthy or topical: *Acting Public Prosecutor v Barry Blythe Holloway* (1981) N298(M) (Miles J).

See *Susan Moru v Tikeling Sakin* (1981) N362(M), regarding the need to frame the grounds of appeal with some particularity.

The duty of the appeal court is to know all it can about what actually happened at the hearing, and consequently it is the duty of the court appealed from to include, in as much detail as possible, everything that did happen – but not in an argumentative way, or (*McCallum v Buibui* [1975] PNGLR 439 at 444 (Frost CJ)) by rewriting the judgment so as to recast the issues in dispute: *Torni Orabi v Benson Tarnean* (1981) N323(M) (Quinlivan AJ).

220. Institution of appeal.

(1) An appeal under Section 219 shall be instituted –

(a) by notice of appeal; and

(b) by entering into a recognizance on appeal, or by giving other security as prescribed by Section 222.

(2) An appellant shall give notice of his intention to appeal by lodging, within one month after the day when the decision is pronounced, a notice of appeal with the clerk of the court by which the conviction, order or adjudication was made.

Appeals from the District Court to the National Court are created by statute and, as such, are mandatory provisions and must be complied with strictly: *Kiau Nikints v Moki Rumints* [1990] PNLGR 123.

221. Notice of appeal.

(1) A notice of appeal under Section 220 shall be in writing, and shall state the nature of the grounds of appeal.

(2) Within one month after the day on which the decision was pronounced, a

copy of the notice of appeal shall be served by or on behalf of the appellant upon –

(a) the respondent, or upon each of the respondents if more than one; and

(b) the Registrar of the National Court.

"I will refuse to hear appeals framed in such meaningless terms as 'the decision is against the weight of evidence' or 'the sentence is manifestly excessive'. When the grounds of appeal are framed with some particularity, not only does opposing counsel know exactly what it is that is being complained of, but the court is immediately apprised of those matters which are under attack. This has the double benefit of first confining, and rightly confining, an appellant to the matters with which he is aggrieved at the time he lodges the appeal, and secondly to allow the Court and opposing counsel to examine the issues before they come into court. Thirdly, magistrates are required to furnish reports and reasons when such have not been given. It is quite unreasonable to expect them to waste time and energy 'covering the field' simply because the appellate will not frame his complaints about conviction with some degree of particularity."[57]

A recognisance under this section is not a condition precedent to a right to appeal under these sections. The waiver provisions under s 231 therefore do not apply: *Kiau Nikints v Moki Rumints* [1990] PNLGR 123.

223. Release of appellant from custody.

Where an appellant is in custody and is not detained for any other cause, a Magistrate, on the certificate of the Clerk of the Court by which the conviction, order or adjudication was made that a copy of the notice of appeal has been served upon him and that the appellant has entered into a recognizance or deposited a sum of money in accordance Section 222, may, by written order, release the appellant from custody.

See s 6 of the *Bail Act*.

It is necessary for an applicant for bail pending appeal to establish exceptional or unusual grounds, but this concept encompasses a wide variety of matters: *Paul Verol Aisi v Malkom Bai* (1976) N52.

224. Disposition, etc, to be forwarded to Registrar of National Court.

(1) The Clerk of the Court the decision of which is appealed against, immediately after notice of appeal is lodged with him, shall forward to the Registrar of the National Court a copy, certified by him to be a true copy –

(a) of the conviction, order or adjudication; and

(b) of the reasons given by the court for the making of the conviction, order or adjudication, if any reasons were given at the time when the decision was pronounced; and

(c) of the complaint; and

[57] *Susan Moru v Tikeling Sakin* (1981) N362(M) (Pratt J).

(d) of the depositions; and

(e) of all other proceedings before the court relating to the conviction, order or adjudication,

(2) together, subject to Subsection (2), with the original exhibits (if any) relating to the conviction, order or adjudication.

(3) Where, in the opinion of the clerk, it is impracticable to forward the exhibits required under Subsection (1), the Clerk may forward to the Registrar of the National Court, instead of the exhibits, a list and description of those exhibits.

225. Report by magistrate.

(1) Where no reasons were given by the Court for the making of the conviction, order or adjudication, the Clerk of the Court the decision of which is appealed against, immediately after the notice of appeal is lodged with him, shall notify the Magistrate who constituted the court by which the conviction, order or adjudication was made, of the notice of appeal.

(2) Immediately after being notified of a notice of appeal under Subsection (1), the Magistrate shall forward to the Registrar of the National Court a written report setting out the reasons for the making of the conviction, order or adjudication.

This section is intending not so much to set out exclusive conditions on which a report of reasons might be forwarded and considered, but rather to ensure that when no reasons have been given, they are later forthcoming: *Paul Papalamnan v Samso Nuakona* (1973) N771.

On appeal in *Benson Bareto v Donatus Kilimito* [1990] PNGLR 125, the magistrate's notes were inadequate and made it impossible to conduct an appeal properly. Hinchliffe J stated that "[m]agistrates should ensure that they record proceedings adequately. Without a proper transcript, the judge or judges on appeal will not know what happened in the court below".

226. Appellant to set down appeal and give notice.

Within 40 days after the institution of an appeal, the appellant shall enter the appeal for hearing on a date to be fixed by the Registrar of the National Court.

An entry shall be made by delivering to the Registrar of the National Court a memorandum in the prescribed form, signed by the appellant or by his lawyer and containing the prescribed particulars.

227. Failure to enter appeal for hearing.

If, within 40 days after the institution of an appeal, the appellant does not enter the appeal for hearing, a Court or Magistrate has the same authority to enforce the conviction, order or adjudication as if it had not been appealed against.

The filing of an entry of appeal for hearing automatically stays the execution of any order or decision for which the appeal is lodged: *Sangam Mote v Alkan Tololo* [1996] PNGLR 404.

228. Notice of hearing.

(1) Notice of hearing of an appeal shall be given by the Registrar of the National Court to the respondent and to each of the respondents if more than one and to the Clerk of the Court the decision of which is appealed against, not less than seven days before the day fixed for the hearing of the appeal.

(2) Notwithstanding anything in Section 238(1), the Registrar of the National Court may in any case give notice by telegram of the hearing of the appeal, and a notice of hearing so given shall be deemed to comply with the requirements of that subsection.

229. Other evidence not to be received on hearing.

Evidence other than the evidence and proceedings before the Court by which the conviction, order or adjudication was made shall not be received on the hearing of an appeal, except by consent of the parties or by order of the National Court.

See also, on fresh evidence, ss 6 and 20-22 of the *Supreme Court Act*.

Fresh evidence may be presented on appeal only when that evidence could not with reasonable care have been discovered previously. Where all the defendant's witnesses were in court at the original trial it is most unlikely that the defendant can bring the case within the well known principles guiding the reception of fresh evidence: *Moses Aikaba v Ephraim Tami* [1971-1972] PNGLR 155 (Raine L).

On appeal from a sentence of the District Court, the National Court may, in its discretion, admit fresh character evidence, particularly where the appellant was unrepresented in the court below: *John Kemai v Symonds* [1975] PNGLR 81 at 82.

In so far as there is a contest as to what took place in the court below, the general rule is that the appellate court should accept the statement of the magistrate: *Yamore Memera v Matthew Bisang* [1976] PNGLR 419.

230. Power of National Court on appeal.

(1) Upon the hearing of an appeal, the National Court shall inquire into the matter, and may–

(a) adjourn the hearing from time to time; and

(b) mitigate or increase a penalty or fine; and

(c) affirm, quash or vary the conviction, order or adjudication appealed from, or substitute or make a conviction, order or adjudication which ought, on the evidence before the National Court, to have been made by a District Court;

(d) remit the case for hearing or for further hearing before the court which made the conviction, order or adjudication or any other competent court;

(e) exercise a power that the Court that made the conviction, order or adjudication might have exercised; and

(f) make such further or other order as to costs or otherwise as the case requires.

(2) An appeal shall be allowed only if it appears to the National Court that there has been a substantial miscarriage of justice.

Where a defendant is convicted on several indictments, and sentence is not allotted to one specific offence or apportioned (as an accumulation), it would seem to constitute on its face an irregularity. However, such irregularity may not constitute a substantial miscarriage of justice within the meaning of this section if the overall sentence is not excessive: *Wama Ul v Jansen* (1975) N834.

There is need for special care on the part of a magistrate hearing a case that has generated much newspaper publicity. The publicity itself, however, is not a ground for holding that the trial miscarried: *Kereku v Dodd* [1969-1970] PNGLR 176 at 189.

Note the import of s 37(13) of the *Constitution*, which allows the court to avoid undue publicity in certain cases.

> "That is a proper consideration so long as it does not result in a convicted man being made the scapegoat of other people who have committed similar crimes but have not been caught and convicted."[58]

To do so constitutes an unsound exercise of discretion and amounts to a substantial miscarriage of justice: *Wilkeson, Stephens and Michalov v Grant* [1967-1968] PNGLR 112 at 117 and 118.

> "It is well established in law (*O'Neill v Graham, Ex Parte Graham* (1952) QSR 79) that there must be something wrong with a judgment before an appeal Court will interfere."[59]

The National Court will not set aside a conviction of a lower court merely because upon a consideration of the evidence it would have come to a different conclusion, or that there appears to be, on any particular finding, oral evidence both ways. The court will not normally interfere with the finding of a magistrate who has had the advantage of seeing and hearing witnesses: *Al Bovell v Peter John Lenehan* (1972) N721.

The National Court, having found a miscarriage of justice under s 236(2), has power to substitute for the sentence of the District Court the sentence it thinks proper: *Gomara Gahusi v Malcolm Stanley Baker* (1970) N601.

The National Court has a discretion regarding costs and may award costs to a successful defendant: *Clive Wissman v Collector of Customs* [1977] PNGLR 324.

The power to award costs mean party and party costs, and in summary jurisdiction are normally the costs of prosecuting the charge: *Aruru Antar v Pius S Nime* [1975] PNGLR 296.

The meaning of "substantial miscarriage of justice" has generally been considered from the point of view of the accused person: see, for example, *Mraz v The Queen* (1955) 93 CLR 493 at 514. In *Secretary for Law v Nash* [1974] PNGLR 45 it was held that the test to be applied where the Secretary for Justice appeals is whether the magistrate, properly directing himself on the law, would have come to the same conclusion as that to which he came.

Where the National Court is satisfied, within the meaning of s 236(2), that a substantial miscarriage of justice has occurred, it may send the matter back to the District Court or it may itself exercise a power which the District Court might have exercised: *Moses Aikaba v Ephraim Tami* [1971-1972] PNGLR 155 at 161.

---

[58] *R v Withers* (1935) 25 Cr App R 53 at 54.
[59] *Masuwe v Thackeray* (1966) N392.

The appearance of a police prosecutor in a case in which his wife was the victim is not unlawful or improper and does not amount to a "substantial miscarriage of justice". It was held, in *Fidelis Agai v Buckly Yarume* [1987] PNGLR 124, that a prosecutor, be he a police prosecutor or a lawyer, should not appear in a case in which he is likely to appear as a witness – unless he is an informant conducting a private prosecution. The facts of the present case did not fall within such a situation, as the police prosecutor was not going to be a witness.

In *Fidelis Agai v Buckly Yarume* [1987] PNGLR 124, a further ground of appeal was the existence of a reasonable suspicion of bias in favour of the prosecution, as the prosecutor and the presiding magistrate were from the same province. Bredmeyer J, cited with approval Lord Widgery CJ in *R v Altricham Justices; Ex Parte Pennington* [1975] 2 All ER 78, who stated that in such circumstances it is not necessary to prove that the judicial officer was biased. It is enough to show a real likelihood of bias, or at all events that a reasonable person advised of the circumstances might reasonably suspect that a judicial officer was incapable of being impartial and detached. However, Bredmeyer J distinguished *R v Altricham Justices; Ex Parte Pennington* from *Fidelis Agai v Buckly Yarume*, on the basis that in the case before Lord Widgery, the connection between the magistrate and victim was proved. In *Fidelis Agai v Buckly Yarume* the connection was not proved. To say that the victim and the magistrate are from the same province, that they live in a small town, and that therefore it should be inferred that they knew each other well and see each other often socially, is merely suspicion, not evidence. As this connection was not proved, it was held that there was no substantial miscarriage of justice.

> "The administration of justice would come to a standstill if every time a prosecutor and victim (or, for that matter – defence counsel and defendant) came from the same province as the magistrate, a party could apply to have the magistrate barred for bias ... The test is whether there is a real likelihood or reasonable suspicion of bias".[60]

In so far as a conviction is based on a plea of guilty, an appellate court may properly entertain an appeal against such conviction where the appellant did not appreciate the nature of the charge. Indeed, it is clearly incumbent on an appellate court to entertain the appeal, since a decision to convict as on a plea of guilty which has been wrongly accepted is a nullity: *Leonard Eliza v Mandina* [1971-1972] PNGLR 422 at 425 and 426.

To deprive a citizen of the right to drive a motor vehicle, where that right is required for carrying out the daily duties of the citizen's occupation, is a penalty which, if wrongly imposed, amounts to a substantial miscarriage of justice: *Wilkeson, Stephens and Michalov v Grant* [1967-1968] PNGLR 112 at 117 and 118.

Where the accused has been in custody for some time and has no legal representation, great care should be taken by the court to ensure that the accused is able to properly present his or her case. Failure of the court to allow the accused to cross-examine a witness (itself a violation of s 137 of the *District Courts Act*), and failure to allow the accused to seek out a witness who would testify as to a material aspect of the defence, constituted a substantial miscarriage of justice: *Kereku v Dodd* [1969-1970] PNGLR 176. Note the more specific provisions of ss 37(3), 37(4)(e), 37(4)(f) and 37(14) of the *Constitution* on an individual's basic rights to speedy trial, legal representation and rights to cross-examine witnesses.

---

[60] *Kavali v Hoihoi* (1986) SC 321.

Raine J held that there was a substantial miscarriage of justice when a magistrate, on a charge of dangerous driving where the defendant has pleaded guilty, in passing sentence relied on his own knowledge of the condition of the road concerned, where that condition was not established by evidence or set out in the statement of facts: *Gomara Gahusi v Malcolm Stanley Baker* (1970) N601.

See discussion of *Kereku v Dodd* [1969-1970] PNGLR 176 (*Criminal Code*, s 544(5)) regarding the error of a court in holding a joint or "lumped" hearing, that is, a hearing where two or more prisoners arraigned upon separate indictments are tried together, without the consent of the accused.

Where evidence is wrongly admitted by a magistrate, a conviction will not necessarily be set aside on that ground if the court is of the opinion that there is sufficient other evidence to support a conviction and that the evidence wrongly admitted did not influence the decision. The test has been expressed as "Is it reasonably probable that the evidence influenced the decision": *Leonard Eliza v Mandina* [1971-1972] PNGLR 422.

The court may allow an appeal only when satisfied that a substantial miscarriage of justice has occurred. In *Pius Embari v S/Const Wangiwa* (1973) N751, imposition of the maximum punishment, where the magistrate was entitled to entertain the view that the stealing involved came within the worst category of stealing, did not constitute such a miscarriage. Imposition of five cumulative sentences, totalling two years and four months imprisonment upon summary conviction for stealing, where the accused was a first offender and pleaded guilty, **is** manifestly harsh and excessive and discloses a substantial miscarriage of justice.

The imposition of a penalty in excess of the maximum pecuniary penalty provided by statute must be regarded as substantial miscarriage of justice: *Joseph Kembu v Eko, Mason* [1971-1972] PNGLR 407 at 413.

In *Samuel Goliath v Vincent Nemil* [1976] PNGLR 522, the court, on appeal from the sentences, proffered the view that it would have been preferable for the second lot of offences, which occurred during the same period, to have been brought to the magistrate's attention on the first occasion. With regard to the sentences imposed, the court found that there was a substantial miscarriage of justice in that there was no apparent justification for the imposition of a greater penalty in respect of the second (lesser) offence, and substituted a sentence of four months imprisonment cumulative upon that of the five months sentence.

See ss 560 and 563 of the *Criminal Code* and ss 128 and 129 of the *Districts Courts Act* 1963 regarding pleas. See ss 37 and 42(1)(a) of the *Constitution* and ss 20 and 596 of the *Criminal Code* regarding sentence.

Where a magistrate stated that as a matter of policy in theft cases all first-offenders would receive a three months term of imprisonment and all repeat-offenders would receive the maximum sentence, this constituted a miscarriage under this section: *Vagi Gau v Kenkone Eava* (1976) N67.

Some of the factors to be taken into consideration in the exercise of the court's discretion to award costs are referred to by Saldanha J in *Clive Wissman v Collector of Customs* [1977] PNGLR 324. One such factor is that in this country we should not slavishly follow the tendency that may exist elsewhere for costs to follow the event in cases of summary prosecution: *Acting Public Prosecutor v Barry Blythe Holloway* (1981) N298 (M).

231. Dispensing with conditions precedent.

The National Court may –

(a) dispense with compliance with a condition precedent to the right of appeal prescribed by this Act, if, in its opinion, the appellant has done whatever is reasonably practicable to comply with the provisions of this Act; and

(b) on application made ex parte by the party appealing – extend the time for compliance with a condition precedent to the right of appeal prescribed by this Act.

For the principles which apply in the exercise of discretionary power to dispense with conditions precedent to the right of appeal, see *Strutt v Haram* (1963) N276.

Thus, where a magistrate decides to convert the hearing of a complaint for an indictable offence into a summary court hearing, the statutory conditions of conversion must be strictly complied with. In *Strutt v Haram* (1963) N276, as the magistrate had not begun any hearing, his refusal to hear the matter meant that no jurisdiction had ever been exercised.

The waiver provisions under s 231 do not apply to recognisances under s 222: *Kiau Nikints v Moki Rumints* [1990] PNLGR 123.

Chapter 3

THE CRIMINAL CODE

The Papua New Guinea Criminal Code 1974 and its antecedents

British New Guinea was established as a British protectorate in late 1884, and formally annexed in 1888, as a result of pressure placed upon Britain by its Australian colonies fearful of German expansionism in the area. The English common law, including the law of crimes, was received "so far as the same are applicable to the circumstances of the Territory and are not repugnant to or inconsistent with [any written law]" by virtue of s 4 of the *Courts and Laws Adopting Ordinance* 1889.

In 1902 the *Criminal Code Ordinance* (No 7 of 1902), s 1, adopted Queensland's *Criminal Code Act* 1899 (63 Vic No 9) into the Territory. The Queensland *Criminal Code*, also known as the "*Griffith Code*" after its draftsman, Sir Samuel Griffith, was intended as a progressive codification of the common law of crimes incorporating the related scattered statutes, and is still used in Queensland and Western Australia. The Code was exported to Nigeria as well, although the Indian *Penal Code* of 1860 was more widely used in colonial Anglophone Africa. The adoption of the Code in British New Guinea (which became the Australian Territory of Papua following the *Commonwealth Papua Act* 1905), was unaccompanied by any qualification as to circumstantial applicability. In *R v Ebulya* [1964] PNGLR 200 at 221-222, the Supreme Court noted that:

> "It is to be observed that the *Criminal Code* of Queensland was adopted as and to be the law of [Papua] without the qualification of circumstantial applicability or of repugnancy to existing laws."

The court went on to say, however, that parts of the Code were clearly inapplicable and unenforceable, such as those referring to trial by jury, or granting rights of appeal to a "Full Court" which did not exist in the Territory at the time of the adoption.

To the north, New Guinea (Kaiser Wilhelm's land) was under German rule from the early 1880s until 1914, and under British military rule from 1914-1921, when it was made a class "C" League of Nations mandate under Australian administration. The Queensland *Criminal Code* was adopted in New Guinea in 1921 by the *Laws Repeal and Adopting Ordinance* (No 1 of 1921), s 16 and Sch 2. The Code was subsequently repealed and then re-adopted with some minor amendments, by the *Laws Repeal and Adopting Ordinance* 1924 (No 1 of 1924). Unlike its Papuan counterpart, the Queensland *Criminal Code (Adopted)* (New Guinea) was subject to circumstantial applicability, although in practice this distinction made little or no difference as no substantive portion of the Code was ever ruled inapplicable: see O'Regan, "*Codes and Common Law in Papua and New Guinea*" (1970) 1 MLJ 1 at 5.

As a result of work done by the Law Reform Committee of the Justice Department during the period of self-government in preparation for Independence, the two adopting enactments, together with all subsequent amendments, were repealed and replaced by the *Criminal Code Act* 1974 (No 78 of 1974), which established, at Sch 1, the *Criminal Code* of Papua New Guinea.

The major substantive changes to the Code were the addition of 12 new sections (ss 158-159, 161-169 and 632) dealing with counterfeiting currency, none of which have been the subject of an indictment since, and the elimination of offences relating to railways, which do not exist in Papua New Guinea. Oysters likewise are not found in Papua New Guinea, but there is still a crime of unlawfully dredging for oysters under s 428. No changes at all were made to ss 22-36 of the Code, which deal with the fundamental issues of criminal responsibility.

The 1974 Code was retained after Independence in 1975 by virtue of Sch 2.6(2) of the *Constitution*, which adopted all pre-Independence laws as Acts of Parliament.

Amendments to the Criminal Code to 1985

Between the Papua New Guinea *Criminal Code* 1974 and 1985 there were several significant amendments to the principal Act.

A major legislative change was to the punishment for the offence of wilful murder. Under s 305 of the *Criminal Code* (Qld), a person convicted of wilful murder was liable to be sentenced to death, unless there were extenuating circumstances operating, in which case the trial judge could impose a sentence of life imprisonment or less. The last death sentence imposed by a trial judge in Papua New Guinea was in 1971, but that sentence was overturned on appeal, with the Full Court substituting life imprisonment. That case also highlighted the difficulties that the courts have in determining whether "extenuating circumstances exist such as to warrant the mitigation of sentence": see *R v Peter Ivoro* [1971-1972] PNGLR 374. Section 309 of the Papua New Guinea *Criminal Code* 1974 (now s 299 in the Revised Laws) abolished the death penalty for wilful murder and replaced it with a mandatory sentence of life imprisonment. Murder simpliciter and manslaughter were punishable by up to life imprisonment, although a lesser punishment could be imposed.

Following the recommendations of the Papua New Guinea Law Reform Commission in its Report No 3, *Report on Punishment for Wilful Murder* (October 1975), the Parliament passed the *Criminal Code (Amendment) Act* 1976 (Act No 2 of 1976), which eliminated the mandatory aspect of the life sentence as punishment for wilful murder. As the Law Reform Commission wrote (at p 5 of Report No 3):

> "The major defect of the mandatory life sentence is that it fails to distinguish between the different situations in which wilful murders occur. Very few of the wilful murders in Papua New Guinea are examples of premeditated crime or cold-blooded apparently motiveless killings. Most can be explained in terms of cultural norms and pressures and the offenders and their clansmen may feel that the killings were justified. If a judge is required by law to impose a sentence of life imprisonment despite the attitudes of the people towards a particular offence

there will be many instances where the sentence will be considered inappropriate and unacceptable in the eyes of the people and the reputation of the courts and of the government will suffer because of this."

The *Criminal Code (Arrest) Act* 1977 (Act No 13 of 1977) also followed recommendations from the Law Reform Commission, this time contained in Ch 2 of its Report No 4, *Report on Arrest, Search and Bail* (March 1976). Basically the new legislation repealed most of the references to arrest scattered throughout the *Criminal Code* and replaced them with the new *Arrest Act*.

The *Criminal Code (Amendment) Act* 1979 (Act No 27 of 1979) amended two sections of the Code. The wording of s 19(f) regarding good behaviour bonds as a sentencing option was altered to allow for the bonds to be made subject to conditions imposed at the court's discretion. Section 553 (now s 541) was also amended to remedy what appears to be an earlier drafting error. Whereas the section, which is in the portion of the Code dealing with alternative verdicts, was entitled "Charge of Rape and Like Offences", in fact the text of the section referred only to indictments alleging unlawful carnal knowledge of a girl under the age of 12 years. The new wording made the section applicable upon an indictment for rape as well.

In its Report No 8, *Indictable Offences Triable Summarily* (August 1978), the Law Reform Commission recommended amendments to the law permitting senior magistrates to summarily hear a range of offences which were previously only triable by a judge upon indictment. Accordingly, Parliament in 1980 approved legislation amending the *District Courts Act* (by the *District Courts (Hearing of Indictable Offences) Act* 1980 (Act No 32 of 1980)) and the *Criminal Code* (by the *Criminal Code (Indictable Offences) Act* 1980 (Act No 28 of 1980)). Sections 432-433 of the *Criminal Code* (now ss 420-421) were repealed and replaced, and ss 467-468 (now ss 455-456) repealed, to conform with the new approach. Most significantly, a new Schedule was added to the *Criminal Code* which listed over 60 indictable offences which may be tried summarily by a Magistrate Grade V in the District Court. The jurisdiction of Grade V Magistrates in relation to indictable offences triable summarily was considered by the Supreme Court in *Supreme Court Reservation No 4 of 1985; Re Omaro Garo v The Police* [1985] PNGLR 320.

Problems relating to the statutory scheme covering the various theft offences surfaced in a number of cases. See, for example, *John Kasaipwalova v The State* [1977] PNGLR 257. In particular, it became apparent that there were gaps in the legislation with respect to the misappropriation of a chose in action, such as bank credit. In response to this situation the Parliament enacted the *Criminal Code (Misappropriation of Property) Act* 1981 (Act No 10 of 1981), which added a new s 395A (now s 383A) entitled "Misappropriation of Property".

The *Criminal Code (Amendment) Act* 1982 (Act No 12 of 1982) was a "tidying-up" piece of legislation. It contained amendments to ss 420, 421, 525 and 561 and added a new s 421A, all relating to the new procedures for trying indictable offences summarily. It also amended ss 32-33 on the defences of compulsion and marital coercion, which were available to all offences except those punishable by death. As a result of the abolition of the death penalty for wilful murder, the Parliament saw fit to amend those sections to provide a further exception in the case of a trial for wilful murder.

The *Criminal Code (Amendment) Act* 1982 also added a new s 313A to the Code, entitled "Genocide". This section fulfilled one of Papua New Guinea's international obligations as a party to the International Convention on the Prevention and

Repression of the Crime of Genocide, and made the commission of, attempted commission of, and conspiracy to commit, genocide an offence punishable by life imprisonment (subject to s 19).

Probably the most sweeping and contentious changes to the *Criminal Code* were effected by the *Criminal Code (Minimum Penalties) (Amendment) Act* 1983 (Act No 10 of 1983), part of a package of legislation which also amended the penal provisions of the *Summary Offences Act* and the *Inter-Group Fighting Act*. With respect to the Code, 25 sections (ss 64-67, 70-74, 76, 78, 395-402, 410, 412, 422 and 510-512) were altered to provide for new and increased maximum sentences, and also to provide for mandatory minimum custodial sentences. (Section 420 was purportedly amended as well, but the 1983 Act did not take into account the effect on this section of amendments in 1980 and 1982, and it appears that the 1983 change was ineffective.) For example, entering a dwelling with intent to commit a crime under s 397(2) was previously punishable by up to 14 years imprisonment. Following amendment, it was punishable by up to 20 years, with a minimum term of imprisonment of seven years. The maximum penalties for the receiving stolen property offences under s 420 were not raised, but the new amendments imposed mandatory minimum sentences of three or five years jail, depending upon the circumstances (ie whether the conviction was under s 410(1) or s 410(2)).

The new legislation came about as the result of private member's bills sponsored by Mr Thomas Negints MP (Tambul-Nebilyer), although they also had the support of the government, according to statements in Parliament by the Deputy Prime Minister, Mr Wingti (*Hansard*, 19 May 1983, p 24/11/1) and the Minister for Justice, Mr Bais (p 29/11/1). In introducing the legislation, Mr Negints told Parliament:

> "The widespread [breakdown] of law and order ... is a sickening epidemic which is hindering the country's total social, economic and political development. It is therefore indeed timely to amend the *Criminal Code* now. The present penalties are too low and weak. Honourable members will also note that amendments increasing the penalty provisions relate to matters in the nature of public order, safety and protection of property in the home. There are many others, such as killing, arson, and what are commonly called 'white collar crimes' crimes committed by public servants, company directors, etc that are left untouched. Therefore, the amendments are only related to matters of immediate concern in society today, such as, unlawful assembly, assault, tribal fighting, stealing vehicles, damaging properties, unlawfully on premises, break and enter, and many others."[61]

The bills were debated only very briefly, moved through all the required readings on the same day (with leave granted), and were passed on the voices. Almost all the speakers were in favour of the bills. Mr Joseph Aoae MP (Kairuku-Hiri), a former Secretary for Justice, was the only speaker to directly oppose the bills, on the grounds that they would be "tying the hands of the judges, giving very little discretion to the judges" in sentencing, even where special circumstances existed in a particular case, such as with respect to youthful first offenders: (*Hansard*, 19 May 1983, pp 25/11/1-3). Mr Anthony Anugu MP (South Bougainville) spoke in support of the bills, but expressed strong reservations nevertheless that the bill provided only "short-term solutions".

The question still remained, however, whether the minimum custodial sentence

---

[61] *Hansard*, 19 May 1983, pp 22/11/2 and 23/11/1-3.

provisions could be properly circumvented in an appropriate case by resorting to other relevant provisions, such as s 19 of the Code. In *Henderson v Blackwell* [1973] PNGLR 223, Frost SPJ decided that, notwithstanding the provision in s 7(1)(d) of the *Dangerous Drugs (Possession) Act* 1970 that upon conviction a prisoner shall be liable to a penalty of "[i]mprisonment for not less than three months or more than two years", ss 138 and 206(2) of the *District Courts Act* still conferred a power on the court to exercise its discretion to impose a fine when a penalty of imprisonment only is provided for "if it considers that the justice of the case would be better met by a fine than by imprisonment". See also *Makin v Kelly* [1963] PNGLR 127 (Ollerenshaw J).

In *Richard Cheong v Vincent Nemil* [1981] PNGLR 472, however, Kearney DCJ did not follow *Henderson v Blackwell*, expressing the obiter dicta view that it is very arguable that the legislative intent in enacting the minimum punishment provision (in this case, s 7 of the *Dangerous Drugs Act* 1952) was to impliedly exclude the power of the court to impose an alternative punishment under s 206(2) (now s 200(2)).

In *Laho Kerekere v Robin Miria* [1983] PNGLR 277, the applicant jumped over a fence at the Murray Barracks in Port Moresby in order to attend a rock concert. He was convicted by a magistrate of an offence under s 20 of the *Summary Offences Act* (unlawfully being on the premises) which now carries a penalty of "imprisonment for a term not less than one year and not exceeding two years". The applicant was a young man, employed, with no prior convictions. The magistrate, in his brief reasons for decision, indicated that the new penalty provision removed his discretion on sentence, and he imposed the minimum of one year's imprisonment.

On appeal, Amet J considered the local precedents and the Australian High Court decision in *Cobiac v Liddy* (1969) 43 ALJR 257, and followed the *Henderson-Makin-Cobiac* line of authority, holding that the sentencing tribunal retained discretion under s 206(2) of the *District Courts Act* to impose a fine. Specifically, Amet J ruled that the later minimum penalties legislation did not expressly, or by necessary implication, repeal the discretion vested by s 206(2):

> "[G]iven the authority of the Papua New Guinea cases, although pre-Independence, the draftsman of the minimum penalty provisions is presumed to have known what the law is or the courts rulings in relation to similar laws have been, so that I would expect to see specific express provisions in an amending Act if the intention were to repeal provisions which had been held to be available to the courts."

In *Lucas Nep Kororo v Moses Jaruka* [1983] PNGLR 392, the Chief Justice, Sir Buri Kidu, considered on appeal a sentence of three years – the new minimum – for a breach of s 399 of the *Criminal Code* (breaking into a building with intent to commit a crime). The appeal was uncontested by the Public Prosecutor's representative. The Chief Justice held that the minimum penalty provisions were not applicable in this case because the indictable offence had been heard summarily by a magistrate under Sch 1A of the Code:

> "There is absolutely no provision in the amending legislation which says that these minimum penalties are to apply equally to the relevant offences dealt with by way of indictment or summarily. It is my view that if any Sch 1A offences in the Code are dealt with by the Grade 5 Magistrates, the question of minimum penalties provided for the same offences in the body of the *Criminal Code* is irrelevant."

A similar case arose before Pratt J in *Sai Isara v Johnathan Klei* (1983) N445. The applicant had pleaded guilty to break, enter and steal. He was found to have come in search of food, but then stole a jacket and some shoes. The magistrate referred the matter of sentence to the National Court, on the basis that the minimum sentence of five years called for under s 398 exceeded his jurisdictional limit of four years. His Honour commented on "the present morass created in the criminal law by the recent legislation", and then followed the judgment in *Kororo v Jaruka*, returning the matter to the magistrate with the direction that the minimum penalty provisions did not apply to indictable offences heard summarily under Sch 1A.

In *Peter Kekai v Munagun* [1984] PNGLR 5, the Deputy Chief Justice, Mari Kapi, considered an appeal from a prisoner convicted of assault and sentenced to the mandatory minimum of six months' jail under s 6 of the *Summary Offences Act*.

Consistent with the previous cases, Kapi DCJ found that the alternative sentencing provisions of the Code and the *District Courts Act* were not ousted by the minimum penalties legislation. However, in this case the sentencing magistrate and Kapi DCJ both agreed that this was a relatively serious offence which required a more serious punishment than a fine. As a custodial sentence was warranted, the magistrate was correct in applying the minimum penalty:

> "[I]f I had the discretion, as previously existed in the law, I would have imposed a term of much less than six months. This is beside the point. I must apply the law as directed by the Parliament. I cannot allow my disagreement with the policy of the law to affect my discretion ... That is to say, if I do not agree with the minimum penalty, I must impose a fine in order to avoid it. In my view, that would be a wrong exercise of discretion in law."

The Supreme Court considered the matter of the minimum penalties and their effect on discretion in *The State v Danny Sunu, Namabai Walter, Iku Gagoro and Philip Haro; Reservations on Points of Law under s 21 Supreme Court Act (Ch 37)* [1983] PNGLR 396. By a 3-2 decision, the court ruled that the judge does have that discretion – that is, that the alternative sentences under s 19 of the Code are not ousted by the minimum penalties provisions.

The majority judges (Kapi DCJ and McDermott and Amet JJ) relied on the Australian High Court cases of *Rose v Huric* (1963-1964) 37 ALJR 1, *Cobiac v Liddy* (1969) 43 ALJR 257 and *Sillery v R* (1981) 35 ALJR 227 for guidance in the careful task of statutory interpretation.

Section 19 of the Code is prefaced by the phrase "In the construction of this Code it is to be taken that, **except when it is expressly provided**" [that seven alternative punishments are available to the sentencing tribunal] (emphasis supplied). The court had to consider whether the new minimum penalty formulations amounted to **express** removal of the discretion conferred by s 19. The majority judges concluded that the minimum penalty provision did not expressly, or by necessary implication, achieve this.

The Parliament's response was to pass another piece of legislation, the *Criminal Code (Amendment) Act* 1983 (Act No 29 of 1983), which was intended to countermand the majority decision in *Supreme Court Reference No 5 of 1983* (1983) SC 264. The amendment Act added s 19(8) of the Code, which provided that:

> "Where a minimum penalty is prescribed for an offence, nothing in this section authorises a court to impose any penalty other than that minimum penalty on a person convicted of that offence."

The amendment Act also added subsections to ss 601 and 602 of the Code, which provided that the normal provisions on discharge of first offenders (s 601) and discharge of offenders in minor property matters where restitution is made (s 602) are inapplicable where a minimum penalty is prescribed.

The amendment Act, and a further piece of legislation, the *Criminal Code (Minimum Penalties) (Amendment) Act* 1984 (Act No 11 of 1984), added a number of new offences to the list of those carrying minimum penalties, including rape and attempted rape (ss 347-348), robbery and robbery with wounding (ss 386-387), and various sexual assaults (ss 213, 215, 216, 217 and 349). Interestingly, wilful murder (s 309), which once was the only offence in the Code which did carry a mandatory sentence (of life imprisonment, before the 1976 amendment), was not added to the increasing number of minimum penalty provisions. As a result of the amendments, rape had a minimum penalty of 10 years of imprisonment, attempted rape had a five year minimum, robbery had a 10 year minimum, and attempted robbery had five or seven year minimum depending upon the presence of certain aggravating factors.

The 1983 amendment Act also altered the administration of the system of indictable offences triable summarily by amending ss 420, 421, 525, 561 and Sch 1A, and by repealing s 421A. The amendment Act also amended s 12 so as to give the *Criminal Code* extra-territorial effect in connection with the *Offences (Overseas) Act* 1983.

On 7 December 1983, the Morobe Province Premier, Mr Utula Samana, was found guilty of an offence under s 7 of the *Summary Offences Act*, for using insulting language likely to cause a breach of the peace. As a result of the minimum penalties legislation the offence carried a mandatory minimum sentence of three months imprisonment with hard labour, and Mr Samana was given this sentence by a senior magistrate of Lae District Court. The matter of the constitutional validity of the minimum penalties legislation was referred directly to the Supreme Court by the Morobe Provincial Government, under the special reference provisions of s 19 of the *Constitution*. Counsel for the Morobe Provincial Government initially submitted that the minimum penalties legislation offended against three sections of the *Constitution*: ss 32(1), 36(1) and 37(3). By a 4-1 majority, with McDermott J dissenting, the Supreme Court, in *Supreme Court Reference No 1 of 1985* (1984) SC 280, held that the minimum penalties were valid under the *Constitution*. Much was made of the need to uphold the principle of the separation of powers, found in the Papua New Guinea *Constitution* in, inter alia, ss 99(3) and 109. As Kapi DCJ wrote (at 19):

> "[Parliament's] power of prescribing punishment for an offence is only limited to the extent that punishments which are prescribed are not of a kind that affect the inherent dignity of the human person ... It has nothing to do with the proportionality of the punishment imposed for a particular criminal act. To read the principle of proportionality into s 36 is to allow the courts to exercise a power which is given to the Parliament to determine in relation to punishment of criminal offences. Such an interpretation, in my view, violates the principle of separation of powers of the legislature and the judiciary."

Despite upholding the validity of the minimum penalties legislation, some of the majority judges did express some disquiet with the new scheme. Bredmeyer J ended his opinion (at 47-48) with a "cautionary tale" about the ineffectiveness of the death penalty provisions in 18th and early 19th century England. Kaputin J, although finding that the Parliament's actions reflected community standards and values (at

57), was nevertheless concerned about the creation of "a lot of peripheral injustice" (at 58) and urged the Parliament to grade the minimum penalties to take account of the circumstances of first offenders.

In his dissenting judgment, McDermott J wrote (at 73) that:

> "What the challenged legislation here effectively does is treat all offences as equally reprehensible up to an arbitrarily set level of punishment. It is only when above that level can the punishment be proportioned to the offence. In many cases, the minimum level of punishment is simply not called for. This crudely applied, across-the-board approach denies to the person being punished any consideration of the [many relevant factors usually taken into account in sentencing]."

On the question of the applicability of s 41 of the *Constitution* in particular cases, the Supreme Court ruled by a 3-2 majority that the provision could not be used by the courts to circumvent the specified minimum penalty.

Section 41 of the *Constitution* provides as follows:

41. Proscribed acts.

(1) Notwithstanding anything to the contrary in any other provision of any law any act that is done under a valid law but in the particular case –

(a) is harsh or oppressive; or

(b) is not warranted by, or is disproportionate to, the requirements of the particular circumstances or of the particular case; or

(c) is otherwise not, in the particular circumstances, reasonably justifiable in a democratic society having a proper regard for the rights and dignity of mankind,

is an unlawful act.

(2) The burden of showing that Subsection (1)(a), (b) or (c) applies in respect of an act is on the party alleging it, and may be discharged on the balance of probabilities.

(3) Nothing in this section affects the operation of any other law under which an act may be held to be unlawful or invalid.

Supreme Court Reference No 1 of 1985 (1984) SC 280 was the first case in which the Supreme Court was asked to construe s 41 of the *Constitution*. The provision, which appears to give the courts another special power in addition to its prerogative powers and supervisory powers (on appeal), is unique to Papua New Guinea. A narrower formulation which specifically related to arrests, detention, searches and interrogation was recommended by the Constitutional Planning Committee in its 1974 Report, but was not accepted by the Constituent Assembly. The (fourth) draft of this provision was accepted without debate and became s 41 of the *Constitution*.

In ruling out the relevance of s 41 to the minimum penalties legislation, the three majority judges (Kidu CJ, Bredmeyer and McDermott JJ) stressed that the sentencing tribunal was bound by the legislation and was acting without discretion. As Bredmeyer J wrote (at 46):

> "When a judge sentences a man to a minimum penalty term of imprisonment, his action involves no discretion. To say that the judge's action is harsh or

oppressive or disproportionate to the circumstances of a particular case etc is really to challenge the statute and not the judge's actions."

Kapi DCJ, in his dissent on this point, found (at 27-28) that the trial court was bound by the minimum penalties legislation, but that a separate application could then be lodged with the Supreme Court under s 41. In an appropriate case the court could find that the minimum penalty was harsh or oppressive or disproportionate to the circumstances and that the sentence was invalid.

Thus, in conclusion, the Supreme Court ruled that the minimum penalties were constitutionally valid and that they could not be circumvented by reference to the courts' uncertain special power to intervene in harsh or oppressive cases under s 41 of the *Constitution*.

For a more detailed discussion of the minimum penalties statutes, cases, and implications, see Weisbrot, "*Papua New Guinea Minimum Penalties Legislation*", (September 1985), ANZJ Crim.

The Revised Laws of Papua New Guinea

In 1973, the Papua New Guinea House of Assembly (the precursor of the post-Independence Parliament) enacted the *Revision of the Laws Act* (Act No 105 of 1973, amended by the *Revised Edition of the Laws Act* 1976). Unlike the consolidations of colonial legislation which had taken place earlier, with the publication of the *Laws of the Territory of Papua* 1888-1945 and the *Laws of the Territory of New Guinea* 1921-1945, the Revision of the Laws project was meant to go beyond merely reprinting the laws in updated form (that is, as amended).

Thus the Revised Laws amount to "a revision and a re-statement" of the statute law in Papua New Guinea, which, in the words of Mr CJ Lynch, the Commissioner for the Revised Edition of the Laws, "cannot, therefore, be approached or used in the same way as more orthodox compilations of statutes": Preface to the Revised Edition, p 5. Whereas consolidations are only prima facie evidence of the law, the Revised Laws are meant to conclusively state the law as at the effective date. Section 13 of the 1973 Act provides that the Revised Laws are "the sole authentic text of the laws of Papua New Guinea": see also s 20.

The Revised Laws of Papua New Guinea are organised into chapters, with each chapter containing the relevant principal act, any regulations or subsidiary legislation, and an appendix indicating the history of the legislation (previous legislation, and tables showing the relationship between old and new section numbers where such numbers have changed in the revision process). Thus, since the Revised Laws replace all previous legislation, there is no need to refer back to the *Criminal Code Act* 1974 by way of citation. It is now correct simply to refer to "Chapter No 262 – the *Criminal Code*".

Some examples of alterations to the *Criminal Code* include the collapsing of three sections relating to perjury (old ss 122-124) into one large section (s 121 of the Revised Laws version); the rationalisation of two sections on alternative verdicts in homicide cases (old ss 551-552), restated as one section (now s 539); the break-up of one section on trial venues (old s 534) into two sections (now ss 522-523); and the elimination of the old s 309, which provided the penalties for wilful murder and murder, by adding the penalty provisions to the definition sections (ss 299 and 300, respectively).

The first edition of the Revised Laws, stating the law as at 1 January1976, came into force on 1 January 1982, by virtue of the *Revised Laws (Commencement) Act* 1981.

Amendments to the Criminal Code since 1985

During the early 1980s, there was a continuing perception of increasing "law and order" problems in Papua New Guinea. Typical of this perception was an editorial in "*Hammer the Criminals*", *Post-Courier* (28 June 1983), p 4. In fact, Sinclair Dinnen has suggested that law and order remained the single most important issue on the agenda of public debate after independence: Dinnen "*Crime, Law and Order in Papua New Guinea*" (1989) 17 MLJ 10. This focussed attention on the criminal law in both its procedural and substantive aspects. During the 1980s there were a number of ad hoc attempts to address these problems, such as the minimum sentencing legislation, as well as plans for a more comprehensive review of the whole of the *Criminal Code* and cognate legislation: Dinnen "*Crime, Law and Order in Papua New Guinea*" (1989) 17 MLJ 10; Dinnen, "*Minimum penalties in Papua New Guinea – a Case Study in Crime and Development*" (1985) 13 MLJ 25.

The Law Reform Commission of Papua New Guinea had a long-standing (since 21 August 1975) reference on the Criminal Justice System, which included reform of the *Criminal Code*. The Commission has from this time been considering undertaking a full review of the Code, but this has not been done to date. In addition, shortly after becoming Minister for Justice in August 1982, Mr Tony Bais announced that the government was committed to a review of the Code, and this was referred to a new Criminal Law Review Committee.

Also at this time, the National Executive Committee established a Committee to Review Policy and Administration on Crime and Law and Order. The Committee was chaired by Mr Leo Morgan, and consisted of representatives from the Departments of the Prime Minister, Justice, Police, Corrective Services, Finance, the National Planning Office and the Public Service Commission, with consultant services from Mr BD Brunton of the University of Papua New Guinea Law Faculty.

No major amendments flowed from these initiatives. The long promised revision of the Code has not eventuated. There has still been no comprehensive review of the *Criminal Code*. Since 1985 there have been a number of piecemeal amendments to the Code, which have not been substantial. The *Criminal Code* remains largely the same as its formulation in 1974.

Although the death penalty for wilful murder was abolished by an amendment to s 299(2) by the *Criminal Code (Amendment) Act* 1976 (Act No 2 of 1976), public concerns over perceptions of rising violent crime led to its re-introduction in 1991. Section 299(2) was repealed and replaced by s 2 of the *Criminal Code (Amendment) Act* 1991 (Act No 25 of 1991).

The general provision under s 19 in relation to the construction of the Code as to punishments has been amended in two major respects. First, s 19(1)(aa) was inserted by s 1 of the *Criminal Code (Amendment) Act* 1991 (Act No 25 of 1991) to make a person sentenced to death liable for imprisonment for life or for any shorter term. This was an amendment consequent on the reintroduction of the death penalty and clarified the power of a judge in relation to the death penalty. A judge has the discretion to impose imprisonment as an alternative to the death penalty. Secondly, s 19(9) and (10) were added by the *Criminal Code (Restriction of Movement) Act* 1986 (Act No 18 of 1986), s 2. These subsections were inserted to address concerns about the relationship of punishment sections to provisions of the *Constitution*, particularly ss 42 and 52. Incidentally, s 19(8) was repealed by *Criminal Code (Amendment No 2) Act* 1986 (Act No 17 of 1986), s 1.

The amendments dealing with the re-introduction of the death penalty were considered in the decision of Woods J in *The State v Yapes Paege and Relya Tanda* [1994] PNGLR 65 at 66. This decision considered the appropriate circumstances for not imposing the death penalty and imposing the alternative prison sentence. There was further discussion of the death penalty for wilful murder in *The State v John Waiyake Komane* [1992] PNGLR 524 at 547. This case discussed the practicalities of imposing sentence in absence of regulations of facilities for carrying out sentence. These and other cases are annotated under s 299 of the Code.

Towards the end of the 1980s public concerns shifted to issues of honesty and integrity in the public service. The *Criminal Code Amendment Act* 1989 (Act No 2 of 1989) introduced a raft of amendments aimed at improving standards of public accountability and honesty. In particular, new offences (under ss 97A-97D) were introduced relating to:

(a) corruptly procuring withdrawal of tenders;

(b) bribery of member of public service;

(c) duty of person offered gratification; and

(d) evidentiary provisions relating to this division.

In addition, a new Div 2 was introduced that criminalised the receipt of secret commissions by those in public office. Interestingly, custom is not of itself a sufficient excuse for any indictment under this new division: s 97O.

Less controversial than the death penalty, but of greater impact on the administration of justice, have been two developments in relation to the District Courts. First, the jurisdiction has been extended for senior magistrates to hear indictable offences summarily. Under the system that operated until 1980, relatively few indictable offences were triable summarily before a magistrate. This resulted in overcrowded National Court calendars and sometimes long delays in bringing an accused, who may be in custody, to trial. There was a transfer of some cases in 1991 allowing senior magistrates to try some indictable offences summarily. The provisions of the Code dealing with indictable offences triable summarily have been amended and expanded. The former senior magistrates (Grade V) have now been restyled as "Principal Magistrates" with additional powers. The relevant section is s 420.

420. Indictable offences that may be dealt with summarily.

(1) When a person is charged before a District Court constituted by a Magistrate Grade V [now referred to as a Principal Magistrate] with an offence specified in Schedule 2, the Court may deal with the charge summarily according to the procedure set out in Section 421.

(2) Subject to Section 421(4), where -

(a) a charge for an offence is dealt with under Subsection (1); and

(b) the maximum penalty provided in this Code for that offence is imprisonment for a term exceeding 10 years,

the maximum penalty which may be imposed by a [Principal] Magistrate is imprisonment for a term not exceeding 10 years, notwithstanding anything to the contrary in this Code.

Schedule 2, which lists the various indictable offences triable summarily, replaced the old Sch 1A, and was inserted by *Criminal Code (Amendment No 2) Act* 1991 (Act No 18 of 1991), s 2. The title of "Grade V Magistrate" was abolished and replaced by the title of "Principal Magistrate" by amendments to the *District Courts Act* in 2000. The National Court decision in *The State v Kenny Lau* (1990) N863 discusses the new Sch 2 in relation to the *Criminal Code Act* and s 420. The *Criminal Code (Amendment No 2) Act* 1986 (Act No 17 of 1986) also included some procedural amendments to ss 420, 421, 525 and 526, all relating to the procedures for trying indictable offences summarily. For example, a new s 525(5) was added, which removed the need to prefer an indictment where a Principal Magistrate transfers an indictable offence triable summarily for greater penalty under s 421(4).

Secondly, as foreshadowed in the first edition of this book in 1978, the long-planned moves to rationalise the courts of summary jurisdiction has occurred with the abolition of the Local Courts. The importance of the role of the District Courts has become consequentially more pronounced.

CRIMINAL CODE ACT

Chapter No. 262

249.Sentence or process or warrant without jurisdiction.

250. Arrest of wrong person [Repealed].

251. Irregular process or warrant.

252. Force used in executing process or in arrest.

253. Duty of persons arresting [Repealed].

254. Police officer preventing escape from arrest [Repealed].

255. Other cases of preventing escape from arrest [Repealed].

256. Preventing escape or rescue after arrest [Repealed].

257. Examination of person of accused persons in custody [Repealed].

258. Preventing a breach of the peace.

259. Suppression of riot.

260. Suppression of riot by magistrates and police officers.

261. Suppression of riot by person acting under lawful orders.

262. Suppression of riot by person acting without order in case of emergency.

263. Riot: Persons subject to military law.

264. Prevention of crimes and offences for which an offender may be arrested without warrant: Prevention of violence by persons of unsound mind.

265. Defence of dwelling-house.

266. Provocation.

267. Defence of provocation

268. Prevention of repetition of insult.

269. Self-defence against unprovoked assault.

270. Self-defence against provoked assault.

271. Aiding in self-defence.

272. Defence of movable property against trespassers.

273. Defence of movable property with claim of right.

274. Defence of movable property without claim of right.

275. Defence of premises against trespassers: Removal of disorderly persons.

276. Defence of possession of real property or vessel with claim of right.

277. Exercise of right of way or easement.

278. Domestic discipline.

279. Discipline of ship or aircraft.

280. Surgical operations.

281. Excessive force.

282. Consent to death immaterial.

Division 2 - Duties Relating to the Preservation of Human Life

283. Duty to provide necessaries.

284. Duty of head of family.

285. Duty of masters.

286. Duty of persons doing dangerous acts.

287. Duty of persons in charge of dangerous things.

CRIMINAL CODE ACT

Chapter No 262

Being an Act to establish a code of criminal law.

1. Interpretation.

In this Act, unless the contrary intention appears -

"the Code" means the Code of Criminal Law contained in the Schedule;

"the commencement date" means 1 November 1975 (being the date of commencement of the pre-Independence *Criminal Code Act* 1974).

Where the strict interpretation of the *Criminal Code* would give rise to an anomalous and unjust situation, the Supreme Court can and should, on the authority of the *Constitution* itself and s 158(2) in particular, remedy it so as to do what Parliament would have done had they the situation in mind. The courts have power to reject the natural or ordinary or prima facie meaning of a word or phrase on the ground that it leads to some result which cannot reasonably be supposed to have been intended by the legislature. Under s 21 and Sch 2 of the *Constitution*, the Supreme Court has, and should accept, a special responsibility to "assist in the development of our indigenous jurisprudence, adapted to the changing circumstances of Papua New Guinea": *Principal Legal Advisors Request No 1 of 1980* [1980] PNGLR 326.

The High Court of Australia was once, but is no longer, in the curial hierarchy of the jurisdiction of Papua New Guinea. Under the *Constitution*, foreign precedents may be persuasive and may be accorded a degree of deference: *Principal Legal Advisors Request No 1 of 1980* [1980] PNGLR 326 (Andrew J).

See Sch 2 of the *Constitution* regarding the adoption of the pre-Independence common law, and the underlying law. See generally the *Interpretation Act*.

The majority decision of the High Court of Australia in *Kaporonovski v The Queen* (1973) 133 CLR 209 is based first and foremost upon a common law principle of statutory interpretation which is inappropriate to the circumstances of Papua New Guinea at this time. The common law principle variously described as the "literal" rule, the "prima facie" meaning rule, the "plain meaning" rule, the "narrow" rule or the "restricted" rule, contrasts with the "fair and literal meaning" rule, the "purposive" rule, the "ample meaning rule", the "substantial meaning" rule, the "broad meaning" rule, the "extensive operation" rule or the "generous meaning" rule. Why is the "literal" rule of statutory interpretation inappropriate? There is no place in a developing country where the courts, as well as the Law Reform Commission, are given special responsibilities in the process of development, for the narrow interpretation of statutes without adequate regard to the social purpose of particular legislation. Development is difficult to achieve if courts adopt too conservative an approach to the interpretation of statutes, the recognition of the general legislative purpose, as well as the obligations laid down under s 158(2) of the *Constitution*, such as, for example, the obligation upon the courts in interpreting the law to give "paramount consideration to the dispensation of justice": *Principal Legal Advisors Request No 1 of 1980* [1980] PNGLR 326 (Wilson J with Andrew J agreeing).

"The correct approach to the interpretation of a section of the Code is that stated by Dixon and Evatt JJ in *Brennan v The King* (1936) 55 CLR 253, 263, as follows: '... it forms part of a code intended to replace the common law, and its language should be construed accordingly to its natural meaning and without any presumption that it was intended to do no more than restate the existing law. It is not the proper course to begin by finding how the law stood before the Code, and then to see if the Code will bear an interpretation which will leave the law unaltered.'... If the Code is thought of as 'written on a palimpsest, with the old writing still discernible behind' (to use the expressive metaphor of Windeyer J in *Vallance v The Queen* (1961) 108 CLR 56, 76), it should be remembered that the first duty of the interpreter of its provisions is to look at the current text rather than at the old writing which has been erased, if the former is clear, the latter is of no relevance."[62]

See s 37(2) of the *Constitution*.

5. Contempt of court.

(1) Subject to Subsection (2), this Act or the Code does not affect the authority of any court of record to punish a person summarily for the offence commonly known as "Contempt of Court".

(2) A person shall not be punished under Subsection (1) and under the Code for the same act or omission.

See s 37(2) of the *Constitution*.

See also *Public Prosecutor v Nahau Rooney (No 1)* [1979] PNGLR 403 and *Public Prosecutor v Nahau Rooney (No 2)* [1979] PNGLR 448.

6. Saving of powers of courts under other acts.

This Act does not limit or affect in any way any provision of any other Act conferring on a court a power to pass a sentence or impose a punishment or make an order in addition to or instead of a sentence or punishment prescribed by the Code, or otherwise to deal with an offender.

Schedule One

THE CRIMINAL CODE

Part I – Introductory

Division 1 – Interpretation

1. Interpretation.

(1) In this Code, unless the contrary intention appears –

"aircraft" includes any machine or apparatus designed to support itself in the atmosphere, whether or not –

[62] *Stuart v The Queen* (1974) 48 ALJR 517 at 521 (Gibbs J). See also *John Kasaipwalova v The State* [1977] PNGLR 257 (Kearney J dissenting).

(a) it is incapable of use through mechanical defect; or

(b) any part or parts of it have been removed for any purpose or by any person;

"bodily harm" means any bodily injury that interferes with health or comfort;

"circumstances of aggravation" includes any circumstances by reason of which an offender is liable to a greater punishment than that to which he would be liable if the offence were committed without the existence of that circumstance;

"clerk" includes -

(a) any person employed for any purpose as or in the capacity of a clerk or servant, or as a collector of money, even if temporarily only, or if -

(i) employed also by other persons than the person alleged to be his employer; or

(ii) employed to pay as well as receive money; and

(b) any person employed as or in the capacity of a commission agent for the collection or disbursement of money, or in any similar capacity, although he has no authority from his employer to receive money or other property on his account; and

(c) any person who acts in the capacity of an officer of a Friendly Society or branch of a Friendly Society;

"company" means an incorporated company;

"criminally responsible" means liable to punishment as for an offence;

"Department of Posts and Telegraphs" means the Department responsible for posts and telegraphs;

"dwelling-house" includes any building or structure, or part of a building or structure, that is for the time being kept by the owner or occupier for the residence of himself, his family, or servants, or any of them, whether or not it is from time to time uninhabited;

"explosive substance" includes a gaseous substance in such a state of compression as to be capable of explosion;

"genocide" means any of the following acts committed with intent to destroy, in whole or in part, a national, ethnical, racial or religious group as such: –

(a) killing members of that group; or

(b) causing serious bodily or mental harm to members of that group; or

(c) deliberately inflicting on that group conditions of life calculated to bring about its destruction in whole or in part; or

(d) imposing measures intended to prevent births within that group; or

(e) forcibly transferring children of that group to another group.

"gratification" includes –

(a) money, loans, rewards or an interest in property; or

(b) an office or employment; or

(c) a payment of or release from a loan or liability; or

(d) valuable consideration of any kind; or

(e) forbearance to demand money or money's worth; or

(f) aid, a vote, consent or influence; or

(g) a service, favour or advantage of any description whatsoever; or

(h) an offer or promise of any kind of gratification as described in Paragraphs (a) to (g) inclusive;

"grievous bodily harm" means any bodily injury of such a nature as to endanger or be likely to endanger life, or to cause or be likely to cause permanent injury to health;

"have in possession" includes having under control in any place, whether for the use or benefit of the person of whom the term is used or of another person, whether or not another person has the actual possession or custody of the thing in question;

"indictment" means a written charge preferred against an accused person in order to his trial before some court other than a court of summary jurisdiction;

"knowingly", when used in connexion with an expression denoting uttering, implies a knowledge of the character of the thing uttered or used;

"liable", used alone, means liable on conviction on indictment;

"mail" includes anything sent by post that is in actual course of transmission from one place to another;

"mail conveyance" includes –

(a) any conveyance of any kind by which a mail is carried; and

(b) any vessel employed by or under the Department of Posts and Telegraphs or the postal authority of any other country, or the Admiralty, for the conveyance of mails, whether under contract or not; and

(c) a ship of war or other vessel in the service of Her Majesty in respect of letters conveyed by it;

"money" includes bank notes, bank drafts, cheques, and any other orders, warrants, authorities, or requests for the payment of money;

"motor vehicle" includes -

(a) any machine or apparatus designed for propulsion wholly or partly by gas, motor spirit, oil, electricity, steam or other mechanical power; and

(b) a motor cycle; and

(c) a caravan, caravan trailer or other trailer designed to be attached to a motor vehicle

whether or not the machine or apparatus –

(d) is incapable of use through mechanical defect; or

(e) has had any part or parts of it removed for any purpose or by any person;

"night" means the interval between 9 pm and 6 am;

"night-time" has the same meaning as "night";

"owner", and other like terms, when used with reference to property, include -

(a) a corporation; and

(b) any other association of persons capable of owning property; and

(c) the State;

"person employed in the Public Service" includes officers and men of the Defence Force, members of the Police Force and persons employed to execute any process of a court of justice;

"Postmaster-General" means the Departmental Head of the Department of Posts and Telegraphs;

"post office" means any structure, room, place or receptacle, appointed by authority of the Postmaster-General for the receipt, despatch or delivery of anything sent by post, or for the transaction of the business of the Department of Posts and Telegraphs relating to posts;

"property" includes every thing, animate or inanimate, capable of being the subject of ownership;

"public body" means –

(a) the State; or

(b) a province; or

(c) a provincial government; or

(d) a The State Service established under or by authority of Section 188 (Establishment of The State Services) of the *Constitution*; or

(e) a constitutional institution, being any office or institution established or provided for by the *Constitution* including the Head of State, a Minister or the National Executive Council; or

(f) a body or corporation established by statute;

"registered brand" means a brand that is registered under a law relating to brands;

"registered mark" means a mark that is registered under a law relating to brands;

"servant" has the same meaning as "clerk";

"ship" includes every kind of vessel used in navigation not propelled by oars;

"summary conviction" means conviction by a court of summary jurisdiction;

"telegram" means a thing sent by telegraph, and includes any written message delivered at a telegraph office or post office for transmission by telegraph, or delivered or prepared for delivery from a telegraph office or post office as a message transmitted by telegraph for delivery;

"telegraph" includes a telephone;

"telegraph office" means any structure, room, place or receptacle appointed by authority of the Postmaster-General for the receipt, dispatch or delivery of anything sent by telegraph, or for the transaction of the business of the Department of Posts and Telegraphs relating to telegraphs;

"thing sent by post" includes -

(a) any letter, newspaper, packet, parcel or other thing authorized by law to be transmitted by post, that -

(i) has been posted or received at a post office for delivery or transmission by post; and

(ii) is in course of transmission by post; and

(b) any moveable receptacle that -

(i) contains any such thing; and

(ii) is in course of transmission by post;

"uncorroborated testimony", in relation to an accused person, means testimony that is not corroborated in some material particular by other evidence implicating him;

"utter" means –

(a) use or deal with; or

(b) attempt to use or deal with; or

(c) attempt to induce any person to use, deal with, or act on, the thing in question;

"valuable security" includes any document that -

(a) is the property of any person; and

(b) is evidence of the ownership of any property or of the right to recover or receive any property;

"vessel" includes a ship or boat, and every other kind of vessel used in navigation.

[Definition of "genocide" insrt Act No 12, 1982 (*Criminal Code (Amendment) Act* 1982), s 4; definition of "gratification" insrt Act No 2, 1989 (*Criminal Code (Amendment) Act* 1989), s 1(a); definition of "public body" insrt Act No 2, 1989 (*Criminal Code (Amendment) Act* 1989), s 1(b)]

(2) A flight of an aircraft shall be deemed to commence

(a) at the time of the closing of the external door of the aircraft last to be closed before the aircraft first moves for the purpose of taking off from any place; or

(b) if Paragraph (a) is not applicable – at the time at which the aircraft first moves for the purpose of taking off from any place,

and shall be deemed to end –

(c) at the time of the opening of the external door of the aircraft first to be opened after the aircraft comes to rest after its next landing after the commencement of the flight; or

(d) if Paragraph (c) is not applicable – at the time at which the aircraft comes to rest after its next landing after the commencement of the flight,

or, if the aircraft is destroyed, or the flight is abandoned, before either Paragraph (c) or (d) becomes applicable, at the time at which the aircraft is destroyed or the flight abandoned, as the case may be.

(3) A building or structure adjacent to, and occupied with, a dwelling-house shall be deemed to be part of the dwelling-house if there is a communication between the building or structure and the dwelling-house, either immediate or by means of a covered and enclosed passage leading from the one to the other, but not otherwise.

(4) For the purposes of the definition "thing sent by post" in Subsection (1) –

(a) a thing shall be deemed to be in course of transmission by post or telegraph from the time of its being delivered to a post office or telegraph office to the time of its being delivered to the person to whom it is addressed; and

(b) a delivery at the house or office of the person to whom anything sent by post or telegraph is addressed, to him or to some person apparently authorized to receive it according to the usual manner of delivering that person's letters or telegrams, shall be deemed a delivery to the person addressed.

(5) In this Code, unless the contrary intention appears, a reference to the Queen and Head of The State includes a reference –

(a) to the successor, by virtue of Section 83 (Queen's successors) of the *Constitution* to the Queen and Head of State; and

(b) as appropriate, to a person or persons referred to in Sec Sch 1.21 (the Head of State: the Governor-General) of the *Constitution*.

"circumstances of aggravation"

On circumstances of aggravation see s 538.

"criminal responsibility"

"Criminal responsibility" is to be determined not by the common law doctrine of *mens rea* or the requirement of a "guilty mind" of some kind, but under Pt 1, Div 5: *Heduru Transport Pty Ltd v Gairo Vegoli* (1977) N99.

"money"

Money ceases to exist as such a thing in the hands of the person receiving it upon payment into a bank account; all that remains is a chose in action: *John Kasaipwalova v The State* [1977] PNGLR 257 (Frost CJ).

Theft of goods given to friends or other persons with customary obligations to repay the gift is not equivalent to theft of money as the term is defined by the Code: *R v Eric Oakari* [1974] PNGLR 182.

> "There is no reason why the fact that credit at the bank is at law characterised as a chose in action thereby excludes it from being 'money'... 'money' is used in various senses in the law. Undoubtedly, in the understanding of the ordinary man, the amount of his credit at a bank would be regarded as 'money'. And the law conceives that 'money' may be of that character."[63]

"Money" includes bank notes and cheques, particularly cheques payable to "cash or bearer", which are as good as bank notes, provided there is a credit to meet them: *R v Gordon Reid McKay* (1954) N56.

See s 367 regarding money held under a direction.

"uncorroborated testimony"

In relation to the definition of "uncorroborated testimony", see cases relating to the sections on offences against sexual morality (Pt IV, Div 2).

In determining whether there is corroboration, it is a matter for the judge to determine whether the facts could constitute corroboration and a matter for the jury to determine whether the facts do constitute corroboration: *R v Clark* (1949) N8. In Papua New Guinea the judge fulfils both functions of judge and of jury.

The rule of practice in a sexual charge that the tribunal of fact should be warned of, or take into account, the risk of acting upon the uncorroborated evidence of the

[63] *John Kasaipwalova v The State* [1977] PNGLR 257 (Kearney J dissenting).

woman as to the elements of the charge, is to be applied in the hearing and determination of offences of a less serious character, such as offensive behaviour, where the behaviour relied on to constitute the offence is offensive because of its sexual nature: *McCallum v Buibui* [1975] PNGLR 439.

A person should not be convicted on the uncorroborated testimony of an accomplice: *R v Clark* (1949) N8.

See also *R v John Henry Jones* (1949) N27 regarding uncorroborated testimony in a rape case, and see *The State v Kalabus* [1977] PNGLR 87, regarding corroboration generally.

2. Definition of offence.

An act or omission that makes the person doing or making it liable to punishment is called an offence.

The definition of "person" does not indicate an intention that the definition of "person" in the *Acts Interpretation (Interim Provisions) Act* 1975 should not apply to the provisions of Ch V (now Pt 1, Div 5). It follows that a corporation, like a natural person, is not criminally responsible for an act which occurs independently of the exercise of its will (s 23), including an act done by a servant in violation of his or her instructions: *Heduru Transport Pty Ltd v Gairo Vegoli* (1977) N99.

See s 37(7) of the *Constitution*.

3. Division of offences.

(1) Offences are of three kinds -

(a) crimes; and

(b) misdemeanours; and

(c) simple offences.

(2) Crimes and Misdemeanours are indictable offences for which offenders, unless otherwise expressly stated, shall be prosecuted or convicted –

(a) on indictment; or

(b) in accordance with Section 420; or

(c) in accordance with any other law.

[Subs (2) am Act No 28, 1980 (*Criminal Code (Indictable Offences) Act* 1980), s 1]

(3) An offence not otherwise designated is a simple offence.

(4) Subject to any other law, a person guilty of a simple offence maybe summarily convicted before a court of summary jurisdiction.

4. Attempts to commit offences.

(1) When a person, intending to commit an offence –

(a) begins to put his intention into execution by means adapted to its fulfilment; and

(b) manifests his intention by some overt act, but does not fulfil his intention to such an extent as to commit the offence, he is said to attempt to commit the offence.

(2) It is immaterial, except so far as regards punishment whether -

(a) the offender does all that is necessary on his part for completing the commission of the offence; or

(b) the complete fulfilment of his intention is prevented by circumstances independent of his will; or

(c) he desists of his own motion from the further prosecution of his intention.

(3) It is immaterial that by reason of circumstances not known to the offender it is impossible in fact to commit the offence.

(4) The same facts may constitute one offence and an attempt to commit another offence.

This section does not merely require that the intention be manifest by some overt act; it requires the commencement of the execution of the intention itself. The cases still draw the distinction between a mere act of preparation and an act of the character required to satisfy s 4: *R v Kopi-Kami* [1965-1966] PNGLR 73 at 77 and 79.

The requirement that the accused has begun to put the intention into execution by means adapted to its fulfilment, provides a rule which the common law has expressed in the terms that "the *actus reus* of an attempt must be sufficiently proximate to the crime attempted. The act must be something more than mere preparation for the commission of the offence": *R v Joseph-Kure* [1955-1966] PNGLR 161 at 166.

It is immaterial, except so far as regards punishment, whether the offender does all that is necessary on his or her part for completing the commission of the offence, or whether the complete fulfilment of the intention is prevented by circumstances independent of the offender's will, or whether the offender desists of his or her own motion from the further prosecution of the intention. It is immaterial that by reason of circumstances not known to the offender it is impossible in fact to commit the offence: *R v Joseph-Kure* [1955-1966] PNGLR 161 at 165.

The "equivocality" which suggests that the *actus reus* of an attempt is sufficiently proximate to the crime attempted only if it indicates beyond reasonable doubt what is the end towards which it is directed, cannot be read into the terms of the Code. It is sufficient if the act relied upon is consistent with the intention confessed by the accused or inferred from all the facts. The Code does not require that the prosecution go further and show that the acts relied upon should be referable, independently of any intention confessed or inferred, unequivocally to an intention to commit the particular crime: *R v Joseph-Kure* [1955-1966] PNGLR 161 at 166 and 167.

See the note under s 210 regarding conviction for an attempt to have carnal knowledge of a dog: *R v Paita Mireseika* (1959) N138.

Corroboration is necessary in cases of attempted rape: *R v Gorogo-Gari* (1958) N127. See also s 340.

In *R v Gorogo-Gari* (1958) N127, on a charge of attempted rape the accused desisted from continuing the attack, but this was only a factor in mitigation of sentence, as the attempt was proved.

See also *R v William Robert Albert* (1953) N1; *R v Bena Forepe* [1965-1966] PNGLR 329; and *R v Kuipa Napai* (1968) N472.

See ss 47(c), 48(c), 62(1)(b), 109, 136, 189(4), 210(2), 213(2), 215, 216, 223(2), 304, 311, 348, 439, 441, 445, 447, 450 and 476 of the Code regarding set notions in which an attempted act constitutes the offence in itself. See ss 509-513 regarding attempts to commit offences, punishment of attempts to commit crimes and misdemeanours, reduction of punishment (where the accused desisted of his or her own volition), and attempts to procure commission of criminal acts.

5. Arrest without warrant.

[S 5 rep *Criminal Code Arrest Act* 1977.]

See ss 57(2) and 42(1)(b) of the *Constitution*.

See the *Arrest Act*.

6. Carnal knowledge.

When the expression "carnal knowledge" or "carnal connexion" is used in the definition of an offence, the offence, so far as regards that element of it, is complete on penetration.

Only the slightest penetration is necessary. It is irrelevant that the hymen is not ruptured: *R v Yoka Kiok* (1970) N607. See also *The State v Kalabus* [1977] PNGLR 87.

Under s 30 there is a rebuttable presumption that a male child under 14 years of age lacks the capacity to have carnal knowledge. See ss 210, 213, 214, 215, 216, 218-224 and 347 for offences for which carnal knowledge is a principal ingredient.

Division 2 – Parties to Offences

7. Principal offenders.

(1) When an offence is committed, each of the following persons shall be deemed to have taken part in committing the offence and to be guilty of the offence, and may be charged with actually committing it -

- (a) every person who actually does the act or makes the omission that constitutes the offence; and
- (b) every person who does or omits to do any act for the purpose of enabling or aiding another person to commit the offence; and
- (c) every person who aids another person in committing the offence; and
- (d) any person who counsels or procures any other person to commit the offence.

(2) In Subsection (1)(d), the person may be charged with –

- (a) committing the offence; or
- (b) counselling or procuring its commission.

(3) A conviction of counselling or procuring the commission of an offence entails the same consequences in all respects as conviction of committing the offence.

(4) Any person who procures another to do or omit to do any act of such a nature that, if he had himself done the act or made the omission, it would have constituted an offence on his part, is -

(a) guilty of an offence of the same kind; and

(b) liable to the same punishment,

as if he had done the act or made the omission, and may be charged with himself doing the act or making the omission.

As to the matter of separate trials of principals, see s 568 and the cases annotated.

As to offences committed in the prosecution of a common purpose, see s 8. For counselling another to commit an offence, see s 9.

Under s 532, where there are several parties to an offence or offences arising out of the same or closely related facts, the parties may be charged in the same indictment and tried together. The court may, however, order separate trials under s 568.

See s 545 regarding alternative verdicts for procuring the commission of a crime.

There is ample authority for the proposition that mere presence at the scene of a crime is not sufficient to create criminal liability; there must be participation in the act. However, if the physical presence of the accused at the scene bespeaks encouragement of, and support to, those engaged in the actual crime, the accused may be regarded as a principal: *R v Potosi* (1973) N730.

Motive alone does not establish responsibility either as principals or accessories: *R v Fum Boto (No 2)* [1967-1968] PNGLR 448.

This section substantially reproduces the common law on principals in the first and second degree. If presence at the commission of the crime is relied on, as distinct from any act or words of assistance, the presence must be willed, not accidental, and with the intention of encouraging or assisting the commission of the crime charged. In some circumstances the fact that a person was voluntarily and purposely present at the commission of a crime and offered no opposition to it, although that person might reasonably be expected to do so or at least to express dissent, might afford cogent evidence that he or she wilfully encouraged the commission of the crime: *R v Tovarula* [1973] PNGLR 140 (Minogue CJ).

When several persons together attack the same man at the same time, using similar weapons or directing similar blows with the common intention to injure, and that man dies as a result of injuries so inflicted, each of the attackers is guilty of wilful murder, murder or manslaughter, according to the intent proved, because each of those several persons is acting in concert with the others at the time, each did the acting constituting the offence under s 7(1)(a), and aided the others under s 7(1)(c). However, if it is not proved that there was any other plan or preconcert to which those several persons were parties, and the hypothesis has not been excluded that the deceased died because of injuries inflicted during a later assault by another person or persons acting alone or together in a common design or concert to which those several persons were parties, and at a time when the original several persons were not shown to be present or participating in the attack or keeping watch or using any dangerous weapon, then those persons who were parties to the first assault are not criminally responsible in any degree for the death. The reason for this is that it has not been shown that those several persons did the act under s 7(1)(a) or aided another person committing the offence under s 7(1)(c) or, there being no preconcert, that they counselled or procured any other person to commit the offence under s 7(1)(d). The position under the Code goes further than the common law, for under the Code a person may be convicted as a principal for counselling or procuring the offence, whereas at common law for the accused to be guilty as a principal in the first or second degree, the accused must be shown to be actively or constructively present at the scene: *R v Sapulo Masuve* (1973) N732.

In *The State v John Badi Woli and Pengas Rakam* [1978] PNGLR 51 both accused were responsible in law for death resulting from an attack where both, in the presence of each other and with intent to harm, were aiding and abetting each other in the attack. It was not to the point that it could not be elicited whose blow caused death.

In *R v Hame Manga* (1970) N596 persons present in a raiding party were aiding by their presence and readiness to assist.

Where two persons participate in a crime, each is responsible for the act of the other: *Awap Omowo and Warsa Yirihim v The State* [1976] PNGLR 188.

If it is established beyond reasonable doubt that the accused was present at the scene with the intention of encouraging or assisting in the killing of the deceased, and thereby aiding in the commission of the offence, the accused would then be guilty of wilful murder: see s 304 regarding wilful murder: *The State v Nataemo Wanu* [1977] PNGLR 152.

In *Porewa Wani v The State* [1979] PNGLR 593, the conclusion is irresistible that, by being present when the deceased was murdered and by knowing of the other party's intention to kill him and by saying (in Motu) "kill him, kill him", the accused was encouraging intentionally by words intended to signify approval and was, therefore, wilfully encouraging.

The position of counsellor and procurer in s 7(1)(d) is very similar to that of the aider or counsellor in common law. However, unlike the situation in common law, "he is a principal offender and he does not cease to be a counsellor or procurer because he is near or at the scene of the crime": *R v Solomon* (1959) Qd R 123 at 129 (Philip J).

> "It is not the proper course to begin by finding how the law stood before the Code, and then to see of the Code will bear an interpretation which will leave the law unaltered".[64]

Regarding wilful encouragement to another person to commit a crime, see the following overseas cases which have been cited in Papua New Guinea: *The Queen v Coney* (1881-1882) 8 QBD 534 at 557-558; *R v Clarkson* [1971] 3 All ER 344; *R v Allan* [1963] 3 WLR 677 at 683; and *R v Russell* [1933] VLR 59 at 66.

A mere assent or acquiescence that a killing should be carried out by others does not amount to an encouragement. An accused person who relies on dissociation from any mutual aiding of another person must be able to point to evidence which shows distinctly that dissociation. Thus, if an accused had first assented in circumstances constituting aiding, there must be evidence that the accused made an unequivocal "timely communication" of his or her intention to abandon that assent: *R v Witrasep Binengim* [1975] PNGLR 95.

---

[64] *Brennan v The Queen* (1936) 55 CLR 253 at 263 (Dixon and Evatt JJ), quoted in *Imiyo Wamela v The State* [1982] PNGLR 269.

Mere prior knowledge of what is intended is in itself not sufficient to bring the accused within this section. A mere consent or acquiescence by the accused does not amount to an encouragement: *R v Umarum* [1969-1970] PNGLR 190 at 191 and 192.

Mere presence at the commission of a crime does not in itself constitute a person an aider and abettor: *R v Opu Anuma* (1974) N801.

It is not enough that the presence of the accused has, in fact, given encouragement. It must be proved that the accused intended to give encouragement and that the accused wilfully encouraged. There must be an intention to encourage and encouragement in fact: *Agiru Aieni v Paul T Tahian* [1978] PNGLR 37.

In *The State v Albert Ugunnie, Matin Tauma and Matthew David Moroua* [1988-1989] PNGLR 101, regarding a charge of mutiny, although the accused were not on duty, their presence at the protest meetings was deliberate and willed, and their participation in those meetings aided and encouraged those who were supposed to be on duty. It was held that this constitutes mutiny.

To be an "aider", "one must aid with a full appreciation of what the active party may be doing and with intention to aid him": *R v Turan* (1952) N211.

It is generally accepted that there can be no aiding for the purpose of s 7(1)(c) where a person merely stands by and does nothing to aid in the commission of the offence: *R v Witrasep Binengim* [1975] PNGLR 95.

In *The State v Laiam Kiala and Meiri Gomosi* [1977] PNGLR 470, two accused assaulted a victim. Their proximity to each other, their previous actions and continuing presence must have encouraged, facilitated, and shielded the assault from interruption and therefore rendered each an aider.

To come within s 7(1)(c), intentional encouragement of the crime is sufficient, whether by word, action or even by mere presence. Where presence is prima facie not accidental, it is evidence, but no more. However, if some of the accused had joined in the common purpose to kill and did no physical act other than that of being present and walking about the scene, findings of fact, depending on the circumstances, may be open that they aided by their presence and readiness to assist: *R v Abia Tambule* [1974] PNGLR 250 following *R v Wendo* [1963] PNGLR 217.

If a person encourages another to commit an offence, the person is liable only for the actual offence which he or she has consciously encouraged under s 7(1)(d): *Sebulon Wat v Peter Kari (No 2)* [1975] PNGLR 339.

On a charge of being a counsellor, it is not enough to show that the defendant knew that some illegal venture was intended. However, it is not necessary that knowledge of intention to commit the particular crime, which was in fact committed, should be shown. The prosecution must show that the defendant knew that an offence of the kind that was committed was intended, and with that knowledge the defendant did something to help the offender commit it: *Imiyo Wamela v The State* [1982] PNGLR 269.

The counsellor or procurer must know that what he or she has counselled or procured is an offence: *Sebulon Wat v Peter Kari* [1975] PNGLR 325.

If the procurer of a felony repents and, before the felony is actually committed, countermands the order, and the principal, notwithstanding, commits the felony, the original procurer is not an accessory: *R v Palwaskit* (1949) N35.

When two persons plan to commit a certain offence, each counsels, and if the plan is executed, procures the other to commit the offence: *R v Sapulo Masuve* (1973) N732.

See s 532 regarding cases in which several accused may be joined and charged in the same indictment.

Evidence of young boys who might be regarded as accomplices must be looked at with the greatest caution and reserve because of the need for corroboration: *R v Barker* (1956) N96.

There is no definition of accomplice and person akin to accomplice in the Code, but *Davies v DPP* provides the common law test of who is an accomplice. The House of Lords held that persons who participate in the actual crime charged, whether as principals or accessories before or after the fact, are to be treated as accomplices within the rule in *Davies v DPP* [1954] AC 378: *The State v Nataemo Wanu* [1977] PNGLR 152.

That a person cannot be convicted of an offence on the uncorroborated testimony of an accomplice has long ceased to be part of the law of this country. The usual justification for the requirement of caution in such a case is the danger that the accomplice will minimise his or her own role in the crime and exaggerate that of the accused, or make false accusations. This rule of practice is not limited to jury cases, but should at common law be applied to any legal tribunal: *The State v Nataemo Wanu* [1977] PNGLR 152.

In Papua New Guinea the law permits conviction on the evidence of an accomplice alone. In Papua New Guinea the evidence of accomplices, in the experience of the judges, is usually given not in a spirit of vindictiveness, but with a sense of justice very much in mind. It is more than possible that in many cases it is done also with intent to avoid a pay-back upon the unconvicted person's family or clan. Nevertheless, it is still regarded as dangerous to convict on an accomplice's evidence alone: *The State v Titeva Fineko* [1978] PNGLR 262.

In Papua New Guinea the case is different from *Davies v DPP* [1954] 2 WLR 343. The law permits conviction on the evidence of the accomplice alone: *The State v Titeva Fineko* [1978] PNGLR 262. Nevertheless, where the magistrate or judge fails to direct properly, the conviction may be quashed: *The State v Amoko-Amoko* [1981] PNGLR 373.

8. Offences committed in prosecution of common purpose.

Where -

(a) two or more persons form a common intention to prosecute an unlawful purpose in conjunction with one another; and

(b) in the prosecution of such purpose an offence is committed of such a nature that its commission was a probable consequence of the prosecution of the purpose,

each of them shall be deemed to have committed the offence

See s 7 regarding parties.

Section 8 does not apply where each accused took part actively or directly in the assault on the deceased, as s 7 directly covers such a situation: *R v Kiandari* [1967-1968] PNGLR 31.

The phrase "probable consequence" includes an inevitable consequence. Thus, where the accused formed a common intention to kill all the residents of a particular village, it was not merely a probable but an inevitable consequence of the fulfilment of the common purpose that a single villager was killed: *R v Wendo* [1963] PNGLR 217 at 241.

It was held, in *R v Korea-Menene* (1968) N479, that where a group of persons form a common intention to assault any policeman, liability under s 8 attaches to all those who form the intention and take part. To justify a conviction of wilful murder pursuant to s 8, there must be proof beyond reasonable doubt that the intention to kill was the common purpose which was shared by all involved, or that it was a probable consequence of their common purpose. Where the common purpose is to attack a person with the intention merely of causing grievous bodily harm, but death results, the proper conviction is murder, even though one of the assailants may form the intention to actually kill. Accordingly, in *Goya v The State* [1987] PNGLR 51, Kapi DCJ, Woods and Barrett JJ held that a conviction of murder should be substituted for a conviction of wilful murder where four persons together attacked two other men with stone, feet and fists and with such force as to cause death from internal injuries, and where the trial judge found that at least one person in the group of four had an intention to kill. To support a defence of withdrawal from a common purpose, the accused must show not only that he or she had withdrawn from the prosecution of the common purpose, but had also communicated that fact to the other accused in such circumstances that any subsequent criminal act by the other accused was that person's separate act. The accused must also show that he or she expressly countermanded or revoked any advising, counselling, procuring or abetting which had previously been given. This is not to alter the onus of proof, but to demonstrate that any influence exercised on the mind of the persons who actually performed the acts in question had been removed, and that the accused had severed the connection or departed from the agreed contract. In *R v Hanjau-Aikolo* (1967) N456, the accused were part of a raiding party which set out to kill an intended victim in a pay-back situation. The intended victim was not present at the time, and the raiding party decided to kill his wife instead. The two accused stood aside, as the wife was a blood relative of theirs and they were not permitted to kill her under their pay-back custom. Although the accused did not expressly announce their withdrawal from the common purpose, the relationship between the accused and the woman was well known to all concerned and their withdrawal was expected and understood.

R v Hanjau-Aikolo (1967) N456 was followed by *The State v Tamang Sem* [1988-89] PNGLR 430.

> "Silence does not imply participation in the common purpose but, in view of the need for withdrawal from the common purpose to be communicated to the other co-accused persons, silence may for purpose of s 8, depending on the circumstances, imply acceptance of the actions of a co-accused in the prosecution of a common purpose."[65]

> "In my respectful view, it is the duty of the courts to develop the principles of the underlying law so as to give effect to the intention of Parliament when it passed s 8 into law. By doing so, the courts would give effect to the wishes and aspirations of the majority of our people to control or reduce crime."[66]

---

[65] *The State v John Waiyake Komane* [1992] PNGLR 524 at 541 (Jalina J).
[66] *The State v John Waiyake Komane* [1992] PNGLR 524 at 543-544 (Jalina J).

Where the case for the prosecution is founded on a common purpose and no eyewitness account of the incident is available, an admission by one accused must generally not be used against the other accused. Such an admission may, however, become admissible as evidence against a companion in a common purpose where it relates to directions, instructions, or arrangements or to utterances accompanying acts: *R v Gemai* [1974] PNLGR 1.

On the formation of a common intention to prosecute the unlawful purpose of wilful murder, see *R v Manganapi-Sandepi* (1969) N537. See s 532 regarding cases in which several accused may be joined and charged in the same indictment. See also the note to *Imeyo Wamela v The State* [1982] PNGLR 269 under s 9.

9. Mode of execution immaterial.

(1) Where -

(a) a person counsels another to commit an offence; and

(b) an offence is actually committed under that counsel by the person to whom it is given,

it is immaterial whether -

(c) the offence actually committed is the same as that counselled or a different one; or

(d) the offence is committed in the way counselled, or in a different way,

if the facts constituting the offence actually committed are a probable consequence of carrying out the counsel.

(2) The person who gave the counsel shall be deemed to have counselled the other person to commit the offence actually committed by him.

See s 7(1)(d) regarding counselling and procuring another to commit an offence.

The word "offence" used in s 9 is the same implied in s 8.

> "It is clear from the words of s 8 that when that section speaks of 'an offence' it cannot mean simply an act or omission viewed in isolation. In most cases an act or omission alone does not render a person liable to punishment; whether it does so may depend on the quality of the act, the intention which accompanied it, its consequences or other circumstances".[67]

See also the annotation of *Imeyo Wamela v The State* [1982] PNGLR 269 under s 7.

10. Accessories after the fact.

(1) A person who receives or assists another who is, to his knowledge, guilty of an offence, in order to enable him to escape punishment, is an accessory after the fact to the offence.

(2) A married woman does not become an accessory after the fact to an offence of which her husband is guilty -

(a) by receiving or assisting him in order to enable him to escape punishment; or

[67] *Stuart v The Queen* (1974) 134 CLR 426 at 440 (Gibbs J). See also *Imiyo Wamela v The State* [1982] PNGLR 269.

(b) by receiving or assisting, in her husband's presence and by his authority, another person who is guilty of an offence in the commission of which her husband has taken part, in order to enable that other person to escape punishment.

(3) A married man does not become an accessory after the fact to an offence of which his wife is guilty by receiving or assisting her in order to enable her to escape punishment.

See ss 510-511 regarding punishment of accessories after the fact.

The common law authorities on accessories after the fact provide the definition for this section: *R v Angie-Ogun* [1969-1970] PNGLR 36 (Ollerenshaw, J).

A person who carries out the general instructions of a thief to dispose of stolen goods, either by hiding the goods or by throwing them away, with the intention of assisting the thief to escape detection and punishment, may become an accessory after the fact to theft under this section, though the accused may also have had the purpose of making personal gain and of avoiding his or her own detection: *R v Angie-Ogun* [1969-1970] PNGLR 36.

The Code provides an exclusive definition of "accessory after the fact" for the purposes of s 519. McDermott AJ stated, in *The State v Roy Nana* [1986] PNGLR 83 at 87, "I have come to the view that s 10 provides an exclusive definition." For the purposes of being charged as an accessory after the fact, an accused must do some act in order to enable the principal offender to escape detection and punishment: *The State v Roy Nana* [1986] PNGLR 83 at 87 (McDermott AJ).

11. Effect of changes in law.

(1) A person cannot be punished for doing or omitting to do an act unless -

(a) the act or omission constituted an offence under the law in force when it occurred; and

(b) doing or omitting to do the act under the same circumstances would constitute an offence under the law in force at the time when he is charged with the offence.

(2) If the law in force when the act or omission occurred differs from that in force at the time of the conviction, the offender cannot be punished to any greater extent than was authorized by the former law, or to any greater extent than is authorized by the latter law.

See s 37(7) of the *Constitution*.

On the effect of the Revised Laws, see *Ando Kenene v Gabriel Samon, Alois Gabour and George Tapu* [1983] PNGLR 179.

In *Avona v The State* [1986] PNGLR 148 the following principles apply:

- Section 11(2) need not be read together with s 11(1). Section 11(2) can only apply where a penalty or penalty aspect of a particular offence has been altered.
- In order to give s 11(2) its proper meaning, the addition of the words "whichever is the lesser" must be implied at the end.
- Properly construed, the effect of s 11(2) is that if the punishment to which a person would be subjected in real terms under the former law is substantially greater than that to which the person would be subjected under

the latter law, ie, under the changed law, then the punishment under the changed law should apply.

- Having regard to the substance of its provisions in changing the minimum penalties, the *Criminal Code (Amendment No 2) Act* 1986 was to be treated as an amending Act and not a repealing Act for the purposes of s 63 of the *Interpretation Act*.
- Accordingly, the provisions of the amendment Act apply to any offence which was committed prior to its commencement.

12. Territorial application of the code.

(1) This Code applies to every person who is in Papua New Guinea at the time of his doing any act or making any omission which constitutes an offence.

(2) Where offences are of such a nature that they comprise several elements, if -

(a) any acts, omissions or events actually occur which, if they all occurred in Papua New Guinea, would constitute an offence; and

(b) any of the acts, or omissions or events occur in Papua New Guinea,

then -

(c) if the act or omission that, in the case of an offence wholly committed in Papua New Guinea, would be the initial element of the offence, occurs in Papua New Guinea, the person who does that act or makes that omission is guilty of an offence of the same kind, and is liable to the same punishment, as if all the subsequent elements of the offence had occurred in Papua New Guinea; and

(d) if the act or omission occurs outside Papua New Guinea, and the person who does the act or makes the omission afterwards comes into Papua New Guinea, he is by coming into Papua New Guinea guilty of an offence of the same kind, and is liable to the same punishment, as if -

(i) the act or omission had occurred in Papua New Guinea; and

(ii) he had been in Papua New Guinea when it occurred.

(3) In a case referred to in Subsection (2)(d), it is a defence to the charge to prove that the accused person did not intend that the act or omission should have effect in Papua New Guinea.

(4) Subject to Subsection (5) this section does not extend to a case in which the only material event that occurs in Papua New Guinea is the death of a person whose death is caused by an act done or omitted to be done outside Papua New Guinea, and at a time when he was not in Papua New Guinea.

(5) The Code shall have extra-territorial effect so as to give effect to the *Offences (Overseas) Act* (Chapter 406).

[Subs (5) insrt *Criminal Code (Amendment) Act* 1983, s 2]

13. Offences procured or counselled by persons outside.

(1) A person who -

(a) while outside Papua New Guinea procures another person to do or omit to do an act in Papua New Guinea of such a nature that, if he had himself done the act or made the omission, in Papua New Guinea, he would have been guilty of an offence; and

(b) afterwards comes into Papua New Guinea,

is by coming into Papua New Guinea guilty of an offence of the same kind, and is liable to the same punishment, as if he had himself done the act or made the omission in Papua New Guinea.

(2) A person who -

(a) while outside Papua New Guinea counsels or procures the commission of an offence that is actually committed in Papua New Guinea; and

(b) afterwards comes into Papua New Guinea,

is guilty of an offence of the same kind, and is liable to the same punishment, as if he had been in Papua New Guinea when the offence was committed.

See ss 7(1)(d) and 9.

14. Offences procured in Papua New Guinea to be committed outside Papua New Guinea.

(1) A person who, while in Papua New Guinea, procures another person to do an act or make an omission at a place outside Papua New Guinea of such a nature that -

(a) if he had himself done the act or made the omission in Papua New Guinea, he would have been guilty of an offence; and

(b) if he had himself done the act or made the omission, he would have been guilty of an offence under the law in force in the place where the act or omission is done or made,

is guilty of an offence of the same kind, and is liable to the same punishment, as if the act had been done or the omission had been made in Papua New Guinea.

(2) The punishment for an offence by virtue of Subsection (1) shall not exceed the punishment that the offender would have incurred under the law in force in the place where the act was done or the omission was made, if he had himself done the act or made the omission.

(3) A prosecution cannot be instituted under this section except at the request of the Government of the State having jurisdiction in the place where the act or omission occurs.

See ss 7(1)(d) and 9.

See also ss 176-177, Sch 1.19 and Sch 1.20 of the *Constitution*.

15. Defence Force.

Officers and men of the Defence Force are, while on duty or in uniform, subject to the special laws relating to that Force, but are not exempt from the provisions of this Code.

See s 203 of the *Constitution* and the *Defence Act* (Ch No 74), especially the Schedule (Code of Military Discipline).

See *The State v Albert Ugunnie, Martin Taumu and Matthew David Moroua* [1988-1989] PNGLR 101.

16. Person not to be punished twice for same offence.

(1) Subject to Subsection (2), a person cannot be punished twice under the provisions of this Code or under the provisions of any other law for the same act or omission.

(2) Subsection (1) does not apply where an act or omission is such that by means of it the offender causes the death of another person, in which case he may be convicted of the offence of which he is guilty by reason of causing the death, notwithstanding that he has already been convicted of some other offence constituted by the act or omission.

See s 37(8) of the *Constitution*. See also s 17 of the Code. As to the plea of *autrefois convict*, see ss 560(c) and 564.

Upon a motion to quash an indictment under s 558, alleging the indictment to be formally defective in that it lays open the possibility of a violation of s 16, the court may only consider whether or not there is a likelihood of double punishment at the close of the evidence. Any attempt to call in s 16 at the start of a trial is premature, for it is possible that the accused might be acquitted of one or both of the charges joined in the indictment: *R v Yofia Abone* [1967-1968] PNGLR 277 at 282.

Section 16 is a very different provision from s 17, which provides a defence to show that an accused has already been convicted. However, s 16 can also be seen as defence, for if the evidence discloses that the act or omission relied upon to establish the offence is the same act or omission of which the accused has already been punished, it is no longer an act or omission rendering the accused liable to punishment under this section and therefore no longer an offence within the definition of "offence" under s 2. The consequence is that the accused cannot be convicted: *Tapopwa Thomas v The State* [1979] PNGLR 140.

In that case, on convictions for rape and unlawful carnal knowledge, the question before the court was whether this amounted to double punishment under this section. In approving of the remarks of Minogue J in *Gaiari-Ganereba v Giddings* [1967-1968] PNGLR 346, it was held:

> "the section seems to intend to include a conviction standing alone, as a punishment – certainly where it can clearly as a matter of English meaning, be seen to 'punish'. Without wishing to decide that every conviction must necessarily of itself amount to a punishment and potentially give rise to the application of s 16; I consider that the second conviction in such a case as this must be considered a 'punishment' at least in so far as it becomes established on the man's criminal record".[68]

The considerations to which the court must turn are suggested in *Gaiari-Ganereba v Giddings* to be "the substance of the offence, that is, of the ingredients that go to make up the act or omission which renders the doer of the act or the maker of the omission liable to punishment." This section, in saying that a person cannot be twice punished for the same act or omission, must be referring to

[68] *Tapopwa Thomas v The State* [1979] PNGLR 140 (Prentice CJ).

punishable acts or omissions; and the prohibition applies though the act or omission would constitute two different offences. The proper test to decide whether "the same act or omission" was being punished twice is that the court should consider whether the same wrongful act or omission which previously resulted in conviction and punishment is the central theme to the basic act or omission in the latest offence charged. If it is, then, except in the case of resulting death, in terms of the exception in s 16 a person may not be twice punished for the same act or omission. Each set of situations should be considered on their own particular "acts or omissions": *Tapopwa Thomas v The State* [1979] PNGLR 140, following *R v Gordon; Ex parte Attorney-General* [1975] Qd R 301.

It seems that the section intends to include a conviction standing alone as a punishment - certainly where it can clearly, as a matter of English meaning, be seen to "punish" - without wishing to decide that every conviction must necessarily amount to a punishment and potentially give rise to the application of s 16. The second conviction in such a case as this (ie a conviction for rape and unlawful carnal knowledge) must be considered a punishment at least in so far as it becomes established on the man's criminal record: *Tapopwa Thomas v The State* [1979] PNGLR 140 (Prentice CJ).

The correct procedure where an accused is indicted on two charges arising out of one and the same incident, and where the accused is technically guilty of both, is that the charges should be treated as alternative charges. It would be wrong for two convictions to appear on the record in respect of exactly the same incident. There is no conviction recorded on the second count and it is, in effect, left alive: *Tapopwa Thomas v The State* [1979] PNGLR 140 (Andrew J).

A conviction and sentence both for rape and for carnal knowledge of a girl under 16 (both charges arising out of the one act of intercourse) amounts to the accused being punished twice for the one act or omission within the meaning of s 16: *Tapopwa Thomas v The State* [1979] PNGLR 140.

With regard to *R v Cowdell* [1962] Crim LR 262, where the accused was charged with unlawful wounding and assault occasioning actual bodily harm, the court held that since the charges arose out of the same incident, they should be treated as alternative. Accordingly, the practice of alternative charges ought to be adhered to, for it would be wrong for two convictions to appear on the record with respect of the same incident. The jury ought to have been discharged from giving a verdict on the second alternative count. If this was done and if the first count was quashed on appeal it would be open to the appeal court to substitute a verdict of assault occasioning actual bodily harm under the provisions of s 5(2) of the *Criminal Appeal Act* 1907. A conviction of assault occasioning actual bodily harm was quashed, which, in effect, left the second count alive. Andrew J said, in *Tapopwa Thomas v The State* [1979] PNGLR 140:

> "In my opinion the procedure as laid down in *Cowdell's* case is the correct one and applicable to the conditions of Papua New Guinea (the *Constitution* Sch 2.2) and in my opinion s 25(2) of our *Supreme Court Act* 1975 gives this court the same powers on appeal to substitute the conviction for an alternative offence that the Court of Appeal in England has when exercising jurisdiction over the now *Criminal Appeals Act* 1968 s 3(1). Alternatively, the trial judge could make findings on the second charge without proceeding to conviction."

In *The State v Tokai Koweri* [1976] PNGLR 468, in relation to the test applicable and appropriate to the circumstances of Papua New Guinea, it was stated:

> "It is only necessary to look at the words 'the same act or omission' to say, that when it is alleged that acts referred to in two indictments are the same, there is implied a unity, at least, of time and place."

In *R v Carl Joseph Magr* [1969-1970] PNGLR 165, the defence of *autrefois convict* was rightly rejected where the accused had been convicted of stealing involving a fraudulent conversion with an intent to deprive a person of his property in a vehicle. The acts constituting this offence were different from the acts constituting the elements of the offence of obtaining money by false pretences, namely the making of a false representation to another person that the vehicle was the accused's complete and unencumbered property and thereby obtaining a sum of money with intent to defraud. It is necessary to distinguish, for the purpose of s 16, between the acts which were the elements of the offence and the particular evidence which was adduced to prove the acts. When it is alleged that acts referred to in two indictments are the same, there is implied a unity at least of time and place.

In *The State v Tokai Koweri* [1976] PNGLR 468 the accused was convicted of being in possession of goods reasonably suspected of being stolen, contrary to the *Police Offences Act*, and was subsequently charged with housebreaking and stealing certain goods, which were the goods that were the subject matter of the original conviction. The court found that this section is not a defence available to the accused as:

> "It is clear that the acts in the first place of breaking and entering the dwelling house and of stealing, the latter being complete once the goods were taken by the accused, are quite different from the later 'acts' of being found in possession of the sale goods reasonably suspected of being stolen."

Where the accused unleashed a stream of abuse against a person, it was a clear breach of this section to impose punishment in respect of both "behaving in a threatening manner" and "behaving in an insulting manner": *Wama Ul v Jansen* (1975) N834.

Neither an assault nor an element of that offence is a necessary element of the offences created by ss 64 and 65, namely taking part in an unlawful assembly and in a riot. Thus, an accused could be convicted of assault as well as under s 64 or s 65, and s 16 does not prevent punishment for both offences: *R v Korea-Menene* (1968) N479.

> "[T]he intention of s 16 is to direct consideration of the substance of an offence, that is, the ingredients ... which renders the doer ... liable to punishment"[69]

The words "same offence" in the heading and "the same act or omission" in the section apply to double punishment for offences coming within one of the three categories of offences established by s 3. Therefore, disciplinary proceedings (as, in *The State v Yomba Gende*, for "disgraceful conduct under the *Police Force (Interim Arrangement) Act* 1973"), contemplates punishment being imposed upon conviction for an offence. The word "act" refers to an act which constitutes the essential element of our offence. Before an "act" can be punished it must constitute the

---

[69] *Gaiari-Ganereba v Giddings* [1967-1968] PNGLR 346 at 352 (Minogue J).

element of the offence which results in conviction. If there is no conviction there is no punishment: *The State v Yomba Gende* (1980) N247 (Kapi J), approving the test of Williams J in *R v Gordon; Ex parte Attorney-General* [1975] Qd R 301 at 323.

In *Sudi Yaku v Commissioner for Police; Ex parte The State* [1980] PNGLR 27 it was stated:

> "In the final result it seems to me that the proper test is whether the same wrongful act or omission which previously resulted in conviction and punishment, is the central theme, the focal point or ... perhaps more appropriately the basic act or omission in the later offence charged."

17. Former conviction or acquittal.

It is a defence to a charge of any offence to show that the accused person has already been-

(a) tried, and convicted or acquitted, on an indictment on which he might have been convicted of the offence with which he is charged, or

(b) acquitted on indictment, or convicted, of an offence of which he might be convicted on the indictment or complaint on which he is charged.

See *Constitution*, s 37(8). See *Criminal Code*, ss 16, 560(c) and 564.

The accused cannot raise the defence of *autrefois convict* in relation to offences which have been taken into account in sentencing under s 603. Nevertheless, the accepted practice has been that the prosecution will not proceed on offences which have been taken into account: *R v Emere Gabua* (1960) N156.

In *Sapuro Masuve v Bryant* [1974] PNGLR 61 the accused was acquitted on wilful murder and subsequently convicted of riotous manner. It was held that the accused had not been acquitted upon indictment of an offence of which he might have been convicted upon the information. Section 17 did not assist.

Expulsion from the police force under disciplinary proceedings does not constitute a previous conviction or acquittal: *Sudi Yaku v Commissioner for Police; Ex parte The State* [1980] PNGLR 27.

Division 4 – Punishments

18. Kinds of punishment.

The punishments that may be inflicted under this Code are -

(a) death; or

(b) imprisonment with hard labour; or

(c) imprisonment without hard labour; or

(d) detention in an industrial or reformatory school; or

(e) fine; or

(f) finding security to keep the peace and be of good behaviour; or

(g) restriction of movement.

[Subs (g) insrt Act No 18, 1986 (*Criminal Code (Restriction of Movement) Act* 1986), s 1]

Customary compensation is now a recognised form of punishment under the *Criminal Law (Compensation) Act* 1991.

In relation to sentencing, see ss 596 and 600-601 and the cases there annotated.

19. Construction of provisions of Code as to punishments.

(1) In the construction of this Code, it is to be taken that, except when it is otherwise expressly provided –

(aa) a person liable to death may be sentenced to imprisonment for life or for any shorter term; and

(a) a person liable to imprisonment for life or for any other period, may be sentenced to imprisonment for any shorter term; and

(b) a person liable to imprisonment may be sentenced to pay a fine not exceeding K2,000.00 in addition to, or instead of, imprisonment; and

(c) a person sentenced on conviction on indictment to pay a fine may be sentenced-

(i) to be imprisoned until the fine is paid, in addition to any other punishment to which he is sentenced; and

(ii) instead of being sentenced to be imprisoned until the fine is paid – to be imprisoned for a term (not exceeding the term provided for in Subparagraph (i)) if the fine is not paid within a specified period (which period may be extended as the court thinks fit); and

(d) a person convicted on indictment of an offence not punishable with death may -

(i) instead of, or in addition to, any punishment to which he is liable - be ordered to enter into his own recognizance with or without sureties, in such amount as the court thinks proper, to keep the peace and be of good behaviour for a time fixed by the court; and

(ii) be ordered to be imprisoned until the recognizance, with sureties if so directed, is entered into; and

(e) a person convicted of any offence on summary conviction may, instead of being sentenced to any punishment to which he is liable, be discharged on his entering into his own recognizances, with or without sureties, in such amount as the court thinks proper, to keep the peace and be of good behaviour for a term not exceeding one year; and

(f) when a person is convicted of an offence not punishable with death, the court may instead of passing sentence, discharge the offender on his entering into his own recognizance with or without sureties, in such sum as the court thinks proper, conditioned that –

(i) he shall appear and receive judgement at some future sittings of the court or when called on within a period specified by the court; and

(ii) if the court thinks fit, he shall in the meantime keep the peace and be of good behaviour and comply with such other conditions as the court, in its discretion, imposes.

[Subs (1)(aa) insrt Act No 25, 1991 (*Criminal Code (Amendment) Act* 1991), s 1; subs (l)(f) am Act No 27, 1979 (*Criminal Code (Amendment) Act* 1979), s 1]

(2) Imprisonment in accordance with Subsection (1)(c)(i), for non-payment of the fine -

(a) shall not extend for a term longer than two years; and

(b) shall not together with the fixed term of imprisonment (if any)extend for a term longer than the longest term for which he might be sentenced to be imprisoned without fine.

(3) In a case to which Subsection (l)(c) applies, the court may give such directions as it thinks proper as to the enforcement of the sentence of imprisonment, including a direction that the person sentenced appear at some future sittings of the court or when called on, by notice in the prescribed form, to show cause why the sentence of imprisonment should not be executed because of the non-payment of the fine within the specified period or any extension of that period.

(4) If under Subsection (3) a person directed to appear, or called on by notice in the prescribed form, to show cause why the sentence of imprisonment should not be executed because of the non-payment of the fine within the specified period, or any extension of that period, does not appear at the required time and place, a Judge may issue a warrant to arrest him and to bring him before a Judge.

(5) Imprisonment under Subsection (l)(d) for not entering into a recognizance -

(a) shall not extend for a term longer than one year; and

(b) shall not together with the fixed term of imprisonment (if any) extend for a term longer than the longest term for which he might be sentenced to be imprisoned without fine.

(6) When a court sentences any person convicted under Subsection (l)(d) to a term of imprisonment, it may further order that -

(a) the offender be imprisoned for such portion of that term as it thinks proper; and

(b) the execution of the sentence for the remaining portion of the sentence be suspended on his entering into a recognizance, with sureties if so directed, in accordance with Subsection (l)(d) but further conditioned that, if called on, he shall appear and receive judgement in respect of his service of the portion of the sentence.

(7) A Judge may, on being satisfied that the offender has committed a breach of any of the conditions of a recognizance under Subsection (6), forfeit the recognizance and commit him to prison to undergo the suspended portion of his sentence or any part of it.

(8) ...

[Subs (8) insrt Act No 29, 1983 (*Criminal Code (Amendment) Act* 1983), s 2; rep Act No 17, 1986 (*Criminal Code (Amendment No 2) Act* 1986), s 1]

(9) Notwithstanding that restriction of movement is not specified as a punishment for an offence, a court may, in addition to any other punishment or punishments imposed, also impose restriction of movement in accordance with Section 600.

[Subs (9) insrt Act No 18, 1986 (*Criminal Code (Restriction of Movement) Act* 1986), s 2]

(10) When a court is considering the punishment or punishments to be imposed in any case it shall also consider whether, in the circumstances of the case, restriction of movement is an appropriate punishment.

[Subs (10) insrt Act No 18, 1986 (*Criminal Code (Restriction of Movement) Act* 1986), s 2]

See ss 18, 596 and 601.

See s 37(2) of the *Constitution* regarding the requirement that nobody may be convicted of an offence that is not defined by, and the penalty for which is not prescribed by, a written law (except in the case of contempt of court).

Under the legal system adopted in Papua New Guinea, a person may not be punished until that person is found guilty of an offence according to law. Under s 37(2) of the *Constitution*, "nobody may be convicted of an offence that is not defined by, and the penalty for which is not prescribed by, a written law". A "written law" refers to an Act of Parliament (including any law made under the Act), organic laws and the *Constitution*. The term has been used to distinguish it from what may be called the unwritten laws, custom as adopted under Sch 2.1 of the *Constitution*, common law as adopted under Sch 2.2 and the underlying law as developed under Schs 2.3 and 2.4: *Acting Public Prosecutor v Uname Aumane Aluma Koku, Luku Wapulae and Piope Kone* [1980] PNGLR 510.

Where an accused is convicted of an offence, the penalty for which is prescribed by the *(Minimum Penalties) Amendment Act* 1983, any period spent in custody awaiting trial cannot be deducted from the minimum penalty: *The State v Peters* [1984] PNGLR 387.

In *R v Kaupa* (1973) N765 the prisoner was convicted of dangerous driving causing death, while intoxicated. Despite the seriousness of the offence, the court discharged the prisoner on his own recognisance on a two-year bond, with conditions including abstaining from consuming alcohol; driving only to and from work; and paying compensation to the kin of the deceased. Mitigating factors included that it was a first offence, the prisoner had an excellent record, he had promised to pay compensation, he was largely influenced by another man to drink and drive, and he had spent four months in jail awaiting trial.

See s 615 of the Code regarding release on licence, and ss 151-152 of the *Constitution* regarding the granting of a pardon.

See s 4 of the *Customs Recognition Act* regarding the circumstances in which customary law may be taken into account in a criminal case. Section 4(e) particularly relates to sentence.

Regarding youthful offenders, see s 36 of the *Child Welfare Act*, and annotations to s 596 of the Code.

For remarks on the appropriateness of the imposition of a fine in Papua New Guinea, and the deterrent effect of a fine having regard to the customary way of life where relatives contribute towards the payment of the fine, see *The State v Keputong Nagong* (1980) N225, discussed under s 596 below.

For principles of appellate review of a decision to suspend sentence, see *Acting Public Prosecutor v Clement Maki and Tom Kasen* (1981) SC 205, discussed under s 596 of the Code.

As a matter of law, a court can only impose the penalty provided by statute[70] and has no power to impose any customary punishment. The adoption, application and enforcement of customary law, under Sch 2.1 of the *Constitution*, is subject to, amongst other things, an Act of Parliament which regulates the use of customary law (Sch 2.1(3)(b)), such as the *Customs Recognition Act*. Under s 4(e) of this Act, custom may be taken into account in punishment, to mitigate or aggravate the sentence to be imposed. However, ultimately, the penalty to be imposed is as provided for under the Code (in this case of wilful murder) and there is no power in the court to impose customary punishment. Further, there is no room for developing the underlying law in this case. The development of an underlying law under Sch 2.3 arises only when there appears to be no rule of law that is applicable. In this case the *Criminal Code* is applicable. As to what the role of customary law should be in such cases, these are matters not for the court but for the legislature. Such proposals for amendment of the Code have been put forward by the Law Reform Commission, but so far the Parliament has not enacted them.[71] Note, however, that the *Criminal Law (Compensation) Act* allows the court to impose customary compensation.

Under this section, a judge may impose any of the lesser punishments prescribed (except upon a conviction for wilful murder under s 299 where there is a maximum penalty of death). The crime of wilful murder is a statutory offence and the only punishment that can be imposed is set out under the Code. A judge has no power to impose any other punishment. Under s 4(e) of the *Customs Recognition Act*, custom shall be taken into account in determining the penalty (if any) to be imposed on a guilty party. This means that a particular custom (defined by s 4 of that Act, and recognised and enforced under s 6 of that Act and Sch 2.1 of the *Constitution*) may be taken into account to explain the guilty party's behaviour; for example, the guilty party may have committed the offence under customary pressure. Custom used in this sense becomes a mitigating factor (see Clarkson J in *R v Asis* (1970) N559, and *R v Iu Ketapi* [1971-1972] PNGLR 44; see also *R v Lakalyo Neak* (1971) N632), providing a cultural justification of the offenders' behaviour, which reduces their culpability or blameworthiness. In some instances the custom may increase the seriousness of the offenders' behaviour. For instance, in incest cases, custom may regard it is immoral and may call for severe punishment. A court may also take into account customary punishment in the same way, for example, whether the offender is liable to pay compensation whatever the court's decision might be: see *R v Kaupa* (1973) N765. All of this means that a judge may increase or decrease the sentence depending on whether custom mitigates or aggravates the offence, and may impose the appropriate sentence within the range given by law. Section 4(e) of the *Customs Recognition Act* does not enlarge the power of the court under ss 19 and 299 of the Code; it may only operate within the range provided by those sections.[72]

---

[70] *Acting Public Prosecutor v Uname Aumane Aluma Koku, Luku Wapulae and Piope Kone* [1980] PNGLR 510. (In this case, ss 19 and 299 of the Code.)

[71] *Acting Public Prosecutor v Uname Aumane Aluma Koku, Luku Wapulae and Piope Kone* [1980] PNGLR 510 (Kapi J, with Kearney DCJ agreeing).

[72] *Acting Public Prosecutor v Uname Aumane Aluma Koku, Luku Wapulae and Piope Kone* [1980] PNGLR 510 (Kapi J, with Kearney DCJ agreeing).

Section 19(1)(f) of the *Criminal Code* does not empower a trial court which has found an offence proved, to dismiss it without convicting: *Supreme Court Reference No 2 of 1981; Re s 19(1)(f) Criminal Code (Ch 262)* [1982] PNGLR 150.

For considerations governing the choice between a fine and a sentence of imprisonment, see *John Rumet Kaputin v The State* [1979] PNGLR 559.

A portion of a sentence may be suspended under s 19(1)(f) upon the offender entering into a recognisance. The terms of the recognisance may be acceptable to the offender or they may not. If the offender declines to enter into a recognisance, he or she is obliged to serve the whole of the term of the sentence. Suspending part of the sentence is a permissible device designed to foster the reformation of a young person: *Acting Public Prosecutor v John Airi* (1981) SC 214.

The suspension of sentence under s 19(1)(f) is only effective upon the offender entering into the recognisance proposed, so it would normally be advisable for the sentencing judge to give the offender the opportunity of entering into the recognisance before commencing to serve the portion of the term ordered to be served. If an offender declines to enter into the recognisance, he or she will of course be committed to prison for the entire term: *Public Prosecutor v Thomas Vola* [1981] PNGLR 412.

Since Independence, the National Parliament has amended s 19(1)(f) and thereby enlarged the powers of a sentencing judge to order an offender to enter into a recognisance to comply with conditions. The fact is that in recent times sentencing judges have made increasingly frequent use of the power to suspend a portion of a sentence. Until now the Supreme Court has not been called upon to examine this practice. To suspend part of a prison sentence upon the offender complying with conditions has something of the character of placing on probation. The *Probation Act* 1980 applies only to Lae and the National Capital District at this time, on a pilot program basis. However, it is still a perfectly proper procedure for a sentencing judge in a suitable case, no matter where the judge happens to be sitting, to exercise discretion under s 19(1)(f) where the judge feels that there is some chance of rehabilitation on the part of the offender. The offender then ought to be given the chance of showing that ability to rehabilitate over an appropriate period of time after release from a relatively short portion of a term of imprisonment, although the offender will lack supervision by a professional probation officer. Part of the sentence may be suspended for other valid reasons, for instance to enable the payment of compensation or a fine, or to keep employment opportunities open. It is timely to remind ourselves that the experience in Papua New Guinea has not shown that imprisonment has been any more successful in this country than in others. After a lengthy and comprehensive inquiry into the New South Wales prison system, the Royal Commissioner, Mr Justice Nagle concluded:

> "In all countries, Marxist or otherwise, imprisonment is used as a punishment for offences against society. There is, however, an increasing awareness of the harmful nature of imprisonment and that it should be used as a last resort."[73]

Section 19 has no application in the District Court – there is no power in the magistrate to suspend a sentence: *Public Prosecutor v Barry Holloway* [1981] PNGLR 482 (Kapi DCJ).

For a discussion of theory and history of the punishment of solitary confinement, see *Tom Amaiu v Commissioner of Corrective Institutions and the State* [1983]

---

[73] *Acting Public Prosecutor v Clement Maki and Tom Kasen* (1981) SC205 (Miles J).

PNGLR 87. Regulation 111(4) of the *Corrective Institutions Regulations* expressly prohibits solitary confinement.

Technical breach is a good reason not to prosecute. However, the most that a trial judge can do is to apply s 19(1)(f) of the *Criminal Code*. Unfortunately, that leaves the accused with the stain of a conviction for what was, on the facts, an offence of a trivial nature: *Supreme Court Reference No 2 of 1981; Re s 19(1)(f) Criminal Code (Ch 262)* [1982] PNGLR 150 at 159 (Kearney DCJ).

It is considered to be of the essence of the legislative function of Parliament in a democracy to provide both for the type of behaviour which will be subject to criminal sanction, and the punishment which conviction will attract. It is of the essence of judicial power, as regards the criminal law, to decide whether an accused has contravened the law, and if so, to assess the proper disposition within whatever range and type of disposition Parliament permits. The *Criminal Code Act* 1974 is an adopted Act of the Parliament under Sch 2.6 of the *Constitution*. It provides exhaustively for the punishment of Code offences: see s 2 of the Act, and ss 18, 19 and many provisions of the Code. The principle of separation of powers permeates the *Constitution*: *Supreme Court Reference No 2 of 1981; Re s 19(1)(f) Criminal Code (Ch 262)* [1982] PNGLR 150 at 158-159 (Kearney DCJ).

On the establishment of a system of probation, see Macpherson and O'Collins, "*Probation in Papua New Guinea: A Fundamental Re-Orientation of Attitudes and Institutions*" (1978) 6 MLJ 97.

Whether or not subsequent conduct should be treated as a breach of bond is a matter within the court's discretion. It is essential for all details of the original conviction and sentence and subsequent conviction to be before the trial judge: *The State v Robert Romba* (1981) N365 (Pratt J).

In *Public Prosecutor v William Bruce Tardrew* [1986] PNGLR 91 the court held that suspension of part of a sentence under s 19(6) is, or may be, appropriate in three broad categories, which are not exhaustive:

- where suspension will promote the personal deterrence, reformation or rehabilitation of the offender.
- where suspension will promote the repayment or restitution of stolen money or goods.
- where imprisonment would cause an excessive degree of suffering to the particular offender, for example because of bad physical or mental health.

In that case, on conviction for charges of forging and uttering where the total amount involved, being K82,202.73, had been recovered, and the total head sentence imposed was five years imprisonment, it was held that suspension of nine-tenths of the sentence on the grounds of alleged ill-health should be quashed on the findings that the respondent would not suffer special or excessive hardships in prison on account of his condition of health.

In *The State v William Peter Colin Welford* [1986] PNGLR 253 the defendant pleaded guilty to misappropriation, stealing and 30 other counts. He was sentenced to 18 months imprisonment and was likely to return to his family in the UK following his jail term. The court held that the case was not one in which the provisions of s 19(6) of the Code, regarding suspended sentences, were appropriate, because any aspect of a suspended sentence linked to a period of time imposed upon a recognisance to be of good behaviour would have no impact as the defendant would no doubt leave Papua New Guinea as soon as his sentence was completed: *Public Prosecutor v William Bruce Tardrew* [1986] PNGLR 91 was applied.

Where a child is to be sentenced by the National Court for an offence punishable by death or imprisonment for life, and the court has no power to declare the child a ward of the Director of Child Welfare under the *Child Welfare Act*, the child must be sentenced in the usual way with resort to the normal discretionary powers under s 19 and the inherent power of the National Court under s 155(4) of the *Constitution* to do justice in the circumstances of the particular case: *The State v S* [1987] PNGLR 271.

20. Calculation of term of sentence: Cumulative sentences: Escaped prisoners.

(1) Where a person who is convicted of an offence is undergoing, or has been sentenced to undergo, for another offence, a sentence involving deprivation of liberty, the punishment to be inflicted on him for the first-mentioned offence may be directed to take effect from the expiration of the deprivation of liberty for the last-mentioned offence.

(2) Subject to Subsection (1), a sentence of imprisonment -

(a) on a conviction on indictment – takes effect from the first day of the sittings of the court at which the offender is convicted; and

(b) on a summary conviction – takes effect from the commencement of the offender's custody under the sentence.

(3) A person who escapes from lawful custody while undergoing a sentence involving deprivation of liberty is liable on recapture to undergo the punishment that he was undergoing at the time of his escape, for a term equal to the period during which he was absent from prison after the escape and before the expiration of the term of his original sentence whether or not at the time of his recapture the term of that sentence had or has not expired.

See s 596 of the Code regarding sentencing generally, and ss 18, 19, 600 and 601 regarding types of punishments that may be inflicted. In *Tremellan v The Queen* [1973] PNGLR 116, Minogue CJ and Frost SPJ said:

> "Generally speaking sentences should be made concurrent where a congeries of offences is committed in the prosecution of a single purpose or the offences arise out of the same or closely related facts."

In that case 38 offences of larceny and making fraudulent entries in accounts over a period of six months were held to be inseparably connected.

Whether cumulative sentences are imposed is a question of the individual circumstances of each case. There is not a fixed principle of law that sentences for a series of offences in the prosecution of a single purpose ought to be served concurrently: *Wari Mugining v R* [1975] PNGLR 352.

It is incorrect to impose more than two sentences cumulative upon a first. This is so especially where there were a number of offences of a similar character in a particular short period: *John Sil Kawage v Gagorine Yube and Stephen Tifai* [1976] PNGLR 604.

In cases before the lower courts, normally not more than two sentences ought to be made cumulative upon another, unless there are exceptional circumstances. In *Pius Embari v Wangiwa* (1973) N751 the magistrate made five sentences cumulative upon another, totalling two years and four months imprisonment, for stealing. The court found that the magistrate was purporting to exercise sentencing powers statutorily reserved for judges. As the appellant was a first offender who pleaded guilty to all charges, the totality of the sentences was manifestly harsh and excessive, disclosing a substantial miscarriage of justice: *Pius Embari v Wangiwa* (1973) N751 (Prentice J).

Were it not for the provision in s 20(3), it is clear that at common law the sentence would still run notwithstanding the escapee's being at liberty. There is nothing in this section, however, which operates to stay or suspend the sentence of an accused who has been released on bail or recognisance pending the outcome of an appeal: *Wong v Gannon* (1969) N544. See ss 222-223 of the *District Courts Act* regarding release from custody pending appeal, and s 236 of the *District Courts Act* regarding the power of the court to enforce a decision after appeal.

In *R v Doriga-Mahuru* (1961) N257 the accused was suspected of having committed a number of forgeries over a short period of time: Because of the state of the available evidence, the prosecution proceeded with only one charge of attempting to obtain by false pretences, and secured a conviction. Subsequently the accused was charged with, and pleaded guilty to, four counts of forgery. In passing sentence, the court used its discretion to treat all five cases as if they were heard or taken into account at the same time for the purposes of allowing the sentences to run concurrently.

It is only in special cases that more than two cumulative sentences should be passed: *Akai Yama v McCombe* (1972) N666.

The totality principle requires that when consecutive sentences are imposed, a final review of the sentence is to be made to ensure that the total is not excessive: *Public Prosecutor v Terrence Kaveku* [1977] PNGLR 110.

It is not enough for the sentence to be merely expressed as "cumulative". This section must be strictly followed, and reference specifically made to the previous offence upon which the instant offence is to be made cumulative: *Akai Yama v McCombe* (1972) N666.

The first paragraph of the section is directed to enlarge the discretion which the sentencing court exercises at the time of the infliction of punishment. The words "who is convicted of an offence" are apt to describe the person who can be punished or, put in another way, to set out the necessary pre-requisite for punishment, ie conviction: *Secretary for Law v Malum* [1973] PNGLR 228 at 229 (Minogue CJ).

This section is to be construed as authorising the imposition of more than two sentences to be served cumulatively, and as authorising sentences imposed at the same time to be served cumulatively. In Papua New Guinea, especially in courts of summary jurisdiction, it is not unusual to see more than two cumulative sentences imposed. The second sentence is made cumulative on the first, and the third on the second. When the third sentence is imposed, the offender, by reference to the second sentence, either "has been sentenced to undergo for another offence a sentence" or "is undergoing for another offence a sentence". To what extent the court in its discretion should limit the number of sentences to be served consecutively is, of course, a different consideration: *Secretary for Law v Malum* [1973] PNGLR 228 (Clarkson and Prentice JJ).

There is power to make sentences cumulative and there is power to make more than two sentences cumulative, but the latter power should be exercised only in exceptional cases. Cases will arise where it will be quite proper to award more than two cumulative sentences, but they will be rare, and they will need to be very bad cases: *Passingan v Beaton* [1971-1972] PNGLR 206 at 210-211.

For principles on sentencing generally, see Raine J in *Kore v Alan Carling* and *Jackson Iavoi v Alan Carling* (1972) N722.

For a consideration of the question of cumulative sentences in a rape-murder, see *The State v Kwamo Bawai* (1981) N304 (Kidu CJ).

For principles of cumulative sentencing in a robbery-manslaughter case see *The State v Mek Keroa Nentepa* (1990) N878, where it was held that sentences for manslaughter and robbery, though committed in the one transaction of robbery, should be cumulative as being two separate serious offences in character: Amet J at 878, applying *Acting Public Prosecutor v Konis Haha* [1981] PNGLR 205.

It is clear that the term of a sentence of imprisonment imposed by the National Court (other than a sentence directed to be served cumulatively) must be calculated from the first day of the sittings of the court, notwithstanding what the terms of the warrant of commitment may provide. In other words, the requirements of s 20(2) must be observed: *Saki v The State* [1980] PNGLR 33.

For considerations on imposing cumulative sentences, see *Tomi Orabi v Benson Tamean* (1981) N323(M).

In prescribing sentences for more than one offence, the court must treat each offence separately, regardless of their relationship in time or kind: *Tremellan v The Queen* [1973] PNGLR 116. The court should consider whether or not the offences:

(a) arise out of the same or closely related facts;

(b) are different in character and involve different subject matter; or

(c) form part of each other in the manner they were committed.

The court should consider the aggregate effect of the sentences and allow some proportionality between the sentences and the offences and the circumstances surrounding them: *Acting Public Prosecutor v Konis Haha* [1981] PNGLR 205 at 216-217.

For a discussion of the "totality principle" see Miles J in *Acting Public Prosecutor v Konis Haha* [1981] PNGLR 205 at 219:

> "It is permissible and in most cases necessary that if the totality principle shows the aggregate to be excessive, then the head sentence is adjusted upwards to some extent. It must not be increased however to take it beyond any statutory maximum, nor indeed should it be extended beyond what might be regarded as the top of the range for that particular offence in the circumstances of the particular case".

A cumulative sentence may be imposed under s 20(1) of the Code. However, except where such cumulative sentence has been imposed specifically, in all other cases the sentence will run from the first day of the sittings (for the National Court) or from the date of the offender's custody under that sentence (for courts of summary jurisdiction). Section 20 is quite clear. If the sentence is to be cumulative to a period already being served, the court must say so: *The State v Aur Sivi* [1981] PNGLR 514.

With one exception, unless a sentence is expressed to be cumulative to another sentence, it will automatically run concurrently. In such cases the cumulative sentence must specify with utmost particularity the existing sentence which is to be extended by adding on the new sentence: *The State v Beig Walbo* (1981) N382(M).

It is wrong in principle to impose a series of fines and cumulative default sentences when in reality there is no prospect of the offender being able to pay the fines. The fixing of consecutive sentences of imprisonment for non-payment of fines is still the imposition of consecutive sentences and is subject to certain well-known principles. These include that, usually, consecutive sentences are inappropriate where several offences arise out of the same incident and that, even where they are appropriate, the court should consider whether the totality of the sentence is not excessive having regard to the totality of the criminal activity: *Ando Kenene v Gabriel Simon, Alois Gabour and George Tapu* [1983] PNGLR 179.

21. Prerogative.

Nothing in this Code affects the prerogative of mercy.

See ss 151 and 152 of the *Constitution*.

Division 5 – Criminal Responsibility

22. Application of Division 5.

This Division applies to all persons charged with offences against any law.

See s 1 of the Code for the definition of "criminally responsible".

Division 5 is to be read together with the other penal statutes that are set out below.

Division 5 of the *Criminal Code* provides a statutory freedom from criminal responsibility which "cannot be destroyed by express enactment of the legislature or by language in a latter statute so clear and unequivocal in its meaning that one must necessarily conclude from it that the legislature intended to destroy that freedom."[74]

Criminal responsibility is to be determined not by the Common Law doctrine of *mens rea* or the requirement of a "guilty mind" of some kind, but under Pt 1, Div 5: *Heduru Transport Pty Ltd v Gairo Vegoli* (1977) N99.

It was doubtless considered that such standards, beliefs, customs and so forth could and would be taken into consideration by the judges upon the question of the proper punishment in each case: *R v Womeni-Nanagawo* [1963] PNGLR 72.

See s 24: *Thick v Hoeter* [1963] PNGLR 87 at 94-95.

23. Ignorance of law, bona fide claim of right.

(1) Subject to Subsection (2), ignorance of the law does not afford an excuse for an act or omission that would otherwise constitute an offence, unless knowledge of the law by the offender is expressly declared to be an element of the offence.

(2) A person is not criminally responsible, as for an offence relating to property, for an act done or omitted to be done by him with respect to any property in the exercise of an honest claim of right and without intention to defraud.

This provision is the Code's counterpart of the common law doctrine of *mens rea*; to succeed, the claim needs only to be honest, it need not be reasonable: *Tiden v Tokavanamur-Topaparik* [1967-1968] PNGLR 231 at 236.

Ignorance of the law affords no excuse: *The State v Aubafo Feama, Nama Auri, Kafidiri Kududebe Hagima* [1978] PNGLR 301.

---

[74] *Sebulon Wat v Peter Kari (No2)* [1975] PNGLR 339.

Section 23 does not speak of an honest and reasonable claim of right: *Sebulon Wat v Peter Kari* [1975] PNGLR 325.

When the defence of claim of right is raised, the onus is on the prosecution to negative it: *R v Whitaker* (1969) N516.

In setting up a claim of right it is sufficient to eliminate one element only of the offence: *R v Joseph Mai* [1975] PNGLR 230.

A claim of right can involve mistakes both as to facts founding a right and as to the legality of the claim of right: *Prosecutor's Request No 4, 1974* [1975] PNGLR 365.

In *R v Magalu* [1974] PNGLR 188, Frost ACJ said (at 199):

> "[A] claim of right sufficient to relieve a person of criminal responsibility need only be honest and need not be reasonable ... But the section does not excuse an offender whose act was done in the mistaken belief that it was not unlawful, which is a mistake of law and no defence to any criminal prosecution."

Mann CJ stated, in *R v Alder* (1962) N228:

> "A claim of right may extend beyond proprietary rights into the field of rights in person and in relation to property or rights to commandeer, manage, control, occupy or exclude occupation of property, but not to a power to destroy property for the public protection as distinct from any personal interest in or in relation to it."

To show intent to defraud it is not sufficient to establish merely that the accused intended to obtain the property by false pretences: s 416. There must also be an intent to divert or use the property obtained in a dishonest way: *Prosecutor's Request No 4, 1974* [1975] PNGLR 365.

On a substantive charge of incitement, if a defence under this section is raised the issue is not whether the person encouraged acted under an honest claim of right, but whether the accused knew that the person encouraged did not have an honest claim of right: *Sebulon Wat v Peter Kari* [1975] PNGLR 325.

By virtue of the definition of property in s 1, the offences of forging and uttering a document are offences "relating to property" within the meaning of that phrase (see ss 460 and 463-464): *R v Magalu* [1974] PNGLR 188.

In *R v Magalu* [1974] PNGLR 188 it was held that where the state of mind of the accused was one of hope that forgeries would not be detected, and if they were that no action would be taken, and when the accused admitted knowing that forging signatures was wrong and that he could get into serious trouble if found out, he could not be excused on charges of forgery and uttering.

See note to s 433 discussing *R v Alder* (1962) N228.

24. Intention: Motive.

(1) Subject to the express provisions of this Code relating to negligent acts and omissions, a person is not criminally responsible for –

- (a) an act or omission that occurs independently of the exercise of his will; or
- (b) an event that occurs by accident.

(2) Unless the intention to cause a particular result is expressly declared to be an element of the offence constituted, in whole or part, by an act or omission, the result intended to be caused by an act or omission is immaterial.

(3) Unless otherwise expressly declared, the motive by which a person is induced –

(a) to do or omit to do an act; or

(b) to form an intention,

is immaterial so far as regards criminal responsibility.

See ss 286-287 of the Code regarding criminal negligence.

Section 24 is intended to make it clear that, subject to the express provisions of the Code relating to negligent acts and omissions, where a person is charged with the commission of a crime, criminal liability shall not attach where the alleged acts or omissions which are said to amount to the commission of the crime charged have occurred independently of the will of the accused, or where, in association with some act or omission of the accused, there has occurred some accidental event which has substantially brought about the final result: *Mamote-Kulang of Tamagot v The Queen* (1964) 111 CLR 62.

This section cannot be relied on to avoid liability where the accused argues intoxication. Section 29 is the sole basis for a defence based on intoxication: *R v Evi* [1975] PNGLR 30.

This section is a general controlling provision but does not necessarily apply to and govern every section. However, clearly it governs ss 289, 291, 298 and 302: *Timbu Kolian v The Queen* [1967-1968] PNGLR 320 at 325.

This section has no relevance when criminal negligence is involved. Similarly, if the unlawfulness of the act of the accused is to be measured according to whether or not the accused is in breach of the duty imposed by s 287, then s 24 has no application: *R v Yofia Abone* [1967-1968] PNGLR 277 at 286, 288 and 289.

The authorities are clear that this section has no relevance to a case where the offence charged rests upon the omission of a duty of the character specified in s 287: *R v Peck* (1971) N650.

Section 24 has no application on the trial of a person for manslaughter based upon a breach of the duty imposed by s 287: *R v Tsagaroan-Kagobo* [1965-1966] PNGLR 122 at 130.

The s 24 defence is made "subject to the express provisions of this Code relating to negligent acts and omissions", so that, in a charge of manslaughter where death is alleged to have resulted from a failure to use reasonable care or take reasonable precautions as required by s 287, liability is determined without resort to s 24: *Beraro v The State* [1988-89] PNGLR 562 at 573 (Amet J).

For the relationship between accident and criminal negligence (ss 286-287), see *Evgeniou v The Queen* [1964] PNGLR 45; (1964) 37 ALJR 508; *The State v Kaiwa Iasumi* (1978) N163.

Sir Samuel Griffith, the draftsman of the Code, said, and his remark has been often repeated, that as a result of s 24 it is now never necessary to have recourse to the old doctrine of *mens rea*: *Timbu Kolian v The Queen* [1967-1968] PNGLR 320.

In general, criminal responsibility is today attached to moral blameworthiness, and according to deeply rooted beliefs blameworthiness does not depend simply on what a person did, or on the results caused by those actions. It depends upon the person's knowledge and intentions when he or she acted. The doctrines of *mens rea* in the common law and of *dole* in the law of Scotland express this element of guilt. There is no reason to think that s 24 demands any departure from the basic concept or that it at all attenuates it. The words used reflect the accepted dominant and orthodox view of psychological processes and must be read literally: *Timbu Kolian v The Queen* 1967-1968] PNGLR 320 at 337 (Windeyer J).

The section "applies to unwilled acts in the sense that the physical actions involved were not due to the conscious mental activity of the person performing them; ... [the accused] would need to be hypnotised or in some other way deprived of conscious volition to come within s 24": *R v Yigwai* [1963] PNGLR 40 (Mann CJ).

It is difficult indeed to draw a satisfactory line between pleas that raise insanity within the M'Naghten rules and pleas that raise mental irresponsibility falling outside them. Nevertheless, a defence of so-called "automatism" has grown up in appropriate cases. This defence is separate and distinct from the defence of insanity. See s 28 regarding the defence of insanity: *R v Hembopi Nakipi* (1971) N646.

It is the absence of the will to act, or more precisely of its exercise, rather than a lack of knowledge or consciousness, which decides criminal liability. A distinction must be made between an unwilled act and a willed act that is the product of a diseased mind which knows not the nature or quality of the willed act: *R v Warago Waiyape* (1974) N796.

The defence of automatism exists in the common law concurrently with the defence of insanity. Under the Code the position is the same, as s 24 is there more or less cheek by jowl with ss 27 and 28, although the onus is not upon the accused person as in a case of "unsoundness of mind". The question is, does the defence fairly arise upon the evidence, and if it does, is there a reasonable doubt that the accused was acting independently of her or his will: *R v Hatenave-Tete* [1965-1966] PNGLR 336.

It is clear upon the authorities that the defence of automatism is not to be considered unless the defence lays a proper foundation for it. The presumption of mental capacity:

> "does not put the legal burden on the defence in the same way as the presumption of sanity does. It leaves the legal burden on the prosecution, but nevertheless, until it is displaced, it enables the prosecution to discharge the ultimate burden of proving that the act was voluntary. In order to displace the presumption of mental capacity, the defence must give sufficient evidence from which it may reasonably be inferred that the act was involuntary. The evidence of the man himself will rarely be sufficient unless it is supported by medical evidence which points to the cause of the mental incapacity".[75]

In *Hill v Baxter* [1958] 1 QB 277, Devlin J said:

> "There are genuine cases of automatism and the like, but the lay man cannot safely attempt without the help of some medical or scientific evidence to distinguish the genuine from the fraudulent."

[75] *Bratty v Attorney-General for Northern Ireland* [1963] AC 386 (Lord Denning); *R v Hembopi Nakipi* (1971) N646.

The fact that the evidence disclosed no motive for the attack does not support any inference of mental incapacity on the part of the accused: *R v Hembopi Nakipi* (1971) N646.

In *The State v Hekavo* [1991] PNGLR 394 Doherty J (at 396) said that:

> "Automatism was defined in *Bratty's* case (at 527) as connoting the state of a person who, though capable of action, 'is not conscious of what he is doing ... It means unconscious involuntary action, and it is a defence because the mind does not go with what is being done.'"

Also in *The State v Hekavo* [1991] PNGLR 394 (at 396-397), Doherty J said:

> "If the defence that automatism rendered an act non-voluntary or not the conscious exercise of the will is to be established the foundation must be first laid and that foundation is not forthcoming merely by making a statement that the defendant's reason was defective due to disease of the mind or a defect of reason. As Lord Goddard said, in *Hill v Baxter* [1958] 1 QB 277, proving that the defendant was in a state of automatism is on him because automatism is akin to insanity and further is a state exclusively within his knowledge. In considering that proof – (as said in *R v Foy* [1960] Qd R 225) – there has to be evidence fit to be left to the jury and it must be evidence after 'one subtracts the medical evidence directed to the establishment of a psychomotor epilepsy'.
>
> As I have noted the standard of proof in establishing automatism is on the balance of probabilities as has been held by *R v Hatenave-Tete* [1965-66] PNGLR 336 at 341 (where it is referred to 'on a preponderance of probability'), and in *Goi v The State* [1991] PNGLR 161. Nevertheless the over-riding principle remains that the State must prove every element of an offence charged and that includes the state of mind of the defendant."

He further stated:

> "Precedents show the defence must produce at least prima facie evidence of the defendant's condition (*Bratty* at 535) adopting *R v Cottle*) and if that proper foundation is not laid the defence of automatism need not be left to the jury (here to the Court as the tribunal of law and fact)."[76]

Doherty J also said:

> "[C]ase law, which reflects a common sense approach, indicates that there must be a foundation of facts coupled with medical expert evidence in order to determine whether a defendant was insane or that his actions were not willed because of automatism or neurological defect. There must be a foundation laid for this."[77]

In *The State v Enakuan Salaiau* [1994] PNGLR 388 Doherty J (at 390-391) held:

> "It is clear from the case law in Papua New Guinea and in other countries that to raise automatism there must be a proper basis. It involves two things: first, that the person suffers from the mental incapacity from time to time and, second, that he suffered it at that time the offence was committed.
>
> Further, the Court must distinguish the genuine cases of automatism and the fraudulent. The layman cannot safely, without the help of medical or scientific evidence, distinguish the genuine from the fraudulent."

---

[76] *The State v Hekavo* [1991] PNGLR 394 at 397 (Doherty J).
[77] *The State v Hekavo* [1991] PNGLR 394 at 400 (Doherty J).

Whereas by the common law misadventure excused only a homicide which was not associated with an unlawful act, the Code provides that an accidental event is never of itself punishable, and it is immaterial whether it arose out of the doing of an unlawful act or of a lawful act: *Timbu Kolian v The Queen* [1967-1968] PNGLR 320.

It is for the state to prove that the accused were not acting independently of their will once it is fairly raised: *R v Warago Waiyape* (1974) N796.

When a defence of accident is raised, there is no onus on the defence to prove accident, but there is an onus on the prosecution to refuse the defence beyond all reasonable doubt: *R v Johnson* (1951) N26.

The correct view seems to be that the prosecution must negative accident if there is evidence in the course of the trial suggesting such a defence: *Thick v Hoeter* [1963] PNGLR 87 at 96.

In a homicide, the defence that the death occurred by accident because the deceased, due to some peculiar constitutional defect (such as an enlarged spleen) unknown to the accused, was more susceptible to death than a person in normal health, will not be maintained when the accused intended the blow and death was a direct result of the blow: *Mamote-Kulang of Tamagot v The Queen* (1964) 111 CLR 62.

The unintended death of a person suffering from a peculiar latent weakness (such as an enlarged spleen) is not an event that occurs by accident if such death is caused by violence which could not have killed but for such weakness. *R v Manga Gabi* [1963] PNGLR 97.

In light of the decision in *Vallance v The Queen* (1961) 108 CLR 56, it can now be said that an event occurs by accident if it was not intended, not foreseen, and unlikely and is one that is not reasonably to be foreseen as a consequence of a person's conduct: (Windeyer J); *Timbu-Kolian v The Queen* [1967-1968] PNGLR 320.

In *R v Kaim Kaim* (1957) N108, Mann CJ said:

> "There is no irrebuttable presumption of law that a person intends the natural result of his actions however obvious ... There cannot be inconsistent intentions where an intention exists at all. The court must ascertain by inference or otherwise what the real intention was and where such an inference is indicated by clear course of conduct, some apparently conflicting intention may on analysis become relegated to a mere wish or desire which cannot replace the inferred intention. If however the evidence shows that the contrary intention is real and not merely a conflicting wish or desire the inference must fail."

While civil standards of negligence should not be applied in the case of criminal negligence, the civil test enunciated in *Overseas Tankship UK Ltd v Morts Dock & Engineering Co Ltd (The Wagon Mound)* [1961] AC 388 may not be all that different from the test of foreseeability for the purposes of this section. In other words, would an ordinary person in like circumstances have foreseen that injury was likely to be sustained in the manner it was in fact sustained as a result of some act or omission. An event occurs by accident if it is not "intended, not foreseen and unlikely, (and is one) that is not reasonably to be foreseen as a consequence of a man's conduct": *R v Aivei Ieme* [1973] PNGLR 1.

This section is applicable where the "precise cause of death was something not intended, not willed, not foreseen and foreseeable". Thus, an accused is saved by the section where although the accused was the cause of death within the meaning of s 291, he or she caused an unforeseeable event to take place which in turn caused the death. There must be an intervening separate event or an indirect cause for this section to be applicable: *R v Marabura-Lama* (1967) N410.

Smithers J held, in *R v Dimi* (1962) N267:

> "It is not intended by [this] section that an event is to be treated as an accident merely because the doer being blinded to its consequences by hate and rage fails to foresee the consequences that would be present to his mind if he thought rationally about the matter ... [A]n event which occurs by accident is one which the person doing the act did not foresee as a possibility substantial enough to be worthy of attention in deciding whether or not to do the act, and the event was so unlikely to result from the act that no ordinary person similarly circumstanced could fairly have been expected to take it into account."

Criminal responsibility rests on "whether there was a break in the chain of causation, and a new cause": *Mamote-Kulang of Tamagot v The Queen* (1964) 111 CLR 62 (Windeyer J).

It is clear that the fact that an act is unlawful does not prevent it from coming within this section: *R v Tsagaroan-Kagobo* [1965-1966] PNGLR 122.

In *Timbu-Kolian v The Queen* [1967-1968] PNGLR 320, it was held that where the accused aimed a blow at his wife, but in the dark struck and killed the infant she was holding, the accused was not guilty of manslaughter, as the child's death was an accident within the meaning of this section and was the result of a willed act by the accused.

While perhaps it cannot be categorically asserted that the two branches of s 24 (the unwilled act and the accidental event) are in all their applications mutually exclusive, so that what falls within the one can never at the same time fall within the other, the total operation of the section in general is that an act which falls within the first part of the section and is accompanied by the will of the actor may bring a consequence which is accidental: see *Vallance v The Queen* (1961) 108 CLR 56 at 61. It is the consequences of the act of the applicant falling within the first part to which the second part of the section is directed. Death as a consequence of such an act cannot be relevantly an event. An unintended, unforeseeable, fortuitous death which results from an act which is a willed act causally related to that death, may be an event which occurs by accident or by chance: *Timbu-Kolian v The Queen* [1967-1968] PNGLR 320 (Barwick CJ).

Barwick CJ further said, in *Timbu-Kolian v The Queen*:

> "The exercise of the will to which this section refers is not identical with the presence of intention, nor is it the equivalent of voluntariness or the presence of volition. Of course, an intended act, in the sense that the actor intended by his action to achieve the full operation of that action as it proved to be in fact, must necessarily, in my opinion, be a willed act within the section. On the other hand, that the applicant by an act of volition wielded the stick (with the intention of hitting his wife), does not mean that the striking of the child was his willed act ... the exercise of will involves the making of a choice to do that which the physical activity of the applicant in fact does: eg in this to land the blow on the head of the child. The relevant act in this case was the striking of the child on the head; it was not an exercise of the will of the applicant, was not his willed act: and from a point of view of criminal responsibility was not his act at all."

The aiming of a blow at the wife was intentional, but before it reached its target a wholly unexpected and unforeseeable event intervened. The child's head intercepted the blow aimed at the wife. In these circumstances the fact that the blow struck the child was an "event" which occurred by accident: *Timbu-Kolian v The Queen* [1967-1968] PNGLR 320 (Owen J).

An event occurs by accident if it is caused by a happening that is not foreseen by the actor and is not reasonably foreseeable by an ordinary person, the onus being on the state to exclude the provisions of this section relating to accident. In *Timbu-Kolian v The Queen* [1967-1968] PNGLR 320 at 343 the accused, after some provocation, threw a stick at his wife in their darkened house and struck and killed their infant son. The court held that the father of an infant in that situation should have been concerned for the safety of the child, and his neglect involved such a rejection of his parental responsibilities that his omission involved a very high degree of moral culpability: *R v Tsagaroan-Kagobo* [1965-1966] PNGLR 122.

In *Timbu-Kolian v The Queen*, the case of *Mamote-Kulang of Tamagot v The Queen* (1964) 111 CLR 62 was distinguished on the facts. In the latter case there was no room to question whether the act of striking the deceased was an exercise of the will of the applicant, nor was any step in the delivery or the landing of the blow or in the circumstances which led to the death fortuitous.

In *The State v Kaiwa Iasumi* (1978) N163, where the accused fired an arrow at a chicken underneath a house and the arrow struck and killed a child whose presence was not known to the accused, this event was unintended, unforeseen and unforeseeable, and the accused had a defence under this section.

It was said in *R v Tsagaroan-Kagobo* [1965-1966] PNGLR 122 that if A shoots at B with or without intent, and kills C, he cannot say that he was acting lawfully towards C. Unexplained, it would be murder. His actual intent or other mental element, if relevant, is transferred to the actual victim.

Where the accused attacked his wife with an axe handle, which accidentally dislodged firewood suspended from the roof, which fell on and killed the wife, this section provides no defence. All that can be said is that the intended injury was inflicted, although not precisely in the manner intended: *R v Kipali-Ikarum* [1967-1968] PNGLR 119 at 134-135.

The s 2 definition of "person" does not indicate an intention that the definition of "person" in the *Acts Interpretation Act* should not apply to the provisions of Ch V. It follows that a corporation, like a natural person, is not criminally responsible for an act which occurs independently of the exercise of its will, including an act done by a servant in violation of instructions. In general, a principal, whether a natural person or a company, cannot be held criminally responsible for the unauthorised acts of a mere servant, on the ground that acts done without the knowledge of the principal are done independently of its will: *Heduru Transport Pty Ltd v Gairo Vegoli* (1977) N99.

In *Hunt v Moloney* (1959) 53 QJPR 109, the Full Court of Queensland held that the operation of this section could not be excluded merely by the objects of the statute against which an offence is charged, and that it can only be indirectly excluded by the clear language of a later statute. All the judges took the view that s 22 applies s 24 to every statutory offence irrespective of type: see *Thick v Hoeter* [1963] PNGLR 87 at 94-95.

See s 22 regarding application of the criminal responsibility sections.

The operation of s 24 cannot be excluded merely by the objects of the statute creating an offence. The section should not be held to be excluded in relation to a statutory offence unless a statute uses clear and unequivocal language to that effect, and establishes strict liability: *Heduru Transport Pty Ltd v Gairo Vegoli* (1977) N99.

The pattern of modern statutes dealing summarily with such subjects as health and public safety shows a legislative intention to displace the presumption of *mens rea*. In *Thick v Hoeter* [1963] PNGLR 87 the statutes referred to were the *Motor Traffic Act* and *Motor Traffic Regulations*.

An act may create an absolute offence, and there may be an implied exclusion of s 24. Also, it may be no defence that the act complained of was committed by a servant on behalf of the appellant without the knowledge of the company. Companies have become recognised as legal "persons", (*Interpretation (Interim Provisions) Act* 1975) but this does not mean that they acquire all human attributes of thought and decision-making. A distinction can be validly drawn between minor offences of a regulatory kind, where no criminal intent is an ingredient, and other offences where it is. In other words, it is appropriate to strengthen the concept of strict responsibility. It was held in *Bromley & Manton Pty Ltd v Eremas Andrew* [1978] PNGLR 498 that the requirement to display prices under s 109(4) of the *Constitution* is an absolute one, and the appellant company could not rely on s 24 to evade prosecution on the basis that its "corporate mind" is elsewhere or because it had instructed its employees to display prices. The company's officer had the "effective management" of the appellant's business and thus the appellant company could not rely on s 24. The offence of failing to display prices did not occur "independently of the will" of the appellant.

For an illustration of the operation of this section, see *R v Kalit* [1971] PNGLR 124. See also *Sebulon Wat v Peter Kari* [1975] PNGLR 325, and *R v Cakic* (1968) N493.

25. Mistake of fact.

(1) Subject to Subsection (2), a person who does or omits to do an act under an honest and reasonable, but mistaken, belief in the existence of any state of things is not criminally responsible for the act or omission to any greater extent than if the real state of things had been such as he believed to exist.

(2) The operation of Subsection (1) may be excluded by the express or implied provisions of the law relating to the subject.

Mistake under the Code is not a defence but a matter which exonerates criminal responsibility. Accordingly, the prosecution must negative the existence of honest and reasonable belief: *R v Ulel* [1973] PNGLR 254.

Where mistake of fact is raised, it is the duty of the court to consider whether it applies. Where there is some evidence of operative mistake, the onus is on the prosecution to satisfy the court of its non-existence: *Anide v Denehy* [1973] PNGLR 215.

If there is some evidence of a mistaken belief, the onus is on the Crown to establish beyond reasonable doubt that the accused did not have such a belief: *R v Yoka Kiok* (1970) N607.

"Honestly held" involves a subjective test, and "reasonably held" involves an objective test applying the standard of the ordinary man coming from the accused's environment: *R v Yoka Kiok* (1970) N607.

To act under a mistaken belief in the existence of a state of things means something more than to act merely in ignorance of the state of things which in fact exists. It requires that a mistaken belief be held and that the act be done under the influence of that belief. Also, a belief in what might subsequently occur is not a belief in the existence of a state of things: *R v Timbu-Kolian* [1967-68] PNGLR 310 at 319.

Section 25 is limited to the existence of a state of things, not to the probable future consequences of that existing state: *R v Korongia* (1961) N204.

If the accused had an honest and reasonable, although mistaken, belief that the force in fact used was necessary for self-defence, the accused is no more criminally responsible than if that force was in fact necessary for defence: *R v Kaiwor Ba* [1975] PNGLR 90. See the note on this case at s 269.

It was held in *R v Kapoi Joharumba* (1972) N679 that where the accused believed on honest and reasonable, yet mistaken, grounds that an act of sorcery had taken place, then s 20 of the *Sorcery Act* came into play. As the accused acted suddenly and at a time when deprived of the power of self-control within s 263, then s 299 operated to reduce a charge of wilful murder to manslaughter.

This section is impliedly excluded from the considerations of provocation such as would reduce a charge of wilful murder or murder to manslaughter under s 303. If a lawful act cannot constitute provocation under s 266, it appears completely inconsistent to hold that a non-existent (an imagined) act can constitute provocation. The test of whether an act constitutes provocation is objective – not what the effect is on a particular individual, which would seem to exclude questions of imagination.[78] The concept of provocation is obviously intended to reduce culpability (s 303) or eliminate it (s 267), because of the fault of the provoker. It is restricted to excusing only actions against the provoker. It is therefore completely anomalous to find excuse in an imagined "provocation" for an assault upon an "innocent" (inoffensive) person: *R v KJ* [1973] PNGLR 93 at 106-107.

There is no authority as to whether this section may operate with s 266. Minogue CJ and Kelly J said, in *R v KJ* [1973] PNGLR 93 at 101:

> "We would venture to say that that may well be because the position has always been thought to be clear, namely that mistake of fact as set out in this section could apply in relation to provocation as defined in s 266. In our view this is so."

In *The State v Akain Tomalom* [1976] PNGLR 512, where the accused asserted that he was entitled to be held not criminally responsible for any false assumption of authority (s 96), on the grounds that he held an honest and reasonable mistake of fact that the activities of his unofficial court had been recognized and legalised by statute, such a mistake would have been a mistake of law and not of fact.

This section has no operation with respect to mistakes relating to the age of the girl in a prosecution under s 216 for unlawful carnal knowledge of a girl under the age of 16. Section 216 provides its own "defence" of mistake, with the onus on the accused to prove the defence on a balance of probabilities: *R v Schulze* (1971) N657.

Where the defence failed in relation to a charge of bigamy, see *The State v Paul Nangsi Kamang* (1975) N12.

As to a mistake of fact with regard to consent in charges of rape, see the note on *R v Kalabus* [1977] PNGLR 87 under s 347. See also *The State v Peter Yama* (1990) N817, where it was held that mistaken belief as to consent may have been honest but was not reasonable, in a situation where the victim was abducted late at

---

[78] *R v KJ* [1973] PNGLR 93 at 106-107 (Prentice J dissenting).

night by the accused and two others and taken to a secluded spot, where she was threatened with a pistol even though she did not see it, and was then repeatedly placed in a situation where the accused refused to take her to her aunt's house unless she submitted to intercourse.

The applicability of this section as a defence to a motor traffic charge is clear: *Exton v Nordfelt* (1965) N349.

If the accused kills believing the deceased to be a sorcerer, that is a mistake, but only as to identity and not as to the intention to terminate a human life: *The State v Yale Gesie and Buamuwe Guluwe* (1980) N254.

Where a particular crime requires intent, as in wilful murder, a mistake of fact may negative that intent and absolve the accused. Reasonableness and honesty in the defence are elements relating to the credibility of witnesses to be determined on the basis of available evidence. *The State v Yale Gesie and Buamuwe Guluwe* (1980) N254.

26. Extraordinary emergencies.

Subject to the express provisions of this Code relating to acts done on compulsion or provocation, or in self-defence, a person is not criminally responsible for an act or omission done or made under such circumstances of sudden or extraordinary emergency that an ordinary person possessing ordinary power of self-control could not reasonably be expected to act otherwise.

Sir Samuel Griffiths in speaking of this section stated:

> "It gives effect to the principle that no man is expected (for the purposes of the criminal at all events) to be wiser or better than all mankind. It is conceived that it is a rule of common law, as it undoubtedly is a rule upon which any jury would desire to act".[79]

In *Viro v The Queen* (1978) 141 CLR 88, a police officer, acting in the performance of his duties, encountered a suspect who had earlier threatened police with what looked like a firearm. Honestly believing that the suspect had a pistol or firearm which he was going to draw, and knowing that he himself had one shot in his shotgun, he shot the suspect in the legs. The suspect later died from the injury and the police officer was charged with wilful murder. Because mere apprehension that a firearm was about to be produced did not constitute an assault, the defence of self-defence under s 268 of the Code was not available. The court held that in such circumstances a "court is entitled to say that this accused is not criminally responsible. In other words he has not acted in a criminal manner, he has acted reasonably in the circumstances as he saw it at the time, not in the circumstances as we now know later". As the High Court, in that case said (at 88):

> "[T]he accused ... reasonably believed that an unlawful attack which threatened him with death or serious bodily harm was being or was about to be made upon him ... By the expression 'reasonably believed' is meant, not what a reasonable man would have believed, but what the accused himself might reasonably believe in all the circumstances in which he found himself."

In *The State v Joseph Ampi* [1988] PNGLR 116, Woods J held (at 119-120) that s 26 applied as:

[79] *R v Pius Piane* [1975] PNGLR 52 at 56.

> "the accused was faced with a sudden emergency and his actions were not unreasonable, they were the actions of an ordinary person possessing ordinary power of self-control in the circumstances that he believed he was in."

In *Abel Pagawa v Frederick Mathew* [1986] PNGLR 154 a person from Irian Jaya had entered Papua New Guinea without an entry permit in contravention of s 16(1)(a) of the *Migration Act*. He stated the reason for this was "because the Indonesians have killed all of us ... I was in prison so I was frightened and ran away". The court held that the defences of sudden or extraordinary emergency under s 26 of the Code, and the defence of compulsion under s 32, were available and had been made out. Kidu CJ stated (at 155-156):

> "I cannot see that the *Migration Act* in making it an offence for a non-citizen to enter Papua New Guinea without an entry permit meant to penalise those who enter the country as a result of being forced into doing so either by being chased into the country or by fleeing another country as a result of military conflict in their country ... Any person who finds himself under threat of being shot is justified in coming into Papua New Guinea to evade being killed."

See s 28 for the test of insanity, s 569 regarding unfitness to plead, s 590 regarding insanity during trial, and s 592 regarding acquittal on grounds of insanity.

Ollerenshaw J said, in *R v Hatenave-Tete* [1965-66] PNGLR 336:

> "Under the Code the position is the same, as s 24 is there more or less cheek by jowl with ss 27 and 28, although the onus is not upon the accused person as in a case of 'unsoundness of mind'. The question is, does the defence fairly arise upon the evidence and if it does is there a reasonable doubt that she was acting independently of her will".

The onus is on the state to prove capacity where an affirmative case, on the balance of probabilities, is set up by the accused: *R v Mako* (1960) N183.

28. Insanity.

(1) A person is not criminally responsible for an act or omission if at the time of doing the act or making the omission he is in such a state of mental disease or natural mental infirmity as to deprive him of capacity -

(a) to understand what he is doing; or

(b) to control his actions; or

(c) to know that he ought not to do the act or make the omission.

(2) A person –

(a) whose mind, at the time of his doing or omitting to do an act is affected by delusions on some specific matter or matters; and

(b) who is not otherwise entitled to the benefit of the provisions of Subsection (1),

is criminally responsible for the act or omission to the same extent as if the real state of things had been such as he was induced by the delusions to believe to exist.

See s 27, which establishes a presumption of sanity, s 569 regarding unfitness to plead, s 590 regarding insanity during trial, and s 592 regarding acquittal on grounds of insanity.

In an inquiry under s 569 an accused was found fit to plead, but in an inquiry as to soundness of mind under s 590 during the course of trial the trial judge directed that the accused be examined by a psychiatrist: *R v Koiyari-Iyeva* [1965-66] PNGLR 284.

The expression "not of sound mind" is not a term of art. There is no comprehensive or exclusive definition: *R v Koiyari-Iyeva* [1965-66] PNGLR 284.

"Not of sound mind" in s 590 bears a different meaning to that in s 592, for in the latter section the term is directed to the situation where the accused is to be freed from criminal responsibility and it must clearly be interpreted by reference to s 28. Section 590 is not directed to such a case, but to the accused's condition at the time of trial: *R v Koiyari-Iyeva* [1965-66] PNGLR 284.

In *Goi v The State* [1991] PNGLR 161, Kidu CJ, Salika and Jalina JJ (at 169) stated:

> "[I]n a defence based on s 28 ..., it must be shown by the defence that the accused person's capacity to understand what he was doing or to control his actions or to know that he ought not to commit the act was taken away from him by the state of his mental disease or natural mental infirmity ... Deprivation of capacity to understand or control actions is not the same as mere impairment of such capacity".

Doherty J held, in *The State v Enakuan Salaiau* [1994] PNGLR 388 at 390:

> "A finding under s 28 is a very drastic one. Once such a finding is made, it brings into play, s 592. This provides that once a court finds a person is not of sound mind, it must find him not guilty and order him to be kept in strict custody at a place and in a manner as it thinks proper pending a decision of the Head of State. It is a mandatory provision and is an open sentence without a specific end. It is normally a life sentence. It is open to review from time to time on advice given to the Head of State. In practical terms, there has been no such review for quite some years at the Laloki psychiatric hospital."

In the same case, Doherty J also said (at 390):

> "Insanity provision under s 28 means that a person did not will or could not make a decision about what he was doing because of the diseased mind. Such a finding obliges a court to hold him indefinitely. An unwilled act because of automatism or some other state under s24 can lead to an acquittal."

A finding that an accused is fit to plead under s 569 does not preclude an inquiry as to "unsoundness of mind" under s 590: *R v Koiyari-Iyeva* [1965-66] PNGLR 284.

Section 590 is designed, in part at least, for the protection of the community and in aid of the mental health legislation: *R v Koiyari-Iyeva* [1965-66] PNGLR 284.

The beliefs of primitive people in the power of sorcery and witchcraft are not delusions within the meaning of s 28: *R v Korongia* (1961) N204. See now *Sorcery Act* in Ch 4 of this book.

There is a presumption of sanity, and the onus is on the defence to establish insanity on the balance of probabilities: *R v Agana Guguna* (1965) N364.

A whole range of emotional disturbances, such as jealousy, anger, revenge or lack of self-control are excluded from this section – these are typical of matters affecting mental stability or balance, as distinct from insanity: *R v Brigitta Asamakan* [1964] PNGLR 193 at 198.

The phrase "natural mental infirmity" is in this section to embrace forms of insanity or unsoundness of mind not comprehended by the phrase "mental disease" per se: *R v Womeni-Nanagawo* [1963] PNGLR 72.

Although it is the state of mind at the time of the commission of the offence which is exclusively important, in considering whether the defence is established on the balance of probabilities one may consider the accused's conduct "before, at the time of, and after the event" in addition to the medical evidence. The medical evidence cannot be conclusive but must be "regarded with much respect": *R v Nicholas Lagit* (1961) N207; *The State v Bakau Kaija* (1980) N213.

The onus of proof required to set aside the statutory presumption of sanity (s 27) is that required in a civil trial, namely on a balance of probabilities, and lies upon the defence: *The State v Bakau Kaija* (1980) N213.

The law in Papua New Guinea, as expressed in this section, does not make diminished responsibility the equivalent of insanity. Deprivation of capacity to control actions is not coincident with more impairment of capacity to control – which may be of a slight or greater degree in different cases: *The State v Joseph Makapi* (1980) N214.

The insanity defence must be established by the accused's counsel on the balance of probabilities: *The State v Joseph Makapi* (1980) N214.

Medical evidence relating to the accused's mental capacity cannot be conclusive, but must be regarded with respect: *The State v Joseph Makapi* (1980) N214.

Diminished responsibility is not a defence under the Code: *Kutapa Keapu v The State* [1994] PNGLR 135 at 137 (Kapi DCJ and Hinchcliffe J).

29. Intoxication.

(1) Section 28 applies to the case of a person whose mind is disordered by intoxication or stupefaction caused, without intention on his part, by drugs or intoxicating liquor or by any other means.

(2) Section 28 does not apply to the case of a person who has intentionally caused himself to become intoxicated or stupefied.

(3) When an intention to cause a specific result is an element of an offence, intoxication, whether complete or partial, and whether intentional or unintentional, may be regarded for the purpose of ascertaining whether such an intention in fact existed.

See ss 3-5 of the *Summary Offences Act* regarding offences related to drunkenness.

This section is the basis for all defences of intoxication. If a defence under s 29 is rejected, no defence is available under s 24: *R v Evi* [1975] PNGLR 30.

In that case it was also held that the accused has the onus of proving on the balance of probabilities the requirements of the defence, including that the accused had no intent to cause his or her own intoxication.

The prosecution must prove the guilt of the accused beyond a reasonable doubt, otherwise the accused is entitled to an acquittal. It follows from this that the state must negative any defence open to the accused except insanity. Insanity may be produced by excessive consumption of alcohol, and it lies upon the defence to establish that defence, but upon the balance of the probabilities rather than with the high standard of proof required of the prosecution: *R v John Henry Jones* (1949)

N27. Drunkenness is a defence only to an offence of which intent is an essential ingredient: *Terrence Leonard Detton v Verdun Brien McNeil* (1960) N174.

The condition of the accused from drink must be taken into account for the purpose of ascertaining if the necessary intention existed: *R v Bena-Forepe* [1965-66] PNGLR 329.

Once the defence of intoxication is raised, it is incumbent upon the prosecution to negative the defence beyond reasonable doubt by showing that the accused had the relevant intent, taking into account the accused's condition in relation to alcohol: *The State v Joseph Evara* (1979) N201.

30. Immature age.

(1) A person under the age of seven years is not criminally responsible for any act or omission.

(2) A person under the age of 14 years is not criminally responsible for an act or omission, unless it is proved that at the time of doing the act or making the omission he had capacity to know that he ought not to do the act or make the omission.

(3) A male person under the age of 14 years is presumed to be incapable of having carnal knowledge, but this presumption is rebuttable.

See s 6 regarding carnal knowledge.

In *R v Iakapo* [1965-66] PNGLR 147 the accused was charged with wilful murder for helping her mother bury a newborn child from an incestuous (according to local custom) relationship. The accused well knew that her mother's authority was not to be challenged by her, and knew that the action ordered, though most distasteful to her, would be accepted by most of her people as a practicable solution to the problem. She did not have the capacity to understand that her duty was to deny her mother's authority and disobey. Accordingly, she was excused from all criminal responsibility under this section.

A boy over seven and under 14 may be an accomplice in first degree offences, such as rape or offences involving carnal knowledge, if the presumption of his lack of criminal responsibility is rebutted by clear proof of his having a "mischievous discretion", ie a capacity to know that he ought not to have committed the offence: *R v Bradley* (1948) N5.

Section 63 of the *Evidence Act* provides that in any proceeding the court may, having seen the accused, determine his age if there is insufficient evidence on the subject: *R v Womeni-Nanagawo* [1963] PNGLR 72.

Where a court concludes that a child does not sufficiently comprehend the nature of an oath or affirmation but does understand the consequences of giving untruthful evidence, the court may take an unsworn statement: *R v Bradley* (1948) N5.

The common law was addressed directly to malice, but operated as a defence for the otherwise criminal acts of the accused. If it only concerned intent, the rule might leave an accused person guilty of manslaughter upon a charge for wilful murder or murder, but such an operation was not intended by this section. Similarly, the accused may not be guilty of aiding and abetting another to commit an offence: *R v Iakapo* [1965-66] PNGLR 147.

The evidence of young boys who might be regarded as accomplices must be looked at with the greatest caution and reserve, and corroboration is generally needed: *R v Barker* (1956) N96.

Capacity to know that an act ought not be done is different from actual knowledge that it is contrary to the law: *R v Womeni-Nanagawo* [1963] PNGLR 72.

See s 63 of the *Evidence Act* regarding evidence of age.

31. Judicial officers.

Except as expressly provided by this Code, a judicial officer is not criminally responsible for anything done or omitted to be done by him in the exercise of his judicial functions, even if -

(a) an act done is in excess of his judicial authority; or

(b) he is bound to do an act omitted to be done.

See ss 119-120 and 132 of the Code regarding offences specifically directed at judges and judicial officers.

32. Justification and excuse: Compulsion.

(1) A person is not criminally responsible for an act or omission done or made -

(a) in execution of the law; or

(b) in obedience to the order of a competent authority that he is bound by law to obey, unless the order is manifestly unlawful; or

(c) when the act is reasonably necessary in order to resist actual and unlawful violence threatened to him, or to another person in his presence; or

(d) when he does or omits to do the act -

(i) in order to save himself from immediate death or grievous bodily harm threatened to be inflicted on him by some person actually present and in a position to execute the threats, and

(ii) believing himself to be unable otherwise to escape the carrying of the threats into execution,

but this protection does not extend to an act or omission that would constitute an offence, punishable with death or the offence of wilful murder, or an offence of which grievous bodily harm to the person of another, or an intention to cause such harm, is an element, nor to a person who has by entering into an unlawful association or conspiracy rendered himself liable to have such threats made to him.

(2) Whether an order is or is not manifestly unlawful is a question of law.

[S 32 am Act No 12, 1982 (*Criminal Code (Amendment) Act* 1982), s 2]

See s 35 of the *Constitution*.

See s 26 of the Code regarding emergency, and s 49 regarding compulsion as a defence to sedition.

In *R v Lupalupa Sisarowe* [1967-68] PNGLR 455, Frost J expressed obiter view that s 32(1)(c) only excuses an act done for the purpose of defence, and its provisions cannot derogate from the specific provisions of ss 269-271.

The proviso under s 32(1) applies to all the circumstances dealt with in s 32(1)(a)-(d) and applies only where the offence charged is punishable by death, or is an offence in the definition of which, or in the commission of which, the causing or intention to cause grievous bodily harm is an element: *The State v Laura (No 1)* [1988-89] PNGLR 92 (Kidu CJ).

As to compulsion in the case of a sodomy charge, see *R v MK* [1973] PNGLR 204, noted under s 210, which construes s 32(1)(d) broadly.

The provisions excuse acts done for the purposes of defence but not covered under s 269. There need not be a prior assault to invoke the defence. Section 32(1)(c) offers defence for an "act ... reasonably necessary" to "resist actual ... violence threatened". The test for what is reasonably necessary is subjective: see *Tapea Kwapena v The State* [1978] PNGLR 316 at 321. The word "actual" for the purposes of violence threatened means "physical": *The State v Angela Colis Towavik* [1981] PNGLR 140 at 145 (Miles J).

Pratt J, in *The State v Angela Colis Towavik* [1981] PNGLR 140, said:

> "Section 32(1)(c), despite the heading of the section in the terms 'Justification and Excuse: Compulsion', is not restricted to an act compelled by actual or threatened violence in the sense of an act of the accused directed towards the victim and carried out under duress brought about by violence or threats on the part of a third party directed towards the accused. For what it is worth, I think that para (1)(d) should be read in the same way."

He further said:

> "With respect to the view expressed by Frost J (as he then was) in *R v Lupalupa-Sisarowe* [1967-68] PNGLR 455, it seems to me that s 32(1)(c) may be regarded as extending to acts which are not covered by the provisions of the Code relating to self-defence. For example s 32(1)(c) specifically refers to threatened violence whereas s 269 requires a prior assault by the victim for self-defence to become available. Of course a threat of violence may constitute an assault (but not a battery) depending on the circumstances. The word 'actual' in s 32(1)(c) is somewhat confusing but I accept the submission that it means 'physical'".

It has been held in Queensland that the proviso appearing under s 32(1)(d) applies to all the circumstances dealt with in the section and is not limited to subs (1)(d): see *R v Silk* [1973] Qd R 298 (Kelly AJ). Whether this is so or not, the proviso applies only where the offence charged is punishable by death, or is an offence in the definition of which, or in the commission of which the causing or intention to cause grievous bodily harm is an element. Where the offence alleged is unlawful wounding (under s 322), the case is taken outside the proviso: *The State v Angela Colis Towavik* [1981] PNGLR 140.

In construing the words "reasonably necessary" in s 32(1)(c), the test is a subjective one. The Supreme Court has decided that the test is subjective in cases of self-defence: *Tapea Kwapena v The State* [1978] PNGLR 316 at 321. The same test should be applied in cases of compulsion under s 32(1)(c): *The State v Angela Colis Towavik* [1981] PNGLR 140.

The issue of compulsion or justification and excuse under s 32 of the Code is a defence and must be raised by the defendant as part of the evidence in defence. It cannot be argued on a no case submission where it is raised before the court as part of a record of interview tendered by the prosecution: *The State v Gigere Undamu* [1990] PNGLR 151 (Doherty AJ).

In *R v MK* [1973] PNGLR 204 at 209, Minogue CJ and Kelly J stated:

> "There may be cases where the accused suffered the commission of the act under such threats of violence that s 32(1)(d) would operate to relieve him of criminal responsibility; or there may be cases where, whilst s 32(1)(d) would not apply, the accused had resisted to an extent that even though an act of sodomy had subsequently been committed on him the court could not be satisfied that it could be said that he had 'allowed' the act. On the other hand if in circumstances where s 32(1)(d) does not apply the accused because, for instance, of fear of suffering some harm, physical or otherwise, does not resist and simply suffers the act to be committed upon him, the tribunal might well find that he had 'allowed' it and so was guilty of the offence. It seems to us that the operation which we have held this section to have may in some circumstances be too harsh and that consideration should be given to allowing for a defence of coercion of lesser degree than that provided for in s 32(1)(d)."

See s 26 of the Code regarding emergency.

This section is concerned only with the marriage relationship, but Mann CJ, in *R v Yigwai* [1963] PNGLR 40, said:

> "in native society a father may have more power over his daughter than was contemplated in European society when s 33 was drafted ... Her position was that of the domestic woman servant in his power and in native society it matters little whether the term 'wife' is used or whether some form of marriage is involved".

See Pt VII, Div 2 (ss 515-518) of the Code on conspiracy.

35. Offences by partners and members of companies with respect to partnership or corporate property.

A member of a co-partnership, corporation or joint stock company who does or omits to do any act with respect to the property of the co-partnership, corporation, or company that would, if he were not a member, constitute an offence is criminally responsible to the same extent as if he were not a member.

See ss 370 and 433(3) of the Code.

As to indictments, see s 530(6), (8) and (9).

36. Liability of husband and wife for offences to the other's property.

(1) In this section, "property", in relation to a wife, means her separate property.

(2) When a husband and wife are living together, neither of them incurs any criminal responsibility for doing or omitting to do any act with respect to the property of the other, except -

- (a) an act or omission of which an intention to injure or defraud some other person is an element; or
- (b) an act done by either of them when leaving or deserting, or when about to leave or desert, the other.

(3) Subject to Subsection (2), a husband or wife is criminally responsible for any act done by him or her with respect to the property of the other that would be an offence if they were not husband and wife, to the same extent as if they were not husband and wife.

(4) A husband or wife cannot institute criminal proceedings against the other with respect to the property of the other while they are living together.

(5) On the prosecution -

(a) of a husband on the complaint of his wife for an offence committed with respect to her property; or

(b) of a wife on the complaint of her husband for an offence committed with respect to his property,

the complainant is a competent and compellable witness.

See s 385 of the Code.

Part II – Offences Against Public Order

Division 1 – Treason and Other Offences against the Queen's Person and Authority

37. Treason.

A person who -

(a) kills the Queen and Head of State, or does Her any bodily harm tending to Her death, maiming, wounding, imprisonment or restraint; or

(b) kills the eldest son and heir-apparent for the time being of the Sovereign, or, if the successor, by virtue of Section 83 of the *Constitution* (Queens successors), to the Queen and Head of The State is a male, the Queen Consort of the reigning King; or

(c) forms an intention to do an act referred to in Paragraph (a) or (b), and manifests such intention by any overt act; or

(d) conspires with any other person to kill the Queen and Head of The State or to do Her any bodily harm tending to Her death, maiming, wounding, imprisonment or restraint; or

(e) levies war against the Queen and Head of The State -

(i) with intent to depose the Queen and Head of The State from the style, honour, and royal name of the Crown of the United Kingdom of Great Britain and Northern Ireland, or of any other of Her Majesty's dominions; or

(ii) in order, by force or constraint, to compel the Queen and Head of The State to change Her measures or counsels, or in order to put any force or constraint on, or to intimidate or overawe, any House of Parliament of any of Her Majesty's dominions; or

(f) conspires with any other person to levy war against the Queen and Head of State, with any intent or purpose referred to in paragraph (e); or

(g) instigates a foreigner to make an armed invasion of any part of Her Majesty's dominions; or

(h) assists by any means whatever a public enemy at war with the Queen and Head of State; or

(i) violates, whether with her consent or not, a Queen Consort, or the wife of the eldest son and heir-apparent for the time being of the successor (being a male) of the Queen and Head of State,

is guilty of the crime of treason.

Penalty: Death.

See s 579 of the Code regarding evidence on charge of treason.

See s 227 of the *Constitution* regarding a declaration of war.

38. Concealment of treason.

A person who -

(a) becomes an accessory after the fact to treason; or

(b) knowing that any person intends to commit treason, does not -

(i) give information of it with all reasonable despatch to a magistrate; or

(ii) use other reasonable endeavours to prevent the commission of the crime,

is guilty of a crime.

Penalty: Subject to Section 19, imprisonment for life.

39. Treasonable crimes.

(1) Any person who forms an intention -

(a) to depose the Queen and Head of The State from the style, honour, and royal name of the Crown of the United Kingdom of Great Britain and Northern Ireland, or of any other of Her Majesty's dominions; or

(b) to levy war against the Queen and Head of The State within any part of Her dominions in order, by force or constraint, to compel the Queen and Head of The State to change Her measures or counsels, or in order to put any force or constraint on, or to intimidate or overawe, any House of Parliament of any of Her Majesty's dominions; or

(c) to instigate a foreigner to make an armed invasion of any of Her Majesty's dominions,

and manifests such intention by any overt act, is guilty of a crime.

Penalty: Subject to Section 19, imprisonment for life.

(2) A person charged with an offence against Subsection (1) is not entitled to be acquitted on the ground that any act proved to have been committed by him constitutes the crime of treason, but a person who has been tried and convicted or acquitted, on a charge of any such crime shall not be afterwards prosecuted for treason in respect of the same facts.

40. Charges of treason or concealment of treason.

(1) A person cannot be tried for treason or for an offence against Section 38 or 39 unless the indictment is presented within two years after the crime is committed.

(2) A person charged with treason or with an offence against Section 38 or 39 shall not be convicted, except -

(a) on his own plea of guilty; or

(b) on the evidence in open court of at least two witnesses to one overt act of the kind of treason alleged; or

(c) on the evidence of one witness to one overt act, and one other witness to another overt act of the same kind of treason.

(3) This section does not apply where the overt act of treason alleged is -

(a) the killing of the Queen and Head of State; or

(b) a direct attempt to endanger the life or injure the person of the Queen and Head of State.

41. Inciting to mutiny.

(1) A person who advisedly attempts -

(a) to seduce any person serving in the Defence Force by sea, land or air from his duty and allegiance; or

(b) to incite any such person to commit an act of mutiny or any traitorous or mutinous act; or

(c) to incite any such persons to make or endeavour to make a mutinous assembly,

is guilty of a crime.

Penalty: Subject to Section 19, imprisonment for life.

(2) A person who has been tried, and convicted or acquitted, on a charge of an offence against Subsection (1) shall not be afterwards prosecuted for any other offence against this Division in respect of the same facts.

See *The State v Albert Ugunnie, Martin Taumu and Matthew David Moroua* [1988-89] PNGLR 101.

42. Assisting escape of prisoners of war.

A person who -

(a) knowingly and advisedly aids an alien enemy of the Queen and Head of The State who is a prisoner of war in Papua New Guinea, whether he -

(i) is confined in a prison or elsewhere; or

(ii) is suffered to be at large on his parole,

to escape from his prison or place of confinement, or, if he is at large on his parole, to escape from Papua New Guinea; or

(b) being a person who owes allegiance to the Queen and Head of State, after any such prisoner has escaped by sea from any part of Her Majesty's dominions, knowingly and advisedly aids him, on the high seas within the territorial waters of Papua New Guinea, in his escape to or towards any place,

is guilty of a crime.

Penalty: Subject to Section 19, imprisonment for life.

43. Overt act.

In the case of an offence against this Division of which the manifestation by an overt act of an intention to effect any purpose is an element -

(a) every act of conspiring with any person to effect that purpose; and

(b) every act done in furtherance of the purpose by any of the persons conspiring,

shall be deemed to be an overt act manifesting the intention.

Division 2 – Sedition

44. Definition of seditious intentions.

Subject to Section 45, an intention -

(a) to bring the Queen and Head of The State into hatred or contempt; or

(b) to excite disaffection against -

(i) the Queen and Head of State, the National Government or the *Constitution* as by law established; or

(ii) the Parliament; or

(iii) the administration of justice; or

(c) to excite the inhabitants of Papua New Guinea to attempt to procure the alteration of any matter in Papua New Guinea as by law established otherwise than by lawful means; or

(d) to raise discontent or disaffection amongst the inhabitants of Papua New Guinea; or

(e) to promote feelings of ill-will and enmity between different classes of the inhabitants of Papua New Guinea,

is a seditious intention.

See s 46 of the *Constitution* on freedom of expression.

See s 54 of the Code.

Political views alone, considered apart from any tendency which they may reveal to become involved in political violence, are not admissible as evidence to establish seditious intention: *R v Cooper* (1959) N219.

By "Government", s 44(b) means the executive branch of the government: *R v Cooper* (1959) N219.

45. Innocent intentions.

It is lawful for any person -

(a) to endeavour in good faith to show that the Queen and Head of The State has been mistaken in any of Her Counsels; or

(b) to point out in good faith errors or defects in -

(i) the government or *Constitution* of Papua New Guinea as by law established; or

(ii) legislation; or

(iii) the administration of justice,

with a view to the reformation of such errors or defects; or

(c) to excite in good faith the inhabitants of Papua New Guinea to attempt to procure by lawful means the alteration of any matter in Papua New Guinea established by law; or

(d) to point out in good faith for the purpose of their removal any matters that are producing or have a tendency to produce feelings of ill-will and enmity between different classes of the inhabitants of Papua New Guinea.

46. Seditious, enterprises, etc.

(1) A seditious enterprise is an enterprise that is undertaken in order to the carrying out of a seditious intention.

(2) Seditious words are words expressive of a seditious intention.

(3) The expression "seditious writing" includes anything intended to be read, and any sign or visible representation, that is expressive of a seditious intention

47. Unlawful oaths to commit capital offences.

A person who -

(a) administers, or is present at and consents to the administering of, any oath or engagement in the nature of an oath, purporting to bind the person who takes it to commit a crime punishable with death; or

(b) takes any such oath or engagement, not being compelled to do so; or

(c) attempts to induce any person to take any such oath or engagement,

is guilty of a crime.

Penalty: Subject to Section 19, imprisonment for life.

As to s 47(c), see s 4 on attempts.

48. Unlawful oaths to commit offences.

A person who -

(a) administers, or is present at and consents to the administering of, any oath or engagement in the nature of an oath, purporting to bind the person who takes it -

(i) to engage in a mutinous or seditious enterprise; or

(ii) to commit an indictable offence not punishable with death; or

(iii) to disturb the public peace; or

(iv) to be of any association, society, or confederacy, formed for the purpose of doing any act referred to in Subparagraph (i), (ii) or (iii); or

(v) to obey the order or commands of any committee or body of men not lawfully constituted, or of any leader or commander or other person not having authority by law for that purpose; or

(vi) not to inform or give evidence against any associate, confederate, or other person, or

(vii) not to reveal or discover -

(A) any unlawful association, society, or confederacy; or

(B) any illegal act done or to be done; or

(C) any illegal oath or engagement that may have been administered or tendered to or taken by himself or any other person, or the import of any such oath or engagement; or

(b) takes any such oath or engagement, not being compelled to do so; or

(c) attempts to induce any person to take any such oath or engagement,

is guilty of a crime.

Penalty: Imprisonment for a term not exceeding seven years.

As to subs (c), see s 4 of the Code on attempts.

49. Compulsion as a defence.

A person who takes any oath or engagement referred to in Section 47 or 48 cannot set up as a defence that he was compelled to do so unless within 14 days after taking it, or if he is prevented by actual force or sickness, within 14 days after the termination of the prevention, he declares -

(a) by information on oath before some member of the National Executive Council or justice of the peace; or

(b) if he is on actual service in the Defence Force by sea, land or air -

(i) by such information; or

(ii) by information to his commanding officer,

the whole of what he knows concerning the matter, including -

(c) the person or persons by whom; and

(d) in whose presence; and

(e) the place where; and

(f) the time when,

the oath or engagement was administered or taken.

See s 31 of the Code regarding compulsion generally.

50. Effect of prosecution.

A person who has been tried, and convicted or acquitted, on a charge of an offence against any of the preceding provisions of this Division shall not be afterwards prosecuted on the same facts for the crime -

(a) of treason; or

(b) of failing, when he knows that a person intends to commit treason, to give information of it with all reasonable despatch to a magistrate or use other reasonable endeavours to prevent the commission of the crime.

See s 200 of the *Constitution*.

51. Raising of unauthorized forces.

(1) A person who -

(a) establishes or organizes; or

(b) assists any person to establish or organize; or

(c) equips or assists any person to equip by any means (including equipping with traditional weapons); or

(d) takes part in or associates with,

a military force, para-military force, police force, body of persons purporting to exercise military, para-military or police powers or functions or any force similar in nature to a military, para-military or police force, except as provided for by law, is guilty of a crime.

Penalty: Imprisonment for a term not exceeding 14 years.

(2) A person who -

(a) plans or prepares for; or

(b) assists in the planning or preparation for,

the raising of a military force, para-military force, police force, body of persons purporting to exercise military, para-military or police powers or functions, or any force similar in nature to a military, para-military or police force, except as provided for by law, is guilty of a crime.

Penalty: Imprisonment for a term not exceeding 14 years.

See ss 199-200 and 203 of the *Constitution*.

In *Koniel Alar and Hosea Biu v The State* [1979] PNGLR 300, the Premier and Deputy Speaker of the Provincial Assembly of East New Britain had established a force known as the "Security", similar in constitution to a police force, and were charged under this section. They pleaded guilty and were sentenced to one year imprisonment with hard labour. On appeal against excessiveness of sentence, the Supreme Court held (Andrew J dissenting) that in view of the seriousness of the offence, a deterrent sentence was necessary in the interests of national unity and security. Deterrence and retribution is more properly applied to people in high public positions as an additional deterrent.

In that case, the appellants had established an illegal police force and had not acted in ignorance of the law. The maximum sentence was 14 years. A custodial sentence of one year was held not to be manifestly excessive.

Wilson J stated:

> "There are offences where the notions of deterrence and retribution must take priority and where sentences of imprisonment may properly be imposed even on men in high public positions to mark the disapproval by the law of the conduct in question and in the hope that other people will be deterred from like behaviour. This offence with its implications for national unity, public safety and the authority of the National Police Force, legitimately falls into this category."

In the same case, Andrew J, dissenting, said:

> "The distinguishing feature of this case is that nowhere on the material before the Court is it shown that the conduct of the appellants was in any way sinister. It was undoubtedly unwise but I cannot see that it was anything but misguided zeal. The purpose was to aid the police force and assist in imposing law and order. It was not clandestine ... taking ... into account ... the appellants' prior good backgrounds and their history of service to the people, I believe that sentences of imprisonment were not warranted."

See ss 199-200 and 203 of the *Constitution*.

On s 52(5), see ss 176-177 of the *Constitution*.

It has been held that s 52(5) is unconstitutional as being in conflict with s 176 and Sch 1.19 of the *Constitution*. In performing his or her constitutional role, including that relating to the prosecution of criminal offences, the Public Prosecutor is not subject to direction or control by any person or authority, subject to two exceptions contained in the *Constitution* itself, namely, s 176(3)(b), which provides that the Head of The State acting with, and in accordance with, the advice of the National Executive Council has power to give directions on any matter that might prejudice the security, defence or international relations of Papua New Guinea; and Sch 1.19, which provides for "regulation" under a constitutional law or an Act of Parliament: *Supreme Court Reference No 1 of 1989; In the matter of the State v Patrick Saul* [1988-89] PNGLR 337 (Kidu CJ, Kapi DCJ, Amet, Los and Barnett JJ).

In *Supreme Court Reference No 1 of 1989; In the matter of the State v Patrick Saul* [1988-89] PNGLR 337 at 341, Kidu CJ, Kapi DCJ, Amet, Los and Barnett JJ stated:

> "Subsection (5) is a very distinct section. The rest of s 52 can stand without it."

See s 44 of the Code, and see s 46 of the *Constitution* on freedom of expression.

The courts have said many times before, and it is important to say it again, that the offence of sedition was not created for the purpose of limiting peoples' political thinking, or their participation in lawful activities designed to improve every aspect of government. One of our most cherished and most valuable civil liberties is freedom of political opinion, and expression of political ideals and ideas. The offence of sedition is concerned with subversive activities against properly constituted authority and with utterances designed to destroy the protection which the community is entitled to enjoy in consequence of the establishment of lawful authority: *R v Cooper* (1959) N219.

55. Defamation of foreign Princes.

A person who, without such justification or excuse as would be sufficient in the case of the defamation of a private person, publishes -

(a) anything intended to be read; or

(b) any sign or visible representation,

tending to expose to hatred or contempt in the estimation of the people of any foreign State any Prince or person exercising sovereign authority over that State is guilty of a misdemeanour.

Penalty: Imprisonment for a term not exceeding two years.

Division 3 – Offences against the Executive and Legislative Power

See generally the *Parliamentary Powers and Privileges Act.*

56. Interference with the Head of The State or Ministers.

(1) Any person who advisedly does any act calculated to interfere with the free exercise -

(a) by the Head of The State of the duties or authority of his office; or

(b) by a member of the National Executive Council of the duties or authority of his office as -

(i) a member of the National Executive Council; or

(ii) a Minister of the Parliament

is guilty of a misdemeanour.

Penalty: Imprisonment for a term not exceeding three years.

(2) ...

[Subs (2) rep Act No 13, 1977 (*Criminal Code (Arrest) Act* 1977), s 3]

57. Interference with the Legislature.

(1) A person who advisedly, by force or fraud, interferes or attempts to interfere with the free exercise -

(a) by the Parliament of its authority; or

(b) by any member of the Parliament of his duties or authority -

(i) as a member; or

(ii) as a member of a Committee of the Parliament,

is guilty of a misdemeanour.

Penalty: Imprisonment for a term not exceeding three years.

(2) ...

[Subs (2) rep Act No 13, 1977 (*Criminal Code (Arrest) Act* 1977), s 4]

58. Disturbing the Legislature.

(1) Any person who advisedly -

(a) disturbs the Parliament while in session; or

(b) commits any disorderly conduct in the immediate view and presence of the Parliament while in session, tending to interrupt its proceedings or to impair the respect due to its authority,

is guilty of a misdemeanour.

Penalty: Imprisonment for a term not exceeding three years.

(2) ...

[Subs (2) rep Act No 13, 1977 (*Criminal Code (Arrest) Act* 1977), s 5]

59. False evidence before Parliament.

(1) A person who in the course of an examination before the Parliament or a Committee of the Parliament, knowingly gives a false answer to any lawful and relevant question put to him in the course of the examination is guilty of a crime.

Penalty: Imprisonment for a term not exceeding seven years.

(2) A person shall not be arrested without warrant for an offence against Subsection (1).

(3) A person shall not be convicted of the offence defined in this section on the uncorroborated testimony of one witness.

60. Witnesses refusing to attend or give evidence before the Parliament or a Committee of the Parliament.

A person who -

(a) being duly summoned to attend as a witness, or to produce any book, document or other thing in his possession, before the Parliament, or a Committee of the Parliament authorized to summon witnesses or to call for the production of that thing, refuses or neglects without lawful excuse -

(i) to attend in accordance with the summons; or

(ii) to produce any thing that he is summoned to produce, and that is relevant and proper to be produced; or

(b) being present before the Parliament, or a Committee of the Parliament authorized to summon witnesses, refuses to answer a lawful and relevant question,

is guilty of a misdemeanour.

Penalty: Imprisonment for a term not exceeding two years.

61. Member of the Parliament receiving bribes.

(1) A member of the Parliament who asks, receives or obtains, or agrees or attempts to receive or obtain, any property or benefit for himself or any other person on any understanding that his vote, opinion, judgement, or action in the Parliament, or any Committee of the Parliament will -

(a) be influenced by it; or

(b) be given in any particular manner or in favour of any particular side of any question or matter,

is guilty of a crime.

Penalty: Imprisonment for a term not exceeding seven years.

(2) A person who commits an offence against Subsection (1) is disqualified from sitting or voting as a member of the Parliament for seven years.

(3) A person shall not be arrested without warrant for an offence against Subsection (1).

See ss 50 and 103 of the *Constitution*.

62. Bribery of member of the Parliament.

(1) A person who -

(a) in order -

(i) to influence a member of the Parliament in his vote, opinion, judgement or action on any question or matter arising in the Parliament or in any Committee of the Parliament; or

(ii) to induce a member to absent himself from the Parliament or from a Committee of the Parliament,

gives, confers or procures, or promises or offers to give or confer, or to procure or attempt to procure, any property or benefit to, on, or for the member, or to, on, or for, any other person, or

(b) attempts, directly or indirectly, by fraud, threats or intimidation of any kind, to influence a member of the Parliament in his vote, opinion, judgement or action on any such question or matter, or to induce him to so absent himself,

is guilty of a crime.

Penalty: Imprisonment for a term not exceeding seven years.

(2) A person shall not be arrested without warrant for an offence against Subsection (1).

(3) Where a person is convicted of an offence against this section, all property that has been tendered or produced in evidence at the trial of the offender, as being the property or part of the property which the offender in the course of the commission of the offence gave, conferred or procured, or promised or offered to give, confer or procure, or to attempt to procure, to, on, or for a member of the Parliament, or to, on, or for any other person, is forfeited to the State, whether the property is the property of the offender or of any other person.

As to s 62(1)(b), see s 4 of the Code.

Division 4 – Unlawful Assemblies: Breaches of the Peace

63. Unlawful assembly, "riot".

(1) Subject to Subsection (3), where three or more persons, with intent to carry out some common purpose -

(a) assemble in such a manner; or

(b) being assembled, conduct themselves in such a manner,

as to cause persons in the neighbourhood to fear on reasonable grounds that they will -

(c) tumultuously disturb the peace; or

(d) by the assembly needlessly and without any reasonable occasion provoke other persons tumultuously to disturb the peace,

they are an unlawful assembly.

(2) It is immaterial that the original assembling was lawful if, being assembled, they conduct themselves with a common purpose in the manner referred to in Subsection (1).

(3) An assembly of three or more persons who assemble for the purpose of protecting the house of any one of them against persons threatening to break and enter the house in order to commit an indictable offence in it is not an unlawful assembly.

(4) When an unlawful assembly has begun to act in so tumultuous a manner as to disturb the peace, the assembly is called a riot, and the persons assembled are said to be riotously assembled.

See s 7 of the *Summary Offences Act* regarding provoking a breach of the peace.

See generally the *Inter-Group Fighting Act*.

Kelly J stated, in *R v Toigen Tiolo* [1969-70] PNGLR 285:

> "When the words 'tumult', 'tumultuous' or 'tumultuously' are applied to an assembly of persons the impression is that the assembly should be of considerable size; that it should be an assembly in which the persons taking part are indulging in agitated movement, an excited emotionally aroused assembly; and generally, though not necessarily, accompanied by noise."

As an illustration of problems of identification of participants in a riot, see *R v Teta Tupi* (1958) N115.

Regarding a motion to quash indictments of riot see *R v Edward Tolikun Kisian* (1970) N580.

To constitute the offence of behaving in a riotous manner, proof is required that the accused disturbed the peace in a disorderly or noisy manner causing considerable commotion: *Eliza v Mandina* [1971-72] PNGLR 422 at 430. This case was heard under the summary offence of riotous behaviour.

See also *Yamore Memera v Mathew Bisang* [1976] PNLGR 419 and *Agiru Aieni v Paul T Tahian* [1978] PNGLR 37.

Sections 63 and 64 are directed at the maintenance of public order and peace. They do not restrict or regulate the rights guaranteed under ss 45, 46, 47 and 52 of the *Constitution*. These guaranteed rights are given on the condition that they will be exercised peacefully. Kidu CJ said, in *The State v John Kosi* (1981) N306, that "[w]hen a meeting or rally or demonstration goes outside the scope of peaceful exercise of rights and freedoms, the *Constitution* ceases to protect."

For an unlawful assembly to become a riot, it is sufficient for persons in the neighbourhood to fear that persons would tumultuously disturb the peace: *R v Korea-Menene* (1968) N479.

In *The State v John Kosi* (1981) N306, where a convoy of buses was stopped by police and, as a result, a crowd gathered, this did not amount to an unlawful assembly in the absence of evidence that the accused incited any of the crowd to do anything or provoked any disturbance of the peace. People have the right to demonstrate peacefully. While the accused and others may have breached traffic laws, this is irrelevant for the purpose of deciding whether there was an unlawful assembly.

64. Punishment of unlawful assembly.

(1) A person who takes part in an unlawful assembly is guilty of a misdemeanour.

Penalty: Imprisonment for a term not exceeding one year.

(2) ...

[Subs (2) rep Act No 13, 1977 (*Criminal Code (Arrest) Act* 1977), s 6]

[S 64 am Act No 10, 1983 (*Criminal Code (Minimum Penalties) (Amendment) Act* 1983), s 1; am Act No 17, 1986 (*Criminal Code (Amendment No 2) Act* 1986), s 3]

This offence is also punishable summarily. See Sch 2.

65. Punishment of riot.

(1) A person who takes part in a riot is guilty of a misdemeanour.

Penalty: Imprisonment for a term not exceeding three years.

(2) ....

[Subs (2) rep Act No 13, 1977 (*Criminal Code (Arrest) Act* 1977), s 7]

[S 65 am Act No 10, 1983 (*Criminal Code (Minimum Penalties) (Amendment) Act* 1983), s 2; am Act No 17, 1986 (*Criminal Code (Amendment No 2) Act* 1986), s 3]

See ss 259-263 of the Code on suppression of riot.

66. Rioters remaining after command ordering them to disperse.

(1) Whenever any persons, to the number of five or more, are riotously assembled together, it is the duty of a commissioned officer of the Police Force to go amongst them, or as near as he can safely come to them, and to give, or cause to be given in his presence, in a loud voice the following command -

> "All persons here assembled are by law commanded to disperse and go peacefully about their lawful business, or they will be liable to be imprisoned with hard labour for a maximum of five years."

(2) A person who wilfully and knowingly, and by force, opposes, obstructs or hurts any person who goes to give, or begins to give a command under Subsection (1), and by so doing prevents the command from being given, is guilty of a crime.

Penalty: Imprisonment for a term not exceeding five years.

(3) Any persons who, being so assembled, continue together to the number of five or more, and do not disperse themselves as soon as practicable after the giving of the command referred to in Subsection (1) are guilty of a crime.

Penalty: Imprisonment for a term not exceeding five years.

(4) When the giving of the command referred to in Subsection (1) is prevented, any persons who, being so assembled, and to whom the command would or ought to have been given if the giving of the command had not been prevented, and who, knowing of the prevention, continue together to the number of five or more, and do not disperse themselves as soon as practicable after the time of the prevention, are guilty of a crime.

Penalty: Imprisonment for a term not exceeding five years.

(5) A prosecution for an offence against this section shall be begun within one year after it is committed.

(6) It is a defence to a charge of an offence against Subsection (3) if the defendant proves that he did not know that the command had been given or did not understand what was said.

[S 66 am Act No 10, 1983 (*Criminal Code (Minimum Penalties) (Amendment) Act* 1983), s 3; penalty provisions subst Act No 17, 1986 (*Criminal Code (Amendment No 2) Act* 1986), ss 4(a), (b) and (c)]

Frost J held that the section does not apply where the unlawful group had a genuine but disputed claim to land: *R v Lupalupa-Sisarowe* [1967-68] PNGLR 455.

67. Rioters demolishing buildings, etc.

(1) Any persons who, being riotously assembled together, unlawfully pull down or destroy, or begin to pull down or destroy -

(a) a building; or

(b) any machinery, whether fixed or moveable; or

(c) any structure used in farming land, in carrying on any trade or manufacture, or in conducting the business of a mine, or

(d) any bridge, wagon-way or trunk for conveying materials from a mine,

are each guilty of a crime.

Penalty: Subject to Section 19, imprisonment for life.

(2) Any persons who, being riotously assembled together, unlawfully damage any of the things referred to in Subsection (1), are each guilty of a crime.

Penalty: Imprisonment for a term not exceeding seven years.

[S 67 am Act No 10, 1983 (*Criminal Code (Minimum Penalties) (Amendment) Act* 1983), s 4; am Act No 17, 1986 (*Criminal Code (Amendment No 2) Act* 1986), ss 5(a) and (b)]

68. Smuggling or rescuing goods under arms.

Any persons who assemble together, to the number of three or more, armed with firearms or other dangerous or offensive weapons, in order to effect or aid in -

(a) the unlawful shipping, unshipping, loading, moving or carrying away of any goods -

(i) the importation of which is prohibited; or

(ii) that are liable to duties of customs that have not paid or secured; or

(b) the rescuing or taking of any such goods from -

(i) any person authorized to seize them; or

(ii) any person employed by such a person or assisting him; or

(iii) any place where such a person has put them; or

(c) the rescuing of a person who has been arrested on a charge of any crime relating to the Customs; or

(d) the prevention of the arrest of a person guilty of any such crime, or of any person aiding in effecting any of the purposes referred to in this section,

are each guilty of a crime.

Penalty: Imprisonment for a term not exceeding seven years.

69. Smuggling under arms or in disguise.

Any persons who are found assembled together, to the number of six or more -

(a) having with them any goods liable to forfeiture under any law relating to the Customs; and

(b) carrying firearms or other dangerous or offensive weapons, or disguised,

are each guilty of a crime.

Penalty: Imprisonment for a term not exceeding seven years.

70. Going armed so as to cause fear.

(1) A person who goes armed in public without lawful occasion in such a manner as to cause terror to any person is guilty of a misdemeanour.

Penalty: Imprisonment for a term not exceeding two years.

(2) ...

[Subs (2) rep Act No 13, 1977 (*Criminal Code (Arrest) Act* 1977), s 8]

[S 70 am Act No 10, 1983 (*Criminal Code (Minimum Penalties) (Amendment) Act* 1983), s 5; am Act No 17, 1986 (*Criminal Code (Amendment No 2) Act* 1986), s 6]

See s 12 of the *Summary Offences Act* (Ch 2 of this book) for the summary offence of carrying weapons.

71. Forcible entry.

(1) A person who, in a manner likely to cause a breach of the peace or reasonable apprehension of a breach of the peace, enters on land that is in the actual and peaceable possession of another person is guilty of a misdemeanour.

Penalty: Imprisonment for a term not exceeding one year.

(2) It is immaterial whether the person entering is entitled to enter on the land or not.

[S 71 am Act No 10, 1983 (*Criminal Code (Minimum Penalties) (Amendment) Act* 1983), s 6; am Act No 17, 1986 (*Criminal Code (Amendment No 2) Act* 1986), s 7]

72. Forcible detainer.

A person who, being in actual possession of land without colour of right, holds possession of it, in a manner likely to cause a breach of the peace or reasonable apprehension of a breach of the peace, against a person entitled by law to the possession of the land is guilty of a misdemeanour.

Penalty: Imprisonment for a term not exceeding one year.

[S 72 am Act No 10, 1983 (*Criminal Code (Minimum Penalties) (Amendment) Act* 1983), s 7; am Act No 17, 1986 (*Criminal Code (Amendment No 2) Act* 1986), s 8]

73. Affray.

A person who takes part in a fight -

(a) in a public highway; or

(b) of such a nature as to alarm the public in any other place to which the public have access,

is guilty of a misdemeanour.

Penalty: Imprisonment for a term not exceeding one year.

[S 73 am Act No 10, 1983 (*Criminal Code (Minimum Penalties) (Amendment) Act* 1983), s 8; am Act No 17, 1986 (*Criminal Code (Amendment No 2) Act* 1986), s 9]

See s 243 of the Code on assault, and s 10 of the *Summary Offences Act* (Ch 2 of this book) regarding fighting.

74. Challenge to fight a duel.

A person who -

(a) challenges another; or

(b) attempts to provoke another; or

(c) attempts to provoke any person to challenge another,

to fight a duel, is guilty of a misdemeanour.

Penalty: Imprisonment for a term not exceeding three years.

[S 74 am Act No 10, 1983 (*Criminal Code (Minimum Penalties) (Amendment) Act* 1983), s 9; am Act No 17, 1986 (*Criminal Code (Amendment No 2) Act* 1986), s 10]

75. Prize fight.

A person who fights in a prize fight, or subscribes to or promotes a prize fight, is guilty of a misdemeanour.

Penalty: Imprisonment for a term not exceeding one year.

76. Threatening violence.

(1) A person who -

(a) with intent to intimidate or annoy any person – threatens to break or injure a dwelling-house; or

(b) with intent to alarm any person in a dwelling-house – discharges loaded firearms or commits any other breach of the peace,

is guilty of a misdemeanour.

[Subs (1) penalty provision rep Act No 17, 1986 (*Criminal Code (Amendment No 2) Act* 1986), s 11(a)]

(2) If an offence against Subsection (1) is committed in the night, the offence is a crime, and the offender shall be imprisoned for a term not exceeding one year.

[Subs (2) am Act No 17, 1986 (*Criminal Code (Amendment No 2) Act* 1986), s 11(b)]

[S 76 am Act No 10, 1983 (*Criminal Code (Minimum Penalties) (Amendment) Act* 1983), s 10]

See s 28(2) of the *Summary Offences Act* regarding the discharging of a firearm with intent to injure, annoy or frighten any person, and s 26 of that Act regarding unlawfully disturbing house-holders.

77. Assembling for the purpose of smuggling.

Any persons who assemble together, to the number of three or more, for the purpose of unshipping, carrying or concealing any goods subject to duties of Customs and liable to forfeiture under any law relating to the Customs are each guilty of an offence.

Penalty: A fine not exceeding K200.00, or to imprisonment for a term not exceeding six months.

78. Unlawful processions.

(1) Any persons who assemble together, to the number of three or more -

(a) bearing or wearing or having amongst them any firearms or other offensive weapons; or

(b) publicly exhibiting any banner, emblem, flag, or symbol, the displaying of which is calculated to promote animosity between people of different religious faiths; or

(c) being accompanied by any music of a like nature or tendency,

and, being so assembled, join in any parade or procession for the purpose of -

(d) celebrating or commemorating any festival, anniversary or political event relating to or connected with any religious or political distinction or difference between any classes of people; or

(e) demonstrating any such religious or political distinction or difference,

are each guilty of an offence.

Penalty: Subject to Subsection (2), imprisonment for a term not exceeding one month.

(2) If the offender is himself bearing or wearing firearms or any other offensive weapon, he is guilty of an offence.

Penalty: Imprisonment for a term not exceeding six months.

(3) When three or more persons are assembled together in a manner referred to in Subsection (1), it is the duty of a commissioned officer of the Police Force to give, or cause to be given in his presence, in a loud voice, to the persons assembled, the following command-

> "All persons here assembled are by law commanded to disperse and go peacefully about their lawful business, or they will be liable to be imprisoned for a maximum of three months."

(4) Any persons who, being so assembled, continue together to the number of three or more, and do not disperse themselves as soon as practicable after the giving of the command referred to in Subsection (3) are each guilty of an offence.

Penalty: Imprisonment for a term exceeding three months.

(5) It is a defence to a charge of an offence against Subsection (4) if the defendant proves that he did not know that the command had been given or did not understand what was said.

[S 78 am Act No 10, 1983 (*Criminal Code (Minimum Penalties) (Amendment) Act* 1983), s 11; penalty provisions subst Act No 17, 1986 (*Criminal Code (Amendment No 2) Act* 1986), ss 12(a), (b) and (c)]

See s 62 of the Code for the definition of unlawful assembly.

Division 5 – Offences Against Political Liberty

79. Interfering with political liberty.

(1) A person who, by violence, threats or intimidation of any kind, hinders or interferes with the free exercise of any political right by another person is guilty of a misdemeanour.

Penalty: Subject to Subsection (2), imprisonment for a term not exceeding two years.

(2) If a person who commits an offence against Subsection (1) is a public officer, and commits the offence in abuse of his authority as such an officer, he is liable to imprisonment for a term not exceeding three years.

Division 6 – Piracy

80. Interpretation of Division 6.

(1) In this Division -

"piracy" means the act of a pirate;

"pirate" includes any person who -

(a) on the high seas commits, otherwise than as an act of war and under the authority of some foreign Prince or State, any act with respect to a ship, or any goods or merchandise belonging to a ship or laden on a ship, that, if the act were committed on land, would constitute robbery as defined in Section 384; and

(b) having on the high seas obtained possession of a ship by means of any such act, retains possession of the ship; and

(c) is declared by any law to be a pirate.

(2) A person who -

(a) at any place within the jurisdiction of the National Court commits -

(i) under colour of a commission from a foreign State or Prince, whether or not the State or Prince is at war with the Queen and Head of State; or

(ii) under pretence of authority from any person,

any act of hostility, or any act that if it were committed on land, would be robbery as defined in Section 384, against another person; or

(b) during a war, adheres to or gives aid to the enemies of Papua New Guinea at any place within the jurisdiction of the National Court; or

(c) forcibly enters a ship at any place within the jurisdiction of the National Court, and throws overboard or destroys any part of the goods or merchandise belonging to the ship or laden on it; or

(d) being on board a ship at any place within the jurisdiction of the National Court -

(i) turns pirate, enemy or rebel, and piratically runs away with the ship, or any boat, ordnance, ammunition, or goods belonging to it or laden on it; or

(ii) voluntarily yields up the ship or any thing referred to in Subparagraph (i) to a pirate; or

(iii) brings a seducing message from a pirate, enemy or rebel; or

(iv) consults or conspires with, or attempts to corrupt, any master or officer of a ship, or any seaman, with intent that he should run way with or yield up any ship, goods or merchandise, turn pirate or go over to pirates; or

(v) lays violent hands on the master of the ship, with intent to hinder him from fighting in defence of the ship and goods committed to his trust; or

(vi) confines the master of the ship; or

(vii) makes, or endeavours to make, a revolt in the ship; or

(e) being on board a ship, knowingly -

(i) trades with a pirate; or

(ii) furnishes a pirate with ammunition, provisions or stores; or

(iii) fits out a ship or vessel with a design to trade with or supply, or to correspond with, a pirate; or

(iv) conspires or corresponds with a pirate,

is a pirate.

81. Punishment of piracy.

(1) A person who, within the territorial jurisdiction of Papua New Guinea, commits piracy is guilty of a crime.

Penalty: Subject to Subsection (2) and to Section 19, imprisonment for life.

(2) If piracy is committed with respect to a ship, and if at or immediately before or immediately after the time of committing the crime the offender -

(a) assaults any person on board of or belonging to the ship with intent to kill him or to kill any other person; or

(b) wounds any such person; or

(c) unlawfully does any act by which the life of any such person is endangered,

the offender is liable to the punishment of death.

82. Attempted piracy with personal violence.

A person who, within the territorial jurisdiction of Papua New Guinea, with intent to commit the crime of piracy with respect to a ship -

(a) assaults any person on board, or belonging to, the ship, with intent to kill him or to kill any other person; or

(b) wounds any such person; or

(c) unlawfully does any act by which the life of any such person is endangered,

is guilty of a crime.

Penalty: Death.

83. Aiding pirates.

A person who -

(a) brings a seducing message from a pirate; or

(b) consults or conspires with, or attempts to corrupt, any master or officer of a ship or any seaman, with intent that he should run away with or yield up any ship, goods, or merchandise, or turn pirate, or go over to pirates,

is guilty of a crime.

Penalty: Subject to Section 19, imprisonment for life.

Part III – Offences Against the Administration of Law and Justice and Against Public Authority

Division 1A – Interpretation

83A. Interpretation.

In this Part, unless the contrary intention appears -

"person employed in the Public Service" includes -

(a) a member of any of the State Services established under or by authority of Section 188 (Establishment of the State Services) of the *Constitution*; and

(b) a constitutional office-holder as defined in Section 221 (Definitions) of the *Constitution*; and

(c) a member of or person employed by a constitutional institution, being any office or institution established or provided for by the *Constitution* including the Head of State, a Minister or the National Executive Council; and

(d) a member of the National Parliament or of a provincial assembly; and

(e) a person employed under the *Official Personal Staff Act* (Chapter 383) of the *Parliamentary Members' Personal Staff Act* 1988; and

(f) a person employed by a provincial government; and

(g) a member, officer or employee of a body or corporation established by statute;

[S 83A insrt Act No 2, 1989 (*Criminal Code (Amendment) Act* 1989), s 2]

Division 1 – Disclosing Official Secrets

84. Disclosure of secrets relating to defences by public officers.

(1) A person employed in the Public Service who communicates to any person otherwise than in the course of his official duty any plans documents or other information relating to any battery, field work or fortification in Papua New Guinea, or relating to any other defence of Papua New Guinea, is guilty of misdemeanour.

(2) If an offence against Subsection (1) is committed advisedly the offender is liable to imprisonment for a term not exceeding three years.

(3) If an offence against Subsection (1) is committed by negligence, the offender is liable to a fine not exceeding K400.00 or imprisonment for one year.

85. Obtaining disclosure of secrets relating to defences.

A person who -

(a) procures a person employed in the Public Service to make a communication referred to in Section 84; or

(b) without lawful authority obtains information as to any matter referred to in that section,

is guilty of a misdemeanour.

Penalty: Imprisonment for a term not exceeding three years.

86. Disclosure of other official secrets.

A person employed in the Public Service who publishes or communicates, otherwise than to some person to whom he is bound to publish or communicate it -

(a) any fact that comes to his knowledge by virtue of his office; or

(b) any document which comes to his possession by virtue of his office,

that it is his duty to keep secret, is guilty of a misdemeanour.

Penalty: Imprisonment for a term not exceeding two years.

Division 2 – Corruption and Abuse of Office

87. Official corruption.

(1) A person who -

(a) being -

(i) employed in the Public Service, or the holder of any public office; and

(ii) charged with the performance of any duty by virtue of employment or office, (not being a duty touching the administration of justice),

corruptly asks, receives or obtains, or agrees or attempts to receive or obtain, any property or benefit for himself or any other person on account of any thing done or omitted to be done, or to be done or omitted to be done by him in the discharge of the duties of his office; or

(b) corruptly gives, confers or procures, or promises or offers to give or confer, or to procure or attempt to procure, to, on or for any person, any property or benefit on account of any such act or omission on the part of a person in the Public Service or holding a public office,

is guilty of a crime.

Penalty: Imprisonment for a term not exceeding seven years, and a fine at the discretion of the court.

(2) A person shall not be arrested without warrant for an offence against Subsection (1).

See s 37(2) of the *Constitution*.

Where a public servant is charged with the offence of corruptly asking, receiving or obtaining any property or benefit of any kind for himself on account of anything done or to be done by him in the discharge of the duties of this office, proof is required of the duty imposed by the holding of the particular office and the corrupt use of the particular office held for gain: *The State v Kirivi* [1987] PNGLR 489; *R v*

David [1931] QWN 2, followed; see also *The State v Waesa Mollo* [1988] PNGLR 49.

In *The State v Waesa Mollo* [1988] PNGLR 49 a public servant, being a member of the Defence Force, was charged with corruptly receiving moneys in connection with his duties as chairman of the Papua New Guinea Defence Force Savings and Loan Society, a body established under the *Savings and Loan Societies Act* (Ch 141). It was held that the charge had not been made out because his duties as chairman were not those of a public servant, but rather those of an official of a private corporation, and the receipt of moneys was not in connection with the corrupt use of any office held in the public service.

In *The State v Kiap Bonga* [1988-1989] PNGLR 360, an accused who was arrested for a minor traffic offence offered a five kina bribe to the arresting officer to influence him not to lay a charge, and the accused subsequently challenged the admissibility of his statement whilst in custody on the ground that the arrest on the corruption charge was without a warrant as required by s 87(2). It was held that the statement was admissible into evidence, as s 87(2) had been repealed by the subsequent enactment of the *Arrest Act* Ch No 339 and, as such, no warrant was required and the arrest was therefore lawful.

88. Extortion by public officers.

A person employed in the Public Service who takes or accepts from any person, for the performance of his duty as an officer of the Public Service any reward beyond his proper pay and emoluments, or any promise of such a reward, is guilty of a misdemeanour.

Penalty: Imprisonment for a term not exceeding three years.

Where a public servant is charged with the offence under s 88 of taking or accepting from any person, for the performance of his or her duty as an officer, any reward beyond the officer's proper pay and emoluments, proof is required that the public servant has the power to do something or to perform a public duty that he or she is entrusted with as a public servant, and is bribed by someone to perform that duty or not to perform it. Obtaining or attempting to obtain a reward beyond one's pay or emoluments will not satisfy the charge: *The State v Kirivi* [1987] PNGLR 489 (Kidu CJ).

89. Public officers interested in contracts.

A person employed in the Public Service who knowingly acquires or holds, directly or indirectly, otherwise than as a member of a registered joint stock company consisting of more than 20 persons, a private interest in any contract or agreement that is made on account of the Public Service with respect to any matter concerning the Department of the Public Service in which he is employed, is guilty of a misdemeanour.

Penalty: Imprisonment for three years, and a fine at the discretion of the court.

See s 37(2) of the *Constitution*.

90. Officers charged with administration of property of a special character or with special duties.

A person, employed in the Public Service, who -

(a) is charged by virtue of his employment with any judicial or administrative duties respecting -

(i) any property of a special character; or

(ii) the carrying on of any manufacture, trade or business of a special character; and

(b) has acquired or holds, directly or indirectly, a private interest in any such property, manufacture, trade, or business; and

(c) discharges any such duties with respect to -

(i) the property, manufacture, trade or business in which he has the interest; or

(ii) the conduct of any person in relation to it,

is guilty of a misdemeanour.

Penalty: Imprisonment for one year, and a fine at the discretion of the court.

See s 37(2) of the *Constitution*.

91. False claims by officials.

A person employed in the Public Service in such a capacity as to require him or to enable him to furnish returns or statements touching -

(a) any remuneration payable or claimed to be payable to himself or to any other person; or

(b) any other matter required by law to be certified for the purpose of any payments of money or delivery of goods to be made to any person,

who makes a return or statement touching any such matter that is, to his knowledge, false in any material particular, is guilty of a misdemeanour.

Penalty: Imprisonment for a term not exceeding three years.

See *Arthur Gilbert Smedley v The State* [1980] PNGLR 379, for an appeal from a conviction under this section.

See also s 418 of the Code regarding fraudulent false accounting.

92. Abuse of office.

(1) A person employed in the Public Service who, in abuse of the authority of his office does, or directs to be done, any arbitrary act prejudicial to the rights of another is guilty of a misdemeanour.

Penalty: Subject to Subsection (2), imprisonment for a term not exceeding two years.

(2) If an act prohibited by Subsection (1) is done, or directed to be done, as the case may be, for purposes of gain, the offender is liable to imprisonment for a term not exceeding three years.

93. Corruption of valuator.

A person who, being duly appointed under any law to be a valuator for determining the compensation to be paid to any person for land compulsorily taken from him under any law, or for injury done to any land under any law -

(a) acts as valuator while he has, to his knowledge, an interest in the land in question; or

(b) executes unfaithfully, dishonestly, or with partiality, the duty of making a valuation of the land or of the extent of the injury,

is guilty of a misdemeanour.

Penalty: Imprisonment for a term not exceeding three years.

94. False certificates by public officers.

A person who, being authorized or required by law to give any certificate touching any matter by virtue of which the rights of any person may be prejudicially affected, gives a certificate that is, to his knowledge, false in any material particular is guilty of a misdemeanour.

Penalty: Imprisonment for a term not exceeding three years.

95. Administering extra-judicial oaths.

(1) A person who administers an oath, or takes a solemn declaration, an affirmation or an affidavit, concerning any matter with respect to which he has not by law authority to do so is guilty of a misdemeanour.

Penalty: Imprisonment for a term not exceeding one year.

(2) Subsection (1) does not apply to an oath, declaration, affirmation, or affidavit, administered or taken -

(a) before a justice in any matter relating to -

(i) the preservation of the peace or the punishment of offences; or

(ii) inquiries respecting sudden death; or

(b) in proceedings before the Parliament or a Committee of the Parliament; or

(c) for some purpose that is lawful under the laws of another country; or

(d) for the purpose of giving validity to an instrument that is intended to be used in another country.

96. False assumption of authority.

A person who -

(a) not being a magistrate or justice assumes to act as a magistrate or justice, as the case may be; or

(b) without authority assumes to act as a person having authority by law to administer an oath or take a solemn declaration, an affirmation or an affidavit, or to do any other act of a public nature that can only be done by persons authorized by law to do so; or

(c) represents himself to be a person authorized by law to sign a document testifying -

(i) to the contents of any register or record kept by lawful authority; or

(ii) testifying to any fact or event,

and signs such a document as being so authorized when he is not, and knows that he is not, so authorized,

is guilty of misdemeanour.

Penalty: Imprisonment for a term not exceeding three years.

In *The State v Akain Tomalom* [1976] PNGLR 512, the accused issued a "summons" for a person to appear before the Warkurai Ni Gunan (an unofficial court based on custom, in the Gazelle Peninsula), and the summons made reference to the District Court and the *District Courts Act*, and "commanded" the summoned person to appear and answer a complaint "dealt with according to Law". Such a summons was deemed to be intended to mislead recipients into believing the issuer had magisterial powers according to the laws of Papua New Guinea, in violation of this section. Further, s 17 of the *Gazelle Peninsula Affairs (Temporary Provisions) Act* 1973 does not give the Warkurai Ni Gunan any powers to summons, charge, adjudicate or enforce decisions against non-Mataungans, even assuming that it gives the Warkurai Ni Gunan arbitral powers by consent among its own members.

See also *R v Bogina* (1961) N216, for another case involving establishment of false courts.

97. Personating public officers.

(1) A person who -

(a) personates any person employed in the Public Service on an occasion when the latter is required to do any act or attend in any place by virtue of his employment; or

(b) falsely represents himself to be a person employed in the Public Service, and assumes to do any act or to attend in any place for the purpose of doing any act by virtue of that employment,

is guilty of a misdemeanour.

Penalty: Imprisonment for a term not exceeding three years.

(2) ...

[Subs (2) rep Act No 13, 1977 (*Criminal Code (Arrest) Act* 1977), s 9]

97A. Corruptly procuring withdrawal of tenders.

A person who -

(a) with intent to obtain a contract from, or provide a service to, a public body, offers a gratification to another person, to induce that person to refrain from making a tender or withdraw or alter a tender; or

(b) solicits or accepts a gratification as an inducement or reward for refraining from making a tender or withdrawing or altering a tender made for such contract,

is guilty of an offence.

Penalty: A fine at the discretion of the Court or imprisonment for a term not exceeding seven years, or both.

[S 97A insrt Act No 2, 1989 (*Criminal Code Amendment Act* 1989), s 3]

97B. Bribery of member of Public Service.

(1) A person who offers to a person employed in the Public Service, or being a person employed in the Public Service, solicits or accepts a gratification as an inducement or reward for -

(a) the person employed in the Public Service voting or abstaining from voting at any meeting in favour of or against any measure; or

(b) the person employed in the Public Service performing or abstaining from performing or aiding in procuring or hindering the performance of an official act; or

(c) the person employed in the Public Service aiding in procuring or preventing the passing of any vote or granting of any contract in favour of any person; or

(d) the person employed in the Public Service showing or refraining from showing any favour of disfavour in his capacity as a person employed in the Public Service,

is guilty of an offence.

Penalty: A fine at the discretion of the Court or imprisonment for a term not exceeding seven years, or both.

(2) An offence under Subsection (1) is committed notwithstanding that the person employed in the Public Service had no right or opportunity to show or refrain from showing favour or that the inducement was not in relation to the affairs of the public body.

[S 97B insrt Act No 2, 1989 (*Criminal Code Amendment Act* 1989), s 4]

97C. Duty of person offered gratification.

(1) A person who is corruptly offered or given a gratification shall report the offer or gift at the earliest opportunity to a commissioned police officer.

(2) A person who, without reasonable excuse, fails to comply with the provisions of Subsection (1) is guilty of an offence.

Penalty: A fine not exceeding K1,000.00 or imprisonment for a term not exceeding 12 months, or both.

[S 97C insrt Act No 2, 1989 (*Criminal Code Amendment Act* 1989), s 5]

97D. Evidentiary provisions relating to this Division.

(1) In proceedings for an offence under this Division evidence is not admissible to show that a gratification is customary in any trade, vocation or calling.

(2) A gratification received or solicited by -

(a) a relative of; or

(b) a partner, clerk or employee of,

an agent from a person having business relations with the principal of such agent, is deemed to have been received or solicited by the agent, unless the agent proves that the gratification was received without his consent or knowledge.

(3) A gratification given or offered to -

(a) a relative of; or

(b) a partner, clerk or employee of,

an agent with the consent or knowledge of the agent, or given or offered at the request of the agent to a person having business relations with the principal of the agent, is deemed to have been offered or given to the agent.

(4) In proceedings under this Division, where a person accused -

(a) is in possession of property or pecuniary resources disproportionate to his known sources of income, for which he cannot satisfactorily account; or

(b) at or about the time of the alleged offence obtained an accretion to his property or pecuniary resources for which he cannot satisfactorily account,

that fact may be -

(c) proved and taken into account by the court; and

(d) considered as corroboration of the evidence of a witness that the accused person accepted or obtained gratification as an inducement or reward.

(5) Where the resources or property referred to in Subsection (4)(a) or an accretion thereto referred to in Section (4)(b) are held by a person whose relationship to the accused gives reasonable cause for believing that he is holding the resources, property or accretion thereto in trust or as a gift from the accused, then the accused shall be deemed to be in possession of those resources or that property or that accretion thereto.

(6) Where, in any proceedings under this Act, it is proved that a gratification has been paid to or received by a person employed in the Public Service, that gratification is deemed to have been paid and received corruptly, as an inducement or reward, unless the contrary is proved.

[S 97D insrt Act No 2, 1989 (*Criminal Code Amendment Act* 1989), s 6]

Division 2A – Secret Commissions

[Div 2A insrt Act No 2, 1989 (*Criminal Code Amendment Act* 1989), s 7]

97E. Interpretation.

In this Division, unless the contrary intention appears -

"advice given", or words to the like effect includes every report, certificate, statement and suggestion intended to influence the person to whom the same is made or given and every influence deliberately or expressly exercised by one person over another;

"agent" includes a person (whether natural or corporate) acting or having been acting, or desirous or intending to act, for or on behalf of a person (whether natural or corporate) whether as agent, partner, co-owner, clerk, servant, employee, banker, broker, auctioneer, architect, clerk of works, charterer, master mariner, purser or any crew of a vessel, engineer, lawyer, surveyor, buyer, salesman, foreman, trustee, official assignee, executor, administrator, liquidator, trustee in bankruptcy or of a deed of assignment, receiver, director, manager, or other officer or member of the committee or governing body of a corporation, club, partnership or association, or in any other capacity, either alone or jointly with any other person (whether natural or corporate) and whether in his own name or in the name of his principal or otherwise, a Minister and a person employed in the Public Service;

"contract" includes a contract of sale or employment or any other contract whatsoever, including an order for any commodity;

"in relation to the affairs or business of his principal" implies the additional words "whether within the scope of his authority or course of his employment as agent or not;

"person having business relations with the principal" includes -

(a) the State, a Minister, a corporation representing the State, a local authority, public body or any Board or authority established under an Act of Parliament; and

(b) a person (whether natural or corporate), whether as principal or agent, carrying on or having carried on or desirous of carrying on or intending to carry on any negotiation or business with a principal, or engaged or interested or having been engaged or interested in the performance of a contract with or in the execution of any work for or business in the supply of any goods or chattels to a principal; and

(c) an agent or employee of any person or body referred to in Paragraph (a);

"principal" includes a person (whether natural or corporate) for or on behalf of whom the agent acts, has acted, or is desirous or intending to act, and includes the State, a Minister or corporation representing the State, or any local authority or other public body constituted by or under Act for or on behalf of whom the agent acts, has acted or is desirous or intending to act;

"solicit a valuable consideration" and "valuable consideration solicited" and words to the like effect shall be construed with the following directions, namely, that an agent who diverts, obstructs, gives untruthful reports or interferes with the proper course of business or manufacture or impedes or obstructs, or fails to use due diligence in the prosecution of any negotiation or business with the intent to obtain the gift of a valuable consideration from any other person interested in that negotiation or business, or with intent to injure any such person, is deemed to have solicited a valuable consideration from a person having business relations with the principal of such agent;

"trustee" includes the public curator, an executor, administrator, liquidator, official assignee, trustee in bankruptcy, receiver, committee of the estate of an insane person, person having power to appoint a trustee, person entitled to obtain probate of the will or letters of administration to the estate of a deceased person, or any other person occupying a fiduciary position;

"valuable consideration" includes any real or personal property, money, loan, office, place, employment, agreement to give employment, benefit or advantage whatsoever, commission or rebate, payment in excess of the actual value of the goods or service, deduction or percentage, bonus or discount, forbearance to demand money or money's worth or valuable thing, detriment, loss or responsibility given, suffered or taken, the refraining from carrying out or doing something which lawfully should be carried out or done and the acceptance of any of the foregoing which shall be deemed the receipt of valuable consideration;

97F. Prohibition of indirect acts.

An act or thing prohibited by this Division is prohibited whether done directly or indirectly by the person mentioned or by or through any other person.

97G. Receipt or solicitation of secret commission by an agent, etc.

(1) An agent who corruptly receives or solicits from any person for himself or for another person a valuable consideration -

(a) as an inducement or reward for or otherwise on account of doing or forbearing to do, or having done or forborne to do, any act in relation to the affairs or business of the principal of the agent; or

(b) the receipt or any expectation of which would in any way tend to influence him to show, or to forbear to show, favour or disfavour to a person in relation to the affairs or business of the principal of the agent,

is guilty of an offence.

(2) A person who corruptly gives or offers to an agent a valuable consideration -

(a) as an inducement or reward for or otherwise on account of the agent doing or forbearing to do, or having done or forborne to do, any act in relation to the affairs or business of the principal of the agent; or

(b) the receipt or any expectation of which would in any way tend to influence the agent to show, or to forbear to show, favour or disfavour to a person in relation to the affairs or business of the principal of the agent,

is guilty of an offence.

97H. Secret gifts.

(1) A valuable consideration received or solicited by -

(a) a parent, spouse or child; or

(b) a partner, clerk or employee,

of an agent, from a person having business relations with the principal of such agent, is deemed to have been received or solicited by the agent, unless it is proved that the valuable consideration was so received or solicited without the consent, knowledge or privity of the agent.

(2) A valuable consideration -

(a) given or offered to -

(i) a parent, spouse or child; or

(ii) a partner, clerk or employee,

of an agent and so given or offered without the consent, knowledge or privity of the agent; or

(b) given or offered, at the request of the agent, to a person by a person having business relations with the principal of such agent,

is deemed to have been given or offered to the agent.

97I. False or misleading receipt or account.

A person who, with intent to deceive or defraud the principal, gives to an agent, or an agent who receives or uses or gives to the principal, a receipt, invoice, account or document in respect of which, or in relation to a dealing, transaction or matter in which, the principal is interested and which -

(a) contains a statement which is false or erroneous or defective in any important particular, or contains an overcharge or is in any way likely to mislead the principal; or

(b) omits to state explicitly and fully the fact of a commission, percentage, bonus, discount, rebate, repayment, gratuity or deduction having been made, given, or allowed, or agreed to be made, given or allowed,

is guilty of an offence.

97J. Secret commission for advice given, etc.

(1) Where advice is given by one person to another, and such advice is in any way intended or likely to induce or influence the person advised -

(a) to enter into a contract with a third person; or

(b) to -

(i) appoint, or join with another in the appointment; or

(ii) vote for, or aid in obtaining the election or appointment; or

(iii) authorize, or join with another in authorizing the appointment,

of a third person as trustee, director, manager or official,

and a valuable consideration is, without the assent of the person advised, given by such third person to the person giving the advice, the gift or receipt of the valuable consideration is an offence.

(2) Subsection (1) does not apply where -

(a) the person giving the advice was, to the knowledge of the person advised, the agent of such third person; or

(b) the valuable consideration was not given in respect of such advice.

(3) An offer or solicitation of a valuable consideration in respect of advice given, or to be given, by one person to another with a view to induce or influence the person advised -

(a) to enter into a contract with the person offering or solicited; or

(b) to -

(i) appoint, or join with another in appointing; or

(ii) vote for, or aid in obtaining the election or appointment; or

(iii) authorize, or join with another in authorizing the appointment,

of the person offering or solicited as trustee, director, manager of official,

and with the intent that the gift or receipt of such valuable consideration is not to be made known to the person advised, is an offence.

(4) Subsection (3) does not apply where the person first-mentioned in that subsection is the agent of the person offering or solicited.

97K. Secret commission to trustee in return for substituted appointment.

A -

(a) person who offers or gives a valuable consideration to a trustee; or

(b) trustee who receives or solicits a valuable consideration for himself or for another person,

without the consent of the persons beneficially entitled to the estate or of a Judge, as an inducement or reward for -

(c) appointing, or having appointed; or

(d) joining, or having joined with another in appointing; or

(e) authorizing, or having authorized or joining with another in authorizing,

a person to be appointed in his stead or instead of him and any other person as trustee, is guilty of an offence.

97L. Liability of Director, etc, acting without authority.

A director, manager or officer of a company, or an officer or member of the crew of a vessel, or a person acting for another, who -

(a) knowingly takes part in; or

(b) is in any way privy to doing; or

(c) attempts to do,

an act or thing without authority, which if authorized, would be in contravention of a provision of this Division, is guilty of an offence.

97M. Penalty on conviction.

A person guilty of an offence against this Division is -

(a) liable -

(i) if a corporation, to a fine not exceeding K2,000.00; and

(ii) if a natural person, to a fine not exceeding K2,000.00 and to imprisonment for a term not exceeding one year or to both such fine and imprisonment; and

(b) in addition, liable to be ordered to pay to such person and in such manner as the court directs the amount or value, according to the estimation of the court, of any valuable consideration received or given by him, or any part thereof, and such order shall be enforceable as an order of the court.

97N. Court may order withdrawal of trifling or technical offences.

Where, in a prosecution under this Division it appears to the court that the offence charged is, in the particular case, of a trifling or merely technical nature, or that in the particular circumstances it is inexpedient to proceed to a conviction, the court may in its discretion and for reasons stated in the application of the accused, dismiss the case, but the court may, if it thinks fit, make an order under Section 97M(b).

97O. Custom of itself no defence.

In a prosecution under this Division it does not amount to a defence to show that the receiving, soliciting, giving or offering of a valuable consideration mentioned or referred to in the prosecution is customary in any trade, business or calling.

97P. Burden of proof that gift is not a secret commission.

Where, in a prosecution under this Division, it is proved that a valuable consideration has been -

(a) received or solicited by an agent from; or

(b) given offered to an agent by,

a person having business relations with the principal of that agent, without the assent of the principal, the burden of proving that such valuable consideration was not received, solicited, given or offered in contravention of a provision of this Division is on the accused.

Division 3 – Corrupt and Improper Practices at Elections

98. Interpretation of Division 3.

In this Division -

"ballot-box" includes any receptacle in which voting-papers are put before being counted at an election;

"election" includes any election held under the authority of any law providing for the choice of persons to fill any office or place of a public character;

"elector" includes any person entitled to vote at an election;

"local election" includes any election held under any law relating to local government;

"polling-booth" includes any room or place in which voting at an election is conducted or in which the votes are counted.

For other electoral offences see Pt XVII (Offences) of the *Organic Law on National Elections* 1996.

99. Personation.

A person who votes or attempts to vote in the name of another person at an election, whether the name is that of a person living or dead or of a fictitious person, is guilty of a crime.

Penalty: Imprisonment for a term not exceeding two years.

100. Double voting.

A person who, being an elector, votes or attempts to vote at an election more often than he is entitled to vote at the election is guilty of a crime.

Penalty: Imprisonment for a term not exceeding two years.

101. Treating.

(1) A person who, before, during or after an election, corruptly provides, or corruptly pays in whole or part the expense of providing, any food, drink or lodging to or for any person on account of anything done or omitted to be done, or omitted to be done, by an elector at the election in the capacity of an elector, is guilty of a misdemeanour.

(2) An elector, who corruptly receives any food, drink, or lodging, on account of an act or omission referred to in Subsection (1) is guilty of a misdemeanour.

Penalty: A fine not exceeding K400.00 or imprisonment for a term not exceeding one year.

102. Undue influence.

A person who -

(a) uses or threatens to use any force or restraint, or does or threatens to do any temporal or spiritual injury, or causes or threatens to cause any detriment of any kind to an elector -

(i) in order to induce him to vote or refrain from voting at an election; or

(ii) on account of his having voted or refrained from voting at an election; or

(b) by force or fraud prevents or obstructs the free exercise of the franchise by an elector, or by any such means compels or induces an elector to vote or refrain from voting at an election,

is guilty of a misdemeanour.

Penalty: A fine not exceeding K400.00 or imprisonment for a term not exceeding one year.

103. Bribery.

A person who -

(a) gives, confers or procures, or promises or offers to give or confer or to procure or attempt to procure, to, on, or for, any person any property or benefit of any kind -

(i) on account of anything done or omitted to be done, or to be done or omitted to be done, by an elector at an election in the capacity of an elector; or

(ii) on account of any person acting or joining in a procession during an election; or

(iii) in order to induce any person to endeavour to procure the return of any person at an election, or the vote of any elector at an election; or

(b) being an elector, asks, receives or obtains, or agrees or attempts to receive or obtain, any property or benefit for himself or any other person on account of anything done or omitted to be done, or to be done or omitted to be done, by him at an election in the capacity of an elector; or

(c) asks, receives or obtains, or agrees or attempts to receive or obtain, any property or benefit for himself or any other person, on account of a promise made by him or any other person to endeavour to procure the return of any person at an election, or the vote of any person at an election; or

(d) advances or pays any money to or to the use of any other person with the intent that the money will be applied for any of the purposes referred to in Paragraph (a), (b) or (c) or in discharge or repayment of money wholly or in part applied for any such purpose; or

(e) corruptly transfers or pays any property or money to any person for the purpose of enabling that person to be registered as an elector, and so influencing the vote of that person at a future election; or

(f) is privy to the transfer or payment referred to in Paragraph (e) that is made for his benefit; or

(g) being a candidate at an election, convenes or holds a meeting of electors or of his committee in a house licensed for the sale of fermented or spirituous liquors,

is guilty of a misdemeanour.

Penalty: A fine not exceeding K400.00 or imprisonment for a term not exceeding one year.

In the case of *In the Matter of the Organic Law on National Elections and in the matter of the Election for the Moresby South Open Electorate; Raymond Agonia v Albert Karo and Electoral Commission* [1992] PNGLR 463, Sheehan J said (at 469):

"Without analysing [s103] exhaustively, it is clearly a section that is designed to prohibit improper inducements to persons, to electors, or candidates in an election. Whether those inducements are made to an elector – defined as any person entitled to vote at any election – or other persons, the corrupt practices aimed at are those inducements offered or sought, with the intention of interfering with the lawful process of an election.

It is also clear that there is in s 103 no general definition of bribery standing apart from the specific instances set out, which does not include an intention to induce a course of action of corrupt practice. It is clear, therefore, that intention is an integral part of the offence. Such phrases as offering gifts, benefits, or inducements on 'account of', or 'in order to induce', or 'with the intent that', are all phrases that show that the purpose of offering the inducement is an element of the offence."

See ss 50, 103, 126 and 168 of the *Constitution*.

105. Illegal practices.

(1) A person who -

(a) being prohibited by law from voting at an election, and knowing that he is so prohibited – votes at the election; or

(b) procures any person who is, and whom he knows to be, prohibited from voting at an election – to vote at the election; or

(c) before or during an election, and for the purpose of, promoting or procuring the choice of any candidate at the election – knowingly publishes a false statement of the withdrawal of another candidate at the election; or

(d) before or during an election, and for the purpose of affecting the return of a candidate at the election – knowingly publishes a false statement of fact respecting the personal character or conduct of the candidate; or

(e) being a candidate at an election – withdraws from being a candidate in consideration of a payment or promise of payment; or

(f) being a candidate or the agent of a candidate at an election – corruptly procures any other person to withdraw from being a candidate at the election in consideration of any payment or promise of payment,

is guilty of a misdemeanour.

Penalty: A fine not exceeding K400.00 or imprisonment for a term not exceeding one year.

(2) If an offence under Subsection (1) was committed with respect to a parliamentary election, the offender also becomes incapable, for two years from the date of the conviction -

(a) of being registered as an electorate for which the election with reference to which the offence was committed was held; and

(b) of voting at any election held for that electorate.

See ss 50, 103, 126 and 168 of the *Constitution*.

106. Other illegal practices.

(1) A person who -

(a) knowingly provides money for any payment that is contrary to any law relating to elections, or for replacing any money that has been expended in any such payment, and that is not allowed by law to be an exception; or

(b) prints, publishes or posts any bill, placard or poster that has reference to an election and does not bear on the face of it the name and address of the printer and publisher; or

(c) hires or uses for a committee-room at an election -

(i) any part of a house licensed for the sale of fermented or spirituous liquors; or

(ii) any part of any premises where any intoxicating liquor is sold or supplied to members of a club, society or association that is not a permanent political club, unless it is a part that -

(A) has a separate entrance; and

(B) has no direct communication with any part of the premises in which intoxicating liquor is sold; and

(C) is ordinarily let for the purpose of chambers or offices or for holding public meetings or arbitrations; or

(d) knowing that it is intended to be used as a committee-room at an election, lets for such use any part of any such premises, not being a part excepted under Paragraph (c)(ii) (A), (B) or (C),

is guilty of an offence.

Penalty: A fine not exceeding K200.00.

(2) If an offence under Subsection (1) was committed with respect to a parliamentary election, and the offender was a candidate or the agent of a candidate at the election, he also incurs the same incapacity as a person convicted of an offence against Section 105 committed with respect to a parliamentary election.

107. Prosecution for corrupt and illegal practices.

(1) A prosecution for an offence against any of the preceding provisions of this Division must be begun -

(a) within one year after the offence is committed; or

(b) if it is committed with respect to a parliamentary election with respect to which a petition is tried by the National Court, within three months after the report of the National Court is made,

whichever period last expires, but in any event it must be begun within two years after the offence is committed.

(2) For the purposes of Subsection (1), the service or execution of process on or against the alleged offender is the commencement of the prosecution, unless the service or execution is prevented by some act on his part, in which case the issue of the process is the commencement of the proceeding.

108. Interference at elections.

(1) A person who -

(a) intrudes into a polling-booth, not being lawfully entitled to be in it; or

(b) wilfully interrupts, obstructs, or disturbs, any proceedings at an election,

is guilty of a misdemeanour.

Penalty: Imprisonment for a term not exceeding three years.

(2) A person found committing an offence against Subsection (1) may be arrested without warrant by direction of the presiding officer.

See *The State v Manessah Voeto* [1978] PNGLR 119.

109. Electors attempting to violate secrecy of ballot, etc.

(1) A person who, having received a ballot-paper from the presiding officer at an election -

(a) wilfully makes on the ballot-paper any mark or writing not expressly authorized by law; or

(b) wilfully fails to fold up the ballot-paper in such a manner as to conceal the names of the candidates; or

(c) wilfully fails to deposit the ballot-paper in the ballot-box in the presence of the presiding officer,

is guilty of a misdemeanour.

Penalty: Imprisonment for a term not exceeding three years.

(2) A person who -

(a) takes or attempts to take a ballot-paper out of the polling booth; or

(b) whilst an elector is preparing his ballot-paper in a compartment provided for the use of electors actually voting, wilfully intrudes into the compartment,

is guilty of a misdemeanour.

Penalty: Imprisonment for a term not exceeding three years.

(3) A person found committing an offence against Subsection (2) may be arrested without warrant by direction of the presiding officer.

See s 4 of the Code regarding attempts.

110. Stuffing ballot-boxes.

(1) A person who places, or is privy to placing, in a ballot-box a ballot-paper that has not been lawfully handed to and marked by an elector is guilty of a crime.

Penalty: Imprisonment for a term not exceeding seven years.

(2) Proof that, at the conclusion of a poll, a greater number of ballot-papers -

(a) is found in a ballot-box in use at a polling-booth; or

(b) is returned by the person who acted as presiding officer at a polling-booth as having been received at the polling-booth,

than the number of electors who voted at that polling-booth is sufficient evidence, until the contrary is shown, that the person who acted as presiding officer at the polling-booth was guilty of either offence.

111. Offences by presiding officers at elections.

A presiding officer at an election who -

(a) on being called on, in the case of an elector who is blind or is unable to read, to mark a ballot-paper against the name of the candidate or candidates for whom the elector says that he desires to vote, wilfully fails to do so in the polling-booth, and in the presence and sight of the persons then lawfully present; or

(b) whilst an elector is preparing his ballot-paper in a compartment provided for the use of electors actually voting, wilfully allows any other person to be in the compartment,

is guilty of a misdemeanour.

Penalty: Imprisonment for a term not exceeding three years.

112. False answers to questions at elections.

(1) A person who at an election -

(a) wilfully makes a false answer to any question that is lawfully put to him by the presiding officer, and that he is required by law to answer; or

(b) being lawfully required to make a declaration before voting, wilfully makes a false declaration,

is guilty of a crime.

Penalty: Imprisonment for a term not exceeding seven years.

(2) A person shall not be arrested without warrant for an offence against Subsection (1) except by direction of the presiding officer.

113. Interfering with secrecy at elections.

(1) Subject to Subsection (2), a person who -

(a) at or after an election, knowingly and wilfully, and without the lawful command of a court or tribunal – unfastens the fold on a ballot-paper within which the number of an elector is written, which fold has been made in accordance with a law; or

(b) being a person required by law to discharge duties at an election at which the voting is by ballot – attempts to ascertain or discover, or aids in ascertaining or discovering, the candidate for whom the vote of any person is given at the election, except in the case of a person voting openly; or

(c) having in the exercise of his office at an election obtained knowledge, or the means of knowledge, of the candidate for whom any person has voted at the election – discloses or aids in disclosing that knowledge otherwise than in answer to a question put in the course of proceedings before a court or tribunal; or

(d) being a person required by law to discharge duties at an election – places on a ballot-paper any mark or writing not authorized by law,

is guilty of a misdemeanour.

Penalty: Imprisonment for a term not exceeding two years.

(2) Subsection (1) does not apply with respect to a member of the Police Force acting with lawful authority in the course of his duty.

114. Breaking seal of packets used at elections.

(1) Subject to Subsection (2), a person who knowingly and wilfully, and without the lawful command of a court or tribunal, opens or breaks the seal of a sealed parcel that has been sealed up under the provisions of any law relating to elections, is guilty of a misdemeanour.

Penalty: Imprisonment for a term not exceeding two years.

(2) Subsection (1) does not apply with respect to a member of the Police Force acting under lawful authority in the course of his duty.

115. Offences at elections when voting is by post.

A person who, at an election at which the voting is by post -

(a) knowing that he is not entitled to vote at the election, signs his name as a voter to a voting-paper; or

(b) signs the name of another person to a voting-paper; or

(c) attests the signature to a voting-paper of a person who is, to his knowledge, not entitled to vote by means of that voting-paper,

is guilty of a misdemeanour.

Penalty: A fine not exceeding K400.00 or imprisonment for a term not exceeding one year.

116. False electoral claims.

(1) A person who -

(a) makes in a claim to be inserted in a list of electors any statement that is, to his knowledge, false in any material particular; or

(b) makes, orally or in writing, to a court or tribunal having jurisdiction to deal with the claims of persons to be registered as electors, or as persons claiming to be electors, a statement relating to the qualification of any person as an elector that is, to his knowledge, false in any material particular,

is guilty of a crime.

Penalty: Imprisonment for a term not exceeding seven years.

(2) A person who commits an offence against Subsection (1) shall not be arrested without warrant for the offence.

(3) A person shall not be convicted of an offence against Subsection (1) on the uncorroborated testimony of one witness.

Division 4 – Selling and Trafficking in Offices

117. Bargaining for offices in Public Service.

A person who -

(a) corruptly asks, receives or obtains, or agrees or attempts to receive or obtain, any property or benefit for himself or any other person on account of anything already done or omitted to be done, or to be done or omitted to be done, by him or by any other person, with regard to -

(i) the appointment or contemplated appointment of any person to any office or employment in the Public Service; or

(ii) any application by any person for employment in the Public Service; or

(b) corruptly gives, confers or procures, or promises or offers to give or confer, or to procure or attempt to procure, to, on, or for any person any property or benefit on account of any such act or omission,

is guilty of a misdemeanour.

Penalty: Imprisonment for a term not exceeding three years, and a fine at the discretion of the court.

See s 37(2) of the *Constitution*.

Division 5 – Offences Relating to the Administration of Justice

118. Interpretation of Division 5.

In this Division, "judicial proceeding" includes any proceeding had or taken in or before any court, tribunal or person, in which evidence may be taken on oath.

119. Judicial corruption.

(1) In this section, "holder of a judicial office" includes an arbitrator or umpire.

(2) A person who -

(a) being the holder of a judicial office, corruptly asks, receives, or obtains, or agrees or attempts to receive or obtain, any property or benefit for himself or any other person on account of any thing done or omitted to be done, or to be done or omitted to de done, by him in his judicial capacity; or

(b) corruptly gives, confers or procures, or promises or offers to give or confer, or to procure or attempt to procure, to, on, or for any person holding a judicial office, or to, on, or for any other person, any property or benefit on account of any such act or omission on the part of a person holding the judicial office,

is guilty of a crime.

Penalty: Subject to Subsection (3), imprisonment for a term not exceeding 14 years, and a fine at the discretion of the court.

(3) In the case of an offence committed by or with respect to an arbitrator or umpire the longest term of imprisonment that may be imposed for an offence against Subsection (2) is seven years.

(4) A person who commits an offence against Subsection (2) shall not be arrested without warrant for the offence.

(5) A prosecution for an offence against Subsection (2)(a) cannot be begun except by the direction of the Public Prosecutor.

See s 177 of the *Constitution*, which seems to make s 119(5) ineffective, and s 176(3) of the *Constitution* with which s 119(5) seems to be inconsistent.

See s 31 of the Code on judicial immunity, and s 35 on abuse of office.

For a discussion of the considerations and authorities relevant to sentencing a person convicted of judicial corruption under this section, see the judgment of Amet J in *The State v Robert Kaki Yabara* (unreported, National Court, 22 February 1984). Here, the circumstances (a Member of Parliament seeking to pay a magistrate K140.00 to show him favour in relation to criminal charges) warranted a substantial exemplary sentence, and the prisoner received four years jail cumulative upon his other sentences.

In *Yabara v The State* [1984] PNGLR 378, Pratt, Bredmeyer and Kaputin JJ held that:

1. For the purposes of establishing the offence of "giving" a benefit or attempting to "give a benefit" under s 119 of the Code, it is the state of mind of the accused at the time of the alleged offence which is determinative. The state of mind of the recipient is irrelevant.

2. Accordingly, the fact that money in an envelope was placed on the table before a magistrate was sufficient evidence of a complete offence, regardless of whether the magistrate accepted the money or not.
3. For the purposes of s 119, a magistrate of the District Court hearing committal proceedings is a person holding "judicial office" and acting in a "judicial capacity".
4. For the purposes of establishing the offence under s 119, not only must the person approached hold "judicial office", but that person must be asked to effect some end favourable to the accused by acting in his or her judicial capacity, that it, carrying out judicial functions.
5. In the circumstances, the conviction had been properly recorded.
6. The fact that the appellant was a Member of Parliament and had a heavy responsibility to maintain the law outweighed other sentencing considerations, and the sentence could not be said to be inadequate.

120. Official corruption not judicial but relating to offences.

(1) A person who -

(a) being a justice not acting judicially, or being a person employed in the Public Service in any capacity not judicial for the prosecution or detention or punishment of offenders, corruptly asks, receives or obtains, or agrees or attempts to receive or obtain any property or benefit for himself or any other person, on account of anything done or omitted to be done, or to be done or omitted to be done, by him, with a view to -

(i) corrupt or improper interference with the due administration of justice; or

(ii) the procurement or facilitation of the commission of an offence; or

(iii) the protection of an offender or intending offender from detection or punishment; or

(b) corruptly gives, confers or procures, or promises or offers to give or confer, or to procure or attempt to procure to, on, or for any person, any property or benefit on account of any such act or omission on the part of the justice or other person so employed,

is guilty of a crime.

Penalty: Imprisonment for a term not exceeding 14 years, and a fine at the discretion of the court.

(2) A person shall not be arrested without warrant for an offence against Subsection (1).

See ss 31, 119 and 132 of the Code.

In *The State v Jackson Tita Toamara* [1988-89] PNGLR 253, Brunton AJ said (at 256):

"[In the context of s 120(1)(iii)], the words 'with a view to' mean 'for the purpose of', that is the acts or omissions of the accused must be for the purpose of allowing the alleged offenders to escape punishment. It seems proper that the purpose of an act can be found in both objective and subjective reality. The acts themselves create a certain objectivity that can indicate their purpose. But the subjective state of mind may also indicate the purpose of an act ... Intention, and the purpose of our acts, is not established by the objective consequences of the acts, but by an examination of all the circumstances."

In the same case, Brunton AJ further said (at 256-257):

"The meaning of the word 'corruptly' in law is confused. It is an undefined adverb ... There is one line of English cases which says that 'corruptly' means dishonestly ... There is another line of English cases which says that 'corruptly' does not mean dishonestly 'but in purposely doing an act which the law forbids' ... The ordinary meaning of the adverb 'corruptly' is wider than 'dishonestly'. Dishonesty may certainly be an ingredient of corruption, but the concept is wider. Corruption can be achieved by pollution, subversion, or the undermining of a concept, institution, or material. When the word 'corruptly' is used with persons, as in s 120(1) – 'A person who ... corruptly ... receives' – then the ordinary use of the word implies immorality, depravity and dishonesty. When the word is linked with the taking of bribes, 'corruptly' is closer to dishonesty as a concept than it is to immorality or depravity ... [T]he State ... must prove an element of dishonesty. Dishonestly is a somewhat firmer concept than corruptly, although it, too, is an undefined adverb, and can lead itself to circularity."

See s 60 of the *Summary Offences Act* regarding obstruction of a police officer in the execution of his or her duty.

In *R v Iki Lida* (1973) N764 the accused was convicted under this section for conspiring to wrongly identify two men as the defendants in a proceeding for behaving in a riotous manner. The sham defendants had agreed to "stand in" for the real defendants because they felt sorry for the latter, who had previously been to jail, and also in exchange for having their council tax paid for them.

In *The State v Tanedo* [1975] PNGLR 395, Prentice DCJ said (at 418):

"The prosecution must in such a case prove not only an agreement between the alleged conspirators to carry out an unlawful purpose (or a lawful purpose by unlawful means) as signified by words or other means of communication between them, but also an intention in the mind of any alleged conspirator to carry out the purpose. Their agreement may be seen as an advancement of the intention which each has conceived in his mind, which then passes from a secret intention to the overt act of mutual consultation and agreement."

In the same case, Prentice DCJ stated further (at 418):

"If two or more persons agree together to do something contrary to law, ... or wrongful and harmful towards another person, ... or to use unlawful means in the carrying out of an object not otherwise unlawful, the persons who so agree commit the crime of conspiracy ... So long as the design to do such an act rests on intention only it is not criminal, but as soon as two or more agree to carry it into effect, then their act becomes punishable."

An agreement to conspire may be implied or inferred from the acts or behaviour of the alleged conspirators: *The State v Sebulon Wat and Miskus Maraleu* [1994] PNGLR 582 (Doherty J).

129. Compounding crimes.

(1) A person who asks, receives or obtains, or agrees or attempts to receive or obtain, any property or benefit for himself or any other person on any agreement or understanding that he will -

(a) compound or conceal a crime; or

(b) abstain from, discontinue or delay a prosecution for a crime; or

(c) withhold any evidence of a crime,

is guilty of an offence.

(2) If the crime the subject of an offence against Subsection (1) is such that a person convicted of it is liable to be sentenced to death or imprisonment for life – the offender is guilty of a crime.

Penalty: Imprisonment for a term not exceeding seven years.

(3) In a case, other than that referred to in Subsection (2), the offender is guilty of a misdemeanour.

Penalty: Imprisonment for a term not exceeding three years.

(4) A person shall not be arrested without warrant for an offence against Subsection (1).

130. Compounding penal actions.

A person who, having brought, or under pretence of bringing, an action against another person on a penal law in order to obtain from him a penalty for any offence committed or alleged to have been committed by him, compounds the action without the order or consent of the court in which the action is brought or is to be brought, is guilty of a misdemeanour.

Penalty: Imprisonment for a term not exceeding one year.

131. Advertising reward for the return of stolen property, etc.

A person who -

(a) publicly offers a reward for the return of any property that has been stolen or lost, and in the offer makes use of any words purporting that -

(i) no question will be asked; or

(ii) the person producing the property will not be seized or molested; or

(b) publicly offers to return to any person who may have brought or advanced money by way of loan on any stolen or lost property the money so paid or advanced, or any other sum of money or reward for the return of the property; or

(c) prints or publishes any such offer,

is guilty of an offence.

Penalty: A fine not exceeding K100.00.

132. Magistrate acting oppressively or when interested.

A magistrate who -

(a) being required or authorized by law to admit an accused person to bail, without reasonable excuse, and in abuse of his office, requires excessive and unreasonable bail; or

(b) wilfully and perversely exercises jurisdiction in any matter in which he has a personal interest,

is guilty of a misdemeanour.

Penalty: Imprisonment for a term not exceeding three years, and a fine at the discretion of the court.

See s 37(2) of the *Constitution* regarding the penalty.

See ss 31 and 119-120 of the Code.

133. Delay to take person arrested before magistrate.

A person who, having arrested another person on a charge of an offence, wilfully delays taking him before a magistrate to be dealt with according to law is guilty of a misdemeanour.

Penalty: Imprisonment for a term not exceeding two years.

134. Bringing fictitious action on penal law.

A person who, in the name of a fictitious plaintiff, or in the name of a real person but without his authority, brings an action against another person on a penal law for the recovery of a penalty for an offence committed or alleged to have been committed by him is guilty of a misdemeanour.

Penalty: Imprisonment for a term not exceeding two years.

135. Inserting advertisement without authority of court.

A person who, without authority, or knowing the advertisement to be false in any material particular, inserts or causes to be inserted in the National Gazette or in a newspaper an advertisement purporting to be published under the authority of a court or tribunal is guilty of a misdemeanour.

Penalty: Imprisonment for a term not exceeding two years.

136. Attempting to pervert justice.

A person who attempts, in any way not specially defined in this Code, to obstruct, prevent, pervert or defeat the course of justice is guilty of a misdemeanour.

Penalty: Imprisonment for a term not exceeding two years.

See s 4 regarding attempts.

It was stated in *The State v Geyame Kiliki* [1990] PNGLR 216 at 218:

> "The ordinary English usage of the verb 'pervert' is to turn aside a thing from its proper use; to lead astray a person, or a person's mind from a right opinion, or conduct: *Concise Oxford English Dictionary*. ... it is proper that words be given their natural meaning, and I was unable to find any case law to suggest that the word pervert had any special legal meaning, or was a term of art ... [A]n attempt to pervert the course of justice should be evidenced by an attempt to turn aside the course of justice from its proper direction; or to influence a tribunal or court so as to lead it astray from its proper conduct, its duty under the law."

In the same case, it was further stated (at 220):

> "The essence ... of the offence, whether its facts are rooted in time before a trial, that is, in the police investigation, or are part of the trial-process such as

interfering with witnesses, or trying to persuade a judge or magistrate to do something, or not to do something, is that the conduct might lead to a miscarriage of justice, whether or not a miscarriage actually occurred. There must be an act which attempts to 'turn aside' the course of justice, and the act must also have that tendency."

This offence is also punishable summarily: see Sch 2 of the Code.

139. Escape by prisoner.

(1) A person who, being a prisoner in lawful custody, escapes from that custody is guilty of a crime.

Penalty: A term of imprisonment of not less than five years.

(2) An offender under Subsection (1) may be tried, convicted, and punished, notwithstanding that at the time of his apprehension or trial the term of his original sentence (if any) has expired.

[Penalty provision subst Act No 12, 1993 (*Criminal Code (Amendment) Act* 1993), s 2]

This is the only remaining offence carrying a minimum penalty

In *The State v Inema Yawok* (1998) N1766 it was held that as s 139 carries a mandatory minimum penalty of five years, there is no discretion for the court to impose a lesser sentence. Kirriwom J stated that:

"The essence of the legislature prescribing both a minimum term and maximum term for an offence is the same as defining the area of a playing field. The Court is required by law to impose punishment within that area, and move upwards or downwards depending on the gravity of the offence and the circumstances of the offender, but within that playground. The minimum penalty does not deprive the Court of its power to give just and fair consideration to each case on its own merits and impose sentence as the justice of the case requires but not below the minimum ... It would be nonsensical to expect a life sentence or even death as maximum penalty for escaping from custody and Parliament naturally would not have intended this to be so ... Considering this provision in the light of the rest of the sections both before and after s 139, it is obvious that there is an ambiguity in the law that the Parliament must rectify. The Supreme Court [in *The State v Aruve Waiba* (1994) CR1/94] thus came to the conclusion that a more lenient interpretation must be given to the law in the light of this ambiguity and decided that the court can suspend the sentence in whole or in part after imposing the minimum sentence prescribed."

In *The State v Jack Moge* [1995] PNGLR 246, Jalina J held that under the amended penalty provision there is no discretion available to courts under s 19 of the Code:

"in the new penalty the words 'imprisonment of not less than 5 years' means that a court or judge may not impose a period of imprisonment of less than 5 years. A court or a judge has no discretion. The fact that a court or a judge has no discretion is clear from the fact that the penalty prescribed in section 139(1) as amended is not subject to section 19 of the Code."

In *The State v Thomas Waim, Tala Gena & Alois Wanpis* (1998) N1750 on the issue of whether to suspend the minimum sentence provided for in s 139 (the court has a discretion under s 19(1)(d) of the Code), Injia J held that:

"although this was a mass breakout, this was an ordinary escape, in that the 3 accused and others simply climbed over the security fence and escaped. There is no evidence that these 3 accused were the main perpetrators. No weapon was used. No CIS staff member was threatened or injured ... I consider that to impose the minimum sentence of 5 years per se would be manifestly excessive in the circumstances. Nevertheless, a strong punitive sentence is warranted because this offence is becoming far too prevalent in this country. Escapes from lawful custody is an affront to the judicial system and law enforcement and it must be met with an equally stern punishment."

This offence is also punishable summarily: see Sch 2 of the Code.

141. Harbouring escaped prisoners.

A person who harbours, maintains or employs a person who is, to his knowledge, a prisoner who has escaped from custody, and is illegally at large, is guilty of a misdemeanour.

Penalty: A fine not exceeding K400.00, or imprisonment for a term not exceeding two years.

This offence is also punishable summarily: see Sch 2 of the Code.

Where an accused pleads not guilty to harbouring "prohibited immigrants", it is essential that the prosecution give formal evidence tending to show that those who might have been "harboured" were "prohibited immigrants". A failure by the prosecution to prove an essential element of the offence cannot be cured by reliance on hearsay statements: *Fred Eiserman v J Nanatsi* [1978] PNGLR 457.

Maintaining and employing clearly involve some act or something positive, as distinct from something passive. With regard to harbouring, what must be shown is that the accused did some act towards concealing the escapee or assisting the escapee in remaining at large. An example of this would be allowing the escapee to occupy the person's house, or providing the escapee with clothing and food. However, if knowing that another were an escapee, the person merely did nothing, or did something which did not assist the escapee to remain at large, the person could not be convicted of harbouring an escapee: *The State v Kuri Wembra* [1977] PNGLR 23.

The prosecution must lead evidence to prove the elements of the offence, namely:

(a) that a prisoner was in lawful custody;

(b) that the prisoner had escaped;

(c) that the accused had knowledge

  (i) of the prisoners escape; and

  (ii) that the prisoner was still unlawfully or without lawful excuse at large; and

(d) that there had been some act or conduct on behalf of the accused which constitutes harbouring within the meaning of the section.

The evidence must show that the accused engaged in "some act towards concealing the escapee or assisting him to remain at large. If he merely did nothing or did something which did not assist, then no offence has been committed ... mere moral support is not sufficient. There must be proof of some active participation". Giving food or shelter may of themselves amount to harbouring: *The State v Lupam Lau* (1981) N309(M), following *The State v Kuri Wembra* [1977] PNGLR 23; *John Tolna v Paul Ari* [1980] PNGLR 23.

Following *The State v Kuri Wembra*, the case of *The State v Lyanda Aken and Kenepia Tuink* (1980) N238 held that the accused must do some act towards concealing the escapee or assisting him or her to remain at large. In that case, shelter was given to avoid detection.

"Prisoner" includes those persons held legally in custody whether by arrest, committal or sentence, and who have not been released by due process of law. Accordingly, the escapee from custody awaiting trial is a "prisoner": *The State v Alan Bekau* [1982] PNGLR 119 (McDermott J).

142. Rescuing persons of unsound mind.

A person who -

(a) rescues any person during -

(i) his conveyance as a person of unsound mind to -

(A) a hospital or reception house for persons of unsound mind; or

(B) a house licensed under the laws relating to persons of unsound mind for the reception of patients; or

(C) a prison; or

(ii) his confinement as a person of unsound mind in any such place; or

(b) being in charge of a person during his conveyance as a person of unsound mind to any such place, wilfully permits him to escape from custody; or

(c) being a superintendent of, or person employed in, any such place wilfully permits a person confined in it to escape from it; or

(d) conceals any such person who has, to his knowledge -

(i) been rescued during such conveyance or confinement; or

(ii) escaped during such conveyance or from such confinement,

is guilty of a misdemeanour.

Penalty: Imprisonment for a term not exceeding three years.

143. Removing, etc, property under lawful seizure.

A person who, when any property has been attached or taken under the process or authority of any court, knowingly, and with intent to hinder or defeat the attachment or process, receives, removes, retains, conceals, or disposes of the property is guilty of a misdemeanour.

Penalty: Imprisonment for a term not exceeding three years.

This offence is also punishable summarily: see Sch 2 of the Code.

144. Obstructing officers of courts of justice.

A person who wilfully obstructs or resists any person lawfully charged with the execution of an order or warrant of a court is guilty of a misdemeanour.

Penalty: On conviction on indictment – a fine not exceeding K400.00 or imprisonment for a term not exceeding one year.

On summary conviction – a fine not exceeding K200.00 or imprisonment for a term not exceeding six months.

Division 7 – Offences Relating to Currency

See also *Central Banking Act*.

145. Interpretation of Division 7.

In this Division, unless the contrary intention appears -

"coin" includes -

(a) coin made in whole or in part out of material other than metal; and

(b) the coin of any country or place outside Papua New Guinea;

"coining instrument" includes any stamp, mould, press for coinage, tool, instrument, appliance or machine -

(a) adapted to make the resemblance of both or either of the sides of any coin; or

(b) adapted or intended to be used for marking coin round the edges with marks or figures apparently resembling those on any genuine coin; or

(c) adapted for making blanks in the shape of genuine coin;

"copy of a note" includes -

(a) a reproduction or negative of a current note or part of a current note in any size, scale or colour; and

(b) a copy of a current note or part of a current note in any size, scale or colour;

"counterfeit", in relation to coin, means -

(a) coin that is not genuine but resembles, or is apparently intended to resemble or pass for, genuine coin; and

(b) genuine coin that has been prepared or altered so as to resemble, or to be apparently intended to resemble or pass for, coin of a higher denomination; and

(c) genuine coin that -

(i) has been clipped or filed, or the size or weight of which has otherwise been diminished; and

(ii) has been prepared or altered so as to conceal the clipping, filing or diminution,

and includes any such coin whether or not it is –

(d) in a fit state to be uttered; or

(e) the process or preparation or alteration is complete;

"current", in relation to notes and coins, means any note or coin that is currently legal tender, with or without restriction as to amount, in Papua New Guinea or in any country or place outside Papua New Guinea;

"forgery", in relation to a note, means -

(a) a note that is not genuine but resembles, or is intended to resemble or pass for, a genuine note; or

(b) a genuine note that has been altered so as to resemble, or to be apparently intended to resemble or pass for, a note of a higher denomination; or

(c) a genuine note that has been split or otherwise tampered with in such a manner as to sever from the note any material part,

and in a case referred to in Paragraph (c) includes both the note and the part severed from it;

"form of a note" means any form of a note, not being a genuine note, intended or likely to pass for a current note, and includes a part of such a form;

"note" includes any bill or note payable to bearer on demand that is used or intended to be used as equivalent to money, whether immediately on issue or at any time after issue;

"utter" includes -

(a) use, deal with or act on; and

(b) attempt to use, deal with, or act on; and

(c) attempt to induce any person to use, deal with, or act on,

the thing in question as if it were genuine.

146. Gilding, etc, metal or other material with intent to make counterfeit coin.

A person who -

(a) gilds or silvers any piece of metal or other material of a fit size or figure to be coined, or colours any piece of metal or other material of such size so as to make it look like gold or silver, with intent that it shall be coined into counterfeit coin; or

(b) makes, or begins to make, any piece of metal or other material into a fit size or figure to facilitate the coining from it of any counterfeit coin with intent that any counterfeit coin shall be made from it,

is guilty of a crime.

Penalty: Imprisonment for a term not exceeding 10 years.

147. Making, etc, coining instruments.

A person who, without lawful excuse (proof of which is on him) -

(a) makes or mends; or

(b) begins or prepares to make or mend; or

(c) has in his possession; or

(d) receives; or

(e) disposes of,

any coining instrument is guilty of a crime.

Penalty: Imprisonment for a term not exceeding seven years.

148. Making counterfeit coin.

A person who makes or begins to make any counterfeit current coin is guilty of a crime.

Penalty: Imprisonment for a term not exceeding 10 years.

149. Buying or selling of counterfeit coin.

A person who, without lawful excuse (proof of which is on him) -

(a) buys, sells, receives, pays or disposes of any counterfeit coin at a lower rate than it imports or is apparently intended to import, or offers to do so; or

(b) brings or receives into Papua New Guinea any counterfeit coin, knowing it to be counterfeit,

is guilty of a crime.

Penalty: Imprisonment for a term not exceeding seven years.

150. Possession of counterfeit coin, etc.

A person who has in his possession -

(a) any counterfeit coin, knowing it to be counterfeit, with intent to utter it or with intent that it may be uttered by any other person; or

(b) any bullion, metal, material, substance or article intending to use it, or knowing that it is intended to be used, in or in connexion with the making of counterfeit coin,

is guilty of a crime.

Penalty: Imprisonment for a term not exceeding three years.

151. Uttering counterfeit coin.

A person who utters any counterfeit coin, knowing it to be counterfeit, is guilty of a crime.

Penalty: Imprisonment for a term not exceeding three years.

152. Uttering metal, etc, as coin.

A person who, with intent to defraud, utters as and for current coin -

(a) any coin that is not current coin; or

(b) any metal or piece of metal or other material, whether a coin or not, that is of less value than the current coin as and for which it is uttered,

is guilty of a crime.

Penalty: Imprisonment for a term not exceeding two years.

153. Clipping or sweating coins.

A person who deals with any current coin in such a manner as to diminish its weight, with intent that when so dealt with it may pass as current coin, is guilty of a crime.

Penalty: Imprisonment for a term not exceeding 10 years.

154. Possession of clippings, etc.

A person who, without lawful excuse (proof of which is on him), has in his possession or disposes of any metal or other material or substance that, to his knowledge, was obtained by dealing with current coin in such a manner as to diminish its weight, whether that metal, material or substance -

(a) consists of filings, clippings, dust or bullion; or

(b) is in solution; or

(c) is in any other form,

is guilty of a crime.

Penalty: Imprisonment for a term not exceeding seven years.

155. Making, possessing or selling tokens, etc, resembling coins.

A person who, without lawful excuse (proof of which is on him), makes, or begins to make, sells, offers for sale or has in his possession for sale any medal, metal, cast, token or other like thing, not being a genuine coin, that -

(a) resembles in size, figure and colour any current coin; or

(b) bears a device resembling a device on a current coin; or

(c) is so formed that it can, by gilding, silvering, colouring, washing or other like process, be so dealt with as to resemble a current coin and is capable, or would if so dealt with be capable, of being passed for a genuine coin,

is guilty of a misdemeanour.

Penalty: Imprisonment for a term not exceeding one year.

156. Defacing coins.

A person who defaces any current coin by stamping on it any name or word, whether or not the weight of the coin is diminished, is guilty of a misdemeanour.

Penalty: Imprisonment for a term not exceeding one year.

157. Defacing or destroying coins.

(1) In this section, "authorized person" means the Head of State, acting on advice, or a person authorized in writing by the Head of State, acting on advice, to grant consents for the purposes of this section.

(2) A person who, without the consent of an authorized person -

(a) destroys, by melting or otherwise, a current coin; or

(b) in the course of carrying on any trade or business, defaces a current coin,

is guilty of a misdemeanour.

Penalty: Imprisonment for a term not exceeding six months.

158. Possession of forged notes.

A person who, without lawful excuse (proof of which is on him), purchases or receives from any person, or has in his possession, a forgery of a current note is guilty of a crime.

Penalty: Imprisonment for a term not exceeding four years.

Once the state has established possession of a forged note at the material time, the onus is on the accused to satisfy the court on the balance of probabilities that he or she had a lawful excuse for having possession of it: *The State v Magracia* [1984] PNGLR 116.

In *The State v Magracia* [1984] PNGLR 116, Kaputin J said:

> "[W]here a man can only show that he did not know that the note was a forgery, that, in itself, is not a lawful excuse: he must go further and show that he acquired them lawfully; for unless he acquired them lawfully he will not have a lawful excuse."

Winkle v Wiltshire [1951] 1 KB 684 was applied in *The State v Magracia* [1984] PNGLR 116. There Lord Goddard CJ held that:

> "a person who proves that he innocently bought fictitious insurance stamps from an unauthorised or unlicensed seller does not establish a 'lawful excuse' ... for having the stamps in his possession. ... [H]e must further show that he acquired the stamps as a result of a lawful transaction between himself and a seller legally entitled to deal in the stamps."

Kirriwom J stated, in *The State v Okun John* (2000) N1977:

> "The phrase 'without lawful excuse' ... can be read to mean that possession per se does not create the offence because the section goes on to qualify what it means in that phrase by stating 'proof of which is on him' meaning that the accused carries the onus of proving that he had lawful excuse for being in possession of the note in question, implies that there must be knowledge that the note was not a valid legal tender or a current note but a forged one or a fake. In other words the physical act of the *actens resis* which is being in possession must be accompanied by the relevant *mens rea* which is knowledge."

In the same case, it was also said:

> "Accepting the High Court case of *He Kaw Teh v R* [(1985) 187 CLR 523] as correctly stating the law on statutory interpretation of section 158 of the *Criminal*

Code, then to the extent that section shifts the onus of proving 'lawful excuse' on the accused is in contravention of the *Constitution* s 37(4)(a) which states that 'a person charged with an offence (a) shall be presumed innocent until proven guilty according to law but a law may place upon a person charged with an offence the burden of proving particular facts which are or would be peculiarly within his knowledge.' This is not one of such offence where the burden shifts. ... Therefore to the extent that the section contradicts the *Constitution* on the burden of proof, it is unconstitutional. It must be struck down in my view to the extent of its inconsistency with the *Constitution*."

See s 37(8) of the *Constitution*.

163. Seizure of counterfeit coin, tool for coining, etc.

Where any person finds in any place, or in the possession of any person who has it or them without lawful excuse -

(a) any counterfeit coin; or

(b) any coining instrument adapted and intended for making any such counterfeit coin; or

(c) any filings or clippings of gold or silver, or any gold or silver in bullion, dust, solution, or any other state, that are or is suspected, on reasonable grounds, to have been obtained by dealing with any current gold or silver coin in such a manner as to diminish its weight; or

(d) a forged current note; or

(e) a tool, instrument or machine adapted and intended for making a forged current note,

the person who finds it or them may seize it or them, and take it or them immediately before a magistrate to be dealt with according to law.

164. Forfeiture of coining instruments.

The following things are forfeit to the State -

(a) all coining instruments made by, or in the possession of, a person without lawful authority; and

(b) any metal or other material or substance intended to be made into counterfeit coin; and

(c) all counterfeit coins, whether partly made or finished; and

(d) any material, substance or article used or intended to be used in or in connexion with the making of counterfeit coin.

165. Forfeiture of forged notes.

All forged current notes are forfeit to the State.

166. Forfeiture of illicit forms.

(1) A form of a current note, and an instrument or thing that may be used in making a form of a current note, made by, or in the possession of, a person without the authority of the Central Bank is forfeited to the State.

(2) A member of the Police Force may, at any time, seize an article forfeited under this section, or an article that he has reasonable ground to believe is forfeited under this section, and bring it before a District Court.

(3) A District Court may order an article seized under this section to be condemned or returned to the person from whom it was seized.

(4) An article condemned under this section shall be dealt with as the Minister directs, and pending his direction, may be held in such custody as the court directs.

167. Counterfeit notes to be marked.

A person charged with the receipt or disbursement of public moneys, and an officer of a bank shall stamp or write in plain letters the words "counterfeit", "altered" or "worthless" on every counterfeit or forged note in the form of a current note that is presented to him at his place of business.

168. Dealing, etc, forfeited goods.

A person who, without lawful authority (proof of which is on him) deals with, moves, alters or interferes with anything that under this Division is forfeit to the State is guilty of a misdemeanour.

Penalty: Imprisonment for a term not exceeding one year.

Division 8 – Offences Relating to Posts and Telegraphs

See s 1 definitions of "Department of Posts and Telegraphs", "mail", "mail conveyance", "money", "Postmaster-General", "Post Office", "Telegraph Office", "property", "telegraph", "telegram" and "thing sent by post".

169. Stopping mails.

A person who -

(a) stops a mail conveyance; or

(b) stops any person engaged in conveying or delivering a mail,

with intent to search the mail, is guilty of a crime.

Penalty: Subject to Section 19, imprisonment for life.

170. Intercepting things sent by post or telegraph.

A person who unlawfully secretes or destroys any thing that is in course of transmission by post or telegraph, or any part of any such thing, is guilty of a crime.

Penalty: Imprisonment for a term not exceeding seven years.

This offence is also punishable summarily: see Sch 2 of the Code.

171. Tampering with things sent by post or telegraph.

A person who, being employed by or under the Department of Posts and Telegraphs -

(a) does with respect to any thing that is in course of transmission by post or telegraph any act that he is not authorized to do by virtue of his employment; or

(b) knowingly permits any other person to do any such act with respect to any such thing,

is guilty of a misdemeanour.

Penalty: Imprisonment for a term not exceeding three years.

This offence is also punishable summarily: see Sch 2 of the Code.

172. Wilful misdelivery of things sent by post or telegraph.

A person who, being charged, by virtue of his employment or a contract with the delivery of any thing sent by post or telegraph, wilfully delivers it to a person other than the person to whom it is addressed, or his authorized agent for that purpose, is guilty of a misdemeanour.

Penalty: Imprisonment for a term not exceeding three years.

This offence is also punishable summarily: see Sch 2 of the Code.

173. Obtaining letters by false pretences.

A person who, by means of a false pretence, induces a person employed by or under the Department of Posts and Telegraphs to deliver to him any thing sent by post or telegraph that is not addressed to him is guilty of a misdemeanour.

Penalty: Imprisonment for a term not exceeding two years.

This offence is also punishable summarily: see Sch 2 of the Code.

174. Secreting letters.

A person who wilfully secretes or detains any thing sent by post or telegraph that -

(a) is found by him; or

(b) is wrongly delivered to him,

and that ought, to his knowledge, to have been delivered to another person, is guilty of a misdemeanour.

Penalty: Imprisonment for a term not exceeding two years.

This offence is also punishable summarily: see Sch 2 of the Code.

175. Fraudulent issue of money orders and postal notes.

A person who being -

(a) employed by or under the Department of Posts and Telegraphs; and

(b) charged by virtue of his employment with any duty in connexion with the issue of money orders or postal notes,

unlawfully, and with intent to defraud, issues a money order or postal note is guilty of a crime.

Penalty: Imprisonment for a term not exceeding seven years.

This offence is also punishable summarily: see Sch 2 of the Code.

176. Fraudulent messages respecting money orders.

A person who being -

(a) employed by or under the Department of Posts and Telegraphs; and

(b) charged by virtue of his employment with any duty in connexion with money orders,

sends to any other person, with intent to defraud, a false or misleading letter, telegram or message concerning -

(c) a money order; or

(d) money payable under a money order,

is guilty of a misdemeanour.

Penalty: Imprisonment for a term not exceeding three years.

This offence is also punishable summarily: see Sch 2 of the Code.

177. Sending dangerous or obscene things by post.

A person who knowingly sends, or attempts to send, by post any thing that -

(a) encloses any thing, whether living or inanimate, of such a nature as to be likely to injure -

(i) any other things in the course of conveyance; or

(ii) any person; or

(b) encloses an indecent or obscene print, painting, photograph, lithograph, engraving, book, card or article; or

(c) has on it, in it or on its cover any indecent, obscene or grossly offensive words, marks or designs,

is guilty of a misdemeanour.

Penalty: Imprisonment for a term not exceeding one year.

This offence is also punishable summarily: see Sch 2 of the Code.

178. Retarding delivery of mails, etc.

A person who -

(a) being required by law or by virtue of his employment to do any act with respect to the receipt, despatch or delivery of any thing that is or may be transmitted by post or telegraph -

(i) neglects or refuses to do the act; or

(ii) wilfully detains or delays, or permits the detention or delay, of, any such thing; or

(b) being employed by or under the Department of Posts and Telegraphs negligently -

(i) loses; or

(ii) detains or delays, or permits the detention or delay of,

anything sent by post or telegraph, is guilty of an offence.

Penalty: A fine not exceeding K200.00.

179. Obstructing mails.

A person who wilfully obstructs or delays the conveyance or delivery of any mail is guilty of an offence.

Penalty: A fine not exceeding K100.00.

180. Penalty on mail-coach driver or guards loitering.

A person who, being a driver of a vehicle used for the conveyance of mails, or being a person in charge of a mail -

(a) loiters on the road; or

(b) wilfully misspends or loses time; or

(c) is under the influence of intoxicating liquor; or

(d) unless prevented by some cause beyond his control (proof of which is on him) – does not convey the mail at the speed fixed by the Minister responsible for posts and telegraphs for its conveyance,

is guilty of an offence.

Penalty: A fine not exceeding K20.00.

181. Fraudulently removing stamps.

(1) A person who, with intent to defraud -

(a) removes from any thing sent by post any stamp affixed on it; or

(b) removes from a stamp previously used, any mark made on it at a post office; or

(c) knowingly uses a postage stamp that has been obliterated or defaced by a mark made on it at a post office,

is guilty of an offence.

Penalty: A fine not exceeding K400.00, or imprisonment for a term not exceeding one year.

(2) Until the contrary is shown on the trial of a person charged with an offence against Subsection (1)(c), proof that the person charged is the writer of the address of any thing sent by post on which the stamp is affixed is sufficient evidence that he is the person who used the stamp.

182. Fraudulent evasion of postal laws.

A person who -

(a) knowingly and fraudulently puts into a post office any thing in or on which, or in or on the cover of which, there is a letter, newspaper or other thing, or any writing or mark, not allowed by law to be placed there; or

(b) wilfully subscribes on the outside of any thing sent by post a false statement of its contents; or

(c) knowingly and fraudulently puts into a post office anything that falsely purports to be a thing falling within any exemption or privilege declared by the laws relating to posts and telegraphs,

is guilty of an offence.

Penalty: A fine not exceeding K100.00.

183. Carrying letters otherwise than by post.

(1) A person who, not being authorized by the Minister responsible for posts and telegraphs to do so -

(a) sends or conveys a letter for hire or reward otherwise than by post; or

(b) takes charge of a letter for conveyance for hire or reward,

is guilty of an offence.

Penalty: A fine not exceeding K100.00.

(2) Until the contrary is proved, every letter sent, conveyed or taken charge of to be conveyed otherwise than by post shall be deemed to have been sent, conveyed or taken charge of for hire or reward.

(3) Subsection (1) does not apply to a letter -

(a) exceeding the weight prescribed by law for letters sent by post; or

(b) concerning goods sent and to be delivered with it; or

(c) containing -

(i) process of, proceedings or pleadings in, a court of justice; or

(ii) briefs or cases or instructions for counsel and their opinions on such briefs and instructions; or

(iii) a deed, affidavit or power of attorney; or

(d) sent by a special messenger and concerning the private affairs of the sender; or

(e) sent or carried to or from the nearest post office.

184. Illegally conducting postal business or obstructing Post Office.

A person who -

(a) without lawful excuse (proof of which is on him) -

(i) makes any envelope, wrapper, card, form or paper -

(A) in imitation of one issued by or under the authority of the Minister responsible for posts and telegraphs or of the postal authority of any other country; or

(B) on which there is any word, letter or mark, that signifies or implies, or may reasonably induce a person receiving it to believe, that a letter, newspaper, packet, or parcel bearing that word, letter, or mark is sent on the service of the National Government, or on the public service of another country; or

(ii) makes on any envelope, wrapper, card, form, or paper, for the purpose of its being issued or sent by post or otherwise -

(A) any stamp or mark in imitation of a stamp or mark of any post office under the control of the Minister responsible for posts and telegraphs or of the postal authority of any other country, or

(B) any other stamp or mark, or any word or letter, that signifies or implies, or may reasonably induce a person receiving it to believe, that a letter, newspaper, packet or parcel bearing that stamp, mark, word, or letter is sent on the service of the National Government, or on the public service of another country; or

(iii) issues or sends by post, or otherwise, any envelope, wrapper, card, form, or paper, so marked; or

(b) without the authority of the Minister responsible for posts and telegraphs (proof of which is on the person charged) -

(i) places or maintains, or permits to be placed or maintained or to remain in, on, or near any place under his control the words "post office", or any word, letter, or mark that signifies or implies, or may reasonably induce any person to believe, that the place is a post office; or

(ii) places, or permits to be placed or to remain, on a vehicle under his control the words "Royal Mail", or any word, letter or mark that signifies or implies, or may reasonably induce any person to believe, that the vehicle is used for the conveyance of mails; or

(c) without the licence of the Minister responsible for posts and telegraphs (proof of which is on the person charged) -

(i) sells, or offers or exposes for sale, a postage stamp; or

(ii) places, or permits to be placed or to remain, on or near his house or premises the words "licensed to sell stamps", or any word, letter or mark that signifies or implies, or may reasonably induce any person to believe, that he is duly licensed to sell postage stamps,

is guilty of an offence.

Penalty: A fine not exceeding K10.00.

185. Destroying or damaging letter receivers.

A person who -

(a) wilfully destroys or damages -

(i) any receptacle provided by the authority of the Minister responsible for posts and telegraphs for the reception of any thing intended to be sent by post; or

(ii) any card or notice relating to the postal service or telegraph service set up by authority of that Minister; or

(b) obliterates any letter or figure on any such thing,

is guilty of an offence.

Penalty: A fine not exceeding K100.00.

186. Placing injurious substances in or against letter boxes.

A person who places in or against any receptacle provided by the authority of the Minister responsible for posts and telegraphs for the reception of any thing intended to be sent by post or telegraph -

(a) any fire or match; or

(b) any explosive, dangerous, noxious, or deleterious substance; or

(c) any fluid or filth,

is guilty of an offence.

Penalty: A fine not exceeding K40.00.

187. Obstructing post and telegraph offices.

A person who, by stopping or loitering opposite to or on the premises of a post office or telegraph office, obstructs -

(a) the business of the office; or

(b) any person lawfully going to the office,

is guilty of an offence.

Penalty: A fine not exceeding K10.00.

188. Obstructing post and telegraph officers in the execution of duty, etc.

(1) A person who -

(a) wilfully obstructs a person employed by or under the Department of Posts and Telegraphs in the execution of the duties of his employment; or

(b) being in a post or telegraph office, or within any premises appertaining to, or used with, a post office or telegraph office, wilfully obstructs the business of the office,

is guilty of an offence.

Penalty: A fine not exceeding K4.00.

(2) A person employed by or under the Department of Posts and Telegraphs

may require any person committing an offence against Subsection (1) to leave the post office, or telegraph office or premises.

(3) A person who refuses or fails to comply with a request made under Subsection (2) is guilty of an offence.

Penalty: A fine not exceeding K10.00.

(4) A person who refuses or fails to comply with a request made under Subsection (2) may be removed by the person authorized to make the request, and all members of the Police Force shall, on demand, remove, or assist in removing, that person.

189. Interference with telegraphs.

(1) A person who wilfully and unlawfully -

(a) destroys, damages or removes any part of any apparatus used in the working of, or in connexion with, an electric telegraph under the control of the Minister responsible for posts and telegraphs; or

(b) prevents or obstructs the sending or delivering of a communication by any such telegraph,

is guilty of a misdemeanour.

Penalty: Subject to Subsection (2), imprisonment for a term not exceeding three years.

(2) A magistrate before whom a person is charged with an offence under Subsection (1) may, if he thinks fit, direct the charge to be dealt with summarily, in which case the offender is liable to a fine not exceeding K100.00 or imprisonment for a term not exceeding three months.

(3) A person found committing or attempting to commit an offence against Subsection (1) may be arrested without warrant.

(4) A person who attempts to commit an offence against Subsection (1) is guilty of an offence.

Penalty: A fine not exceeding K100.00, or imprisonment for a term not exceeding three months.

190. Negligently injuring telegraphs.

A person who negligently destroys or damages any post, wire or material used in connexion with an electric telegraph under the control of the Minister responsible for posts and telegraphs is guilty of an offence.

Penalty: A fine not exceeding K4.00.

191. Violation of secrecy.

A person employed in a telegraph office who publishes or communicates the contents or substance of a telegram, otherwise than to a person to whom he is authorized to deliver the telegram, is guilty of an offence.

Penalty: A fine not exceeding K200.00 or imprisonment for a term not exceeding six months.

192. Making charges for use of telegraph line without authority.

A person who, having become entitled under an agreement with the Minister responsible for posts and telegraphs to the use of a telegraph line, demands or receives any payment or valuable consideration from any other person for the use of the line is guilty of an offence.

Penalty: A fine not exceeding K100.00.

193. Obstructing possession of posts and telegraphs officers, etc.

A person who -

(a) wilfully obstructs or delays any person who, as duly authorized by the Minister responsible for posts and telegraphs, enters into a post office or telegraph office, or takes possession of anything in it that belongs or appertains to the Department of Posts and Telegraphs; or

(b) wilfully interferes with any such person who has so entered and is in the post office or telegraph office, or on the premises where the post office or telegraph office is situated, for a reasonable time for the purpose of taking such possession,

is guilty of an offence.

Penalty: A fine not exceeding K40.00.

194. Resisting officers.

A person who resists a person employed by or under the Department of Posts and Telegraphs who is engaged in the execution of his duty under the laws relating to posts and telegraphs is guilty of an offence.

Penalty: A fine not exceeding K100.00, or imprisonment for a term not exceeding three months.

Division 9 – Miscellaneous Offences against Public Authority

195. False declaration as to execution of sentence of death.

A person who subscribes a certificate or declaration as to the execution of a sentence of death that is to his knowledge false in a material particular is guilty of a crime.

Penalty: Imprisonment for a term not exceeding 14 years.

196. False statements required to be under oath or solemn declaration.

(1) A person who, on any occasion on which a person making a statement concerning any matter -

(a) is required by law to make it on oath or under some sanction that may by law be substituted for an oath; or

(b) is required to verify it by solemn declaration or affirmation,

makes a statement concerning the matter that is to his knowledge false in a material particular, and verifies it on oath or under such other sanction or by solemn declarations or affirmation, is guilty of a crime.

Penalty: Imprisonment for a term not exceeding seven years.

(2) A person cannot be convicted of an offence against Subsection (1) on the uncorroborated testimony of one witness.

(3) ...

[Sub (3) rep Act No 12, 1993 (*Criminal Code (Amendment) Act* 1993), s1]

197. False declarations and statements.

(1) A person who, on any occasion on which he is permitted or required by law to make a statement or declaration before a person authorized by law to permit it to be made before him, makes a statement or declaration before that person that is to his knowledge false in a material particular is guilty of a misdemeanour.

Penalty: Imprisonment for a term not exceeding three years.

(2) A person cannot be convicted of an offence against Subsection (1) on the uncorroborated testimony of one witness.

198. Shooting at Customs boats or officers.

A person who -

(a) shoots at a vessel that is in use by an officer of Customs who is engaged in the execution of his duty as such an officer; or

(b) shoots at, wounds or causes any grievous bodily harm to an officer of Customs who is engaged in the execution of his duty in the prevention of smuggling, or a person acting in aid of an officer of Customs who is so engaged,

is guilty of a crime.

Penalty: Imprisonment for a term not exceeding 14 years.

See s 559 of the Code on evidence in customs cases.

199. Resisting officers engaged in preventing smuggling.

A person who, with violence, assaults, obstructs or resists -

(a) an officer of Customs, or any person duly employed for the prevention of smuggling, who is engaged in the execution of his duty in the prevention of smuggling; or

(b) any person acting in aid of any such officer or person while he is so engaged,

is guilty of a crime.

Penalty: Imprisonment for a term not exceeding three years.

200. Resisting Customs officers generally.

A person who -

(a) assaults or obstructs -

(i) an officer of Customs, or any person duly employed for the prevention of smuggling, who is engaged -

(A) in the execution of his duty under any law relating to the Customs; or

(B) in the seizure of any goods claimed to be liable to forfeiture under any such law; or

(ii) a person acting in aid of any such officer or person while he is so engaged; or

(b) rescues or attempts to rescue any goods that have been seized under any such law; or

(c) before, at, or after the seizure of any goods under any such law -

(i) staves, breaks or destroys the goods with intent to prevent the seizure or the securing of the goods; or

(ii) attempts to do any such act,

is guilty of an offence.

Penalty: A fine not exceeding K200.00.

201. Resisting public officers, etc.

A person who obstructs or resists -

(a) any public officer who is engaged in the discharge or attempted discharge of the duties of his office under any law; or

(b) any person who is engaged in the discharge or attempted discharge of any duty imposed on him by any law,

is guilty of a misdemeanour.

Penalty: Imprisonment for a term not exceeding two years.

202. Refusal by public officer to perform duty.

A person employed in the Public Service, or as an officer of a court or tribunal, who perversely and without lawful excuse omits or refuses to do any act that it is his duty to do by virtue of his employment is guilty of a misdemeanour.

Penalty: Imprisonment for a term not exceeding two years, and a fine at the discretion of the court

203. Neglect of police officers to suppress riot.

A member of the Police Force who, having notice that there is a riot in his neighbourhood, without reasonable excuse omits to do his duty in suppressing the riot is guilty of a misdemeanour.

Penalty: Imprisonment for a term not exceeding two years.

See ss 259-263 of the Code on suppression of riots.

204. Neglect to aid in suppressing riot.

A person who, having reasonable notice that he is required to assist a member of the Police Force in suppressing a riot, without reasonable excuse omits to do so, is guilty of a misdemeanour.

Penalty: Imprisonment for a term not exceeding one year.

See ss 259-263 of the Code on suppression of riots.

205. Neglect to aid in arresting offenders.

A person who, having reasonable notice that he is required to assist a commissioned officer of the Police Force in arresting a person, or in preserving the peace, without reasonable excuse omits to do so is guilty of a misdemeanour.

Penalty: Imprisonment for a term not exceeding one year.

206. Disobedience to lawful order issued by statutory authority.

(1) Subject to Subsection (2), a person who without lawful excuse (proof of which is on him), disobeys a lawful order issued by any court, or by any person authorized by any law to make the order, is guilty of a misdemeanour.

Penalty: Imprisonment for a term not exceeding one year.

(2) Subsection (I) does not apply if some other mode of proceeding against the defaulter is expressly provided for by any law, and intended to be exclusive of all other punishment.

It was held in *The State v John Rumet Kaputin* [1979] PNGLR 554 that disobedience to the orders of the National Court is rare, and it is not necessary to stress the general deterrent aspect of the penalty in this case. There should be a substantial personal deterrent, and punishment. In addition, the penalty must be such as will appear to the people of this country to be adequate having regard to the extent of the disobedience (annual returns ordered by the National Court to be filed in accordance with the requirements of the *Companies Act* were not filed until more than 10 months after the date limited by the Order had expired) that has taken place. A fine, even a very substantial one, would not sufficiently reflect the seriousness of this matter. The sentence in this case was 10 weeks jail with hard labour.

Without attempting to exhaustively define the term "lawful excuse", it would include the various exculpations provided within Ch V (now Div 5) of the Code, which deals generally with criminal responsibility, and may extend to excuses which are provided or arise under some other statute or provision of the law: *The State v John Rumet Kaputin* [1979] PNGLR 554.

There is no basis for reading the section as though the word "wilfully" appeared before the word "disobeys". The *Criminal Code* is a code, and if the section had meant "wilfully disobeys" it would have contained that expression: *The State v John Rumet Kaputin* [1979] PNGLR 554.

Under this section, the burden of proving that the accused disobeyed a lawful order issued by the court is on the state, and such proof must be proof beyond a reasonable doubt: *Woolmington v DPP* [1935] AC 462. However, the words of the section specifically cast the persuasive burden on the accused of proving lawful excuse. The accused is required to establish a defence only on the balance of probabilities, the ordinary civil burden of proof: *The State v John Rumet Kaputin* [1979] PNGLR 554. See also *Bishop v Bishop Brothers Engineering Pty Ltd* [1988-1989] PNGLR 433, on onus and standard of proof.

A person against whom an order is made has an obligation to obey even where the person believes the order to be irregular or void: *Yap v Tan* [1987] PNGLR 227.

Part IV – Acts Injurious to the Public in General

Division 1 – Offences Relating to Religious Worship

207. Offering violence to officiating ministers of religion.

A person who -

(a) by threats or force -

(i) prevents or attempts to prevent any minister of religion from -

(A) lawfully officiating in any place of religious worship; or

(B) performing his duty in the lawful burial of the dead in any cemetery or other burial place; or

(ii) obstructs or attempts to obstruct any minister of religion while so officiating or performing that duty; or

(b) assaults, or, on the pretence of executing any civil process, arrests any minister of religion who -

(i) is engaged in; or

(ii) is, to the knowledge of the offender, about to engage in,

any of the offices or duties referred to in Paragraph (a), or who is, to the knowledge of the offender -

(iii) going to perform them; or

(iv) returning from performing them,

is guilty of a misdemeanour.

Penalty: Imprisonment for a term not exceeding two years.

This offence is also punishable summarily: see Sch 2 of the Code.

208. Disturbing religious worship.

A person who wilfully and without lawful justification or excuse (proof of which is on him) -

(a) disquiets or disturbs any meeting of persons lawfully assembled for religious worship; or

(b) assaults -

(i) any person lawfully officiating at any such meeting; or

(ii) any of the persons assembled, at any such meeting,

is guilty of an offence.

Penalty: A fine not exceeding K50.00, or imprisonment for a term not exceeding two months.

Division 2 – Offences Against Sexual Morality

See s 621 of the Code regarding custody of girls under the age of 18.

209. Knowledge of age immaterial.

Except as otherwise expressly Stated, it is immaterial, in the case of any of the offences specified in this Division committed with respect to a woman or girl under a specified age, that the accused person did not know that the woman or girl was under that age, or believed that she was not under that age.

210. Unnatural offences.

(1) A person who -

(a) has carnal knowledge of any person against the order of nature; or

(b) has carnal knowledge of an animal; or

(c) permits a male person to have carnal knowledge of him or her against the order of nature,

is guilty of a crime.

Penalty: Imprisonment for a term not exceeding 14 years.

(2) A person who attempts to commit an offence against Subsection (1) is guilty of a crime.

Penalty: Imprisonment for a term not exceeding seven years.

(3) ...

[Sub (3) rep Act No 12, 1993 (*Criminal Code (Amendment) Act* 1993), s 3]

See s 6 of the Code regarding carnal knowledge.

In *R v Paita Mireseika* (1959) N138 the accused was charged with attempting to have carnal knowledge of a dog. He was observed kneeling with his penis exposed in erection in near proximity to the rear of the dog which he was holding with his left hand under the dog's back legs. In these circumstances, the accused had gone beyond mere preparation and his conduct fell within the definition of attempt in s 4. He had begun to put his intention into execution by means adapted to its fulfilment, and manifested his intent by overt acts such that he was in the process of having intercourse with the dog though something remained to be done when he was disturbed.

The word "permits" in this section means no more than "allows" without any qualification: *R v MK* [1973] PNGLR 204 at 209 (Minogue CJ and Kelly J).

The word "permit" or "permits" is used in a number of sections of the Code (such as ss 178, 184, 222, 224 and 225), some dealing with a physical act done to the person of the accused or to some other person. On the other hand, the word "consent" or "consents" is also used in a number of sections, two of which (ss 243, assault, and 347, rape) deal with a physical act done to a person other than the accused. This analysis supports the view that in the Code permission and consent are two separate concepts, and where the requirement is consent, or the lack of it, that word is used: *R v MK* [1973] PNGLR 204 at 207 (Minogue CJ and Kelly J).

The state must show that there was permission, in that the accused consented in the sense of acting of his or her own free will. You cannot permit without consenting, and consent involves a consciousness or understanding of the act or conduct to which it is directed: *R v Mamo Kamzo* (1972) N671.

Sakora J, in *The State v Stuart Hamilton Merriam* [1994] PNGLR 104 at 112, said that "[c]onsent is no defence under s 210."

The legislature having shown itself alive to the necessity for exceptions as to duress in certain cases, should not be construed as having intended this section to say "freely permits" or "willingly permits", or to have intended the appendix "unless his action in so doing was a result of his being in any way forced to submit". That the word "permit" is to be construed in its ordinary meaning – that is, "allow, suffer, not prevent" – appears not only from the context of the section as a whole, but also from the other parts of the statute. Once a person allowed, suffered or did not prevent (permitted) intercourse, having perceived what was about to take place and the character of the act, that person would be committing an offence under s 210: *R v MK* [1973] PNGLR 204 at 213 (Prentice J).

In offences of this nature, there is a strong concern, which should be reflected in the sentence, of the people of Papua New Guinea not only for the general care of children, but that young children should not be exposed to sexual treatment such as in this case, which is regarded throughout the country as a matter of gravity: *Secretary for Law v Kabua Dewake* [1975] PNGLR 100.

Where the circumstances of the offence would have amounted to rape if the victim had been female, the relevant aggravating factors set out in *John Aubuku v The State* [1987] PNGLR 267 when considering sentence for rape of a female, can be justifiably applied. However, the sentencing guidelines set down in that case cannot be fully adopted due to the difference in maximum penalties provided for rape and unnatural offences respectively: *The State v Raphael Kuengu* [1993] PNGLR 124 (Doherty J).

For observations on the need for deterrent punishment when sodomy has been committed by a prisoner on a fellow prisoner without the latter's consent, see *The State v Titus Philip Pos* [1991] PNGLR 208.

For considerations that may be necessary in sentencing offenders from village backgrounds, see *R v Clemence Mandoma Kau Sigor; R v Piki Piliu* (1969) FC3.

211. Indecent treatment of boys under 14.

(1) In this section, "deal with" includes doing any act that, if done without consent, would constitute an assault as defined in Section 243.

(2) A person who unlawfully and indecently deals with a boy under the age of 14 years is guilty of a crime.

Penalty: Imprisonment for a term not exceeding seven years.

The unsworn evidence of a child in a case involving indecent assault must be accepted with caution and ought to be corroborated by other independent evidence implicating the accused. Such evidence should be direct or circumstantial and confirm in some material particular that not only has the crime been committed, but that the accused committed it: *R v Bradley* (1948) N5.

This section is intended to protect boys under the age of 14, therefore the boy involved may not be charged as an accomplice or principal offender notwithstanding s 7 of the Code, but could be guilty of indecent practices between males under s 212, which sets no age limits: *R v Barker* (1956) N96 (affirmed (1957) N96A).

On appeal to the High Court of Australia it was held that there was nothing on the facts to show that the boys in question were in fact accomplices to a s 212 offence: *Barker v The Queen* (1957) N96A.

In offences of this nature, there is a strong concern, which should be reflected in the sentence, of the people of Papua New Guinea not only for the general care of children, but that young children should not be exposed to sexual treatment such as in this case, which is regarded throughout the country as a matter of gravity: *Secretary for Law v Kabua Dewake* [1975] PNGLR 100.

Assault is defined in s 243 of the Code. See also s 337 regarding indecent assaults.

See s 63 of the *Evidence Act* regarding evidence of age.

212. Indecent practices between males.

(1) A male person, who whether in public or private -

(a) commits an act of gross indecency with another male person; or

(b) procures another male person to commit an act of gross indecency with him; or

(c) attempts to procure the commission of any such act by a male person with himself or with another male person,

is guilty of a misdemeanour.

Penalty: Imprisonment for a term not exceeding three years.

(2) ...

[Sub (2) rep Act No 13, 1977 (*Criminal Code (Arrest) Act* 1977), s 10]

See s 337 of the Code regarding indecent assaults on males.

Acts committed by one male upon another in the absence of consent at least by that other may be said to be committed with that other, and thus fall within the purview of s 212: *R v Hancox* (1960) N173.

See notes on *R v Barker* under s 211 regarding boys under the age of 14.

It is not necessary for the court to ascertain the exact words used by the accused in his attempt to procure the commission of an indecent act. In *R v Bates* (1962) N255, the court determined that he did use words of a kind and in a context which were intended to convey a request to commit an act of gross indecency and an offer or promise of a financial reward for the sexual gratification he required, and accordingly convicted the accused.

In *R v Finch* (1959) N146 it was stated:

> "[C]harges of a sexual nature ... are notoriously easy to make and difficult to refute. There is a salutary role of practice that it is dangerous to convict on uncorroborated testimony in such cases."

As an illustration of sufficiency of corroboration under this section, see *R v Edward Thomas Glennon* (1962) N236.

213. Defilement of girls under 12.

(1) A person who has unlawful carnal knowledge of a girl under the age of 12 years is guilty of a crime.

Penalty: Subject to Section 19, imprisonment for life.

(2) A person who attempts to have unlawful carnal knowledge of a girl under the age of 12 years is guilty of a misdemeanour.

Penalty: Imprisonment for a term not exceeding seven years.

(3) In the case of an offender whose age does not exceed 16 years the court, instead of sentencing him to any term of imprisonment, may order him to be sent to an industrial or reformatory school for a period not exceeding three years.

(4) A person cannot be convicted of an offence against Subsection (1) or (2) of the uncorroborated testimony of one witness.

(5) The wife of the accused person is a competent but not a compellable witness.

[S 213 am Act No 11, 1984 (*Criminal Code (Minimum Penalties) (Amendment) Act* 1984), s 1; am Act No 17, 1986 (*Criminal Code (Amendment No 2) Act* 1986), ss 13(a) and (b)]

"Uncorroborated testimony" is defined by s 1 of the Code. See s 4 regarding attempts. As to carnal knowledge, see s 6.

In *The State v John Saganu* [1994] PNGLR 308 at 313, Doherty J said that evidence capable of being corroborative for the purposes of s 213(4) "is evidence corroborative of the accused's guilt and must be independent – it cannot come from one witness alone. Hence, recent complaint – whilst showing credibility – emanates from the witness making the initial allegations."

Doherty J further stated, in *The State v John Saganu* [1994] PNGLR 308 at 313:

> "Since the legislature, when enacting this [sic] provisions, was well aware that people do not have carnal knowledge of children before eye witnesses, it must have intended corroborative evidence other than direct eye witnesses' evidence."

In that case it was held that evidence placing the accused and the prosecutrix in the same place and time and in a sexual context together, a medical report indicating that penetration by force had taken place, and the evidence of the accused which was indicative of his lack of truth and credibility, were all corroborative of the prosecutrix's story.

Brunton AJ, in *The State v Thomas Pipon* [1988-1989] PNGLR 179, said that the following guidelines may be taken as appropriate to sentencing for the offence of defilement of girls under 12 years contrary to s 213 of the Code, for which the maximum prescribed penalty is life imprisonment:

1. Defilement is not just a repugnant, offensive and unnatural offence against a particular child, but may be also seen as part of a wider oppressive structure. Sentencing policy needs not only "to protect the public and in particular, young girls", but also to address the offence in its social context.
2. Because the offence involves unlawful sexual intercourse and a maximum term of life imprisonment, the principles of sentencing for the offence of

rape should be applied. This is particularly so where consent is not present.

3. On a plea of not guilty, where the accused is mature and there are no aggravating or mitigating circumstances, a sentence of five years should be taken as the starting point.

4. Where the age gap between the victim and the accused is narrow, a sentence appropriate to a juvenile offender may be appropriate.

5. The actual sentence imposed may vary depending on the facts, such as, the frequency of the acts, the duration of the relationship and whether or not any permanent physical or psychological damage has been done to the victim or the family.

6. The sentence may be increased for aggravating circumstances such as: offences committed over a long period of time; offences where the accused is pathologically driven to sex with young children; resulting pregnancy; the infliction of sexually transmitted diseases; and offences involving very young children; any of the above in combination with the status of the accused as a person in *loco parentis* to a child, or to whom the child gives its complete trust; acts of group sex involving children and a number of adults; and organised child prostitution (including conspirators, aiders, abettors and counsellors).

See *Secretary for Law v John Sibulewa Kwauga* [1974] PNGLR 135, and *The State v John Lauriston Birch* [1978] PNGLR 79.

Compensation under the *Criminal Code (Compensation) Act* 1991 is inappropriate where children are victims of crime. However, where such compensation has already been paid to relatives of the victim, it may be a mitigating factor in sentence: *The State v William Muma* [1995] PNGLR 161. Ssee criticism of this case by Kalinoe and Twivey in (1996) 24 MLJ 117.

See s 63 of the *Evidence Act* regarding evidence of age.

214. Householder permitting defilement of young girls on his premises.

(1) A person who -

(a) being the owner or occupier of any premises; or

(b) having, or acting or assisting in, the management or control of any premises,

induces, or knowingly permits, any girl under the age of 16 years to resort to or be in or on the premises for the purpose of being unlawfully carnally known by any man (whether a particular man or not) is guilty of an indictable offence.

(2) Subject to Subsection (3), an offender against Subsection (1) is guilty of a misdemeanour, and is liable to imprisonment for a term not exceeding two years.

(3) If the girl is under the age of 12 years, an offender against Subsection (1) is guilty of a crime, and is liable, subject to Section 19, to imprisonment for life.

(4) It is a defence to a charge of an offence against Subsection (1) to prove that the accused person believed, on reasonable grounds, that the girl was of or above the age of 16 years.

(5) The husband or wife of the accused person is a competent but not a compellable witness.

See s 6 of the Code on carnal knowledge.

See s 63 of the *Evidence Act* regarding proof of age.

215. Attempt to abuse girls under 10.

(1) A person who attempts to have unlawful carnal knowledge of a girl under the age of 10 years is guilty of a crime.

Penalty: Imprisonment for a term not exceeding 14 years.

(2) ...

[Subs (2) rep Act No 12, 1993 (*Criminal Code (Amendment) Act* 1993), s 4]

(3) The wife of the accused person is a competent but not a compellable witness.

[S 215 am Act No 11, 1984 (*Criminal Code (Minimum Penalties) (Amendment) Act* 1984), s 2; am Act No 17, 1986 (*Criminal Code (Amendment No 2) Act* 1986), s 14]

See s 63 of the *Evidence Act* regarding proof of age.

In *The State v Sugueri Sipi* [1987] PNGLR 357, on a charge of attempting to have unlawful carnal knowledge of a girl under the age of 10 years, the victim, aged eight years, did not give evidence. The mother of the victim gave evidence of what she had seen, and that evidence was accepted by the court. King AJ held that the evidentiary rule to the effect that, in sexual cases, it is prudent to require corroboration of the evidence of the complainant/victim was not relevant where the complainant/victim did not herself give evidence, and was not to be applied to the eyewitness evidence of the mother.

216. Defilement of girls under 16 and of idiots.

(1) A person who -

(a) has or attempts to have unlawful carnal knowledge of a girl under the age of 16 years; or

(b) knowing a woman or girl to be an idiot or imbecile, has or attempts to have unlawful carnal knowledge of her,

is guilty of a misdemeanour.

Penalty: Imprisonment for a term not exceeding five years.

(2) It is a defence to a charge of an offence against Subsection (1)(a) to prove that the accused person believed, on reasonable grounds, that the girl was of or above the age of 16 years.

(3) A person cannot be convicted of an offence under this section on the uncorroborated testimony of one witness.

(4) The wife of the accused person is a competent but not a compellable witness.

[S 216 am Act No 11, 1984 (*Criminal Code (Minimum Penalties) (Amendment) Act* 1984), s 3; am Act No 17, 1986 (*Criminal Code (Amendment No 2) Act* 1986), s 15]

This offence is also punishable summarily: see Sch 2 of the Code.

"Uncorroborated testimony" is defined by s 1.

See s 4 regarding attempts.

As to carnal knowledge, see s 6.

See s 63 of the *Evidence Act* regarding proof of age.

The onus of establishing that the accused believed on reasonable grounds that the girl was of or above age is on the defence, which must prove this on the balance of probabilities: *R v Ulel* [1973] PNGLR 254.

Where the accused's defence is based on reasonable belief that the girl was above the age of consent, "regard must be held for the society in which the parties lived and for the fact that one could not expect a person in that society to have any real appreciation of chronological age as opposed to apparent physical development as a test of maturity": *R v Ulel* [1973] PNGLR 254 (Clarkson J).

In pressing a defence under this section that the accused believed on reasonable grounds that the girl was of or above the age of 16 years, it is insufficient to show that the accused believed the girl to be big enough to admit of intercourse without sustaining physical harm, or that she was old enough for marriage in native custom. The accused's reasonable belief must be as to her chronological age under the section: *R v Wanigu* [1973] PNGLR 330 at 332-333 (Prentice J).

In *R v Tagum Wakis* (1975) N826, Prentice DCJ in dicta reaffirmed his holding that reasonable but mistaken belief must go to the girl's chronological age. Here, the court found that in any event the accused could not have entertained a reasonable belief that the girl was even of marriageable age according to custom.

In a prosecution under this section, it is well established that strict proof of the girl's age is required. There are two questions. The first is whether there is some evidence of age which, if accepted, would either prove the girl's age directly or enable it to be inferred that the girl was under 16. The other question is, whilst there may be some evidence on which the judge could lawfully convict, whether there is sufficient evidence which ought reasonably to satisfy the judge that it has established that the girl is under 16: *The State v Peter Joseph Hayden* [1976] PNGLR 509.

In a prosecution under this section, the court may, in the absence of evidence to determine the age of the girl, determine the question itself, under s 63 of the *Evidence Act*, having then seen the girl. In *The State v Peter Joseph Hayden* [1976] PNGLR 509, the court refused to do so, commenting that the age of the girl was difficult to judge, and that even a national doctor called as a witness was not prepared to make an estimate.

It has been clearly held in the common law system of criminal law, as developed by statute, that it is not necessary for the Crown to negative the "defence" of reasonable and honest belief that the girl is over the age of consent. This section of the Code has merely applied the standard enactments as to exculpation so well known in common law jurisdictions, and the same principles should and do apply in determining that the onus of proof of the "defence" is upon the accused, and that the onus is that of proof on a balance of probabilities. Section 25 has no operation in respect to mistakes relating to a matter of the age of the girl: *R v Schulze* (1971) N657.

On the exclusion of s 25 see also *R v Ulel* (1969) N533.In cases of unlawful carnal knowledge, lack of consent is not an element of the offence: *R v Karibe-Puni* [1967-1968] PNGLR 388.

Evidence of an early complaint is admissible to show consistency, notwithstanding that consent is not in issue: *R v Ulel* (1969) N533.

The onus is on the accused on the balance of probabilities to prove first that he had the requisite belief, and second that the belief was based on reasonable grounds. An accused may not articulate all the reasons for holding a belief, yet circumstances may indicate other factors which are likely to influence the belief: *The State v Leo Nimo* [1980] PNGLR 129.

What is required under the defence provision of this section is a belief, based on reasonable grounds, by the defendant that he is dealing with an adult as opposed to a child, and that he believes she is of an age to consent. The approach that restricts belief to chronological age is completely unrelated to the facts of life in many of the situations from which a charge of this nature arises. What has to be established is that at some subsequent time, usually when the man finds himself confronted by a police officer, there are factors which he can point to which illustrate a belief that he was not committing any criminal offence at the time intercourse took place; ie that the girl was "old enough", "grown up", "adult", "mature", and so on: *The State v Kami Pongua* [1980] PNGLR 41.

The principles enunciated in *R v Ulel* [1973] PNGLR 254, (regarding that section of Melanesian society with little or no knowledge of chronological age or the relevance of chronological age to the criminal laws of Papua New Guinea) are logically just as relevant to a case where no reference to age is made in the mind of the accused for reasons other than education or knowledge of the Gregorian calendar, as they are to members of a society to whom such references are utterly meaningless. Whether the defence will be successful or not because of the accused's education and background in the former case, is another matter. He will certainly have a harder row to hoe: *The State v Kami Pongua* [1980] PNGLR 41, not following *R v Paul Wanigu* [1973] PNGLR 330 (Prentice J).

Miles J stated, in *The State v Leo Nimo* [1980] PNGLR 129 at 136, that, following *R v Waningu*, and disapproving *The State v Kami Pongua*, the accused must show:

> "that he held certain beliefs from which it may be inferred that had he consciously turned an enlightened mind to the precise question, he would have concluded that she was of or over the age permitted by law ... [It is not] sufficient for the accused to have a general belief in the maturity of the girl (either in the sense of physical aptitude or ... being permitted by custom to engage in intercourse), unless there is some nexus with the age laid down specifically in the statute".

The facts that no force was used and that sexual intercourse took place by mutual agreement is not relevant to the charge itself. The allegation is not one of rape, but it does have some bearing on the defence, that is the belief held by the accused and the factors which formed the basis of that belief: *The State v Kami Pongua* [1980] PNGLR 41.

Brunton AJ, in *The State v Sottie Apusa* [1988-1989] PNGLR 170, stated that the following guidelines may be taken as appropriate to sentencing for the offence of unlawful carnal knowledge of a girl under 16 years contrary to s 216(a) of the Code, for which the maximum prescribed penalty is five years imprisonment:

(a) a lower range from discharge up to 20 months, for cases where the accused and the victim are of similar age, where the accused is a young offender and the victim between 14 and 16 years, and where the offender is disabled, or physically or mentally handicapped and the victim a consenting party;

(b) a middle range from 20 months to 40 months, for cases where the accused is a mature man and there are no circumstances of aggravation; and

(c) an upper range from 40 months to the maximum of five years, for cases where there are circumstances of aggravation, such as: cases where there is a relationship of trust and dependency between the accused and the victim, for example, teacher and pupil, medical carer and patient, and step-father/uncle relationships.

217. Indecent treatment of girls under 16.

(1) In this section, "deal with" includes doing any act that, if done without consent, would constitute an assault as defined in Section 243.

(2) A person who unlawfully and indecently deals with a girl under the age of 16 years is guilty of a misdemeanour.

Penalty: Subject to Subsection (3), imprisonment for a term not exceeding two years.

(3) If the girl is under the age of 12 years, an offender against Subsection (2) is liable to imprisonment for a term not exceeding five years.

(4) It is a defence to a charge of an offence against Subsection (2) to prove that the accused person believed, on reasonable grounds, that the girl was of or above the age of 16 years.

(5) The wife of the accused person is a competent but not a compellable witness.

[S 217 am Act No 11, 1984 (*Criminal Code (Minimum Penalties) (Amendment) Act* 1984), s 4; am Act No 17, 1986 (*Criminal Code (Amendment No 2) Act* 1986), s 16]

This offence is also punishable summarily: see Sch 2 of the Code.

An act of intercourse consented to by a woman is not indecent behaviour toward her, even in a case where the woman was 14 years old: *Ikiap v Lingnoge* (1972) N673.

Where the complainant's evidence is clear and relates to matters clearly within her knowledge or observation, corroboration is not essential though highly desirable: *R v Hiroro* (1961) N215.

It is a rule of practice in such cases for a judge not to convict without corroboration: *R v Clark* (1949) N8.

See s 63 of the *Evidence Act* regarding proof of age.

218. Procuring girl or woman.

(1) A person who procures, entices or leads away any girl or woman, whether with her consent or not, with intent that some other person may have carnal knowledge of her, whether inside or outside Papua New Guinea is guilty of an offence, notwithstanding that some one or more of the acts constituting the offence may have been committed outside Papua New Guinea.

Penalty: Imprisonment for a term not exceeding three years.

(2) A person cannot be convicted of any offence under this section on the uncorroborated testimony of one witness.

"Uncorroborated testimony" is defined by s 1 of the Code.

As to carnal knowledge, see s 6.

In *R v Gill* (1948) N23 the accused, a kiap, forced a man and woman to have sexual intercourse in public (in the centre of a village) before he would marry them (which in any case he was not lawfully entitled to do). Thus the accused procured by abuse of authority a woman with the intent that another might have carnal knowledge of her.

219. Procuring girl or woman by drugs, etc.

(1) A person who -

(a) by means of any fraud, violence, threat or abuse of authority; or

(b) by the use of any drug or intoxicating liquor,

procures, entices or leads away any girl or woman, with intent that some other person may have carnal knowledge of her whether inside or outside Papua New Guinea is guilty of an offence notwithstanding that some one or more of the acts constituting the offence may have been committed outside Papua New Guinea.

Penalty: Imprisonment for a term not exceeding seven years.

(2) A person cannot be convicted of any offence under this section on the uncorroborated testimony of one witness.

220. Abduction of girl under 18 with intent to have carnal knowledge.

(1) A person who, with intent that an unmarried girl under the age of 18 years may be unlawfully carnally known by any man (whether a particular man or not) takes her or causes her to be taken out of the custody or protection of her father or mother or other person having the lawful care or charge of her, and against the will of that father or mother or person, is guilty of a misdemeanour.

Penalty: Imprisonment for a term not exceeding two years.

(2) It is a defence to a charge of an offence against Subsection (1) to prove that the accused person believed, on reasonable grounds, that the girl was of or above the age of 18 years.

(3) The husband or wife of the accused person is a competent but not a compellable witness.

As to carnal knowledge, see s 6 of the Code. See s 351, regarding abduction.

Each of the elements of the offence of taking an unmarried girl under the age of 18 out of lawful protection with intent to have unlawful carnal knowledge must be proved by prosecution, ie unmarried, under 18 years, under care of someone, carnal knowledge: *R v Harry Pascoe Lawry* (1958) N126.

It is a defence of this section to show that the accused believed on reasonable grounds that the girl was of or above 18 years. In this case it was not reasonable grounds for accused to merely contend that he had never thought about the girl's age: *R v Harry Pascoe Lawry* (1958) N126.

See s 63 of the *Evidence Act* regarding proof of age.

221. Unlawful detentions with intent to defile or in a brothel.

(1) A person who -

(a) detains a woman or girl against her will in or on any premises for the purpose of her being unlawfully carnally known by a man (whether a particular man or not); or

(b) detains a woman or girl against her will in a brothel,

is guilty of a misdemeanour.

Penalty: Imprisonment for a term not exceeding two years.

(2) The husband or wife of the accused person is a competent but not a compellable witness.

(3) For the purposes of this section, when a woman or girl is in or on any premises for the purpose of her being unlawfully carnally known by a man (whether a particular man or not), or is in a brothel, a person shall be deemed to detain her in or on the premises for the purposes of her being so unlawfully carnally known, or to detain her in the brothel, if -

(a) with intent to compel or induce her to remain in or on the premises or in the brothel, he withholds from her any wearing apparel or other property belonging to her; or

(b) after wearing apparel has been lent or otherwise supplied to her by or by the direction of that person or any other person, he threatens her with legal proceedings if she takes the wearing apparel away with her.

(4) It is lawful for a woman or girl to take any such wearing apparel as is necessary to enable her to leave a brothel or any premises in or on which she is for the purpose of her being unlawfully carnally known by a man.

222. Conspiracy to defile.

A person who conspires with another to induce any woman or girl, by means of any false pretence or other fraudulent means, to permit a man to have unlawful carnal knowledge of her is guilty of a misdemeanour.

Penalty: Imprisonment for a term not exceeding three years.

223. Incest by man.

(1) A person who carnally knows a woman or girl who is, to his knowledge -

(a) his daughter or other lineal descendant; or

(b) his sister; or

(c) his mother,

is guilty of a crime.

Penalty: Subject to Section 19, imprisonment for life.

(2) A person who attempts to have carnal knowledge of a woman or girl who is to his knowledge -

(a) his daughter or other lineal descendant; or

(b) his sister or his mother,

is guilty of a crime.

Penalty: Imprisonment for a term not exceeding seven years.

(3) It is immaterial that the carnal knowledge was had, or that the attempt was made, with the consent of the woman or girl.

(4) The wife of the accused person is a competent but not a compellable witness.

See s 4 of the Code regarding attempts.

As to carnal knowledge, see s 6.

See s 582 regarding evidence of relationship.

Kearney J expressed the opinion that probably the true rationale for the existence of the offence is the view that the criminal law exists for the enforcement of moral beliefs and that severe sentences reflect these moral beliefs and public abhorrence: *The State v MKB* [1976] PNGLR 197.

The evidence of a daughter that she had committed incest only because of threats requires corroboration: *R v Minai* [1963] PNGLR 195.

The act of intercourse between parent and adopted child is not an offence within the section: *The State v Misimb Kais* [1978] PNGLR 241.

The term "daughter or other lineal descendant" in the section means "daughter of the blood" and imports consanguinity (a descendant "of the blood") and does not extend to a customarily adopted daughter. Section 37(2) of the *Constitution* provides that a "person may not be convicted of an offence that is not defined by ... a written law". Thus, where s 223 of the Code does not extend by definition to an adopted daughter, then custom may not be applied, adopted and enforced as part of the underlying law: Sch 2.1. A custom that could be shown to regard sexual intercourse between customary-adopting father and adopted daughter as equivalent to "incest" as defined, would be inconsistent with the provision of s 223: *Sangamu Wauta v The State* [1978] PNGLR 326.

In determining the meaning of the word "sister", which is not defined in the *Criminal Code*, for the purposes of s 223(1)(b), the court may consider evidence of the custom of the community in question. In *The State v Peter Burin* [1994] PNGLR 15, involving an accused and prosecutrix who were cousins, customary law regarded them as brother and sister and prohibited sexual intercourse between them. It was held that a sister under s 223(1)(b) includes a cousin sister, and that such a finding depended on custom whether a first cousin has the status of a sister for the purposes of the section.[80]

"Incest" with a niece is not an offence: *In Re Emmanuel Lavaki* (1982) N324(M).

Brunton AJ said, in *The State v Mitige Neheya* [1988-1989] PNGLR 174 at 177:

> "An incestuous act with a child is a circumstance of aggravation of the most severe kind. It is a gross betrayal of the most sacred relationship of father and daughter. When young girls are the victims, it is difficult to imagine that the girls will not be scarred emotionally, perhaps for life."

In the same case it was further stated (at 178):

> "Previously incest has been a hidden crime, but with more public awareness and increased public concern, incest, particularly involving the father-daughter relationship, is now known to be far more widespread and devastating than was thought in the past. These offences on young girls are seen as part of a larger total oppressiveness that pervades the lives of women. ... The courts should deal with cases of incest, as with rape, clearly and decisively, so that there can be no doubt as to sentencing policy."

In *The State v Mitige Neheya* [1988-1989] PNGLR 174, Brunton AJ said that the following guidelines may be taken as appropriate to sentencing for the offence of incest:

1. Because the offence involves unlawful sexual intercourse and a maximum term of life imprisonment, the principles of sentencing for the offence of rape should be applied.

[80] *The State v Peter Burin* [1994] PNGLR 15 (Doherty J).

2. On a plea of not guilty where the accused is a mature person and there are no aggravating or mitigating circumstances, a sentence of five years should be taken as the starting point.
3. The sentence may be increased for aggravating circumstances such as physical or psychological damage to the victim, resulting pregnancy and infection of the victim with sexually transmitted diseases.
4. The lower range of sentences should be reserved for young offenders where there is little disparity in ages, or for consensual acts involving adults.

The following are matters relevant to the assessment of punishment for incest:

(a) the relationship of the parties;
(b) their comparative ages;
(c) the age of the victim;
(d) whether it was consensual between adults (as in a brother and sister close in age);
(e) the number of times sexual relations took place;
(f) the period of time (if there was more than one incident) over which the incidents took place; and
(g) the degree of force used.

The following are aggravating factors, whatever the age of the victim:

(a) evidence that the victim has suffered physically or psychologically from the incest;
(b) that the incest has continued at frequent intervals over a long period of time;
(c) that the victim has been threatened or treated violently by, or was terrified by, the accused;
(d) that the incest has been accompanied by perversions abhorrent to the victim, for example, buggery or fellatio;
(e) that the victim has become pregnant by reason of the accused failing to take contraceptive measures; or
(f) that the defendant has committed similar offences against more than one girl.[81]

In *The State v Arthur Maradi Tamti* (1999) N1878, a case of non-consensual incest between father and daughter, Jalina J commented on the increasing prevalence of incest:

> "This year alone I have dealt with a number of incest cases. In *The State v John Elei* ... I sentenced the prisoner who forced his sister to commit incest with him to 6 years imprisonment in hard labour. In *The State v Pikah Ndrohas* ... I sentenced the prisoner who consensually committed incest with his sister and who had a prior conviction for incest with the same sister to 7 years imprisonment in hard labour. In *The State v Francis Liro* ... I sentenced the prisoner to a total of 13 years imprisonment for incest with two separate daughters. In *The State v David Daniel and Polin Daniel* ... I sentenced the son to 8 years imprisonment and the mother to 2 years and 6 months imprisonment. ... [These cases] demonstrate that incest is becoming prevalent and must be stamped out through imposition of stiff penalties."

---

[81] *Mitige Neheye v The State; Martin Gawi v The State* [1994] PNGLR 71 at 76 (Doherty J), following *Attorney General's Reference No 1 of 1989* [1989] 3 All ER 571.

For the purposes of the crime of incest by a man with his "sister" contrary to s 223 of the Code, "sister" includes a half-sister: *The State v Luke Aidou* [1985] PNGLR 292. Barnett AJ looked to the customs of Siassi Island, which forbade half-brothers and sisters from having sexual intercourse. Custom could be applied under Sch 2 of the *Constitution* since the custom was not inconsistent with a constitutional law or statute, or repugnant to the general principles of humanity and so is not constrained by Sch 2.1(2). This is consistent with *R v Thompson* [1933] QJPR 93, which held that "sister" included a half-sister who was from the same mother but of a different father, and in which the High Court of Australia refused leave to appeal: *R v Thompson* (1934) 52 CLR 750.[82]

For the range of sentences where a father commits incest with his daughter, see *Grayson Andowa v The State* (1998) SC 576, and for a range where the incest is between brother and sister see *Joel Samson v The State* (1998) SC 575.

224. Incest by adult female.

(1) A woman or girl of or above the age of 18 years who permits -

(a) her father or other lineal ancestor; or

(b) her brother; or

(c) her son,

to have carnal knowledge of her, knowing him to be her father or other lineal ancestor, her brother or her son, as the case may be, is guilty of a misdemeanour.

Penalty: Imprisonment for a term not exceeding three years.

(2) It is a defence to a charge of an offence against Subsection (1) that the woman or girl was, at the time when she permitted her father or other lineal ancestor, her brother or her son to have carnal knowledge of her, acting under this coercion.

(3) The husband of the accused person is a competent but not a compellable witness.

As to carnal knowledge, see s 6 of the Code.

225. Attempts to procure abortion.

(1) A person who, with intent to procure the miscarriage of a woman, whether or not she is pregnant, unlawfully administers to her or causes her to take any poison or other noxious thing or uses force or any other means, is guilty of a crime.

Penalty: Imprisonment for a term not exceeding 14 years.

(2) A woman who, with intent to procure her own miscarriage, whether or not she is pregnant -

(a) unlawfully administers to herself any poison or other noxious thing, or uses force or any other means; or

(b) permits any such thing or means to be administered or used to her,

[82] *The State v Luke Aidou* [1985] PNGLR 292.

is guilty of a crime.

Penalty: Imprisonment for a term not exceeding seven years.

See ss 280 and 286 of the Code, regarding surgical operations and the duty of persons doing dangerous acts.

See Weisbrot and Ottley, "*Law and Medicine in Papua New Guinea: Licensing and Liability of Practitioners*" (1977) 5 MLJ 175 at 212-225.

Regarding abortion, see McRae, "*Law Relating to Fertility Control and Family Planning in Papua New Guinea*" (1980) 8 MLJ 5 at 36ff.

226. Supplying drugs or instruments to procure abortion.

A person who unlawfully supplies to or procures for any person any thing, knowing that it is intended to be unlawfully used to procure the miscarriage of a woman, whether or not she is pregnant, is guilty of a misdemeanour.

Penalty: Imprisonment for a term not exceeding three years.

227. Indecent acts.

(1) A person who -

(a) wilfully and without lawful excuse does an indecent act in a place to which the public are permitted to have access, whether or not on payment of a charge for admission; or

(b) wilfully does an indecent act in a place with intent to insult or offend a person, or by which any person is reasonably insulted or offended

is guilty of a misdemeanour.

Penalty: Imprisonment for a term not exceeding two years.

(2) For the purposes of Subsection (1), the uttering of indecent words or the making of an indecent suggestion shall be deemed to be an indecent act.

(3) ...

[Subs (3) rep Act No 13, 1977 (*Criminal Code (Arrest) Act* 1977), s 11]

This offence is also punishable summarily: see Sch 2 of the Code.

228. Obscene publications and exhibitions.

(1) A person who knowingly, and without lawful justification or excuse -

(a) publicly sells or exposes for sale -

(i) an obscene book or other obscene printed or written matter; or

(ii) an obscene picture, photograph, drawing or model; or

(iii) any other object tending to corrupt morals; or

(b) exposes to view in a place to which the public are permitted to have access, whether or not on payment of a charge for admission -

(i) an obscene picture, photograph, drawing or model; or

(ii) any other object tending to corrupt morals; or

(c) publicly exhibits any indecent show or performance, whether or not on payment of a charge for admission to see the show or performance; or

(d) for the purposes of, or by way of, trade or sale, or for distribution or public exhibition, makes, produces or has in his possession an obscene writing, drawing, print, painting, picture, poster, emblem, photograph or cinematograph film, or any other obscene object; or

(e) for a purpose referred to in Paragraph (d) -

(i) imports, conveys, or exports; or

(ii) causes to be imported or exported; or

(iii) puts into circulation,

any obscene matter or thing referred to in that paragraph; or

(f) carries on or takes part in a business (whether public or private) concerned with any obscene matter or thing referred to in this section, or deals in, distributes, exhibits publicly or makes a business of lending any such obscene matter or thing; or

(g) with a view to assisting in an act made punishable by this section, advertises or makes known by any means that a person is engaged in any such act, or how or from whom any obscene matter or thing referred to in this section can, directly or indirectly, be procured,

is guilty of a misdemeanour.

Penalty: Imprisonment for a term not exceeding two years.

(2) It is a defence to a charge of an offence against Subsection (1) to prove that it was for the public benefit that the act complained of should be done.

(3) Whether the doing of an act referred to in Subsection (1) is not for the public benefit is a question of fact.

This offence is also punishable summarily: see Sch 2 of the Code.

See ss 24 and 25 of the *Summary Offences Act* as to indecent writings and indecent drawings.

229. Search, seizure and destruction.

(1) If it appears to a magistrate on a complaint made on oath that there are reasonable grounds for suspecting that there is in a house, vessel or place an obscene matter or thing referred to in Section 228, he may issue his warrant directing a member of the Police Force named in the warrant, or all members of the Police Force -

(a) to search the house, vessel or place; and

(b) to seize any such obscene matter or thing it found and take it before a magistrate to be dealt with according to law.

(2) A warrant under Subsection (1) must be executed by day unless, by the warrant, the magistrate specially authorizes it to be executed by night.

(3) Any obscene matter or thing seized under Subsection (1) may be detained by a magistrate, and when it is no longer required as evidence may be destroyed under an order of a magistrate.

Division 3 – Nuisances: Misconduct Relating to Corpses

230. Common nuisances.

A person who -

(a) without lawful justification or excuse (proof of which is on him) does any act, or omits to do any act with respect to any property under his control, by which act or omission danger is caused to the lives, safety, or health, of the public; or

(b) without lawful justification or excuse, (proof of which is on him) does any act, or omits to do any act with respect to any property under his control, by which act or omission -

(i) danger is caused to the property or comfort of the public or the public are obstructed in the exercise or enjoyment of any right common to all inhabitants of Papua New Guinea; and

(ii) injury is caused to the person of some person,

is guilty of a misdemeanour.

Penalty: Imprisonment for a term not exceeding two years.

This offence is also punishable summarily: see Sch 2 of the Code.

See s 287 for the duty of persons in charge of dangerous things.

231. Bawdy houses.

A person who keeps a house, room, set of rooms or place of any kind for purposes of prostitution is guilty of a misdemeanour.

Penalty: Imprisonment for a term not exceeding three years.

This offence is also punishable summarily: see Sch 2 of the Code.

See s 55 of the *Summary Offences Act* regarding living on the earnings of prostitution, s 56 regarding keeping a brothel, and s 57 regarding knowingly permitting one's premises to be used for a brothel.

232. Gaming houses.

(1) A person who -

(a) keeps for gain a place to which persons resort for the purpose of playing at a game of chance; or

(b) keeps a place that is kept or used for playing in it a game of chance, or a game of mixed chance and skill, and in which -

(i) a bank is kept by one or more of the players exclusively of the others; or

(ii) a game is played the chances of which are not alike favourable to all the players, including the banker or other persons by whom the game is managed, or against whom the other players stake, play, or bet,

is said to keep a common gaming house.

(2) A person who keeps a common gaming house is guilty of a misdemeanour.

Penalty: Imprisonment for a term not exceeding three years.

This offence is also punishable summarily: see Sch 2 of the Code.

See s 51 of the *Summary Offences Act* regarding playing an unlawful game, s 52 regarding gaming in places of public resort, and s 53 regarding possession of instruments of gaming.

See s 583 regarding evidence of gaming. See also the *Gaming Act*.

233. Betting houses.

(1) A house, room or place that is used -

(a) for the purpose of bets being made in it between persons resorting to it and -

(i) the owner, occupier or keeper of the place; or

(ii) any person using the place; or

(iii) any person procured or employed by or acting for or on behalf of the owner, occupier or keeper of the place, or a person using the place; or

(iv) any person having the care or management, or in any manner conducting the business, of the place; or

(b) for the purpose of any money or other property being paid or received in it by or on behalf of the owner, occupier or keeper of the place or a person using the place, as or for the consideration -

(i) for an assurance, undertaking, promise, or agreement, express or implied, to later pay or give any money or other property on any event or contingency of or relating to any horse race, or other race, fight, game, sport or exercise; or

(ii) for securing the paying or giving by some other person of any money or other property on the event or contingency,

is called a common betting house.

(2) A person who opens, keeps or uses a common betting house is guilty of a misdemeanour.

Penalty: On conviction on indictment – imprisonment for a term not exceeding three years.

On Summary conviction – a fine not exceeding K1,000.00 and imprisonment for a term not exceeding one year.

(3) A person who -

(a) is the owner or occupier of any house, room or place and knowingly and wilfully permits it to be opened, kept or used, as a common betting house by another person; or

(b) has the use or management or assists in conducting the business, of a common betting house,

is guilty of an offence.

Penalty: A fine not exceeding K1,000.00 and imprisonment for a term not exceeding one year.

This offence is also punishable summarily: see Sch 2 of the Code.

See also the *Gaming Act.*

See s 53 of the *Summary Offences Act* regarding possession of instruments of gaming.

234. Lotteries.

(1) In this section, "lottery" includes any scheme or device for the sale, gift, disposal, or distribution, of any property depending on or to be determined by lot or chance, whether -

(a) by the throwing or casting of dice; or

(b) the drawing of tickets, cards, lots, number or figures; or

(c) by means of a wheel or trained animal; or

(d) by any other means.

(2) Subject to Subsection (3), a person who opens, keeps or uses any place for carrying on a lottery of any kind is guilty of a misdemeanour.

Penalty: Imprisonment for a term not exceeding three years.

(3) The section does not apply to any lottery approved under Section 3 of the *Gaming Act.*

This offence is also punishable summarily: see Sch 2 of the Code.

Although this is a penal statute, in construing this section resort **may not** be had to the *ejusdem generis* rule, so as to read down the elements of a lottery to a restricted class in favour of the defendant. The use of the word "includes" in the section indicates that there are other meanings that the legislature wishes it to have as well. The definition, then, is not meant to be exclusive; rather it is intended to enlarge the meaning of "lottery" beyond its natural meanings, and not to restrict it: *R v Harris* [1973] PNGLR 382 at 385-386.

The promotion of a "Spinning Wheel System" scheme, similar in operation to that known as a chain letter, requiring participants to send money to a person at the top of the pyramiding list while adding his or her own name at the bottom, constitutes the operation of a lottery within the meaning of this section. Gain for the participant depends entirely on the chance of others participating in the scheme, and the original participant has no control, nor does he or she exercise any influence in the subsequent course of events: *R v Harris* [1973] PNGLR 382 at 386-387.

235. Acting as keeper of bawdy houses, gaming houses, betting houses and lotteries.

A person who appears, acts or behaves as master, or as the person having the care or management, of any house, room, set of rooms or place referred to in Section 231, 232, 233 or 234, is to be taken to be the keeper of it, whether or not he is the real keeper.

236. Misconduct with regard to corpses.

A person who, without lawful justification or excuse (proof of which is on him) -

(a) neglects to perform any duty imposed on him by law or undertaken by him, whether for reward or otherwise, concerning the burial or other disposition of a human body or human remains; or

(b) improperly or indecently interferes with, or offers any indignity to, any dead human body or human remains, whether buried or not,

is guilty of a misdemeanour.

Penalty: Imprisonment for a term not exceeding two years.

The words "indecently" and "improper" must be construed in their local setting and circumstances. The word "indecent" has no definite legal meaning.

In *R v Noboi-Bosai* [1971-1972] PNGLR 271 at 283-284, it was said:

> "Concepts of decency and proprietary (and obscenity) appear in many places of the ordinances and laws of Papua and New Guinea. Having regard to the multifarious customs, languages, dress, beliefs, degrees of civilisation, and social organisation among the people who live in remote wildernesses ... one cannot conceive that the legislature would have intended to impose uniform blanket standards of decency and proprietary, on all the peoples of the country. In assessing proprietary and decency of behaviour in relation to corpses in the Gabusi area, I should endeavour to apply the standards, so far as I can ascertain them, of the reasonable primitive Gabusi villager ... in early 1971."

Here, the court found that the defendants not guilty, adjudging their behaviour to be "normal and reasonable" for villagers in their remote area.

In that same case, Prentice J said:

> "The funerary customs of the peoples of Papua New Guinea have been, and in many cases remain, bizarre in the extreme. These are matters of notoriety. Can it be said that the Government of Papua in 1902 by adoption of the *Queensland Criminal Code*, and in particular [this section], was intending to make so many varied pious, ritual, strength-seeking practices, indecent and improper? I cannot find so."

Prentice J further held that the section's placement within the:

> "Nuisances: Misconduct grouping of the Code, which deals otherwise with gaming, bawdy houses, gambling and lotteries; the penalty of merely two years; and the inclusion of the words 'without lawful justification or excuse', all lead to the conclusion that cannibalism was not brought under this section by intendment."

The act of cutting the body amounted to an interference. The meaning of the word "improperly" can be determined by examining the conduct in the light of all the circumstances and the subject conduct is to be measured against "the recognised standards of common proprietary" or the "current standards" and "contemporary ... community standards" The question is whether it would offend community standards of propriety in the circumstances when, and the manner in which, it is presented to the average Papua New Guinean. It is the average contemporary Papua New Guinean standard which must be applied: *The State v Aubafu Feama, Nama Auri Kafidiri Kududebe Hagima* [1978] PNGLR 301.

Division 4 – Offences Against Public Health

237. False information as to health on foreign ships.

A person who, being the master or medical officer of a ship arriving from overseas -

(a) neglects or refuses to give to any officer employed in the Public Service any information that he is required by law to give to him; or

(b) gives to any such officer, orally or in writing, any information touching any matter as to which he is required by law to give him information, which information is, to his knowledge, false in a material particular,

is guilty of a misdemeanour.

Penalty: A fine not exceeding K400.00 and imprisonment for a term not exceeding one year.

This offence is also punishable summarily: see Sch 2 of the Code.

238. Exposing for sale things unfit for food.

A person who -

(a) knowingly exposes for sale for the food of man; or

(b) has in his possession with intent to sell it for the food of man, any article that he knows to be unfit for the food of man,

is guilty of a misdemeanour.

Penalty: Imprisonment for a term not exceeding two years.

This offence is also punishable summarily: see Sch 2 of the Code.

See also the *Pure Food Act*.

See s 483 of the Code on false warrants or labels relating to the sale of food.

239. Dealing in diseased meat.

A person who knowingly -

(a) takes into a slaughter-house used for the slaughter of animals intended for the food of man the whole or any part of the carcass of an animal that has died of a disease; or

(b) sells or exposes for sale the whole or part of the carcass of an animal that has died of a disease, or that was diseased when slaughtered, unless the dressing of the animal was authorized under the *Slaughtering Act*,

is guilty of a misdemeanour.

Penalty: Imprisonment for a term not exceeding two years.

This offence is also punishable summarily: see Sch 2 of the Code.

See also s 483 of the Code.

240. Adulterating liquor.

A person who -

(a) puts a deleterious or poisonous substance into any spirituous or fermented liquor, or mixes any such substance with any such liquor; or

(b) sells or otherwise disposes of, or keeps for sale, any spirituous or fermented liquor into which any such substance has been put, or with which any such substance has been mixed,

is guilty of a misdemeanour.

Penalty: A fine not exceeding K400.00 or imprisonment for a term not exceeding one year.

This offence is also punishable summarily: see Sch 2 of the Code.

See s 13 of the *Summary Offences Act* regarding adding matter to food or drink with intent to cause the consumer mental or physical harm.

Division 5 – Miscellaneous Offences

241. Dealing with land fraudulently acquired from the State.

(1) A person who buys or takes on lease any land, or any estate in any land, from any person who has acquired the land or estate by means of a fraudulent evasion of the laws relating to the sale or leasing of Government land knowing that the seller or lessor has so acquired it, is guilty of a misdemeanour.

Penalty: Imprisonment for a term not exceeding one year.

(2) Where a person commits an offence against Subsection (1) in relation to any land, his estate in the land is forfeited to the State.

242. Fraudulent destruction or removal of goods liable to duty.

A person who fraudulently destroys, or takes from their lawful place of deposit or detention, any goods that -

(a) are liable to the payment of duty; and

(b) are deposited or detained for the purpose of securing payment of the duty,

is guilty of a misdemeanour.

Penalty: Imprisonment for a term not exceeding three years.

Part V – Offences Against the Person and Relating to Marriage and Parental Rights and Duties, and Against the Reputation of Individuals

Division 1 – Assaults and Violence to the Person Generally: Justification and Excuse

243. Definition of assault.

(1) A person who -

(a) directly or indirectly strikes, touches or moves, or otherwise applies force to, the person of another, without his consent, or with his consent if the consent is obtained by fraud; or

(b) by any bodily act or gesture attempts or threatens to apply force to the person of another without his consent, under such circumstances that the person making the attempt or threat has actually or apparently a present ability to effect his purpose,

is said to assault that other person, and the act is called an assault.

(2) A reference in Subsection (1) to the application of force includes a reference to the application of heat, light, electrical force, gas, odour, or any other substance or thing in such a degree as to cause injury or personal discomfort.

(3) A male person under the age of 17 years shall be deemed not to be capable of consenting to any act by any other male person that but for such consent would be an indecent assault.

See s 77 of the Code regarding affray.

Punishment of assaults is provided for in ss 335-341.

See s 364 regarding assault with intent to steal.

The great majority of assault cases are tried summarily under Pt V, Div 6, ss 342-346. See s 6 of the *Summary Offences Act* for the analogous summary offence. See s 28(1)(a) and 28(2)(a) of the *Summary Offences Act* regarding the use of firearms, stones, sticks or any missiles with intent to injure or frighten. As to the summary offence of assaulting a police officer, see s 61 of the *Summary Offences Act*. As to adding matter to food or drink with intent to cause the consumer mental or physical harm, see s 13 of the *Summary Offences Act*.

Although not exhaustive, the phrase "applies force" is subject to the *ejusdem generis* rule and the "force" would need to be such as could be detectable by the ordinary senses. Thus, sorcery, although believed in by the parties, is not "force": *R v Ferapo Meata* (1967) N419. This was reversed by the *Sorcery Act* 1971 in so far as it makes an act of sorcery a wrongful act or insult for the purposes of provocation.

Flashing a torch in a man's face at night was not an application of light to such a degree as to cause injury or discomfort so as to constitute an assault: *R v Kampangio* [1969-1970] PNGLR 218.

In *R v Tigel-Giring* (1962) N253 the accused's administration of a concoction containing hydrochloric acid and water with intent to harm the victim constituted an assault.

For a case of indecent assault, where consent to sexual intercourse was obtained by the fraud of the accused, see *The State v Andrew Tovue* [1981] PNGLR 8, discussed under s 349.

244. Assaults unlawful.

(1) An assault is unlawful and constitutes an offence unless it is authorized, justified or excused by law.

(2) The application of force by one person to the person of another may be unlawful, even if it is done with the consent of that other person.

Custom by itself cannot provide a lawful justification or excuse for an assault. Such excuse or justification has to be found under the Code (or the common law as provided by the Code) or some other statutory provision (for example, the *Customs (Recognition) Act*): *R v Misam Wapet* (1970) N602.

It is unlawful assault for an Assistant District Officer acting as a magistrate to forcibly detain and interrogate persons with a view to obtaining information about an alleged crime: *R v Anderson* (1957) N109.

In *R v de Navrancourt* (1958) N114 it was held that no assault had been committed where the accused, headmaster of a mission school, led a Papua New Guinean tied to a rope behind his horse from one village to another as a dramatic disciplinary measure.

See ss 267-269 on excuses to assaults.

245. Execution of sentence.

It is lawful for a person who is charged by law with the duty of executing or giving effect to the lawful sentence of a court to execute or give effect to the sentence.

See ss 32 and 252 of the Code.

246. Execution of process.

It is lawful for a person who is -

(a) charged by law with the duty of executing the lawful process of a court; and

(b) required to arrest or detain another person under such process,

and for every person lawfully assisting a person so charged, to arrest or detain the other person according to the terms of the process.

See ss 32 and 252 of the Code.

247. Execution of warrants.

[S 247 rep Act No 13, 1977 (*Criminal Code (Arrest) Act* 1977), s 12]

248. Erroneous sentence or process or warrant.

Where -

(a) a sentence was passed, or the process was issued, by a court having jurisdiction under any circumstances to pass the sentence or to issue the process; or

(b) a warrant was issued by a court, or person having authority under any circumstances to issue the warrant,

it is immaterial whether or not the court or person had authority to pass the sentence or issue the process or warrant in the particular case, unless the person executing it knows that the sentence, process or warrant was in fact passed or issued without authority.

249. Sentence or process or warrant without jurisdiction.

A person who -

(a) executes, or assists in executing, any sentence, process or warrant that purports to be passed or issued by a court or person; and

(b) would be justified, under Section 245, 246, 247 or 248 in executing it if it had been passed or issued by a court or person having authority to pass or issue it,

is not criminally responsible for any act done in such execution, notwithstanding that the court or person had no authority to pass the sentence or issue the process or warrant, if in the execution he acted in good faith and in the belief that the sentence, process or warrant was that of a court or person having such authority.

250. Arrest of wrong person.

[S 250 rep Act No 13, 1977 (*Criminal Code (Arrest) Act* 1977), s 13]

251. Irregular process or warrant.

When any process or warrant is bad in law by reason of some defect in substance or in form apparent on the face of it, a person who, in good faith and believing that it is good in law, acts in the execution of the process or warrant is not criminally responsible for anything done in the execution to any greater extent than if the process or warrant were good in law.

252. Force used in executing process or in arrest.

It is lawful for a person who is engaged in the lawful execution of any sentence, process or warrant, and for any person lawfully assisting him, to use such force as is reasonably necessary to overcome any force used in resisting the execution.

[S 252 am Act No 13, 1977 (*Criminal Code (Arrest) Act* 1977), s 14]

See the *Arrest Act* (Ch 4 of this book).

253. Duty of persons arresting.

[S 253 rep Act No 13, 1977 (*Criminal Code (Arrest) Act* 1977), s 15]

See the *Arrest Act* (Ch 4 of this book).

254. Police officer preventing escape from arrest.

[S 254 rep Act No 13, 1977 (*Criminal Code (Arrest) Act* 1977), s 16]

See the *Arrest Act* (Ch 4 of this book).

255. Other cases of preventing escape from arrest.

[S 255 rep Act No 13, 1977 (*Criminal Code (Arrest) Act* 1977), s 17]

See the *Arrest Act* (Ch 4 of this book).

256. Preventing escape or rescue after arrest.

[S 256 rep Act No 13, 1977 (*Criminal Code (Arrest) Act* 1977), s 18]

See the *Arrest Act* (Ch 4 of this book).

257. Examination of person of accused persons in custody.

[S 257 rep Act No 13, 1977 (*Criminal Code (Arrest) Act* 1977), s 19]

See the *Arrest Act* (Ch 4 of this book).

258. Preventing a breach of the peace.

It is lawful for a person who witnesses a breach of the peace to interfere to prevent the continuance or renewal of it, and to use such force as is -

(a) reasonably necessary for its prevention; and

(b) reasonably proportioned to the danger to be apprehended from its continuance or renewal.

[S 258 subst Act No 13, 1977 (*Criminal Code (Arrest) Act* 1977), s 20]

259. Suppression of riot.

It is lawful for any person to use such force as is -

(a) necessary to suppress a riot; and

(b) reasonably proportioned to the danger to be apprehended from its continuance.

260. Suppression of riot by magistrates and police officers.

It is lawful for a magistrate to use, or order to be used, and for a member of the Police Force to use, such force as -

(a) he believes, on reasonable grounds, to be necessary in order to suppress a riot; and

(b) is reasonably proportioned to the danger that he believes, on reasonable grounds, is to be apprehended from its continuance.

261. Suppression of riot by person acting under lawful orders.

(1) It is lawful for a person, acting in good faith in obedience to orders, not manifestly unlawful, given by a magistrate for the suppression of a riot, to use such force as he believes, on reasonable grounds to be necessary for carrying the orders into effect.

(2) The question, whether or not any particular order referred to in Subsection (1) is manifestly unlawful is a question of law.

262. Suppression of riot by person acting without order in case of emergency.

When any person believes, on reasonable grounds, that serious mischief will arise from a riot before there is time to procure the intervention of a magistrate, it is lawful for him to use such force as -

(a) he believes, on reasonable grounds to be necessary for the suppression of the riot; and

(b) is reasonably proportioned to the danger that he believes, on reasonable grounds, is to be apprehended from its continuance.

263. Riot: Persons subject to military law.

(1) It is lawful for a person who is bound by military law to obey the lawful commands of his superior officer and to obey any command given to him by his superior officer for the purposes of the suppression of a riot, unless the command is manifestly unlawful.

(2) The question, whether or not any particular command referred to in Subsection (1) is manifestly unlawful is a question of law.

264. Prevention of crimes and offences for which an offender may be arrested without warrant: Prevention of violence by persons of unsound mind.

It is lawful for any person to use such force as is reasonably necessary in order to prevent -

(a) the commission of an offence other than an offence specified by law (including this Code) to be an offence for which a person may only be arrested by virtue of a warrant; or

(b) any act from being done that he believes, on reasonable grounds, would amount to such an offence; or

(c) a person whom he believes, on reasonable grounds, to be of unsound mind from doing violence to any person or property.

[S 264 am Act No 13, 1977 (*Criminal Code (Arrest) Act* 1977), s 21]

265. Defence of dwelling-house.

It is lawful for a person who is in peaceable possession of a dwelling-house, and for any person lawfully assisting him or acting by his authority, to use such force as he believes, on reasonable grounds, to be necessary in order to prevent the forcible breaking and entering of the dwelling-house by any person whom he believes, on reasonable grounds, to be attempting to break and enter it with intent to commit an indictable offence in it.

"Dwelling-house" is defined by s 1 of the Code. "Breaking and entering" is defined by s 394. As to forcible entry and detainer, see ss 71-72.

This defence is only available in circumstances where force is used to prevent forcible breaking and entering: *The State v Angela Colis Towavik* [1981] PNGLR 140.

266. Provocation.

(1) Subject to this section, "provocation" used with reference to an offence of which an assault is an element, means a wrongful act or insult of such a nature as to be likely, when done -

(a) to an ordinary person; or

(b) in the presence of an ordinary person to another person -

(i) who is under his immediate care; or

(ii) to whom he stands -

(A) in a conjugal, parental, filial or fraternal relationship; or

(B) in the relation of master or servant,

to deprive him of the power of self-control, and to induce him to assault the person by whom the act or insult is done or offered.

(2) When an act or insult referred to in Subsection (1) is done or offered by one person to another, or in the presence of another to a person who is under the immediate care of that other or to whom the latter stands in a relation referred to in Subsection (1) the former is said to give to the latter provocation for an assault.

(3) A lawful act is not provocation to any person for an assault.

(4) An act that a person does in consequence of incitement given by another person in order to induce him to do the act, and thus to furnish an excuse for committing an assault, is not provocation to that other person for an assault.

(5) An arrest that is unlawful is not necessarily provocation for an assault, but may be evidence of provocation to a person who knows of the illegality.

See ss 25, 267, 269 and 270 of the Code.

The onus is on the prosecution, once there is sufficient evidence to raise provocation, to negative that defence: *The State v Davelambem Yangidao* (1980) N278.

The onus is on the prosecution when a defence of provocation is raised, and the state must prove beyond reasonable doubt that the elements supporting the defence are not present: *R v Agana Guguna* (1965) N364.

See also *R v Kristeff* (1967) N445.

There is no authority as to whether this section may operate with s 25. Minogue CJ and Kelly J said, in *R v KJ* [1973] PNGLR 93 at 101:

> "We would venture to say that that may well be because the position has always been thought to be clear, namely that mistake of fact as set out in s 24 could apply in relation to provocation as defined here. In our view this is so."

Section 25 is impliedly excluded from the considerations of provocation such as would reduce a charge of wilful murder or murder to manslaughter under s 303. If a lawful act cannot constitute provocation under this section, it appears completely inconsistent to hold that a non-existent (an imagined) act can constitute provocation. The concept of provocation is obviously intended to reduce culpability (s 303) or eliminate it (s 268), because of the fault of the provoker. It is restricted to excusing only actions against the provoker. It is therefore completely anomalous to find excuse in an imagined "provocation" for an assault upon an "innocent" (inoffensive) person: *R v KJ* [1973] PNGLR 93 (Prentice J dissenting).

Under the old Code this section posed the problem of whether it provided the definition of provocation for s 303 (killing on provocation). The general view of the bench in Papua New Guinea was that this section supplied the definition of provocation for s 303, although some judges dissented from this view. See O'Regan, "*Provocation and Homicide in Papua New Guinea*" (1971) 10 *Western Australia Law Review* 1, which reviews and analyses the case law on the subject. However, the matter has been settled by the new wording of s 303, which expressly provides that 268 supplies the definition of provocation in cases of killing.

Provocation is available to a charge of unlawful assault under the *Summary Offences Act*. See *Supreme Court Reference No 6 of 1984; Re Provocation* [1985] PNGLR 31.

To ascertain the scope of the partial defence under s 303, there is no justification for going outside the words of this section, even though it may afford a narrower scope for provocation than the common law allows: *The State v Inawai Moroi* [1981] PNGLR 132.

Exculpatory provocation has been found to exist notwithstanding the passage of quite a substantial time from the occurrence of the act constituting the provocation. As well, the passion of a member of a primitive race may remain alive and heated for periods much greater than that of a more sophisticated person: *R v Rumints-Gorok* [1963] PNGLR 81 at 84.

Long before the *Criminal Code* was enacted, provocation existed as a defence to murder to allow for the frailty of human nature. The Code intended not only to preserve that concession to human frailty, but to extend it, as it does in s 269. It is natural that that frailty should increase in times of sickness and that allowance should be made for a person's loss or ability to control his or her emotional responses brought about by normal ills: *R v Iawe-Mama* [1965-1966] PNGLR 96 at 103-104.

R v Terep Komar (1972) N709 provides an example of words spoken by a wife that would be likely, when said to an ordinary Papuan villager of the accused's background and village environment, to deprive him of his power of self-control.

Words alone may amount to provocation. It was held in *R v Kink Abu* (1970) N576 that where the deceased boasted of adulterous affairs and said to her husband, "You come and eat my vagina and the vagina of your sister" and "When I have illicit intercourse will you eat the semen and other liquid for our intercourse", these words – in any community, European or native – would in the circumstance be such as might reasonably be considered to constitute provocation.

An admission of adultery may be provocation, depending on the accused's cultural and social context: *R v Koruapu* (1957) N104A.

The words "with reference to an offence of which an assault is an element" are to be interpreted as "with reference to an offence in the commission of which an assault may be committed": *R v KJ* [1973] PNGLR 93 (Minogue CJ and Kelly J).

The words "an offence of which an assault is an element" used in this section mean "an offence in the commission of which an assault is committed": *Kaporonovski v The Queen* (1973) 133 CLR 209 not followed. Therefore, provocation is available as a complete defence to an accused person on a charge of manslaughter under s 302 of the Code: *Principal Legal Advisors Request No 1 of 1980* [1980] PNGLR 326 (Wilson and Andrew JJ, with Greville Smith J dissenting).

This section can provide a defence to manslaughter and other crimes of violence in the course of which an assault is committed: *R v Nantisantjaba* (1963) N305 (Smithers J).

The law of England appears to have the view that with respect to provocation based upon adultery, only the discovery of a spouse *in flagrante delicto* can be regarded as sufficient to induce loss of control, and that a mere confession of adultery, even if sudden and unexpected, will not be sufficient. In Papua New Guinea, however, subsequent discovery of an adulterous act would quite likely be cause for the ordinary villager to be deprived of the power of self-control and induce him to commit an assault: *R v Rumints-Gorok* [1963] PNGLR 81 at 83.

In *R v Moses-Robert* [1965-1966] PNGLR 180 at 187 it was held that the court may find that the accused was provoked by his wife's unwitnessed adultery, but the provocation must be sudden.

"Wrongful act" or "insult" are not mutually exclusive; an insult may well be by conduct and the speaking of words may constitute provocation by wrongful acts: *R v Korongia* (1961) N204.

The word "wrongful" in this section does not mean "unlawful", nor is it used to qualify the word "insult". The words "ordinary person" refer to an ordinary person of the same community as the accused: *R v Zariai-Gavene* [1963] PNGLR 203 at 214.

The ordinary person who loses the power of self-control and assaults another in the heat of passion will not commit a technical or minor assault. Thus, the accused cannot strictly be held to a response "proportionate" to the victim's provocation: *R v Zariai-Gavene* [1963] PNGLR 203 at 215.

A civil trespass to personal property may be a "wrongful act": *R v Nabai son of Tinip and Atabena son of Nangage and Velipi son of Minum* (1964) N333.

Neither under this section, nor under the common law, does there appear room for the doctrine of transferred malice or misdirected retaliation or indirect retaliation. Therefore, the act of a third person cannot constitute provocation for an assault by the accused upon a victim: *R v Sigo Sasawari* (1975) N825.

See also *R v Hone Dorope* (1970) N608.

In *R v Marumyapusek* [1973] PNGLR 582 the accused was struck by his wife with a piece of taro and he retaliated immediately with no intention of causing her harm. His reaction was that of an ordinary villager, and danger that serious injury to the deceased might result from his blow was not appreciated. The accused had acted under provocation, and the force used was not disproportionate to the provocation and was not intended, nor such as was likely, to cause death or grievous bodily harm.

Where an accused's wife may have provoked the accused, but the accused's act resulted in a lethal blow to the accused's infant son, the accused cannot rely on the defence of provocation: *R v Tsagoroan Kagobo* [1965-1966] PNGLR 122 at 128.

A brother-in-law may stand in a fraternal relationship to the accused within the section. In Papua New Guinea "filial" is not limited to father and son relationships only, but may extend to sons of brothers and even sons of first cousins: *R v Domara-Saope* [1967-1968] PNGLR 71.

A first cousin by native custom (amongst the Kulwango) is regarded as a brother and consequently is in a filial relationship: *R v Iglis Lu'umbat* (1966) N405.

The relationships set out in s 266 should be given their common and general meaning and should extend beyond strictly definable blood relationships. Where evidence of a precise relationship is deficient, the onus is on the Crown to negative the applicability of the relationship contended by the defence: *R v Yanda-Piaua* [1967-1968] PNGLR 482.

For a case considering the proportionality or disproportionality of force used in response to a provocation (by insulting words), see *The State v Marawa Kanaio* [1979] PNGLR 319.

See also the later cases of *R v Kopal Wamme* (1974) N809; *R v KJ* [1973] PNGLR 93; *R v Sigo Sasawari* (1975) N825; *R v Galamu Obu* (1974) N786; and *R v Lipo Maima* [1974] PNGLR 78, on the position under the old Code.

For cases dealing with sorcery and sorcery as provocation, see notes under s 20 of the *Sorcery Act* 1971.

See Narokobi, "*Adaptation of Western Law in Papua New Guinea*" 5 Mel LJ No 1, 51-69 at 61-62; O'Neill, "*Criminal Law – Provocation as a Complete Defence to a Charge of Manslaughter: A Note*" 1 Mel LJ No 1, 58-59.

See O'Regan, "*Provocation and Homicide in Papua New Guinea*" 1 Mel JL No 3, 60-74 and O'Regan, "*Ordinary Man and Provocation in Papua and New Guinea*" (1972) 21 ICLQ 476.

267. Defence of provocation.

(1) A person is not criminally responsible for an assault committed on a person who gives him provocation for the assault, if he -

(a) is deprived by the provocation of the power of self-control; and

(b) acts on it on the sudden and before there is time for his passion to cool,

if the force used is not disproportionate to the provocation, and is not intended to cause, and is not likely to cause, death or grievous bodily harm.

(2) Any question, whether or not -

(a) any particular act or insult is likely to deprive an ordinary person of the power of self-control and to induce him to assault the person by whom the act or insult is done or offered; or

(b) in any particular case, the person provoked was actually deprived by the provocation of the power of self-control; or

(c) any force used is disproportionate to the provocation,

is a question of fact.

In Papua New Guinea, the pre-Independence Supreme Court consistently held that s 267 does make provocation a defence to manslaughter. The overwhelming view in our jurisdiction has been that s 267 had the effect that provocation, as defined in s 266, was, subject to the conditions stated in s 267, a defence to a charge of manslaughter, unlawfully doing grievous bodily harm or unlawful wounding, where the death, grievous bodily harm or wounding has been caused by an assault committed by the accused. The Code, in defining those crimes, does not use the word "assault", and does not make an assault a necessary component part of the offence, but the defence of provocation was nevertheless held applicable where the assault was alleged to have been in fact an element of the offence charged.[83] The conflict of judicial opinion between the Papua New Guinean cases and the majority of the Australian High Court in *Kaporonovski v The Queen* (1973) 133 CLR 209, should be resolved with reference to the whole of the circumstances of this country. It is important to realise that what amounts to provocation here may not be regarded as such in Australia and other jurisdictions. The Papuan New Guinean Supreme Court must also resolve the point of law raised by constitutional requirements (ss 20-21 and Sch 2) to develop the underlying law as appropriate to the circumstances of the country. It was said, in *Principal Legal Advisors Request No 1 1980* [1980] PNGLR 326:

> "With this in mind, I am quite unable to see why this court should now abandon the view which has developed in the indigenous jurisprudence of Papua New Guinea and follow the obiter view of the majority of the High Court in *Kaporonovski*, and thereby abandon consistency and coherency in the development of the law. The view of the law expressed in the Papua New Guinea cases was the correct view of the law and entirely appropriate to the circumstances of Papua New Guinea. Henceforth, *Kaporonovski* should not be used as authority in Papua New Guinea, and provocation is available as a complete defence to manslaughter."

See Wilson, "*Provocation in Papua New Guinea*" (1981) 5 Crim LJ (No 3) 128-135, for a discussion of *Principal Legal Adviser's Reference No 1 of 1980.*

Andrew J said, in *Principal Legal Advisors Request No 1 1980* [1980] PNGLR 326:

> "*Kaporonovski* is to be approached with caution as its findings are based on different legislation (with the amendments to the Papua New Guinean Code) to our own and because it is dealing with the concept of provocation in a different cultural environment."

The absolute defence of provocation under this section is available in appropriate circumstances upon a charge of manslaughter. This section is not limited to cases where the offence charged includes, by definition, assault: *The State v Saiko Norman* [1979] PNGLR 599 (not following the majority of the High Court of Australia in *Kaporonovski v The Queen* (1974-1975) 133 CLR 209, and Greville Smith J in *The State v Marawa Kanaio* [1979] PNGLR 319).

In *The State v Mole Manipe* (1979) N196 it was argued that by virtue of the operation of ss 25, 266, 267, and 303 of the *Criminal Code*, and s 20 of the *Sorcery Act*, the accused had a defence of provocation, in that he honestly and reasonably believed (if mistakenly) that the deceased was a sorcerer who had committed an act of evil sorcery directed at him of such nature, judged by reference to the traditional beliefs of his society, as was likely to deprive him of his power of self-control and induce him to assault the deceased. In this case, however, the evidence indicated that the accused was not in fact deprived of his power of self-control and that he did not retaliate in the heat of passion – rather the accused's retaliation was a planned and controlled act of revenge.

The circumstances or criteria reducing wilful murder or murder to manslaughter under s 303 are different from and less stringent than those applicable to s 267. The use of the word "sudden" is different in both – in s 267 it is the accused who must

[83] See *R v Nantisantjaba* [1963] PNGLR 148 at 151; *R v Iawe-Mama* [1965-1966] PNGLR 96 at 101; *R v Bauoro-Dame* [1965-1966] PNGLR 201 at 204; *R v Panuvo-Inapero* (unreported, 1966); *R v Anton Komalko* (unreported, 1969); *R v Marumyapusek* [1973] PNGLR 582; *R v KJ* [1973] PNGLR 93; and *The State v Saikoro Norman* [1979] PNGLR 599.

act on the provocation "on the sudden", whereas in s 303 it is the provocation itself which must "be sudden". Under s 267, a person (who is charged with an offence) is not criminally responsible for an assault committed on a person who gives provocation for the assault, provided always that the person charged:

(a) is deprived by the provocation of the power of self control; and

(b) acts on the provocation on the sudden; and

(c) before there is time for his or her passion to cool, and **provided further that** the force used by the person charged;

(d) is not disproportionate to the provocation; and

(e) is not intended to cause death or grievous bodily; and

(f) (the force used) is not likely to cause death or grievous bodily harm.

For s 303 to operate in order to reduce wilful murder to manslaughter, three circumstances must exist. The accused must do the act that causes death:

(a) in the heat of passion which must be caused by -

(b) sudden provocation within the meaning of 266; and

(c) before there is the time for that passion to cool.

Under s 303:

(a) the force used by the accused may be disproportionate to the provocation;

(b) it **can** be intended to cause death or grievous bodily harm; and

(c) it **may** be likely to cause death or grievous bodily harm.[84]

See note on *R v Zariai-Gavene* [1963] PNGLR 203 under the preceding section.

In the case of *R v Taimbari-Kesa* (1966) N397, regarding unlawful wounding, provocation was found to exist. It was held that a man retaliating with a knife when kicked had not used force disproportionate to the provocation, according to the proviso in s 267. It was held that each case must depend on its own circumstances.

This section constitutes a departure from the common law, under which provocation, whilst mitigating the penalty, was not an excuse so as to render the assault lawful: *R v Gamumu* [1963] PNGLR 1 at 7.

This section applies to a considerable number of offences where assault is a de facto element in the evidence relied on by the state: *R v Marumyapusek* [1973] PNGLR 572.

What has come to be referred to as the doctrine of proportionate retaliation is specifically incorporated into this section. This is understandable in a section that provides complete exculpation from criminal responsibility for an assault that may bring grievous bodily harm in its train: *R v Iawe-Mama* [1965-1966] PNGLR 96 at 102.

The law in England measures the critical degree of provocation by reference to its likelihood to produce the actual violence used, whereas the Code measures it by its likelihood to induce a mere assault. In addition, this section recognises that mere verbal insults may constitute a sufficient inducement and may thus constitute exculpatory provocation: *R v Rumints-Gorok* [1963] PNGLR 81 at 83.

The doctrine of proportionate retaliation applies in cases of provocation under the Code. Provocation consists of three elements – the act of provocation, the loss of

---

[84] *Rosa Angitai v The State* (1983) SC 252.

self-control, both actual and reasonable, and the retaliation proportionate to the provocation: *R v John* (1971) N659.

There is no stated requirement that the accused shall have been deprived of the power of self-control. It is only stipulated that the wrongful act or insult shall be of a kind which would deprive an ordinary person so stimulated of the power of self-control. The only expressly stipulated condition of the required state of mind of the accused is that he or she shall have acted in the heat of passion caused by sudden provocation. This phrase requires that the accused has acted not only while in a state of extreme anger, but when the passion has caused the accused to cease to be the master of his or her own understanding, ie anger has taken the place of reason: *R v Rumints-Gorok* [1963] PNGLR 81.

The appellate court can draw its own inferences: followed *Karo Gamoga v The State* [1981] PNGLR 443. The inferences (there being no direct evidence) of punches to the spleen and the forceful sitting on the victim could not be supported: followed *R v Marumyapusek* [1973] PNGLR 582. Assault followed by a death with no casual relation between them is not a killing – there is only a killing when the assault causes death, and if the causing of death is justified or excused there is no unlawful causing of death.

Where the accused's assault was excused or justified on the basis of provocation, one could not then find that accused must have objectively appreciated the risks involved in the assault because it is well known that many persons have enlarged spleens. It could not follow that the accused's assault was "likely to cause death or grievous bodily harm": *Benny Baki v The State* (1983) SC 240.

For the purpose of provocation, the "loss of self-control" is not an absolute loss of all control, but a loss related both to the degree of provocation and to the degree and form of retaliation. The "reasonable man", against whose reaction to the provocation the accused's action is to be tested, is an ordinary man in the environment and culture of the accused, but the test is objective and care must be taken that it does not become subjective and that it does not take account of any fact personal to the accused: *R v Hand* [1963] PNGLR 9; (1960) 8 FLR 381.

The reasonable man in Papua New Guinea is the man in the lap lap who takes the place of the man on the Clapham Omnibus, so one must take the ordinary native living the rural life of low standard led by the accused and his relatives and similar lives: *R v Rumints-Gorok* [1963] PNGLR 81 at 83.

The standard is that the act of provocation was "in all the circumstances ... likely to deprive a village native living in the cultural environment of the accused, of the power of self-control and to induce such a person to assault the offender". In *R v Gamumu* [1963] PNGLR 1, the provocateur was an elderly, infirm woman, and the accused, in striking her sharply twice with a digging stick, used force disproportionate to the provocation and was therefore unable to utilise the defence made available by this section.[85]

Where provocation is found to exist, a defence under this section is possible if the force used was not disproportionate to the provocation. Each case must depend on its own circumstances. In measuring the proportion of the force used, the section "requires a man to guide his anger with judgment", but a man who has been provoked to the extent that he has lost control of himself cannot be held to too fine a standard of judgment: *R v Taimbari-Kesa* (1966) N397.

---

[85] *R v Gamumu* [1963] PNGLR 1 at 8.

See s 303 regarding killing on provocation. See s 266 for definition of provocation. See also the assault provision in s 243.

268. Prevention of repetition of insult.

It is lawful for a person to use such force as is reasonably necessary to prevent the repetition of an act or insult of such a nature as to be provocation to him for an assault, if the force used is not intended to cause, and is not likely to cause, death or grievous bodily harm.

269. Self-defence against unprovoked assault.

(1) When a person is unlawfully assaulted and has not provoked the assault, it is lawful for him to use such force to the assailant as is reasonably necessary to make an effectual defence against the assault, if the force used is not intended to cause, and is not likely to cause, death or grievous bodily harm.

(2) If -

(a) the nature of the assault is such as to cause reasonable apprehension of death or grievous bodily harm; and

(b) the person using force by way of defence believes, on reasonable grounds, that he cannot otherwise preserve the person defended from death or grievous bodily harm,

it is lawful for him to use such force to the assailant as is necessary for defence, even if it causes death or grievous bodily harm.

See s 1 definition of "grievous bodily harm", s 243 on assault, s 266 on provocation and s 281 on excessive force.

Where a person is in fear of some future assault by another person, that fear does not constitute lawful justification by way of self-defence for an assault on the person feared. There must be prior assault by the victim for the defence of self-defence to become available: *The State v Angela Colis Towavik* [1981] PNGLR 140.

Contrary to what may be the position at common law, the *Criminal Code* provisions as to self-defence do not excuse a pre-emptive blow unless there is some act on the part of the victim which itself can be regarded as an assault: *The State v Angela Colis Towavik* [1981] PNGLR 140.

Where the evidence suggests self-defence, the onus is on the state to show the absence of any one of the requirements of the section: *R v Paul Maren* (1971) N615.

The prosecution bears the burden of disproving self-defence where the evidence discloses self-defence as a defence: *R v Pari-Parilla* (1969) N527.

Once a ground is disclosed by the evidence on which a plea of self-defence may arise, or provocation, it is essential to a conviction of murder that the jury shall be satisfied beyond reasonable doubt that one or other or all of the ultimate facts which establish those pleas are not present: *R v Kristeff* (1967) N445.

The essence of self-defence is that violence is presently being offered. An actual assault in the terms of s 243 is required. An unknown future threat from sorcery is not enough: *R v Korongia* (1961) N204.

Fear of death or grievous bodily harm on some future occasion does not provide a defence under the section: *R v Yambiwato* [1967-1968] PNGLR 222.

The degree of force which it is lawful for the accused to use for the purpose of defence is set out in *R v Muratovic* [1967] Qd R 15:

"The person using force in self-defence is entitled to use any force which is reasonably necessary to preserve himself from death or grievous bodily harm if (1) the nature of the assault is such as to cause reasonable apprehension of death or grievous bodily harm and (2) the person using the force by way of self-defence believes on reasonable grounds that he cannot otherwise preserve the person defended from death or grievous bodily harm."[86]

The word "otherwise" must in the context of the section mean "otherwise than by using the force which he in fact used": *R v Kaiwor Ba* [1975] PNGLR 90.

If the two conditions specified in the paragraph are satisfied, it does not become necessary for practical purposes to consider a third question, whether the force used was in fact necessary for defence. If the accused had an honest and reasonable, although mistaken, belief that the force in fact used was necessary for defence, the accused is no more criminally responsible than if that force was in fact necessary for defence: s 25.[87]

If the jury consider that the nature of the assault was such as to cause reasonable apprehension of death or grievous bodily harm, and that the accused believed, on reasonable grounds, that he or she could not otherwise preserve the person defended from death or grievous bodily harm, or if the jury is left in doubt on those matters, the issue must be decided in favour of the accused and a verdict of acquittal must be entered. This is because on that hypothesis the jury could not be satisfied that the force used was more than the accused reasonably believed to be necessary to preserve the person defended from death or grievous bodily harm. To find against the accused, the jury would be bound, if they acted reasonably, to find beyond reasonable doubt that:

(a) the nature of the assault on the appellant was not such as to cause reasonable apprehension of death or grievous bodily harm; or

(b) the appellant did not believe that he or she could not preserve himself or herself from death or grievous bodily harm except by using the force in the manner used; or

(c) if the accused had such belief it was not based on reasonable grounds.[88]

In *The State v Takip Palne of Dumbol* [1976] PNGLR 90, O'Leary AJ interpreted "otherwise" in the second paragraph as meaning that the accused believed, on reasonable grounds, that the accused could not preserve himself or herself from death or grievous bodily harm otherwise than by using the force which was in fact used. The consequence of this interpretation is that if the accused did reasonably believe etc it becomes unnecessary for practical purposes to consider whether the force used was in fact necessary for defence.

To retreat before employing force is no longer to be treated as an independent and imperative condition if a plea of self-defence is made out. Whether a retreat could or should have been made is merely an element for the jury to consider as entering into the reasonableness of the conduct of the accused: *R v Kambe-Pare* [1965] PNGLR 321.

For the purposes of utilising this section, even in the absence of an actual assault, it is sufficient if the accused had an honest and reasonable belief that he or she was about to be assaulted. The test is an objective one: *R v Kristeff* (1967) N445.

[86] *R v Kaiwor Ba* [1975] PNGLR 90.
[87] *R v Kaiwor Ba* [1975] PNGLR 90.
[88] *R v Kaiwor Ba* [1975] PNGLR 90.

R v Howe (1958) 100 CLR 448 expressed the common law doctrine that where the defence of self-defence fails merely because the actions of the accused went beyond what was necessary, or what he or she reasonably regarded as necessary in the circumstances, then manslaughter should be available as an alternative verdict on a charge of murder or wilful murder. In *R v Yambiwato* [1967-1968] PNGLR 222 at 230, Clarkson J held that this common law doctrine was not available under the Code and that, in any event, "the principle could not be applied in a case such as the present where the excess of force was applied not in defence against an assault but to forestall a possible future assault". See also *R v Kampangio* [1969-1970] PNGLR 218.

In *R v Amuna* (1954) N59 the victim shot several arrows from a distance at the accused, because of a dispute over ownership of a pig. When the victim was distracted by the accused's son, the accused charged the victim and speared him in the back, causing serious injury. The court found that the father and son had not acted in concert, and acquitted the son. However, the accused violated the conditions for self-defence against unprovoked assault, in that the use of such force was not reasonably necessary to preserve himself or his son from death or grievous bodily harm.

Read together with s 289, s 269 in its second paragraph either provides a complete defence or, if the defence fails by virtue of the matters therein provided for being excluded, the verdict must be either wilful murder, murder or manslaughter, according to the intent proved. The common law position is that where a plea of self-defence to a charge of murder fails because the accused used force going beyond what was necessary in the circumstances of the preservation of the accused, such a homicide is reduced to manslaughter. This position is not, therefore, open on the construction of the Code.

In *The State v Jefferey Bijuma* (1989) N765, in a brief struggle between two men, the accused drew a knife and stabbed the deceased in the throat causing instant death. It was done in self-defence against an unprovoked assault, but the force used was excessive. The accused's intention was to defend himself, and in these circumstances that was a lawful purpose even though the force used was excessive. For this reason it was not a killing done in the course of an unlawful purpose, and he was therefore not guilty of murder. As the force used was excessive, however, and not justified by s 269 of the *Criminal Code*, the killing was unlawful and constituted the crime of manslaughter.

In *R v Hor Mui (Administrative Report)* (1946) N25, although the accused were originally unarmed, their continued striking and stabbing (30 cuts) of the victim were acts which went beyond the force which was necessary for self-defence and therefore were unlawful.

See *R v Woroboi Dese* [1974] PNGLR 23 generally regarding an appeal against a verdict of guilty of manslaughter using the defence of self-defence.

270. Self-defence against provoked assault.

(1) Subject to Subsection (2), when -

(a) a person has unlawfully assaulted another person, or has provoked an assault from another person; and

(b) the other person assaults him with such violence as -

(i) to cause reasonable apprehension of death or grievous bodily harm; and

(ii) to induce him to believe, on reasonable grounds that it is necessary for his preservation from death or grievous bodily harm to use force in self-defence,

the first-mentioned person is not criminally responsible for using any such force as is reasonably necessary for such preservation, even if it causes death or grievous bodily harm.

(2) The protection provided by Subsection (1) does not apply -

(a) where the person using force that causes death or grievous bodily harm -

(i) first began the assault with intent to kill or to do grievous bodily harm to some person; or

(ii) endeavoured to kill or to do grievous bodily harm to some person before the necessity of so preserving himself arose; or

(b) unless, before the necessity arose, the person using such force declined further conflict, and quitted it or retreated from it as far as was practicable.

See s 243 of the Code regarding assault. See the s 1 definition of "grievous bodily harm". See also s 32(1)(c) and (d), regarding compulsion.

Where self-defence is raised on the evidence, the state must exclude it beyond reasonable doubt: *R v David Daure* [1967-1968] PNGLR 1.

The force excused in ss 269 and 270 is force used in self-defence and not the force used by a person who has accepted the challenge of another to engage in a fight. The use of force in such a situation is not excused even by reason of the immediate tactical situation which required the accused to disable a person about to attack. The provisions of the Code are the same as the common law distinction between self-defence and fighting: *R v Lupalupa Sisarowe* [1967-1968] PNGLR 455.

Mann CJ said, in *R v Kambe-Pare* [1965] PNGLR 321:

> "To retreat before employing force is no longer to be treated as an independent and imperative condition if a plea of self-defence is made out. Whether a retreat could or should have been made is merely an element for the jury to consider as entering into the reasonableness of the conduct of the accused."

It was held in *Tapea Kwapena v The State* [1978] PNGLR 316 that where the appellant was in fear of his life, being confronted with a shotgun which he believed to have been loaded, it was unreasonable to expect him to have retreated before he could raise self-defence. Faced with such a weapon, the possibility of retreating even a few feet might well have put him in greater jeopardy. If you are attacked with a deadly weapon you can defend yourself with a deadly weapon or with any other weapon which may protect your life. The law does not concern itself with niceties in such matters. A person in such a situation cannot weigh the exact measure of the necessary defensive action. If:

(a) the assault on the accused had been such as to cause reasonable apprehension of death or grievous bodily harm, and

(b) the accused believed on reasonable grounds that he could not defend himself otherwise than by using the force that he in fact used,

it is unnecessary then to consider a third question, namely whether the force used was in fact necessary for defence.

In *R v Dogwaingikata Miakawo* (1971) N630 a stage was reached during the fight when the accused had the deceased at his mercy and yet continued to act with great violence with a highly lethal weapon (bush knife). The degree of force used by the accused far exceeded that which was reasonably necessary for his preservation, and thus he was not able to use this section to his benefit.

"Likely" means reasonably foreseeable by an ordinary person as probably causing death or grievous bodily harm: *R v Domara-Saope* [1967-1968] PNGLR 71.

271. Aiding in self-defence.

Where it is lawful for a person to use force of any degree for the purpose of defending himself against an assault, it is lawful for any other person acting in good faith in his aid to use force of a like degree for the purpose of defending him.

See s 32(1)(c) and (d) and ss 269 and 270 of the Code.

Where the accused had an honest and reasonable, although mistaken, belief that he was coming to the aid of a person in need of assistance against an unprovoked attack, when in fact that person was the aggressor, s 25 operates together with this section, so that the degree of force permitted to the aider is determined according to the accused's belief, ie s 269. The accused is, therefore, no more criminally responsible than if the degree of force used was in fact necessary for defence: *R v Kaiwor Ba* [1975] PNGLR 90 at 92 and 93.

See also *The State v Aia Peto* (1975) N17.

272. Defence of movable property against trespassers.

It is lawful for a person who is in peaceable possession of any movable property, and for any person acting by the authority of any such person, to use such force as is reasonably necessary in order -

(a) to resist the taking of that property by a trespasser; or

(b) to retake it from a trespasser,

if he does not do him bodily harm.

See s 1 definition of "bodily harm".

273. Defence of movable property with claim of right.

When a person is in peaceable possession of any movable property under a claim of right, it is lawful for him and for any person acting by his authority to use such force as is reasonably necessary in order to defend his possession of the property even against a person who is entitled by law to possession of the property if he does not do him bodily harm.

See s 1 definition of "bodily harm" and s 22 claim of right.

274. Defence of movable property without claim of right.

When a person who is entitled by law to the possession of movable property attempts to take it from a person who-

(a) is in possession of the property; and

(b) neither -

(i) claims right to it; nor

(ii) acts by the authority of a person who claims right,

and the person in possession resists him, it is lawful for the person entitled to possession to use force in order to obtain possession of the property, if he does not do bodily harm to the person in possession.

275. Defence of premises against trespassers: Removal of disorderly persons.

(1) In this section, "place" includes any part of an enclosure or structure, whether or not it is separated from the rest of the enclosure or structure by a partition, fence, rope, or any other means.

(2) It is lawful for a person who is -

(a) in peaceable possession of any land, structure, vessel or place; or

(b) entitled to the control or management of any land, structure, vessel or place,

and for any person acting by the authority of such a person, to use such force as is reasonably necessary in order -

(c) to prevent any person from wrongfully entering on the land, structure, vessel or place; or

(d) to remove from it a person who wrongfully remains on it,

if he does not do bodily harm to that person.

(3) It is lawful for a person who is:

(a) in peaceable possession of any land, structure, vessel or place; or

(b) entitled to the control or management of any land, structure, vessel or place,

and for any person acting by the authority of such a person, to use force in order to remove from it any person who conducts himself in a disorderly manner in it, if he does not do him bodily harm.

"Bodily harm" and "vessel" are defined in s 1. See also ss 70-71 and 265 of the Code.

276. Defence of possession of real property or vessel with claim of right.

When a person is in peaceable possession of any land, structure or vessel, with a claim of right, it is lawful for him, and for any person acting by his authority, to use such force as is reasonably necessary in order to defend his possession, even against a person who is entitled by law to the possession of the property, if he does not do him bodily harm.

See s 1 definition of "bodily harm" and s 22 claim of right.

277. Exercise of right of way or easement.

When a person who is lawfully entitled to enter on land for the exercise of a right of way or other easement, or a profit -

(a) enters on the land for the purpose of exercising the right of way, easement or profit, after notice that his right to use the way or easement or to take the profit is disputed by the person in possession of the land; or

(b) having entered persists in his entry after the notice,

it is lawful for the person in possession, and for any person acting by his authority, to use such force as is reasonably necessary for the purpose of making the person entering desist from the entry, if he does not do him bodily harm.

278. Domestic discipline.

It is lawful for a parent or a person in the place of a parent, or for a schoolmaster, or master, to use, by way of correction, towards a child, pupil or apprentice under his care such force as is reasonable under the circumstances.

279. Discipline of ship or aircraft.

It is lawful for the master or other person in command of -

(a) a vessel on a voyage; or

(b) an aircraft on a flight,

and any person acting by his authority, to use, for the purpose of maintaining good order and discipline on board the vessel or aircraft, such force as -

(c) he believes, on reasonable grounds, to be necessary; and

(d) is reasonable under the circumstances.

"Vessel" and "aircraft" are defined in s 1 of the Code.

280. Surgical operations.

A person is not criminally responsible for performing in good faith and with reasonably care and skill a surgical operation on -

(a) any person for his benefit; or

(b) an unborn child for the preservation of the mother's life,

if the performance of the operation is reasonable, having regard to the patient's state at the time and to all the circumstances of the case.

See s 225 of the Code.

See Weisbrot and Ottley, "*Law and Medicine in Papua New Guinea: Licensing and Liability of Practitioners*" (1977), 5(2) MLJ 175.

281. Excessive force.

Even where the use of force by one person to another is lawful, the use of more force than is justified by law under the circumstances is unlawful.

See generally ss 240-288 of the Code which provide for the lawful use of force in certain circumstances.

In *R v McDonald* (1947) N212 it was held that the use of a sharp knife against the fists of a drunk man was excessive self-defence and unlawful.

See discussion of *R v Kristeff* (1967) N445 at s 274. Where a defence under s 274 fails because of excessive force, the unlawful killing may be wilful murder, murder or manslaughter according to the intent proved.

282. Consent to death immaterial.

Consent by a person to the causing of his own death does not affect the criminal responsibility of any person by whom the death is caused.

See s 244 of the Code.

Division 2 – Duties Relating to the Preservation of Human Life

283. Duty to provide necessaries.

(1) It is the duty of every person having charge of another who -

(a) is unable by reason of age, sickness, unsoundness of mind, detention, or any other cause, to withdraw himself from that charge; and

(b) is unable to provide himself with the necessaries of life,

whether the charge -

(c) is undertaken under a contract; or

(d) is imposed by law; or

(e) arises by reason of any act, whether lawful or unlawful, of the person who has the charge,

to provide for the other person the necessaries of life.

(2) A person on whom a duty is imposed by Subsection (1) shall be deemed to have caused any consequences that result to the life or health of the other person by reason of any omission to perform that duty.

See s 323 of the Code.

284. Duty of head of family.

It is the duty of every person who, as head of a family, has the charge of a child under the age of 14 years who is a member of his household to provide the necessaries of life for the child, and he shall be deemed to have caused any consequences that result to the life or health of the child by reason of any omission to perform that duty, whether or not the child is helpless.

See s 323 of the Code.

285. Duty of masters.

It is the duty of every person who as a master has contracted to provide necessary food, clothing or lodging for any servant or apprentice under the age of 16 years to provide it, and he shall be deemed to have caused any consequences that result to the life or health of the servant or apprentice by reason of any omission to perform that duty.

See s 324 of the Code.

286. Duty of persons doing dangerous acts.

It is the duty of every person who, except in a case of necessity, undertakes -

(a) to administer surgical or medical treatment to any other person; or

(b) to do any other lawful act that is or may be dangerous to human life or health,

to have reasonable skill and to use reasonable care in doing the act, and he shall be deemed to have caused any consequences that result to the life or health of any person by reason of any omission to observe or perform that duty.

See s 24 of the Code regarding the defence of accident. See ss 300 and 302 where a person dies as a result of a breach of the duty imposed by this section. See s 326 regarding man-traps, and s 327 regarding negligent acts causing harm.

The law applicable is as stated in the terms of the section. The only elaboration necessary relates to the degree of negligence required, which is that required by the common law standard in cases where negligence amounts to manslaughter. This is usefully stated in *R v Bateman* (1925) 94 LJ (KB) 791, such that it "went beyond a mere matter of compensation between subjects and showed such disregard for life and safety of others as to amount to a crime against the State and conduct deserving punishment". Thus, in *Prosecutor's Request No 2 of 1974* [1974] PNGLR 317, where an unqualified villager had performed an operation involving the opening of a man's chest by means of a bamboo knife without antiseptic, the standard applicable is better expressed simply as that of the reasonable man. For the purpose of this case, a reasonable man was to be presumed one whose state of knowledge and prudence was such that he appreciated the difference in training and skill between a qualified medical practitioner and a "village surgeon" without any medical qualifications.

Criminal negligence, which is "conduct going beyond a matter of compensation and is conduct deserving of punishment", is a question of degree to be determined by the jury: *R v Abe* (1964) N299A.

R v Wabia Yasi (1970) N577 involved a charge of manslaughter where the accused was charged on the basis of criminal negligence, having administered medical treatment. It was held that the circumstances of the accused as a young man with little education and only limited training for the task he was undertaking, are relevant considerations in deciding whether or not the accused has been criminally negligent.

Where the accused fired an arrow at a hen underneath a house and it missed the hen but killed a child whose presence was not known to the accused, the court held that this event was unintended, unforeseen and unforeseeable and the accused had a defence under s 23.[89] The accused was not criminally responsible if he acted neither intentionally nor recklessly nor negligently. Criminal negligence is the high degree of inadvertence to consequences which will ground a conviction for manslaughter. The degree of negligence has variously been described as "culpable", "criminal", "gross", "wicked", "clear" and "complete": *Andrews v DPP* [1937] AC 576. In *The State v Kaiwa Iasumi* (1978) N163, it was said:

[89] Followed: *Vallance v The Queen* (1961) 108 CLR 56; *Mamote-Kulang v The Queen* (1964) 111 CLR 62; *Ward v The Queen* [1972] WAR 36; *Timbu Kolian v The Queen* (1969-70) 119 CLR 47.

> "Simple lack of care such as will constitute civil liability is not enough: for purposes of the criminal law there are degrees of negligence: and a very high degree of negligence is required to be proved before the felony is established."

Whether the accused was criminally negligent or not must be decided by reference only to the situation prevailing when the accused performed the action in issue, ie when the bow and arrow was aimed and fired, and not by reference to the consequences which brought the accused before the court: followed *Akerele v The King* [1943] AC 255. It was stated in *The State v Kaiwa Iasumi* that "[t]he negligence to be imputed depends on the probable, not the actual result".

See also the interlocutory judgment in *The State v Elias Subang*, otherwise known as *Salia Wangi of Rabaul* [1976] PNGLR 141.

See Weisbrot and Ottley, "*Law and Medicine in Papua New Guinea: Licensing and Liability of Practitioners*" (1977) 5(2) MLJ 175.

287. Duty of persons in charge of dangerous things.

(1) It is the duty of every person who has in his charge or under his control any thing whether living or inanimate, and whether moving or stationary, of such a nature that in the absence of care or precaution in its use or management the life, safety or health of any person may be endangered to use reasonable care and take reasonable precautions to avoid that danger.

(2) A person on whom a duty is imposed by Subsection (1) shall be deemed to have caused any consequences that result to the life or health of any person by reason of any omission to perform that duty.

See s 24 of the Code regarding the defence of accident.

See ss 300 and 302, where the breach of duty imposed by this section results in death.

See s 327 regarding negligent acts.

See s 328 regarding dangerous driving.

See s 64 of the *Summary Offences Act* regarding the summary offence of negligent driving.

The standard of negligence to be established is the criminal standard, which involves showing the accused acted with such a reckless disregard for the lives and safety of others as to make his or her conduct deserving of punishment: *Evgeniou v The Queen* (1964) 37 ALJR 508.

The standard of care required of persons in control of motor vehicles is the same as that required by the common law where negligence causing death is alleged to amount to manslaughter: *R v Druett* [1965-1966] PNGLR 395.

The civil law defence of "volenti" does not apply to breaches of the duty imposed by this section: *R v Druett* [1965-1966] PNGLR 395.

As a further matter of law, it is sufficient if the negligence complained of is a direct cause of death or injury. It is not necessary that it should be the sole direct cause: *R v Bile Lumapa* (1968) N498.

If the negligent actions of another motorist put the accused in a difficult situation, that cannot excuse the accused, so long as the accused's negligence was a substantial cause of the deceased's death: *R v Elly* (1965) N357.

In cases where death results from a failure to use reasonable care or take reasonable precautions as required by this section, liability is determined without resort to s 24: *Evgeniou v The Queen* [1964] PNGLR 45; (1964) 37 ALJR 508.

The authorities are clear that s 24 has no relevance to a case where the offence charged rests upon the omission of a duty of the character specified in this section: *R v Peck* (1971) N650.

If the unlawfulness of an act of the accused is to be measured according to whether or not the accused is in breach of the duty imposed by this section, then s 24 (accident/lack of intent) has no application: *R v Yofia Abone* [1967-1968] PNGLR 277 at 289.

In *R v Aivei Ieme* [1973] PNGLR 1, Prentice J (at 9) expressed the opinion that the defence of accident under s 24 was not applicable where criminal negligence had been proved.

In *R v Druett* [1965-1966] PNGLR 395, Ollerenshaw J adopted the standard of care definition of Hewart CJ in *R v Bateman* (1925) 94 LJ (KB) 791 at 793. That definition provided that to support an indictment for manslaughter, the prosecution must prove a breach of the duty imposed by this section according to the standard of the criminal law and not the civil law. The evidence must show a disregard for human life which goes beyond a mere matter of compensation, but which amounts to a crime against the state deserving punishment.

Criminal negligence is the very high degree of inadvertence to consequences which will ground a conviction for manslaughter. This is a jury question. In *The State v Andrew Amoy* [1978] PNGLR 266, the negligence of the accused in driving at the speed he did and in all the circumstances was of a type variously described as "culpable", "criminal", "gross", "wicked", "clear" and "complete". The question of the criminal negligence has to be answered by reference only to the situation prevailing when the accused performed the actions in issue – the negligence to be imputed depends on the probable not the actual result. There is an apparent conflict between the test of what constitutes dangerous driving as applied in England and that in Australia. In England, in such cases as *R v Evans* (1963) 47 Cr App R 62, and *R v Ball* (1966) 50 Cr App R 266, the view seems to have been taken that dangerous driving may be caused by the "slightest negligence": see also *R v Gosney* (1971) 55 Cr App R 502. The view adopted by the High Court in Australia in *McBride v The Queen* (1966) 115 CLR 44, and by the Supreme Court of South Australia in *R v Mayne* (1975) 11 SASR 583, was that not all departures from due care and attention are necessarily to be classified as dangerous.

The test in *R v Bateman* has been applied in *R v Peck* (1971) N650; *R v Wilson Otto Nuna* (1962) N246; *R v Yafia Abone* [1967-1968] PNGLR 277; *R v Gamumu* [1963] PNGLR 1; *R v Elly* (1965) N357; *R v Pius Tokivung* (1969) N545; *R v Gaiara Gabereba* (1967) N155; *The State v John Koe* [1976] PNGLR 562; *Java Johnson Beraro v The State* [1988-1989] PNGLR 562.

To amount to criminal negligence the conduct of the accused must be able to be characterised as "grossly careless or reckless". There must be an "element of culpability or what an ordinary man would understand as criminality surpassing in a material degree mere failure to measure up to the standard of care of the ordinary reasonable man": *R v Begari-Dubere* (1962) N227 (Smithers J).

In determining whether a juvenile accused has used reasonable care and taken reasonable precautions to avoid danger, within the terms of this section, the test is whether it had been shown beyond reasonable doubt that the actions of the accused fell so far short of what would be expected of a normal boy of his age and in the circumstances as to amount to the degree of criminal negligence variously described by the courts as "gross", "wicked", "clear", "complete", etc: *R v Taperara* [1975] PNGLR 9.

The determination as to whether an accused is "criminally negligent or not ... must be decided by reference only to the situation prevailing when the accused performed the actions in issue and not by reference to the consequences which brought him before the Court": *Java Johnson Beraro v The State* [1988-1989] PNGLR 562 at 575 (Amet J).

In *R v Wilson Otto Nuna* (1962) N246 the accused was driving a tip-truck, carrying a number of passengers on this occasion to the local church. Near the church all the passengers alighted except for the deceased, who was having difficulty getting down whilst holding her baby. The accused, assuming that all the passengers had alighted, began to drive off, and the deceased was flung off the truck, receiving injuries which resulted in her death. The court described this as a "border-line case", but found that the accused should have taken the precaution of checking that all the passengers had safely alighted before starting up the truck. Failure to do so amounted to criminal negligence under this section, and the accused was convicted of manslaughter.

Where an accused fires a loaded shotgun allegedly to "frighten" those whom he believes are about to assault him, the accused is under a duty of care imposed by this section. Given that the accused fired four times in a very confined space with the deceased standing only a few feet away, the killing amounted to criminal negligence as the act went "beyond a mere matter of compensation and showed such disregard for the life and safety of others as to amount to a crime against the State and conduct deserving punishment": *R v Kristeff* (1967) N445.

In a proceeding where the offence charged rests upon the omission of a duty outlined by this section, it is not a question of whether the accused says that he or she considered the actions safe, but whether the ordinary reasonable man would consider them safe: *R v Peck* (1971) N650.

Where a rock was picked up with the intent of being thrown offensively, it was "in the charge and under the control" of the person picking it up, and it was an "object of such a nature that in the absence of care or precaution in its use or management, the life, safety or health of (persons) may be endangered": *R v Aivei Ieme* [1973] PNGLR 1.

The standard required to avoid liability under s 292 is not that of a very careful as well as an overcautious person who has considered all the possibilities however remote. Criminal negligence requires reckless indifference to human life or safety: *R v Hill* (1964) N323.

A policeman acted reasonably where he accidentally shot a bystander while using a shotgun to frighten off a crowd, which was closing in on an overturned truck for stealing: *John Wamala v The State* (1998) SC 581.

288. Duty to do certain acts.

When a person undertakes to do any act the omission to do which is or may be dangerous to human life or health, it is his duty to do that act, and he shall be deemed to have caused any consequences that result to the life or health of any person by reason of any omission to perform that duty.

The section is not to be read as referring to situations where one person is under a contractual or other legal obligation to do certain things: *R v Marabura-Lama* (1967) N410.

Division 3 – Homicide: Suicide: Concealment of Birth

289. Homicide.

It is unlawful to kill a person unless the killing is authorized or justified or excused by law.

See s 35 of the *Constitution* regarding the fundamental right to life, and the exceptions thereto.

As to the "presumption of life", see *Axon v Axon* (1937-1938) 59 CLR 359 at 404-405, referred to in *John Peng v The State* [1982] PNGLR 331 (McDerrnott J).

For complete defences, see ss 22-36 and 245 of the Code. For a partial defence, see s 303.

This section provides that any killing not authorised, justified or excused by law is unlawful. It was said in *Evgeniou v The Queen* (1964) 37 ALJR 508 at 509 (McTiernan and Menzies JJ), in an appeal to the High Court of Australia from Papua New Guinea:

> "There are, however, strong indications that it is only an omission to observe or perform a duty that is to be regarded as giving rise to criminal responsibility: see ss 286-291 and 300. These indications we accept".[90]

It was held, in *R v Palwaskit* (1949) N35:

> "An instance of an 'authorised' killing is a judicial hanging; an instance of a 'justified' killing is a killing, in certain exceptional circumstances and provided there is no other reasonable way, done to prevent the escape of an arrested felon; an instance of a killing 'excused' by law, is that of a killing, in certain exceptional circumstances, in legitimate self-defence".

Where a person strikes an unlawful blow which results in death, the killing is, subject to the general provisions of Ch V of the Code, nonetheless unlawful when it is shown that the person who was struck was not the person at whom the blow was aimed: *R v Timbu-Kolian* [1967-1968] PNGLR 310 at 317.

To attract liability under this section of the Code, proof is required of what amounts to at least criminal negligence at common law: *R v Yofia Abone* [1967-1968] PNGLR 277 at 287-288.

290. When a child becomes a human being.

A child becomes a person capable of being killed when it has completely proceeded in a living state from the body of its mother, whether or not -

(a) it has breathed; or

(b) it has an independent circulation; or

(c) the navel-string is severed.

See ss 292, 301, 312 and 313 of the Code.

[90] *R v Taperara* [1975] PNGLR 9 at 11.

291. Definition of killing.

Subject to the succeeding provisions of this Code, any person who causes the death of another, directly or indirectly, by any means, shall be deemed to have killed the other person.

In *R v Kampangio* [1969-1970] PNGLR 218, Prentice J expressed the opinion that the Code-makers intended to make the Code cover the field as to defences to charges of murder (with the exception of provisions such as ss 24, 25 and 26 which relate to all sections of the Code). He thus took the view that the common law "doctrine of excessive force" was not available in New Guinea.

Section 291 is widely drawn, and a case where the act complained of results in the immediate death of the victim appears to come within its terms, whether or not the victim is at the time diseased, injured, senile, or in danger of immediate death from some other hand: *R v Yambiwato* [1967-1968] PNGLR 222.

Doherty J said, in *The State v Aselin* [1991] PNGLR 408:

> "On a charge of murder where death does not occur immediately the court must be satisfied that the original wounding was the operating and substantial cause of the death. Death following normal medical treatment to deal with the wounding may be regarded as caused by the felonious injury, but the same principle does not apply where the treatment applied is abnormal."

Where two persons are jointly charged with unlawful killing, so long as the court is satisfied that death was caused by the accused acting in concert, it is unnecessary to decide which accused committed the act which actually caused death: *Awap Omowo and Warsa Yirihim v The State* [1976] PNGLR 188.

If there is the intervention of some overwhelming cause following upon a mortal wound (such as if a stranger comes in and shoots the victim dead) so as to reduce the significance of the original wound and make it merely part of the history or the setting, the death does not flow from the wound: *R v Sapulo-Masuve* (1973) N732.

292. Death by acts done at childbirth.

When a child dies in consequence of an act done or omitted to be done by any person before or during its birth, the person who did or omitted to do the act shall be deemed to have killed the child.

See ss 280, 286, 290, 301, 312 and 313 of the Code.

293. Causing death by threats.

A person who, by threats, intimidation or deceit, causes another person to do an act or make an omission that results in the death of that other person shall be deemed to have killed him.

294. Acceleration of death.

A person who does any act or makes any omission that hastens the death of another person who, when the act is done or the omission is made, is suffering from some disorder or disease arising from another cause, shall be deemed to have killed that other person.

Under the common law an act or omission relied upon to support a charge of unlawful killing needed not to be the sole or even the immediate cause of death – it was sufficient if it accelerated the death. This view has been carried into the Code under this section: *R v Tiendeli Pakale* (1970) N565.

"Disorder" should be given a wide meaning so as to include injuries as well as diseases. In this case the disorder had been blows inflicted by the other attacker: *R v Yambiwato* [1967-1968] PNGLR 222.

The true meaning and area of application of this section are difficult to determine. However, it cannot be said that the section operates so that a person who causes the immediate death of a person dying from injuries, as opposed to disease, does not kill him within the meaning of ss 289 and 291: *R v John* (1971) N659.

295. When injury or death might be prevented by proper precaution.

When a person causes a bodily injury to another from which death results it is immaterial that -

(a) the injury might have been avoided by proper precaution on the part of the person injured; or

(b) his death from the injury might have been prevented by proper care or treatment.

296. Injuries causing death in consequence of subsequent treatment.

When -

(a) a person does grievous bodily harm to another; and

(b) the other person has recourse to surgical or medical treatment; and

(c) death results either from the injury or the treatment;

the first-mentioned person shall be deemed to have killed the other person, even if the immediate cause of death was the surgical or medical treatment, if the treatment was -

(d) reasonably proper under the circumstances; and

(e) applied in good faith.

"Grievous bodily harm" is defined by s 1 of the Code.

297. Limitation as to time of death.

(1) A person shall be deemed not to have killed another if the death of the person does not take place within a year and a day of the cause of death.

(2) Subject to Subsections (3) and (4), the period referred to in Subsection (1) shall be calculated inclusive of the day on which the last unlawful act contributing to the cause of death was done.

(3) If the cause of death is an omission to perform a duty, the period referred to in Subsection (1) shall be calculated inclusive of the date on which the omission ceased.

(4) If the cause of death is -

(a) in part an unlawful act; and

(b) in part an omission to perform a duty,

the period referred to in Subsection (1) shall be calculated inclusive of the day on which -

(c) the last unlawful act was done; or

(d) the omission ceased,

whichever last occurred.

298. Unlawful homicide.

A person who unlawfully kills another is guilty of the crime of wilful murder, murder, infanticide or manslaughter, according to the circumstances of the case.

The court has noted the practice in Australian courts of warning juries of the unsafeness of convicting on circumstantial evidence alone, unless no other explanation than guilt is reasonably compatible with the circumstances: *Samuel Peacock v The King* (1911) 13 CLR 619 at 630. The court has noted at the same time the more modern view of the House of Lords that it is unnecessary that such a direction should be given, provided that the jury is directed in plain terms that they must not convict unless satisfied of guilt beyond reasonable doubt. Their Lordships did recognise, however, that the caution in *Peacock* may well on occasions prove a useful guide for a jury: *McGreevy v DPP* [1973] 1 All ER 503 at 510-110, discussed in *The State v John Yaku Earu* (1976) N73.

The fact that a deceased's body was never found is, in itself, no reason for a prosecution for wilful murder to fail: *The State v Nataemo Wanu* [1977] PNGLR 152.

Where evidence of guilt is substantially confessional only, as there is no body, but the tribunal is satisfied as to the death of the person alleged to have been killed, the court must, in relation to the criminal conduct of the accused to which he has confessed, give similar weight to hypotheses more or less reasonably consistent with the confession being untrue: *R v Mon and Debong* [1965-1966] PNGLR 42.

299. Wilful murder.

(1) Subject to the succeeding provisions of this Code, a person who unlawfully kills another person, intending to cause his death or that of some other person, is guilty of wilful murder.

(2) A person who commits wilful murder shall be liable to be sentenced to death.

[Subs (2) am Act No 2, 1976 (*Criminal Code (Amendment) Act* 1976); subst Act No 25, 1991 (*Criminal Code (Amendment) Act* 1991), s 2]

See s 35 of the *Constitution* regarding the fundamental right to life, and the exceptions.

Where an accused is charged with a killing, which with others was part of a single course of conduct, then evidence of such other killings is relevant and admissible evidence to show the intention of the accused: *R v Mondo-Gengegl* (1967) N426.

For the necessity for clear proof of identity where a number of persons were involved in the incident out of which the alleged offence arose, see *R v Pogi-Wap* (1969) N539; *Mek Yambe v Oraka* (1974) N815; and *The State v Angaun Kakas* [1994] PNGLR 20 (Injia AJ).

There is need for special caution when dealing with evidence of identification in situations where observation of the accused is made under "difficult conditions": *John Beng v The State* [1977] PNGLR 115. A case in which two persons escaping from a blazing house, in which both have been badly burnt, and in which they have left their children, are "difficult conditions" for the purposes of making an identification. Where there is no other "evidence of sufficient cogency or probity to support the correctness of the identification", nor any independent forensic evidence of arson, oral testimony alone cannot push the burden beyond reasonable doubt: *The State v Kasave Tabo* (1990) N932.

In a trial for wilful murder, the death of the victim is an essential fact to be established, and it may be proved circumstantially provided the inference leaves no reasonable doubt: *R v Pari-Parilla* (1969) N527.

The fact of death of the victim may be proved circumstantially, even though there is no trace of the body. In *R v Bia-Umeme* (1959) N145, the wildness of the terrain and the youth of the victim were sufficient to conclude that the child was dead.

If it is established beyond reasonable doubt that the accused was present at the scene with the intention of encouraging or assisting in the killing of the deceased, and thereby aiding in the commission of the offence, the accused would then be guilty of wilful murder: *The State v Nataemo Wanu* [1977] PNGLR 152. See s 7 regarding aiding.

If a trial judge is not satisfied of the intention to kill, a conviction of manslaughter only should be made: *R v Woods* (1966) N399.

In *The State v Raphael Kuanande* [1994] PNGLR 512 at 514, Injia AJ said:

> "Intention is a matter which goes to the state of mind of the accused at the time he acted. It may be proven by direct evidence of the accused's expression of intention followed by the act itself or by circumstantial evidence. In either situation, it is necessary to examine the course of conduct of the accused prior, at the time and subsequent to the act constitution the offence."

A distinction must be made between an unwilled act and a willed act the product of a diseased mind which knows not the nature or quality of the willed act: *R v Waiyape* (1974) N796.

Wilful murder has always been regarded as one of the most intrinsically serious of all offences. That is why in most jurisdictions it carries a fixed penalty – sometime death, frequently life imprisonment. The "life" detainee may be discharged through exercise of the power of mercy under s 151 of the *Constitution* or released on license under s 603: *Goli Golu v The State* [1979] PNGLR 653 (Kearney J).

On the length of sentence for wilful murder, see *Nomane v The State* (1995) SCR 2/95 (30 years); *The State v Tola Kini* (1995) N1359 (22 years); *Ure Hane v The State* [1984] PNGLR 105 (15 years); and *The State v Clive Surute, Clive Guvero, Didimus Surute, Redrich Guvero and Harry Estegata* (1999) N1847 (20 Years).

For considerations on sentence where the wilful murder has been prompted by fear of sorcery, see *Acting Public Prosecutor v Uname Aumane* [1980] PNGLR 510, discussed under s 596.

See *Acting Public Prosecutor v Uname Aumane* [1980] PNGLR 510 (Kapi J), discussed under s 596, regarding considerations on sentence in a wilful murder case where aspects of customary law have been raised by the defence in mitigation.

For a case in which exceptional circumstances existed such that upon conviction for wilful murder the accused was sentenced only to the rising of the court (and this sentence was confirmed by a majority of the Supreme Court), see *Public Prosecutor v Panikuiaka Nopi* [1979] PNGLR 536.

Due to the operation of s19 of the *Criminal Code*, which makes the sentence of death discretionary, the maximum penalty of the sentence of death should be imposed only for the worst wilful murder: *The State v John Waiyake Komane* [1992] PNGLR 524 at 547.

In *The State v Yapes Paege and Relya Tanda* [1994] PNGLR 65 at 66, Woods J said:

> "The penalty laid down in *Criminal Code* s 299 for wilful murder is death. So, initially there is no range of sentence for this offence ... And the Court must now be mindful of the fact that the Parliament brought in this penalty by deliberate consideration in 1992, so it is not as though it is a penalty that can be regarded or disregarded lightly. ... Of course, Parliament has also said that the court can act under s 19 of the *Criminal Code* and impose a term of years instead of death. This immediately implies that the penalty in s 299 is not mandatory. There is some discretion. However, this discretion under s 19 cannot be an automatic moderation of the law. The application of s 19 must require appropriate circumstances, but it cannot mean there is a very wide discretion within the range of one year imprisonment to life imprisonment to death. Surely, if there was this automatic wide range, this would have been included in s 299 itself. By putting it specially in s 19, it suggests something special."

See Griffin, "*The Death Sentence in Papua New Guinea*" (1972) 1(3) MLJ 91-92, for the pre-amendment.

In *Ure Hane v The State* [1984] PNGLR 105, Bredmeyer J set out a non-exhaustive list of the most serious instances of the crime:

A wilful murder done in the course of committing a theft, a robbery, a break and enter, or a rape.

A wilful murder of a police officer or prison warden acting in the execution of his or her duty.

A wilful murder done in the course of, or for the purpose of, resisting, avoiding or preventing lawful arrest or in effecting or assisting in an escape from lawful custody.

A wilful murder of a person in police or court custody (Particular to PNG).

A payback killing of a completely innocent person (Particular to PNG).

Any second or third murder.

Any murder where the offender has a long record of violence such that that person is likely to commit such offences in the future.

A wilful murder of the Governor-General, the Prime Minister, the Leader of the Opposition, the Speaker of National Parliament, the Chief Justice, a Bishop, a visiting Prime Minister, the Pope or other VIPs.

Woods J, following *Veen v The Queen* (1979) 53 ALJR 305, stated (at 113-114) that:

> "we should not at this stage fall into the trap of classifying an offender as a danger and a menace to society and thereby sentencing him to life because he may be a menace if he is released after too early a period. The crime itself must warrant the life imprisonment because he has shown his danger to society. We must not imprison for life because we consider he will be a danger."

In *The State v Eliesa Kopeia Madiroto* (1997) N1554, Sevua J stated that:

"[i]n the case of *Ure Hane*, Bredmeyer J categorised different types of the more serious cases of wilful murder, however, with respect, these have changed since this decision was made some thirteen years ago. There are now, in my view, certain classes of wilful murder that fall into the most serious categories of wilful murder that are not mentioned in that judgment. I consider therefore that, that decision needs to be reviewed in the light of some of the most serious homicides occurring in the country … at the present time."

In *The State v Yapes Paege and Relya Tanda* [1994] PNGLR 65 the Public Prosecutor pleaded strongly against sentencing the accused to the penalty of death. Woods J held that "[a]s he is the representative of the people and the State, I must regard his views as the policy of the government and the State" and exercised the discretion under s 19 to impose sentence of life imprisonment.

See also *R v Kiandari* [1967-1968] PNGLR 31; *R v Lupalupa-Sisarowe* [1967-1968] PNGLR 455. See s 300 regarding murder, and s 304 regarding attempted murder. For alternative verdicts, see s 539.

300. Murder.

(1) Subject to the succeeding provisions of this Code, a person who kills another person under any of the following circumstances is guilty of murder -

(a) if the offender intended to do grievous bodily harm to the person killed or to some other person; or

(b) if death was caused by means of an act -

(i) done in the prosecution of an unlawful purpose; and

(ii) of such a nature as to be likely to endanger human life; or

(c) if the offender intended to do grievous bodily harm to some person for the purpose of facilitating -

(i) the commission of a crime other than a crime specified by a law (including this Code) to be a crime for which a person may only be arrested by virtue of a warrant; or

(ii) the flight of an offender who has committed or attempted to commit an offence referred to in Subparagraph (i); or

(d) if death was caused by administering any stupefying or overpowering thing for a purpose specified in Paragraph (c); or

(e) if death was caused by wilfully stopping the breath of a person for a purpose specified in Paragraph (c).

Penalty: Subject to Section 19, imprisonment for life.

[Subs 300(1)(b)(i) am Act No 12, 1982 (*Criminal Code (Amendment) Act* 1982), s 3; Subs 300(1)(c) am Act No 13, 1977 (*Criminal Code (Arrest) Act* 1977), s 22]

(2) In a case to which Subsection (1)(a) applies, it is immaterial that the offender did not intend to hurt the particular person who was killed.

(3) In a case to which Subsection (1)(b) applies, it is immaterial that the offender did not intend to hurt any person.

(4) In a case to which Subsection (1)(c), (d) or (e) applies it is immaterial that

the offender -

(a) did not intend to cause death; or

(b) did not know that death was likely to result.

"Grievous bodily harm" is defined by s 1 of the Code.

See s 299 regarding wilful murder, and s 304 regarding attempted murder. For alternative verdicts, see s 539.

On an indictment for murder, if the evidence would support a verdict of either murder or manslaughter, the onus is on the prosecution to prove that the offence amounts to murder: *R v Koruapu* (1957) N104A.

The test of whether an act is of such a nature as to be likely to endanger human life is an objective one: *R v Koito Kartogati* [1974] PNGLR 225.

To sustain a charge under this section the prosecution must show a separate and distinct unlawful purpose in the course of which a dangerous act is done. Here the act which caused death (an axe blow) was itself the unlawful purpose: *R v Hone Dorope* (1970) N608.

In *The State v Nelson Tuli* (1997) N1534, Batari J stated that: "[f]or the purpose of that provision, the 'act' which is done in prosecution of the unlawful purpose is separate and distinct from the 'unlawful purpose'."

Section 300(1)(b) relates to an act of such a nature as to be likely to endanger human life when the act is done in the prosecution of a further purpose which is unlawful. It is essential that the dangerous act relied upon by the prosecution and the unlawful purpose should be shown to be distinct. It is quite clear that where personal injury to the victim is the unlawful purpose relied upon, that provision is not applicable and the prosecution must rely on s 300(1)(a) if it is contended that the act amounts to murder: *Joseph Maino v The State* [1977] PNGLR 404.

Section 300(1)(b) was held applicable where an old woman was killed by a shot discharged by the accused from a rifle when she surprised him ransacking her house, and the accused had armed himself in the event of being discovered: *Joseph Maino v The State* [1977] PNGLR 404 following *R v Hansen* [1974] Qd R 404.

In *Pasi v The State* [1991] PNGLR 254 at 256, Kapi DCJ said:

> "The applicability of [s 300(1)(b)] ... is set out in the cases of *R v Hone Dorope* [1970] SC 608 and *The State v Joseph Maino* [1977] PNGLR 404. These two cases stand for the proposition that the 'act' which is done in the prosecution of an unlawful purpose is separate and distinct from the 'unlawful purpose'. In the present case, assault on the deceased which constitutes the act cannot also constitute the unlawful purpose. In such circumstances, s 300(1)(b) cannot be applicable".

Where a charge of murder is made under s 300(1)(b) of the Code only, an alternative verdict is not available under s 300(1)(a). The only alternative verdict is that of manslaughter under s 539(2) of the Code: *Pasi v The State* [1991] PNGLR 254.

Kidu CJ proposed the following guidelines as appropriate in sentencing for murder:

(a) on a plea of guilty where there are no special aggravating factors, a sentence of six years;

(b) a sentence of less than six years may be imposed only where there are special mitigating factors, such as the youthfulness or very advanced age of the accused;

(c) on a plea of not guilty, a range of sentences from eight to 12 years or more in a case where aggravating factors are evidenced.[91]

In *Simbe v The State* [1994] PNGLR 38, Woods, Konilio and Sevua JJ said (at 39-40):

"[Section] 300 states that the sentence for murder is life imprisonment. However, usually the Court has acted under s 19 and imposed a term of years. The records show that the term of years imposed in 1991 and 1992 for murder ranged from four years imprisonment to life imprisonment. ... [T]here may be a very wide variation in the circumstances that lead to a person being killed in a s 300 situation ... Each case of murder must be decided on a case-by-case basis, but always remembering that the sentence laid down by s 300 is life imprisonment and the term of years is by virtue of s 19."

In *The State v Drikore Yuana Peter* (2000) N1973, Kirriwom J handed down a 12 year sentence for the killing of one co-wife of a common husband by another co-wife. His Honour referred to the decisions in *The State v Maria Er* (1998) N1749; *The State v Margaret John (No 2)* [1996] PNGLR 298 and *The State v Maria Pung (Yamai)* [1995] PNGLR 173, where:

"their honours took a very stern view of the upsurge of this crime and said that strong deterrent sentences were necessary to deter wives or co-wives involved in domestic disputes with their husbands, or with the husbands' girlfriends or as between co-wives themselves."

See s 596 regarding sentencing generally, but see especially *Public Prosecutor v Tom Ake* [1978] PNGLR 469.

301. Infanticide.

(1) Where -

(a) by a wilful act or omission a woman causes the death of her child under the age of 12 months; and

(b) at the time of the act or omission the balance of her mind was disturbed by reason of -

(i) her not having fully recovered from the effect of giving birth to the child; or

(ii) the effect of lactation consequent on the birth of the child,

she is guilty of infanticide, and may be dealt with and punished as if she had been guilty of the manslaughter of the child.

(2) On an indictment for the offence of infanticide, the accused may be convicted of an offence under Section 313.

(3) On an indictment for wilful murder, murder or manslaughter, a woman may be convicted of infanticide.

This section was originally in the *Infanticide Act* 1953-1956 before being incorporated in the Code in 1974.

This provision cuts across the general principles of criminal responsibility and was intended to do so. It is purely statutory in origin, and was introduced to overcome a practical situation in which public opinion regarded this as an unnatural offence and was so adverse to inflicting capital punishment on mothers who

[91] *The State v Eddy Kava Laura (No 2)* [1988-1989] PNGLR 98.

destroyed their own infants in these circumstances, that many escaped conviction or sentence in varying degree. Thus, this section is designed to give more effective and realistic legal protection to recently born infants, and at the same time, to admit a reduced degree of criminal responsibility in the cases specified. Provocation is a precise parallel: *R v Brigitta Asamaken* [1964] PNGLR 193 at 198.

This section applies where persons, not insane at the time, are so emotionally disturbed that the normal state of mental balance or stability is not fully present to help them resist influences which a person is normally expected by law to resist. It is also relevant, of course, to consider whether the lack of balance (but seemingly not the killing) was due to the effect of childbirth or lactation: *R v Brigitta Asamaken* [1964] PNGLR 193.

An accused can rely on this section, provided the mental state exists, even if as a matter of causation such mental state is not the reason for the accused's actions: *R v Yigwai-Aku and Aku-Gobis* [1963] PNGLR 40.

Where the facts disclose a possible partial defence of infanticide, the onus is on the prosecution to satisfy the court, beyond reasonable doubt, that the elements of the crime of infanticide are either absent, or, at least, not wholly present, and that each ingredient of wilful murder is present and not negatived by any other defence which may be raised by the evidence in the particular case: *R v Brigitta Asamaken* [1964] PNGLR 193 at 198.

Where infanticide is alleged, the s 27 presumption of sanity does not operate to shift the onus to the defence to prove, on the balance of probabilities, that the person was not of sound mind. Section 27 must be read together with s 28, which gives some assistance in determining the nature and quality of unsoundness of mind for the purposes of the defence of insanity. This section expressly applies to cases where the "balance of mind" is "disturbed". These words are not appropriate to describe the kind of insanity which relieves a person from criminal responsibility for his or her actions. A whole range of emotional disturbances, such as jealousy, anger, revenge or lack of self-control are excluded from s 28, and these are typical of matters affecting mental stability or balance, as distinct from insanity: *R v Brigitta Asamaken* [1964] PNGLR 193.

Infanticide is available as an alternative verdict to a charge of wilful murder, murder or manslaughter or as a charge in its own right. In every case the same facts and degree of proof need to be established by the prosecution: *R v Yigwai-Aku and Aku-Gobis* [1963] PNGLR 40.

Jalina J said, in *The State v Fambin Diofilia Joseph* [1992] PNGLR 238 at 242:

> "Although this offence is not prevalent, ... [c]ontinued leniency may lead to the object of s 301 of the *Criminal Code* being defeated. Women must be made to realise that a child, once born and alive, has a right to life whether she likes it or not. When a child is born ... the mother should think twice before she kills the child, and if she does so, she must face severe consequences, including imprisonment."

See s 540(a) regarding infanticide as an alternative verdict upon an indictment for wilful murder or murder.

The following guidelines were suggested as appropriate to sentencing for the offence in *The State v Fambin Diofilia Joseph* [1992] PNGLR 238:

(1) The kind of infanticide in *Imiyo Wamela v The State* [1982] PNGLR 269, where the mother killed her child by "breaking its head with a stone",

should attract a penalty of at least four to five years, not 10 months imprisonment, as imposed.

(2) Infanticide by strangulation should attract a penalty of three to four years.

(3) Infanticide by abandonment should attract a penalty of two to three years.

See ss 290, 292, 312 and 313.

302. Manslaughter.

A person who unlawfully kills another under such circumstances as not to constitute wilful murder, murder on infanticide is guilty of manslaughter.

Penalty: Subject to Section 19, imprisonment for life.

See s 24 of the Code regarding the defence of accident, and “the spleen cases”.

See ss 286-287 regarding manslaughter as a result of criminal negligence.

See s 303 regarding killing on provocation reduced to manslaughter.

See s 328 and *The State v John Koe* [1976] PNGLR 562, regarding the difference in degree of criminal responsibility between manslaughter and dangerous driving causing death.

Provocation (ss 266-267) is available as a complete defence to an accused person on a charge of manslaughter: *PLAR No 1 of 1980* [1980] PNGLR 326.

Amet J said, in *The State v Rex Lialu* [1988-1989] PNGLR 449 at 452:

> “I consider that our sentences for manslaughter must reflect the serious view which the legislature took over loss of human life in fixing the maximum sentence as life imprisonment. This is also a refection of the community’s view against unwanton killing. I repeat my view that sentences for manslaughter must be relatively higher than sentences for rape and robbery to reflect the importance and sanctity of the life given by God which no man has the right to take or deprive prematurely. A life has been taken which cannot be restored, quite unlike rape and robbery.”

See also *The State v Polin Pochalon Lopai* [1989-1989] PNGLR 48 and *The State v Mek Keroa Nentepa* (1990) N878.

Los J stated, in *Kesino Apo v The State* [1988] PNGLR 182 at 18:

> “As a rule, ... a custodial sentence is a starting point for the fundamental reason that all human lives must be protected. ... In the unlawful killing area, generally speaking the sentences have varied from two years to nine years. I have noticed that in some instances a charge of manslaughter is laid as a result of plea bargaining. In this type of case any further reduction of sentences would be irrational. But in my respectful view where a manslaughter charge against an offender is laid on the merit of the case all mitigating factors must be applied in favour of the offender.”

In sentencing for manslaughter, the court must have careful regard to the circumstances of death and the way in which death was actually caused: *R v Phillips* (1985) 7 Cr App R(S) 235 at 237.

In considering the nature of the act of the offender in causing death, the following matters should be taken into account:

(a) the nature and frequency of the attack or assault on the deceased;

(b) whether the injury which caused death arose directly from the assault, or whether the injury was caused by an object when the deceased subsequently fell;

(c) whether death was caused by a fist or weapon;

(d) whether the offender deliberately set out to hurt anyone;

(e) whether there was any provocation in the non-legal sense;

(f) whether the deceased had a thin skull; or

(g) whether the deceased had an enlarged spleen.[92]

In *Jack Tanga v The State* (1999) SC 602 the appellant's sentence of 12 years imprisonment for unlawfully killing his wife was confirmed. Jalina, Injia and Kirriwom JJ held that:

> "[t]he offence of manslaughter is a serious offence. This is reflected by the maximum punishment which is life imprisonment. This reflects the value the society places on human life and its total condemnation of one person's unlawful taking of another's life under any circumstances. The approach to be adopted in determining the punishment is set out by the Supreme Court in *Rex Lialu v The State* [1990] PNGLR 487; and that is to have regard to the aggregate effect of all the relevant considerations, factors which aggravate or mitigate the seriousness of the offence, and then to determine the appropriate penalty for that particular offence."

In *The State v Polin Pochalon Lopai* [1989] PNGLR 48 the accused was sentenced to six years imprisonment after pleaded guilty to the manslaughter of his wife by one kick which ruptured her spleen. Bredmeyer J balanced the aggravating features, namely, that the victim's spleen was of normal size and therefore not easy to rupture, and the victim was only 24 years old, with the mitigating factors, that the accused pleaded guilty, it was his first offence, and that he had children.

In *Jack Tanga v The State* (1999) SC 602, it was stated:

> "Many sentences for manslaughter cases imposed by the National Court and in some cases confirmed on appeal by the Supreme Court have in fact ranged between 6 – 10 years: See *The State v Maria Er* (1998) N1749 *The State v James Make & Others* [1998] N1748. To our knowledge, the highest sentence in a manslaughter case confirmed on appeal by the Supreme Court is *Antap Yala v The State* (1996) unreported judgment SCR 69/96."

Amet CJ, Salika and Injia JJ said in *Antap Yala v The State* (unreported, SCR 69/96, 1996):

> "The maximum punishment for the offence of manslaughter is life imprisonment. Whilst sentences for manslaughter will normally be lower than sentences for murder and wilful murder, there are those cases which will justify the imposition of heavy punishment and even the maximum punishment. ... The sentence in any given case will of course depend on its own peculiar facts. We are unable to prescribe any particular range of sentences for this offence as it is all too difficult to fix any range of sentences with some degree of precision. However, we would suggest that in an unintentional killing case which is uncontested, whatever the extenuating and mitigating circumstances may be, the application of vicious force, with or without the use of a weapon, causing serious bodily injury resulting in death may attract sentences between 10 years and above

[92] *Rex Lialu v The State* [1990] PNGLR 487.

and in some cases, even life imprisonment. ... The National Court (has) been far too lenient in the past in relation to men who are belting their wives. And in some instances wives belting their husbands. So let (us) warn everyone right now that the sentences are going to go up."

The views in *Antap Yala v The State* were supported in *Jack Tanga v The State* (1999) SC 602 and *John Tapil Tapi v The State* (2000) SC 635. *Jack Tanga v The State* (12 years) and *John Tapil Tapi v The State* (16 years) represent the top range of sentences for manslaughter.

The State v Steven Kenny (1999) N1881 was a "spleen killing" case related to domestic violence. Kirriwom J held that:

"[m]en who physically assault their wives or women generally must realise by now that spleen-related deaths are common and frequent where men indiscriminately batter their women-folk without the slightest regard for their health and life. Resorting to physical violence to resolve one's anger is not the right behaviour of decent and respectable men. Men who expect respect and support from their women must earn that respect by their conduct deserving of praise and dignity. ... The prisoner simply lost his self-control and as the consequence an innocent life is lost. ... Counsel for the prisoner referred to the case of *Rex Lialu v The State* [1990] PNGLR 487 ... I must say categorically that *Rex Lialu* is out of date and in view of the prevalence and the rising trend of violent deaths in totally unacceptable circumstances, reliance on this authority is no longer of any force or effect. That was a time when a sentence of six and half years was held to be excessive on appeal and reduced to four and half years imprisonment. Constant reliance on *Rex Lialu* gives clear impression that sentences of manslaughter fall within the category of four (4) years. But the tide has changed. Manslaughter cases with no aggravating circumstances can now attract up to 6 or 7 years imprisonment on a plea or more on trial. Where there are aggravating circumstances and on a plea matter, the prisoner should expect nothing less than 8 years."

In that case the prisoner was sentenced to six years imprisonment.

For an illustration of sentencing principles applied to a spleen type death where loss of a foetus may become an aggravating factor depending on the stage of pregnancy, see *The State v John Anthony Lesley* (1990) N927.

In *The State v John Gapaiho* (1990) N880, Brunton J distinguished *The State v Polin Pochalon Lopai* [1989] PNGLR 48, on the basis that the latter case dealt with domestic violence and spleen killings and therefore did not have general applicability to all manslaughter cases.

303. Killing on provocation.

Where a person who unlawfully kills another under circumstances that but for this section, would constitute wilful murder or murder, does the act that causes death in the heat of passion caused by sudden provocation within the meaning of Section 266 and before there is time for his passion to cool, he is guilty of manslaughter only.

See *PLAR No 1 of 1980* [1980] PNGLR 326, annotated under s 267.

The absolute defence of provocation under s 267 is available in appropriate circumstances upon a charge of manslaughter. The killing would not be unlawful where the act was excused by law (s 267): *The State v Saikoro Norman* [1979] PNGLR 599.

Where there has been a series of incidents culminating in a struggle causing a death, the court is entitled to consider all of the incidents as setting the stage for what is alleged to have been the sudden provocation: *R v Manga-Kitai* [1967-1968] PNGLR 1.

In *R v Borauda Sem* (1964) N311, murder was reduced to manslaughter by provocation. A wife had repeatedly insulted her husband who stabbed her and threw her out of the house.

In *R v Dogwaingikata Miakawo* (1971) N630 ill-will existed between the accused and the deceased for several months. The accused was armed and sought out the deceased with aggressive intent. The acts of the deceased in picking up his bow and arrow and tightening his bow string did not constitute acts of provocation to the accused.

In determining whether that act is done in the heat of passion, consideration must be given to the total effect on the accused of the facts surrounding the killing. In *The State v Tresca Waime* (1981) N305 the accused's bride price had not been paid by the husband as required by custom; no payment to her family was made upon the birth of her three children as required by custom; the accused had supported the deceased for years; the deceased had often physically and verbally abused the accused; and just prior to the killing the deceased had carnal knowledge of the accused against custom and by force. The circumstances clearly satisfy the section.

The state must negative beyond reasonable doubt that the accused did the killing "in the heat of passion caused by sudden provocation". For the act to be done in the heat of passion, the accused must have ceased to be the master of his or her own understanding. Mere anger is not sufficient; there must be passion taking the place of reason: *R v Moses-Robert* [1965-1966] PNGLR 180 at 185.

See also *R v Kink Abu* (1970) N576.

Acting while "very angry" is not acting in the "heat of passion": *R v Oa* [1967-1968] PNGLR 26.

The defence of provocation may exist even where an intent to kill exists: *R v Manga-Kitai* [1967-1968] PNGLR 1.

The "reasonable relationship" rule, discussed in *R v Kopal Wamne* (1974) N809, is not a separate legal element of provocation. It is a misdirection for a judge to withdraw consideration of provocation from the court as a tribunal of fact on the basis merely that a "reasonable relationship" between the provocative act and the retaliatory act does not appear. The question of law for the judge is whether there is any evidence on which the court as a tribunal of fact might entertain a reasonable doubt that provocation in terms of s 266 exists. Where there is such evidence, it is for the court as tribunal of fact to consider, and give such weight as it thinks proper, to "reasonable relationship" when deciding whether or not it has a reasonable doubt as to the existence of provocation in terms of s 266. Neither s 266, which comprehensively defines "provocation", nor this section, makes any mention of "reasonable relationship" as an element. See, by marked contrast, s 267. There is no warrant for reading the common law rule in *Mancini v DPP* as an independent necessary legal requirement. To do so would be contrary to the principles by which a Code is to be construed: *The State v Inawai Moroi* [1981] PNGLR 132.

The fact that the accused retaliated to an unarmed provocation with a lethal weapon, used with such violence as to indicate a plain intention to kill, does not negative the objective requirements of the section if it is shown that the ordinary peaceful citizen in the accused's cultural environment would retaliate in such a manner: *R v Yanda-Piaua* [1967-1968] PNGLR 482.

The act provoked must bear some reasonable relation to the provocative act: *R v Kopal Wamne* (1974) N809.

The mere admission of a crime unaccompanied by any act or words threatening or reflecting on the bearer does not amount to provocation: *R v Oa* [1967-1968] PNGLR 26.

Where provocation under s 303 is raised as a defence, the prosecution must discount three elements: an act of provocation; the loss of self-control (actual and reasonable); and a retaliation proportionate to the provocation: *R v Kopal Wamne* (1974) N809.

Failure of an accused to testify to loss of self-control is not fatal to a defence of provocation. Loss of self-control can be shown by inference from the surrounding facts: *R v Sarufa* [1974] PNGLR 173.

At a drunken brawl at a party where the deceased had continually threatened to fight the accused, the accused was acquitted of unlawful killing on the ground of provocation: *R v Ryan* (1954) N143.

See Narokobi, "*Adaptation of Western law in Papua New Guinea*" 5(1) MLJ 61-62; O'Neill, "*Criminal Law Provocation as a Complete Defence to a Charge of Manslaughter: A Note*" 1(1) MLJ 58-59; O'Regan, "*Provocation and Homicide in Papua New Guinea*" 1(3) MLJ 314-325; O'Regan, "*Ordinary Men and Provocation in Papua and New Guinea*" (1972) 21 ICLQ 476; Weisbrot, "*Integration of Laws in PNG: Custom and the Criminal Law in Conflict*" in Weisbrot et al, *Law and Social Change in PNG* (1982), pp 78-79.

304. Attempted murder, etc.

A person who -

(a) attempts unlawfully to kill another person; or

(b) with intent unlawfully to kill another person does any act, or omits to do any act that it is his duty to do, the act or omission being of such a nature as to be likely to endanger human life,

is guilty of a crime.

Penalty: Subject to Section 19, imprisonment for life.

In a case of attempted murder, the state must prove an intent actually to kill. The other elements of the crime to be proved by the state are to be found in s 4, which defines attempts. Thus, the state must prove beyond a reasonable doubt that:

(a) the accused intended actually to kill the deceased;

(b) the accused put his or her intention into execution by means adapted to its fulfilment; and

(c) the accused had manifested his or her intention by some overt act.[93]

This charge places upon the Crown the obligation to prove an intent to kill: *R v Bena Forepe* [1965-1966] PNGLR 329.

Specific intent (to kill) is a necessary ingredient of this offence, and must be proved beyond reasonable doubt: *R v Kiki Kau'Au* (1970) N557.

[93] *R v Kiki Kau'Au* (1970) N557.

Attempted murder, insofar as it involves the specific (though unsuccessful) intent to kill, may be regarded as potentially more serious than that of murder and than many cases of manslaughter which involve intents to do less serious things, but produce, without intending, death: *Peter Naibiri, Kutoi Soti Apia v The State* (1978) SC 137.

Provocation as a defence (s 267) is inapplicable to a charge under this section for attempted murder: *R v Bauoro-Dame* [1965-1966] PNGLR 201 at 204.

The position under the Code is the same as in England, and no alternative verdict is open upon a proceeding under this section. That is, s 539 is not relevant by analogy. The usual course is to include in the indictment an alternative count under s 315, or even some lesser offence: *R v Kiki Kau'Au* (1970) N557.

See s 4 discussion of attempts, particularly *R v Kopi-Kami* [1965-1966] PNGLR 73 at 77 and 79.

Under s 539, a verdict of unlawfully wounding with intent to do grievous bodily harm (s 315) is open on an indictment of attempted murder: *The State v Wanaepe Warara* [1977] PNGLR 458.

305. Accessory after the fact to murder, etc.

A person who becomes an accessory after the fact to wilful murder or murder is guilty of a crime.

Penalty: Subject to Section 19, imprisonment for life.

See s 519 of the Code, regarding accessories after the fact to crimes generally.

306. Written threats to kill.

A person who, knowing its contents directly or indirectly causes any person to receive a writing threatening to kill any person is guilty of a crime.

Penalty: Imprisonment for a term not exceeding seven years.

307. Conspiring to kill.

A person who conspires with any other person to kill any person, whether that other person is in Papua New Guinea or elsewhere, is guilty of a crime.

Penalty: Imprisonment for a term not exceeding 14 years.

308. Urging, etc unlawful killing.

(1) A person who -

(a) incites, encourages, urges, counsels or commands the unlawful killing of another person; or

(b) does or omits to do any act for the purpose of facilitating, enabling or assisting the unlawful killing of another

(c) person,

is guilty of a crime.

Penalty: Imprisonment for a term not exceeding seven years.

(2) For the purposes of Subsection (1), it is immaterial that -

(a) no specific person was incited, encouraged, urged, counselled, commanded, enabled or assisted to kill; or

(b) the killing of no specific person was incited, encouraged, urged, counselled, commanded, facilitated, enabled or assisted; or

(c) no person was in fact killed.

See s 7(1)(c) and (d) of the Code regarding aiding, counselling or procuring another person to commit an offence.

The section "seems to be directed towards the situation where the prosecution is unable to prove an attempt to kill or an aiding under s 7 or a conspiracy to murder under s 307": *Mauwe Anatape v The State* [1981] PNGLR 68 at 70 (Miles J). "It exists to enable the prosecution of 'behind the scenes' persons who plan and organise payback killings": Kearney DCJ at 69.

Although the legislature might like to consider the matter, under the present scheme a conviction under this section is not open as an alternative verdict upon a charge of wilful murder, because it is not expressly provided for in ss 539-540 (old s 552) or otherwise. There is an anomaly in the Code where the maximum sentences for two different crimes (s 308 in contrast with aiding a wilful murder under ss 7(1)(c) and 299) with either of which a person might be charged, are so different. It is anomalous if chance dictates which of two crimes is charged and which of the two differing maximum penalties apply: *Porewa Wani v The State* [1979] PNGLR 593.

In an appeal against sentence under this section, the appellant has to show that an error occurred which has the effect of vitiating the trial judge's discretion on sentencing. Where such an error is not identifiable, the appellant has to show that the sentence is manifestly excessive or out of all reasonable proportion to the circumstances of the crime. There is no pattern of sentencing established under the section. The court may therefore seek assistance from sentences normally prescribed for homicide cases. It is proper for a heavy sentence to be imposed where an extended killing takes advantage of and interferes with the administration of justice. In cases where the offence is prevalent, heavy sentences are considered desirable, since they are more likely to be widely known and deter potential offenders: *Mauwe Anatape v The State* [1981] PNGLR 68.

309. Failure to report killing or intended killing.

(1) Subject to Subsections (3) and (4), a person who -

(a) knowing that a person intends to kill, or has expressed the intention of killing, another person and has taken active steps to put his intention into effect; or

(b) knowing that a person has done an act or omission of a kind referred to in Section 308; or

(c) knowing that a person has killed another person,

fails to take reasonable steps to report the matter as soon as practicable to a magistrate, a member of the Police Force or some other person in authority is guilty of an offence.

Penalty: On summary conviction – imprisonment for a term not exceeding six months.

On conviction on indictment – imprisonment for a term not exceeding two years.

(2) For the purposes of Subsection (1), it is immaterial that -

(a) the person killed or intended to be killed was unknown, or that no specific person was intended to be killed; or

(b) any steps taken to put an intention of unlawfully killing into effect did not, as a matter of law, amount to an attempt to kill or a preparation to kill.

(3) It is a defence to a charge of an offence against Subsection (1) if the accused person proves that he believed, on reasonable grounds, that the matter -

(a) had already been reported, or was being reported to a magistrate, a member of the Police Force or some other person in authority; or

(b) had come to the knowledge of a magistrate, a member of the Police Force or some other person in authority.

(4) An offence against Subsection (1) is not committed when the person failing to take reasonable steps to report-

(a) is under the age of 14 years; or

(b) would not, at the time when the failure occurred, have been a compellable witness against the person referred to in Subsection (1)(a), (b) or (c) in a prosecution of the latter for murder under this Code.

310. Aiding suicide.

A person who -

(a) procures another to kill himself; or

(b) counsels another to kill himself and so induces him to do so; or

(c) aids another in killing himself, is guilty of a crime.

Penalty: Subject to Section 19, imprisonment for life.

311. Attempting to commit suicide.

A person who attempts to kill himself is guilty of a misdemeanour.

Penalty: Imprisonment for a term not exceeding one year.

In many jurisdictions, attempted suicide is no longer an offence and, although it is an offence under the *Criminal Code*, in conformity with current thinking it appears that the Public Prosecutor does not prosecute an offender who attempts to take his or her own life: *Public Prosecutor v Panikuiaka Nopi* [1979] PNGLR 536 (Saldanha J).

312. Killing unborn child.

A person who, when a woman is about to be delivered of a child, prevents the child from being born alive by any act or omission of such a nature that, if the child had been born alive and had then died, he would be deemed to have unlawfully killed the child is guilty of a crime.

Penalty: Subject to Section 19, imprisonment for life.

See ss 290, 292, 301 and 313 of the Code.

See s 540 regarding alternative verdicts.

313. Concealing the birth of children.

A person who, when a woman is delivered of a child, endeavours, by any secret disposition of the dead body of the child, to conceal the birth, is guilty of a misdemeanour whether the child died before at or after its birth.

Penalty: Imprisonment for a term not exceeding two years.

The major reason for the existence of this section is to provide a possible alternative verdict under ss 540: *The State v Meli Heti* [1977] PNGLR 173.

Under this section, the offspring delivered must be proved to be a "child" and not only a foetus or the unformed subject of a premature discharge. It does not matter whether the child died before, at, or after its birth. A "child" must be such that, if in fact it died at or after birth it had, at the time it died, and setting aside altogether the cause of that death, a capacity in the ordinary course for a continued existence independent of its mother; and if it died before birth, it must be such that, had it been born immediately prior to its death, and setting aside altogether the cause of that death, it also had that capacity. One means of proving that the child was in fact viable is to show that the woman, at the material time, had been pregnant for 28 weeks. Below that period it may properly be presumed not to have been viable: *The State v Meli Heti* [1977] PNGLR 173.

There is no rule of law which compels a woman to proclaim her own lack of chastity, and if she had miscarried at a time when the foetus was but a few months old, and therefore could have had no chance of life, you could not convict her upon this charge: *The State v Meli Heti* [1977] PNGLR 173.

See ss 290, 292, 301 and 312 of the Code.

There are three elements to this offence:

(a) it must be a child and not a mere foetus (*The State v Meli Heti* [1977] PNGLR 173, followed);

(b) there must be a disposition which is secret; and

(c) such disposition must be for the purpose of concealing the birth of the child, be it then dead or alive.

It is the degree of effort at concealment which so often affects the nature of the disposition. Temporary concealment may be sufficient: *The State v Margaret Torovel* [1982] PNGLR 242.

313A. Genocide.

A person who -

(a) commits genocide; or

(b) conspires to commit genocide; or

(c) incites a person to commit genocide; or

(d) attempts to commit genocide; or

(e) takes part in the commission of genocide,

is guilty of a crime.

Penalty: Subject to Section 19, imprisonment for life.

[S 313A insrt Act No 12, 1982 (*Criminal Code (Amendment) Act* 1982), s 4, pursuant to international treaty obligations]

Division 4 – Offences Endangering Life or Health

314. Disabling or stupefying in order to commit indictable offence.

(1) A person who, by any means calculated to choke, suffocate, or strangle, and with intent -

(a) to commit or to facilitate the commission of an indictable offence; or

(b) to facilitate the flight of an offender after the commission or attempted commission of an indictable offence,

makes, or attempts to make, any person incapable of resistance is guilty of a crime.

(2) A person who, with intent -

(a) to commit or to facilitate the commission of an indictable offence; or

(b) to facilitate the flight of an offender after the commission or attempted commission of an indictable offence,

administers, or attempts to administer, a stupefying or overpowering drug or thing to any person, is guilty of a crime.

Penalty: Subject to Section 1 9, imprisonment for life.

315. Acts intended to cause grievous bodily harm or prevent apprehension.

A person who, with intent -

(a) to maim, disfigure, or disable any person; or

(b) to do some grievous bodily harm to any person; or

(c) to resist or prevent the lawful arrest or detention of any person,

does any of the following things is guilty of a crime -

(d) unlawfully wounding or doing a grievous bodily harm to a person; or

(e) unlawfully attempting to strike a person with a projectile; or

(f) unlawfully causing an explosive substance to explode; or

(g) sending or delivering an explosive substance or other dangerous or noxious thing to a person; or

(h) causing any substance or thing referred to in Paragraph (g) to be taken or received by a person; or

(i) puts a corrosive fluid or destructive or explosive substance in any place; or

(j) unlawfully casts or throws a fluid or substance referred to in Paragraph (i) at or on a person, or otherwise applies any such fluid or substance to the person of a person.

Penalty: Subject to Section 19, imprisonment for life.

It is clear by the operation of s 542 that a person indicted under this section may be convicted under s 319 (causing grievous bodily harm) if the evidence establishes it: *R v Meauri* [1969-1970] PNGLR 254 at 259.

See also *R v Bawai-Pesoi* [1965-1966] PNGLR 210.

It is not necessary for the prosecution to prove that at the time of the alleged offence some person actually then had a present intention to effect such an arrest. The only intent with which the section is concerned is that of the accused to prevent an arrest: *Reference No l of 1976* [1976] PNGLR 377.

The police have a very important duty to perform in the preservation of law and order in the community and, whilst acting in a proper manner in the discharge of their functions, are entitled to expect and should receive the protection of the law from unwarranted actions: *Secretary for Law v Amuna Kaniel Peter and Kanior Iamur Beilum* [1974] PNGLR 99.

The policy of the legislature in regard to offences of this character is illustrated by the maximum penalty of life imprisonment. There would rarely be instances of this kind of offence which could be met with other than a substantial sentence of imprisonment in the current conditions in Papua New Guinea: *Public Prosecutor v Terrence Kaveku* [1977] PNGLR 110. See s 596 regarding sentencing generally.

"Grievous bodily harm" and "explosive substance" are defined in s 1.

For a case on doing grievous bodily harm (s 315(a)), see *The State v Andrew Temo* (1981) N293.

316. Taking or sending dangerous goods on aircraft.

(1) In this section, "dangerous goods" means -

(a) firearms, ammunition, weapons and explosive substances; and

(b) substances and things that by reason of their nature or condition may endanger the safety of an aircraft or of a person on board an aircraft.

(2) A person who -

(a) carries or places dangerous goods on board an aircraft; or

(b) delivers dangerous goods to another person for the purpose of their being placed on board an aircraft; or

(c) has dangerous goods in his possession on board an aircraft,

is guilty of a crime.

Penalty: Imprisonment for a term not exceeding seven years.

(3) It is a defence to a charge of on offence against Subsection (2) to prove that the act constituting the offence -

(a) was lawfully consented to by the owner or operator of the aircraft with knowledge by him of the nature of the goods concerned; or

(b) was done by authority or permission of or under a law.

"Aircraft" is defined by s 1 of the Code.

317. Endangering safety of persons travelling by aircraft.

A person who, with intent to injure or to endanger the safety of any person (whether or not a particular person) whilst he is on board an aircraft -

(a) deals with -

(i) the aircraft; or

(ii) anything on or near the aircraft; or

(iii) anything directly or indirectly connected with the guidance, control or operation of the aircraft,

in such a manner as to affect or endanger, or be likely to affect or endanger, the free and safe use of the aircraft or the safety of any such person; or

(b) by any omission to do any act that it is his duty to do causes the safety of any such person to be endangered,

is guilty of a crime.

Penalty: Subject to Section 19, imprisonment for life.

"Aircraft" is defined by s 1 of the Code.

318. Preventing escape from wreck.

A person who unlawfully -

(a) prevents or obstructs a person who is on board of, or is escaping from, a vessel that is in distress, or wrecked or cast ashore, in his endeavours to save his life; or

(b) obstructs a person in his endeavours to save the life of any person so situated,

is guilty of a crime.

Penalty: Subject to Section 19, imprisonment for life.

"Vessel" is defined by s 1 of the Code.

319. Grievous bodily harm.

A person who unlawfully does grievous bodily harm to another person is guilty of a crime.

Penalty: Imprisonment for a term not exceeding seven years.

When the offence is defined, as it is in this section, by its result, and there is no other over-riding guide to its meaning, the conclusion is that the offender is the person who unlawfully does an act or makes an omission that causes that result. Thus, to sustain a charge under this section, the prosecution must prove that, for example, the accused was in breach of the duty imposed on him by s 287 (duty of person in charge of dangerous things) or that he committed an assault (s 243) which was not authorised, justified or excused by law (s 244), or that his act or omission was otherwise made unlawful by other provisions of the Code or other statute law: *R v Yofia Abone* [1967-1968] PNGLR 277 at 287.

On a charge of unlawfully doing grievous bodily harm, an alternative verdict of unlawfully wounding under s 322 is available: *R v Bawai-Pesoi* [1965-1966] PNGLR 210.

The Code retains the position apparently applicable previously at common law, that on a charge of doing grievous bodily harm, without alternative counts, no lesser offence could be found against an accused: *R v Polhill* (1973) N734. See ss 542 and 547.

It is clear that by the operation of s 542, if a person is indicted under s 315(1) for unlawful wounding with intent to do some grievous bodily harm, that person may be convicted under this section if the evidence establishes it: *R v Meauri* [1969-1970] PNGLR 254 at 259.

See the definition of grievous bodily harm in s 1. See s 315. See s 340 regarding bodily harm.

320. Attempting to injure by explosive substances.

A person who unlawfully, and with intent to do bodily harm to another, puts any explosive substance in any place is guilty of a crime.

Penalty: Imprisonment for a term not exceeding 14 years.

"Explosive Substances" are defined in s 1 of the Code.

321. Maliciously administering poison with intent to harm.

A person who unlawfully, and with intent to injure or annoy another person, causes any poison or other noxious thing to be administered to, or to be taken by, any person, and by doing so -

(a) endangers his life; or

(b) does him some grievous bodily harm,

is guilty of a crime.

Penalty: Imprisonment for a term not exceeding 14 years.

In *R v Tigel Giring* (1962) N253 the accused administered a concoction containing hydrochloric acid to the victim, intending temporary, although serious, injury. The victim in fact suffered pain and nausea over several weeks but was left with no permanent injury. Therefore the accused would not be guilty of this offence, but rather of assault, as grievous bodily harm was not done.

322. Wounding and similar acts.

(1) A person who -

(a) unlawfully wounds another person; or

(b) unlawfully, and with intent to injure or annoy any person, causes any poison or other noxious thing to be administered to, or to be taken by, any person,

is guilty of a misdemeanour.

Penalty: Imprisonment for a term not exceeding three years.

(2) ...

[Subs (2) rep Act No 13, 1977 (*Criminal Code (Arrest) Act* 1977), s 23]

This offence is also punishable summarily: see Sch 2 of the Code.

There is no definition of the word "unlawful" in the *Criminal Code*. However, s 244 states that an assault is unlawful and constitutes an offence unless it is authorised or justified or excused by law. In accordance with the views expressed by the Supreme Court in *PLAR No 1 of 1980* [1980] PNGLR 326, it seems that if the facts proved to support a charge of unlawful wounding indicate that the offence was committed by an act or acts which constitute an assault, then the so-called defences to a charge of assault which establish justification or excuse, such as provocation, self-defence and the like, are available as defences to unlawful wounding, and the onus is on the prosecution to exclude such a defence fairly raised beyond reasonable doubt: *The State v Angela Colis Towavik* [1981] PNGLR 140.

Unlawful wounding requires evidence that the whole skin was severed. An abrasion which merely breaks the outer skin is not evidence of unlawful wounding: *R v Richard Hutchings* (1972) N710.

There may be an alternative verdict under this section upon a charge under s 315 (intent to cause grievous bodily harm) through the operation of s 538: *R v Bawai-Pesoi* [1965-1966] PNGLR 210.

323. Failure to supply necessaries.

A person who is charged with the duty of providing for another person the necessaries of life and, without lawful excuse, fails to do so, so that the life of that other person is, or is likely to be, endangered, or his health is, or is likely to be, permanently injured, is guilty of a misdemeanour.

Penalty: Imprisonment for a term not exceeding three years.

See ss 288 and 284 of the Code regarding duty to provide necessaries and duty of head of family.

324. Endangering life or health of apprentices or servants.

A person who, being charged as a master with the duty of providing necessary food, clothing or lodging for a servant or apprentice under the age of 16 years -

(a) unlawfully fails to perform that duty; or

(b) does any bodily harm or causes any bodily harm to be done to the servant or apprentice,

so that -

(c) the life of the servant or apprentice is, or is likely to be, endangered; or

(d) his health is, or is likely to be, permanently injured,

is guilty of a misdemeanour.

Penalty: Imprisonment for a term not exceeding three years.

See s 285 of the Code regarding the duty of masters.

325. Endangering life of children by exposure.

A person who unlawfully abandons or exposes a child under the age of two years so that -

(a) the life of the child is, or is likely to be, endangered; or

(b) his health is or is likely to be, permanently injured,

is guilty of a misdemeanour.

Penalty: Imprisonment for a term not exceeding three years.

See ss 284-285 of the Code.

326. Setting man-traps.

(1) A person who -

(a) sets or places any spring-gun, man-trap or other contrivance calculated to destroy human life or to inflict grievous bodily harm, in any place with the intent that it may kill or inflict grievous bodily harm on a trespasser or other person coming in contact with it; or

(b) causes any such thing to be so set or placed; or

(c) places any such thing in such a place and in such a manner that it is likely to cause any such result,

is guilty of a misdemeanour.

Penalty: Imprisonment for a term not exceeding three years.

(2) A person who knowingly permits any spring-gun, man-trap or other contrivance that has been set or placed by another person in such a place and in such a manner that it is likely to cause any result referred to in Subsection (1), to continue so set or placed in any place that is then in, or afterwards comes into, his possession or occupation, shall be deemed to have set and placed the gun, trap or contrivance with the intent referred to in Subsection (1) .

(3) Subsection (1) does not make it unlawful -

(a) to set any gun or trap such as is usually set for the purpose of destroying vermin; or

(b) to set any spring-gun, man-trap or engine at night in a dwelling-house for the protection of the dwelling-house.

"Grievous bodily harm" and "dwelling-house" are defined by s 1 of the Code.

See s 286 regarding the duty of persons doing dangerous acts.

327. Negligent acts causing harm.

(1) A person who unlawfully does any act, or omits to do any act that it is his duty to do, by which act or omission bodily harm is actually caused to a person is guilty of a misdemeanour.

Penalty: Imprisonment for a term not exceeding two years.

(2) ...

[Subs (2) rep Act No 13, 1977 (*Criminal Code (Arrest) Act* 1977), s 24]

See ss 286-287 of the Code.

"Bodily harm" is defined by s 1.

328. Dangerous driving of a motor vehicle.

(1) For the purposes of this section -

"driving a motor vehicle on a road or in a public place dangerously"- includes the driving of a motor vehicle at a speed or in a manner dangerous to the public, having regard to all the circumstances of the case, including -

(a) the nature, condition, and use of the road or public place; and

(b) the amount of traffic that -

(i) is on the road or in the public place at the time; or

(ii) might reasonably be expected to be on the road or in the public place;

"public place" -

(a) includes every place of public resort open to or used by the public as of right and any field, ground, park, reserve, garden, wharf, pier, jetty, market, passage or any other place for the time being used for a public purpose or open to access by the public by the express or tacit consent or sufferance of the owner, whether or not it is at all times so open; but

(b) does not include a track that is used for the time being as a course for the racing or testing of motor vehicles, and from which other traffic is excluded at the time.

(2) A person who drives a motor vehicle on a road or in a public place dangerously is guilty of a misdemeanour.

Penalty: Subject to the succeeding provisions of this section -

On summary conviction – a fine not exceeding K200.00 or imprisonment for a term not exceeding six months, or both.

On conviction on indictment – a fine not exceeding K1,000.00 or imprisonment for a term not exceeding two years, or both.

(3) If the offender has been previously convicted, on indictment or summarily, of an offence against Subsection (2) he is liable on summary conviction to a fine not exceeding K400.00 or to imprisonment for a term not exceeding 12 months, or both.

(4) If the offender has been twice previously convicted on indictment or summarily (or once on indictment and once summarily) of an offence against Subsection (2), the court shall, on conviction, impose, as the whole or part of the punishment, imprisonment.

(5) If the offender causes the death of or grievous bodily harm to another person he is liable on conviction on indictment to imprisonment for a term not exceeding five years.

(6) ...

[Subs (6) rep Act No 13, 1977 (*Criminal Code (Arrest) Act* 1977), s 25]

The offence of dangerous driving causing death (s 328(5)) is also punishable summarily: see Sch 2 of the Code.

"Motor vehicle" is defined by s 1.

See ss 335 and 292.

See ss 64-65 of the *Summary Offences Act* regarding the summary offences of negligent and dangerous driving.

See s 574 of the Code regarding the discretion of the court to view the scene of the accident.

This offence is not intended to be used as an alternative and second charge to manslaughter, but is intended to be used as a substitute for it.[94] Most charges of vehicular homicide should be preferred under this section, except in "most serious" cases, for example a car thief knocking down a policeman to effect his escape: *R v Kombora Rabura* (1973) N768.

By virtue of this section, an alternative finding of dangerous driving causing death is open on a charge of manslaughter. The court should ask itself whether facts show such a very high degree of negligence as should result in a finding of manslaughter, or do they show such a high but lesser degree of negligence (going at least beyond that required to establish civil liability in tort) as would warrant a finding of the lesser offence of dangerous driving causing death: *The State v John Koe* [1976] PNGLR 562. On same point see *R v Bile Lumapa* (1968) N498.

In *The State v Dela Tami* [1977] PNGLR 57 it was stated that the following rule of law in the English cases is entirely appropriate and applicable to the circumstances of Papua New Guinea:

> "Fault involves a failure; a falling below the care or skill of a competent and experienced driver, in relation to the manner of the driving and to the relevant circumstances of the case. If the dangerous driving occurs, however, as a result of some sudden overwhelming misfortune suffered by the driver for which he is in no way to blame – if, for example, he suddenly has an epileptic fit or passes into a coma, or is attacked by a swarm of bees or stunned by a blow on the head from a stone – then he is not guilty of driving in a manner dangerous to the public".

It is well established that to convict an accused under this section there must have been some fault on his or her part. Under the Code, the question of fault is more accurately analysed in terms of the excusatory defences under Pt I, Div 5, particularly ss 24 and 26, that is, "accident" and "sudden emergency": *Migi Barton v The State* (1981) SC 213(M).

The standard of driving required to secure a conviction for dangerous driving causing death must go beyond the civil standard required to establish negligence, but is not to be confused with the much higher standard required for manslaughter: *The State v Kevin Marcellin Daniel* (1980) N283. Contrast ss 286, 287 and 302.

---

[94] Archbold (37th ed), para 2818.

In cases involving dangerous driving causing death, the state has to prove, beyond a reasonable doubt, that death was a result of the dangerous driving. A standard of care beyond the civil standard is necessary and that standard is judged objectively: *The State v Peter Kepolo* (1980) N243.

The court must take care lest the seriousness of the outcome overshadow its consideration of the actual negligence at the time, but nevertheless the quality of the driving may be deduced from resultant facts: *The State v John Koe* [1976] PNGLR 562.

Evidence of the driver's prior consumption of liquor is admissible provided it really bears to a significant extent upon his or her condition at the time of the alleged offence: *R v Himson Mulas* [1969-1970] PNGLR 1.

The statement of the law by the High Court of Australia in *R v Coventry* (1937-1938) 59 CLR 633 is appropriate to the circumstances of Papua New Guinea and is certainly not at odds with anything stated by the Court of Appeal in England. In the words of the joint judgment of Latham CJ, Rich, Dixon and McTiernan JJ (at 637-638):

> "The driver may have honestly believed that he was driving very carefully and yet may be guilty of driving in a manner which is dangerous to the public ... The standard is an objective standard, 'impersonal and universal, fixed in relation to the safety of other users of the highway' ... The standard is impersonal in the sense that it does not vary with individuals, and it is universal in the sense that it is applicable in the case of all persons who drive motor vehicles."

These principles must be applied in conjunction with the overall statement of the English Court of Criminal Appeal in *R v Gosney* [1971] 2 QB 674 at 680, which states accurately the general framework applicable to offences under this section as much in Papua New Guinea as in England:

> "In order to justify a conviction there must be, not only a situation which, viewed objectively, was dangerous, but there must also have been some fault on the part of the driver, causing that situation. 'Fault' certainly does not necessarily involve deliberate misconduct or recklessness ... Fault involves a failure, a falling below the care or skill of a competent experienced driver, in relation to the manner of the driving and to the relevant circumstances of the case. A fault in that sense, though normally no danger would have arisen from it, is sufficient. The fault need not be the sole cause of the dangerous situation. It is enough if it is, looked at sensibly, a cause."[95]

It is not an essential element of this offence that the accused should have adverted to the possible consequences of the manner of driving and been indifferent to them. In short, recklessness is not necessary; inadvertent negligence if sufficiently serious enough. Though this is so with regard to the question of guilt or innocence, the distinction between heedlessness and recklessness is highly relevant to the question of penalty. In England the former is normally punished with a fine and the latter with a custodial sentence: see *R v Guilfoyle* [1973] 2 All ER 844. This distinction conjoins common sense and fairness and is equally applicable in Papua New Guinea: *Karo Gamoga v The State* [1981] PNGLR 443 (Andrew J).

See also *Anna Saunsbury v Jack Wartovo* (1982) N402(M), decided on the facts, following *Karo Gamoga v The State*.

[95] *Karo Gomoga v The State* [1981] PNGLR 443 (Pratt J).

Simson v Peat [1952] 2 QB 24 sets out the correct tone for considering mechanical defects as defences to cases involving dangerous driving. Certainly where the accused is aware of a defect he or she cannot rely on it, unless it is relatively minor or insignificant. This principle can be extended to say that even if the defect was not known, there are cases where a reasonably experienced driver, exercising reasonable prudence, should have discovered such a defect. As stated in *Spurge* (1961) 45 Cr App R 191 at 197, "the essence of the defence is that the danger has been created by a sudden total loss of control in no way due to any fault on the part of the driver": *The State v Kevin Marcellin Daniel* (1980) N283.

Charges alleging dangerous driving, in which matters such as mechanical defect or intervention by other persons are raised as issues, necessarily involve consideration of those concepts of foreseeability and degrees of probability which bedevil or enrich the law of tortious negligence. These considerations are not free from difficulty, and that may be one of the reasons why this offence has been abolished in England and replaced by the offence of reckless driving: *Miji Barton v The State* (1981) SC 213(M) (Miles J).

On a charge of dangerous driving it is not necessary to establish that the accused actually hampered, threatened or collided with another vehicle: *Secretary for Law v Godwin* (1974) N821 (dicta of Prentice J).

In *R v Coventry* (1937-1938) 59 CLR 633 at 638 it was said:

> "Sudden, even though mistaken, action in a critical situation may not, in all the circumstances of a case, constitute driving to the danger of the public."

In *R v Pias Piane* [1975] PNGLR 52, the driver was startled as a result of loud banging on the roof of the cab, and diverted his attention momentarily from the road, to ascertain the cause of the commotion which he believed to be a serious accident. The resulting accident was held not to be the product of dangerous driving under this section.[96]

The standard of driving set out in the section is an objective one and not subjective to the driver. However, it is not sufficient for the state to produce evidence which merely shows that the driving of the accused was objectively dangerous: *R v Pias Piane* [1975] PNGLR 52.

On a charge of dangerous driving causing death the prosecution must prove that the dangerous driving on the part of the accused was a substantial cause of death but not that it was the sole substantial cause. A substantial cause will be something more than *de minimis*: *The State v Elias Subang (No 2)* [1976] PNGLR 179.

Upon a charge of dangerous driving causing death there is no issue of breach of duty towards the deceased. The questions in issue are:

(a) whether the accused person was driving dangerously, that is dangerously towards the other persons who might reasonably be expected to be on or near the road; and if so,

(b) whether the accused thereby cause the death of another person.[97]

In the determination of the question of whether driving constitutes a danger, it is well established (see *R v Coventry* 59 CLR 633; *McBride v The Queen* (1966) 115 CLR 44 at 49-50 (Barwick CJ)) that the test is an objective one. The test of objectivity does not exclude as irrelevant an issue of fault or culpability: *Karo Gamoga v The State* [1981] PNGLR 443 (Andrew J).

---

[96] *R v Pias Piane* [1975] PNGLR 52 at 56-57

[97] *R v Himson Mulas* [1969-1970] PNGLR 1.

"Dangerous to the public" within the meaning of this section applies to passengers of the accused as well as to other road users: *The State v Kevin Marcellin Daniel* (1980) N283.

The words of the section are to be given their natural meaning, and the expression "driving ... in a manner dangerous to the public" includes, in "the public", passengers in the vehicle being driven by the person concerned: *R v Moses Tango* (1973) N755.

The case of *R v Messulam Wauta* (1973) N785 is relevant to the joinder of counts. Where it was alleged that the accused's driving resulted in the deaths of several persons, the causing of death of a single person is a circumstance of aggravation and not an element of the offence, hence where two acts of dangerous driving were alleged causing deaths in both cases, the state had to elect which act or omission constituting dangerous driving it would proceed on.

The "excusatory defences" set out in Pt I, Div 5 of the Code apply to this offence, and likewise criminal responsibility must be established within those terms: *R v Pius Piane* [1975] PNGLR 52 at 54.

The offence of dangerous driving causing death has reached staggering proportions in Papua New Guinea over recent years and this calls for a stern view to be taken of this crime. Only in the most exceptional of cases may the necessity for public deterrence against this offence be overriden by the circumstances of a particular case to the extent that the offender not be jailed: *Public Prosecutor v Sima Kone* [1979] PNGLR 294. However, see *Karo Gamogo v The State* [1981] PNGLR 443, where this case is discussed and explained, such that the judicial discretion in relation to sentence is not removed to the extent that a sentence of imprisonment is mandatory in every case of dangerous driving causing death.

This charge is one where the punitive and deterrent aspects of punishment may well prevail over the reformative, and where it may well be appropriate to sentence even a first offender of unimpeachable character to imprisonment for example's sake. These principles are well established (see *Public Prosecutor v Willy Moke Soki* [1977] PNGLR 165; *Public Prosecutor v Sima Kone* [1979] PNGLR 294; and *The State v Alphonse Raphael* [1979] PNGLR 47) but nevertheless they do not remove the judicial discretion in relation to sentence to the extent that a sentence of imprisonment is mandatory in every case of dangerous driving causing death. There is a distinction between cases of heedlessness and recklessness or, expressed in another way, between cases of incompetence and error of judgment on the one hand, and cases involving circumstances of aggravation which characterise the more serious breaches of the section (such as high speed, intoxication, overtaking in the face of oncoming traffic, cutting corners, and other such examples of recklessness involved in deliberately taking unjustifiable risks) on the other hand: *Karo Gamoga v The State* [1981] PNGLR 443 (Andrew J).

The aggravating factors commonly encountered in dangerous driving cases, especially when conjoined with the ever-present possibility of payback killing and tribal fighting resulting from a road accident death in many areas, carry with them the consequence that an offender could normally expect to receive a custodial sentence. Nevertheless, there are individual instances where such a course is not warranted: *Karo Gamoga v The State* [1981] PNGLR 443 (Pratt J).

See *Public Prosecutor v Willy Moke Soki* [1977] PNGLR 165, discussed under s 596 of the Code, regarding sentencing policy for offences under this section.

See also *The State v Aina Uwantuna* (1989) N726, for sentencing considerations where a truck driver collided with a bus killing 12 people, where there was no evidence of recklessness or excessively aggravating circumstances.

329. Additional power to convict for dangerous driving.

(1) On an indictment charging a person with an offence in connexion with or arising out of the driving of a motor vehicle by him (other than an offence against Section 328), he may be convicted of an offence against that section (with or without a circumstance of aggravation specified in Section 328(5)) if such offence is established by evidence.

(2) Subsection (1) applies notwithstanding the provisions of Section 539.

330. Cancellation of driver's licence to operate motor vehicle.

(1) In this section, "driver's licence" includes any driving licence or driving permit deemed to be equivalent in Papua New Guinea to, and accepted in place of, a driver's licence for the purpose of authorizing the holder to drive in Papua New Guinea any vehicle of the type or class to the driving of which the driving licence or driving permit is applicable.

(2) Where a person is convicted on indictment of an offence in connexion with or arising out of the driving of a motor vehicle by him, the court may, in addition to any sentence that it may pass, order that the offender be, from the date of conviction, disqualified -

(a) absolutely; or

(b) for such period as the court shall specify in its order,

from holding or obtaining a driver's licence to operate a motor vehicle.

(3) A copy of an order under Subsection (2) shall be transmitted by the proper officer of the court to the Commissioner of Police.

331. Sending or taking unseaworthy ships to sea.

(1) Subject to Subsections (2) and (3), a person who -

(a) sends or attempts to send a ship to sea in such an unseaworthy state that the life of any person

(b) is likely to be endangered; or

(c) being a master of a ship, knowingly takes or attempts to take the ship to sea in such an unseaworthy state that the life of any person is likely to be endangered,

is guilty of a crime.

Penalty: Imprisonment for a term not exceeding 14 years.

(2) It is a defence to a charge of an offence against Subsection (1) to prove that the going of the ship to sea in such unseaworthy state was, under the circumstances, reasonable and justifiable.

(3) It is a defence to a charge of an offence against Subsection (1)(a) to show that the accused person used all reasonable means to ensure the ship being sent to sea in a seaworthy state.

"Ship" is defined by s 1 of the Code.

332. Endangering steamships by tampering with machinery.

(1) A person who -

(a) has actual control over -

(i) a steam vessel; or

(ii) any part of the machinery of a steam vessel; and

(b) does any act or makes any omission or is privy to any act or omission with respect to the machinery of the vessel by which, to his knowledge, the safety of any person on board the vessel is, or is likely to be, endangered,

is guilty of a misdemeanour.

Penalty: Imprisonment for a term not exceeding three years.

(2) A person who is the engineer, or one of the engineers, in charge of the machinery of a steam vessel when any act is done or omitted to be done by any other person with respect to the machinery of the vessel by which the safety of any person on board the vessel is, or is likely to be, endangered is guilty of an offence.

Penalty: A fine not exceeding K200.00.

(3) It is a defence to a charge of an offence against Subsection (2) to prove that the act or omission was done or made without the knowledge of the accused person, and without any neglect or default on his part.

"Vessel" is defined by s 1 of the Code.

333. Evading laws as to equipment of ships and shipping dangerous goods.

A person who -

(a) has actual control over a vessel on which any article has been placed with his knowledge or consent, for the purpose of obtaining permission or authority to leave a port, and removes, or allows the removal or, the article from the vessel after the permission or authority has been obtained; or

(b) knowingly sends by a vessel, or carries in a vessel,

(i) any explosive substance; or

(ii) any acid or other thing of a dangerous or destructive nature, under a false description of the substance or thing, or with a false description of the sender,

is guilty of a misdemeanour.

Penalty: Imprisonment for a term not exceeding three years.

"Vessel" is defined by s 1 of the Code.

334. Landing explosives.

A person who -

(a) being charged by law with any duty respecting the landing or delivery of any explosive substance, or of an acid or other thing of a dangerous or destructive nature, from a vessel fails to perform that duty; or

(b) being concerned in the landing of any such substance or thing from a vessel, violates the provisions of the laws relating to such landing,

is guilty of a misdemeanour.

Penalty: Imprisonment for a term not exceeding three years.

"Explosive substance" is defined by s 1 of the Code.

Division 5 – Assaults

335. Common assault.

A person who unlawfully assaults another person is guilty of a misdemeanour.

Penalty: If no greater punishment is provided, imprisonment for a term not exceeding one year.

This offence is also punishable summarily: see Sch 2 of the Code.

See s 243 for the definition of assault.

See *R v Kirkland* (1954) N61.

336. Assault with intent to commit unnatural offence.

A person who assaults another person with intent to have carnal knowledge of him against the order of nature is guilty of a crime.

Penalty: Imprisonment for a term not exceeding 14 years.

337. Indecent assault on males.

A person who unlawfully and indecently assaults a male person is guilty of a misdemeanour.

Penalty: Imprisonment for a term not exceeding three years.

This offence is also punishable summarily: see Sch 2 of the Code.

See s 212 regarding indecent practices between males.

See s 349 regarding indecent assault on females.

R v Harry Edward Hamilton (1948) N24 was a case concerning unlawful and indecent assault on a male by a kiap. The kiap struck the victim on the genitals for a sexual assault on an eight year old girl and encouraged his police-boys to do likewise, culminating in ordering a woman to masturbate the victim.

338. Assaults on persons protecting wrecks

A person who unlawfully assaults and uses actual violence to any person acting in the execution of his duty in or concerning the preservation of –

(a) a vessel in distress; or

(b) any vessel or goods -

(i) wrecked; or

(ii) stranded; or

(iii) cast on shore; or

(iv) lying under water,

is guilty of a crime.

Penalty: Imprisonment for a term not exceeding seven years.

339. Assaults of member of crew on aircraft.

A person who while on board an aircraft -

(a) unlawfully assaults a member of the crew of the aircraft; or

(b) threatens a member with any violence, injury or detriment to be caused to him or any other person on the aircraft by the offender or by any other person,

with the intention of -

(c) affecting the performance by the member of his functions or duties in connexion with the operation of the aircraft; or

(d) lessening the member's ability to perform those functions or duties,

is guilty of a crime.

Penalty: Imprisonment for a term not exceeding 14 years.

340. Assaults occasioning bodily harm.

(1) A person who unlawfully assaults another and by doing so does him bodily harm is guilty of a misdemeanour.

Penalty: Imprisonment for a term not exceeding three years.

(2) ...

[Subs (2) rep Act No 13, 1977 (*Criminal Code (Arrest) Act* 1977), s 26]

This offence is also punishable summarily: see Sch 2 of the Code.

341. Serious assaults.

A person who -

(a) assaults another with intent -

(i) to commit a crime; or

(ii) to resist or prevent the lawful arrest or detention of himself or of any other person; or

(b) assaults, resists or wilfully obstructs -

(i) a member of the Police Force while acting in the execution of his duty; or

(ii) any person acting in aid of a member of the Police Force while so acting; or

(c) unlawfully assaults, resists or obstructs a person who is engaged in the lawful execution of any process against any property, or in making a lawful distress; or

(d) assaults, resists or obstructs a person engaged in such a lawful execution of process, or in making a lawful distress with intent to rescue any property lawfully taken under the process or distress; or

(e) assaults a person on account of an act done by him in the execution of a duty imposed on him by law; or

(f) assaults a person in pursuance of an unlawful conspiracy respecting -

(i) a manufacture, trade, business or occupation; or

(ii) any person or persons concerned or employed in a manufacture, trade, business or occupation; or

(iii) the wages of any such person or persons,

is guilty of a misdemeanour.

Penalty: Imprisonment for a term not exceeding three years.

This offence is also punishable summarily: see Sch 2 of the Code.

"Police Officer" is defined by s 1.

As to s 341(b), see ss 60-61 of the *Summary Offences Act* regarding obstructing and assaulting a member of the police force.

In *The State v Herman* (1997) N1656 a gang of young people invaded a home and seriously assaulted the occupants. A near maximum sentence of two years imprisonment with hard labour was handed down.

In relation to a charge under this section, and when considering the possible illegality of any force used by the police officer in arresting or preventing escape from arrest at the relevant time, regard must be had to the provisions of both ss 252 and 254: *R v Erico Aufe* [1974] PNGLR 331.

Division 6 – Assaults Punishable on Summary Conviction

342. Summary jurisdiction.

(1) Subject to this Division, a person who unlawfully assaults another may be summarily convicted before a court of summary jurisdiction.

(2) Where the court -

(a) finds that the assault complained of was accompanied by an attempt to commit a crime; or

(b) is of opinion that the charge is a fit subject for prosecution by indictment,

it shall abstain from dealing with the case summarily.

(3) This section does not authorise a court to deal summarily with a charge of assault on which a question arises as to-

(a) the title to land, an estate in land or an interest in or accruing from land; or

(b) an insolvency; or

(c) the execution of the process of a court.

343. Common assaults.

Any person who unlawfully assaults another is liable on summary conviction to a fine not exceeding K200.00, inclusive of costs, and in default of payment to imprisonment for a term not exceeding six months unless the fine and costs are sooner paid, or to imprisonment for a term not exceeding six months in the first instance.

344. Aggravated assaults.

(1) If the person assaulted is a male child whose age does not, in the opinion of the court exceed 14 years, or is a female, and the court is of opinion that the assault is of such an aggravated nature that the offender cannot be sufficiently punished under Section 343, the offender is liable to a penalty of a fine not exceeding K400.00, inclusive of costs, and in default of payment to imprisonment for a term not exceeding 12 months unless the fine and costs are sooner paid, or to imprisonment for a term not exceeding 12 months, in the first instance.

(2) The court may also, if it thinks fit, require the offender to enter into a recognizance to keep the peace and be of good behaviour for any term not exceeding six months from the expiration of the sentence.

345. Effect of summary conviction or dismissal.

(1) If on complaint by or on behalf of the party aggrieved -

(a) a complaint of an assault has been heard on the merits before a court, under Section 343 or 344; and

(b) the court dismisses the complaint,

the court shall immediately make out a certificate of the fact of the dismissal and give it to the accused person.

(2) A person who has obtained a certificate of dismissal under Subsection (1), or who has been convicted on a complaint to which Subsection (1) applies and has paid the fine and costs or has endured the punishment adjudged (if any) is released from all further proceedings, civil or criminal, for the same cause.

346. Assaults in interference with freedom of trade or work.

A person who assaults another with intent to hinder or prevent him from -

(a) working at or exercising his lawful trade, business or occupation; or

(b) buying, selling or otherwise dealing with any property intended for sale,

is guilty of an offence.

Penalty: Imprisonment for a term not exceeding three months.

Division 7 – Assaults on Females: Abduction

347. Definition of rape.

A person who has carnal knowledge of a woman or girl, not being his wife -

(a) without her consent; or

(b) with her consent, if the consent is obtained -

(i) by force; or

(ii) by means of threats or intimidation; or

(iii) by fear of bodily harm; or

(iv) by means of false and fraudulent representations as to the nature of the act; or

(v) in the case of a married woman, by personating her husband,

is guilty of the crime of rape.

Penalty: Subject to Section 19, imprisonment for life.

[S 347 am Act No 29, 1983 (*Criminal Code (Amendment) Act* 1983), s 3; am Act No 11, 1984 (*Criminal Code (Minimum Penalties) (Amendment) Act* 1984), s 5; am Act No 17, 1986 (*Criminal Code (Amendment No 2) Act* 1986), s 17]

See s 6 of the Code regarding carnal knowledge.

The proper construction of this section is that it covers the field in the sense that the crime is committed if the state proves that the accused had carnal knowledge of the prosecutrix without her consent, or with her consent but only in the circumstances set out in the section. This means that common law principles relating to circumstances in which the consent is vitiated are not to be imported: *R v Merembu Bongab* [1971-1972] PNGLR 433 at 439.

As to drunkenness (s 29) as a defence to a charge of rape, see *R v Evi* [1975] PNGLR 30.

The question of whether consent has been given is an essential issue of fact, and the onus is on the Crown. It is not correct to say that as a matter of law a child of tender years cannot consent. It is a question of whether she did or did not. It is otherwise in the case of other offences involving unlawful carnal knowledge or indecent dealing with young girls, because in those cases lack of consent is not an element of the offence: *R v Karibe-Puni* [1967-1968] PNGLR 388.

In *R v Paiovi Aravapo* (1954) N60 the evidence adduced by the prosecution failed to prove beyond a reasonable doubt that the act of sexual intercourse occurred without the woman's consent. Factors giving rise to doubt included the fact that the time and place did not seem propitious for such an offence; the evidence given by the complainant as to the removal of her pants was conflicting; no cry was heard from the woman; eyewitnesses did not call to the accused to desist; the accused removed his boots before, and replaced them after, the act of intercourse; and the accused did not hasten his departure even after becoming aware of the presence of onlookers.

In *R v Merembu Bongab* [1971-1972] PNGLR 433 the prosecutrix consented to the accused having sexual intercourse with her in the mistaken belief that he was her de facto husband. The court held that such consent is not vitiated on the grounds that the accused impersonated her husband within the meaning of this section, as those words refer to a married woman's lawful husband. It may be said that such a construction is too restricted, due possibly to the more rigid moral attitudes of the late 19th century towards sexual relationships when the Code was formulated. However, it has the advantage of certainty in prescribing the precise circumstances in which a man's conduct is punishable as rape in this type of case.

Where marriage to the prosecutrix is raised as a defence to a charge of rape, the defence must prove, on the balance of probability, that there exists a valid subsisting marriage between the accused and the prosecutrix. If there is no evidence to support a customary or a general law marriage, the accused must subsequently be found guilty of the charge of rape: *The State v Paul Ben Kuman* (1996) CR 954 of (Lenalia AJ).

Where the victim's consent to acts of sexual intercourse was obtained by the fraud of the accused, who led her to believe that these were "treatments" according to traditional medicine, the accused was guilty of indecent assault under s 349 of the Code: *The State v Andrew Tovue* [1981] PNGLR 8.

Upon a charge of rape where there is no dispute that penetration has taken place and the only issue is consent or non-consent, the alternative verdict of guilty of indecent assault is not available. See ss 541 and 547 regarding alternative verdicts: *R v Merembu Bongab* [1971-1972] PNGLR 433.

In *The State v Terry Charles* [1990] PNGLR 63, Doherty AJ said:

> "Consent (either express or implied) to sexual intercourse may be given in such a way that it is dependent on certain conditions, non-fulfilment of which will imply revocation of consent. Accordingly, in circumstances where the prosecutrix agreed to go with the accused to his parents' house for the night but was taken instead to a broken-down and deserted house nearby where sexual intercourse was forced upon her by the accused and four others, any implied consent to sexual intercourse in the safety of the parents' house was revoked when the accused sought to take her to a place that exposed her to danger."

In the generality of cases, as a matter of common sense and reasonable inference, if no force was used then it follows that there was no resistance, and if there was no resistance then there was consent. However, absence of consent may be shown to be due to fraud or to the fact, for example, that the woman was asleep. There is no closed category of alternatives to physical resistance permitting, as a matter of reasonable inference, a finding of non-consent: *The State v John Lauriston Birch* [1978] PNGLR 79.

The House of Lords, in *DPP v Morgan* [1975] 2 All ER 347, held by a majority that the crime of rape consists in having sexual intercourse with the woman with intent to do so without her consent or with indifference whether or not she consented. It could not be committed if that essential *mens rea* were absent. Accordingly, if an accused in fact believed that the woman had consented, whether or not that belief was based on reasonable grounds, he could not be found guilty of rape. Rape is defined in s 347. The definition contains no words indicating that intent is an ingredient of the crime. Upon a charge of rape no element of intent to cause a specific result is involved. Belief in the fact of consent is a matter which is dealt with by s 25 of the Code, which requires the formation of an honest and reasonable but mistaken belief: *The State v John Kalabus and Aita Sanangkepe* [1977] PNGLR 87.

Doherty J said, in *The State v Michael Rave, James Maien and Philip Baule* [1993] PNGLR 85 at 91-92:

"*Holman v R* [1970] WAR 2, holds that 'a woman's consent to intercourse may be hesitant, reluctant, grudging or tearful but if she consciously permits it (providing her permission is not obtained by force, threats, fear or fraud) it is not rape', however, we cannot adopt the culture and the cultural attitude of another country into ours. In Papua New Guinea, tears can indicate reluctance and even refusal, or at least the will of the person being overborne. Certainly, that definition does not sound like consent, it sounds like a person's spirit being broken."

There is no requirement that the state call any medical evidence as to the condition of the prosecutrix's genital organs; such evidence would not be helpful where there is no allegation of violence or ejaculation on the part of the accused: *R v Merembu Bongab* [1971-1972] PNGLR 433 at 434-435.

Prentice CJ stated, in *Birch v The State* [1979] PNGLR 75:

"If it be the law of the United Kingdom as at Independence Day, properly understood, that lack of fresh complaint is evidence of consent (contrast the law in Australia set out in *Kilby v R* (1973) 1 ALR 283); such is my experience of trials for rape and sexual offences in Papua New Guinea, that I have no hesitation in asserting and holding that such a principle of the common law (if it be such) is totally unsuited to the conditions of and present organisation of Papua New Guinean Society. In this country questions of shame and irrational parental reaction by way of instinctive punishment of the complaining child who has been unwillingly 'spoilt' (to adopt the pisin phrase) might well, and in my experience of court trials, commonly do, render children reluctant to make an immediate complaint."

Failure to make fresh complaint is not evidence of consent, but evidence relevant to the credibility of the prosecutrix: *Birch v The State* [1979] PNGLR 75 (Kearney J).

In *Kaina v The State* [1990] PNGLR 292 a customary marriage to the prosecutrix was raised as a defence to a charge of rape. The trial judge accepted and relied upon, as evidence of dissolution of the marriage, an order of the local Village Court on a complaint to it which appeared to relate to compensatory proceedings for the behaviour of the husband to the wife. On appeal, the court held that it could not be satisfied of the fact that at the date of trial the prosecutrix was not then married to the accused. Further, the trial judge's reliance on the Village Court decision was held to be wrong as it was in conflict with the principle in *Hollington v Hewthorne & Co Ltd* [1943] 1 KB 587, that evidence in such prior civil or administrative decisions would be inadmissible in a criminal action.

Hinchliffe and Brown JJ said, in *Kaina v The State* [1990] PNGLR 292 at 297-298:

"The prior Village Court determination was not only pursuant to a different complaint, but involves customary considerations in lieu of statutory offences and more importantly involves different standards of proof. The Village Court may be equated in this instance with a quasi-administrative tribunal, making a decision in a civil field while the trial judge under the *Criminal Code* must be satisfied on the criminal standard."

Hinchliffe and Brown JJ further stated (at 299):

> "So far as we are aware, the States in Australia have legislated to recognise the possibility of a conviction for rape by a husband notwithstanding a subsisting marriage. The implied common law consent arising from the marriage contract has been abolished so that for instance, if the spouses are living separate and apart, a wife may negative consent. It is this implied consent which is enshrined in s 347 of the *Criminal Code*. ... Legislative amendment to s 347 to afford married women in the circumstances of this case, greater protection under the law is long overdue."

Corroboration in sexual offence cases

There is a rule of practice that corroboration is necessary in rape cases in some material particular by other evidence implicating the accused person, that is, evidence which confirms the commission of the offence and the identification of the accused person as its perpetrator. It is not necessary that it should confirm the prosecutrix in every detail of the crime: *R v Yoka Kiok* (1970) N607.

It has always been held that in rape cases the tribunal should be alert to the danger of convicting unless corroboration is available of the complainant's charge. This rule of practice, falling short of a rule of law, is neither inconsistent with a constitutional law or statute, nor inapplicable nor inappropriate to the circumstances of the country, nor inconsistent with established custom. It is consistent with the principles of natural justice. It was said in *The State v Kewa Kai* [1976] PNGLR 481:

> "Its continued application would ... be in keeping with the development of the underlying law that is imposed as a duty upon the courts (by Sch 2.3 of the *Constitution*)."

The failure of a judge or magistrate sitting alone to advert properly and clearly to the rule of practice that the tribunal of fact should be very cautious before acting on the uncorroborated evidence of the complainant, will constitute an error of law sufficient to ground an appeal against conviction: *McCallum v Buibui* [1975] PNGLR 439.

While it is not a requirement of law that the prosecutrix's version be corroborated, it is nevertheless the general rule of practice that in cases involving an issue of consent there should be evidence corroborating that of the prosecutrix. For there to be corroboration there must be evidence independent of the complainant, which confirms in some material particular not only the evidence that the crime was committed, but also that the prisoner committed it. To look separately at each element said to constitute corroboration may lead to error, particularly as corroboration need not be, and rarely is, direct evidence that the accused committed the crime. It may be merely circumstantial evidence of the accused's connection with the crime. Mere opportunity to commit the crime does not provide corroboration, yet, taking the circumstances surrounding the opportunity, they may be of such nature as to lead to the inference that it was probable that advantage would be taken of the opportunity. External evidence concerning the nature of the place and the circumstances under which sexual relations admittedly occurred, may provide corroborative evidence, of a circumstantial type, of lack of consent, even though the only direct evidence thereof is from the complainant: *The State v John Kalabus and Aita Sanangkepe* [1977] PNGLR 87.

The fact that there is no fresh complaint by a woman alleging rape is not evidence of consent: followed *Kilby v The Queen* [1973] ALR 283. The failure of a supposedly outraged woman to complain, or her having had the complaint, as it were, wrung from her, is a jury matter, going to the consistency or inconsistency of her alleged non-consent to the intercourse. Evidence of distress can be corroboration of the version given by the prosecutrix. It is evidence that has to be viewed warily: *Bernard Touramasong, Thomas Painuk, George Valavun and Joseph Muruna v The State* [1978] PNGLR 337.

On a charge of assault indicating a sexual nature, evidence from a witness or witnesses, other than the prosecution or complainant, of a "fresh complaint" is admissible. However, it does not amount to corroboration. In order that evidence may amount to corroboration, it must be extraneous to the witness who is to be corroborated. Where evidence admitted is not corroborated, the judge should state and record that he or she understands the dangers of convicting upon the uncorroborated evidence: *Peter Townsend v George Oika* [1981] PNGLR 12, following *Thomas Arthur McCallum v Gregory Buibui* [1975] PNGLR 439.

In *The State v Bikhet Ngurares Paulo* [1994] PNGLR 335, Doherty J criticised the common law rule relating to corroboration in sexual offence cases, particularly that of "fresh complaints":

> "Why should this rule of corroboration apply to a sexual offence when it does not apply to other serious offences eg – murder and burglary. The comment 'it was easy to accuse and hard to deny' can be said in regard to such crimes; where the Courts are equally obliged to direct the normal rules of evidence assessing facts, credibility and weight."

Evidence of complaints may enhance the reliability of the prosecutrix's story but it does not constitute corroboration. Corroboration must come from a source independent of the witness: *Thomas Arthur McCallum v Gregory Buibui* [1975] PNGLR 439.

False denials by the accused to the police in the course of an investigation may amount to corroboration: *R v Bauwai Giava* (1964) N331.

Except in exceptional circumstances, evidence of distressed condition will carry little weight as corroborative evidence: *Thomas Arthur McCallum v Gregory Buibui* [1975] PNGLR 439. However, in *The State v Dickson Wape* [1994] PNGLR 558, the court allowed evidence of the appearance of the victim in the morning, looking somewhat distraught, wearing only her panties and her torn skirt. This, along with the evidence that after she was abducted and taken away a search was conducted to locate her without any success, was corroborative evidence.

In *Didei v The State* [1990] PNGLR 458 at 460-461, Kapi DCJ, Sheehan and Salika JJ said:

> "[T]here is no need of a 'formula' type of pronouncement regarding corroboration where there is in fact obvious and substantial corroboration, and the trial judge points to it as being relied on to support a prosecutrix's story. But when there is no corroborative evidence the warning must be given and recorded."

In *The State v Anton Kumak* (1990) N835 the three accused were each charged with rape. The issue at trial was whether there was consent. In relation to the need for corroboration, Ellis J stated:

> "Sexual offences of [this] kind represent a category of cases where there is a general rule of practice that there should be evidence corroborating that of the victim. This arises from the fact that the rape is a serious charge; easy to allege and difficult to refute: see *The State v Kalabus & Another* [1977] PNGLR 87 and

R v Finch (1959) N146. As to the practical application of that general rule of practice, I note the decision in *R v Yoka Kiok* (1970) N607 which suggests that what is required is some evidence, independent of the victim, which confirms the commission of the offence and the identification of the accused: 'it is not necessary that it should confirm the prosecutrix in every detail of the crime' (ibid, p 2). In the present case, corroboration is potentially available from any of four sources: the evidence of the victim's 'sister', the evidence of that victim's 'brother-in-law', the medical report and the accused's record of interview to the extent that that record of the interview contains admissions."

For the rules on corroboration in a case of indecent assault on a female, see the discussion of *The State v Andrew Tovue* [1981] PNGLR 8, under s 349 of the Code.

On the issue of rape in marriage see Luluaki "*When Rape is not Rape: the Marital Rape Exemption Rule under the Papua New Guinea Criminal Code and Related Issues*" (1994) 22 MLJ 59.

Sentencing

Rape is a crime of violence and, like other offences of violence, calls for a deterrent sentence. Parliament has seen fit to provide substantial penalties for crimes of violence, clearly to ensure that the people will come to learn that violence cannot be tolerated in any organised society and that those who offend will be dealt with sternly. Only in this way will the incidence of violence be reduced: *Public Prosecutor v Arape Etape; Public Prosecutor v Poso Tapo; Public Prosecutor v Petrus Mombi* [1977] PNGLR 416.

Guidelines for gang rape sentencing were set out as an eight year starting point in *John Aubuku v The State* [1987] PNGLR 267, and a 12 year recommendation in *The State v Peter Kaudik* [1987] PNGLR 201. However, there have been changes in the policy of the courts since those leading cases. It was stated in *Thomas Waim v The State* (1997) SC 519:

> "Those cases where decided 10 years ago, and there has been an escalation in the prevalence and seriousness of the commission of rapes and multiple gang rapes over the period ... Thus, 12 years for gang rape is now, in our respectful opinion, inadequate and inappropriate. Some recent decisions of the National Court have properly reflected the community's concerns and imposed sentences of 14, 15 and 16 years."

Other recent cases have shown that aggravating factors such as the young age of the victim, injury to the victim, abduction and the use of force or threatened force may attract sentences in the range of 14 to 18 years. See *Matagal v St* (1996) SCRA No 95 and *Lawrence Hindemba v The State* (1998) SC 593.

The breach of a position of trust may warrant a heavier sentence. Positions of trust are not limited, and may extend to such de facto situations as a vehicle operator and his passengers: *Meaoa v The State* [1986] PNGLR 280.

Injia AJ said, in *The State v Kenneth Penias* [1994] PNGLR 48 at 51:[98]

> "Rape constitutes an invasion of the privacy of the most intimate part of a woman's body. Women become objects of sex, and sex alone, to men like the prisoner, who prey upon them and rape them. But women are, after all, human

[98] Adopted in *Meaoa v The State* [1986] PNGLR 280.

beings just like men. They have rights and opportunities equal to men, as guaranteed to them under our *Constitution*. They are entitled to be respected and fairly treated. They have all the right to travel freely alone or in groups, in any place they choose to be, at any time of the day. At times, because of their gender, with which comes insecurity, they need the protection of men. Unfortunately, rape has become a prevalent offence in this country. Women in towns and in villages are living in fear because of the pervasive conduct of men like the prisoner. Our women in the small communities, in the villages and remote islands, and in small towns and centres, who once enjoyed freedom and tranquillity, are living under fear and feel restricted. That is why the Supreme Court in *Aubuku's case* said that people who commit rape must be punished with a strong punitive sentence."

Civil action

Rape is actionable in the tort actions of battery and assault whether the accused is prosecuted or not, and whether the prosecution leads to a conviction or acquittal: *Dalin More v Chief Inspector Onopia* (1998) N1736.

348. Attempt to commit rape.

A person who attempts to commit the crime of rape is guilty of a crime.

Penalty: Imprisonment for a term not exceeding 14 years.

[S 348 am Act No 29, 1983 (*Criminal Code (Amendment) Act* 1983), s 4; am Act No 17, 1986 (*Criminal Code (Amendment No 2) Act* 1986), s 18]

See s 4 of the Code regarding attempts.

Rape is defined by s 347.

Reading this section together with s 4, in order to establish an attempted rape, the prosecution must prove that -

(a) the accused intended to have carnal knowledge of the complainant without her consent, or obtaining her consent by force or by means of threats or intimidation, or by fear of bodily harm, etc;

(b) the accused had begun to put his intention into execution by means adapted to its fulfilment; and

(c) the accused had manifested his intention by some overt act.[99]

It was said in *R v Joseph-Kure* [1965-1966] PNGLR 161:

"When the victim is physically resisting the fulfilment of her assailant's proved intention to rape her one thing needed for its fulfilment is the overcoming of her resistance, so that force used for that immediate purpose is most obviously a means adapted to the fulfilment of the ultimate and compound purpose of achieving penetration without consent. There is nothing in the definition of 'attempt' requiring that the act said to constitute the means of executing the intention should be directed towards the performance of one rather than another element of a compound offence the other element being penetration."

To establish an attempt to rape, the prosecution must prove beyond reasonable doubt an intention by the accused to have carnal knowledge without consent of the

[99] *R v Joseph-Kure* [1965-1966] PNGLR 161 at 166.

complainant, and that the accused tried more than to seduce her by displaying some overt act to put his intention into execution by means adapted to its fulfilment: *R v Chan* (1964) N312.

Where in the course of a rape the accused has made several unsuccessful attempts at penetration, these should not be charged as separate and distinct counts of attempted rape: *R v Evi* [1975] PNGLR 30.

Rape is a compound crime, which consists not merely in achieving penetration, but in achieving it without consent or with consent obtained by force, fear or threat. In the s 4 definition of attempts, the expression "appears to put his intention into execution by means adapted to its fulfilment", where the offence attempted is a compound one, points to the beginning of the execution of the crime rather than to the bringing of the final element of it: *R v Kuipa Nopai* (1968) N472.

349. Indecent assaults on females.

A person who unlawfully and indecently assaults a woman or girl is guilty of a misdemeanour.

Penalty: Imprisonment for a term not exceeding two years.

[S 349 am Act No 11, 1984 (*Criminal Code (Minimum Penalties) (Amendment) Act* 1984), s7; am Act No 17, 1986 (*Criminal Code (Amendment No 2) Act* 1986), s 19]

This offence is also punishable summarily: see Sch 2 of the Code.

See s 243 for the definition of assault. See s 347 regarding rape.

See s 337 regarding indecent assaults on males.

In *The State v Andrew Tovue* [1981] PNGLR 8, it was held that the accused worked a trick upon the victim and her husband, both unsophisticated people, and convinced them that he was a traditional medicine man with the ability to make pregnant women give birth more quickly. The "treatment" included acts of sexual intercourse. It is clear that the victim would not have consented to the acts of sexual intercourse with the accused had she not been led by him to believe that these acts were part of his traditional medicine. In these circumstances, the victim's consent was obtained by the fraud of the accused, and his penetration of her body in the acts of sexual intercourse amounted to assaults upon her, under s 243 of the Code.

Kearney DCJ said, in *The State v Andrew Tovue* [1981] PNGLR 8:

> "What amounts to 'indecency' depends upon the standards of modesty of the ordinary citizen of the area at the time the act occurred. Standards of decency vary from place to place and from time to time. I respectfully agree with view expressed by Prentice J in *R v Noboi Bosai* [1971-1972] PNGLR 271, 283, that there is no uniform blanket standard of decency yet applicable throughout the country, and respectfully disagree with the contrary view expressed by Wilson J in *The State v Aubafo Feama, Nama Auri, Kafidiri Kudebebe Hagima* [1978] PNGLR 301, 308. Clearly, what is indecent at one time and place or under one set of circumstances may not be indecent at another time and place or in different circumstances."

Corroboration is not required by law, but in practice persons are not usually convicted on the testimony of a complainant woman in criminal proceedings for a sexual offence unless her testimony is corroborated by independent evidence implicating the accused. Nevertheless, an accused may be convicted upon the uncorroborated evidence of the complainant, provided the court is satisfied it is true.

In cases where such corroboration is lacking, it is necessary that the trial judge or magistrate makes it quite clear that the danger of convicting upon such uncorroborated evidence is very much to the fore of his or her mind. This is more than a rule of prudence – failure to do so will result in the conviction being set aside on appeal: *The State v Andrew Tovue* [1981] PNGLR 8.

It is a rule of practice, though not a rule of law, not to convict on the uncorroborated testimony of the woman in criminal proceedings for a sexual offence. The rule derives from experience that allegations of sexual misbehaviour are very easy to make but may be very difficult to refute, however innocent the person accused may be: *Re Appeal by Toboromilat* (1953) N46.

In *The State v Paul Talip Kambio Wasma Sic* (1995) N1327 the issue before the court was whether a six-year-old alleged victim of indecent and unlawful assault was fit to give evidence against the accused. Injia J held that an infant prosecutrix need not give evidence before the accused can be convicted of an offence under s 349. The evidence of the mother of the prosecutrix's complaint about the indecent assault alone is sufficient to convict, as long as the evidence of the mother is of good quality, and where necessary, corroborated by other credible witnesses. *The State v Sugeri Sipi* [1987] PNGLR 357 was considered: see annotation under s 215 above.

On a charge of this kind, judges, as a matter of practice, warn juries not to convict unless there is some corroboration of the evidence of the complainant: *R v Mumford* (1953) N48.

350. Abduction.

(1) A person who -

(a) with intent -

(i) to marry or carnally know a woman; or

(ii) to cause her to be married or carnally known by any other person,

takes her away, or detains her, against her will; or

(b) from motives of gain, and with an intent referred to in Paragraph (a), takes or entices away, or detains, a woman who is under 21 years, and who -

(i) has any interest, whether legal or equitable, present or future, absolute, conditional, or contingent, in any property; or

(ii) is a presumptive heiress or co-heiress, or the presumptive next of kin, or one of the presumptive next of kin, to any person who has such an interest,

out of the custody of her father or mother, or other person having the lawful care or charge of her, and against the will of the father or mother or other person,

is guilty of a crime.

Penalty: Imprisonment for a term not exceeding seven years.

(2) A person who is convicted of an offence against Subsection (1) that was committed with respect to a woman referred to in Subsection (1)(b), is incapable of taking any estate or interest, legal or equitable, in any property of the woman, or in which she- has any interest, or that comes to her as an heiress, co-heiress, or next of kin, and if he has married the woman, all such property shall, on his conviction, be settled in such manner as the National Court, on application by the Principal Legal Adviser, orders.

351. Abduction of girls under 16.

(1) A person who unlawfully takes an unmarried girl under the age of 16 years out of the custody or protection of her father or mother, or other person having the lawful care or charge of her, and against the will of the father, mother or other person, is guilty of a misdemeanour.

Penalty: Imprisonment for a term not exceeding two years.

(2) It is immaterial in the case of a charge of an offence against Subsection (1) that -

(a) the offender believed the girl to be of or above the age of 16years; or

(b) the girl was taken with her own consent or at her own suggestion.

See s 220 of the Code.

See *R v Taurino* (1960) N160.

352. Rule of evidence.

On a charge of an offence against any provision of this Division, the wife of the accused person is a competent but not a compellable witness.

Division 8 – Offences against Liberty

353. Kidnapping.

A person who forcibly takes or detains another with intent to compel that other person to work for him against his will is guilty of a crime.

Penalty: Imprisonment for a term not exceeding seven years.

354. Kidnapping for ransom.

(1) A person who -

(a) takes or entices away or detains, a person with intent to -

(i) extort or gain anything from; or

(ii) to procure anything to be done or omitted to be done by,

any person by a demand containing threats of injury or detriment, to be caused to the person taken, enticed or detained either by the offender or any other person, if the demand is not complied with; or

(b) receives or harbours the person in respect of whom threats referred to in Paragraph (a) are made, knowing that person to have been so taken or enticed away, or detained,

is guilty of the crime of kidnapping for ransom.

Penalty: Subject to Subsection (2), imprisonment for a term not exceeding 14 years.

(2) If the person kidnapped has been set at liberty without having suffered grievous bodily harm the offender is liable to imprisonment for a term not exceeding 10 years.

(3) A person who attempts to commit the crime of kidnapping for ransom is guilty of a crime.

Penalty: Imprisonment for a term not exceeding seven years.

(4) The wife of the accused person is a competent but not a compellable witness.

As to s 354(1)(a)(i), see s 361 of the Code.

As to s 354(1)(b), see s 390.

The words "any person" in the section may include the person detained as well as any third person. The words "kidnapping" and "ransom" do not have established meanings so as to provide a construction of the phrase "kidnapping for ransom": *The State v Kwalimu Goina* [1982] PNGLR 112 (Followed *R v Campbell and Brennan* [1981] Qd R 516).

The intent to extort, and threats of injury which accompany extortion demands, give the act of detaining its serious quality, and a short duration of detention does not affect that serious quality: *The State v Kwalimu Goina* [1982] PNGLR 112.

The word "anything" in s 354(1)(a) is not limited to something tangible. The "detaining" (however affected) and the "procuring" do not have to involve separate and distinct acts: *The State v Kwalimu Goina* [1982] PNGLR 112.

Under this section, the person detained need not be a different person from the person of whom the extortion demands are made: *The State v Kwalimu Goina* [1982] PNGLR 112.

Kidnapping is considered similar to robbing with violence and other offences involving violence against the person. The deterrent aspect of the punishment for the offence is of primary importance and is calculated to protect society from similar deliberate attacks. Even though an increase in sentence may take effect after the accused persons believed they had completed their punishments, the seriousness of the offence must outweigh such a consideration, although it may be taken into account: *The State v Kwalimu Goina* [1982] PNGLR 112.

355. Deprivation of liberty.

A person who unlawfully -

(a) confines or detains another in any place against his will; or

(b) deprives another of his personal liberty,

is guilty of a misdemeanour.

Penalty: Imprisonment for a term not exceeding three years.

See ss 42 and 43 of the *Constitution*.

"Unlawful" means that a detention is unlawful unless it is authorised or excused by law: *McKenzie v The State* (1998) SC 596. At common law, a confinement is illegal if the person confined is not informed of the reason why he or she is seized and detained. In Papua New Guinea it is further specially provided that "[n]o person shall be deprived of his personal liberty except as authorised by law in certain specified cases", and that "[a] person who is arrested or detained shall be informed promptly, in a language that he understands, of the reasons for his arrest and detention and of any charge against him": *Constitution*, s 42(1) and 42(2)(a) (formerly *Human Rights Act* 1972, s 11(1) and (2)); *R v Besia* [1975] PNGLR 74 at 77.

Where the accused, an Officer-in-Charge of a rural police station, placed persons in confinement and allegedly ordered that they be formally charged, but after several weeks they remained in confinement without being charged, the accused could not use s 24 as a defence. The court found that his degree and length of dereliction of duty as Officer-in-Charge amounted to recklessness that would disentitle his being able to urge that his will did not go with the actual unlawful imprisonment as it continued. Further, the reasonably prudent Officer-in-Charge would have foreseen the possibility that the persons would not be charged for some time, and that their confinement would therefore be unlawful unless he carried out his responsibility of seeing that his subordinates did their work properly. Similarly, the accused could not have entertained an honest and reasonable mistake over such a long period of time that the persons had been charged, in order to utilise the defence of mistake: *R v Besia* [1975] PNGLR 74.

The state has the onus of proof to negative the existence of exculpatory circumstances – the position under the Code is other than that in the United Kingdom, where Archbold (38th ed) states (at p 2798) that once an imprisonment is shown, the defence must justify it: *R v Besia* [1975] PNGLR 74.

The practice of confinement of a woman, not charged with an offence, pending the arrest of her husband who is the actual suspect, is unlawful both at common law or by failure to comply with s 11 of the *Human Rights Act* 1972 (now s 42 of the *Constitution*): *R v Besia* [1975] PNGLR 74.

In *R v John William MacGregor* (1957) N110 a patrol officer committed a "technical" deprivation of liberty by handcuffing a man to a flagpole for half an hour.

By virtue of s 32 of the *Criminal Code* in conjunction with s 355, it is a defence to a charge under s 355 that the person making a citizen's arrest and subsequent detention under the *Arrest Act* was doing so in execution of the law: *McKenzie v The State* (1998) SC 596.

356. False certificates by officers charged with duties relating to liberty.

A person who -

(a) being required by law to give a certificate concerning any matter by virtue of which the liberty of any person may be affected, gives a certificate that is, to his knowledge, false in a material particular; or

(b) not being a person authorised by law to give such a certificate, gives such a certificate, and represents himself to be a person authorised to give it,

is guilty of a misdemeanour.

Penalty: Imprisonment for a term not exceeding three years.

357. Concealment of matters affecting liberty.

A person who -

(a) being required by law to keep any record concerning any matter relating to a person in confinement -

(i) refuses or neglects to keep the record; or

(ii) makes in the record an entry that is, to his knowledge, false in a material particular; or

(b) being required by law to give any information to any person touching any person in confinement, or to show to any person any person in confinement, or any place in which a person is confined -

(i) refuses or neglects to give the information, or to show the person or place, to any person to whom he is required to give the information or show the person or place; or

(ii) gives to any person to whom he is required to give it information concerning any such matter that is, to his knowledge, false in a material particular,

is guilty of a misdemeanour.

Penalty: Imprisonment for a term not exceeding three years.

358. Unlawful custody of person of unsound mind.

A person who detains or assumes the custody of a person of unsound mind contrary to the provisions of the laws relating to such person is guilty of a misdemeanour.

Penalty: Imprisonment for a term not exceeding two years.

See Pt VIII of the *Public Health Act* regarding "persons of unsound mind".

359. Threats.

A person who threatens to do any injury or cause any detriment, to another person with intent -

(a) to prevent or hinder the other person from doing an act that he is lawfully entitled to do; or

(b) to compel him to do an act that he is lawfully entitled to abstain from doing,

is guilty of a misdemeanour.

Penalty: A fine not exceeding K400.00 or imprisonment for a term not exceeding one year.

This offence is also punishable summarily: see Sch 2 of the Code.

See s 243(1)(b) regarding assault by threat. See ss 389-392 regarding extortion by threats.

Division 9 – Bigamy and Offences Relating to Parental Rights and Duties

360. Bigamy.

(1) Subject to this section, a person who is married who goes through a form or ceremony of marriage with another person is guilty of an indictable offence.

Penalty: Imprisonment for a term not exceeding five years.

(2) It is a defence to a prosecution for an offence against Subsection (1) if the defendant proves that -

(a) at the time of the alleged offence, he believed that his spouse was dead; and

(b) his spouse had been absent from him for such time and in such circumstances as to provide, at the time of the alleged offence, reasonable grounds for presuming that his spouse was dead.

(3) For the purposes of Subsection (2) proof by a defendant that -

(a) his spouse had been continually absent from him for the period of seven years immediately preceding the date of the alleged offence; and

(b) he had no reason to believe that his spouse had been alive at any time within that period,

is sufficient proof of the matters referred to in Subsection (2)(b).

(4) Subject to Subsections (5) and (8) a person who goes through a form or ceremony of marriage with a person who is married, knowing, or having reasonable grounds to believe, that the latter person is married, is guilty of an indictable offence.

Penalty: Imprisonment for a term not exceeding five years.

(5) It is not an offence against this section for a person to go through a form or ceremony of marriage with that person's own spouse.

(6) In a prosecution for an offence against this section, the spouse of the accused person is a competent and compellable witness for the prosecution or the defence.

(7) In a prosecution for an offence against this section, the fact that, at the time of the alleged offence, a person was married shall not be taken to have been proved if the only evidence of the fact is the evidence of the other party to the alleged marriage.

(8) This section does not apply to or in relation to a customary marriage entered into by a person who is a party to a subsisting customary marriage, where the custom applying to each of those marriages recognises the other marriage as being, or continuing to be, valid.

See s 5(f) of the *Custom Recognition Act* regarding recognition of customary family law.

See s 25 of the *Criminal Code* regarding mistake of fact as a defence.

See s 63 of the *Marriage Act* 1963, which also creates an offence of bigamy.

A "Christian" marriage solemnised under the provisions of Pt IV of the *Marriage Act* 1963, followed by a "customary" marriage to another person as defined by Pt V of the *Marriage Act* (s 55), would, if proved, amount in law to the offence of bigamy (s 55(1)). Whether or not that is desirable is not for the court to say. There may well be a feeling in the community that where the law recognises polygamous and potentially polygamous marriages by virtue of the recognition of the validity of native customary marriages, then an offence of bigamy is hardly appropriate to the circumstances of the country: *The State v Boas Gugu* [1981] PNGLR 5 (Andrew J).

In *R v Sagoo* [1975] 2 All ER 926, the court held that for the purposes of the criminal law the relevant time for determining the question of whether the accused was within the meaning of the words "being married" ["is married" in Papua New Guinea] was the time of the alleged bigamous ceremony of marriage and not the time of contracting the marriage. Thus, where a potentially polygamous marriage still subsisted but had become monogamous in character at the time of the alleged bigamous ceremony of marriage, the accused was held to have been correctly convicted of bigamy: *The State v Boas Gugu* [1981] PNGLR 5.

The validity of the second marriage does not affect the question. It is the appearing to contract a second marriage, and the going through the ceremony, which constitutes the crime of bigamy. Otherwise it could never exist in the ordinary cases, as a previous marriage always renders null and void a marriage that is celebrated afterwards by either of the parties to an existing marriage: *The State v Boas Gugu* [1981] PNGLR 5.

In *The State v Paul Nangsi Kamang* (1975) N12 the accused was charged under s 63(1) of the *Marriage Act*. He had undergone two marriages under the *Marriage Act*. His defence was that the first marriage was invalid because at the time of marriage his wife was already married by way of custom. It was held that s 55(2) of the *Marriage Act* provides that if a customary marriage is valid and if it were proved that the first wife had, at the time of her marriage to the accused, previously been married by custom, or a reasonable doubt raised whether such a marriage might have taken place, the accused would have a complete defence to a charge of bigamy. It was held on the facts that this had not been shown. The accused was sentenced to imprisonment for six months.

In *The State v Floyd Robinson* [1992] PNGLR 205, the accused, having entered into a church-solemnised marriage with JA, obtained a Certificate of Dissolution of Marriage from the Local Court. He then organised a new marriage by way of a civil ceremony at the Registrar General's Office after making a false declaration of his marriage status. It was held that as the Local Court had no jurisdiction to dissolve a statutory marriage, the accused remained legally married to his first wife and had a de facto relationship with the other woman. Although there was no evidence to suggest that the accused learned prior to his second marriage that the Local Court had set aside the order to issue a certificate of dissolution when it realised it was a statutory marriage, the accused was held responsible for fixing the problems he had created. He was given a two year suspended sentence on the charge of bigamy and fined K300 for false declaration.

See Kassam "*When is a Customary Law Marriage not Customary in Papua New Guinea? A Comment*" 1(3) MLJ 92-97.

361. Child-stealing.

(1) A person who, with intent to deprive a parent or guardian of a child under the age of 14 years, or any other person who has the lawful care or charge of such a child, of the possession of the child, or with intent to steal any article on or about the person of any such child -

(a) forcibly or fraudulently takes or entices away, or detains, the child; or

(b) receives or harbours the child, knowing it to have been so taken or enticed away or detained,

is guilty of a crime.

Penalty: Imprisonment for a term not exceeding seven years.

(2) It is a defence to a charge of an offence against Subsection (1) to prove that the accused person -

(a) claimed in good faith a right to the possession of the child; or

(b) in the case of an illegitimate child (not being a child who has been adopted) is its mother or claimed (in good faith) to be its father.

(3) The husband or wife of the accused person is a competent but not a compellable witness.

Compare with kidnapping in ss 353 and 354 of the Code.

362. Desertion of children.

A parent of a child under the age of 14 years who is able to maintain the child and who wilfully and without lawful or reasonable cause deserts the child and leaves it without means of support is guilty of a misdemeanour.

Penalty: Imprisonment for a term not exceeding one year.

This offence is also punishable summarily: see Sch 2 of the Code.

Remedies are also available under s 22 of the *Deserted Wives and Children Act.*

Part VI – Offences Relating to Property and Contracts

Division 1 – Stealing and Similar Offences

Subdivision A. – Introductory

363. Interpretation of Division 1.

(1) In this Division, unless the contrary intention appears -

"animals" includes all living creatures other than man;

"stealing" has the meaning attributed to it by the succeeding provisions of this Division;

"thing capable of being stolen" has the meaning attributed to it by Section 364.

(2) For the purposes of this Division, an animal wild by nature shall be deemed to be in a state of confinement only as long is it is in a den, cage, sty, tank or other small enclosure, or is otherwise so placed that it cannot escape and its owner can take possession of it at pleasure.

364. Things capable of being stolen.

(1) The following things are capable of being stolen -

(a) all inanimate things that -

(i) are the property of any person; and

(ii) are movable; and

(b) subject to Subsection (4), all tame animals (whether tame by nature or tamed) that are the property of any person; and

(c) animals wild by nature of a kind that is not ordinarily found in Papua New Guinea in a condition of natural liberty, that -

(i) are the property of any person; and

(ii) are usually kept in a state of confinement (whether they are actually in confinement or have escaped from confinement); and

(d) animals wild by nature, of a kind that is ordinarily found in Papua New Guinea in a condition of natural liberty, that -

(i) are the property of any person; and

(ii) are -

(A) in confinement; or

(B) actually being pursued after escaping from confinement; and

(e) the dead bodies of wild animals; and

(f) all things that are produced by or form part of an animal that is capable of being stolen; and

(g) oysters and oyster brood while in oyster beds, layings or fisheries that -

(i) are the property of any person; and

(ii) are sufficiently marked out, or are known by general repute to be his property.

(2) An animal in the enjoyment of its natural liberty is not capable of being stolen.

(3) An inanimate thing that -

(a) is the property of any person; and

(b) being capable of being made movable, becomes movable (even if it is made movable in order for it to be stolen),

becomes capable of being stolen as soon as it becomes movable.

(4) A tame pigeon is not capable of being stolen unless it is in a pigeon-house or on its owner's land.

"Property" is defined by s 1 of the Code.

See ss 428-429 regarding exploitation of oysters and fish.

A chose in action, such as a debt, is incapable of being stolen: *John Kasaipwalova v The State* [1977] PNGLR 257 (Frost CJ).

Cheques paid into a bank are not capable of being stolen; they become a chose in action, an asset of the bank not subject to larceny: *R v Jamieson* [1975] PNGLR 216.

A bank credit, being an intangible chose in action, would not have been capable of being stolen at common law, and is not within the requirements of this section. However, "the money and proceeds" referred to in ss 367-369 form a special category of property capable of being stolen in addition to that defined by s 364: *John Kasaipwalova v The State* [1977] PNGLR 257 (Kearney J, dissenting).

A thing capable of being stolen, at common law, had to have some physical substance. Accordingly, property rights which had no tangible subject matter – that is, choses in action – could not, as such, be stolen. This obvious defect in the law of theft was met in part only by statute, until eventually, by the *Theft Act* 1968 (UK), choses in action were made capable of theft. A cheque has a dual nature; as a piece of paper it has physical substance, and it is regarded by the law as a chose in action. As a piece of paper it may have been capable of being stolen, at common law, or if, like other written instruments included in the definition of "valuable security" in the *Larceny Act* 1861, it lacked the minimal value required by the common law, it became larcenable by s 27 of that Act. Though the mode of stealing is a conversion which involves cashing the cheque, it remains nevertheless the cheque itself, and not its proceeds, which are stolen: *John Kasaipwalova v The State* [1977] PNGLR 257 (Kearney J, dissenting).

See *The State v Wilfred Timon Bai* [1980] PNGLR 216, and *R v Jamieson* [1975] PNGLR 216, annotated under s 365 below.

365. Definition of stealing.

(1) In this section –

"owner" in relation to a thing, means -

(a) the owner or a part-owner of the thing; or

(b) any person having possession or control of, or a special property in the thing;

"special property includes -

(a) any charge or lien on the thing in question; and

(b) any right arising from or dependent on holding possession of the thing in question, whether by the person entitled to the right or by some other person for his benefit.

(2) Subject to the succeeding provisions of this Code, a person who fraudulently takes anything capable of being stolen, or fraudulently converts to his own use or to the use of any other person anything capable of being stolen, is said to steal that thing.

(3) The act of stealing is not complete until the person taking or converting the thing actually moves it or otherwise actually deals with it by some physical act.

(4) A person who takes or converts anything capable of being stolen shall be deemed to do so fraudulently if he does so with intent -

(a) to permanently deprive the owner of the thing of it; or

(b) to permanently deprive any person who has any special property in the thing of that property; or

(c) to use the thing as a pledge or security; or

(d) to part with it on a condition as to its return that the person taking or converting it may be unable to perform; or

(e) to deal with it in such a manner that it cannot be returned in the condition in which it was at the time of the taking or conversion; or

(f) in the case of money, to use it at the will of the person who takes or converts it, even if he intends to afterwards repay the amount to the owner.

(5) In the case of a conversion, it is immaterial -

(a) whether the thing converted is taken for the purpose of conversion, or is at the time of the conversion in the possession of the person who converts it; and

(b) that the person who converts the property -

(i) is the holder of a power of attorney for the disposition of it; or

(ii) is otherwise authorised to dispose of it.

(6) A taking or conversion may be fraudulent, even if it is effected without secrecy or attempt at concealment.

(7) When a thing converted has been lost by the owner and found by the person who converts it, the conversion shall not be deemed to be fraudulent if at the time of the conversion the person converting the thing -

(a) does not know who is the owner; and

(b) believes, on reasonable grounds, that the owner cannot be discovered.

See s 364 of the Code regarding things capable of being stolen, and s 367 regarding funds held under direction. See s 372 for punishment of theft offences.

In *Tom Amaiu v The State* [1979] PNGLR 576 it was alleged that the appellant could not have been convicted of stealing a cheque which was awaiting collection because no property in the cheque had ever passed to the payee. It was held that it was unnecessary to decide whether property in the cheque had passed to the payee, because the definition of "owner" in s 365(1) includes the owner, any part owner or any person having possession or control of or a special property in the thing in question and, at the very least, the payee had a special property in the cheque.

It is not always necessary in order to support a charge of or involving larceny to prove the name of the owner of the property or to prove the ownership of the property: *Tom Amaiu v The State* [1979] PNGLR 576 at 580, citing *Lodge v Lawton* [1978] VR 112, and *R v King* (1978) 19 SASR 118.

An essential element of stealing is an asportation involving some physical removal, however small it may be: *R v Albert* (1953) N1.

For stealing to be constituted there must be an actual moving, or in the case of conversion, an actual dealing by some physical act, of a thing capable of being stolen. Where money is paid into a bank, that money becomes at once the money of the banker, and all that the customer has is a chose in action. Thus, there can be no stealing unless the payment of the money into the bank constitutes a taking or fraudulent conversion of the money, as all that remains is a chose in action, and the physical acts of operating upon the account by cheque or otherwise cannot constitute an actual moving or other dealing with a thing capable of being stolen:, *John Kasaipwalova v The State* [1977] PNGLR 257 (Frost CJ).

On carrying away goods, see also *R v Harbour* (1954) N135.

The court is entitled to view the evidence of all the transactions as a whole, rather than to consider each transaction in isolation as a separate and individual one, in order to rebut any defence of simple mistake or inadvertence on the part of the accused: *R v Walsh* [1971] PNGLR 293.

Frost CJ said, in *The State v Alpen Popo* [1977] PNGLR 18:

> "It is a well-known rule that recent possession of stolen property is evidence, either that the person in possession of it stole the property, or received it knowing it to have been stolen, according to the circumstances of the case. Prima facie, the presumption is that he stole it himself, but if the circumstances are such as to show it to be impossible that he stole it, it may be inferred that he received it, knowing that someone else had stolen it."

See s 410 regarding receiving stolen property.

In *R v Maraga Gomora* (1953) N31 a few months had passed between the time of the alleged theft and the disappearance of the goods, stretching the doctrine to its limit so far as falling within the description of "recently" stolen. The lapse of time must affect the strength of any presumption from the possession to be drawn by a jury.

In *R v Griffin* [1971] PNGLR 72 Prentice J, at 75, gave this explanation of the doctrine of recent possession:

> "Under the doctrine of recent possession, where there has been a robbery and part of the stolen property is found soon after in the possession of a person not the owner, a presumption of fact may therefore be raised against that person to the effect that he stole the articles, where he does not give a reasonable account of how he got the property. If an explanation is given by that person and it appears to be a reasonable one, the tribunal should acquit, even if it does not positively accept the explanation. But when an accused 'on being questioned has given an explanation of his possession which is admittedly untrue ... the presumption of guilt does arise.' This is a presumption which may be rebutted and, if the subsequent explanation of the prisoner satisfies the jury, or raises a reasonable doubt, he is still entitled to an acquittal."

R v Griffin [1971] PNGLR 72 provides an application of the doctrine of recent possession which is a presumption of fact rather than of law. In that case, possession was considered recent, as the accused gave unsatisfactory and contradictory explanations on how he came into possession of 49 crocodile skins the day after they disappeared from a warehouse.

Where the accused converted moneys from a social club to his own use, it is immaterial that the moneys initially came into his possession lawfully, the accused being treasurer of the social club: *R v McKay* (1954) N56.

At early common law, the offence of larceny could only be committed of a specific thing belonging to another person. It was necessary to prove a taking or carrying away (asportation), coupled with an intention to deprive the owner of the property taken. Consequently, in the case of a bailment, there could be no larceny because there was no wrongful taking. To meet this gap in the law, in some jurisdictions legislation was passed to constitute the offence of larceny as a bailee:

see, for example, the *Crimes Act* 1900 (NSW), s 125. Under the Code the same result was achieved by extending the definition of stealing to cover the case of fraudulent conversion of the thing by a person to that person's own use or the use of another person (365(2)): *John Kasaipwalova v The State* [1977] PNGLR 257 (Frost CJ).

Kearney J, in dissent, stated in *John Kasaipwalova v The State* [1977] PNGLR 257:

> "'Fraudulent conversion' appears as one mode of stealing, in s 365(2). Three aspects may be noted: it is not limited to, although it includes, conversion by bailees; it does not extend, in its terms, to proceeds of a thing bailed; and it has no application where both possession and property are obtained with the consent of the owner."

Taking moneys with an intention of paying them back later does not prevent a charge from amounting to theft under s 365(4)(f): *The State v Alphonse Joseph Sema* [1977] PNGLR 289.

It is sufficient proof of fraud under s 365(4)(f) that the person intends to take or convert money, even though that person may afterwards intend to repay the amount: *The State v Wilfred Timon Bai* [1980] PNGLR 77.

No judicial definition of conversion has been attempted which would cover every possible case. The civil law definition is inappropriate, because a claim for damages for conversion cannot succeed unless the owner has suffered damage, which is not the case in a criminal prosecution for fraudulent conversion. At common law a prisoner must be shown to have possession of the goods, and generally the prosecution must prove some conduct on the part of the prisoner setting up a full title to the property or asserting a right to pass the property. Under s 365(3) any physical act amounting to a disposal of the thing would appear to constitute an instance of a conversion if the thing is not held in the bailee's possession: *John Kasaipwalova v The State* [1977] PNGLR 257 (Frost CJ).

In *R v Gahoso Simbane* [1975] PNGLR 257 the accused broke into the dwelling of another and removed a suitcase out of spite; this taking being tortious but not felonious. However, the accused later opened the suitcase and found a moneybox, the contents of which he converted to his own use. At this point it became larceny:

> "If the original possession be rightful, subsequent misappropriation does not make it a felony; but if the original possession be wrongful, although not felonious, and then a man disposes of the chattel *animo furandi* it is larceny."

In *Watau v Purcell* (1956) N95 the accused found a cigarette lighter at a hotel. Larceny by finding involves questions of some nicety and depends upon the whole circumstances, and this makes it imperative for the court, when the original possession was innocent, to be quite sure that the possession changed from an innocent one to guilty or fraudulent one. There was no duty on the appellant to report the find and there was no evidence that the owner could be discovered, especially in the circumstances where the lighter had been found in a public hotel.

Where an accused finds property belonging to the government (postage stamps), but forgets to return them, he is not deemed to have converted the property: *R v Basengke* (1954) N58.

In *R v Jamieson* [1975] PNGLR 216 the accused, acting as a debt collector, received cheques in the course of his business which were paid into his own account, but he failed to account to his client creditor company. The court held that there was no evidence that the accused had taken anything "capable of being stolen": s 364. There was no evidence of any actual movement or dealing: s 365(3). The mere negotiation of the cheque would not be conversion. The money paid into the bank means the depositor has only a chose in action. The money deposited becomes an asset of the bank and not subject to larceny, although it might be the subject of misappropriation. The subsequent disposal of the moneys could not amount to larceny. There was nothing to relate the moneys actually withdrawn to the proceeds of the cheque paid in as compared with other moneys posted to the working account.

In *R v McKay* (1954) N56 the accused was obliged to bank social club moneys in a Samarai bank agency, and he did not do so. He later brought the moneys with him to Port Moresby, and after five days did not deposit the moneys at the central bank. The accused was said to have dealt with the moneys for the purposes of s 365(3).

In *The State v Wilfred Timon Bai* [1980] PNGLR 77 Miles J held, at 84-85:

> "'fraudulent conversion' relates to 'anything capable of being stolen'. The word 'stolen' ... must be read subject to s 363 ... which ... does not include a chose in action. I cannot see that the accused by signing and depositing the cheques can be regarded as fraudulently converting the money any more than he can be regarded as stealing in the common law sense".[100]

There cannot be larceny of a chose in action, namely the debt owed by a bank to its customer, ie moneys in the bank: *R v Jamieson* [1975] PNGLR 216 following *Croton v The Queen* (1967) 117 CLR 326 and *R v Davenport* [1954] 1 WLR 567; ER 602.

It appears that an allegation in an indictment that an accused stole three sums of money is not satisfied by finding that the accused stole three cheques in specie.

Where there is no evidence of how the accused disposed of the proceeds of the cheques, nor evidence of whether the cash had been put to the accused's own purposes, larceny under the Code cannot be constituted: *The State v Wilfred Timon Bai* [1980] PNGLR 77.

In *R v Jamieson* [1975] PNGLR 216 evidence of similar facts went to establish a fraudulent intent as required in s 365 and to rebut defences of innocent dealing, inadvertence, mistake or mishap.

The distinction between larceny by trick and the statutory offence of obtaining property by false pretences is that if a person being the owner of a chattel, or having authority from the owner to alienate it, is induced by the fraud of another person to part with it that person, and that person at the time of taking it intends to misappropriate it as his or her own, then, if the person who parted with the property intended to part with property in the chattel to the taker as well as possession, the offence is not larceny but false pretences. However, if the person intended to part only with possession of the chattel to the taker, the offence is larceny: *Tom Amaiu v The State* [1979] PNGLR 576 at 580, citing *R v Ward* (1938) 38 SR (NSW) 308.

In *Tom Amaiu v The State* [1979] PNGLR 576 a sentence of five years was held not to be manifestly excessive where a large sum was involved and where the appellant was a Member of Parliament who deceived his own people in order to steal their money. This was a case of the educated and well placed preying on the uneducated and less well placed.

As to alternative verdicts of false pretences or cheating, see s 544.

---

[100] Following *R v Jamieson* [1975] PNGLR 216.

366. Special cases relating to stealing.

(1) When a wild animal in the enjoyment of its natural liberty has been killed by any person, the taking of the dead body of the animal by that person, or by any person acting under his orders, before it has been reduced into actual possession by the owner of the land on which the animal was killed or on which it died, is not stealing.

(2) When a factor or agent pledges or gives a lien on any goods or documents of title to goods entrusted to him for any sum of money not greater than the sum of the -

(a) amount due to him from his principal at the time of pledging or giving the lien; and

(b) the amount of any bill of exchange or promissory note accepted or made by him for or on account of his principal,

that dealing with the goods or document of title is not stealing.

(3) When a servant, contrary to his master's orders, takes from his possession any food in order that it may be given to an animal belonging to or in the possession of his master, that taking is not stealing.

See s 364 of the Code for the definition of "animal". See s 376.

367. Funds, etc, held under direction.

(1) Subject to Subsection (2), where a person receives, alone or jointly with another person, any money or valuable security, or a power of attorney for the sale, mortgage, pledge or other disposition of any property, whether capable of being stolen or not, with a direction that -

(a) the money or any part of it; or

(b) any other money received in exchange for it, or any part of it; or

(c) the proceeds or any part of the proceeds of the security, or of the mortgage pledge, or other disposition,

shall be applied to any purpose or paid to any person specified in the direction, the money and proceeds shall be deemed to be the property of the person from whom the money, security, or power of attorney was received until the direction has been complied with.

(2) Where in a case to which Subsection (1) applies the person receiving the money, security or power of attorney, and the person from whom he receives it, ordinarily deal with each other on the term that in the absence of any special direction all money paid to the former on account of the latter would be properly treated as an item in a debtor and creditor account between them, the former cannot be charged with stealing the money or any such proceeds unless the direction is written.

"Money" and "valuable security" are defined by s 1 of the Code. See s 372(9) regarding the punishment for this offence. See s 364 regarding things capable of being stolen.

The reason underlying the enactment of this section was "to extend the definition of stealing, which includes a fraudulent conversion, to the proceeds of property converted **under a bailment** by treating the bailor as the owner of the proceeds **to**

the same extent as he was of the property originally bailed." (emphasis in original): *John Kasaipwalova v The State* [1977] PNGLR 257 (Williams J).

This section applies only where a person receives property which is limited to three categories:

(a) any money, which by definition under s 1 includes cheques; or

(b) valuable security; or

(c) a power of attorney for the sale, mortgage, pledge or other disposition of any property, whether capable of being stolen or not.

Thus, in Queensland it has been held to have no application where chattels such as potatoes are received for sale (*R v Smalley* [1963] Qd R 508): *John Kasaipwalova v The State* [1977] PNGLR 257 (Frost CJ).

Frost CJ said, in *John Kasaipwalova v The State* [1977] PNGLR 257:

> "[T]he method of dealing with the case of money or property received with a direction has this effect, that s 367 must be read with s 365 so that for criminal responsibility to be established the offence remains that of stealing, and not the wider statutory offence found in some jurisdictions of misappropriations, and to enable proof of one element, the money or proceeds must remain a thing capable of being stolen, in relation to which therefore an actual dealing by some physical act remains possible ... money ceases to exist as such a thing in the hands of the person receiving it upon payment into a bank account. It is true that such an application of the law of banking may limit the effect of s 367, but that follows from the method adopted by the legislature of bringing the objects to be achieved by s 367 into the law of stealing, and indeed the whole structure of Subdiv A, as it now is."

In *John Kasaipwalova v The State*, Kearney J, dissenting, quoted from Sir Samuel Griffith's explanatory letter of 29 October 1897 to the Attorney-General, accompanying the Draft Code:

> "Property held under such circumstances [under a direction or received by agents for sale] shall be deemed to be the property of the person beneficially entitled to it. A fraudulent conversion of the property then falls within the general definition of stealing."

Under this section the deemed property is not expressed to include any valuable security or the power of attorney or deed or instrument, if any, relating to the mortgage, pledge or other disposition. Frost CJ said, In *John Kasaipwalova v The State* [1977] PNGLR 257:

> "The mischief to which the section is directed is theft of money or money received in exchange for it or the proceeds of the two strictly limited categories of property, where that money or property is received by a person under a direction as provided for in the section, irrespectively whether the money, valuable security or power of attorney is the subject of a bailment, or the property therein has passed to that person."

He further stated that, therefore, the:

> "conclusion is that the operation of the section does extend to the case of the receipt of money with an appropriate direction in which, in the circumstances of the case, apart from s 367 the property in the money would pass to the person receiving it. By the legal fiction which the section creates, that money remains the property of the person from whom it was received."

There are three elements in a bailment, namely that a specific thing is delivered, the thing delivered remains the property of the bailor, or at least it does not become the property of the bailee, and that the thing itself, or something for which it has been exchanged under the contract of bailment, is to be restored or delivered: *John Kasaipwalova v The State* [1977] PNGLR 257 (Williams J).

A direction given after the receipt of the money would be outside the section. It is true that the section seems to contemplate a receipt accompanied by a direction, perhaps to ensure certainty in its application. It does not say money received "following" a direction. However, a prior direction is not excluded; it is sufficient if the receipt is identified with an earlier direction: *John Kasaipwalova v The State* [1977] PNGLR 257 (Frost CJ).

Frost CJ (quoting from *R v Ward* 38 SR (NSW) 308 (Jordan, CJ)) said, in *John Kasaipwalova v The State* [1977] PNGLR 257:

> "When the money is handed over by one person to another to be applied for a particular purpose, it is a question of fact whether it is intended that the very coins, notes or cheques shall be retained by the recipient until they are so applied and then applied in specie; or whether it is intended that the recipient shall, or may, if he choose, become a debtor for the amount so received and assume an obligation to pay an equivalent amount for the prescribed purpose. In the former case, the specific money remains the property of the person who handed it over, until it is so applied ... But the initial question must always be determined; was the money to remain the property of the person paying it until it had been applied by the payee, or was it to become, or might it become, the payee's property subject to a liability to account? This depends entirely on the facts of the particular case."

If a person hands a boy a 20 toea coin with instructions to buy him a newspaper and bring back the change, the inference that no more than a bailment is intended is overwhelming. However, where money in the form of coins, notes or a cheque is given by one to another with instructions to use it for a specific purpose, in ordinary circumstances, and particularly if the amount is large and the contemplated expenditure is to take place over a period of time, the inference is that the person receiving the money acquires the property in the money subject, at most, to a liability to account for a corresponding sum. If the person receiving the money then converts it at common law, he or she could not be guilty of either fraudulent conversion (for that offence involves the conversion to one's own use of the property of another) or of the simple taking of the money (as it had become his or her own property). For criminal responsibility to be established in those circumstances, the offence of obtaining goods by false pretence or wilfully false promise with intent to defraud under s 404 would have to be proved: *John Kasaipwalova v The State* [1977] PNGLR 257 (Frost CJ).

There is nothing in the section requiring its operation to be limited to cases where there is an existing relationship between the parties, say, of principal and agent, or a bailment is created. Frost CJ stated, in *John Kasaipwalova v The State* [1977] PNGLR 257:

> "I would not go farther than to hold that the section requires an instruction or direction as defined, which may be implied from the circumstances and conditional, but free from ambiguity and uncertainty, and understood to be binding between the parties. Further, there can be a direction within the meaning of s 367 even though the purpose specified is of a general nature. Otherwise, for

> example, a person who received a cheque with a direction to apply it for the purpose of establishing a school for traditional dancing and who then cashed the cheque and fraudulently applied the money to the use of another, say, by paying off hire purchase arrears on his brother's car, would not be guilty of an offence, a result unlikely to have been intended by the legislature."

In *R v Jamieson* [1975] PNGLR 216 the accused, acting as a debt collector, received cheques in the course of his business which were paid into his own account, but he failed to pass them on to his client credit company. The court held that there was no evidence that the accused had taken anything "capable of being stolen". Money paid into the bank means that the depositor has only a chose in action. The money deposited becomes an asset of the bank and not subject to larceny, although it might be the subject of misappropriation. There was nothing to relate the moneys actually withdrawn to the proceeds of the cheque paid in as compared with other moneys posted to the working account. There was no specific direction that would have prevented the accused banking the cheque in his own account. While these facts might show a case of fraudulent misappropriation of money or fraudulent failure to account, there was no case to answer on the counts of stealing.

Kearney J, dissenting, stated in *John Kasaipwalova v The State* [1977] PNGLR 257:

> "The question arises whether the phrase 'any other money received in exchange for it' comprehends a credit in a bank account. I consider it does; I see no reason why the fact that the credit at the bank is at law characterised as a chose in action thereby excludes it from being 'money' [within the broad definition of 'money' in s 1]."

The effect of this section is that the bank credit is deemed as against the receiver to be the property of the person from whom the original money was received. This has no effect on the law of banking, but it may operate so as to expose the customer to criminal liability under s 365, should that person fail to comply with the direction and fraudulently convert the amount of the credit to his or her own use. Whether or not this is so depends upon whether money in s 367, constituted by a bank credit, is comprehended by the words "anything capable of being stolen" in s 365. A bank credit would not have been capable of being stolen at common law, but the "money and proceeds" referred to in ss 367-369 form a special category of property capable of being stolen, in addition to that defined by s 364: *John Kasaipwalova v The State* [1977] PNGLR 257 (Kearney J dissenting).

368. Funds, etc, received by agents for sale.

(1) Subject to Subsection (2), where a person receives, alone or jointly with another person, any property from another person on terms -

(a) authorising or requiring him to sell it or otherwise dispose of it; and

(b) requiring him -

(i) to pay or account for the proceeds of the property, or any part of the proceeds; or

(ii) to deliver any thing received in exchange for the property, to the person from whom it is received or to some other person, then the proceeds of the property, and any thing received in exchange for it, shall be deemed to be the property of the person from whom the property was received until they have been disposed of in accordance with the terms on which the property was received.

(2) Subsection (1) does not apply where it is a part of the terms on which the property was received that-

(a) the proceeds (if any) will form an item in a debtor and creditor account between him and the person to whom he is to pay them or account for them; and

(b) the relation of debtor and creditor only will exist between them in respect of the proceeds.

369. Money received for another.

Where a person receives, alone or jointly with another person, any money on behalf of another, the money shall be deemed to be the property of the person on whose behalf it is received, unless it is received on the terms that -

(a) it will form an item in a debtor and creditor account; and

(b) the relation of debtor and creditor only will exist between the parties in respect of it.

The section does not assist in the constitution of the offence of stealing; it can operate only to deem property to be that of another person: *R v Jamieson* [1975] PNGLR 216 at 223.

"Money" is defined by s 1.

370. Stealing by persons having an interest in the thing stolen.

Where a person takes or converts any thing capable of being stolen under such circumstances as would otherwise amount to stealing, it is immaterial that he -

(a) has a special property or interest in the thing; or

(b) is the owner of the thing taken or converted subject to some special property or interest of some other person in the thing; or

(c) is lessee of the thing; or

(d) is one of two or more joint owners of the thing; or

(e) is a director or officer of a corporation or society that is the owner of the thing.

See ss 35 and 433(2) of the Code.

As to indictment, see s 530(6)-(10).

Where the accused was a member and treasurer of the club from which he was alleged to have stolen money, it is immaterial that he may himself have had an interest in the money: *R v McKay* (1954) N56.

371. Husband and wife.

A person who, while a man and his wife are living together, procures either of them to deal with any thing that is to his knowledge, the property of the other in a manner that would be stealing if they were not married shall be deemed to have stolen the thing, and may be charged with stealing it.

Subdivision B – The Offence of Stealing

372. Stealing.

(1) Any person who steals anything capable of being stolen is guilty of a crime.

Penalty: Subject to this section, imprisonment for a term not exceeding three years.

(2) If the thing stolen is a testamentary instrument, (whether the testator is living or dead), the offender is liable, subject to Section 19, to imprisonment for life.

(3) If the thing stolen is anything in course of transmission by post, the offender is liable, subject to Section 19 to imprisonment for life.

(4) If the thing stolen is an aircraft, the offender is liable to imprisonment for a term not exceeding 14 years.

(5) If -

- (a) the thing is stolen from the person of another person; or
- (b) the thing is stolen in a dwelling-house, and -
  - (i) its value exceeds K10.00; or
  - (ii) the offender at or immediately before or after the time of stealing uses or threatens to use violence to any person in the dwelling-house; or
- (c) the thing is stolen from a vessel, vehicle or place of deposit used for the conveyance or custody of goods in transit from one place to another; or
- (d) the thing is stolen from a vessel that is in distress or wrecked or stranded; or
- (e) the thing is stolen from a public office in which it is deposited or kept; or
- (f) the offender, in order to commit the offence, opens a locked room, box or other receptacle by means of a key or other instrument,

the offender is liable to imprisonment for a term not exceeding seven years.

(6) If the offender is a person employed in the Public Service, and the thing stolen -

- (a) is the property of the State; or
- (b) came into the possession of the offender by virtue of his employment,

he is liable to imprisonment for a term not exceeding seven years.

(7) If the offender is a clerk or servant, and the thing stolen -

(a) is the property of his employer; or

(b) came into the possession of the offender on account of his employer,

he is liable to imprisonment for a term not exceeding seven years.

(8) If the offender is a director or officer of a corporation and the thing stolen is the property of the corporation, he is liable to imprisonment for a term not exceeding seven years.

(9) If the thing stolen is -

(a) property that has been received by the offender with a power of attorney for its disposition; or

(b) money received by the offender with a direction that it should be applied or paid to a person specified in the direction; or

(c) the whole or part of the proceeds of a valuable security that was received by the offender with a direction that the proceeds of it should be applied to a purpose or paid to a person specified in the direction; or

(d) the whole or part of the proceeds arising from a disposition of any property that have been received by the offender by virtue of a power of attorney for such disposition, the power of attorney having been received by the offender with a direction that the proceeds be applied to a purpose or paid to a person specified in the direction,

the offender is liable to imprisonment for a term not exceeding seven years.

(10) If the thing stolen is of the value of K1,000.00 or upwards, the offender is liable to imprisonment for a term not exceeding seven years.

(11) If the thing stolen is a fixture or chattel let to the offender to be used by him with a house or lodging, and its value exceeds K100.00, he is liable to imprisonment for a term not exceeding seven years.

(12) If the offender before committing the offence -

(a) had been convicted on indictment of an indictable offence against any provision of this Division; or

(b) had been twice previously summarily convicted of an offence against any such provision punishable on summary conviction whether or not each of the convictions was in respect of an offence of the same character,

he is liable to imprisonment for a term not exceeding seven years.

[S 372 am Act No 13, 1977 (*Criminal Code (Arrest) Act* 1977), s 26A]

This offence is also punishable summarily: see Sch 2 of the Code.

In *R v Gahoso Simbane* [1975] PNGLR 257 the accused broke into the dwelling of another and removed a suitcase out of spite. In later opening the suitcase in the garden, the accused discovered a moneybox, which he feloniously converted under s 365(5). It was held that the accused could not be punished for the more serious offence of stealing something valued in excess of K10.00 (s 372(5)(b)) from a dwelling-house, as the crime was committed outside the dwelling, and may not be related back to the original taking.

It is a necessary ingredient in offence under s 372(6) to prove, in addition to the stealing, that the accused is employed by the public service and that the thing stolen is the property of the government or came into the accused's possession by virtue of his or her employment: *The State v Wilfred Timon Bai* [1980] PNGLR 77.

A substantial individual and general deterrent sentence was required where the accused was a mature educated person in a substantial position of trust who stole government funds, an offence (under s 372(6)) which is particularly prevalent in outstations because of staff inefficiency, shortage of trained police and disarray of records: *The State v Herman Kagl Diawo* [1980] PNGLR 148.

Where the government operates an agency of a bank in the name of the bank, a public servant who embezzles bank funds may be punished under s 372(6): *Susuve Hahari v Fyfe* (1967) N439.

Evidence of good character may not go far in mitigation of sentence in such cases, because good character will usually be required of persons filling positions of trust anyway: *R v Mary Josephine Harley* [1971-1972] PNGLR 399.

For principles on sentencing offenders under s 372(6), see *The State v Keputong Nagong* (1980) N225, discussed under s 596.

The legislative intention is that the special cases set out in this section require an increased sentence: *Public Prosecutor v Sam Minimo* [1977] PNGLR 226.

See s 420(d) for summary conviction. As to s 372(2), see Pt III, Div 8 of the Code.

Subdivision C – Offences Analogous to Stealing

373. Concealing registers.

A person who with intent to defraud, conceals or takes from its place of deposit -

(a) a register that is authorised or required by law to be kept for -

(i) authenticating or recording the title to any property; or

(ii) recording births, baptisms, marriages, deaths or burials; or

(b) a copy of any part of any such register that is required by law to be sent to any public officer,

is guilty of a crime.

Penalty: Imprisonment for a term not exceeding 14 years.

374. Concealing wills.

A person who, with intent to defraud, conceals a testamentary instrument (whether the testator is living or dead) is guilty of a crime.

Penalty: Imprisonment for a term not exceeding 14 years.

375. Concealing deeds, etc.

A person who, with intent to defraud, conceals the whole or part of a document that is evidence of title to any land is guilty of a crime.

Penalty: Imprisonment for a term not exceeding three years.

376. Killing animals with intent to steal.

A person who kills an animal capable of being stolen with intent to steal the skin or carcass or any part of the skin or carcass, is guilty of a crime, and is liable to the same punishment as if he had stolen the animal.

This offence is also punishable summarily: see Sch 2 of the Code.

See s 364 regarding animals, and s 366 regarding special case thefts.

377. Severing with intent to steal.

A person who makes anything moveable with intent to steal it is guilty of a crime, and is liable to the same punishment as if he had stolen the thing after it became movable.

This offence is also punishable summarily: see Sch 2 of the Code.

378. Using registered brands with criminal intention.

A person who, with intent to facilitate the commission of a crime, brands or marks an animal with a registered brand or registered mark without the permission of the owner of the brand or mark is guilty of a misdemeanour.

Penalty: Imprisonment for a term not exceeding three years.

379. Fraudulently dealing with minerals in mines.

A person who takes, conceals or otherwise disposes of any ore of any metal or mineral in or about a mine, with intent to defraud any person, is guilty of a misdemeanour.

Penalty: Imprisonment for a term not exceeding two years.

380. Bringing stolen goods into Papua New Guinea.

(1) A person who, having at any place outside Papua New Guinea obtained any property by any act that-

(a) if it had been done in Papua New Guinea, would have constituted the crime of stealing; and

(b) is an offence under the laws in force in the place where it was done,

brings the property into Papua New Guinea, or has it in his possession in Papua New Guinea, is guilty of a crime, and, subject to Subsection (2), is liable to the same punishment as if he had stolen it in Papua New Guinea.

(2) The punishment imposed for an offence against Subsection (1) shall not exceed the punishment that would be incurred for the same act under the laws in force in the place where the act by which the offender obtained the property was done.

381. Fraudulent disposition of mortgaged goods.

(1) In this section, "mortgaged goods" includes -

(a) any goods and chattels; and

(b) any live animals; and

(c) any progeny of any animals; and

(d) any crops or produce of the earth, whether growing or severed,

that are subject to the provisions of any instrument by which a valid charge or lien is created on them by way of security for any debt or obligation.

(2) A mortgagor of mortgaged goods who removes or disposes of the goods -

(a) without the consent of the mortgagee; and

(b) with intent to defraud,

is guilty of a misdemeanour.

Penalty: Imprisonment for a term not exceeding three years.

(3) The consent of the mortgagee may be implied from the nature of the property mortgaged.

See s 408 of the Code regarding frauds on sale or mortgage of property.

382. Fraudulent appropriation of power.

A person who fraudulently abstracts or diverts to his own use or to the use of any other person any mechanical, illuminating or electrical power derived from any machine, apparatus or substance that is the property of another person is guilty of a crime.

Penalty: Imprisonment for a term not exceeding three years.

The words "abstract" and "divert" are used disjunctively, creating two separate actions for which a person may be liable. In *The State v Thomas Paipua* [1982] PNGLR 402 the accused had broken a seal, unscrewed the meter box and reconnected the wire inside. This did not amount to a "diversion" but to an "abstraction".

Illegal wiring which by-passed the Electricity Commissioner's meter, enabling the operation of air-conditioners without cost, constituted diverting to one's own use: *The State v Anthony Sim* [1980] PNGLR 424.

"Machine" comprehends an electricity generator. "Property of another person" is not an element which must be proved as laid in the indictment, for every ordinary person may reasonably be presumed to know that the Commission generates electricity: *The State v Anthony Sim* [1980] PNGLR 424.

383. Unlawfully using motor vehicles, etc.

(1) In this section, "unlawfully uses" includes the unlawful possession by any person of any motor vehicle or aircraft -

(a) without the consent of the owner or of the person in lawful possession of it; and

(b) with intent to deprive the owner or person in lawful possession of it of the use and possession of it temporarily or permanently.

(2) A person who unlawfully uses a motor vehicle or aircraft without the consent of the owner or of the person in lawful possession of the vehicle or aircraft is guilty of a crime.

Penalty: Imprisonment for a term not exceeding five years.

(3) This section applies without prejudice to any provision relating to the unlawful use of motor vehicles or aircraft of any other law, but an offender is not liable to be convicted under both this section and such a provision in respect of any one and the same unlawful use.

This section was to have been repealed and replaced by the *Criminal Code (Amendment) Act* 1977 (No 42 of 1977), s 1. However, that Act has never been brought into force.

This offence is also punishable summarily: see Sch 2 of the Code.

See s 422 regarding unlawful use of a motor vehicle, bicycle, boat or canoe.

"Motor vehicle" is defined by s 1.

For a proceeding under s 25 of the *Motor Traffic Act*, Ch 234 (driving a motor vehicle without the owner's consent), see *Nabo Tiambo v Gideon Lari* [1979] PNGLR 525.

For a consideration of principles relating to a default penalty of imprisonment for non-payment of a fine imposed under s 25(1) of the *Motor Traffic Act* Ch 234, see *Garry Kulau v Kevin Alile* (1990) N869.

383A. Misappropriation of property.

(1) A person who dishonestly applies to his own use or to the use of another person -

(a) property belonging to another; or

(b) property belonging to him, which is in his possession or control (either solely or conjointly with another person) subject to a trust, direction or condition or on account of any other person,

is guilty of the crime of misappropriation of property.

(2) An offender guilty of the crime of misappropriation of property is liable to imprisonment for five years except in any of the following cases when he is liable to imprisonment for ten years -

(a) where the offender is a director of a company and the property dishonestly applied is company property;

(b) where the offender is an employee and the property dishonestly applied is the property of his employer;

(c) where the property dishonestly applied was subject to a trust, direction or condition;

(d) where the property dishonestly applied is of a value of K2,000 or upwards.

(3) For the purposes of this section -

(a) property includes money and all other property real or personal, legal or equitable, including things in action and other intangible property;

(b) a person's application of property may be dishonest even although he is willing to pay for the property or he intends to restore the property afterwards or to make restitution thereof to the person to whom it belongs or to fulfil his obligations afterwards in respect of the property;

(c) a person's application of property shall be taken not to be dishonest, except where the property came into his possession or control as trustee or personal representative, if when he applies the property he does not know to whom the property belongs and believes on reasonable grounds that such person cannot be discovered by taking reasonable steps;

(d) persons to whom property belongs include the owner, any part owner, any person having a legal or equitable interest in or claim to the property and any person who, immediately before the offender's application of the property, had control of it.

[S 383A insrt Act No 10, 1981 (*Criminal Code (Misappropriation of Property) Act 1981*) s 1]

In order to convict an accused of a charge under s 383A of the Code, the state must prove beyond reasonable doubt that the accused:

(a) dishonestly;
(b) applied to his own use or use of another;
(c) property belonging to another.[101]

Whether an accused person has a particular state of mind is a question of fact which has to be decided by the jury when there is a trial on indictment and by justices when there are summary proceedings: *Lawi v The State* [1987] PNGLR 183, followed in *The State v Napilye Kuri* [1994] PNGLR 371 at 375 (Woods J).

Salika J held, in *The State v Gabriel Ramoi* [1993] PNGLR 390 at 392:

> "[The] word 'dishonestly' in s 383A of the *Criminal Code* relates only to the state of the mind of the person who does the act which amounts to misappropriation. The state of mind when a person applies property is a question of fact for the trial judge to determine on all of the facts presented before him. And when the judge considers the facts on how the property was applied, he uses the 'ordinary standards of reasonable and honest people' test to determine whether or not the property so applied was dishonestly applied. ... 'Dishonest' is defined in the *Oxford Advanced Learners Dictionary of Current English* as 'intended to cheat, deceive or mislead'".

The question of whether the accused acted dishonestly is an objective one. Injia AJ said, in *The State v Francis Natuwohala Laumadava* [1994] PNGLR 291 at 293:

> "At the same time, it is also a subjective one. The Court must look into the mind of the accused and determine whether, given his intelligence and experience, he would have appreciated, as right-minded people would have done, that what he was doing was dishonest."

Injia AJ held, in *The State v Francis Natuwohala Laumadava* [1994] PNGLR 291 at 302, that where the accused instructed a subordinate to make a payment on his behalf, it is immaterial that the accused did not pay the money in person. The point was that the money was applied to the personal use of the accused in paying his loan debt.

[101] *The State v Gabriel Ramoi* [1993] PNGLR 390 at 392 (Salika J).

In *The State v James Makario* (1990) N862, on a charge that the accused dishonestly applied to the use of another person property belonging to another, and for false pretences, it was held that as the application of property of another to the use of another person is an essential element of an offence under s 383A(1)(a), in addition to the element of dishonesty, it must be strictly proved that the property was used or applied for the use of no other person than the person specified in the indictment.

Where moneys are granted for a particular public purpose, the grantor has a legal and equitable proprietary interest in them until they are expended on the purpose for which they were granted: *Joseph Rokpa v The State* [1994] PNGLR 535 (Kapi DCJ, Woods and Los JJ) following *Lawi v The State* [1987] PNGLR 183.

In *The State v Francis Kumo Gene* [1991] PNGLR 33 the court held that the words in s 383A(3)(d) "any person having a legal or equitable interest in or claim to the property" refer to persons who have proprietary rights in property such as bailors, mortgagees, lessors, trustees etc. Further, the phrase "or claim to the property" also indicates a proprietary nature, in the context of the foregoing phrase. Brunton J (at 39) accepted that it appears that choses in action could include debts or the rights to sue on a contract. Money had been granted by the state, to persons who represented an unincorporated provincial youth council, on condition that the money be used for a particular purpose, namely, a bookkeeping project. An allegation in the indictment charging misappropriation under s 383A that the money was "the property of the State" was held to be at variance with the evidence, and the variance between the indictment and the evidence was "material to the merits of the case" within s 535.

The courts have laid down sentencing guidelines. *Wellington Belawa v The State* [1988-1989] PNGLR 496 recommended a base term of two years to be adjusted upward or downward where the amount taken is between 1,000 kina and 10,000 kina, and where the amount is between K40,000 and K150,000, a term of imprisonment between three to five years is appropriate. Bredmeyer and Barnett JJ discussed the factors to be considered:

(a) the amount taken;

(b) the degree of trust held by the offender;

(c) the period over which the offence was committed (a case of sudden impulse would carry a lesser sentence than a planned scheme over a period of time);

(d) the use to which the money was put to;

(e) the effect on the victims;

(f) the effect on the offender himself; and

(g) whether restitution was made to the victims.[102]

It has been recently suggested that while these factors are still relevant, the tariff laid out in *Wellington Belawa v The State* is now outdated. Sawong J noted, in obiter in *The State v Paroa Kaia* (1995) N1401, that circumstances have changed considerably, and the fact that misappropriation has increased consistently should be reflected by increased sentences.

---

[102] Applied in *The State v Bygonnes Tuse Nae* (1996) N1474.

Subdivision D – Stealing with Violence: Extortion by Threats

384. Definition of robbery.

A person who steals any thing, and, at, immediately before or immediately after, the time of stealing it, uses or threatens to use actual violence to any person or property in order to obtain the thing stolen or to prevent or overcome resistance to its being stolen is said to be guilty of robbery.

Robbery is punished under s 386 of the Code.

See s 365 for the definition of "steals".

See s 243 regarding assaults.

385. Loaded arms.

For the purposes of this Subdivision, any arms that are loaded in the barrel or chamber with -

(a) an explosive substance; and

(b) a solid substance capable of being projected,

shall be deemed to be loaded arms, even if an attempt to discharge the same may fail from want of proper appliances or from any other cause.

"Explosive substance" is defined by s 1 of the Code.

See the definition of "firearm" in s 28(4) of the *Summary Offences Act*.

386. The offence of robbery.

(1) A person who commits robbery is guilty of a crime.

Penalty: Subject to Subsection (2), imprisonment for a term not exceeding 14 years.

(2) If a person charged with an offence against Subsection (1) -

(a) is armed with a dangerous or offensive weapon or instrument;

(b) is in company with one or more other persons; or

(c) at, immediately before or immediately after, the time of the robbery, wounds or uses any other personal violence to any person,

he is liable subject to Section 19, to imprisonment for life.

[S 386 am Act No 29, 1983 (*Criminal Code (Amendment) Act* 1983), s 5; am Act No 17, 1986 (*Criminal Code (Amendment No 2) Act* 1986), s 20]

See s 384 of the Code for definition of robbery.

In *Gimble v The State* [1988-1989] PNGLR 271, Bredmeyer, Los, and Hinchliffe JJ discussed the following guidelines to be taken as appropriate to sentencing for aggravated robbery contrary to s 386(2) of the Code, for which the maximum prescribed penalty is life imprisonment:

1. On a plea of not guilty by young first offenders carrying weapons and threatening violence for:-

   (a) robbery of a house – a starting point of seven years;

(b) robbery of a bank – a starting point of six years;

(c) robbery of a store, hotel, club, vehicle on the road or the like – a starting point of five years; and

(d) robbery of a person on the street – a starting point of three years.

2. Features of aggravation such as actual violence, a large amount stolen, or where the robber is in a position of trust towards the victim may justify a higher sentence.

3. A plea of guilty may justify a lower sentence.

In *Public Prosecutor v Don Hale* (1998) SC 564, the Supreme Court considered that the minimum sentences in *Gimble v The State* may no longer be appropriate:

> "We first of all find that the trial judge erred in considering the appropriate tariff to start with in considering the appropriate sentence. *Gimble's case* suggests starting with 7 years but the trial judge started even lower than that. We find that with the prevalence of violent crime involving the use of guns the ranges of sentences recommended in *Gimble's* case are having no effect and are no longer relevant. *Gimble's* case was decided in 1989 and crimes of violence have definitely increased with the use of guns being more prevalent and the community is calling for heavier punishments as a deterrence. We feel that the starting point to an appropriate sentence involving the robbery of home owners at night with the use of firearms to threaten victims should be 10 years."

Public Prosecutor v Don Hale was followed in a number of cases including *The State v Steward Pariwan* (1999) N1834, *The State v Paul Wagira and Alphonse Mause* (1999) N1836, *The State v Jonathan Wellington* (1999) N1837, and *John Arua Peter v The State* (2000) SC 638.

In *Tau Jim Anis v The State* (2000) SC 642 the appellants were convicted of armed robbery and each sentenced to 10 years imprisonment. Sheehan, Jalina and Kirriwom JJ held that was excessive in all the circumstances. Their Honours held that:

> "we are of the view that a sentence of 10 years for first time young offenders like the two young appellants in this case, who, according to the guidelines in *Gimble v The State* [1988-89] PNGLR 271 would be sentenced to five years on a trial as the starting point seems to be a big jump. We make this observation notwithstanding the current upward sentencing trend for armed robbery as observed in the *Public Prosecutor v Don Hale* (1998) SC 564."

There is nothing in *Public Prosecutor v Don Hale* laying down a blanket authority superseding the more detailed and categorically evolved principles in *Gimble v The State*. The Supreme Court, in *Public Prosecutor v Don Hale*, was referring to robbery of a dwelling-house in the context of *Gimble* guidelines. Sheehan, Jalina and Kirriwom JJ said, in *Tau Jim Anis v The State* (2000) SC 642:

> "It seems that that discussion had been read out of that context and in doing so already offends against the principles established in *Gimble v The State* which in our view is still good law."

In *The State v Robert Bandi* (1989) N802 the fact that the perpetrator of a robbery was the sole breadwinner in the family, played only a minor role in the offence, and had no prior convictions, did not amount to "special circumstances" which may have given rise to a suspended sentence, as referred to in *Gimble v The State*.

For the armed robbery of mailbags containing cash being transferred by a bank, where there has been co-operation or mitigating circumstances to reduce the sentence or to give any special consideration, it is appropriate to impose the highest term of years in the range of sentences applicable, that being 12 years: *The State v Biwa Geta* [1988] PNGLR 153.

Where an offender, who committed a robbery with threats of actual violence, received a broken arm after villagers who had witnessed the robbery chased him and hit him with an axe, it was held appropriate to reduce a four year sentence to three years to account for the punishment received by the offender when the villagers took the law into their own hands and administered "jungle justice": *The State v Smith James Ondari* (1990) N 867. See *Acting Public Prosecutor v Andrew Lalaiva of Honi and Angela Ume* [1981] PNGLR 148, reported in [1981] PNGLR 148, but only as to appeal practice point.

387. Attempted robbery accompanied by wounding, or in company.

(1) A person who assaults a person with intent to steal any thing, and, at, immediately before or immediately after, the time of the assault, uses or threatens to use actual violence to any person or property in order -

(a) to obtain the thing intended to be stolen; or

(b) to prevent or overcome resistance to its being stolen,

is guilty of a crime.

Penalty: Imprisonment for a term not exceeding seven years.

(2) If the offender -

(a) is armed with a dangerous or offensive weapon or instrument; or

(b) is in company with one or more other persons,

he is liable to imprisonment for a term not exceeding 14 years.

(3) If the offender -

(a) is armed with any loaded arms; and

(b) at, immediately before or immediately after, the time of the assault wounds any person by discharging the loaded arms,

he is liable subject to Section 19, imprisonment for life.

[S 387 am Act No 29, 1983 (*Criminal Code (Amendment) Act* 1983), s 6; am Act No 17, 1986 (*Criminal Code (Amendment No 2) Act* 1986), s 21]

See s 243 of the Code regarding assault, and s 365 regarding stealing.

388. Assault with intent to steal.

A person who assaults any person with intent to steal any thing is guilty of a crime.

Penalty: Imprisonment for a term not exceeding three years.

See s 243 of the Code regarding assault, and s 365 regarding stealing.

389. Demanding property with menaces with intent to steal.

A person who, with intent to steal any thing, demands it from any person with threats of injury or detriment to be caused to him, by the offender or by any other person, if the demand is not complied with is guilty of a crime.

Penalty: Imprisonment for a term not exceeding ten years.

See s 359 of the Code regarding threats.

390. Demanding property by written or oral threats.

(1) In this section, "writing" includes any gramophone record, wire, tape, or other thing by which words or sounds are recorded and from which they are capable of being reproduced.

(2) A person who, with intent to extort or gain any thing from any person -

(a) knowing the contents of the writing, causes any person to receive a writing -

(i) demanding, without reasonable or probable cause, anything from, or that any thing be procured to be done or omitted to be done by, any person; and

(ii) containing threats of injury or detriment to be caused to any person, by the offender or any other person, if the demand is not complied with; or

(b) orally demands, without reasonable or probable cause, any thing from, or that any thing be procured to be done or omitted to be done by, any person, with threats to be caused to any person, by the offender or any other person, if the demand is not complied with,

is guilty of a crime.

Penalty: Imprisonment for a term not exceeding 14 years.

As to s 390(2)(b), see s 354(1)(a) of the Code regarding kidnapping for ransom.

390A. Demands for compensation or other payment.

A person who, with intent to extort or gain any thing, payment, or compensation from any person -

(a) demands the thing, payment or compensation; and

(b) in order to obtain compliance with the demand -

(i) causes or threatens to cause injury to any person or damage to any property; or

(ii) does or threatens to do any act which renders, or is likely to render any public road, bridge, navigable river or navigable channel, natural or artificial, impassable or less safe for travelling or conveying property; or

(iii) otherwise unlawfully threatens or intimidates any person,

is guilty of a crime.

Penalty: Imprisonment for a term not exceeding seven years.

[S 390A insrt Act No 18, 1991 (*Criminal Code (Amendment No 2) Act* 1991), s 1]

391. Attempts at extortion by threats.

(1) A person who, with intent to extort or gain any thing from any person -

(a) accuses, or threatens to accuse, any person of -

(i) committing an indictable offence; or

(ii) offering or making a solicitation or threat to a person as an inducement to commit or permit the commission of an of an indictable offence; or

(b) threatens that any person will be accused by any other person of an indictable offence or of any such act; or

(c) knowing the contents of the writing, causes any person to receive any writing, containing any such accusation or threat,

is guilty of a crime

Penalty: Subject to Subsection (2), imprisonment for a term not exceeding three years.

(2) If the accusation or threat of accusation is of -

(a) an offence for which the punishment of death or imprisonment for life may be inflicted; or

(b) an offence against any provision of Division IV.2, or an attempt to commit any such offence; or

(c) an assault with intent to have carnal knowledge of a person against the order of nature; or

(d) an unlawful and indecent assault on a male person; or

(e) an attempt to commit the crime of rape, or an assault with intent to commit the crime of rape; or

(f) an unlawful and indecent assault on a woman or girl; or

(g) a solicitation or threat offered or made to any person as an inducement to commit or permit the commission of any of the offences referred to in the preceding provisions of this subsection,

the offender is liable to imprisonment for a term not exceeding 14 years.

(3) It is immaterial whether the person accused or threatened to be accused has or has not committed the offence or act of which he is accused or threatened to be accused.

See s 359 of the Code regarding threats.

392. Procuring execution of deeds, etc, by threats.

A person who, with intent to defraud, and by means of -

(a) any unlawful violence to, or restraint of, the person of another;

(b) a threat of violence or restraint to be used to the person of another; or

(c) accusing, or threatening to accuse, a person of -

(i) committing an indictable offence; or

(ii) offering or making any solicitation or threat to any person as an inducement to commit or permit the commission of any indictable offence,

compels or induces any person -

(d) to execute, make, accept, endorse, alter or destroy the whole or any part of any valuable security; or

(e) to write, impress or affix any name or seal on or to any paper or parchment, so that it may be afterwards made or converted into, or used or dealt with as, a valuable security,

is guilty of a crime.

Penalty: Imprisonment for a term not exceeding 14 years.

"Valuable security" is defined by s 1 of the Code.

See s 359 regarding threats.

393. Taking unlawful control of aircraft.

(1) A person who, directly or indirectly, unlawfully takes or exercises control of an aircraft is guilty of a crime.

Penalty: Subject to Subsections (2) and (3), imprisonment for a term not exceeding seven years.

(2) If, at, immediately before or immediately after, the time of taking or exercising such control, the offender -

(a) uses or threatens to use actual violence to any person or property in order -

(i) to take or exercise control of the aircraft; or

(ii) to prevent or overcome resistance to such control being taken or exercised; or

(b) is armed with a dangerous or offensive weapon or instrument; or

(c) is in company with one or more other persons; or

(d) takes or exercises such control by any fraudulent representation, trick, device or other means,

he is liable, subject to Section 19, to imprisonment for life.

(3) If another person who is not an accomplice of the offender is on board the aircraft, the offender is liable to imprisonment for a term not exceeding 14 years.

"Aircraft" is defined by s 1 of the Code.

This offence is uncommon in Papua New Guinea, and when it is committed for a second time it must be met with a punitive and deterrent sentence. See *The State v Michael Kompie* (1996) N1471 and *The State v John Michael Awal* (2000) CR 905/98.

Subdivision E – Burglary: Housebreaking and Like Offences

394. Breaking: Breaking and entering.

(1) A person who -

(a) breaks any part, external or internal, of a building; or

(b) opens, by unlocking, pulling, pushing, lifting or any other means, any door, window, shutter, cellar, flap, or other thing, intended to close or cover an opening in a building, or an opening giving passage from one part of a building to another,

shall be deemed to break the building.

(2) A person is said to enter a building as soon as any part of his body or any part of any instrument used by him is within the building.

(3) A person who -

(a) obtains entrance into a building by means of -

(i) any threat or artifice used for that purpose; or

(ii) collusion with any person in the building; or

(b) enters any chimney or other aperture of the building permanently left open for any necessary purpose, but not intended to be ordinarily used as a means of entrance,

shall be deemed to have broken and entered the building.

In *R v Daugamani-Adamanika* [1965-1966] PNGLR 80 at 88 the court held that the further opening of two doors, which were left partly opened, did not constitute a housebreaking at common law and does not come within the first part of the definition of "breaking" as set out in this section of the Code. The word "opens" in the second part of the definition means "opens something which heretofore was closed", meaning "fully closed".

Whether the operation of a latch, catch or lock constitutes an actual breaking should be considered with reference to the mechanical design of these devices which constitute functionally a complete bar to entry while in the set position, but incorporate in their design mechanical means for repeated release and re-setting of the mechanism. It was decided in many early cases that the removal of such a mechanical bar constituted an actual breaking. The mechanical device need not constitute a lock; it is sufficient if it has a latch which merely has to be lifted. Generally, the lifting of a closure, such as a flap which is not fitted with a lock or latch and was merely held down by its own slight weight, did not constitute housebreaking. However, where the closure was especially heavy, requiring substantial force to move it, and was not a normal entrance, the occupier was entitled to assume that law-abiding people would not choose this as a mode of entry, and the weight of the flap was in itself a "security": *R v Daugamani-Adamanika* [1965-1966] PNGLR 80 at 86-87.

On the authorities, the word "break" is used, in the context of housebreaking, prima facie in the sense of "actual fracture by the application of force". The nature of the required breaking must be clearly borne in mind in Papua New Guinea, to avoid miscarriage of justice, in that the Tok Pisin expressions "em i brukim banis" or "em i brukim dor" etc are frequently used merely to indicate that the person burst on the scene, without necessarily implying damage or physical breaking: *R v Daugamani-Adamanika* [1965-1966] PNGLR 80 at 85.

395. Housebreaking: Burglary.

(1) A person who -

(a) breaks and enters the dwelling-house of another with intent to commit a crime in it; or

(b) having -

(i) entered the dwelling-house of another with intent to commit a crime in it; or

(ii) committed a crime in the dwelling-house of another

breaks out of the dwelling-house; or

(c) breaks and enters the dwelling-house of another and commits a crime in it,

is guilty of a crime.

Penalty: Subject to Subsection (2), imprisonment for a term not exceeding 14 years.

(2) If the offence is committed in the night, the offender is liable, subject to Section 19, to imprisonment for life.

[Penalty provision and subs (2) subst Act No 10, 1983 (*Criminal Code (Minimum Penalties) Amendment Act* 1983), s 12; am Act No 17, 1986 (*Criminal Code (Amendment No 2) Act* 1986), s 22]

This offence is also punishable summarily: see Sch 2 of the Code.

"Dwelling-house" and "night" are defined by s 1. As to what constitutes breaking and entering, see s 394.

The crime of burglary was developed in the common law as a premium offence carrying much heavier penalties than the larceny which is generally involved, because of the extremely dangerous situation created by intruders found in dwelling-houses at night time. The heavier penalty was not readily imposed in cases where the house was not securely locked, apparently in recognition of the obligation of the householder to make premises secure against intruders: *R v Daugamani-Adamanika* [1965-1966] PNGLR 80 at 85.

Under this section, the prosecution must prove beyond a reasonable doubt the intention of committing a crime – a crime demonstrably under one of the sections of the Code. In *R v Ori Ais'* (1953) N34 the accused broke and entered the dwelling through a latched door, but did not manifest his intention by an overt act. Note that this case was decided prior to the insertion into the Code of s 396, which would now be the relevant section in these circumstances.

In order to prove that the accused broke and entered with intent to commit rape, the state must prove either that the accused was aware that the woman would not consent to his advances, or else that he realised that she might not be consenting and determined to have sexual intercourse with her whether she was consenting or not: *R v Merembu Bongab* [1971-1972] PNGLR 433 at 440.

In *R v Gahoso Simbane* [1975] PNGLR 257 the accused admitted breaking and entering into the victim's dwelling-house and carrying away a suitcase full of goods. The accused asserted, however, that he did not break and enter with intent to steal, but was merely venting his spite against the victim, whose brother (also the accused's brother-in-law) had sent the accused's wife from the village to marry another man. The court acquitted, finding reasonable doubt that the accused had the requisite intent at the time of the break and entry.

A servant who is a member of the complainant's household may nevertheless be a trespasser in or on the "dwelling-house of another" where the servant goes to a part of that house for an entirely unlawful purpose. The principle in *Harrison v Duke of Rutland* [1893] 1 QB 142 applies: *R v Kaim Kaim* (1957) N108.

Where the only evidence was a fingerprint on a louvre blade, which established that the accused had attempted to break and enter, there could be no evidence of intention within the meaning of s 395(1)(a): *R v Iata Kara* (1974) N777.

Lord Goddard stated, in *R v James Loughlin* (1951) 35 Cr App R 69, that too often where a man is charged with housebreaking and the evidence shows recent possession of stolen property:

> "the Court directs the jury that there is no evidence that he broke and entered and tells the jury to concentrate on the receiving. That is not the law. If it is proved that premises have been broken into, and that certain property has been stolen from those premises, and that very shortly afterwards a man is found in possession of that property, that is certainly evidence from which the jury can infer that he is the housebreaker or shopbreaker and; if he is, it is inconsistent to find him guilty of receiving, because a man cannot receive from himself".

This statement of the significance of the doctrine of recent possession is entirely applicable and appropriate to the circumstances of Papua New Guinea; see s 398 regarding shop-breaking, and s 410 regarding possession of stolen property: *The State v Alpen Popo* [1977] PNGLR 18.

The offence created under s 395 is that provided for by s 396, with the addition of the circumstances of aggravation of "intent to commit a crime", and thus s 538 is applicable, regarding alternative verdicts: *R v Mai* [1975] PNGLR 230.

At common law, housebreaking and burglary were regarded as aggravated forms of entering a dwelling-house with intent to commit a crime (s 397), and both may be regarded as highly aggravated forms of stealing. When looking at the form in which the two neighbouring offences are now expressed in ss 389 and 397 of the Code, it is clear that the legislature intended that these two offences should be regarded as similar in character and differing only in degree depending upon whether or not the aggravated ingredient of housebreaking was present. Thus, s 538 would permit an accused indicted under this section to be convicted under s 397: *R v Daugamani-Adamanika* [1965-1966] PNGLR 80 at 89-90.

Circumstances of aggravation do not appear in a charge under s 395(1)(a). However, if "in the night" is inserted in the body of the charge, these are circumstances of aggravation, and if this is not proved, s 538 comes into play and the accused may be convicted of housebreaking with intent "simpliciter": *R v Gahoso Simbane* [1975] PNGLR 257.

In *The State v Joseph Evara* (1979) N201, Prentice CJ seemed to accept the defence submission that offences under this section are crimes of specific intent, and thus intoxication may be available as a defence. However, the evidence in this case did not sustain the defence. Breaking, entering and stealing is one indivisible offence. If one of the ingredients is missing, the offence is not proven: *The State v Joe Ivoro and Gemora Yavura* [1980] PNGLR 1.

Where a District Court deals summarily with an indictable offence listed in Sch 2 to the Code which is also a minimum penalty offence, and where the defendant is aged between 16 and 21 years, the court is required to impose the minimum penalty subject to s 138 of the *District Court Act*: *John Worofang v Patrick Wallace* [1984] PNGLR 144.

In *Tai Kenang v Simon Kasper* [1984] PNGLR 102 it was held that on a charge of breaking, entering and stealing under s 395 of the Code, an accused may be convicted under s 538 of the Code of the lesser alternative charge of stealing simpliciter, because breaking, entering and stealing and is an aggravated form of stealing. Bredmeyer J expressed approval for *R v Short* [1928] St R Qd 246:

> "In *Short's* case the court was concerned about fairness to the accused; if the alternative lesser charge of stealing had been explained to the jury, the accused may have been convicted of that lesser offence. In other cases, as in the instant one, where the elements of breaking and entering were not proved, it produces a fairness to the State."

This offence is also punishable summarily: see Sch 2 of the Code.

As to breaking and entering, see s 394.

"Dwelling-house" is defined by s 1.

While persons without a real criminal intent should not be categorised as "rogues and vagabonds" from mere attendance on property without legal right, nevertheless in *R v Kepo* [1975] PNGLR 226, where there was an ingredient of interference with the integrity of another's property, then no lawful purpose had been demonstrated.

In *R v Mai* [1975] PNGLR 230, despite the fact that the accused had acted under an honest claim of right and without an intent to defraud, he was nevertheless without a lawful excuse where he was acting under a sense of grievance in an attempt at self-help.

In *R v Gahoso Simbane* [1975] PNGLR 257 the accused broke down the door and entered into the dwelling of another as an act of vengeance, because he was angry with the owner's brother. In convicting the accused, the court noted that the door was forced, in the absence of the owner, without the owner's permission and with no possible excuse for what was done. The accused was therefore guilty under this section even though he had no intent to commit a specific crime.

A conviction under this section is possible where the accused was charged under s 395, by operation of s 538: *R v Iata Kara* (1974) N777.

A conviction under this section is possible, rather than that available under s 395(c), on the basis that stealing can be regarded as a "circumstance of aggravation" to breaking and entering under s 538: *The State v Joseph Evara* (1979) N201.

397. Entering dwelling-house with intent to commit crime.

(1) A person who enters or is in the dwelling-house of another with intent to commit a crime in it is guilty of a crime.

Penalty – Subject to Subsection (2) imprisonment for a term not exceeding seven years.

(2) If the offence is committed in the night, the offender shall be imprisoned for a term not exceeding 14 years.

[Penalty provision and subs (2) subst Act No 10, 1983 (*Criminal Code (Minimum Penalties) Amendment Act* 1983), s 14; am Act No 17, 1986 (*Criminal Code (Amendment No 2) Act* 1986), s 24]

This offence is also punishable summarily: see Sch 2 of the Code.

See s 394 regarding "enters". See the definition of "dwelling-house" in s 1.

A person may be convicted of a crime under this section upon a charge under s 395, by operation of s 538, where the elements are proved. Legislative intent is clear that these two offences should be regarded as similar in character and differing only in degree, depending upon whether or not the aggravated ingredient of housebreaking is present: *R v Daugamani-Adamanika* [1965-1966] PNGLR 80 at 89-90.

398. Breaking into buildings and committing crime.

A person who -

(a) breaks and enters -

(i) a schoolhouse, shop, warehouse, counting-house, office, store, vehicle, garage, hangar, pavilion, factory, workshop, tent, caravan, petrol-station, ship, aircraft, vessel or club; or

(ii) a building that is adjacent to a dwelling-house and occupied with it, but is not part of it,

and commits a crime in it; or

(b) having committed a crime in -

(i) a schoolhouse, shop, warehouse, counting-house, office, store, vehicle, garage, hangar, pavilion, factory, workshop, tent, caravan, petrol-station, ship, aircraft, vessel or club; or

(ii) a building that is adjacent to a dwelling-house and occupied with it, but is not part of it,

breaks out of it,

is guilty of a crime.

Penalty: Imprisonment for a term not exceeding 14 years.

[Penalty provision subst Act No 10, 1983 (*Criminal Code (Minimum Penalties) Amendment Act* 1983), s 15; am Act No 17, 1986 (*Criminal Code (Amendment No 2) Act* 1986), s 25]

This offence is also punishable summarily: see Sch 2 of the Code.

As to breaking and entering, see s 394.

"Ship", "aircraft", "vessel" and "dwelling-house" are defined by s 1.

See also *Paulus Mandatitip v The State* [1978] PNGLR 126.

For considerations on sentence in breaking, entering and stealing (from business premises) involving a youthful offender, see *Bakiri Pena v The State* (1980) SC 183.

There is no definition of "shop" in the Code. The ordinary meaning of the word "shop" is a building which is in fact used as a shop, and the particular mode of use may determine whether a temporary absence or cessation of business amounts to a cessation of the character of a shop. The definition of dwelling-house in the Code is analogous, and a temporary non-use of the building for the purpose of a shop is immaterial: *R v Kingston-Kapoli* (1960) N175.

Upon an indictment under this section, it is open to the court to convict under s 399: *R v Kingston-Kapoli* (1960) N175. However, compare *R v McCoy and McCaskel* (1938) St R Qd 249, *R v Johnson* [1973] Qd R 303, *Trainer v The King* (1906) 4 CLR 126 and *R v Kelly* [1963] 3 All ER 588.

399. Breaking into building with intent to commit crime.

A person who breaks and enters –

(a) a schoolhouse, shop, warehouse, counting-house, office, store, vehicle, garage, hangar, pavilion, factory, workshop, tent, caravan, petrol-station, ship, aircraft, vessel or club; or

(b) a building that is adjacent to a dwelling-house and occupied with it, but is not part of it,

with intent to commit a crime in it, is guilty of a crime.

Penalty: Imprisonment for a term not exceeding seven years.

[Penalty provision subst Act No 10, 1983 (*Criminal Code (Minimum Penalties) Amendment Act* 1983), s 16; am Act No 17, 1986 (*Criminal Code (Amendment No 2) Act* 1986), s 26]

This offence is also punishable summarily: see Sch 2 of the Code.

As to breaking and entering, see s 394.

"Ship", "aircraft", "vessel" and "dwelling-house" are defined by s 1.

See discussion of *R v Kingston-Kapoli* (1960) N175, under s 398 above.

400. Breaking into place of worship and committing crime.

A person who -

(a) breaks and enters a building ordinarily used for religious worship and commits a crime in it; or

(b) having committed a crime in any such building breaks out of it,

is guilty of a crime.

Penalty: Imprisonment for a term not exceeding 14 years.

[Penalty provision subst Act No 10, 1983 (*Criminal Code (Minimum Penalties) Amendment Act* 1983), s 17; am Act No 17, 1986 (*Criminal Code (Amendment No 2) Act* 1986), s 27]

This offence is also punishable summarily: see Sch 2 of the Code.

As to breaking and entering, see s 394.

401. Breaking into place of worship with intent to commit a crime.

A person who breaks and enters a building ordinarily used for religious worship, with intent to commit a crime in it, is guilty of a crime.

Penalty: Imprisonment for a term not exceeding seven years.

[Penalty provision subst Act No 10, 1983 (*Criminal Code (Minimum Penalties) Amendment Act* 1983), s 18; am Act No 17, 1986 (*Criminal Code (Amendment No 2) Act* 1986), s 28]

This offence is also punishable summarily: see Sch 2 of the Code.

As to breaking and entering, see s 394.

402. Persons found armed, etc, with intent to commit crime.

(1) A person who is found -

(a) being armed with a dangerous or offensive weapon or instrument, with intent to break or enter a dwelling-house, and to commit a crime in it; or

(b) being armed by night with a dangerous or offensive weapon or instrument, with intent to break or enter any building, and to commit a crime in it; or

(c) having in his possession by night without lawful excuse (proof of which is on him) an instrument of house-breaking; or

(d) having in his possession by day an instrument of house-breaking with intent to commit a crime; or

(e) having his face masked or blackened or being otherwise disguised, with intent to commit a crime; or

(f) being in a building by night with intent to commit a crime in it,

is guilty of a crime.

Penalty: Subject to Subsection (2), imprisonment for a term not exceeding three years.

(2) If the offender has been previously convicted of a crime relating to property, he shall be imprisoned for a term not exceeding seven years.

[Penalty provision and subs (2) subst Act No 10, 1983 (*Criminal Code (Minimum Penalties) Amendment Act* 1983), s 19; am Act No 17, 1986 (*Criminal Code (Amendment No 2) Act* 1986), s 29]

As to breaking and entering, see s 406 of the Code. "Dwelling-house", "have in possession", and "night" are defined by s 1.

As to s 402(1)(a) and (b), see s 12 of the *Summary Offences Act* regarding the summary offence of carrying offensive weapons.

As to s 402(1)(c), see s 18 of the *Summary Offences Act* regarding possession of housebreaking implements.

As to s 402(1)(e), see s 17 of the *Summary Offences Act* regarding the summary offence of wearing, or possessing on the person, a disguise with intent to commit an offence. See also Thompson, *Whigs and Hunters: The Origins of the Black Act* (1975).

As to s 402(1)(f), see ss 19-20 of the *Summary Offences Act*.

In *The State v Minambkali Asu, Lakap Erape and John Koipiu* (1980) N236, the court considered that a prior offence relating to property (in this case, pig theft) committed when the prisoner was a child need not be given weight as aggravating circumstances, so that the prisoner need not be sentenced under s 402(2).

Subdivision F – Obtaining Property by False Pretences: Cheating

403. False pretence: Wilfully false promise.

(1) A representation made by words or otherwise of a matter of fact, past or present that -

(a) is false in fact; and

(b) the person making it knows to be false or does not believe to be true,

is a false pretence.

(2) A promise made by words or otherwise to do or omit to do any thing by a person who at the time of making the promise -

(a) does not intend to perform it; or

(b) does not believe he will be able to perform it,

is a wilfully false promise.

404. Obtaining goods or credit by false pretence or wilfully false promise.

(1) A person who by a false pretence or wilfully false promise, or partly by a false pretence and partly by a wilfully false promise, and with intent to defraud -

(a) obtains from any other person any chattel, money or valuable security; or

(b) induces any other person to deliver to any person any chattel, money or valuable security,

is guilty of a crime.

Penalty: Imprisonment for a term not exceeding five years.

(2) It is immaterial that the thing is obtained or its delivery is induced through the medium of a contract induced by the false pretence or the wilfully false promise, or partly by the false pretence and partly by the wilfully false promise, as the case may be.

(3) A person incurring a debt or liability who obtains credit by a false pretence or wilfully false promise, or partly by a false pretence and partly by a wilfully false promise, or by any other fraud, is guilty of a misdemeanour.

Penalty: Imprisonment for a term not exceeding one year.

(4) ...

[Subs (4) rep Act No 12, 1993 (*Criminal Code (Amendment) Act* 1993), s 5]

This offence is also punishable summarily: see Sch 2 of the Code.

"False pretence" and "wilfully false promise" are defined in s 403. See ss 488-491 below, regarding personation.

As to indictments, see s 530(17) and (18).

As to alternative verdicts, see s 544.

See s 14 of the *Summary Offences Act* regarding the passing of valueless cheques.

See s 15 of the *Summary Offences Act* for the analogous offence triable summarily.

The intention to defraud is a separate element of the charge and, while the intent may be inferred from the fact of the accused's false pretences, the intention to defraud is not necessarily established by proof of these elements alone: *Prosecutor's Request No 4 of 1974* [1975] PNGLR 365.

See the discussion of *John Kasaipwalova v The State* [1977] PNGLR 257 (at s 367 above) regarding conversion of funds held under a direction. Frost CJ held that where the amount is large and contemplated expenditure is to take place over a period of time, the inference is that the person receiving the money acquires the property in the money subject, at most, to a liability to account for a corresponding sum. If the money is then converted, the person could not be guilty of fraudulent conversion or simple theft, as the property is that person's. However, criminal responsibility would have to be proved under s 404 for the offence of obtaining goods by false pretence or wilfully false promise with intent to defraud.

The false representation must be to material existing facts and not a promise to do something in the future or a representation by the representor as to the existence of an intention to do something in the future: *Albert Alexander Age v The State* [1979] PNGLR 589.

One must assume as a matter of common-sense that, in requiring information as to the purpose of the loan, the assets and creditworthiness of the apparent borrower, the bank is not requiring valueless information, but material which it will use in deciding whether a loan will be granted. Misrepresentations which deceive the bank into granting the loan, which, if the truth had been known, would never have been granted at all, come within this section: *Albert Alexander Age v The State* [1979] PNGLR 589 at 592.

As to why a bogus bank loan application, in this case, amounted to a misrepresentation of material existing facts rather than a representation to do something in the future, see *Albert Alexander Age v The State* [1979] PNGLR 589 at 590-591.

It is enough for the accused to have been dishonestly seeking an advantage for himself. It is not essential to establish that economic loss to the representee would necessarily have resulted: *Albert Alexander Age v The State* [1979] PNGLR 589 at 592. See also *Prosecutor's Request No 4 of 1974* [1975] PNGLR 365 and *Balcombe v De Simoni* (1972) 126 CLR 576 at 583-584.

Bredmeyer J said, in *Wellington Belawa v The State* [1988-1989] PNGLR 496 at 500-501:

> "There are numerous factors which should be taken into account on sentence [for an offence involving dishonesty where the offender is in a position of trust] ... and I have been assisted by the guidelines given by the English Court of Criminal Appeal in *Barrick's* case (1985) 82 Cr App R 78 at 82. With some adaptation from that list I set out the major factors as follows:
>
> - The amount taken.

- The degree of trust placed in the offender including his rank. The higher the position of trust the greater the culpability. Thus if the offender holds a very senior position on the public service or in a company, the greater the punishment that will be imposed. The principle here is that 'from whom much is given, much is expected'. The person who enjoys a high position of trust and respect and enjoys high salary and other perquisites should be expected to carry out his duties honestly and to set an example to others.
- The period over which the fraud or theft was perpetrated. Did the offender take the money on one day or was his guilty intention put into effect over a longer period of time?
- The impact of the offence on the public and public confidence.
- The use to which the money was put. Was the money put to some worthwhile purpose or was it wasted on luxuries or idle living?
- The effect upon the victim. Was theft covered by insurance, for example, or was the money stolen from a widow and children waiting for their late husband's pension? Was theft from family members etc?
- Restitution of the money whenever paid is always a mitigating factor because it restores the victim to the position he was in before the commission of the offence.
- Remorse. This is related to (7) and (9). If restitution is made, it may or may not show remorse. The sooner the restitution is made after the commission of the offence, or after the detection of the offence, the more clearly it shows remorse. If it is made on the eve of the trial immediately after conviction, it does not show remorse.
- A plea of guilty or not guilty. A discount is usually given for a plea of guilty. In some cases a plea shows remorse especially where the State evidence may have some weakness; in other cases it may not show remorse but purely submission to the overwhelming weight of the State case.
- Any prior record. I consider the absence of any record of little relevance in this kind of serious theft. Normally the offender has no prior convictions; if he did have prior convictions, he would be unlikely to be holding the position from which he committed theft.
- The effect on the offender. The principal factors to consider here are: did he lose his job and is he likely to obtain another job?
- Matters of mitigation special to the accused such as illness, being placed under a great strain by excessive responsibility, or perhaps a long delay in being confronted with his dishonesty and the start of his trial."

Bredmeyer J also said, in *Wellington Belawa v The State* [1988-1989] PNGLR 496:

"The following scale of sentences may usefully be accepted as a base to be then adjusted upwards or downwards according to the various factors above:

- where the amount misappropriated is between K1 and K1,000, a gaol term should rarely be imposed;
- where the amount misappropriated is between K1,000 and K10,000, a gaol term of up to two years is appropriate;
- where the amount misappropriated is between K10,000 and K40,000, two to three years imprisonment is appropriate;

- where the amount misappropriated is between K40,000 and K150,000, three to five years imprisonment is appropriate."

On the distinction between larceny by trick and obtaining property by false pretences, see the note on *Tom Amaiu v The State* [1979] PNGLR 576 at 580, under s 365 above.

405. Obtaining execution of valuable security by false pretence or wilfully false promise.

(1) A person who, by false pretence or wilfully false promise, or partly by a false pretence and partly by a wilfully false promise, and with intent to defraud, induces any person -

(a) to execute, make, accept, endorse, alter or destroy the whole or part of a valuable security; or

(b) to write, impress or affix a name or seal on or to a paper or parchment in order that it may be afterwards made or converted into or used or dealt with as a valuable security,

is guilty of a crime.

Penalty: Imprisonment for a term not exceeding three years.

(2) ...

[Subs (2) rep Act No 12, 1993 (*Criminal Code (Amendment) Act* 1993), s 6]

"False pretence" and "wilfully false promise" are defined in s 403.

406. Cheating.

(1) A person who, by means of any fraudulent trick or device -

(a) obtains from any other person any thing capable of being stolen; or

(b) induces any other person -

(i) to deliver to any person any thing capable of being stolen; or

(ii) to pay or deliver to any person any money or goods, or any greater sum of money or greater quantity of goods than he would have paid or delivered but for the trick or device,

is guilty of a misdemeanour.

Penalty: Imprisonment for a term not exceeding two years.

(2) ...

[Subs (2) rep Act No 13, 1977 (*Criminal Code (Arrest) Act* 1977), s 27]

This offence is also punishable summarily: see Sch 2 of the Code.

As to things capable of being stolen, see s 364 above.

As to indictments, see s 530(17) and (18) below.

As to alternative verdicts, see s 542 below.

Offences of dishonesty relating to false accounting and to making of false entries, under ss 418 and 406 respectively, call for strong deterrence, not only to the people involved but to members of the public generally. These types of offences are becoming more prevalent throughout the country and the tariff must inevitably rise: *Phipps v The Queen* (1975) FC 76.

On the distinction between larceny by trick and obtaining property by false pretences, see the hnote on *Tom Amaiu v The State* [1979] PNGLR 576 at 580, under s 365 above.

407. Conspiracy to defraud.

(1) A person who conspires with another person -

(a) by deceit or any fraudulent means to affect the market price of any thing publicly sold; or

(b) to defraud the public, or any person (whether or not a particular person); or

(c) to extort property from any person,

is guilty of a crime.

Penalty: Imprisonment for a term not exceeding seven years.

(2) A person shall not be arrested without warrant for an offence against Subsection (1).

As to conspiracies generally, see ss 515-517 below.

"Property" is defined by s 1.

See *The State v Tanedo* [1975] PNGLR 395.

408. Frauds on sale or mortgage of property.

A seller or mortgagor of any property, or the lawyer or agent of a seller or mortgagor of any property who, with intent to induce the purchaser or mortgagee to accept the title offered or produced to him, and with intent to defraud -

(a) conceals from the purchaser or mortgagee an instrument material to the title, or an incumbrance; or

(b) falsifies a pedigree on which the title depends or may depend,

is guilty of a misdemeanour.

Penalty: Imprisonment for a term not exceeding two years.

"Property" is defined by s 1 of the Code.

See s 381 regarding fraudulent disposition of mortgaged goods.

409. Pretending to exercise witchcraft or tell fortunes.

A person who -

(a) pretends to exercise or use any kind of witchcraft, sorcery, enchantment or conjuration; or

(b) undertakes to tell fortunes; or

(c) pretends from his skill or knowledge in any occult science to discover where or in what manner any thing supposed to have been stolen or lost may be found,

is guilty of a misdemeanour.

Penalty: Imprisonment for a term not exceeding one year.

This offence is also punishable summarily: see Sch 2 of the Code.

See the *Sorcery Act* 1971.

Subdivision G – Receiving Property Stolen or Fraudulently Obtained and Like Offences

410. Receiving stolen property, etc.

(1) A person who receives any thing that has been obtained by means of -

(a) any act constituting an indictable offence; or

(b) any act done at a place outside Papua New Guinea that -

(i) if it had been done in Papua New Guinea would have constituted an indictable offence; and

(ii) is an offence under the laws in force in the place where it was done,

knowing it to have been so obtained, is guilty of a crime.

Penalty: Subject to Subsection (2), imprisonment for a term not exceeding seven years.

(2) If the offence by means of which the thing was obtained is a crime, the offender shall be imprisoned for a term not exceeding 14 years.

(3) Where a thing referred to in Subsection (1) has been -

(a) converted into other property; or

(b) mortgaged, pledged or exchanged for any other property,

a person knowing that -

(c) the property is wholly or in part the property into which the thing so obtained has been converted or for which it has been mortgaged or pledged or exchanged; and

(d) the thing so obtained was obtained under such circumstances as to constitute an offence against Subsection (1),

receives the whole or any part of the property into which the thing so obtained has been converted, or for which it has been mortgaged or pledged or exchanged, is guilty of an offence against Subsection (1).

(4) For the purpose of proving the receiving of any thing for the purpose of this section, it is sufficient to show that the accused person -

(a) has, alone or jointly with some other person, had the thing in his possession; or

(b) has aided in concealing it or disposing of it.

[Penalty provision and subs (2) subst Act No 10, 1983 (*Criminal Code (Minimum Penalties) Amendment Act* 1983), s 20; am Act No 17, 1986 (*Criminal Code (Amendment No 2) Act* 1986), s 30]

This offence is also punishable summarily: see Sch 2 of the Code.

"Property" is defined by s 1.

See s 532(5)-(7) regarding joining the thief and receiver on the same indictment.

The elements of the offence of receiving are that the thing must have been stolen, the defendant must have received it, and he or she must have known that it was stolen. The first element of theft may be proved solely from the defendant's admissions if the circumstances of the receiving justify an inference that the property was stolen: *Zimbin David v Yapu David* [1988] PNGLR 178. A receiver may or may not be an accessory after the fact. In Papua New Guinea the receiver is an accomplice. The rule in the common law case of *R v Ready and Manning* [1942] VLR 85, is not followed. The test is whether the accused can be put on the same indictment as the principal offender: *The State v Amoko-Amoko* [1981] PNGLR 373.

Where all elements of this offence may not be provable, for example where there is no evidence as to ownership of the goods in question, resort may be had to s 16 of the *Summary Offences Act* which relates to property reasonably suspected of having been stolen.

The crime of receiving has always been regarded as a very serious offence. The legislature has marked out the crime of receiving because the receiver is the carefully concealed instrument which makes theft on a wholesale scale possible: *R v Barry Ilett* (1974) FC69.

Generally the guilty knowledge must be at the time of receiving the goods and not acquired afterwards, for innocent receipt followed by fraudulent appropriation is not receiving. However, if the acts of the accused already in possession of the goods constitute a fresh receiving or the completion of an incomplete receiving, then receiving is made out: *R v Angie- Ogun* [1969-1970] PNGLR 36 at 42.

In *R v Angie-Ogun* [1969-1970] PNGLR 36 at 39, the surreptitious conduct of the thief and the very nature of the articles, which would not have honestly come into the thief's possession under normal circumstances, did or should have put the receiver on notice that the goods were stolen.

In that same case (at 42) it was held that a person who is informed that goods have been hidden or otherwise left in his or her room or house may thereafter receive them in a number of ways without actually handling them. For example, if the person decided to leave the goods where they have been put until police interest has waned, with the intention of subsequently disposing of them, the act of receiving would occur when the decision to retain was made.

It is immaterial whether the accused received the goods for profit, to assist the thief, or merely for the purpose of concealment: *R v Angie-Ogun* [1969-1970] PNGLR 36 at 41.

Conviction of the thief is not evidence, on the trial of the receiver, that the goods were stolen. However, the circumstances in which the accused received the goods may of themselves establish that the goods were obtained by means of an act constituting an indictable offence: *R v Angie-Ogun* [1969-1970] PNGLR 36 at 39.

Possession of recently stolen property is really no more than one of the many items of evidence which may be adduced by the prosecution. In the application of the rule, the onus of satisfying the tribunal of fact of the accused's guilt always rests with the prosecution; it never changes: *The State v Alpen Popo* [1977] PNGLR 18.

It was stated in *R v Garth* [1949] 1 All ER 773 at 774:

"Possession of property recently stolen where no explanation is given is evidence which can go to the jury that the prisoner received the property knowing it to have been stolen, but ... the onus is always on the prosecution; if the prisoner gives an explanation which raises a doubt in the minds of the jury whether or not he knew the property was stolen ... he is entitled to be acquitted."

This statement is adopted as applicable to Papua New Guinea: *The State v Alpen Popo* [1977] PNGLR 18.

In the case of *Zimbin David v Yapu David* [1988] PNGLR 178 at 179, it was stated:

"The only issue in this case is: did the prosecution prove that the money was stolen? In some cases the prosecution can prove theft of goods found on the defendant by direct evidence ... In most cases no direct evidence of theft is available but the circumstances in which the property is received may be in themselves sufficient proof that the goods were stolen. The defendant's admission of the circumstances in which he got the goods may allow an inference to be drawn that they were stolen."

Everleigh LJ said, in *R v Korniak* (1982) 76 Cr App R 145 at 150:

"Statements made by a defendant charged with handling stolen goods must be carefully analysed. The statement may be relevant to establish that he knew or believed that the goods were stolen or to establish that the goods **were in fact** stolen. Statements of fact must be distinguished from statements of belief. The latter do not prove that the goods were in fact stolen. On the other hand statements of fact which are within the defendant's knowledge are clearly admissible to prove that the goods were stolen."

This was followed in *Zimbin David v Yapu David* [1988] PNGLR 178 at 180. In that case, where the accused was drinking in an hotel with K who was unemployed, when K placed K100 cash in his shirt pocket and in reply to the question "Whose money was it?" said "It is your money, take it and keep your mouth shut", the inference was clearly open that the money was stolen. It was stated (at 181):

"Where [the money] was stolen from ... is not an essential element of the offence based on the cases. In many cases the Crown gets a conviction without being able to prove from whom the goods were stolen."

In *Zimbin David v Yapu David* [1988] PNGLR 178 it was further said (at 182):

"[R]eceiving is regarded by the law as very serious, eg, 14 years maximum imprisonment against three years imprisonment for simple stealing and this is so for two reasons. The first, is that the receiver is very often 'the fence', the one who sells the stolen property, and without him, in some types of theft there would be no thieves, eg, the receiver of stolen car parts. Secondly, ... the receiver runs less risk of being caught. The first reason has no application to theft of money. A man who steals money does not need a receiver to help him dispose of it, and hence a receiver of money does not encourage theft of money."

See also discussion of *The State v Alpen Popo* [1977] PNGLR 18, under s 395 above.

411. Receiving after change of ownership.

Where a thing has been obtained by means of -

(a) any act constituting an indictable offence; or

(b) an act done at a place outside Papua New Guinea that -

(i) if it had been done in Papua New Guinea would have constituted an indictable offence; and

(ii) is an offence under the laws in force in the place where it was done,

and -

(c) another person has acquired a lawful title to the thing; or

(d) if the thing has been converted into other property, mortgaged, pledged or exchanged for other property in the circumstances referred to in Section 410(3) another person has acquired a lawful title to the other property or to the proceeds or part proceeds of the conversion, mortgage, pledge or exchange,

a subsequent receiving of the thing, or of that other property or proceeds or part-proceeds, as the case may be, is not an offence even if the receiver knows that the thing has previously been so obtained.

"Property" is defined by s 1 of the Code.

412. Taking reward for recovery of property obtained by means of indictable offences.

A person who corruptly -

(a) receives or obtains; or

(b) agrees to receive or obtain,

any property or benefit on an agreement or understanding that he will help any person to recover any thing that has been obtained by means of -

(c) any act constituting an indictable offence; or

(d) any act done at a place outside Papua New Guinea that -

(i) if it had been done in Papua New Guinea would have constituted an indictable offence; and

(ii) is an offence under the laws in force in the place where it was done,

is, unless he has used all due diligence to cause the offender to be brought to trial for the offence, guilty of a crime.

Penalty: Imprisonment for a term not exceeding seven years.

[Penalty provision subst Act No 10, 1983 (*Criminal Code (Minimum Penalties) Amendment Act* 1983), s 21; am Act No 17, 1986 (*Criminal Code (Amendment No 2) Act* 1986), s 31]

Subdivision H – Frauds by Trustees and Officers of Corporations: False Accounting

413. Trustees fraudulently disposing of trust property.

(1) In this section the term “trustee” means -

(a) a trustee on an express trust created by a deed, will or instrument, whether for a public or private or charitable purpose; or

(b) a trustee appointed by or under the authority of a law of Papua New Guinea for any such purpose; or

(c) a person on whom the duties of a trust referred to in Paragraph (a) or (b) devolve; or

(d) an executor or administrator; or

(e) a liquidator, trustee or other like officer, acting under any law relating to joint-stock companies or to insolvent debtors.

(2) Subject to Section 416, a trustee of any property who, with intent to defraud -

(a) destroys the property; or

(b) converts the property,

is guilty of a crime.

Penalty: Imprisonment for a term not exceeding seven years.

(3) A person cannot be arrested without warrant for an offence against Subsection (2).

(4) If civil proceedings have been taken against a trustee in respect of an act done by him that is an offence against Subsection (2), he shall not be afterwards prosecuted for the same cause, as for an offence, on the complaint of the person by whom the civil proceedings were taken, without the sanction of the court or Judge before whom the civil proceedings were had or are pending.

“Property” is defined by s 1 of the Code.

414. Directors and officers of corporations fraudulently appropriating property, keeping fraudulent accounts or falsifying books or accounts.

(1) Subject to Section 416, a person who -

(a) being a director or officer of a corporation –

(i) receives or possesses himself as such of any of the property of the corporation otherwise than in payment of a just debt or demand; and

(ii) with intent to defraud, omits to -

(A) make a full and true entry of the property in the books and accounts of the corporation; or

(B) cause or direct such an entry to be made; or

(b) being a director, officer or member of a corporation, with intent to defraud –

(i) destroys, alters, mutilates or falsifies –

(A) any book, document, valuable security or account that belongs to the corporation; or

(B) any entry in any such book, document, or account,

or is privy to any such act; or

(ii) makes, or is privy to making, any false entry in any such book, document, or account; or

(iii) omits, or is privy to omitting, any material particular from any such book, document, or account,

is guilty of a crime.

Penalty: Imprisonment for a term not exceeding seven years.

(2) ...

[Subs (2) rep Act No 12, 1993 (*Criminal Code (Amendment) Act* 1993), s 8]

"Company" is defined in s 1 of the Code. See also *Companies Act*, Ch 146.

415. False statements by officials of companies.

(1) Subject to Section 416, a promoter, director, officer or auditor of a corporation, existing or intended to be formed, who makes, circulates or publishes, or concurs in making, circulating or publishing, any written statement or account that is, to his knowledge, false in a material particular, with intent by doing so -

(a) to deceive or defraud any member, shareholder or creditor of the corporation, whether or not a particular person; or

(b) to induce any person, whether or not a particular person -

(i) to become a member of, or to entrust or advance any property to, the corporation; or

(ii) to enter into any security for the benefit of the corporation,

is guilty of a crime.

Penalty: Imprisonment for a term not exceeding seven years.

(2) ...

[Subs (2) rep Act No 12, 1993 (*Criminal Code (Amendment) Act* 1993), s 9]

"Company" is defined in s 1 of the Code. See also *Companies Act*, Ch 146.

416. Prior disclosure.

(1) It is a defence to a charge of an offence against any of the preceding provisions of this Subdivision to prove that the accused person, before being charged with the offence and -

(a) in consequence of the compulsory process of a court in an action or proceeding instituted in good faith by a party aggrieved; or

(b) in a compulsory examination or deposition before a court,

disclosed on oath the act alleged to constitute the offence.

(2) A person is not entitled to refuse to answer any question or interrogatory in any civil proceedings in any court on the ground that his doing so might tend to show that he had committed an offence against any of the preceding provisions of this Subdivision.

As to s 416(2), compare s 37(10) of the *Constitution*, which guarantees the right to silence.

417. Misappropriation by members of local authorities.

(1) In this section "Local Authority" includes any corporation or board constituted or appointed under the authority of a law, and charged with the administration of moneys for any purposes of local concern.

(2) A person who, being a member of a Local Authority -

(a) advisedly applies any money forming part of any fund under the control of the Local Authority to any purpose to which, to his knowledge, it cannot lawfully be applied; or

(b) advisedly concurs in any such application of any such money,

is guilty of a misdemeanour.

Penalty: Imprisonment for a term not exceeding two years.

(3) A prosecution for an offence against Subsection (2) cannot be begun except by the direction of the Public Prosecutor.

418. Fraudulent false accounting.

A person who, being a clerk or servant, or being employed or acting in the capacity of a clerk or servant-

(a) destroys, alters, mutilates or falsifies -

(i) any book, document, valuable security or account that belongs to or is in the possession of his employer, or has been received by him on account of his employer; or

(ii) any entry in any such book, document or account,

or is privy to any such act; or

(b) makes or is privy to making any false entry in any such book, document or account; or

(c) omits or is privy to omitting any material particular from any such book, document or account,

with intent to defraud, is guilty of a crime.

Penalty: Imprisonment for a term not exceeding seven years.

"Clerk", "servant", and "valuable security" are defined by s 1 of the Code.

See also s 91 of the Code regarding false claims by government officials.

See s 496 regarding falsification of books by insolvents, and s 506 regarding falsification of books of companies.

See the remarks of the Full Court on deterrence of offences under this section in *Phipps v The Queen* (1975) FC 76 under s 406 above.

This section is designed to attack employees who make false entries, or who falsify documents to hide defalcations or to hide schemes that they have hatched for their own benefit, to the detriment of their employers, but not to the detriment of others. In *The State v Asaoka Kouji of Rabaul* [1976] PNGLR 292 the accused falsified records, which decreased the amount of royalties owed by his employer to the government for logging operations. The situation is not comprehended by the section.

The phrase "intent to defraud" bears the same meaning as it does in the equivalent common law offences. The Crown must establish not merely that the accused acted in excess of whatever the accused's power was, but that he or she did not act honestly: *R v McEachern* [1967-1968] PNGLR 48.

Intent to defraud exists when the false document is brought into existence for no other purpose than that of deceiving a person responsible for a public duty into doing something that he or she would not have done but for the deceit, or not doing something that, but for it, he or she would have done: *R v Kautete Ova* (1969) N552.

In *R v Walsh* (1971) N627, the addition of the word "banked", plus a date, on the otherwise correct cash sales invoices in question did not amount to falsifying the invoices within the meaning of s 418(a). It was probably to meet a case like this that the offence provided in s 418(b) was inserted.

The court is entitled to view the evidence of all the transactions as a whole rather than to consider each transaction in isolation as a separate and individual one, in order to rebut any defence of simple mistake or inadvertence on the part of the accused or to establish that the acts charged were done and that it was accused who did them: *R v Walsh* (1971) N627.

See also *Secretary for Law v Suares* [1974] PNGLR 288.

See *Arthur Gilbert Smedley v The State* [1980] PNGLR 379, for an appeal from a conviction under this section.

419. False accounting by public officer.

An officer charged with the receipt, custody or management of any part of the public revenue or property, knowingly furnishes any false statement or return of -

(a) any money or property received by him or entrusted to his care; or

(b) any balance of money or property in his possession or under his control,

is guilty of a misdemeanour.

Penalty: Imprisonment for a term not exceeding two years.

The prosecution must prove that the officer was charged with the management of public revenue and that the officer furnished a false statement which he or she knew to be so: *R v Collins* (1950) N12.

Public revenue is not defined in the Code, but its meaning is clear enough. It is revenue of the state. Taxes imposed and collected by a local government council pursuant to the *Local Government Act* are not part of the revenue of the state and are therefore not part of the public revenue: *R v Kautete Ova* (1969) N552.

Subdivision I – Summary Trial for Certain Indictable Offences

[Subdiv I subst Act No 28, 1980 (*Criminal Code (Indictable) Offences Act* 1980), ss 2, 3 and 4; subst Act No 17, 1986 (*Criminal Code (Amendment No 2) Act* 1986), s 32]

420. Indictable offences that may be dealt with summarily.

(1) Where a person is charged before a District Court constituted by a Magistrate Grade V with an offence specified in Schedule 2, the Court may deal with the charge summarily according to the procedure set out in Section 421.

(2) Subject to Section 421(4), where -

(a) a charge for an offence is dealt with under Subsection (1); and

(b) the maximum penalty provided in this Code for that offence is imprisonment for a term exceeding 10 years,

the maximum penalty which may be imposed by a Magistrate Grade V is imprisonment for a term not exceeding 10 years, notwithstanding anything to the contrary in this Code.

See generally the *Summary Offences Act* 1977, set out in Ch 2 of this book.

Since summary jurisdiction is entirely a creation of statute, there must be strict compliance with the requirements of the statute conferring the jurisdiction, and a conviction made without strict compliance is a nullity and must be quashed: *Daniel v Stuckey* (1972) N681.

When the allegations appear to be better dealt with by indictment, the magistrate ought to draw this to the attention of the police prosecutor: *Michael Simi v John Bayam* [1980] PNGLR 300.

See *The State v The Principal Magistrate District Court, Port Moresby; Ex Parte Public Prosecutor* [1983] PNGLR 43 on the issue of election to try Sch 2 offences summarily.

It is the duty of police to lay a charge for the most serious offence constituted by the facts. It was held in *Michael Simi v John Bayam* [1980] PNGLR 300 that the police ought not to artificially split one course of conduct into summary offences of being unlawfully on premises and damaging property and the indictable offence (triable summarily) of stealing. A charge under s 398 was more appropriate.

In *Supreme Court Reservation No 4 of 1985; Re Omaro Garo v The Police* [1985] PNGLR 320 it was held that where a District Court constituted by a grade V magistrate deals with an offence specified in Sch 2 of the Code, the court is bound by the penalties provided for in s 720 of the Code, and introduced by the *Criminal Code (Minimum Penalties) Amendment Act* 1983, which provides that the offender shall be fined a sum not less than K100 and not exceeding K200 or imprisoned for a term not less than three months and not exceeding six months. Kidu CJ ascertained that a mistake had been made in the drafting of the 1983 amendments, with Parliament purporting to amend a subsection which had previously been repealed.

After enunciating well-established principles with respect to repealing legislation, he stated (at 322-323) that:

> "it must be assumed that when parliament enacted Act No 10 of 1983 it had before it the *Criminal Code* as amended to date. Quite clearly then parliament meant to delete the penalty provision in subs(1) and not subs(2) ... There is also little doubt that parliament intended, by the same amending provision, to add a completely new subsection to s 420 ... I consider that what parliament intended to do was add a subs(3) to s 420".

Since summary jurisdiction is entirely a creation of statute, there must be strict compliance with the requirements of the statute conferring the jurisdiction, and a conviction made without strict compliance is a nullity and must be quashed: *Daniel v Stuckey* (1972) N681.

Upon a charge under the Code where summary proceedings are possible, it must be clearly explained to the accused that he or she may be tried before the National Court, before the accused is asked to plead. Failure to observe the requirements of the summary procedure renders a conviction a nullity: *Daniel v Stuckey* (1972) N681.

See also *Strutt v Haram* (1963) N276 and *Pori Korene v Kindau Gapi* [1973] PNGLR 272.

If the magistrate is of the opinion that the punishment he or she can impose properly is insufficient, that is surely a very good reason for refusing to deal summarily with charges that can be dealt with on indictment: *Pius Embari v Wangiwa* (1973) N751.

As to disputes involving land appearing in the District Court, see *Thomas Show Sun Men v Topotol* (1958) N123.

421A. Procedure on committal to National Court.

(1) Where an offender is committed under Section 421(4), the committing Magistrate shall, as soon as practicable, arrange for transmission to -

(a) the Registrar of the National Court; and

(b) the Public Prosecutor; and

(c) if requested, the offender or his legal representative,

a copy of -

(d) the information; and

(e) a transcript of the evidence given before him; and

(f) the warrant committing the offender to custody, or the certificate that the offender has been admitted to bail; and

(g) the notice of committal for sentence.

(2) For the purposes of Subsection (1)(g), the notice of committal for sentence shall contain the following particulars -

(a) the name of the offender; and

(b) the particulars of the offence for which the offender has been committed for sentence; and

(c) a statement, signed by the committing Magistrate, stating that he considers the circumstances of the offence warrant a penalty greater than that prescribed as the maximum penalty for indictable offences triable summarily under this Division.

Subdivision J – Offences Analogous to Stealing Punishable on Summary Conviction

422. Unlawfully using motor vehicle, bicycle, boat or canoe.

A person who unlawfully uses a motor vehicle, bicycle, boat or canoe without the consent of the owner or of the person in lawful possession of it is guilty of an offence.

Penalty: A fine not exceeding K400.00 or imprisonment for a term not exceeding one year.

[Penalty provision am Act No 10, 1983 (*Criminal Code (Minimum Penalties) (Amendment) Act* 1983), s 23; am Act No 17, 1986 (*Criminal Code (Amendment No 2) Act* 1986), s 33]

This section was to have been repealed and replaced by the *Criminal Code (Amendment) Act* 1977 (No 42 of 1977), s 2; however, that Act has never been brought into effect.

See s 383 of the Code regarding unlawfully using a motor vehicle.

423. Unlawfully using cattle.

(1) For the purposes of this section, "unlawfully uses" includes the unlawful possession by any person without the consent of the owner or of the person in lawful possession, with intent to deprive the owner or person in lawful possession of use or possession, temporarily or permanently.

(2) A person who unlawfully uses a horse, mare, gelding, ass, mule, camel, bull, cow, ox, ram, ewe, wether, goat or pig, or the young or any such animal, without the consent of the owner, or the person in lawful possession of it, is guilty of an offence.

Penalty: A fine not exceeding K200.00 or imprisonment for a term not exceeding six months, for every animal so used.

424. Suspicion of stealing cattle.

Where a horse, mare, gelding, ass, mule, camel, bull, cow, ox, ram, ewe, wether, goat or pig, or the young of any such animal, is suspected, on reasonable grounds, to have been stolen, any person in whose possession or custody the skin or carcass, or any part of the skin or carcass, of the animal is found is guilty of an offence, unless he proves that he came lawfully by the thing in question.

Penalty: A fine not exceeding K100.00.

425. Committal for trial

If the court before whom any person is brought, charged with an offence against any of the preceding provisions of this subdivision, is of opinion that there ought to be a prosecution for an indictable offence, it may -

(a) abstain from dealing with the case summarily; and

(b) commit the defendant to take his trial for the indictable offence.

426. Unlawful possession of shipwrecked goods.

(1) A person in whose possession or on whose premises there is found any thing that -

(a) belongs to a vessel in distress, wrecked or stranded; and

(b) is suspected, on reasonable grounds, to have been unlawfully taken from the vessel,

is guilty of an offence unless he proves that he came lawfully by the thing in question.

Penalty: A fine not exceeding K200.00 or imprisonment for a term not exceeding six months.

(2) The court shall order the thing, referred to in Subsection (1), to be delivered up to the rightful owner.

427. Offering shipwrecked goods for sale

(1) A person who offers or exposes for sale any thing that is suspected, on reasonable grounds, to have been unlawfully taken from a vessel in distress, wrecked or stranded is guilty of an offence unless he proves that he came lawfully by the thing in question.

Penalty: A fine not exceeding K200.00 or imprisonment for a term not exceeding six months.

(2) Any person employed in the Public Service may seize any thing, referred to in Subsection (1), so offered for sale.

(3) If the accused person is convicted, the court that convicts him shall order the thing referred to in Subsection (1) to be delivered up to its rightful owner on payment of a reasonable reward, to be ascertained by the court, to the person who seized it.

428. Unlawfully dredging for oysters.

A person who unlawfully, and otherwise than in the course of catching or fishing for swimming fish with a net or other instrument adapted for taking only swimming fish -

(a) uses, for the purpose of taking oysters or oyster brood, any net or other instrument within the limits of an oyster bed, laying or fishery, that -

(i) is the property of any other person; and

(ii) is sufficiently marked out, or is known by general repute as his property,

whether any oysters or oyster brood are actually taken or not; or

(b) drags on the ground or soil of any such fishery with any net or instrument,

is guilty of an offence.

Penalty: Imprisonment for a term not exceeding three months.

See s 364 of the Code.

429. Unlawfully taking fish.

A person who unlawfully takes or destroys, or attempts to take or destroy, any fish in any water that is private property, or in which there is a private right of fishery is guilty of an offence.

Penalty: A fine not exceeding K50.00.

See s 364 of the Code.

430. Arrest without warrant.

[S 430 rep Act No 13, 1977 (*Criminal Code (Arrest) Act* 1977), s 28]

431. Warrant in first instance.

[S 431 rep Act No 13, 1977 (*Criminal Code (Arrest) Act* 1977), s 29]

432. Effect of summary conviction and civil proceedings.

(1) A person who has been summarily convicted of an offence against Section 422, 426, 427, 428 or 429, and -

- (a) who has paid the fine or sum adjudged to be paid under the conviction, together with the costs (if any); or
- (b) who has suffered the imprisonment adjudged for non-payment; or
- (c) who has suffered the imprisonment adjudged in the first instance; or
- (d) who has been pardoned; or
- (e) who has been discharged without punishment on making satisfaction to the person aggrieved; or
- (f) whose sentence has been conditionally suspended,

is not liable to any civil proceedings for the same cause at the suit of the person on whose complaint he was convicted.

(2) If civil proceedings have been taken against any person in respect of any act done by him that is an offence against any provision of this subdivision, he cannot be afterwards prosecuted for the same cause, as for an offence, on the complaint of the person by whom the civil proceedings were taken.

Division 2 – Injuries to Property

Subdivision A – Interpretation

433. Unlawful acts.

(1) An act that causes injury to the property of another, and that is done without his consent, is unlawful unless it is authorized or justified or excused by law.

(2) It is immaterial that the person who does the injury is in possession of the property injured or has a partial interest in it.

(3) A person is not criminally responsible for an injury caused to property by the use of such force as is reasonably necessary for the purpose of defending or protecting himself, any other person or any property from injury that he believes, on reasonable grounds, to be imminent.

See s 47 of the *Summary Offences Act* regarding the summary offence of damaging property.

As to s 433(2), see ss 35 and 370 of the Code. For indictments, see s 542(6), (8) and (9).

To be "imminent" the injury must be of a kind actually contemplated by the accused and be an "apparent and immediate or proximate threat of injury": *R v Alder* (1962) N228.

A defence arising under s 433(3) excludes a defence under s 23. If the two sections were read together, a mere subjective belief that danger was imminent would in every case be sufficient, for the accused could honestly claim the right, regardless of the actual existence of reasonable grounds required, by forming the subjective belief that his or her grounds were reasonable: *R v Alder* (1962) N228.

434. Acts done with intent to defraud.

(1) When an act that causes injury to property, and that would otherwise be lawful, is done with intent to defraud any person, it is unlawful.

(2) When an act that causes injury to property is done with intent to defraud any person, it is immaterial that the property in question is the property of the offender himself.

435. Damage.

In relation to a document, or to a writing or inscription, "damage" includes obliterating and rendering illegible, in whole or in part.

Subdivision B – Offences

436. Arson.

A person who wilfully and unlawfully sets fire to -

(a) a building or structure, whether completed or not; or

(b) a vessel, whether completed or not; or

(c) a stack of cultivated vegetable produce; or

(d) a stack of mineral or vegetable fuel; or

(e) a mine, or the workings, fittings or appliances of a mine; or

(f) an aircraft or motor vehicle,

is guilty of a crime.

Penalty: Subject to Section 19, imprisonment for life.

See s 437 of the Code regarding attempt.

See s 48 of the *Summary Offences Act* regarding negligent use of fire.

On the issue of sentence for arson see *The State v Ipu Samuel Yomb* [1992] PNGLR 261 and *The State v Seye Wasea Bukere* (1999) N1848.

In *The State v Ipu Samuel Yomb* the accused pleaded guilty to an act of arson in setting fire to the house occupied by his sister-in-law and her family. This act was in reprisal for the ill treatment of his sister by her husband, who was the brother of the victim of the arson. Doherty J set down factors relevant to the case:

(a) the deliberate or very reckless putting of lives at risk;

(b) the deliberate pouring of kerosene and setting fire to the roof, knowing that people were inside;

(c) the deliberate locking of the door, so preventing escape by the occupants;

(d) the deliberate cold-blooded planning of the offence;

(e) the value of the house and its contents to the occupants; and

(f) the complete lack of provocation offered to the defendant by the occupants and their children.

In *The State v Seye Wasea Bukere* (1999) N1848 the accused set fire to a pre-school classroom at the Indagen Community School. The accused argued that he had two disputes with the school, the first involving the land on which the pre-school classroom was erected and the second was the killing of the accused's pig by the headmaster of the school. Akuram J adopted Doherty J's considerations referred to above as relevant considerations in sentencing arson cases, and imposed a sentence of four years.

In *The State v Ipu Samuel Yomb* [1992] PNGLR 261, a sentence of six to seven years was appropriate. Bearing in mind the defendant's age [19 years at the time of the offence], his plea and his prior good behaviour, Doherty J reduced seven years to five years in hard labour.

437. Attempts to commit arson.

A person who -

(a) attempts unlawfully to set fire to any thing referred to in Section 436; or

(b) wilfully and unlawfully sets fire to any thing that is so situated that any thing referred to in Section 436 is likely to catch fire from it,

is guilty of a crime.

Penalty: Imprisonment for a term not exceeding 14 years.

See s 436 of the Code regarding the completed offence.

See s 4 regarding attempts generally.

438. Setting fire to crops and growing plants.

A person who wilfully and unlawfully sets fire to -

(a) a crop of cultivated vegetable produce, whether standing or cut; or

(b) a crop of hay or grass, whether -

(i) the natural or indigenous product of the soil or not; or

(ii) under cultivation or not; or

(iii) standing or cut; or

(c) any standing trees, saplings or shrubs, whether indigenous or cultivated; or

(d) any heath, gorse, furze, or fern,

is guilty of a crime.

Penalty: Imprisonment for a term not exceeding 14 years.

This offence is also punishable summarily: see Sch 2 of the Code.

439. Attempting to set fire to crops, etc.

A person who attempts unlawfully to set fire to any thing referred to in Section 438 is guilty of a crime.

Penalty: Imprisonment for a term not exceeding seven years.

This offence is also punishable summarily: see Sch 2 of the Code.

See s 4 regarding attempts generally.

440. Casting away ships.

A person who -

(a) wilfully and unlawfully casts away or destroys a vessel, whether complete or not; or

(b) wilfully and unlawfully does any act that tends to the immediate loss or destruction of a vessel in distress; or

(c) with intent to bring a vessel into danger -

(i) interferes with any light, beacon, mark or signal used for -

(A) purposes of navigation; or

(B) the guidance of seamen; or

(ii) exhibits any false light or signal,

is guilty of a crime.

Penalty: Subject to Section 19, imprisonment for life.

"Vessel" is defined by s 1 of the Code.

See s 441 below, regarding the attempted offence.

See s 45(1) of the *Summary Offences Act* for the summary offence of casting boats adrift, and s 45(3) for a definition of "casts adrift".

441. Attempts to cast away ships.

A person who attempts unlawfully -

(a) to cast away or destroy a vessel, whether or not it is complete; or

(b) to do any act tending to the immediate loss or destruction of a vessel in distress,

is guilty of a crime.

Penalty: Imprisonment for a term not exceeding 14 years.

See s 4 of the Code regarding attempts.

442. Endangering the safe use of an aircraft.

(1) A person who, with intent to prejudice the safe use of an aircraft or to injure any property on an aircraft -

(a) deals with the aircraft or with any thing -

(i) on or near the aircraft; or

(ii) directly or indirectly connected with the guidance, control or operation of the aircraft,

in such a manner as to affect or endanger the free and safe use of the aircraft; or

(b) by any omission to do any act that it is his duty to do causes the free and safe use of the aircraft to be endangered,

is guilty of a crime.

Penalty: Subject to Section 19, imprisonment for life.

(2) A person who, while on board an aircraft, wilfully does an act or makes an omission, or is privy to an act or omission, by which to his knowledge the safety of the aircraft is or is likely to be endangered is guilty of a crime.

Penalty: Imprisonment for a term not exceeding seven years.

"Aircraft" is defined by s 1 of the Code.

443. Injuring animals.

(1) A person who wilfully and unlawfully kills, maims or wounds an animal capable of being stolen is guilty of a misdemeanour.

Penalty: Subject to Subsection (2), imprisonment for a term not exceeding two years.

(2) If an offence against Subsection (1) is committed by night, the offender is liable to imprisonment for a term not exceeding three years.

This offence is also punishable summarily: see Sch 2 of the Code.

444. Malicious injuries in general: punishment in special cases.

(1) A person who wilfully and unlawfully destroys or damages any property is guilty of an offence that, unless otherwise stated, is a misdemeanour.

Penalty: If no other punishment is provided by this section – imprisonment for a term not exceeding two years.

(2) If an offence against Subsection (1) is committed by night, the offender is liable to imprisonment for a term not exceeding three years.

(3) If the property destroyed or damaged was a dwelling-house or a vessel, or an aircraft, and the injury is caused by the explosion of any explosive substance, and -

(a) any person is in the dwelling-house or vessel or aircraft; or

(b) the destruction or damage actually endangers the life of any person, the offence is a crime and the offender is liable, subject to Section 19, to imprisonment for life.

(4) If the property destroyed or damaged was a bank or wall of the sea, or of a river, canal, aqueduct, reservoir, or inland water, or a work that appertains to a port, harbour, dock, reservoir or inland water, and the injury causes actual danger or inundation or damage to any land or building the offence is a crime, and the offender is liable, subject to Section 19, to imprisonment for life.

(5) If the property was a bridge, viaduct or aqueduct that was over a highway or canal, or over which a highway or canal passed, and -

(a) was destroyed; or

(b) was damaged and -

(i) the damage was done with intent to make the bridge, viaduct or aqueduct, or the highway or canal, or any part of any of those things, dangerous or impassable; and

(ii) the bridge, viaduct or aqueduct, or the highway or canal, as the case may be, was made dangerous or impassable by the damage,

the offence is a crime, and the offender is liable, subject to Section 19, to imprisonment for life.

(6) If the property destroyed or damaged was -

(a) a testamentary instrument, whether the testator is living or dead; or

(b) a register that is authorized or required by law to be kept for -

(i) authenticating or recording the title to any property; or

(ii) recording births, baptisms, marriages, deaths or burials; or

(c) a copy of any part of any such register that is required by law to be sent to any public officer,

the offence is a crime, and the offender is liable to imprisonment for a term not exceeding 14 years.

(7) If the property destroyed or damaged was a vessel in distress, wrecked or stranded, or any thing that belongs to such a vessel, the offence is a crime, and the offender is liable to imprisonment for a term not exceeding seven years.

(8) If the property destroyed or damaged was an aircraft or any thing directly or indirectly connected with the guidance, control or operation of an aircraft, the offence is a crime, and the offender is liable to imprisonment for a term not exceeding 14 years.

(9) If the property was -

(a) a vessel, whether complete or not, and it is destroyed; or

(b) a vessel, whether complete or not, and it is damaged, and the damage is done with intent to destroy it or make it useless; or

(c) a light, beacon, buoy, mark or signal used for purposes of navigation, or for the guidance of seamen; or

(d) a bank or wall of the sea, or of a river, canal, aqueduct, reservoir or inland water, or a work that -

(i) appertains to a port, harbour, dock, canal, aqueduct, reservoir or inland water; or

(ii) is used for the purpose of loading or unloading goods; or

(e) a bridge, viaduct or aqueduct, that is constructed over a highway or canal, or over which a highway or canal passes, and -

(i) it is damaged; and

(ii) the damage is done with intent to make the bridge, viaduct or aqueduct, or the highway or canal or any part of it, dangerous or impassable; or

(f) any thing in process of manufacture, an agricultural or manufacturing machine, a manufacturing implement or a machine or appliance used or intended to be used for performing any process connected with the preparation of any agricultural or pastoral produce, and it is destroyed; or

(g) any thing, machine, implement or appliance specified in Paragraph (f) and the damage is done with intent to destroy it or to make it useless; or

(h) a shaft or passage of a mine, and the injury is done with intent to damage the mine or to obstruct its working; or

(i) a machine, appliance, apparatus, building, erection, bridge or road appertaining to or used with a mine, whether or not it was completed; or

(j) a rope, chain or tackle that is used in a mine, or on any way or work appertaining to or used with a mine, and it is destroyed; or

(k) a rope, chain or tackle specified in Paragraph (j), and -

(i) it is damaged; and

(ii) damage is done with intent to destroy it or to make it useless; or

(l) a well or bore for water, or the dam, bank, wall, or floodgate of a millpond or pool,

the offence is a crime, and the offender is liable to imprisonment for a term not exceeding seven years.

(10) If the property destroyed or damaged was a document that -

(a) was deposited or kept in a public office; or

(b) was evidence of title to any land or estate in land,

the offence is a crime, and the offender is liable to imprisonment for a term not exceeding seven years.

The offence in general (s 444(1)) is also punishable summarily: see Sch 2 of the Code.

As to alternative verdicts, see s 543.

See s 28(1)(b) and (2)(b) of the *Summary Offences Act* regarding the use of firearms, stones, sticks or any missiles with intent to damage property.

See s 47 of the *Summary Offences Act* regarding the summary offence of damaging property.

"Wilfully" means "intentionally", "deliberately", "recklessly" or "maliciously" but not "accidentally" or "negligently". Thus, for an offence to be committed under this section it is necessary for the accused either to intend to do the particular type of harm in fact done, or having reason to foresee that such harm was likely to be done, for the accused recklessly to take the risk of it. Where the accused tossed a bottle out of the window of a moving bus and smashed the windscreen of a parked car, the test of liability is whether the accused intended the damage or had foreseen the risk involved: *Pukari-Flabu v Hambakon Sma* [1965-1966] PNGLR 348.

A police officer, under a duty to restore law and order, does not "unlawfully destroy or damage" property if acting under an honest belief that such destruction is a necessary means to achieving this object: *R v Alder* (1962) N228.

445. Attempts to destroy property by explosives.

A person who, unlawfully, and with intent to destroy or damage any property, puts an explosive substance in any place, is guilty of a crime.

Penalty: Imprisonment for a term not exceeding 14 years.

See s 4 of the Code regarding attempts.

446. Unlawful deposition of explosives.

(1) A person who wilfully and without reasonable cause or accuse throws, leaves down or otherwise deposits any explosive substance in any place under such circumstances that it may cause -

(a) injury to any person; or

(b) damage to the property of any person,

is guilty of a misdemeanour.

Penalty: Imprisonment for a term not exceeding two years.

(2) ...

[Subs (2) rep Act No 13, 1977 (*Criminal Code (Arrest) Act* 1977), s 30]

447. Attempts to injure mines.

A person who, with intent to injure a mine or to obstruct the working of a mine -

(a) unlawfully, and otherwise than by an act done underground in the course of working an adjoining mine-

(i) causes water to run into the mine or into a subterranean passage communicating with the mine; or

(ii) obstructs any shaft or passage of the mine; or

(b) unlawfully obstructs the working of any machine, alliance or apparatus appertaining to or used with the mine, whether or not it is completed; or

(c) unlawfully, and with intent to make it useless, injures or unfastens a rope, chain or tackle that is used in the mine or on any way or work appertaining to or used with the mine,

is guilty of a crime.

Penalty: Imprisonment for a term not exceeding seven years.

448. Interfering with marine signals.

A person who -

(a) wilfully and unlawfully removes, defaces or makes invisible any light, beacon, buoy, mark or signal used for -

(i) purposes of navigation; or

(ii) the guidance of seamen; or

(b) unlawfully attempts to remove, deface or make invisible any such thing,

is guilty of a crime.

Penalty: Imprisonment for a term not exceeding seven years.

449. Interfering with navigation works.

A person who -

(a) wilfully and unlawfully removes or disturbs any fixed objector materials used for -

(i) securing a bank or wall of the sea, or of a river, canal, aqueduct, reservoir or inland water; or

(ii) securing any work that -

(A) appertains to a port, harbour, dock, canal, aqueduct, reservoir or inland water; or

(B) is used for purposes of navigation or loading or unloading goods; or

(b) unlawfully does any act with intent to obstruct the carrying on completion or maintenance of the navigation of a navigable river or canal, and by doing so obstructs the carrying on, completion or maintenance,

is guilty of a crime.

Penalty: Imprisonment for a term not exceeding seven years.

450. Communicating infectious disease to animals.

A person who wilfully and unlawfully causes, is concerned in causing or attempts to cause an infectious disease to be communicated to or among any animals capable of being stolen is guilty of a crime.

Penalty: Imprisonment for a term not exceeding seven years.

451. Travelling with infected animals.

A person who -

(a) causes any four-footed animal that is infected with an infectious disease to travel; or

(b) being the owner, or one of the joint owners, of any four-footed animal that is infected with an infectious disease, permits or connives at the travelling of any such animal,

contrary to any law relating to infected animals of that kind, is guilty of a misdemeanour.

Penalty: Imprisonment for a term not exceeding two years.

This offence is also punishable summarily: see Sch 2 of the Code.

452. Removing boundary marks.

A person who wilfully and unlawfully, and with intent to defraud, removes or defaces an object or mark that has been lawfully erected or made as an indication of the boundary of any land is guilty of a misdemeanour.

Penalty: Imprisonment for a term not exceeding three years.

453. Sending letters threatening to burn or destroy.

A person who, knowing the contents of the writing, causes a person to receive a writing threatening that-

(a) a building or vessel, whether or not it is complete; or

(b) any stack of cultivated vegetable produce; or

(c) any such produce that is in or under a building,

will be burnt or destroyed is guilty of a crime.

Penalty: Imprisonment for a term not exceeding seven years.

See ss 359 and 389-392 of the Code regarding threats and extortion

454. Arrest without warrant.

[S 454 rep Act No 13, 1977 (*Criminal Code (Arrest) Act* 1977), s 31]

Subdivision C – Summary Conviction for certain offences

455. Offences that may be dealt with summarily.

[S 455 rep Act No 28, 1980 (*Criminal Code (Indictable Offences) Act* 1980), s 5]

See Sch 2 of the Code.

456. Procedure.

[S 456 rep Act No 28, 1980 (*Criminal Code (Indictable Offences) Act* 1980), s 5]

See Sch 2 of the Code.

457. Trivial charges.

If on the trial of any person under this subdivision the court is of opinion that the injury is of so trivial a nature as not to deserve any punishment, it may convict the defendant and discharge him without inflicting any punishment.

See also s 602 of the Code regarding discharge.

458. Effect of summary conviction and of civil proceedings.

(1) A person who has been summarily convicted of an offence against this subdivision and who -

(a) has -

(i) paid the fine or sum (if any) adjudged to be paid under the conviction together with the costs (if any); or

(ii) suffered the imprisonment adjudged for non-payment of it; or

(iii) suffered the imprisonment adjudged in the first instance; or

(iv) been pardoned; or

(v) been discharged without punishment; or

(b) has had his sentence conditionally suspended,

is not liable to any civil proceedings for the same cause at the suit of the person on whose complaint he was convicted.

(2) If civil proceedings have been taken against any person in respect of an act done by him that is an offence of which he might have been convicted under this subdivision, he cannot be afterwards prosecuted for the same cause, as for an offence, on the complaint of the person by whom the civil proceedings were taken.

Division 3 – Forgery and Like Offences: Personation

Subdivision A – Forgery in General

459. Interpretation of Division 3.

(1) In this Division -

"bank note" includes -

(a) any negotiable instrument issued -

(i) by or on behalf of any person or corporation in any part of the world; or

(ii) by the authority of any State, Prince or Government,

and intended to be used as equivalent to money, immediately on issue or at any time afterwards; and

(b) a bank bill or bank post bill;

"document" includes -

(a) a register or register-book, or a part of a register or register-book; and

(b) any -

(i) book; and

(ii) paper, parchment or other material, used for writing or printing,

that is marked with any letters or marks denoting words, or with any other signs capable of conveying a definite meaning to persons conversant with them, but does not include trade marks on articles of commerce;

"resemble" applied to any thing, includes the case where the thing is made to resemble, or is apparently intended to resemble, the object spoken of;

"seal" includes any stamp, die or other thing, from which an impression can be taken by means of pressure or of ink, or by any other means;

"writing" includes a mere signature and a mark of any kind.

(2) A document or writing is said to be false -

(a) in the case of a document that -

(i) is a register or record kept by lawful authority; or

(ii) is an entry in any such register; or

(iii) purports to be issued by lawful authority as testifying -

(A) to the contents of any register or record kept by lawful authority; or

(B) to any fact or event,

if any material particular stated in the document is untrue; or

(b) if the whole or some material part of the document or writing -

(i) purports to be made by or on behalf of some person who did not make it or authorize it to be made; or

(ii) where the time or place of making is material – is, with a fraudulent intent, falsely dated as to the time or place of making even though it is made by or by the authority of the person by whom it purports to be made; or

(c) if the whole or some material part of the document or writing purports to be made by or on behalf of a person who does not, in fact, exist; or

(d) if it is made in the name of an existing person, either by that person himself or by his authority, with the fraudulent intention that it should pass as being made by a person, real or fictitious, other than the person who made it or authorized it to be made.

(3) A seal or mark is said to be counterfeit if it is made without lawful authority, and is in such a form as to resemble a genuine seal or mark, or, in the case of a seal, in such a form as to be capable of producing impressions resembling those produced by a genuine seal.

(4) A representation of the impression of a seal is said to be counterfeit if it is not in fact made by the seal.

460. Definition of forgery.

(1) In this section, "make a false document or writing" includes -

(a) altering a genuine document or writing in a material part, whether by erasure, obliteration, removal or otherwise; and

(b) making a material addition to the body of a genuine document or writing, and

(c) adding to a genuine document or writing a false date, attestation, seal or other material matter.

(2) A person who makes a false document or writing, knowing it to be false, and with intent that it may in any way be used or acted on as genuine, whether in Papua New Guinea or elsewhere -

(a) to the prejudice of a person; or

(b) with intent that a person may, in the belief that it is genuine, be induced to do or refrain from doing any act, whether in Papua New Guinea or elsewhere,

is said to forge the document or writing.

(3) A person who makes -

(a) a counterfeit seal or mark; or

(b) an impression of a counterfeit seal knowing the seal to be counterfeit; or

(c) a counterfeit representation of the impression of a genuine seal; or

(d) without lawful authority, an impression of a genuine seal,

with intent that the thing so made may in any way be used or acted on as genuine, whether in Papua New Guinea or elsewhere -

(e) to the prejudice of any person; or

(f) with intent that a person may, in the belief that it is genuine, be induced to do or refrain from doing any act, whether in Papua New Guinea or elsewhere,

is said to forge the seal or mark.

(4) It is immaterial in what language a forged document or writing is expressed.

(5) It is immaterial that the forger of any thing forged did not intend that a particular person -

(a) should use or act on it; or

(b) should be prejudiced by it; or

(c) be induced to do or refrain from doing any act.

(6) It is immaterial that the thing forged is incomplete, or does not purport to be a document, writing or seal that would be binding in law for any particular purpose, if it is so made, and is of such a kind, as to indicate that it was intended to be used or acted on.

Forgery is punished by s 462 of the Code.

An intent to defraud or to gain advantage is not required by this section. Accordingly, any criminal intention, except as expressly required in ss 460 and 463, is not an element of the offences of forgery and uttering: *R v Magalu* [1974] PNGLR 188.

461. Other immaterial matters.

(1) In the case of an offence that involves the forging or uttering of a document or writing relating to -

(a) the payment of money; or

(b) the delivery or transfer of any property; or

(c) the creation or performance of an obligation,

it is immaterial in what country -

(d) the money or property is, or purports to be, payable, deliverable or transferable; or

(e) the obligation is, or purports to be, performed.

(2) If, under Subsection (1) -

(a) the money or the property purports to be payable, deliverable, or transferable; or

(b) the obligation purports to be an obligation to be performed,

in a country other than Papua New Guinea, it is immaterial whether or not the document or writing is under seal.

Subdivision B – Offences

462. Forgery in general: punishment in special cases.

(1) A person who forges any document, writing or seal is guilty of an offence that, unless otherwise stated, is a crime.

Penalty: If no other punishment is provided – imprisonment for a term not exceeding three years.

(2) If the thing forged -

(a) purports to be, or is intended by the offender to be understood to be or to be used as -

(i) the National Seal; or

(ii) the great seal of the United Kingdom, or of Australia; or

(iii) the privy seal, or any privy signet of the Queen and Head of State; or

(iv) the royal sign manual of the Queen and Head of State; or

(v) the seal of the Head of State or the Governor-General; or

(vi) any public seal lawfully appointed to be used for authenticating an act of State in any part of Her Majesty's Dominions; or

(b) is a document having on it or affixed to it any such seal, signet or sign manual, or any thing that purports to be, or is intended by the offender to be understood to be, any such seal, signet or sign manual,

the offender is liable, subject to Section 19, to imprisonment for life.

(3) If the thing forged purports to be, or is intended by the offender to be understood to be or to be used as -

(a) a document that is -

(i) evidence of title to -

(A) any portion of the public debt of any of Her Majesty's Dominions or of any foreign State; or

(B) any dividend or interest payable in respect of a debt referred to in Clause (A); or

(ii) a transfer or assignment of any document referred to in Subparagraph (i); or

(iii) a receipt or certificate for any interest or money payable or accruing on or in respect of a debt referred to in Subparagraph (i); or

(b) a transfer or assignment of –

(i) a share in any corporation, company or society, whether domestic or foreign; or

(ii) any share or interest in -

(A) the capital stock of any such corporation, company or society; or

(B) the debt of any such corporation, company or society; or

(c) a receipt or certificate for any interest or money payable or accruing on or in respect of any share, interest or debt referred to in Paragraph (b); or

(d) a document acknowledging or being evidence of the indebtedness of the Government or of the Government of any of Her Majesty's Dominions, or of any foreign Prince or State, to any person; or

(e) a document that by the law of Papua New Guinea or of any other country, is evidence of the title to any land or estate in land in Papua New Guinea or that other country, or an entry in any register or book that is such evidence; or

(f) a document that by law is required for procuring the registration of any title to any land or estate in land; or

(g) a testamentary instrument, whether the testator is living or dead, or a probate or letters of administration; or

(h) a bank note, bill of exchange or promissory note, or an acceptance, endorsement, or assignment of a bank note, bill of exchange or promissory note; or

(i) a deed bond or other written obligation, or a warrant, order or other security for -

(i) the payment of money; or

(ii) the delivery or transfer of a valuable security; or

(iii) procuring or giving credit, whether negotiable or not, or an endorsement or assignment of any such document; or

(j) an accountable receipt, or an acknowledgment of the deposit, receipt, payment or delivery of money or goods, or of any valuable security, or an endorsement or assignment of any such document; or

(k) a bill of lading, dock warrant, warehouse-keeper's certificate, warrant or order for the delivery of goods, or any other document used in the ordinary course of business -

(i) as proof of the possession or control of goods; or

(ii) as authorizing, or purporting to authorize, either by endorsement or by delivery, the possessor of the document to transfer or receive the goods represented by the document, or an endorsement or assignment of any such document; or

(l) a charter party, or a shipping document accompanying a bill of lading, or an endorsement or assignment of a charter party or such a document; or

(m) a policy of insurance of any kind; or

(n) a power of attorney or other authority to execute any document referred to in the preceding provisions of this section; or

(o) the signature of a witness to any of the documents referred to in the preceding provisions of this section to which attestation is by law required; or

(p) a register of births, baptisms, marriages, deaths or burials authorized or required by law to be kept, or any entry in any such register; or

(q) a copy of any register or entry referred to in Paragraph (p), that is authorized or required by law to be given or sent to or by any person; or

(r) a seal used by a registrar appointed to keep any register referred to in this subsection, or the impression of any such seal, or the signature of any such registrar,

the offender is liable to imprisonment for a term not exceeding 14 years.

(4) If the thing forged purports to be, or is intended by the offender to be understood to be or to be used as -

(a) the signature of the Head of State, a member of the National Executive Council, the Governor-General of Australia, a member of the Federal Executive Council of Australia, or any of Her Majesty's Principal Secretaries of State or Under Secretaries of State, on any grant, commission, warrant, or order; or

(b) a seal or stamp, used for the purposes of the public revenue in Papua New Guinea or of any part of Her Majesty's Dominions or in any foreign State; or

(c) a document relating to the obtaining or receiving of any money payable on account of the Public Service of Papua New Guinea or any part of Her Majesty's Dominions, or any other property of Her Majesty in any part of Her Dominions, or a power of attorney or other authority to execute any such document,

the offender is liable to imprisonment for a term not exceeding 14 years.

(5) If the thing forged purports to be, or is intended by the offender to be understood to be or to be used as -

(a) the seal of a court of record of Papua New Guinea or in any part of Her Majesty's Dominions, or a seal used at the Chambers of a Judge for stamping or sealing summonses or order; or

(b) a seal or signature by virtue of which any document can by law be used as evidence; or

(c) any process of any court of justice of Papua New Guinea or in any part of Her Majesty's Dominions; or

(d) a document issued or made by or out of or by the authority of a court referred to in Paragraph (c); or

(e) a document or copy of a document of any kind, which document or copy is intended by the offender to be used as evidence in a court referred to in Paragraph (c); or

(f) a record or other document of or belonging to a court of record of Papua New Guinea or in any part of Her Majesty's Dominions; or

(g) a copy or certificate of any record of a court referred to in Paragraph (f); or

(h) an instrument, that is made evidence by any law; or

(i) a document that a justice is required or authorized by law to make, attest or issue, and purporting to be made, attested or issued by a justice; or

(j) a stamp used for denoting the payment of fees or percentages in any court; or

(k) a licence or certificate required or authorized by law to be given for the celebration of a marriage; or

(l) a consent to the marriage of a minor given by a person authorized by law to give it; or

(m) a certificate of marriage given under the laws relating to the solemnization of marriage; or

(n) a copy of the registry of a marriage; or

(o) a stamp issued or made under the laws relating to the Post Office; or

(p) a power of attorney or letter of attorney; or

(q) the signature of a witness to a power of attorney or letter of attorney; or

(r) a contract, or a writing that constitutes, with other writings, a contract, or that is evidence of a contract; or

(s) an authority or request for the payment of money or for the delivery of property; or

(t) an acquittance or discharge, a voucher of having received any property, or any document that is evidence of the receipt of any property; or

(u) any mark that under the authority of a law is impressed on or otherwise attached to or connected with any article for the purpose of denoting -

(i) the quality of the article; or

(ii) the fact that it has been examined or approved by or under the authority of some public body or public officer; or

(v) a certificate given under the laws relating to quarantine,

the offender is liable to imprisonment for a term not exceeding seven years.

(6) If the thing forged purports to be, or is intended by the offender to be understood to be or to be used as, a message to be sent by telegraph, or a message received by telegraph, the offender is liable to the same punishment as if he had forged a document to the same effect as the message.

See the definition of "forgery" in s 460 of the Code.

463. Uttering false documents and counterfeit seals.

(1) In this section, "fraudulently" means with an intention -

(a) that the thing in question shall be used or acted on as genuine, whether in Papua New Guinea or elsewhere, to the prejudice of some person, whether a particular person or not; or

(b) that some person, whether a particular person or not, will, in the belief that the thing in question is genuine, be induced to do or refrain from doing some act, whether in Papua New Guinea or elsewhere.

(2) A person who knowingly and fraudulently utters a false document or writing, or a counterfeit seal, is guilty of an offence of the same kind and is liable to the same punishment as if he had forged the thing in question.

(3) It is immaterial whether the false document or writing, or counterfeit seal, was made in Papua New Guinea or elsewhere.

"Utter" is defined by s 1 of the Code.

"False document", "writing" and "seal" are defined in s 459.

See s 462 regarding punishment for various categories of uttering offences (liable to same punishment as for forgery).

For considerations of sentence upon a conviction for uttering a false document, namely an illicitly altered bank savings passbook, see *Kali Mari v The State* (1980) SC 175.

464. Uttering cancelled or exhausted documents.

A person who knowingly utters as and for a subsisting and effectual document any document -

(a) that has by any lawful authority been ordered to be revoked, cancelled or suspended; or

(b) the operation of which has ceased -

(i) by effluxion of time; or

(ii) by death; or

(iii) by the happening of any other event,

is guilty of an offence of the same kind and is liable to the same punishment as if he had forged the document.

"Utter" is defined by s 1 of the Code.

465. Uttering cancelled stamps.

A person who knowingly utters as and for a valid and uncancelled stamp -

(a) a stamp; or

(b) an impression of a seal,

used for any purpose connected with the public revenue of Papua New Guinea or of any part of Her Majesty's Dominions, that has been already used, or has been cancelled, is guilty of an offence of the same kind and is liable to the same Punishments as if he had forged the stamp or seal.

"Utter" is defined by s 1 of the Code.

466. Procuring execution of documents by false pretences.

A person who, by means of any false and fraudulent representation as to the nature, contents or operation of a document, procures another to sign or execute the document, is guilty of an offence of the same kind and is liable to the same punishment as if he had forged the document.

467. Obliterating crossing on cheques.

A person who, with intent to defraud -

(a) obliterates, adds to or alters the crossing on a cheque; or

(b) knowingly utters a crossed cheque, the crossing on which has been obliterated, added to or altered,

is guilty of a crime.

Penalty: Imprisonment for a term not exceeding seven years.

This offence is also punishable summarily: see Sch 2 of the Code.

468. Making documents without authority.

A person who, with intent to defraud -

(a) without lawful authority or excuse, makes, signs or executes, for or in the name, or on account, of another person, an instrument; or

(b) knowingly utters an instrument so made, signed or executed by another person,

is guilty of a crime.

Penalty: Imprisonment for a term not exceeding seven years.

This offence is also punishable summarily: see Sch 2 of the Code.

As to "intent to defraud", see the note on *R v McEachern* [1967-1968] PNGLR 48, under s 418.

See also *The State v Virgil Dewit Perryman* [1982] PNGLR 5, regarding documents without authority.

469. Demanding property on forged testamentary instruments.

A person who procures the delivery or payment to himself or any other person of any property or money-

(a) by virtue of any probate or letters of administration granted on a forged testamentary instrument, knowing the testamentary instrument to have been forged; or

(b) on or by virtue of any probate or letters of administration obtained by false evidence, knowing the grant to have been so obtained,

is guilty of an offence of the same kind and is liable to the same punishment as if he had forged the document or thing by virtue of which he procured the delivery or payment.

470. Purchasing forged bank notes.

A person who, without lawful authority or excuse (proof of which is on him) -

(a) purchases or receives from any person; or

(b) has in his possession,

a forged bank note, whether filled up or in blank, knowing it to be forged, is guilty of a crime.

Penalty: Imprisonment for a term not exceeding seven years.

471. False certificate of message received by telegraph.

A person who knowingly signs on a document that purports to be a copy of a document the contents of which have been received by telegraph under the laws authorizing the transmission by telegraph of the contents of documents requiring signature or seal, a false certificate that it has been duly received under the provisions of those laws is guilty of an offence of the same kind, and is liable to the same punishment as if he had forged the document of which it purports to be a copy.

"Telegraph" is defined by s 1 of the Code.

472. Falsifying warrants for money payable under public authority.

A person employed in the Public Service who knowingly and with intent to defraud makes out or delivers to any person a warrant for the payment of any money payable by public authority for a greater or less amount than that to which the person on whose behalf the warrant is made out is entitled, is guilty of a crime.

Penalty: Imprisonment for a term not exceeding seven years.

This offence is also punishable summarily: see Sch 2 of the Code.

473. Falsification of registers.

(1) A person who, having the actual custody of any register or record kept by lawful authority, knowingly permits any entry that is to his knowledge false in a material particular to be made in the register or record is guilty of a crime.

Penalty: Imprisonment for a term not exceeding seven years.

(2) ...

[Sub (2) rep Act No 12, 1993 (*Criminal Code (Amendment) Act* 1993), s 10]

This offence is also punishable summarily: see Sch 2 of the Code.

474. Sending false certificate of marriage to Registrar.

A person who signs or transmits to a person authorized by law to register marriages -

(a) a certificate of marriage; or

(b) a document purporting to be a certificate of marriage,

that is to his knowledge false in a material particular, is guilty of a crime.

Penalty: Imprisonment for a term not exceeding seven years.

This offence is also punishable summarily: see Sch 2 of the Code.

475. False statements for the purpose of registers of births, deaths and marriages.

A person who knowingly, and with intent to procure it to be inserted in a register of births, deaths or marriages, makes a false statement concerning a matter required by law to be registered in any such register is guilty of a misdemeanour.

Penalty: Imprisonment for a term not exceeding three years.

This offence is also punishable summarily: see Sch 2 of the Code.

476. Attempts to procure unauthorized status.

A person who -

(a) by a false representation procures any authority authorized by any law to issue certificates testifying that the holders of them are entitled to any right or privilege, or to enjoy any rank or status, to issue to himself or any other person any such certificate; or

(b) falsely represents to any person that he has obtained a certificate issued by any such authority; or

(c) by a false representation procures himself or any other person to be registered on a register kept by lawful authority as a person entitled -

(i) to such a certificate; or

(ii) to any right or privilege; or

(iii) to enjoy any rank or status,

is guilty of a misdemeanour.

Penalty: Imprisonment for a term not exceeding three years.

This offence is also punishable summarily: see Sch 2 of the Code.

477. Counterfeiting trade marks.

(1) In this section -

"counterfeit" includes any imitation of a genuine mark that is not genuine and that resembles the genuine mark;

"trade mark" includes any word or mark of any kind that is lawfully used by any person to denote that any article is -

(a) of his manufacture, workmanship, production or merchandise; or

(b) a thing of a peculiar or particular description made or sold by him.

(2) A person who, with intent to defraud or to enable another person to defraud -

(a) makes a counterfeit trade mark; or

(b) knowingly uses a trade mark, whether genuine or counterfeit, on an article, or on any thing containing or connected with any article, in such a manner that the trade mark signifies or implies, or may reasonably induce any person to believe, contrary to the fact, that the article is such as is designated by the trade mark,

is guilty of a misdemeanour.

Penalty: Imprisonment for a term not exceeding two years and a fine at the discretion of the court.

(3) When a person is convicted under this section -

(a) every thing that he has in his possession to which the trademark or counterfeit trade mark has been applied; and

(b) every instrument that he has in his possession -

(i) by means of which any such mark has been so applied; or

(ii) which is intended for applying any such mark,

is forfeited to the State.

As to the penalty provision of s 477(2), compare s 37(2) of the *Constitution*.

"Registered brand" and "registered mark" are defined by s 1 of the Code.

478. Circulating false copies of rules or lists of members of societies or companies.

A person who knowingly, and with intent to deceive or defraud, or to enable another person to deceive or defraud, utters to any person a document that -

(a) purports to be a copy of the memorandum or articles of association or other constitution of a corporation or joint-stock company, or of the rules or by-laws of any corporation or society, constituted under the authority of any law, but is not a true copy of it; or

(b) purports to be a list of the members of any such corporation, company, or society, but is not a true list of those members,

is guilty of a misdemeanour.

Penalty: Imprisonment for a term not exceeding three years.

"Company" is defined by s 1 of the Code.

Subdivision C – Forgery and Like Offences Punishable on Summary Conviction

479. Application of Subdivision C.

The provisions of this subdivision are in addition to and not in derogation of any other provisions of this Code relating to the same matters, but so that an offender cannot be twice convicted for the same act.

480. Sending false telegrams.

A person who -

(a) knowingly and without the authority of the pretended sender, sends or delivers, or causes to be sent or delivered, to any person employed by or under the Department of Posts and Telegraphs, for the purpose of being transmitted as a telegram, a message or writing purporting to be sent by another person; or

(b) signs a telegram in the name of another person without that person's authority, or in the name of a fictitious person; or

(c) wilfully alters a telegram without the authority of the sender; or

(d) writes, issues or delivers, as and for a telegram received through a telegraph office, a writing purporting to be a telegram so received, that is not a telegram so received,

is guilty of an offence.

Penalty: A fine not exceeding K400.00 or imprisonment for a term not exceeding one year.

"Telegraph" and "telegram" are defined by s 1 of the Code.

481. Forgery of seamen's tickets or documents under Acts controlling factories and shops.

A person who -

(a) forges any document purporting to be, or intended by the offender to be understood to be or to be used as, a document required to be obtained or used under the provisions of the laws relating to -

(i) the engagement or discharge of seamen; or

(ii) the regulation of factories and shops; or

(b) utters any document that is required to be obtained or used under the provisions of those laws, and that has been issued to another person, and falsely represents himself to be the person named in the document,

is guilty of an offence.

Penalty: A fine not exceeding K400.000 or imprisonment for a term not exceeding one year.

482. Fraudulent use of adhesive stamps.

A person who with intent that it may be used again -

(a) fraudulently removes an adhesive stamp, or causes an adhesive stamp to be removed, from any document; or

(b) fraudulently affixes an adhesive stamp that has been removed from any document to another document; or

(c) knowingly utters an adhesive stamp that has been fraudulently removed from any document; or

(d) knowingly utters any document that has on it an adhesive stamp that has been fraudulently removed from another document,

is guilty of an offence.

Penalty: A fine not exceeding K100.00.

483. False warranties or labels relating to the sale of food.

A person who -

(a) knowingly gives to a purchaser a false warranty in writing with respect to an article of food or a drug sold by him, whether as principal or agent; or

(b) knowingly gives with any article of food or drug sold by him a label that falsely describes the article or drug sold; or

(c) in any proceedings under the law relating to the sale of food and drugs knowingly applies to an article of food or a drug a certificate or warranty given with respect to another article or drug,

is guilty of an offence.

Penalty: A fine not exceeding K40.00.

See ss 238-239 of the Code regarding sale of unfit food.

Subdivision D – Preparation for Forgery

484. Instruments and materials for forgery.

A person who, without lawful authority or excuse, (proof of which is on him) -

(a) makes, begins or prepares to make, uses, or knowingly has in his possession or disposes of, any paper resembling any paper that is specially provided by the proper authority for the purpose of being used for making -

(i) any document acknowledging or being evidence of the indebtedness to any person of -

(A) the Government; or

(B) the Government of any of Her Majesty's Dominions; or

(C) any foreign Prince or State; or

(D) any person carrying on the business of banking; or

(ii) a stamp, licence, permit or other document used for the purposes of the public revenue of Papua New Guinea, or of any part of Her Majesty's Dominions; or

(iii) a bank note,

or any machinery, instrument or material -

(iv) for making any such paper; or

(v) capable of producing in or on paper any words, figures, letters, marks or lines resembling any words, figures, letters, marks or lines used in or on any paper specially provided for any such purpose; or

(b) impresses or makes on any plate or material any words, figures, letters, marks or lines the print of which resembles, in whole or part, the words, figures, letters, marks or lines used in any document referred to in Paragraph (a); or

(c) uses, or knowingly has in his possession, or disposes of -

(i) any plate or material on which any words, figures, letters, marks or lines referred to in Paragraph (b) or (c) are impressed or made; or

(ii) any paper on which is written or printed the whole or any part of the usual contents of any document referred to in Paragraph (a),

is guilty of a crime.

Penalty: Imprisonment for a term not exceeding 14 years.

"Have in possession" is defined by s 1 of the Code.

485. Counterfeit stamps.

A person who, without lawful authority or excuse (proof of which is on him) -

(a) makes or mends, begins or prepares to make or mend, uses or knowingly has in his possession, or disposes of any die, plate or instrument capable of making an impression resembling that made by any die, plate or instrument, used for the purpose of making any stamp, whether impressed or adhesive, that-

(i) is used for the purposes of the public revenue or of the Post Office in -

(A) Papua New Guinea; or

(B) any part of Her Majesty's Dominions; or

(C) any foreign State; or

(ii) is capable of producing in or on paper any words, figures, letters, marks or lines resembling any words, figures, letters, marks or lines used in or on any paper specially provided by the proper authority for any such purpose; or

(b) knowingly has in his possession or disposes of -

(i) any paper or other material that has on it the impression of any die, plate or instrument referred to in Paragraph (a); or

(ii) any paper that has on it or in it any words, figures, letters, marks or lines referred to in Paragraph (a); or

(c) fraudulently, and with intent that use may be made of any stamp referred to in Paragraph (a) or of any part of it, removes the stamp from any material in any way; or

(d) fraudulently, and with intent that use may be made of any part of any stamp referred to in Paragraph (a), mutilates the stamp; or

(e) fraudulently fixes or places on any material or on any stamp referred to in Paragraph (a) any stamp or part of a stamp that has been removed from any other material, or out of or from any other stamp; or

(f) fraudulently, and with intent that use may be made of any stamp referred to in Paragraph (a) that has been already impressed on or attached to any material, erases or otherwise removes, either really or apparently from such material anything written on it; or

(g) knowingly has in his possession or disposes of anything obtained or prepared by any unlawful act, referred to in this section,

is guilty of a crime.

Penalty: Imprisonment for a term not exceeding 14 years.

"Have in Possession" is defined by s 1 of the Code.

486. Paper for postal purposes.

A person who, without lawful authority or excuse, (proof of which is on him), knowingly has in his possession or disposes of any paper that has been specially provided by the proper authority for the purpose of being used for postage stamps, money orders or postal notes, before the paper has been lawfully issued for public use, is guilty of a misdemeanour.

Penalty: Imprisonment for a term not exceeding two years.

"Have in possession" is defined by s 1 of the Code.

487. Paper and dies for postage stamps.

(1) For the purposes of this section unless the contrary is shown a stamp purporting to denote a rate of postage of any country is to be taken to be a stamp used for postal purposes in that country.

(2) A person who, without lawful authority or excuse (proof of which is on him) -

(a) makes, begins or prepares to make, uses for any postal purpose, has in his possession or disposes of any imitation or representation on paper or any other material, of any stamp used for denoting any rate of postage of Papua New Guinea or of any part of Her Majesty's Dominions, or of any foreign country; or

(b) makes or mends, begins or prepares to make or mend, uses, has in his possession or disposes of any die, plate, instrument or material for making an imitation or representation referred to in Paragraph (a),

is guilty of an offence.

Penalty: A fine not exceeding K100.00 or imprisonment for a term not exceeding one year.

(3) Any stamps, and any other things that are found in the possession of a person convicted of an offence against this section are forfeited to the State.

"Have in possession" is defined by s 1 of the Code.

Subdivision E – Personation

488. Personation in general.

(1) A person who, with intent to defraud any person, falsely represents himself to be some other person, living or dead, is guilty of an offence that, unless otherwise stated, is a misdemeanour.

Penalty: Imprisonment for a term not exceeding three years.

(2) If the representation referred to in Subsection (1) is that the offender is a person entitled by will or operation of law to any specific property, and he commits the offence with intent to obtain that property or possession of it, the offence is a crime, and the offender is liable to imprisonment for a term not exceeding 14 years.

See ss 97 and 99 of the Code regarding particular offences involving personation.

See ss 403-409 regarding obtaining property by false pretences.

489. Falsely acknowledging deeds, recognizances, etc.

A person who, without lawful authority or excuse (proof of which is on him), makes, in the name of any other person, before any court or person lawfully authorized to take such an acknowledgment, an acknowledgment of liability of any kind, or an acknowledgment of a deed or other instrument, is guilty of a crime.

Penalty: Imprisonment for a term not exceeding seven years.

490. Personation of a person named in certificate.

A person who utters any document that has been issued by lawful authority to another person, and by which that other person is certified -

- (a) to be a person possessed of any qualifications recognized by law for any purpose; or
- (b) to be the holder of any office; or
- (c) to be entitled to exercise any profession, trade or business; or
- (d) to be entitled to any right or privilege, or to enjoy any rank or status,

and falsely represents himself to be the person named in the document, is guilty of an offence of the same kind, and is liable to the same punishment as if he had forged the document.

See s 488 of the Code regarding personation generally.

"Utter" is defined by s 1.

See s 459 regarding the term "document".

See s 476 regarding attempts to procure unauthorised status.

491. Lending certificates for personation.

A person who, being a person to whom any document has been issued by lawful authority, by which he is certified -

(a) to be a person possessed of any qualification recognized by law for any purpose; or

(b) to be the holder of any office; or

(c) to be entitled to exercise any profession, trade or business; or

(d) to be entitled to any right or privilege, or to enjoy any rank or status,

lends the document to another person with intent that that other person may represent himself to be the person named in it, is guilty of a misdemeanour.

Penalty: Imprisonment for a term not exceeding three years.

Division 4 – Offences Connected with Trade and Breach of Contract

Subdivision A – Fraudulent Debtors

492. Interpretation of Subdivision A.

(1) In this subdivision, "an insolvent" means a person with respect to whom any proceedings have been taken under the provisions of the laws relating to insolvent debtors that result in his affairs being administered under the provisions of those laws for the benefit of his creditors.

(2) For the purposes of this subdivision, a person is deemed to have been an insolvent from the time when the proceedings were taken, whether or not the result had happened when the unlawful act in question was done.

493. Absconding with property in contemplation of or immediately after insolvency.

(1) Subject to Subsection (2), a person who -

(a) being an insolvent -

(i) departs from the country and takes with him; or

(ii) attempts or prepares to depart from the country and to take with him,

any part of his property, to the amount of K40.00 that ought by law to be divided amongst his creditors; or

(b) departs from the country and takes with him, or attempts or prepares to depart from the country and to take with him, any part of his property to the amount of K40.00 that ought by law, in the event of his becoming insolvent, to be divided among his creditors, and within four months afterwards becomes an insolvent,

is guilty of a crime.

Penalty: Imprisonment for a term not exceeding three years.

(2) It is a defence to a charge of an offence against Subsection (1) to prove that the accused person had no intent to defraud.

494. Frauds by insolvents.

A person who -

(a) being an insolvent -

(i) fraudulently removes any part of his property to the value of K20.00; or

(ii) fraudulently parts with, alters or makes any omission in or is privy to fraudulently parting with, altering or making an omission in any document affecting or relating to his property or affairs; or

(b) does any act referred to in Paragraph (a), and within four months afterwards becomes an insolvent; or

(c) being an insolvent, attempts to account for any part of his property by alleging fictitious losses or expenses; or

(d) attempts at a meeting of his creditors to account for any part of his property by fictitious losses or expenses, and within four months afterwards becomes an insolvent; or

(e) by any false representation or other fraud obtains any property on credit and does not pay for it, and within four months afterwards becomes an insolvent,

is guilty of a misdemeanour.

Penalty: Imprisonment for a term not exceeding three years.

495. Other frauds by insolvents.

(1) Subject to Subsection (2), a person who -

(a) being an insolvent -

(i) conceals any part of his property to the amount of K20.00; or

(ii) conceals any debt due to or from him; or

(b) does any of the following acts -

(i) conceals any part of his property to the amount of K20.00; or

(ii) conceals any debt due to or from him; or

(iii) obtains any property on credit under the false pretence of carrying on business and dealing in the ordinary way of trade, and does not pay for the same; or

(iv) pawns, pledges or disposes of otherwise than in the ordinary way of trade, any property that he has obtained on credit and has not paid for,

and within four months afterwards becomes an insolvent,

is guilty of a misdemeanour.

Penalty: Imprisonment for a term not exceeding three years.

(2) It is a defence to a charge of an offence against Subsection (1) to prove that the accused person had no intent to defraud.

496. Falsification of books by insolvents.

(1) Subject to Subsection (2), a person who -

(a) being an insolvent -

(i) conceals, destroys, alters, mutilates or falsifies any book, document, valuable security, or account relating to his property or affairs, or any entry in any such book, document or account, or is privy to any such act; or

(ii) makes or is privy to the making of any false entry in any such book, document or account; or

(b) does or is privy to any act referred to in Paragraph (a), and within four months afterwards becomes an insolvent,

is guilty of a misdemeanour.

Penalty: Imprisonment for a term not exceeding three years.

(2) It is a defence to a charge of an offence against Subsection (1) to prove that the accused person had no intent to conceal the state of his affairs or to defraud.

See s 418 of the Code regarding fraudulent false accounting, and s 506 regarding falsification of books of companies.

"Document" is defined by s 459 and "valuable security" is defined by s 1.

497. Frauds by insolvents in course of insolvency proceedings.

A person whose affairs are in course of administration under the provisions of the laws relating to insolvent debtors who -

(a) knowing or believing that a false debt has been proved by any person in the course of the administration, fails for the period of one month to give information of it to the trustee of his property, or

(b) makes any false representation or commits any other fraud for the purpose of obtaining the consent of his creditors or any of them to any agreement with reference to his affairs or to any proceedings taken under or by the virtue of the administration,

is guilty of a misdemeanour.

Penalty: Imprisonment for a term not exceeding three years.

498. Failure by insolvents to discover property.

(1) Subject to Subsection (2), a person whose affairs are in course of administration under the provisions of the laws relating to insolvent debtors who -

(a) fails to fully and truly discover to the trustee of his property, to the best of his knowledge and belief, all his property, and how, and to whom, and for what consideration, and when, he disposed of every part of it, except such part as has been disposed of in the ordinary way of his trade (if any) or laid out in the ordinary expense of his family; or

(b) fails to deliver to the trustee, or as he directs, any part of his property that -

(i) is in his custody or under his control; and

(ii) he is required by law to deliver; or

(c) fails to deliver to the trustee, or as he directs, any book, document, paper or writing that -

(i) is in his custody or under his control; and

(ii) relates to his property or affairs, or

(d) omits or is privy to omitting a material particular from a statement relating to his affairs,

is guilty of a misdemeanour.

Penalty: Imprisonment for a term not exceeding three years.

(2) It is a defence to a charge of an offence against Subsection (1) to prove that the accused person had no intent to conceal the state of his affairs or to defraud.

499. Failure to keep proper books.

(1) Subject to Subsection (2), a person who -

(a) omits to keep proper books of account showing the true state of his affairs; and

(b) within three years afterwards becomes an insolvent,

is guilty of a misdemeanour.

Penalty: Imprisonment for a term not exceeding three years.

(2) It is a defence to a charge of an offence against Subsection (1) to prove that the accused person had no intention to conceal the state of his affairs or to defraud.

500. Concealing documents.

(1) Subject to Subsection (2), an insolvent who prevents the production of a book, document, paper or writing affecting or relating to his property or affairs is guilty of a misdemeanour.

Penalty: Imprisonment for a term not exceeding three years.

(2) It is a defence to a charge of an offence against Subsection (1) to prove that the accused person had no intent to conceal the state of his affairs or to defraud.

501. Receiving insolvent's property with intent to defraud.

A person who, with intent to defraud the creditors of an insolvent -

(a) receives any property from the insolvent; or

(b) fails to deliver to the trustee of the property of the insolvent any property that forms part of the estate of the insolvent,

is guilty of a misdemeanour.

Penalty: Imprisonment for a term not exceeding three years.

502. Making false claim in insolvency.

A person who -

(a) being a creditor of an insolvent, or being a creditor of a debtor who has taken proceedings for a composition with his creditors under the provisions of the laws relating to insolvent debtors, makes in the insolvency, or in the proceedings for a composition, with intent to defraud, a proof of declaration of debt or statement of account that is to his knowledge false in a material particular; or

(b) not being a creditor of an insolvent or of a debtor who has taken proceedings referred to in Paragraph (a) makes in the insolvency, or in the proceedings for a composition, with intent to defraud, a proof or declaration of debt,

is guilty of a misdemeanour.

Penalty: Imprisonment for a term not exceeding one year.

503. Concealing property of insolvents.

A person who conceals any part of the property of an insolvent, and does not, within 42 days after the appointment of a trustee of the property of the insolvent, discover such property to -

(a) the trustee; or

(b) the Registrar of the National Court,

is guilty of an offence.

Penalty: Imprisonment for a term not exceeding six months.

504. Fraudulent dealing with property by debts.

A person who, with intent to defraud his creditors or any of them -

(a) makes a gift, delivery or transfer of his property, or a charge on his property; or

(b) conceals or removes any part of his property after or within two months before the date of any unsatisfied judgment or order for payment of money obtained against him,

is guilty of a misdemeanour.

Penalty: Imprisonment for a term not exceeding one year.

Subdivision B – Other Offences

505. Concealment by officers of companies on reduction of capital.

A person who, being a director or officer of a joint stock company, the capital of which is proposed to be reduced-

(a) conceals the name of a creditor of the company who is entitled to object to the proposed reduction; or

(b) knowingly misrepresents the nature or amount of the debt or claim of a creditor of the company; or

(c) is privy to any such concealment or misrepresentation,

is guilty of a misdemeanour.

Penalty: Imprisonment for a term not exceeding three years.

506. Falsification of books of companies.

A director, officer or contributory of a company that is in course of being wound up under the provisions of the laws relating to joint-stock companies who, with intent to deceive or defraud, or to make another person deceive or defraud -

(a) conceals, destroys, alters, mutilates or falsifies -

(i) a book, document, valuable security or account relating to the affairs of the company; or

(ii) an entry in any such book, document or account,

or is privy to any such act; or

(b) makes or is privy to making any false entry in any book, document or account, belonging to the company,

is guilty of a misdemeanour.

Penalty: Imprisonment for a term not exceeding two years.

See s 418 of the Code regarding fraudulent accounting, and s 496 regarding falsification of books by insolvents.

"Company" is defined by s 1.

507. Mixing uncertified with certified articles.

Where under a law -

(a) a mark has been attached to an article; or

(b) a certificate has been given with respect to an article,

for the purpose of denoting -

(c) the quality of the article; or

(d) the fact that it has been examined or approved by or under the authority of some public body or public officer,

a person who mixes with the article any other article that has not been so examined or approved is guilty of a misdemeanour.

Penalty: Imprisonment for a term not exceeding three years.

508. Intimidation of workmen and employers.

(1) In this section, "industrial dispute" means an industrial dispute within the meaning of the *Industrial Organizations Act*.

(2) Subject to Section 518, where by -

(a) violence to the person or property of another, or by threats or intimidation of any kind; or

(b) besetting the house or place of work of another; or

(c) following another in a disorderly manner in a public highway; or

(d) molesting, or in any way obstructing, another by any physical act in the pursuit of his lawful vocation,

a person -

(e) compels or attempts to compel any person employed in any manufacture, trade, business, or occupation-

(i) to depart from his employment; or

(ii) to return his work before it is finished; or

(f) prevents any person who is not employed from accepting employment from any other person,

he is guilty of an offence.

Penalty: Imprisonment for a term not exceeding three months.

(3) Subject to Section 518, a person who uses violence to the person or property of another, or uses threats or intimidation of any kind to another, or by any physical act molests or in any way obstructs another -

(a) for the purpose of inducing a person -

(i) to belong to a club or association; or

(ii) to contribute to a common fund; or

(iii) to pay a fine or penalty; or

(b) on account of a person -

(i) not belonging to any particular club or association; or

(ii) not having contributed or having refused to contribute to a common fund; or

(iii) having refused to pay a fine or penalty; or

(c) on account of a person not having complied, or refusing to comply, with any rules, orders, resolutions or regulations made or pretended to be made by any person, club or association, in order to obtain -

(i) an advance of wages or to reduce the rate of wages in; or

(ii) to lessen or alter the hours of working in; or

(iii) to decrease or alter the quantity of work done in; or

(iv) to regulate the mode of carrying on,

any manufacture, trade or business or the management of any manufacture, trade or business,

is guilty of an offence.

Penalty: Imprisonment for a term not exceeding three months.

(4) Subject to Section 518, a person who by -

(a) violence to the person or property of another; or

(b) threats or intimidation of any kind; or

(c) molesting or in any way obstructing another,

compels, or endeavours to compel, any person carrying on any manufacture, trade or business -

(d) to make an alteration in his mode of carrying it on; or

(e) to limit -

(i) the number of his apprentices; or

(ii) the number or description of his journeymen, workmen or servants,

is guilty of an offence.

Penalty: Imprisonment for a term not exceeding three months.

(5) It is lawful for any person or persons acting in contemplation of, or during the continuance of, an industrial dispute to attend peaceably and in a reasonable manner at or near a place (other than a private residence, unless the consent of the owner is first obtained) where a person resides, works, carries on business or happens to be, if he or they so attend merely for the purpose -

(a) of obtaining or communicating information; or

(b) of peacefully persuading a person to work or refrain from working,

and such an attending shall not be deemed to be a besetting within the meaning of this section.

(6) Notification or warning of an intention -

(a) to lock-out or strike; or

(b) on the part of any workman or workmen to refuse to enter into or continue in the employment of any employer,

shall not be deemed a threat or intimidation or molestation or obstruction within the meaning of this section.

(7) A person cannot refuse to give evidence on a charge of an offence against this section on the ground that he is liable to punishment under this section, but every person who gives evidence on any such charge is indemnified against any prosecution against himself for having offended in the matter with respect to which he gives evidence.

(8) The action of persons who -

(a) merely agree together to fix -

(i) the rate of wages or prices that they will pay or accept for any work or article; or

(ii) the hours during which they will work in, or carry on, any manufacture, trade or business, in which they are engaged; or

(b) merely meet together and consult for the purpose of making any such agreement,

shall not be deemed to be a physical act for the purposes of this section.

See s 518 of the Code regarding industrial disputes.

Part VII – Preparation to Commit Offences: Conspiracy: Accessories after the Fact

Division 1 – Attempts and Preparation to Commit Offences

509. Attempts to commit offences

(1) A person who attempts to commit an indictable offence is guilty of an indictable offence, that, unless otherwise stated, is a misdemeanour.

(2) When a person who commits an indictable offence is punishable on summary conviction, a person who attempts to commit such an offence may also be summarily convicted.

See s 4 of the Code regarding the definition of "attempts"

510. Punishment of attempts to commit crimes.

(1) A person who attempts to commit a crime of such kind that a person convicted of it is liable to the punishment of death or imprisonment for life or for a term of 14 years or more, with or without any other punishment, is liable, if no other punishment is provided, to imprisonment for seven years.

(2) A person who attempts to commit a crime of any other kind, is liable, if no other punishment is provided, to a punishment equal to one-half of the greatest punishment to which an offender convicted of the crime that he attempted to commit is liable.

[S 510 subst Act No 10, 1983 (*Criminal Code (Minimum Penalties) (Amendment) Act* 1983), s 4; subst Act No 17, 1986 (*Criminal Code (Amendment No 2) Act* 1986), s 34]

See s 4 of the Code regarding attempts generally.

An example of a case where the same punishment is provided for the attempt as for the completed offence is defilement of girls under 16: see s 216.

511. Punishment of attempts to commit misdemeanours.

A person who attempts to commit a misdemeanour, is liable, if no other punishment is provided, to a punishment equal to one-half of the greatest punishment to which an offender convicted of the offence that he attempted to commit is liable.

[S 511 subst Act No 10, 1983 (*Criminal Code (Minimum Penalties) (Amendment) Act* 1983) s 25; subst Act No 17, 1986 (*Criminal Code (Amendment No 2) Act* 1986), s 35]

See s 4 of the Code regarding attempts generally.

512. Reduction of punishment.

(1) Where a person is convicted of attempting to commit an offence, and it is proved that he desisted of his own motion from the further prosecution of his intention, without its fulfilment being prevented by circumstances independent of his will, he is liable to one-half of the punishment to which he would otherwise be liable.

(2) If the punishment referred to in subsection (1) is imprisonment for life, the greatest punishment to which he is liable is imprisonment for seven years.

[S 512 subst Act No 10, 1983 (*Criminal Code (Minimum Penalties) (Amendment) Act* 1983), s 26; subst Act No 17, 1986 (*Criminal Code (Amendment No 2) Act* 1986), s 36]

See s 4 of the Code regarding attempts generally.

513. Attempts to procure commission of criminal acts.

(1) Subject to Subsection (2), a person who attempts to procure another to do any act or make any omission, whether in Papua New Guinea or elsewhere, of such a nature that, if the act were done or the omission were made in Papua New Guinea an offence would be committed under the laws of Papua New Guinea, or the laws in force in the place where the act or omission is proposed to be done or made, whether by himself or by that other person, is guilty of an offence of the same kind and is liable to the same punishment as if he had himself attempted to do the same act or make the same omission in Papua New Guinea.

(2) Subject to Subsection (3), if the act or omission referred to in Subsection (1) is proposed to be done or made at a place not in Papua New Guinea, the punishment cannot exceed that which he would have incurred under the laws in force where the act or omission was proposed to be done or made, if he had himself attempted to do the proposed act or make the proposed omission.

(3) In a case referred to in Subsection (2), a prosecution shall not be instituted except at the request of the Government of the State having jurisdiction in the place where the act or omission was proposed to be done or made.

As to s 513(3), see ss 176 and 177 of the *Constitution* regarding the functions of the Public Prosecutor.

See s 4 of the Code regarding attempts, and s 7 regarding complicity.

514. Preparation to commit crimes with explosives, etc.

A person who makes or knowingly has in his possession any explosive substance, or any dangerous or noxious engine, instrument or thing -

(a) with intent; or

(b) for the purpose of enabling any other person,

to commit a crime by means of it, is guilty of a crime.

Penalty: Imprisonment for a term not exceeding three years.

"Have in possession" and "explosive substance" are defined by s 1 of the Code.

Division 2 – Conspiracy

515. Conspiracy to commit crimes.

A person who conspires with another to commit a crime or to do any act in any part of the world that -

(a) if done in Papua New Guinea would be a crime; and

(b) is an offence under the laws in force in the place where it is proposed to be done,

is guilty of a crime.

Penalty: If no other penalty is provided -

(a) imprisonment for a term not exceeding seven years; or

(b) if the maximum penalty for the crime in question does not exceed imprisonment for a term of seven years – not exceeding that penalty.

See ss 7-9 of the Code regarding parties to an offence.

See Noone, "*Preliminary Crimes: The Reform of Attempt and Conspiracy in Papua New Guinea*" (1973) 2(1) MLJ 66-90.

516. Conspiracy to commit other offences.

A person who conspires with another -

(a) to commit an offence that is not a crime; or

(b) to do an act in any part of the world that if done in Papua New Guinea would be an offence that is not a crime, and that is an offence under the laws in force in the place where it is proposed to be done,

is guilty of a misdemeanour.

Penalty: Imprisonment for a term not exceeding three years.

517. Other conspiracies.

Subject to Section 518, a person who conspires with another -

(a) to prevent or defeat the execution or enforcement of any law; or

(b) to cause any injury to the person or reputation of a person; or

(c) to depreciate the value of any property of a person; or

(d) to prevent or obstruct the free and lawful disposition of any property by its owner for its fair value; or

(e) to injure a person in his trade or profession; or

(f) to prevent or obstruct, by means of any act or acts that if done by an individual person would constitute an offence on his part, the free and lawful exercise by any person of his trade, profession or occupation; or

(g) to effect any unlawful purpose; or

(h) to effect any lawful purpose by any unlawful means,

is guilty of a misdemeanour.

Penalty: Imprisonment for a term not exceeding three years.

See *The State v Tanedo* [1975] PNGLR 395.

518. Industrial disputes.

(1) In this section, "industrial dispute" means an industrial dispute within the meaning of the *Industrial Organizations Act*.

(2) Notwithstanding Section 508 or 517 -

(a) an act done or omission made by any two or more persons in contemplation or furtherance of any industrial dispute; and

(b) an agreement or combination by any two or more persons -

(i) to do any act or make any omission; or

(ii) to procure any act to be done or omission to be made,

in contemplation or furtherance of any industrial dispute,

does not make them guilty of any offence if the act or omission if done or made by an individual person would not have made him guilty of an offence.

See s 508 of the Code.

For a comment on this provision, see Seddon, "*Legal Problems Facing Trade Unions in Papua New Guinea*" (1975) Vol 3(1) MLJ 103.

Division 3 – Accessories After the Fact

519. Accessories after the fact to crimes.

A person who becomes an accessory after the fact to a crime is guilty of a crime.

Penalty: If no other punishment is provided, imprisonment for a term not exceeding two years.

See s 305 of the Code regarding accessories after the fact to murder.

See s 10 regarding the definition of "accessory after the fact".

See *R v Angie-Ogun* [1969-1970] PNGLR 36.

See ss 7-9 regarding parties to offences.

In *The State v Roy Nana* [1986] PNGLR 83 the court held that:

(a) the Code provides an exclusive definition for "accessory after the fact" for the purposes of s 519; and

(b) for the purposes of being charged as an accessory after the fact, an accused must do some act in order to enable the principal offender to escape detection and punishment.

In that case, McDermott J stated (at 87):

> "I have come to the view that s 10 provides an exclusive definition. It is a simple definition of the pre-existing legal concept of 'accessory after the fact' ... What the accused were doing in this case was going around trying to find buyers for the stolen goods. They could not be found guilty of being accessory after the

fact, if this activity was for their own gain and unrelated to giving assistance to the principal to avoid apprehension. There has to be such a connection before one can be considered an accessory."

See references under s 519 of the Code.

Part VIII – Procedure

Division 1 – Place of Trial

521. Interpretation of Division 1.

(1) In this Division, "place of trial" means the place appointed under the *National Court Act* for sittings of the National Court at which the hearing of a charge of an indictable offence is to take place.

522. Place of trial.

(1) Subject to this section, the place of trial shall be -

(a) when the person awaiting trial has been committed for trial or sentence -

(i) the place to which he has been committed for trial or sentence; or

(ii) if no place has been specified – the place appointed under the *National Court Act* for sittings of the National Court nearest to the place at which the person charged was committed for trial or sentence; or

(b) when the person awaiting trial has not been committed for trial or sentence – the place at which the indictment against him was presented.

(2) In relation to any pending matter in which the trial has not yet commenced, the National Court or a Judge may -

(a) on the application of a State Prosecutor or a person awaiting trial or his counsel; and

(b) on good cause being shown,

order that the place of trial be changed to some other place appointed under the *National Court Act* for sittings of the National Court.

(3) This section does not affect the power of the court before which a trial has commenced to adjourn the trial to a different place.

See ss 37(3), 37(4), 37(14) and 42(3) of the *Constitution*.

In *The Matter of an Application for an Order of Transfer of Place of Trial:The State v Theo Yandalan, Japeth Kapalin and Leo Morris* [1994] PNGLR 405, an application was made by the prosecution for the transfer of a trial for wilful murder due to the fear held by the eye witnesses for their safety if they testified and the threats of the accuseds' line made to the people concerned with the investigation. The court ordered that a change of venue take place as the applicants had shown good cause. Further, the court was satisfied that the accuseds' opportunity to test the state case and present evidence on their own account would not be adversely affected by the transfer.

523. Recognizance when place of trial changed.

(1) When an order is made changing the place of trial -

(a) the recognizance of bail of any person awaiting trial; and

(b) the recognizance of any person bound to attend as a witness or otherwise,

applies in respect of the sittings of the court at the new time and place of trial.

(2) A person bound by a recognizance enlarged by virtue of Subsection (1) is not liable to have his recognizance forfeited or be otherwise dealt with for failure to appear unless he has been given notice of the new time and place of trial.

See the *Bail Act*.

Division 2 – Indictments

Apart from the provisions in the Code itself, there are two other Acts which are relevant to the position, powers and functions of the Public Prosecutor. One is s 176 of the *Constitution*, which set up the office of the Public Prosecutor and, inter alia, established that in the performance of his or her functions, the Public Prosecutor will not be subject to direction or control by any person or authority. Because he or she is not subject to the usual checks and balances which would normally apply to an Attorney-General under the common law concerning the filing of "ex officio" indictments and the entry of a nolle prosequi, one must look very closely at the legislation which governs the powers and responsibilities of the Public Prosecutor. Indeed, the Public Prosecutor has almost complete freedom from the normal restraints and checks which would apply to any Attorney-General in the performance of that high office. Consistent with the protection the Public Prosecutor must be given under the *Constitution*, he or she is also much harder to remove from office. Under s 178 of the *Constitution*, the Public Prosecutor may be removed only for inability, misbehaviour, or misconduct in office under the *Leadership Code*. The only other Act which appears to affect the functions of the Public Prosecutor is the *Public Prosecutor (Office and Function) Act* 1977, which is complimentary to that part of the *Constitution* which states that the Public Prosecutor is "to control the exercise and performance of the prosecution function" within the State of Papua New Guinea: *Arthur Gilbert Smedley v The State* [1980] PNGLR 379 at 403-404 (Pratt J).

The provisions of this Division apply to complaints in the Local and District Courts: *Mames-Weviong v Zania* [1967-1968] PNGLR 79.

See s 537 of the Code regarding summary convictions.

See s 616 regarding information by leave of the court in the case of private prosecutors.

See Griffin, *Criminal Procedure in Papua New Guinea* (1977), Ch 10 on indictments generally.

524. Procedure: Preliminary.

(1) No indictment may be presented in the National Court except in accordance with Sections 525 and 526.

(2) The Head of State, acting on advice, may appoint lawyers to be State Prosecutors.

(3) The Public Prosecutor is, ex officio, a State Prosecutor.

Indictments presented after Independence are entitled in the name of "The State": *The State v John Mogo Wonom of Jigi* [1975] PNGLR 311. See Chalmers, "*The Position of Head of The State in an Independent Papua New Guinea*" (1978) 27 ICLQ 672.

The procedure to be followed where a coroner's inquisition charges a person with the offence of wilful murder or manslaughter, is for the coroner to forthwith transmit the inquisition, depositions, statement (if any) and recognisance, with a certificate under the coroner's hand that they have been taken before him or her, to the Registrar of the National Court: *R v Wendo* [1963] PNGLR 217 at 220. See *Coroners Act*.

See Raine J's remarks on this section in *R v Boxtell* (1972) N703.

See ss 176-177 of the *Constitution* regarding the office of the Public Prosecutor.

525. Procedure for indictment.

(1) Where a person is committed for trial or sentence for an indictable offence, the Public Prosecutor or a State Prosecutor shall consider the evidence in the matter and may -

(a) reduce into writing in an indictment a charge of any offence that the evidence appears to him to warrant; or

(b) decline to lay a charge.

(2) An indictment may be presented to the National Court by the Public Prosecutor or any State Prosecutor.

(3) Where the Public Prosecutor or a State Prosecutor declines to lay a charge, he shall, as soon as practicable -

(a) sign a declaration in duplicate to that effect; and

(b) cause the original of the declaration to be filed in the National Court; and

(c) deliver the duplicate of the declaration to the person committed -

(i) if the person is in custody – by sending it by post or messenger to the person having custody of him; or

(ii) if the person is not in custody – by delivering it to him personally or by sending it to him by post to his last-known address.

(4) On receipt of a copy of a declaration under Subsection (3), any person having custody of the person named in it shall immediately release him from custody in relation to the charge to which the declaration relates.

(5) This section does not apply to a committal for sentence under Section 421(4).

[Subs (5) insrt Act No 12, 1982 (*Criminal Code (Amendment) Act* 1982), s 8; rep Act No 29, 1983 (*Criminal Code (Amendment) Act* 1983), s 10; insrt Act No 17, 1986 (*Criminal Code (Amendment No 2) Act* 1986), s 37]

This section is now quite different from the old s 561 of the *Queensland Criminal Code (Adopted)* dealing with "Ex officio informations", and a completely new section, s 526, has been introduced into the 1974 Code: *Arthur Gilbert Smedley v The State* [1980] PNGLR 379.

This section has its roots in the old *Criminal Procedure Acts* of Papua and New Guinea, ss 12 and 3 respectively. Inherent conflicts existed between the provisions of the *Criminal Procedure Acts* and s 561 of the *Queensland Criminal Code (Adopted)*. After *R v Ebulya* [1964] PNGLR 200, the practice developed throughout the country in favour of the view which supported old s 561 of the Code as paramount: *Arthur Gilbert Smedley v The State* [1980] PNGLR 379 (Pratt J).

Historically, the grand jury in England served to ensure that no person could be held for trial unless there was evidence of guilt. Even after the passage of the *Summary Jurisdiction Act* 1848 and *Indictable Offences Act* 1848, which provided for pre-trial examination by Justices of the Peace, the grand jury system was retained as a double safeguard. In Australia, the Attorney-General was given a duty analogous to or replacing that which, under the common law, was performed by a grand jury. The system has the advantage of entrusting the question to a most eminent lawyer, rather than to a panel of laymen. In Papua New Guinea, this power is now in the hands of the Secretary for Justice or a Public Prosecutor: *R v Kapon Top* (1975) N831.

Pratt J stated, in *Arthur Gilbert Smedley v The State* [1980] PNGLR 379 at 407-408:

> "There are only two main forms of indictment, a s 525 indictment and a s 526 indictment. The first is an indictment following on committal proceedings be it for the same charge as that for which the accused was committed, or a completely different charge. Once having decided to reduce the charge to writing, and then in fact having presented the indictment to the court, that is an end to the matter. There is nothing in s 524 which says that having presented the indictment and then subsequently under s 527 presented or filed a nolle prosequi, he may go back to s 525 and draft and present another indictment. Likewise, in the instant case under appeal where the magistrate has refused to commit, the prosecutor has power under s 526 to present an indictment despite the magistrate's refusal to commit, but again having done that, there is nothing in the section which allows him to present a further indictment. That this should be so is really not surprising when a proper historical perspective is adopted. I would expect to find any such suggested power specified in the clearest terms, and not something to be twisted out of the section by reliance on court interpretation, assisted by a clearly misconceived matter of practice over the past few years. Although the positions of Attorney-General and Public Prosecutor are somewhat similar in part, the analogy is one which must be treated with care. Professionally and ethically they are similar but not when it comes to the powers vested in each."

The phrase "[t]he indictment may be presented to" in s 525(2) and s 526 implies a presentation in open court but without a plea being called for: see, for example *R v Topulumar* [1971-1972] PNGLR 320 at 322. Previously, in order for an indictment to be in fact an indictment, it appears that it had to be physically presented in open court. Thus, the prosecutor must reduce the charge to writing (ss 525(1) and 526(1)) and must present such indictment to the National Court (ss 525(2) and 526(2)): *Arthur Gilbert Smedley v The State* [1980] PNGLR 379 at 404-405 (Pratt J).

Section 525 in its proper construction permits only an indictment for an offence for which the accused has been committed, as the words "the offence" occurring in the section should be read as referring to the offence for which the accused has been committed for trial: *R v Angoro Evu* [1969-1970] PNGLR 274.

In *The State v Jack Gola and Mopana Aure* [1990] PNGLR 206, Brunton J stated:

> "The power of the Public Prosecutor and the State Prosecutors deriving from the *Constitution*, s 176 and s 177, the *Public Prosecutor (Office and Functions) Act* (Ch 338), s 4(1) and the Code, ss 524, 525 and 526, to lay indictments is an absolute one; it is for the Prosecutor to choose the charge and to decide what plea will be accepted: the role of the judge is to offer observations on the course of action preposed in the light of which the Prosecutor may reconsider his position."

Brunton J further stated (at 214-215):

> "The essence of the system of law that has developed from English and Australian antecedents, in Papua New Guinea, is that the system of justice must be open, above board, and capable of respect by the public. While the *Constitution* and the statutes vest in the Public Prosecutor the discretion to choose the charge on which to lay an indictment, the exercise of that discretion must be such as to appear to conform with the expectations of society. It may well be that in some cases the State Prosecutors feel that the evidence and witnesses may not be sufficient to obtain a conviction on a trial, and that it is better to accept a plea to a lesser charge, rather than end up with an acquittal. But this has to be balanced against the need to maintain public confidence in the system as a whole. Certainly the appearance of having decisions made out of court between opposing counsel as to what charge is to be preferred, and what charge is to be pleaded to, should be avoided. A proper view may be to present the case to the court on a more serious charge for which there is proper evidence to go to the tribunal of fact, and to let the court decide. If the evidence is there, and if it is proper in the sense of coming from witnesses of truth, then it is for the tribunal of fact to adjudicate upon, rather than for counsel to determine in private discussions."

See also on this point *R v Toigen Tiolo* [1969-1970] PNGLR 285.

An indictment is not formally defective because it is handwritten: *R v Ongasi Wosis* [1971-1972] PNGLR 476.

Technical breach is a good reason not to prosecute. However, the most that a trial judge can do in the absence of some provision such as s 20 of the *Local Courts Act* 1963 or s 657A of the *Queensland Criminal Code* is to apply s 19(1)(f) of the Papua New Guinea Code. Unfortunately, that leaves the accused with the stain of a conviction for, what was on the facts, an offence of a trivial nature: *Supreme Court Reference No 2 of 1981; Re s 19(1)(f) Criminal Code (Ch 262)* [1982] PNGLR 150 at 159 (Kearney DCJ).

526. Indictment without committal.

(1) Where a court of summary jurisdiction has refused to commit a person for trial for an indictable offence, the Public Prosecutor may -

- (a) consider the evidence contained in the depositions taken before the court (and any other relevant evidence); and
- (b) reduce into writing in an indictment a charge of any offence that the evidence appears to warrant.

(2) The indictment may be presented to the National Court by the Public Prosecutor or a State Prosecutor.

(3) Where the Public Prosecutor reduces a charge to writing in an indictment under Subsection (1), he shall cause to be served on the accused person or his lawyer -

(a) copies of the depositions taken at the committal proceedings; and

(b) copies of statements taken from witnesses whom the prosecution intends to call at the trial

within such time before the commencement of the trial as is reasonable in order to allow the accused person to prepare his defence.

See *The State v Peter Painke (No 2)* [1977] PNGLR 141, annotated under s 527.

This section was the major reform in the 1974 Code, enshrining in law the important principle that no person should be brought to trial unless there have first been committal proceedings. It substantially reduced the former power of the Public Prosecutor to indict, as the Public Prosecutor can no longer by-pass the committal process and take a case directly to court. It is thus a power subject to the legislative power of the Parliament, under the *Constitution*, and also subject to control by the court. As the courts have made clear – see, for example *The State v Peter Painke No 2* [1977] PNGLR 141 – they will protect the rights of the accused from abuse: *Arthur Gilbert Smedley v The State* [1980] PNGLR 379 (Kearney DCJ, dissenting).

The presentation of an "ex officio" indictment is an exercise in great power. That it has always been regarded as such is amply demonstrated by even a short survey of the historical development of criminal procedure under the common law: see Edwards, *The Law Officers of the Crown* (1964), Ch 13. The circumstances under the common law where the ex officio information developed were quite different from the circumstances existing in Papua New Guinea before 1974, and certainly so after Independence in 1975: *Arthur Gilbert Smedley v The State* [1980] PNGLR 379 (Pratt J).

Kearney DCJ and Pratt J said, in *Arthur Gilbert Smedley v The State* [1980] PNGLR 379 at 382 and 407, that the term "ex officio" indictment has no meaning in Papua New Guinea and should completely disappear from the language here. The power to indict is purely statutory, and does not inhere in the office in any way.

Pratt J said, in the same case (at 407-408):

> "There are only two main forms of indictment, a s 525 indictment and a s 526 indictment. The first is an indictment following on committal proceedings be it for the same charges as that for which the accused was committed, or a completely different charge. Once having decided to reduce the charge to writing, and then in fact having presented the indictment to the court, that is an end to the matter. There is nothing in s 524 which says that having presented the indictment and then subsequently under s 527 presented or filed a nolle prosequi, he may go back to s 525 and draft and present another indictment. Likewise, in the instant case under appeal where the magistrate has refused to commit, the prosecutor has power under s 526 to present an indictment despite the magistrate's refusal to commit, but again having done that, there is nothing in the section which allows him to present a further indictment. That this should be so is really not surprising when a proper historical perspective is adopted. I would expect to find any such suggested power specified in the clearest terms, and not something to be twisted out of the section by reliance on court interpretation, assisted by a clearly

misconceived matter of practice over the past few years. Although the positions of Attorney-General and Public Prosecutor are somewhat similar in part, the analogy is one which must be treated with care. Professionally and ethically, they are similar but not when it comes to the powers vested in each."

Wilson J also stated, in *Arthur Gilbert Smedley v The State* [1980] PNGLR 379:

"The State can, as of right, present one indictment (and one indictment only) as a result of one committal. This section does not permit a plurality of indictments. This conclusion is arrived at having regard to the intention of the legislature as appears from a reading of ss 524(1) and 526, and the decision of the Court of Appeal in England in *R v Thompson, R v Cleim* [1975] 2 All ER 1028, in which it recognised that principle in circumstances in which the applicable statutory enactments were analogous to those in force in Papua New Guinea. In this country, the Code (s 535) provides for amendment of indictments. If a first indictment is quashed or if, by virtue of the entering of a nolle prosequi, the person named therein is discharged from any further proceedings on the indictment to which it relates or if a first indictment otherwise fails in toto, the Code (s 616) provides for the presentment 'by any person' (including the Public Prosecutor himself) of a subsequent indictment or information by leave of the National Court. Therein lies the remedy for the State if it is decided to pursue the prosecution further. Therein also lies the right of any private person to seek leave to institute criminal proceedings against any other person. The interest of the State in bringing an accused to trial is amply safeguarded."

In *R v Tovarula* [1973] PNGLR 140 it was said:

"There is considerable difference in wording between this section and the old Code equivalent of s 561. In *R v Tovarula* [1973] PNGLR 140, s 561 was held to allow the presentation of an ex officio indictment against a person committed for trial and previously indicted where a nolle prosequi had been entered against that previous indictment. This section is considerably narrower and apparently applies only to situations of refusal to commit by a District Court Magistrate. Query, whether this section now excludes the two traditional uses of ex officio indictments, namely where different charges arise from a reading of the depositions taken at the committal and where a man consents to plead guilty to a charge in respect of which no committal has taken place."

Jalina J stated, in *The State v Esorom Burege (No 1)* [1992] PNGLR 481 at 485:

"Unlike s 525(1), where the Public Prosecutor or a State Prosecutor may consider the evidence in a matter and may reduce to writing in an indictment a charge of any offence that the evidence appears to him to warrant, or to decline to lay a charge, s 526(1) is in very clear terms. It provides only for the Public Prosecutor, after considering the evidence contained in the depositions taken before the court (and any other evidence), to reduce into writing in an indictment a charge of any offence that the evidence appears to warrant. It does not provide for a State Prosecutor to also consider the evidence and reduce in writing in an indictment a charge of any offence that the evidence appears to warrant although, in practice, a State Prosecutor considers the evidence and makes the relevant recommendation to the Public Prosecutor to indict the person. The Public Prosecutor then sends the indictment back to the prosecutor to present to the National Court and prosecute the accused. The exercise, therefore, of the powers of the Public Prosecutor pursuant to s 526(1) does not arise until after a court of summary jurisdiction has refused to commit a person for trial."

Jalina J further stated:

> "An order by a District Court magistrate for the withdrawal of an information does not amount to dismissal of an information and therefore cannot be construed as a refusal to commit a defendant for trial."

In the same case, Jalina J said (at 486):

> "An indictment purported to be signed and presented against the accused by the State Prosecutor was defective and *ultra vires* the powers of the State Prosecutor, who purported to exercised the powers of the Public Prosecutor under s 526(1) of the *Criminal Code*, and further amounted to an abuse of the process of the court."

Indictments presented after Independence are entitled in the name of "The State": *The State v John Mogo Wonom* [1975] PNGLR 311.

As to the background, history and applicability of ex officio indictments in pre-Independence Papua New Guinea, see *R v Burusep* [1963] PNGLR 181, but note Prentice DCJ's remarks on this case in *The State v Tanedo* [1975] PNGLR 395 at 399-401, and Prentice J's views on *R v Burusep* in *R v Baker* [1971-1972] PNGLR 79 at 84.

The old s 561 gave the Crown an uncontrolled power of indictment without prior committal proceedings. In practice, the power was used for two purposes. The first use was when a person had been committed for trial for an offence and the depositions disclosed evidence of a different offence or of other offences. The second use was where a person consented to plead guilty to a charge in respect of which no committal proceedings had been taken: *R v Angoro Evu* [1969-1970] PNGLR 274.

An ex officio indictment may be presented whether a person has been committed for trial or not. Also, irregularities in committal proceedings will not invalidate a subsequent indictment, and an ex officio indictment may be used where there has been a purported committal, even if the proceedings were invalid: *The State v Tanedo* [1975] PNGLR 395.

An indictment may be presented against an accused person in his or her absence: *R v Topulumar* [1971-1972] PNGLR 320 at 322-323.

When a person has been committed for trial for an offence, and the depositions disclose evidence of a different offence or of other offences, it is convenient and just that an indictment should be presented by the prosecutor: R v Toigen Tiolo [1969-1970] PNGLR 285. Note that this case was heard under the old Code s 561.

On the issue of whether or not the state could present an amended indictment bearing the Public Prosecutor's signature, it was held in *The State v Pawa Kombea* (1997) N1518 that:

1. It is only once than an indictment could be preferred on the basis of one committal. This would be both ss 526(2) and 526(2) indictments – *Criminal Code* Ch 262.
2. The power to amend an indictment does not include the power to accept a new but amended bill of indictment either under ss 525 or 526 of the Code.

In that case, Lenalia AJ stated that:

"There are two main types of indictments in our jurisdiction. There are those taken under s 525(2) [of the Code] following committal proceedings under ss 94(B) and 100(1)(3)(a) of the *District Courts Act.* The second type is under s 526(2) [of the Code] where there has been a refusal to commit by the committal magistrate for insufficiency of evidence – see 100(2) *District Courts Act.* I am more inclined to think that once having decided to reduce the charge into writing and then that indictment is in fact presented to the Court, that in my reading of ss 524, 525(2) and 526(2) is the end of the matter and the prosecution cannot thereafter seek to amend by a substitute, and an amended indictment. ... I must refuse acceptance of the amended bill of indictment proposed by the State Prosecutor".

In *R v Topulumar* [1971-1972] PNGLR 320 at 323, it was said that this section (referring to s 561 of the *Queensland Criminal Code*) is wide enough to enable the joinder in one indictment of persons committed for trial and persons indicted without committal ex officio.

See Kassam, "*Ex-officio Indictments: An Aspect of Criminal Justice in Papua New Guinea*" (1974) 2(2) MLJ 248-262.

527. Nolle prosequis.

(1) The Public Prosecutor or a State Prosecutor may at any time inform the National Court that an indictment then pending in the Court will not be further proceeded with, by filing with or presenting to the Court a document under his hand to that effect.

(2) When a document referred to in Subsection (1) is filed or presented the person named in it is to be immediately discharged from any further proceedings on the indictment to which it relates.

Presenting a nolle prosequi before the commencement of the trial does not amount to an abuse of process of the court. The fact that the state has reserved the right to present another indictment is merely the consequence of a nolle prosequi and therefore not improper: *The State v Peter Painke* [1976] PNGLR 210.

McDermott J said, in *The State v Jonah-Jahai* (1982) N391:

"Where the nolle prosequi is presented after commencement of trial, there are considerations of double jeopardy (see s 17 of the Code) and the public interest requiring the proper investigation of alleged crimes. In this case, on balance, the trial had not reached the position where double jeopardy had arisen, and consequently the presentation of a nolle prosequi was accepted."[103]

The entry of a nolle prosequi and/or the giving of an undertaking not to prosecute one conspirator does not amount to an acquittal. Therefore, nothing prevents the court from proceeding to convict the other of two alleged conspirators: *The State v Tanedo* [1975] PNGLR 395.

It is well established that a superior court has the power inherent in its jurisdiction to prevent any abuse of its process and to control its own procedure. If an indictment is preferred and the prosecution subsequently enters a nolle prosequi, it is an abuse of the process of the court for the prosecution to later prefer an indictment containing the same charge. The court has a discretion to stay, and in

[103] *Arthur Gilbert Smedley v The State* [1980] PNGLR 379 was followed. *R v Abia Tambule* [1974] PNGLR 250 was distinguished.

general should stay, a subsequent indictment containing charges founded on the same facts as those on which a previous indictment is based. This rule is fully applicable to the circumstances of Papua New Guinea: *The State v Peter Painke (No 2)* [1977] PNGLR 141.

Clarkson J, dissenting, stated in *R v Abia Tambule* [1974] PNGLR 250 at 256-257:

> "On the plain construction of the section, the State is entitled to present a nolle prosequi while an indictment is still pending. Thus it was open for the State to enter a nolle prosequi at the conclusion of its case when it appeared that the State's evidence was insufficient to sustain the charge. If the presentation of a further indictment then appears to the court to constitute an abuse of its process, the court may utilise its inherent jurisdiction to protect its own processes from misuse."

It was further said in that case (at 252):

> "Other Code sections expressly confer on the court a discretion to make orders to prevent the accused from being prejudiced by the court's procedure. [See, for example ss 531, 535 and 558] This consideration is sufficient to show that the powers conferred on the State prosecutor to enter a nolle prosequi were not intended to be subject to any discretionary control by the court. The power may thus be exercised at any stage of the trial in relation to an indictment so long as it can be said that the indictment remains pending in court."

Frost SPJ and Minogue CJ (Clarkson J dissenting) expressed the view in *R v Abia Tambule* [1974] PNGLR 250 at 253 that if a fair hearing requires upon the evidence a determination of the merits of the case in favour of the accused, that right cannot be defeated by permitting the state to withdraw the charge once the hearing commences, particularly if the nature of the withdrawal does not preclude further proceedings. For the state to enter a nolle prosequi at a stage of a trial when the state had called all the evidence available, and it was insufficient to sustain the charge, was to deny the accused a fair hearing under s 16(2) of the *Human Rights Act* 1971. That section has since been repealed, but was virtually identical to s 37(3) of the *Constitution*.

Brunton J said, in *The State v Daniel Aigal and Gui Robert Kauna* [1990] PNGLR 318 at 320-321:

> "The powers of this Court under s 57 of the *Constitution* are wide and although it appears that the National Court has no statutory power to force the State to exercise its discretion in relation to what charge is laid, or what plea is to be accepted ... a judge is not entirely without powers when confronted with a nolle prosequi ... Here a court, using its powers under s 57 of the *Constitution* can prevent a nolle prosequi from being filed if the filing would jeopardise an accused's right to a fair trial within a reasonable time under s 37(3) of the *Constitution*, particularly if the nolle prosequi would amount to an abuse of process: *R v Abia Tambule* [1974] PNGLR 250; *The State v Jonah-Jakai* (1982) N391 (McDermott J).
>
> In principle, if a court can prevent the filing of a nolle prosequi by using its powers under s 57 of the *Constitution* in respect of breaches of s 37(3), then it should also be able to apply the same power in respect of other rights – certainly s 42 – but perhaps not so obviously s 35 – Right to Life and s 36 – Right to Freedom from Inhuman Treatment."

See s 37(3) of the *Constitution*.

Notwithstanding the responsibility that his or her decision carries with it, the Public Prosecutor is not answerable to anyone, even the presiding judge, in the matter of entering a nolle prosequi: *R v Nere Pundali* (1973) N767.

For discussion comparing the powers to present an ex officio indictment and to enter a nolle prosequi, see *Arthur Gilbert Smedley v The State* [1980] PNGLR 379 at 401-403 (Pratt J).

528. Form of indictment.

(1) An indictment shall be intituled with the name of the court in which it is presented, and must, subject to the succeeding provisions of this Division set forth the offence with which the accused person is charged -

(a) in such a manner; and

(b) with such particulars as to -

(i) the alleged time and place of committing the offence; and

(ii) the person (if any) alleged to be aggrieved; and

(iii) the property (if any) in question,

as is necessary to inform the accused person of the nature of the charge.

(2) Subject to Subsections (3) and (4), if any circumstance of aggravation is intended to be relied on it must be charged in the indictment.

(3) Where the circumstance of aggravation intended to be relied on is a previous conviction, the conviction shall not be charged in the indictment, but written notice of an intention to rely on it as circumstance of aggravation shall be served on the accused person or his lawyer, before the commencement of the trial.

(4) Where a written notice has been served in accordance with Subsection (3) and the accused person has been convicted -

(a) of the offence charged in the indictment; or

(b) of any other offence of which he might be convicted under the indictment,

the prosecution may, after the conviction of the accused person but before sentence is imposed, allege and prove the previous conviction.

(5) On proof of the previous conviction the court may -

(a) convict the accused person of the aggravated offence as if the previous conviction had been charged in the indictment; and

(b) substitute a conviction for the aggravated offence for the conviction already recorded in the trial,

and the accused person is liable to punishment accordingly.

(6) It is sufficient to describe an offence in the words of this Code or the other written law defining it.

(7) The place of trial shall be named in the margin of the indictment.

See s 536 of the Code regarding particulars.

See s 1 for the definition of "circumstances of aggravation".

There appears to be nothing in our *Criminal Code* which bears upon the proof required when an allegation is made that a crime was committed "on or about". From time immemorial a date specified in an indictment has never been a material matter unless it was actually an essential part of the alleged offence. Where the words "on or about" are used to render a verdict of guilty lawful, the offence must be shown to have been committed within some period which has a reasonable approximation to the date mentioned in the indictment: *The State v Titeva Fineko* [1978] PNGLR 262.

An indictment is not formally defective because it does not bear the seal of the court: *R v Ongasi Wosis* [1971-1972] PNGLR 476.

It is not necessary for the person who signs the indictment to present it: *R v Kision* (1976) N580.

The matters set forth in s 395A(2)(a)-(d) of the Code are matters which constitute circumstances of aggravation within the meaning of s 528(2), and must be set out in the indictment where the prosecutor intends to rely upon them as a major matter raising the penalty from a maximum of five years to a maximum of 10 years: *The State v Miseal Butemo Jiregari* [1984] PNGLR 62.

See *Acting Public Prosecutor v Andrew Amona Yongga* [1981] PNGLR 314, discussed under s 603, regarding "sample charges".

529. General rules applicable to indictments.

The following rules are applicable to all indictments -

(a) any document or other thing may be described by any name or designation by which it is usually known, and any document may be described by its purport without setting out a copy or facsimile of the whole or any part of it; and

(b) a trade-mark may be described by that name, and any other mark may be described in any way that will indicate its nature, without setting out a copy or facsimile of it; and

(c) it is not necessary to set out the value of any thing mentioned in an indictment unless the value is an essential element of the offence; and

(d) it is not necessary to set out the means or instrument by which any act is done, unless the means or instrument are an essential element of the offence; and

(e) it is not necessary to set out any particulars -

(i) as to any person or thing that need not be proved; or

(ii) any other matter that need not be proved.

A definition of "document" is found in s 459 of the Code.

530. Particular indictments.

(1) An indictment for treason must state overt acts of the reason alleged.

(2) In an indictment for an offence that relates to -

(a) taking or administering an oath or engagement; or

(b) giving false testimony; or

(c) making a false statement on solemn declaration or otherwise; or

(d) procuring the giving of false testimony or the making of a false statement,

it is not necessary to set out the words of the oath, or engagement, testimony or statement, but it is sufficient to set out the purport of it, or so much as is material.

(3) In an indictment for an offence that relates to -

(a) giving false testimony; or

(b) procuring or attempting to procure the giving of false testimony,

it is not necessary to allege the jurisdiction of the court or tribunal before which the false testimony was given, or was intended or proposed to be given.

(4) In an indictment for an offence committed with respect to -

(a) the Department of Posts and Telegraphs; or

(b) the revenue of that Department; or

(c) anything sent by post or telegraph; or

(d) anything under the control of the Minister responsible for posts and telegraphs,

any property of which the ownership must be alleged may be alleged to be the property of the Minister responsible for posts and telegraphs.

(5) In an indictment under Subsection (4) the Minister responsible for posts and telegraphs may be described by that term alone, without mentioning his name or using any other addition or description.

(6) In an indictment in which it is necessary to mention money, it may be described simply as money, without specifying any particular form of money.

(7) An averment referred to in Subsection (6) will be sustained, so far as regards the description of the property, by proof that the offender obtained or dealt with any coin or anything that is included in the term "money", or any portion of the value of it, in such a manner as to constitute the offence, even if the coin or thing was delivered to him in order that some part of the value of it should be returned to the person who delivered it or to some other person, and has been returned accordingly.

(8) In an indictment in which it is necessary to mention any co-owners of property, it is sufficient -

(a) to name one of such persons, adding the words "and another" or "and others", as the case may be; and

(b) to state that the property belonged to the person so named and another or others, as the case may be.

(9) In an indictment for an offence relating to any property of a company that is authorized to sue and be sued in the name of a public officer, the property may be alleged to be the property of the public officer.

(10) In an indictment for an offence relating to any property that is by law deemed to be the property of an officer of an institution, the property in question may be alleged to be the property of the officer for the time being by his name of office.

(11) In an indictment for an offence relating to a testamentary instrument, it is not necessary to allege that the instrument is the property of any person.

(12) In an indictment for an offence relating to anything -

(a) fixed in a square or street, or in a place dedicated to public use or ornament; or

(b) in or taken from a public office,

it is not necessary to allege that the thing in respect of which the offence is committed is the property of any person.

(13) In an indictment for an offence relating to a document that is evidence of title to land or an estate in land, the document may be described as being evidence of the title of the person or some one of the persons having an estate in the land to which the document relates, the land or some part of it being described in some manner sufficient to identify it.

(14) In an indictment for stealing a chattel or fixture let to the offender, the chattel or fixture may be described as the property of the person who actually let it to hire.

(15) In an indictment against a person employed in the Public Service for an offence committed with respect to any thing that came into his possession by virtue of his employment, the thing in question may be described as the property of the State.

(16) In an indictment for an offence respecting any property, (whether within the meaning of Section 1 or Section 383A), if it is uncertain to which of two or more persons the property belonged at the time when the offence was committed -

(a) the property may be described as being the property of one or other of such persons, naming each of them, but without specifying which of them; and

(b) the indictment will be sustained, so far as regards the allegation of ownership, on proof that at the time when the offence was committed the property belonged to one or other of such persons without ascertaining which of them.

[Subs (16) am Act No 10, 1981 (*Criminal Code (Misappropriation of Property) Act* 1981), s 2]

(17) In an indictment for the offence -

(a) of obtaining or procuring the delivery of any thing capable of being stolen by a false pretence and with intent to defraud; or

(b) of obtaining any property by means of a fraudulent trick or device; or

(c) of inducing by means of any such trick or device the payment or delivery of any money or goods; or

(d) of attempting to commit, or to procure the commission of, any such offence,

it is not necessary to mention the owner of the property in question.

(18) In an indictment for an offence that involves any fraud, fraudulent pretence, trick or device, it is not necessary to set out the details of the fraud, pretence, trick or device.

(19) In an indictment for an offence relating to an insolvent, it is not necessary to set out -

(a) any debt, act of insolvency, adjudication or other proceeding in any court; or

(b) any order, warrant or document made or issued by or out of or by the authority of, any court.

See s 1 of the Code for definitions of "Post and Telegraph Department", "telegraph", "money", "property", "owner", "company", and "person employed in the Public Service".

See s 459 for a definition of "document".

Under s 531(6), moneys including bank notes and cheques may be referred to generally as "money" on the face of the indictment: *R v McKay* (1954) N56.

531. Joinder of charges: General rules.

(1) Subject to this Code, an indictment must charge one offence only and not two or more offences.

(2) Subject to Subsection (3), when several distinct indictable offences are alleged to be constituted -

(a) by the same acts or omissions; or

(b) by a series of acts done or omitted to be done in the prosecution of a single purpose,

charges of such distinct offences may be joined in the same indictment against the same person, and the several statements of the offences may be made in the same form as in other cases, without any allegation of connexion between the offences.

(3) If in a case to which Subsection (2) applies, it appears to the court that the accused person is likely to be prejudiced by the joinder, the court may -

(a) require the prosecutor to elect on which of the several charges he will proceed; or

(b) direct that the trial of the accused person on each or any of the charges be had separately.

(4) This section does not authorize the joinder of a charge of wilful murder, murder or manslaughter with a charge of any other offence.

The general prohibition in s 531 against an indictment charging more than one offence applies where there is no evidence directed to show that on a general reconciliation of the accounts there was an overall deficiency: *R v Walsh* [1971-1972] PNGLR 293.

The words "any other offence" in s 531(4) mean any offence other than wilful murder, murder or manslaughter, and thus it is acceptable to join two or more counts of wilful murder, two or more counts of murder or two or more counts of manslaughter in the same indictment: *The State v Elias Subang (No 1)* [1976] PNGLR 141.

On the meaning of "any other offence", it is not permissible to join a charge of rape with wilful murder, murder or manslaughter in the same indictment: *Charles Bougapa Ombusu v The State* [1996] PNGLR 335.

A joinder of distinct offences on a complaint does not render the complaint a nullity; the accused is only entitled at the hearing to put the prosecutor to election as to what charge will be proceeded upon: *Mames-Weviong v Zania* [1967-1968] PNGLR 79.

A wrongful joinder of counts does not render a trial a nullity unless there is a miscarriage of justice: *Wari Mugining v The Queen* [1975] PNGLR 352 (Williams J).

Where separate acts are charged by separate individuals at different times or places, even though all the parties were acting in concert (in this case a single war raid), the indictment is bad for duplicity: *R v Burusep* [1963] PNGLR 181.

Several different counts may be joined against one single accused under this section, provided the counts arose out of closely related facts and the prosecution of a single purpose: *Wari Mugining v The Queen* [1975] PNGLR 352.

Where the offences alleged could be said to be constituted by a series of acts done in the prosecution of an unlawful purpose, the joinder is good. Joinder of riot and assault was held to be good in *R v Kision* (1976) N580.

The words "constituted by" should bear an extended meaning. In *R v McEachern* [1967-1968] PNGLR 48, 15 counts (forgery, uttering false documents, unauthorised making of documents with intent to defraud and fraudulent false accounting while acting as a servant) were properly joined in one indictment, as the distinct indictable offences alleged to be constituted by the series of acts were done in the prosecution of a single purpose, namely, the unlawful maintenance of a position of control and advantage in the hotel of his employer.

The word "single", as in "done in the prosecution of a single purpose" in s 531(2), bears the meaning not only of "separate" or "individual", but also "undivided" or "one". Acts done or omitted to be done in the prosecution of the same purpose, which is renewed or revived from time to time, are not done or omitted to be done in the prosecution of a single purpose. In *R v Dwyer* [1967-1968] PNGLR 104 at 111, the prosecution tried to join counts of stealing and fraudulent false accounting, which the court found might have had the same or similar purpose, but owing to the lapse of time over a period of more than two years between the acts, joinder was not permitted.

In *R v Toigen Tiolo* [1969] PNGLR 285, regarding assault occasioning bodily harm and riot (the same acts which constitute the one offence may constitute the other), the joinder held to be good.

Where it is alleged that the accused's driving resulted in the deaths of several persons, the causing of death is a circumstance of aggravation and not an element of the offence. Hence, in *R v Messulam Wauta* (1973) N785, where there were two acts of dangerous driving allegedly causing deaths in both cases, the state had to elect which act or omission constituting dangerous driving it would proceed on.

For the relationship of this section to s 532, see *Wari Mugining v The Queen* [1975] PNGLR 352.

For an example of several distinct thefts as a servant, see *R v Walsh* [1971-1972] PNGLR 293.

532. Joinder of charges: Special cases.

(1) In an indictment against a person for stealing money, the accused person may be charged and proceeded against for the amount of a general deficiency, notwithstanding that the general deficiency is made up of any number of specific sums of money the taking of which extended over any space of time.

(1A) In an indictment against a person for misappropriation of property he may be charged and proceeded against for the amount of a general deficiency even although -

- (a) any number of specific applications of property have resulted in the general deficiency; and
- (b) such applications of property have extended over any space of time; and
- (c) the property applied belongs to different persons and has come into the possession or control of the accused person at different times and subject to different trusts, directions, conditions or duties to account.

[Subs (1A) insrt Act No 10, 1981 (*Criminal Code (Misappropriation of Property) Act* 1981), s 3]

(2) In an indictment against a person for stealing, he may be charged with two or three distinct acts of stealing the property of the same person, committed by him within the space of six months from the first to the last of such acts.

(3) If on the trial of a person charged with stealing it appears that property alleged to have been stolen at one time was stolen at different times, the prosecutor is not for that reason required to elect on which act of stealing he will proceed, unless it appears that -

- (a) there were more than three acts of stealing; or
- (b) more than six months elapsed between the first and the last of such acts.

(4) In a case referred to in Subsection (3), the prosecutor must elect to proceed in respect of two or three acts of stealing that appear to have taken place within the period of six months from the first to the last of the acts.

(5) Charges of stealing any property and of receiving the same property, or any part of it, knowing it to have been stolen, may be joined in the same indictment, and the accused person may, according to the evidence, be convicted-

- (a) of stealing the property; or
- (b) of receiving, the property or any part of it, knowing it to have been stolen.

(6) Subject to Subsection (7), when an indictment referred to in Subsection (5) is preferred against two or more persons -

- (a) all or any of the accused persons may be convicted of stealing the property or of receiving it, or any part of it, knowing it to have been stolen; or

(b) according to the evidence, one or more of them may be convicted of stealing the property, and the other or others of them of receiving it, or any part of it, knowing it to have been stolen.

(7) If on an indictment referred to in Subsection (6) the court finds specially that -

(a) the accused person, or all or any of the accused persons, when the indictment is preferred against two or more persons, either stole the property, or received it, or any part of it, knowing it to have been stolen; and

(b) it is unable to say which of those offences was committed by such person or persons as the case may be,

such person or persons are not for that reason entitled to be acquitted, but the court shall enter a conviction for the offence for which the lesser punishment is provided.

(8) Any number of persons charged with -

(a) committing or procuring the commission of the same offence, although at different times; or

(b) being accessories after the fact to the same offence, although at different times; or

(c) receiving, although at different times -

(i) any property that has been obtained by means of -

(A) a crime or misdemeanour; or

(B) an act that if it had been done in Papua New Guinea would be a crime or misdemeanour and that is an offence under the laws in force in the place where it was done; or

(ii) any part of any property so obtained,

may -

(d) be charged with substantive offences in the same indictment; and

(e) be tried together,

notwithstanding that the principal offender or the person who so obtained the property -

(f) is not included in the same indictment; or

(g) is not amenable to justice.

(9) Any number of persons charged with committing different or separate offences arising substantially out of the same facts or out of closely related facts so that a substantial part of the facts is relevant to all the charges may be charged in the same indictment and tried together.

"Money" and "property" are defined by s 1 of the Code.

As to s 532(6)-(9), see s 7 regarding parties. See also s 10.

See s 586 regarding evidence on certain charges of stealing money, and see the note on *R v Eric Oakari* [1974] PNGLR 182 discussed under that section.

The words "general deficiency" in s 532(1) mean the difference in money terms between the amount which, at the end of the period selected for accounting, a person or corporation should possess in cash or deposits, or investments representing cash, and the amount that the person or corporation actually possesses. Proof of a totality of any number of specific sums proved to have been stolen alone does not constitute proof of a general deficiency. In *R v Walsh* [1971-1972] PNGLR 293, where an indictment charged a number of separate offences, failure to prove a general deficiency amounted to a material irregularity, and an appeal against conviction was allowed.

Section 532(1) and (3) do not have application in a case where the charge in the indictment is one of stealing money, not goods and money. In such a case, application should be made to amend the indictment: *R v Eric Oakari* [1974] PNGLR 182.

It was permissible to indict together, under s 532(8), 32 accused persons charged with the wilful murder of the same deceased, some of whom were alleged to have actually killed the deceased, and others who were alleged to be principal offenders by virtue of ss 7 or 8: *R v Wendo* [1963] PNGLR 217 at 218.

When there is objection to a joint or "lumped" hearing, that is, a hearing where two or more prisoners arraigned upon separate indictments are tried together, prohibition would appear to lie. In some cases, even when there has been consent to such a course, it may be possible to show that there has been a mistrial. There is no definite principle as to whether such irregularities vitiate the proceedings. In *Munday v Gill* (1930) 44 CLR 38 at 79-80, Gavan Duffy and Starke JJ said:

> "In some instances the irregularity is so serious that the consent of the accused will not cure it; in others, consent overcomes the irregularity; whilst in yet others, it is very slight and unattended by any serious consequence to the accused, so that no substantial miscarriage of justice takes place. The fact that the accused person has consented to the irregular procedure is weighty, and one that is often decisive; but it is not conclusive of itself and the court must consider the whole of the circumstances."[104]

Section 532(6) has no application to the joinder of counts in an indictment against a single accused, but applies in the case of multiple offenders: see *Wari Mugining v The Queen* [1975] PNGLR 352 and *R v Mesulam Wauta* (1973) N785.

"Facts" in s 532(9) is not limited to the facts in issue in each separate offence, but includes all the evidentiary facts relevant and admissible to prove the crimes charged, and "closely related facts" includes those of a connected series of events.

The question of whether facts are closely related to one another is a question of degree which must be decided having regard to the time, place, nature of the incidents, the similarity of scene, and identity of the victim: *John Rul Nabil v The State* [1979] PNGLR 88.

Applying *Wari Mugining v The Queen* [1975] PNGLR 352, whether irregularity is substantial (as here with a wrongful joinder under s 532(9)) and is a ground for setting aside the proceedings or a conviction, depends on whether there is, or would be, a substantial miscarriage of justice: *The State v Leo Nimo* [1980] PNGLR 129.

---

[104] *Kereku v Dodd* [1969-1970] PNGLR 176 at 183-187.

In Papua New Guinea, a joint trial on two or more separate indictments is an irregularity and not a nullity, although at common law, because of the existence of a jury, such trials were always nullities: *The State v Leo Nimo* [1980] PNGLR 129.

A lack of objection by counsel until two prosecution witnesses have given evidence can cure an irregularity: *The State v Leo Nimo* [1980] PNGLR 129.

See *Acting Public Prosecutor v Andrew Amona Yongga* [1981] PNGLR 314, discussed under s 603, regarding "sample charges".

In *John Rul Nabil v The State* [1979] PNGLR 88 there was an appeal that the joint trial of the four appellants was not authorised by law on the ground that the joint trial of separate offenders was contrary to this section. Three had only aided in the commission of the rape, and therefore the *facta probanda* were not the same. It was held, following the decision of Burbury CJ in *R v Ford* [1967] Tas SR 20, on the equivalent section of the Tasmanian *Criminal Code*, that "facts" in the section is not limited to the facts in issue in each separate offence, but includes all the evidentiary facts relevant and admissible to prove the crimes charged, and "closely related facts" includes those of a connected series of events. A question of whether facts are closely related is a question of degree to be decided with regard to the time, place, nature of the incident, the similarity of scene, and identity of the victim.

Where two or more persons are jointly indicted, and a witness is the wife of one of the jointly accused and is therefore not competent as a witness, the trial judge has a discretionary power to order or refuse a separate trial of that accused. In choosing which course to follow, the trial judge must exercise that discretion in the interests of justice as a whole, and not solely the interest of an individual accused: *Wemp Mapa v The State* [1979] PNGLR 135.

In an order for mistrial upon an application for severance of one accused in a joint trial, a trial judge must give paramount consideration to the dispensation of justice: *Constitution*, s 156(2). Consequently, in exercising his or her discretion upon the question of severance, the judge must consider the interests of justice as a whole and not solely the interests of an individual accused. An appellant who argues that a trial judge has wrongly exercised the discretion in refusing to grant (or in granting) separate trials, faces almost insuperable difficulties: *Wemp Mapa v The State* [1979] PNGLR 135 (Andrew J).

533. Accessories.

A person who –

(a) counsels or procures another person to commit an offence; or

(b) aids another person in committing an offence; or

(c) becomes an accessory after the fact to an offence,

may be -

(d) charged in the same indictment with the principal offender, and may be tried with him or separately; or

(e) indicted and tried separately,

whether or not the principal offender -

(f) has been convicted; or

(g) is amenable to justice.

See s 7 of the Code regarding parties to offences.

534. Formal defects.

(1) An indictment is not open to objection –

(a) by reason of the designation of any person by a name of office or other descriptive title instead of by his proper name; or

(b) for omitting to state the time at which the offence was committed unless the time is an essential element of the offence; or

(c) for stating imperfectly the time at which the offence was committed; or

(d) for stating the offence to have been committed on an impossible day, or on a day that never happened or has not yet happened.

(2) An objection to an indictment for a formal defect apparent on its face must be taken by motion to quash the indictment before the accused person pleads to the indictment.

See ss 558-559 of the Code regarding motion to quash, and misnomer respectively.

535. Amendment of indictments.

(1) If on the trial of a person charged with an indictable offence -

(a) there appears to be a variance between the indictment and the evidence; or

(b) it appears that -

(i) any words that ought to have been inserted in the indictment have been omitted; or

(ii) any words that ought to have been omitted have been inserted,

the court may, if it thinks that -

(c) the variance, omission or insertion is not material to the merits of the case; and

(d) the accused person will not be prejudiced in his defence on the merits,

order the indictment to be amended, so far as it is necessary, on such terms (if any) as to postponing the trial as the court thinks reasonable.

(2) When an indictment has been amended, the trial shall proceed at the appointed time, on the amended indictment, and the same consequences ensue in all respects and as to all persons as if the indictment had been originally in its amended form.

(3) If it becomes necessary to draw up a formal record in any case in which an amendment to an indictment has been made, the record shall be drawn up setting out the indictment as amended, and without taking any notice of the fact of the amendment having been made.

The indictment may be amended based on the evidence placed before the court, without recourse to the depositions: *R v Ah Wong* (1954) N51.

An indictment may be amended by the prosecution after the submission of no case to answer and before the defence presents its case: *The State v Tanedo* [1975] PNGLR 395.

The phrase "the variance is not material to the merits of the case" was intended to show that the correction of the record required by the variance may be made if its making would not affect the merits of the case being made: *The State v Tanedo* [1975] PNGLR 395.

Brunton J said, in *The State v Francis Kumo Gene* [1991] PNGLR 33 at 43:

> "If the court amends the indictment, changes the nature of the charge, after both sides have closed their cases, then the potentiality for oppression or embarrassment is considerable. It may be thought that a way out of the dilemma would be to recall the lawyers, re-open the case, put the issue to them and give the parties an opportunity to address the court. This course has been followed. Proper trial administration and the public interest value finality in the court process. There is value in having cases properly prosecuted. There is value in due process. There is value in finality. But there is also value in having both sides express their views on complicated legal issues."

As a general rule, an indictment should not be amended after the counsel for the defence has addressed the jury: *Simili Kara v The State* [1984] PNGLR 254.

This principle was enunciated in *R v Rymes* (1853) 175 ER 573 at 574 (Vaughan Williams J) and was applied in *Simili Kara v The State* [1984] PNGLR 254. In that case (at 257-258) Kidu CJ quoted the earlier case:

> "I will not allow an indictment to be amended after the counsel for the defence has addressed the jury. The proper course is that when the counsel for the prosecution has given all the evidence that he means to give he should, if he wishes for an amendment, ask for it before he closes his case, and then, if the amendment is allowed, the counsel for the prisoner addresses the jury on the indictment as it is amended."

Kidu CJ (at 258) cited several reasons for applying this general rule, including:

- If an accused person is convicted on this new charge he or she would be convicted on a charge to which he or she was not asked to plead as required by s 557(1) of the Code.
- If he or she did not plead to the new charge then the trial would be deemed not to have commenced, because s 557(2) of the Code states that a criminal trial commences when an accused person is asked to plead to the charge in the indictment.
- Sections 37(4)(a), (b) and (c) of the *Constitution* would have been contravened.

See also *The State v Gelam Koivaku* [1986] PNGLR 217.

536. Particulars.

The court may -

(a) if it thinks fit, direct particulars to be delivered to the accused person of any matter alleged in the indictment; and

(b) adjourn the trial for the purpose of the delivery.

537. Summary convictions.

The provisions of this Division relating to indictments apply to complaints or informations preferred against offenders on their trial before courts of summary jurisdiction on charges of indictable offences that may be dealt with summarily.

The provisions relating to indictments in this Division apply to complaints or informations in the Local and District Courts as well: *Mames-Weviong v Zania* [1967-1968] PNGLR 79.

Division 3 – Effect of Indictments

538. Offences involving circumstances of aggravation.

Subject to this Division, on an indictment charging a person with an offence committed with circumstances of aggravation, he may be convicted of any offence that is -

(a) established by the evidence; and

(b) constituted by any act or omission that is an element of the offence charged,

with or without any of the circumstances of aggravation charged in the indictment.

Upon a charge under s 315 of the Code, for intent to cause grievous bodily harm, the accused may alternatively be convicted under s 319, for doing grievous bodily harm, by operation of this section: *R v Bawai-Pesoi* [1965-1966] PNGLR 210.

To break, enter and steal (under ss 395-399) is not to steal "with circumstances of aggravation" for the purposes of this section: *R v Griffin* [1971] PNGLR 72.

This section is not applicable to a situation where the accused is charged with a break and entry into a dwelling-house with intent to steal (s 395), and the intent element fails, for the purpose of moving towards conviction under s 396 for unlawful break and entry. However, if the words "in the night" were inserted into the body of a charge for housebreaking, these are circumstances of aggravation, and if this element is not proved, s 538 comes into play and the accused may be convicted of housebreaking with intent simpliciter: *R v Gahoso Simbane* [1975] PNGLR 257.

At common law, housebreaking and burglary (s 395) were regarded as aggravated forms of entering a dwelling-house with intent to commit a crime (s 397) (and both may be regarded as highly aggravated forms of stealing (s 365)). When looking at the form in which the two neighbouring offences are now expressed in ss 395 and 397 of the Code, it is clear that the legislature intended those two offences to be regarded as similar in character and differing only in degree, depending upon whether or not the aggravated ingredient of housebreaking was present. Thus, an accused indicted under s 395 may properly be convicted of an offence under s 397: *R v Daugamani-Adamanika* [1965-1966] PNGLR 80 at 89-90.

Bray CJ stated, in *Weaver v Samuels* (1971) SASR 116:

"The rule is that if the defendant desires to dispute circumstances of aggravation alleged in sworn evidence for the prosecution, he must do so by sworn evidence from himself or someone else; but if the aggravating matter is not sworn to, but is only alleged on the hand and denied on the other in an unsworn form, then it is the duty of the court 'to act upon the version of the facts which, within the bounds of reasonable possibility, is most favourable to the accused' (*Maitland's Case* [1963] SASR 332, 355). In addition, I held in *Law v Deed* [1970] SASR 374, that if the defendant alleges circumstances of mitigation peculiarly within his knowledge which the prosecution is not in a position to negative, again his version must be accepted 'within the bounds of reasonable possibility: and if the court is minded to reject it as beyond those bounds, it must at least give him an opportunity to support his story by his oath if he so desires'".[105]

See the annotations to *Topopwa Thomas v The State* [1979] PNGLR 140, under s 16 of the Code.

See also *R v Iata Kara* (1974) N777.

See also ss 542 and 547 regarding alternative verdicts generally, ss 539 and 540 regarding unlawful killings, s 541 regarding sexual offences, ss 543 and 544 regarding property offences, s 545 regarding procuring offences and s 556 regarding attempts.

539. Charge of murder or manslaughter.

(1) On an indictment charging a person with the crime of wilful murder, he may be convicted of the crime of murder or of the crime of manslaughter but not, except as is expressly provided in this Code, of any other offence other than that with which he is charged.

(2) On an indictment charging a person with the crime of murder, he may be convicted of the crime of manslaughter but not, except as is expressly provided in this Code of any other offence other than that with which he is charged.

(3) On an indictment charging a person with the crime of manslaughter he shall not, except as is expressly provided in this Code, be convicted of any other offence.

(4) On an indictment charging a person with wilful murder, murder or manslaughter, the accused person may be convicted of -

(a) unlawfully doing grievous bodily harm to such other person; or

(b) unlawfully assaulting such other person and thereby doing him bodily harm; or

(c) unlawfully wounding such other person; or

(d) unlawfully assaulting such other person.

This section is rightly peculiar to Papua New Guinea, bearing in mind the difficulties in police investigations, the remoteness of qualified medical personnel and the non-availability of facilities to preserve evidence for scientific investigations: *The State v Davelambem Yangidao* (1980) N278.

See offences under Pt III, Div 7 of the Code.

This section complements s 531 which, while permitting in certain circumstances the joinder of charges of distinct offences in one indictment, expressly states that it does not authorise the joinder of a charge of wilful murder, murder or manslaughter

[105] This case was followed in *Koniel Alar and Hosea Biu v The State* [1979] PNGLR 300.

with a charge of any other offence: *R v SM; The Queen v SM, UN, PE* [1973] PNGLR 304.

This section is not relevant by analogy to a charge under s 304 for attempted murder. The usual course is to include in the indictment an alternative count under s 315, or some lesser offence: *R v Kiki Kau'au* (1970) N557.

On an indictment charging a person with assault occasioning bodily harm pursuant to s 340, the alternative verdict of unlawful assault pursuant to s 539(4) is not available. Such an alternative verdict is available on a charge of wilful murder, murder or manslaughter: *The State v John MacKenzie and Apiari* (1990) N861.

See also ss 546 and 548.

See ss 311-312 and 327-328.

The pre-1974 provision referred only to indictments charging "unlawful killing", which may have implied relevance only to manslaughter cases (see *R v Sapulo-Masuve* [1973] PNGLR 304), but the 1974 Code clarified the matter by specifying that indictments charging "wilful murder, murder or manslaughter" are to come under this section.

The second paragraph was added in Papua New Guinea in 1923, and was designed to increase the number of alternative verdicts which could be returned. This unusual provision is not found in Australia or England, and "was probably enacted in Papua New Guinea having regard to the difficulties of proving that death followed injuries proved to be inflicted upon a deceased person, difficulties which would obviously be encountered in criminal investigations from time to time in remote areas, particularly when carried out some time after the death was reported, when the body may have been buried and perhaps no medical officer was available": *R v SM; The Queen v SM, UN, PE* [1973] PNGLR 304 at 310-311(Clarkson J quoting from Frost SPJ's judgment in the court below).[106]

Clarkson J also said, in *R v SM; The Queen v SM, UN, PE* [1973] PNGLR 304:

> "The alternative verdicts of unlawfully doing grievous bodily harm, unlawfully assaulting and thereby doing bodily harm, unlawfully wounding and unlawfully assaulting, described in the second paragraph are available on any indictment for an unlawful killing whether wilful murder, murder or manslaughter. That is, even though the words "unlawfully killing" in paragraph one encompass manslaughter only; the same words in paragraph two are not similarly limited and encompass wilful murder and murder as well as manslaughter, as is the case in ss 298-300 and 302".[107]

In *R v SM; The Queen v SM, UN, PE* there was insufficient medical evidence to prove that the blows of the accused caused the death of the victim. Consequently, the accused were both found guilty on an alternative verdict of unlawfully assaulting the victim.

See also s 313.

See the annotations to *Tapopwa Thomas v The State* [1979] PNGLR 140, under s 16 of the Code.

---

[106] *R v Sapulo-Masuve* [1973] PNGLR 304

[107] See also *R v Marumyapusek* [1973] PNGLR 582.

540. Homicide of child, alternative verdicts.

On an indictment charging the wilful murder, murder or manslaughter of any person, if on the evidence it appears that the person alleged to have been killed was a child of which a woman had recently been delivered, the accused person may be convicted of -

(a) the offence of infanticide; or

(b) the offence of preventing the child from being born alive by an act or omission of such a nature that, if the child had been born alive and had then died, he would be deemed to have unlawfully killed the child; or

(c) the offence of endeavouring by a secret disposition of the dead body of the child to conceal the birth.

See ss 301, 312 and 313 of the Code regarding the offences specified in this section as alternative verdicts to wilful murder, murder or manslaughter.

541. Charge of rape and like offences.

On an indictment charging a person with the crime of rape or having unlawful carnal knowledge of a girl under the age of 12 years, he may be convicted of any offence -

(a) of which the unlawful carnal knowledge of a woman or girl, whether of a particular age or description or not, is an element and blood relationship is not an element; or

(b) of which procuring the woman or girl to have unlawful carnal connexion with any man is an element; or

(c) of administering to the woman or girl, or causing her to take any drug or other thing with intent to stupefy or overpower her in order to enable any man to have unlawful carnal knowledge of her; or

(d) of unlawfully and indecently assaulting the woman or girl; or

(e) of unlawfully and indecently dealing with a girl under the age of 12 years or a girl under the age of 16 years.

[S 541 am Act No 27, 1979 (*Criminal Code (Amendment) Act* 1979), s 2]

See s 213 of the Code for the offence referred to.

See the annotations to *Tapopwa Thomas v The State* [1979] PNGLR 140, and specifically the remarks of Andrew J with regard to separate counts on the one indictment.

Under s 578 of the former Code, unlawful carnal knowledge of a girl under 16 years was an alternative verdict open to the court upon a charge of rape. Under this section, however, that is no longer possible. Despite the heading, this section refers only to alternative verdicts open on a charge of unlawful carnal knowledge of a girl under age. Prentice DCJ commented, in *The State v Kewa Kai* [1976] PNGLR 481, that "[p]erhaps there has been an oversight in the drafting of the new Code." Note that this is no longer so since the 1979 amendment.

542. Charge involving specific result.

(1) On an indictment charging a person with an offence of which the causing of some specific result is an element, he may be convicted of any offence of which an intent to cause that result, or a result of a similar but less injurious nature, is an element.

(2) On an indictment charging a person with an offence of which an intent to cause some specific result is an element, he may be convicted of any offence that is established by the evidence and of which the unlawful causing of that result is an element.

Under this section, if the indictment charges a person with an offence of which an intent to cause some specific result is an element, the person may be convicted of any offence which is established by the evidence and of which the unlawful causing of that result is an element, and without any limitation arising from any other element of the offence charged: *R v Bawai-Pesoi* [1965-1966] PNGLR 210.

The better prosecution practice is to place all the realistically possible counts in the indictment, rather than forcing the court unnecessarily to construe the difficult provisions of this Division, while on circuit: *The State v Wanaepe Warara* [1977] PNGLR 458.

A verdict of intent to do grievous bodily harm (s 315) or doing grievous bodily harm (s 319) is open upon an indictment alleging attempted murder: *The State v Wanaepe Warara* [1977] PNGLR 458.

It is clear from this section that if indicted for unlawful wounding with intent to do some grievous bodily harm under s 315, a person can be convicted under s 319 if the evidence establishes it: *R v Meauri* [1969-1970] PNGLR 254 at 259. See s 559 regarding situations where the evidence discloses an offence of a similar nature.

The Code retains the position apparently previously applicable at common law, that on a charge of doing grievous bodily harm (s 319), without alternative counts, no lesser offence could be found against an accused: *R v Polhill* (1973) N734.

Where an accused is charged with breaking and entering with intent to steal (s 395) and the intent element fails, the accused may still be convicted under s 396 for unlawful break and entry: *R v Gahoso Simbane* [1973] PNGLR 257.

It was said in *Supreme Court Reservation No 4 of 1984; Re The State v James Pah* [1985] PNGLR 188:

> "On an indictment charging the offence of attempting unlawfully to kill as defined in the Code s 304, a verdict of grievous bodily harm with intent under s 315 of the Code is not available as an alternative verdict pursuant to s 542 of the Code. Section 542(1) and (2), which provides for alternative verdicts for charges involving specific results, in referring to an offence of which 'the causing of some specific result is an element' cannot apply to the charge of attempting unlawfully to kill because the **causing** of as distinct from the intending of some specific result (that is, specific injury) is not an element of the charge of attempting unlawfully to kill".

Kidu CJ said in *Re The State v James Pah* [1985] PNGLR 188 at 190:

> "With the greatest respect, s 542(1) applies to an offence which has as one of its elements the causing of a specific result and attempted murder has only two elements: causing of death is not one of them. It is the intention to cause a specific result and attempted murder does not have such an element, that is, the

intention to kill. However the problem under s 542(2) is that where the offence of attempted murder is not proved the alternative offence, grievous bodily harm with intent, has no application because such alternative offence is quite different from attempted murder".

In the same case, Bredmeyer J said (at 192):

"[T]he offence of attempted murder does not involve as an element of it the causing of a specific result (that is, a specific injury). That being so the first part of s 542(1) does not apply to an indictment for attempted murder hence that section cannot be used to bring in an alternative verdict under s 315 of grievous bodily harm with intent to do grievous bodily harm. The opening words of s 542(2) do apply to attempted murder. But the latter part of s 542(2) does not apply because the specific result intended in the offence of attempted murder is death and the 'unlawful causing of that result' (that is, death) is not an element of the offence of causing grievous bodily harm with intent. The result is that a s 315 verdict of grievous bodily harm with intent is not open as an alternative verdict to attempted murder under either subsection of s 542".

"Property" is defined by s 1 of the Code.

See also s 44 regarding malicious injuries in general.

544. Stealing, false pretences, cheating and misappropriation of property.

Upon an indictment charging a person with any of the following, that is to say -

(a) stealing, with or without a circumstance of aggravation; or

(b) obtaining goods by false pretences; or

(c) obtaining goods by a wilfully false promise, or

(d) obtaining goods partly by a false pretence and partly by a wilfully false promise; or

(e) cheating; or

(f) misappropriation of property; or

(g) procuring any other person to commit any such offence,

he may be convicted of any other of those offences committed with respect to the same property, if that other offence is established by the evidence.

[S 544 subst Act No 10, 1981 (*Criminal Code (Misappropriation of Property) Act 1981*), s 4]

"Property" is defined by s 1 of the Code.

It was stated in *Tom Amaiu v The State* [1979] PNGLR 576 at 580-581:

"Owing to the close similarity between stealing (old s 377) and obtaining by false pretences (old s 416), it is often difficult to know which offence should be charged, but since they are materially different they cannot be joined in the same indictment. It is undesirable that one should be able to avoid conviction of either on the ground that he committed the other. To reduce the likelihood of a technical acquittal where it is clear that an accused has committed one of these offences but has been charged with the other, five Australian States and Papua New Guinea have statutory rules that where the accused is charged with stealing but false pretences is proved, he may be acquitted of stealing and convicted of false pretences, and vice versa."

Pratt and Woods JJ held, in *Opai Kunangel v St* [1985] PNGLR 144:

> "On a charge of misappropriation of property brought pursuant to the Code s 383A, as introduced by the *Criminal Code (Misappropriation of Property) Act* (No 10 of 1981), an alternative verdict of false pretences is available pursuant to s 544 of the Code even where the offence was committed before the amendment introducing the offence of misappropriation became effective because a false pretence, once made, continues to remain a false pretence until acted upon".[108]

See ss 7, 9 and 533 of the Code.

546. Conviction for attempt to commit offence.

(1) On an indictment charging a person with committing an offence, he may be convicted -

- (a) of attempting to commit the offence; or
- (b) of attempting to commit any other offence of which he might be convicted on the indictment.

(2) On an indictment charging a person with procuring the commission of an offence, he may be convicted -

- (a) of attempting to procure the commission of the offence; or
- (b) of attempting to procure the commission of any other offence of such a nature that a person may be convicted of it on an indictment charging him with committing the offence of which the accused person is alleged to have procured the commission.

(3) On an indictment charging a person with attempting to commit any offence, he may be convicted of attempting to commit any other offence of such a nature that a person may be convicted of it on an indictment charging him with committing the offence that the accused person is alleged to have attempted to commit.

(4) On an indictment charging a person with attempting to procure the commission of any offence, he may be convicted of attempting to procure the commission of any other offence of such a nature that a person may be convicted of it on an indictment charging him with committing the offence of which the accused person is alleged to have attempted to procure the commission.

(5) On an indictment charging a person with attempting to procure another person to do an act or make an omission of such a nature that if the act had been done or the omission had been made, an offence would have been committed, he may be convicted of attempting to procure that other person to do any other act or make any other omission of such a nature that if the act had been done or the omission had been made an offence would have been committed, if the last-mentioned offence is itself of such a nature that a person may be convicted of it on an indictment charging him with doing the act or making the omission that the accused person is alleged in the indictment to have attempted to procure that other person to do or make.

[108] *R v Greathead* (1878) 14 Cox's CC 108 and *R v Moreton* (1913) 8 Cr App R 214 were followed.

See s 4 of the Code regarding the definition of "attempts".

547. When evidence shows offence of similar nature.

(1) If on the trial of a person charged with an indictable offence the evidence establishes that he is guilty of another indictable offence of such a nature that on an indictment charging him with it he might have been convicted of the offence with which he is actually charged, he may be convicted of the offence with which he is so charged.

(2) In a case to which Subsection (1) applies, the person is not liable to be afterwards prosecuted for the offence established by the evidence, unless the court before which the trial is had directs the accused person to be indicted for that offence, in which case he may be dealt with in all respects as if he had not been put upon his trial for the offence with which he is actually charged.

Upon a charge of rape under s 347, where there is no dispute that penetration has taken place and the only issue is consent or non-consent, the alternative verdict of guilty of indecent assault is not available: *R v Merembu Bongab* [1971-1972] PNGLR 433.

See also s 541.

Does s 547, on its true construction, permit the conviction of a person for the lesser offence of attempt when the evidence in the case shows that the full offence was committed? This question was considered in *The State v Albert Monja* [1987] PNGLR 447, where the accused was charged with attempted rape, but after the close of evidence it was clear that actual sexual intercourse had taken place. King AJ stated that the words "might have been convicted" where they appeared in s 547, referred to the theoretical possibility of a conviction of a similar or lesser offence:

> "When one reads s 547(1) it cannot be doubted that it is an enabling or facultative provision, designed to overcome problems which might emerge in the course of criminal trials, whether technical or substantive, and which are not or cannot be cured by laying alternative charges or amending the indictment. Because it is an enabling provision, it should be construed in the way which will make it most effective in that role. That consideration alone is in my opinion decisive ... Most reasonable people would, I am sure, think it absurd that if the evidence in a given case involving a charge of attempt shows that the full offence was probably committed, the accused should automatically escape conviction of attempt and public funds be wasted on a second trial".

The Code retains the position apparently previously applicable at common law, that on a charge of doing grievous bodily harm (s 319), without alternative counts, no lesser offence could be found against an accused: *R v Polhill* (1973) N734.

By this section, if a person is indicted under s 319 (doing grievous bodily harm) and if the evidence establishes guilt under s 315 (unlawful wounding with intent to do grievous bodily harm), the person may be convicted under s 319 and such conviction carries with it the immunity from a prosecution under s 315 referred to in the second paragraph of s 547: *R v Meauri* [1969-1970] PNGLR 254 at 259.

See s 542 above, regarding alternative verdicts.

See also *R v Manga Gabi* [1963] PNGLR 97 and *R v Kingston-Kapoli* (1960) N175.

548. Effect of conviction.

A person convicted under any of the preceding provisions of this Division is liable to the same punishment as if he had been convicted on an indictment charging him with the offence of which he is actually convicted.

549. Corrupt practices.

If, on the trial of a person charged with an indictable offence relating to elections the evidence establishes that he -

(a) is not guilty of the offence charged; and

(b) is guilty of an offence relating to elections and punishable on summary conviction,

he may be convicted of the last-mentioned offence, and is liable to the same punishment as if he had been summarily convicted of that offence.

550. Illegal practices.

If, on the trial of a person charged with an offence relating to elections and punishable on summary conviction, the evidence establishes that he is guilty of an indictable offence relating to elections, he is not entitled to have the charge dismissed if the evidence also establishes that he did any act or acts such as to constitute the offence with which he is actually charged.

551. Indictment for joint receiving.

On an indictment charging two or more persons jointly with an offence of which the receiving of any property is an element, if the evidence establishes that one or more of them separately received any part or parts of the property under such circumstances as to constitute an offence, he or they may be convicted of the offence or offences so established by the evidence.

Division 4 – Trial: Adjournment: Pleas: Practice

552. Right to be tried.

(1) In this section, "place of trial" means the place appointed under the *National Court Act* for sittings of the National Court at which the hearing of a charge of an indictable offence is to take place.

(2) A person who has been committed for trial or sentence or against whom the Public Prosecutor has laid a charge under Section 526 may make application at any sittings of the National Court to be brought to his trial.

(3) If no indictment has been presented against the applicant -

(a) where the application is made at a sittings of the National Court at the place of trial – before the end of the sittings at which the application is made; or

(b) where the application is made at a sittings of the National Court at some other place – before the end of the next sittings of the court at the place of trial,

the court shall, on application by him, admit him to bail on such terms as the court thinks proper, unless the court is satisfied that there are special reasons why the application should be refused.

(4) If -

(a) a person has made an application under Subsection (2); and

(b) at the end of the sittings of the National Court at his place of trial next following the application -

(i) no indictment has been presented against him; or

(ii) the court is satisfied that the prosecution has not in the circumstances of the case made a genuine attempt to complete its case,

he is entitled to be discharged.

See ss 37(3), 37(4), 37 (14) and 42(3) of the *Constitution*.

See the note on *R v B* (1969) N561, regarding the necessity of trials being open to the public, discussed under s 557 of the Code.

In s 552 the right to be discharged is not intended to apply to an accused who has failed to attend and cannot be tried because of his or her absence: *R v Byrne* [1971-1972] PNGLR 1.

An accused person is "brought to his trial" within the meaning of s 552(2) when the accused is placed in a position where he or she is able to be tried, that is by the presentation of an indictment against the accused and with the state either ready to proceed by having its witnesses to prosecute its case against the accused, or by the Public Prosecutor informing the court that the state will not further proceed upon the indictment, in which event the accused is discharged. If the phrase "brought to his trial" meant that the accused must actually be tried, then it would follow that the court's discretion to adjourn the hearing, under s 555, would be fettered, contrary to the intention of the legislature: *R v Martin Main* [1971-1972] PNGLR 289 at 291-292.

The meaning of the words "brought to trial" have been judicially considered by Kelly J in *R v Byrne* [1971-1972] PNGLR 1 at 5:

> "these words mean placed in a position where he is able to be tried, that is by the presentation of an indictment against him and with the Crown either ready to proceed against him or by the Crown informing the court that the Crown will not further proceed upon the indictment in which event the accused is discharged under [s 527 – nolle prosequis]".

This case was followed in *R v Martin Main* [1971-1972] PNGLR 289. These two cases deal with the old s 590 of the Queensland *Criminal Code (Adopted)*, which is worded slightly differently from our present provisions, but the same meaning for the words "to be brought to his trial" is adopted: *The State v Frank Taso Yasim* [1983] PNGLR 111 (Kapi DCJ).

As to the phrase "he is entitled to be discharged", the words of Kelly J in *R v Byrne* [1971-1972] PNGLR 1 at 5 are adopted:

> "The use of the word 'entitled' seems to imply that it is a right which the accused has in these circumstances if he chooses to avail himself of it."

Kapi DCJ, referring to Kelly J's words, said in *The State v Frank Taso Yasim* [1983] PNGLR 111:

"That is to say that if the circumstances in the provision are proved he should be discharged if he chooses to claim an entitlement. Where an application under s 552(2) is made by an accused, the minimum action the State can take is simply to present an indictment against the accused by the last day of the sittings following the application. By taking this action the State brings the accused person to trial. It does no follow that the State will complete the case at the time of the presentation of the indictment."

In *Lindsay Kivia, Robert N'Draku and Peter Seski v The State* [1988] PNGLR 107 at 111, Amet J stated that an application under s 552(2):

"may be made at any time during the sittings of the National Court by an accused to be brought to his trial. The practice has grown for the application to be made at the end of sittings if the case has not been started or dealt with in that sitting. There is no reason why the application could not be made at the start of sitting or in the course of that sitting. The subsection does not stipulate that the application should be made at the end of sittings. The State can, if application is made prior to the end of the sitting, present an indictment any time after the application, prior to the end of that same sitting."

In that same case, it was said (at 111-112):

"The 'entitlement to be discharged' accrues to or vests in the accused first in time at the end of the sittings next following the application, if he can satisfy the court of the existence of the conditions under subs (b)(i) or subs (b)(ii) ... The time limit of the end of sittings next following the application is within which or by which the State is to act. And if it does not then the entitlement of the accused shall come into existence from that time onwards, and he is entitled to be discharged upon his application, either at that time or afterwards, at the commencement of the next sittings or any other time he chooses to exercise the right to that entitlement. It does not lapse because he chooses not to claim his right to that entitlement, otherwise such a construction would defeat the purpose of the two provisions, if at the end of the sittings next following the application the State did not present an indictment, or if an indictment had earlier been presented but that no genuine attempt was made by the prosecution to complete its case, and the position remanned the same for the next several sittings, the subs (2) application would be quite useless."

It was further said (at 112):

"I do not agree that the State, by simply presenting an indictment on the last day of the sittings next following the sub (2) application brings the accused to his trial. If the State cannot be in a position to proceed by having its witnesses to prosecute the case against the accused, then it cannot fairly be said that the accused was brought to trial. The State must genuinely show that it was ready with all its witnesses to prosecute its case against the accused, but for want of time ... The mere presentation of an indictment by the State in answer to an application ... or in anticipation of an imminent s 552(4) application without being ready to prosecute with witnesses available is not 'bringing to trial' and would amount in my view to an abuse of process".

Properly construed, s 552(4) does not mean that the entitlement to discharge is intended to come to an end with the "sittings next following" the application, but that the grounds contained in s 552(4)(b)(i) or s 552(4)(b)(ii) must be shown to exist at those sittings, so that once the state has failed to present an indictment at the "sitting next following", an accused has an entitlement to a discharge which the accused may at his or her option thereafter exercise: *The State v Yamai* [1987] PNGLR 314 (King AJ).

Where an accused seeks discharge from indictment on the ground of delay in being brought to trial, the onus of showing that the prosecution has not made a genuine attempt to complete its case is on the applicant. Such onus is to be equated with the civil standard: *The State v Alphonse Wohuinangu* (1991) N966.

The common law refusal to recognise the existence of a special right to a speedy trial or to a trial within a reasonable time is displaced by s 552 (4)(b)(ii) of the *Criminal Code Act: The State v Alphonse Wohuinangu* (1991) N966.

There is no automatic right of the accused to have proceedings dismissed for delay alone. It is still for the trial judge to consider the particular reasons for the prosecution's failure to embark on the trial, as evidenced by *R v Main* [1971] PNGLR 290. Where delay in having the accused brought to trial is shown to be owing more to circuit exigencies of the National Court rather than to any distinct failure of the prosecution to bring the applicant to trial, this is a significant factor in the determination of whether the application to dismiss should be granted: *The State v Alphonse Wohuinangu* (1991) N966.

553. Bail generally.

[S 553 rep Act No 13, 1977 (*Criminal Code (Arrest) Act* 1977), s 32]

See the *Bail Act*.

554. Delivery of copy of indictment.

(1) When a charge is laid against a person under Section 525 or 526, a copy of the indictment shall be served on the accused person or his lawyer at a reasonable time before the commencement of his trial.

(2) When the prosecution serves a notice of intention to rely on a previous conviction as a circumstance of aggravation, it shall serve a copy of the notice on the accused person or his lawyer a reasonable time before the commencement of the trial.

(3) If a copy of the indictment or the notice of intention to rely on a previous conviction as a circumstance of aggravation is not so served within such time before the commencement of the trial as is reasonable in order to allow the accused to prepare his defence, the court shall, on application, grant to the accused person an adjournment for such time as it thinks reasonable in the interest of justice.

555. Adjournment of trial.

(1) A court before which a trial has commenced may at any time, in its discretion, adjourn the trial.

(2) A court before which a trial has commenced may at any time, on application by the State Prosecutor or the accused or his lawyer, direct that the trial be continued at a different place, whether or not the place is a place appointed under the National Court Act for sittings of the National Court.

(3) If a court directs that the trial in which no evidence has been taken be continued at a different place, the trial may be continued before a Judge other than the Judge before whom it commenced.

556. Effect of adjournment.

(1) When an order is made under Section 555 adjourning a trial to a different time or place -

(a) the accused person is bound to attend the trial; and

(b) the recognizance of any person bound to attend as a witness or otherwise applies in respect of the new time and place of trial.

(2) A person bound to appear at a trial by virtue of Subsection (1) is not liable to have his recognizance forfeited or be otherwise dealt with for failure to appear unless he has received notice within a reasonable time of the time and place to which the trial has been adjourned.

See s 37(5) of the *Constitution*.

557. Accused person to be called on to plead to indictment.

(1) At the time appointed for the trial of an accused person, he shall be informed in open court of the offence with which he is charged, as set out in the indictment, and shall be called on to plead to the indictment, and to say whether he is guilty or not guilty of the charge.

(2) The trial begins when the accused person is called on in accordance with Subsection (1).

See s 42(1)(a) of the *Constitution*; see also s 557 of the *Criminal Code*.

See also ss 37(3), 37(4), 37(5), 37(14) and 42(3) of the *Constitution*.

This section makes it clear that the accused is to be arraigned in public, although the Code does not go on to provide expressly that the remainder of the trial should be so held. However, English and Australian precedents state that at common law a criminal trial must be held in a public court with open doors. In *R v Dickason* (1913) 17 CLR 50 the High Court of Australia summarised the role as follows:

> "there is no adherent power in a court of justice to exclude the public inasmuch as one of the normal attributes of the court is publicity, that is, admission of the public to attend the proceedings".[109]

However, see the *Child Welfare Act* 1961, which establishes Children's Courts.

The accused must be present at his or her trial in order to plead under s 557, but an indictment may be presented against an accused in his or her absence: *R v Byrne* [1971-1972] PNGLR 1.

558. Motion to quash indictment.

(1) The accused person may, before pleading, apply to the court to quash the indictment on the ground that -

(a) it is calculated to prejudice or embarrass him in his defence to the charge; or

(b) it is formally defective.

(2) On a motion under Subsection (1), the court may -

(a) quash the indictment; or

---

[109] *R v B* (1969) N561.

(b) order it to be amended in such manner as the court thinks just; or

(c) refuse the motion.

See s 534 of the Code regarding defective indictments.

See s 560 regarding pleas generally.

Where an accused person objects to an indictment on the ground that it is a nullity, the accused is entitled to have the objection dealt with as soon as it is raised, and is not required to plead to the indictment first: *R v McEachern* [1967-1968] PNGLR 48.

Upon a motion to quash the indictment pursuant to this section, alleging that the indictment is formally defective in that it lays open the possibility of a violation of the s 16 prohibition on double punishment for the same offence, the court may only consider whether or not there is a likelihood of double punishment at the close of the evidence. Any attempt to call in s 16 at the start of a trial is premature, for it is possible that the accused might be acquitted of one or both of the charges joined in the indictment: *R v Yofia Abone* [1967-1968] PNGLR 277 at 282.

Where the prosecution tried two parties to a joint crime under separate indictments and called each as a witness against the other, thereby eliciting self-incriminating testimony, it was open to the court to quash the indictment on the basis that such a practice constituted a gross abuse of process and had the effect of prejudicing or embarrassing the accused within the meaning of this section, particularly where the accused were unsophisticated and unrepresented: *R v Simbene Dandemb* [1969-1970] PNGLR 207. See also s 37(10) of the *Constitution*.

See s 14 of the *Evidence Act*, regarding the right against self-incrimination.

The case of *R v Angoro Evu* [1969-1970] PNGLR 274 involved a motion to quash the indictment, where the accused was indicted for a different offence from that for which he was committed.

A motion made before plea may be entertained, where the accused seeks to assert that there is no indictment upon which he or she may be tried on the ground that the indictment presented is based on an invalid committal: *R v Little* [1967-1968] PNGLR 63.

R v Nakian Mandiam [1973] PNGLR 135 involved a motion to quash an indictment on the ground that it was formally defective. The basis for this argument was that the committal proceedings were defective, as a statutory declaration setting out injuries received was tendered in evidence, and thus the accused was not given the opportunity to cross-examine. A judge may entertain a motion to quash an indictment arising from alleged irregularities in the committal proceedings where the irregularities are such that the committal proceedings were so defective that there had been no lawful committal. If there has been no lawful committal, then no lawful indictment can be based upon it. In the present case there was a substantial body of evidence correctly taken at the committal proceedings and it was open to the magistrate to form the view that there was a prima facie case, so the acceptance of some inadmissible evidence did not vitiate the whole committal.

A refusal to allow an accused to make a proper application to quash an indictment under s 558 amounts to an error of law warranting a new trial before another judge so that a proper application can be made and an order made thereon: *Alphonse Sapau v The State* [1990] PNGLR 302 (Amet, Hinchliffe and Konilio JJ).

In an application to quash an indictment where the jurisdiction of the committal court was in question, it was held that there is no statutory requirement for the proposition that the court in the area where the offence was committed only should commit the accused to the National Court in the particular area: *The State v Vele Veole* (1990) N902.

On a motion to quash an indictment see *R v Burusep* [1963] PNGLR 181. See also *R v Toigen Tiolo* [1969-1970] PNGLR 285.

559. Misnomer.

If the accused person says that he is wrongly named in the indictment, the court may, on being satisfied by affidavit or otherwise of the error, order the indictment to be amended.

See s 534 of the Code regarding defective indictments.

560. Pleas.

(1) If the accused person does not apply to quash the indictment, he must either plead to it, or demur to it on the ground that it does not disclose any offence cognizable by the court.

(2) If the accused person pleads, he may plead -

(a) that he is guilty of the offence charged in the indictment, or, with the consent of a State Prosecutor, of any other offence of which he might be convicted on the indictment; or

(b) that he is not guilty; or

(c) that he has already been convicted -

(i) on an indictment on which he might have been convicted of the offence with which he is charged; or

(ii) of an offence of which he might be convicted on the indictment; or

(d) that he has already been acquitted on an indictment -

(i) on which he might have been convicted of the offence with which he is charged; or

(ii) of an offence of which he might be convicted on the indictment; or

(e) that he has already been tried and convicted or acquitted of an offence committed or alleged to be committed under such circumstances that he cannot under this Code be tried for the offence charged in the indictment; or

(f) that he has been pardoned for the offence charged in the indictment; or

(g) that the court has no jurisdiction to try him for the offence.

(3) Two or more pleas may be pleaded together, except that the plea of guilty cannot be pleaded with any other plea to the same charge.

(4) An accused person may plead and demur together.

See s 563 of the Code regarding entry of a not guilty plea.

See ss 37(3), 37(4), 37(8), 37(14) and 42(3) of the *Constitution*.

As to s 560(2)(c), see s 564 of the Code.

As to s 560(2)(f), see 37(9) of the *Constitution*.

See s 534 of the Code regarding defective indictments.

See s 558 regarding motions to quash, s 562 regarding standing mute, s 563 regarding entry of plea of not guilty, s 564 regarding plea of autrefois acquit or convict, s 567 regarding demurrer, s 569 regarding want of understanding, and s 578 regarding further pleas.

A plea of not guilty does no more than indicate that the accused relies upon the constitutional presumption of innocence (s 37(4)(a)) and the right to require the prosecution to prove the case alleged against him or her according to law. The Papua New Guinea practice of a trial judge, upon arraignment, putting to the accused the various ingredients of the offence alleged and asking if he or she admits that they are true, is perfectly proper if the judge feels that there is any doubt that the accused will not otherwise understand the nature of the charge. Conversely, it carries with it the attendant danger that the accused may believe that he or she is required to answer the question as to whether the allegations are true. If the accused does labour under that misapprehension, he or she may mistakenly forfeit the right to require the prosecution to prove its case at trial. A trial judge who chooses to seek an answer from the accused as to the truth of the allegations must be particularly careful to not in effect deprive the accused of the right to insist on the presumption of innocence. In order to overcome this problem, a practice grew up in Papua New Guinea, which was later codified (s 563), whereby defence counsel may, with leave of the court, apply to enter a plea of not guilty on behalf of the accused: *Gabriel Laku v The State* [1981] PNGLR 350.

Where the appellant had pleaded guilty, was represented by counsel, and had the plea accepted by the trial judge, it would be most unusual for an appellate court to interfere with the verdict. See *Launce Vetari v The State* (1979) SC 156.

In the courts of Papua New Guinea, each element of the charge must be put to the accused, and if the defendant has any cause to show why he or she should not be convicted or why an order should not be made against him or her, the court is to proceed to hear and to determine the case. The defendant must unequivocally admit every element of the charge: *Wui Wapi v Ludwick Kembu* [1980] PNGLR 7.

In *Gabriel Laku v The State* [1981] PNGLR 350 the trial judge erred in informing the accused, gently or otherwise, that "he must say if the charge was true or not true", although that may be in many instances a convenient procedure for obtaining a plea. An accused person is not obliged to plead one way or the other. Given the circumstances in which the court obtained the plea of guilty from the appellant, when the appellant later denied an essential element of the charge (penetration, in a case of unlawful carnal knowledge) on allocutus, the court should have exercised its discretion in favour of vacating the "tainted" plea of guilty and the conviction. It was held that not having done so, the court could not be satisfied that no miscarriage of justice had occurred. While there will undoubtedly be cases in which it will be proper to refuse to allow a plea of guilty to be withdrawn after conviction (for example, where the application is frivolous or based on a flimsy technicality), nevertheless generally speaking where the discretion is exercised against the prisoner, it will be closely examined by the appellate court. It is well known that persons admit guilt for all sorts of reasons, including the wish to get the case over and done with.

In Papua New Guinea the court has to be very careful to avoid a possible situation in which the accused volunteers responsibility and that others, and perhaps more influential members, of the accused's clan mark him or her out to accept responsibility. In *The State v Yaulipa Bulaim* (1980) N234, it was quite conceivable that the accused would be under some fear or threat if he did not admit to being a party to the crime (of wilful murder).

If an accused person appears to be pleading guilty to the charge, the magistrate should record a plea of guilty provisionally. Only if further inquiry, usually provided by a perusal of the statement of facts, supports such a plea, should the provisional plea be confirmed: *Nabo Tiambo v Gideon Lari* [1979] PNGLR 525.

For a discussion of the various precautions which have traditionally been taken in order to ensure that an accused person pleading guilty does in fact fully understand and appreciate what he or she is doing, see *The State v Manga Kinjip* [1976] PNGLR 86 at 88.

Where the accused does not appear to admit all the ingredients of the state's case, the issues of fact which are not admitted are required to go to trial: *R v Suk Ula* [1975] PNGLR 123.

When, on a plea of guilty, an accused controverts a vital assertion of the police case, if the prosecution seeks to maintain that vital assertion, the issue thereby raised should be decided by the hearing of evidence: *Takovong v Tarera* (1975) N837.

The state may not accept a change of plea without the leave of the court, which has discretion in the matter: *R v Iwari* [1964] PNGLR 175.

A plea of not guilty may, by leave of the court, be withdrawn during the trial and a plea of guilty substituted: *R v Suk Ula* [1975] PNGLR 123.

A plea of guilty is not a conviction. Conviction is indicated by the allocutus being administered to the accused. Thus, if any discretion exists in the acceptance of a plea of guilty, it may be exercised up to this point: *R v Ambaidunga Kinde* (1974) N799.

On the extreme caution to be exercised in accepting a plea of guilty when persons are uneducated and unrepresented, see *Towarli Tokoi v Bryant* (1972) N674, *Laeka Ivarabou v Nanau* [1967-1968] PNGLR 12 at 17, *Jacob Hendrich Prai v An Officer of the State* [1979] PNGLR 1, and *Appeals No 13-34, 44-74, 76-82 of 1979* (unreported, Andrew J, 28 May 1979).

It was held in *The State v Atu Kote* [1978] PNGLR 212 that here can be no conviction on a count to which an accused person pleads guilty until by some act on the part of the court it has indicated a determination of the question of guilt: followed *R v Jerome and McMahon* [1964] Qd R 595. If a plea of guilty once recorded does not rank as a conviction, it only ranks as a conviction when the offender is in fact sentenced: followed *R v Cole* (1965) 2 All ER 29.

There may be occasions when it is proper for a court of appeal to say that the trial judge should have refused to accept a plea of guilty or should have set it aside. In this event, the trial would become a nullity and the correct procedure would be to order a new trial. A plea of guilty does not amount to an admission of all the facts set up in the depositions. Where the accused disputes matters, once put in issue those matters should not be accepted unless proved: *R v Millay* [1971-1972] PNGLR 121.

See *R v Koiyari-Iyeva* [1965-1966] PNGLR 284, and ss 581 and 602 regarding fitness to plead.

Before accepting a plea of guilty in any case in which a police officer is a complainant and the accused is not represented by counsel or solicitor, the court would be well advised to point out to any such accused that the severity of penalties does not depend on whether he or she pleads guilty or not guilty, and to inquire whether anyone connected with the police force has suggested that the accused should plead guilty. It would also be prudent on the part of the magistrate to intimate positively to the person before the court the accused's right to put everything he or she wishes before the court, provided it is relevant to the charge, and then getting down on the record the agreement of the accused that the accused has said all that he or she wishes to say: *Exton v Nordfelt* (1965) N349.

Where a defendant is unrepresented it is essential that the court, where there is a plea of guilty, should make absolutely sure that the defendant understands the elements of the charges to which he or she so pleads. Where a defendant pleads guilty owing to a misstatement of the law by the trial judge, the conviction will be quashed. It is well established that where a plea of guilty has been wrongly or mistakenly entered, the trial judge, in his or her discretion, can permit the accused to proceed to trial or quash the indictment: *Moses Aikaba v Tami* [1971] PNGLR 155.

A judge should only accept a plea of guilty if it is made in plain, unambiguous and unmistakable terms; the plea of guilty to a charge of murder should only be accepted if the court is satisfied that the accused has had explained to him or her, and has understood, the various implications of the accused's course of action: *The State v Manga Kinjip* [1976] PNGLR 86.

Where an accused intends to plead guilty to a charge of wilful murder for which the mandatory penalty is life imprisonment, an appropriate procedure is the presentation to the court of:

(a) a statement signed by the accused setting out clearly what has been explained by counsel and stating unequivocally that, despite that advice, the accused wishes to plead guilty to the charge; and

(b) a certificate, signed by senior counsel appearing for the accused, that counsel has explained to the accused the consequences of the plea of guilty, has taken the accused word by word through the statement, and is satisfied that the accused fully understands everything that counsel has explained to him or her, and further stating, that in so pleading, the accused is not abandoning any defence that might be open to him or her in the light of the accused's knowledge of the case on counsel's instructions.[110]

Leave to withdraw a plea of guilty after conviction is a discretionary matter. It is to be contrasted with the entering of a plea of guilty when the plea has been equivocal. If there is any doubt about whether an accused person intends to plead guilty or not guilty, it should be resolved by recording a plea of not guilty and proceeding to trial. There is a constitutional presumption of innocence up until the time of conviction. Once an unequivocal plea has been entered and the court proceeds to consider sentence, the prisoner is regarded as having been convicted, and it is wholly a matter of the court's discretion as to whether the conviction

[110] *The State v Manga Kinjip* [1976] PNGLR 86.

should be set aside and the plea of guilty vacated. This may be regarded as part of the underlying law of Papua New Guinea. Decisions in other jurisdictions which limit the exercise of this discretion in certain ways should not be followed in this country: *Gabriel Laku v The State* [1981] PNGLR 350.

Quite apart from the discretion vested in the court by s 563 to change a plea from guilty to not guilty upon an application from defence counsel, the court may enter a plea of not guilty upon its own motion. This discretion is derived from the inherent unlimited jurisdiction of the National Court, and from the *Constitution*. In deciding cases, the courts are to give paramount consideration to the dispensation of justice: *Constitution*, s 158(2). Further, (under s 155(4) of the *Constitution*) the National Court has inherent power to make such other orders as are necessary to do justice in the circumstances of a particular case. These provisions enable the court to decline to accept a plea of guilty: *The State v Yaulipa Bulaim* (1980) N234.

A National Court has power, in an appropriate case, to enter a plea of not guilty on behalf of an accused person who pleads guilty but whose lawyer does not make an application under s 563 of the *Criminal Code* for a plea of not guilty to be entered on the accused's behalf. This discretionary power is derived from the power to enforce guaranteed rights and freedoms under s 57 of the *Constitution* and the inherent jurisdiction under s 155(4) of the *Constitution*. Its exercise complies with the direction in s 158(2) of the *Constitution* to give paramount consideration to the dispensation of justice: *The State v Peter Sari* [1990] PNGLR 48 (Jalina AJ).

Jalina AJ said, in *The State v Peter Sari* [1990] PNGLR 48 at 54:

> "It follows from the authorities that if the depositions do not disclose any offence or do not disclose all the elements of the offence charged or disclose possible defences, the entry of a plea of guilty would, in my opinion, be tantamount to denial of the right of the accused to the full protection of law under s 37(1) and his right to be proven guilty according to law under s 37(4)(a) of the *Constitution*. These rights should not be at the whim of lawyers who, perhaps in their plea-bargaining process, or perhaps to reduce the amount of workload, decide to advise the accused to plead guilty. The accused could have been denied his constitutional rights had the court not intervened."

Where a trial judge is asked to disqualify himself or herself for bias after having entered a plea of not guilty on behalf of the accused after having read the depositions, it is appropriate, in the interests of integrity and impartiality, that the judge disqualify himself or herself from further hearing of the case: *The State v Peter Sari* [1990] PNGLR 48 (Jalina AJ).

Where a trial judge, upon perusal of the committal depositions, declines to accept a plea of guilty:

(a) a plea of not guilty should be recorded and the matter should then proceed to trial before another judge of the court; or

(b) where the prosecution elects to accept a plea of guilty to a lesser alternative charge in satisfaction of the indictment, the trial judge must re-arraign the accused on the lesser charge as supported by the depositions.[111]

[111] *Dinge Damane v The State* [1991] PNGLR 244.

Bray CJ (adopted by Raine J) stated in *Weaver v Samuels* [1971] SASR 116 at 119-120:

"The defendant must be given the benefit of any reasonable doubt on matters of penalty, as well as on matters of guilt or innocence, in the absence of any statutory provision to the contrary. The plea of guilty admits no more than the bare legal ingredients of the crime. Any dispute as to anything beyond this must be resolved on ordinary legal principles, including the presumption of innocence."[112]

See also *Fred Eiserman v J Nanatsi* [1978] PNGLR 457.

In England, once an indictment is before the court, the accused must be arraigned and tried thereon unless:

(a) on motion to quash or demurrer pleaded it is held defective in substance or form and not amended;

(b) the matter at bar is pleaded and the plea is tried or confirmed in favour of the accused;

(c) a nolle prosequi is entered by the Attorney-General, not before the indictment is found;

(d) the indictment disclosed an offence which a particular court had no jurisdiction to try; or

(e) there is a gross abuse of process, in which case the court can act to remedy the situation by refusing to allow the indictment to go to trial.

In Papua New Guinea, a gross abuse of process is involved where a national, who is a participant in a joint crime, and who is unsophisticated, ignorant, backward, and generally primitive, is called to give evidence and incriminates himself or herself. No amount of warnings against self-incrimination can possibly cure the situation: *R v Simbene Dandemb* [1969-1970] PNGLR 207 at 215-216.

Insofar as a conviction is based on a plea of guilty, an appellate court may properly entertain an appeal against such conviction where the appellant did not appreciate the nature of the charge; indeed, it is clearly incumbent on an appellate court to entertain the appeal, since a decision to convict as on a plea of guilty which has been wrongly accepted is a nullity: *Eliza v Mandina* [1971-1972] PNGLR 422 at 425-426.

In *The State v Kingsley Doledole* (1997) N1513, Batari AJ stated:

"As to whether or not the State is free to accept the change of plea without leave of the Court, I adopt what in my view is the proper approach as alluded to by Smithers J in *Iwari's case* [*R v Iwari* [1964] PNGLR 175] at 176:

> 'As to this the court in *Soanes'case* [*R v Soanes* (1948) 1 All ER 289; 32 Cr App R 136] said: ... While it is impossible to lay down a hard and fast rule in any class of case as to when a plea for a lesser offence should be accepted by counsel for the Crown – and it must always be in the discretion of the judge whether he will accept it – in the opinion of the court, where nothing appears in the depositions which can be said to reduce the crime from the more serious offence charged to some lesser offence for which, under statute, a verdict may be returned, the duty of counsel for the crown would be to present the offence charged in the indictment, leaving it as a matter for the jury, if they see fit in the exercise of their undoubted prerogative, to find the lesser verdict. In the upshot, the question is entirely for the trial judge to

---

112 *R v Gabia Vagi* [1973] PNGLR 30.

consider and may in his discretion accept or decline the change of plea on the facts admitted at the time of the application. The State is not empowered to accept the change of plea during the course of the trial without leave of the Court and should resist the temptation to do so in line with its duty to 'present the offence charged in the indictment, if they see fit in the exercise of their undoubted prerogative, to find the lesser verdict.'

See *Soanes' case*, supra."

A court should be wary of the dangers of proceeding under this section where the accused is ignorant and has not had legal advice: *R v Ebulya* [1964] PNGLR 200.

See annotations under s 560 of the Code.

See also s 37 of the *Constitution*.

562. Standing mute.

(1) If an accused person, on being called on to plead to an indictment, will not plead or answer directly to the indictment, the court may, if it thinks fit, order a plea of not guilty to be entered on behalf of the accused person.

(2) A plea entered under Subsection (1) has the same effect as if it had been actually pleaded.

See s 560 of the Code regarding pleas generally.

563. Entry of plea of not guilty.

Notwithstanding anything in this Code, counsel for an accused person may, with leave of the court and after the accused person has been -

(a) informed of the offence with which he is charged; and

(b) asked to plead to the indictment,

enter a plea of not guilty on behalf of the accused person.

See ss 37(3), 37(4), 37(14), 42(3) of the *Constitution*.

See s 560 of the Code regarding pleas generally.

This section is intended to provide an additional safeguard to an accused who is unaware of legal defences (such as self-defence and provocation) open to the accused through admitting to certain alleged facts: *Nal'U Limagwe v The State* [1976] PNGLR 382.

A trial judge who chooses to seek an answer from the accused as to the truth of the prosecution allegations during the plea must be particularly careful that he or she is not in effect depriving the accused of the right to insist on the constitutional presumption of innocence until proven guilty. In order to overcome this problem a practice grew up in Papua New Guinea whereby counsel for the accused, with leave of the court, applied to enter a plea of "not guilty" on behalf of the accused. This was later codified in this section of the Code. It was held in *Gabriel Laku v The State* [1981] PNGLR 350 that where the plea of guilty was elicited by a court requirement that the accused say whether the charge was true or not true, it must be regarded as tainted, and in view of the inconsistency of the plea with the later statements of the accused on allocutus, the trial judge should have exercised his discretion to set the guilty plea aside.

The court must, in its discretion, consider whether it is safe to accept a plea of guilty. Obviously in a case where the accused is not represented by counsel, the dangers of accepting a plea are great. In the case where the accused is represented by counsel, the court must satisfy itself, with the help of counsel, that it is safe to accept a plea of guilty to the offence charged. The court must not surrender its duty by relying merely on the word of defence counsel: *The State v Yaulipa Bulaim* (1980) N234.

Once an unequivocal plea has been entered and the court proceeds to consider sentence, the prisoner is regarded as having been convicted, and it is a matter of the court's discretion as to whether the conviction should be set aside and the plea of guilty vacated when the accused, on allocutus, denies an essential element of the charge. (Decision of Kapi J in *The State v Joe Ivoro and Gemora Yavura* [1980] PNGLR 1 adopted.) Generally speaking, where the discretion is exercised against the prisoner, it will be closely examined by the appellate court: *Gabriel Laku v The State* [1981] PNGLR 350.

In *The State v Joe Ivoro and Gemora Yavura* [1980] PNGLR 1, having already accepted pleas of guilty and having administered the allocutus, Kapi J then changed the pleas to not guilty under this section. His Honour chose to disqualify himself from presiding at the trial since he had formed an opinion regarding the evidence to be called by the state at the trial, and thus would not be seen to be impartial.

In *The State v Peter Sari* [1990] PNGLR 48 Jalina AJ was asked to disqualify himself in similar circumstances, and he did so even though he saw no potential bias having read the dispositions. On the other hand, in *The State v Jack Oroko Tepol* (1999) N1941, the court also vacated a plea of guilty by the accused, but as the state did not object to Kirriwom J presiding on the trial, there was no question of bias, and no need for His Honour to disqualify himself.

An application to enter a plea of not guilty should not be made until after the accused has been informed of the offence with which he or she is charged, has been asked to plead to the indictment, and after the plea has been heard: *The State v Nal'U Limagwe* [1976] PNGLR 382.

Leave to enter a plea of not guilty after a plea of guilty has been heard will not be granted unless good grounds are shown. It is not sufficient for counsel for the accused to state that in his or her opinion a plea of not guilty should be entered: *The State v Nal'U Limagwe* [1976] PNGLR 382.

An application under this section should only be made after the accused has been informed of the offence with which he or she is charged and has been asked to plead to the indictment: *The State v Nal'U Limagwe* [1976] PNGLR 382 (Saldanha J).

In *R v Angie-Ogun* [1969-1970] PNGLR 36 at 38, upon being carefully arraigned on one count of receiving stolen property and one count of assisting the thief in escaping punishment, the accused in effect pleaded guilty to each charge. However, upon the application of his counsel and the Crown not objecting, the court granted leave for pleas of not guilty to be entered. The court thereupon entirely disregarded what the accused said in response to the arraignments, and placed the onus upon the prosecution to prove all elements beyond all reasonable doubt.

Where the trial judge has some doubts about whether an indictment discloses wilful murder or manslaughter, the court should not accept a plea of guilty to a charge of wilful murder; the proper course is to vacate the plea and proceed to try the issues of fact: *Public Prosecutor v Yapuna Kaso* [1977] PNGLR 209.

Where the accused had originally admitted the truth of the allegations upon arraignment, and the court, in its discretion, decides to accept a subsequent plea of not guilty, the court may also choose to ignore the accused's admission. The application of this principle should be limited, however, to cases in which the accused is illiterate and entirely ignorant of the processes of the law. In other cases the prosecution would be justified in making use of the words uttered at the time of arraignment, and cross-examining the accused upon them if he or she elected to give evidence. It would not be necessary for the prosecution to prove the admissions, because judges here exercise the dual function of judge and jury. All that would be necessary is for counsel to indicate at the appropriate time that he or she intends to rely upon what was said: *The State v John Mugur Poka* [1977] PNGLR 27.

It is a proper ground for the court to exercise its discretion under this section and allow an accused to change a guilty plea to not guilty, where the accused desires to test the prosecution's case: *The State v John Mugur Poka* [1977] PNGLR 27.

Notwithstanding the fact that an admission of the truth of the allegations has been made upon arraignment, if the court subsequently allows a plea of not guilty to be entered under this section, the whole matter is at large and the accused is not restricted to contesting the case solely upon the ground upon which the judge exercised his or her discretion: *The State v John Mugur Poka* [1977] PNGLR 27.

Where the accused made a voluntary confession of guilt, nevertheless and notwithstanding the accused's admissions and the absence of any retraction, counsel for the accused may submit that the court cannot be satisfied to the necessary degree of the accused's guilt. Strange as this situation may appear, it follows quite naturally from the provisions of this section which, in effect, permits defence counsel with the court's leave to enter a plea of not guilty even though such a course may be directly opposed to the client's instructions: *R v Namiropa Koinbondi* [1969-1970] PNGLR 194 at 198-199.

In *R v Gahoso Simbane* [1973] PNGLR 257, where the accused was arraigned on a charge of stealing, and said "I did", counsel was given leave to plead not guilty.

For circumstances generally where a plea of "not guilty" was entered following an application under s 563 (the accused would find it impossible to understand the notions of impropriety and misconduct with which the charge was concerned and could not differentiate between the external elements of the charge and the other essential ingredients of the charge), it would be unjust and tantamount to a breach of the accused's fundamental human rights as guaranteed by the *Constitution* of Papua New Guinea (s 37) not to enter a plea of not guilty: *The State v Aubafu Feama, Nana Auri, Kafidiri Kududebe Hagima* [1978] PNGLR 301.

Where a plea of not guilty is entered under this section, it is like a plea of not guilty by the accused in the first place, pursuant to s 560. Issues raised in the charge must then be tried according to law, under s 566: *The State v Joe Ivoro and Gemora Yavura* [1980] PNGLR 1.

564. Plea of autrefois convict or autrefois acquit.

In a plea that the accused person has already been convicted or acquitted, it is sufficient to state that he has been lawfully convicted or acquitted, as the case may be, of the offence charged in the indictment, or of the other offence of which he alleges that he has been convicted or acquitted, and in the latter case to describe the offence in any way in which it is commonly known.

See ss 16-17, 547 and 560(2)(c)-(f) of the Code.

See s 560 regarding pleas generally.

The accused cannot raise the plea of *autrefois convict* in relation to offences which have been "taken into account" in sentencing, under s 603. Nevertheless, the accepted practice has been that the prosecution will not proceed on offences which have been taken into account: *R v Emere Gabua* (1960) N156.

Injia AJ said, in *The State v John Nugints* [1994] PNGLR 493 at 495-496:

> "A plea of *autrefois acquit* is a complete defence to a charge, whether the charge be by way of indictment or information. The defence would operate in a situation where the second offence or the facts in support of the second offence with which a person is charged are the same as the first offence on which the same person is convicted or acquitted. I would adopt the test of unity in offence or unity in evidence, as set out by Clarkson J in *Sapuro Masuve v Bryant* [1974] PNGLR 61 at p 65:
>
> > 'It then becomes necessary to consider the degree of identity between the offence of which the appellants were acquitted and that with which they are now charged, that is, to apply the test which has been variously described as being whether the two offences are substantially the same or in effect the same or whether the evidence necessary to support the commission of the second offence would have been sufficient to procure a conviction on the first offence.'"

The accused had been charged with unlawful assault contrary to s 6(1) of the *Summary Offences Act* Ch 264 and acquitted in the District Court. He was subsequently indicted in the National Court on a charge of unlawfully doing grievous bodily harm contrary to s 319 of the *Criminal Code* Ch 262. It was held:

> "[E]ven though the two offences are different, the facts alleged, or the evidence which would have been necessary to prove those alleged facts on a charge of unlawful assault, are substantially the same, if not the same, as the facts alleged or evidence which could be called to support the present charge."

A plea of *autrefois acquit* was upheld: *The State v John Nugints* [1994] PNGLR 493 at 496 (Injia AJ).

Where an accused, through his or her counsel, produces to the court a certificate of dismissal in respect of the same matter involving the same victim and the same accused, the production of the certificate provides a bar to any legal proceedings in any court, insofar as the matter in those proceedings relates to the same matter involving the same accused. This provision applies notwithstanding that "the two offences are different in the sense that they are founded on different legislation, the Courts are different, and the procedures prescribed in those legislation for dealing with the offence are different": *The State v John Nugints* [1994] PNGLR 493 at 496 (Injia AJ).

Injia AJ further stated in that case at 497:

> "[Section] 560(2)(e) and s 564 of the *Criminal Code* and s 162(2) of the *District Courts Act* recognize and re-enforce the accused's right under s 37(8) of the *Constitution*."

See ss 37(3), 37(4), 37(13), 37(14) and 42(3) of the *Constitution*.

It is established that the court has the power, inherent in the court's jurisdiction, to prevent any abuse of its process, and to control its own procedure: *R v Abia Tambule* [1974] PNGLR 250 at 252.

Where the law requires proof of a fact, the court must feel an actual persuasion of the occurrence of that fact. A mere mechanical comparison of probabilities is not enough. There must be a belief in the reality of that fact: *R v Namiropa Koinbondi* [1969-1970] PNGLR 194 at 200.

The proper form of direction where facts are peculiarly within the knowledge of the accused is laid down in *Reg v Guiren* (1962) 79 WN (NSW) 811 at 812:

> "Provided the jury is not directed that the onus is thrown on the accused, it is not a misdirection to tell them that if the truth is not easily ascertainable by the Crown, but is probably well known to the accused, then the fact that no explanation or answer is forthcoming, as might be expected if the truth were consistent with innocence, is a matter the jury may properly consider. They have then to say whether in this state of the evidence they have a reasonable doubt of the accused's guilt."

If they have, they must acquit: *The State v John Kasaipwalova* [1977] PNGLR 257.

Where circumstantial evidence and the accused's false and contradictory accounts of events tend to confirm his or her guilt, the court must ask itself whether there is any reasonable hypothesis consistent with the innocence of the accused: *R v Polhill* (1973) N734.

It was stated in *R v Banji* (1962) N254:

> "[T]he expression 'prove affirmatively' either in statutory provisions or in judgments does not have any bearing on the degree of proof required. It shows merely the direction in which a fact must be established to whatever degree of proof may be appropriate."

It is the province of the magistrate to decide all questions of fact in the lower courts. The magistrate is to decide on questions of credibility, the weight to be given to the evidence of the witnesses and the inferences to be drawn from the evidence he or she accepts as trustworthy: *Basil Morehare Tapora v Holt* (1961) N187.

It is not necessary for every item in a prosecution case to be proved beyond reasonable doubt: see *R v Beble* [1979] Qd R 278. It is necessary that at the end of the whole proceedings one is satisfied of guilt beyond reasonable doubt - that is, that all essential matters, as opposed to ancillary matters, are proved beyond reasonable doubt: *John Peng v The State* [1982] PNGLR 331 (Pratt J, with Kidu CJ agreeing).

567. Demurrer.

(1) When an accused person demurs only and does not plead any plea, the court shall hear and determine the matter immediately.

(2) If the demurrer is overruled, the accused person shall be called on to plead to the indictment.

(3) When an accused person pleads and demurs together, it is in the discretion of the court whether the plea or demurrer is first disposed of.

(4) No joinder in demurrer is necessary.

See s 560 of the Code regarding pleas.

568. Separate trials.

When two or more persons are charged in the same indictment, whether with the same offence or with different offences, the court may, at any time during the trial, on the application of any of the accused persons, direct that the trial of any of the accused persons be held separately from the trial of the other or others of them.

See ss 7 and 532(6)-(9) of the Code regarding parties to offences and joinder of charges.

In a joint indictment where one accused pleads guilty and the other not guilty, the proper course is to postpone sentence on any prisoner who has pleaded guilty until those who have pleaded not guilty have been tried, so that the court may be in possession of the facts relating to all who are convicted and may be able to assess properly their degrees of guilt: followed *R v Payne* (1950) 34 Cr App R 43. The above rule will not apply where a prisoner who has pleaded guilty is to be called as a witness. In such circumstances, it is a proper practice that sentence should be passed forthwith, so that there should be no suspicion of the prisoner's evidence being coloured by the fact that he or she hopes to get a lighter sentence because of the evidence which he or she gives. Where it is proposed to call an accomplice for the state, it is the practice to:

(a) omit him or her from the indictment; or

(b) take a plea of guilty on arraignment; or during the trial if he or she withdraws the plea of not guilty;

or before calling him or her either:

(a) offer no evidence and permit an acquittal; or

(b) enter a nolle prosequi.[113]

Where a common purpose is alleged, prima facie the several accused should be tried together: *R v Kision* (1970) N580.

In a joint trial the court must carefully separate the evidence, for the charge is both joint and several against the accused: *Keko Aparo v The State* (1983) SC 249, following *R v Fenwick* (1953) 54 SR (NSW) 147.

In *Wemp Mapa v The State* [1979] PNGLR 135 at 138, Andrew J queried whether this section operates only upon an application for severance made by an accused.

Doherty J stated, in *The State v Arey Watul* [1992] PNGLR 475 at 477:

> "Section 568 of the *Criminal Code* gives the court the discretion at any time during a trial on the application of any of the accused persons, to direct that their trials should be held separately.
>
> No application has been made to separate this defendant from any other co-accused. The section of the code is not worded to allow a court to separate defendants on its own volition. There has to be an application."

On a question of undue participation by a trial judge, the remarks of Lord Greene MR in *Yuill v Yuill* [1945] 1 All ER 183 at 185-189, are important:

> "But with the utmost respect to the judge it was, I think, unfortunate that he took so large a part as he did ... It is quite plain to me that the judge was endeavouring to ascertain the truth in the manner which at the moment seemed to him most convenient. But he must, I think, have lost sight of the inconveniences which are apt to flow from an undue participation by the judge in the examination of witnesses. It is, of course, always proper for a judge – and it is his duty – to put a question with a view to elucidating an obscure answer or when he thinks that the witness has misunderstood a question put to him by counsel. If there are matters which the judge considers have not been sufficiently cleared up or questions which he himself thinks ought to have been put, he can, of course, take steps to see that the deficiency is made good. It is, I think, generally more convenient to do this when counsel has finished his questions or is passing to a

[113] *The State v Atu Kote* [1978] PNGLR 212.

new subject. It must always be borne in mind that the judge does not know what is in counsel's brief and has not the same facilities as counsel for an effective examination-in-chief or cross-examination. In cross-examination, for instance, experienced counsel will see just as clearly as the judge that, for example, a particular question will be the crucial one. But it is for counsel to decide at what stage he will put the question, and the whole strength of the cross-examination may be destroyed if the judge, in his desire to get at what seems to him to be the crucial point, himself intervenes and prematurely puts the question himself. I think it desirable to throw out these suggestions in case they may be found helpful in the future ... A judge who observes the demeanour of the witness while they are being examined by counsel has from his detached position a much more favourable opportunity of forming a just appreciation than a judge who himself conducts the examination. If he takes the latter course he, so to speak, descends into the arena and is liable to have his vision clouded by the dust of the conflict. Unconsciously he deprives himself of the advantage and dispassionate observation".

In *Birch v The State* [1979] PNGLR 75 at 79-80, the trial judge did not unduly participate in the circumstances of dealing with a very young Papua New Guinean girl as a witness and the problem of inexperienced prosecutors and inexpert evidence gatherers.

In that case, where the trial judge asked 186 questions to the prosecutor's 123, corrected the false impression of counsel that he had to proceed either on an allegation of carnal knowledge or upon rape, required the production of the only available copy from the accused of a signed record of an interview, and recalled three witnesses of the prosecution, this did not constitute undue participation by a judge in the conduct of a trial.

If an appellant escapes custody or jumps bail prior to the hearing of the appeal, the court may in its discretion adjourn the case or dismiss the appeal. The court may hear the appeal although the appellant has escaped or not answered bail, for example, where all the points raised on behalf of the appellant have been raised and fully argued on behalf of the other appellants: *Keko Aparo v The State* (1983) SC 249.

569. Want of understanding of accused person.

(1) If, where the accused person is called on to plead to the indictment it appears to be uncertain whether he is capable of understanding the proceedings at the trial so as to be able to make a proper defence, then before a plea is entered to the indictment the court shall enquire into the matter in order to discover whether or not he is capable.

(2) If the court finds that the accused person is capable of understanding the proceedings, he shall then be called on to plead and the trial shall proceed as in other cases.

(3) If the court finds that the accused person is not capable of understanding the proceedings -

(a) the court shall say whether he is so found by it for the reason that he is of unsound mind or for some other specified reason; and

(b) the finding shall be recorded; and

(c) the court may order the accused person -

(i) to be discharged; or

(ii) be kept in custody in such place and in such manner as the court thinks proper until he can be dealt with according to law.

(4) A person found under this section to be incapable of understanding the proceedings at the trial may be again indicted and tried for the offence.

See s 560 of the Code regarding pleas.

In *R v Koiyari-Iyeva* [1965-1966] PNGLR 284 the accused was found fit to plead, but there was an inquiry as to soundness of mind under s 590 during the course of the trial. The trial judge directed that a psychiatrist examine the accused.

The words "so as to be able to make a proper defence" appearing in s 569(1) should be read into the second part. Also, the section does not require an express finding of insanity. The standard of proof of insanity is similar to that in civil cases: *R v Smith* [1965-1966] PNGLR 220.

570. Defence of accused.

(1) A person charged with an offence is entitled to make his defence at his trial and to have the witnesses examined and cross-examined by his lawyer.

(2) A person charged with an offence may, by leave of the court, have his defence conducted by another person who is not a lawyer.

See s 37(4)(e) and (f) of the *Constitution*.

A report of the General Council of the Bar of England in 1915 approved counsel's conduct of a case when an accused admits his or her guilt. The counsel does not have to withdraw from the case, but may test the evidence put by each witness and argue the sufficiency of the evidence put. Counsel must go no further than putting the state to proof of the charge: *Nal'U Limagwe v The State* [1976] PNGLR 382.

In *The State v Arey Watul* [1992] PNGLR 475 (Doherty J) it was held at the close of the state case that the accuseds had a case to answer in a trial that had proceeded in their absence following their escape from custody during a weekend adjournment. The hearing was adjourned until they were recaptured to allow them to call evidence according to s 570 of the Code.

571. Presence of accused.

(1) Subject to Subsection (2), a trial must take place in the presence of the accused person, unless he so conducts himself as to render the continuance of the proceedings in his presence impracticable, in which case the court-

(a) may order him to be removed; and

(b) may direct the trial to proceed in his absence.

(2) The court may, in any case, if it thinks fit, permit a person charged with a misdemeanour to be absent during the whole or any part of the trial on such conditions as it thinks proper.

(3) If the accused person absents himself during the trial without leave, the court may direct a warrant to be issued to arrest him and bring him before the court.

See s 37(5) of the *Constitution*.

In a proceeding on charges of indecent interference with corpses, the court excused the accused from being present during the balance of the proceedings to obviate the necessity of the court travelling to Daru or requiring the accused to be brought to Port Moresby, which would have delayed the giving of the judgment: *R v Noboi Bosai* [1971-1972] PNGLR 271 at 272.

An accused may stand trial other than from the dock. It is a matter of long-standing practice that an accused person stands trial from the dock. Where an accused is defended by counsel, and wishes to sit in court near his or her counsel, they are entitled to do so. It is not a matter of indulgence by the court. If it should not be a matter of indulgence, then requests to sit near counsel should now be very freely granted in the interests of dispensing justice to the individual: see *Constitution*, s 158(2): *The State v Allan Woila (No 2)* [1978] PNGLR 113.

572. Evidence in defence.

(1) At the close of the evidence for the prosecution, the proper officer of the courts shall-ask the accused person or his counsel whether the accused intends to adduce evidence in his defence or whether he desires to make a statement to the court before he or his counsel addresses the court.

(2) Whether or not the accused intends to adduce evidence in his defence he is entitled to make a statement to the court.

(3) When the accused makes a statement to the court he shall make the statement at the close of the evidence for the prosecution and before adducing any evidence in his defence.

Compare this section with s 96 of the *District Courts Act.*

It has always been a matter of practice to advise an accused of the right to remain silent if he or she wishes. This is especially so if the accused is unrepresented. Although such advice to a defendant does not have a statutory basis, a failure by a court to advise a defendant of that particular right at the time when the court is also advising the defendant of the right to call evidence may well prove fatal to the case if a conviction is subsequently recorded, depending upon all the circumstances of the individual case: *Koi Konom v Nelson Watai* (1981) N297 (M). See s 37(10) of the *Constitution* regarding the right to silence.

Where the accused has not given evidence, this cannot be used as a bolster to a deficient prosecution case. However, there is authority for saying that once there is evidence upon which the court might be satisfied beyond reasonable doubt that the accused is guilty, the fact that the accused has not given evidence, or called evidence in his or her power to call, may lend assurance to any satisfaction the court may feel: *The State v Marawa Kanaio* [1979] PNGLR 319.

For a discussion of the practical application of an assertion of the right to remain silent, see *Paulus Pawa v The State* [1981] PNGLR 498.

Minogue CJ (at 6-7) approved the dicta of the High Court in *May v O'Sullivan* (1955) 92 CLR 654 at 658, that:

> "If the truth is not easily ascertainable by the prosecution, but is probably well known to the defendant, then the fact that no explanation or answer is forthcoming as might be expected if the truth were consistent with innocence, is a matter which the court or jury may properly consider".[114]

[114] *R v Kauka Moru* (1971) N622.

See also *R v Abia Tambule* [1974] PNGLR 250.

Where the truth of a matter can be easily ascertained by the Crown, and the accused has given an explanation adduced before the court, no weight can be attached to the failure of the accused to testify: *R v Lupalupa-Sisarowe* [1967-1968] PNGLR 455.

It is a fundamental principle of the law that if a person makes a statement outside court, that evidence is evidence against that person only and not against anyone else, including any person whom he or she may implicate: *R v Sapulo Masuve* (1973) N732.

Unsworn statements

Kapi J said, in *The State v Nagiri-Topoma* [1980] PNGLR 18:

> "The practice in the National Court has always been that where an accused makes a statement from the dock, that is, an unsworn statement, he is never subjected to cross-examination either by the State or the judge, however he must subject himself to cross examination when he chooses to give sworn evidence from the box."

An unsworn statement from the dock does not have the same weight as sworn testimony. See *The State v Stephen Isaac Awoda* (1983) N416, which follows *R v Ulel* [1973] PNGLR 254; *Frost v Hale* (1964) 48 Cr App R 284; and *Samuel Peacock v The King* (1911) 13 CLR 619.

The right to make an unsworn statement from the dock is not affected by the *Evidence Act*: *R v Kor Gabril, Dots Kundup and Piam Gip* [1973] PNGLR 704.

The defendant may not be cross-examined on a statement from the dock: *Gaude v Gomara* (1956) N180.

On the question of the weight to be attached to unsworn statements by the accused, see generally pp 7-14 of *R v Ulel* [1973] PNGLR 254.

The proper direction to be given to a jury when the accused has made an unsworn statement is that:[115]

> "it is not sworn evidence which can be cross-examined to, but that nevertheless they can attach to it such weight as they think fit, and should take it into consideration in deciding whether the prosecution have made out their case so that they feel sure that the prisoner is guilty"[116]

or that

> "the jury should take the prisoner's statement as prima facie a possible version of the facts and consider it with the sworn evidence, giving it such weight as it appears to be entitled to in comparison with the facts clearly established by evidence".[117]

Where the accused is required to establish a defence, he or she is not obliged to call or give sworn evidence. The accused may establish the defence in an unsworn statement. However, an unsworn statement, although evidence, does not have the same weight as sworn testimony: *R v Ulel* [1973] PNGLR 254.

The practice was noted that where one of a group of accused persons gives sworn evidence and others make application to make unsworn statements, a judge may

---

[115] *The State v John Kasaipwalova* [1977] PNGLR 257.
[116] *R v Anthony David Frost and George Talbot Hale* (1964) 48 Cr App R 284.
[117] *Samuel Peacock v The King* (1911) 13 CLR 619 at 640-641 (Griffith CJ).

direct by consent that such unsworn statements be made: *R v Manganapi-Sandepi* (1969) N537.

Once the stage is reached at which a defendant indicates that he or she wishes to put the matter to trial, the police statement of facts should be destroyed - symbolically if not literally. That is, it should be destroyed to the extent that it is put completely out of the mind of the presiding magistrate. When a person pleads guilty of course, he or she pleads only to those facts which are necessary to sustain the elements of the charge and not to any other facts. In Papua New Guinea the practice has sensibly arisen in the magistrates' court of putting a statement of facts to the accused so that the accused may understand what the charge is all about, and then, having done that, asking if the accused has heard the facts and if he or she agrees with the facts. That state of affairs is, of course, something over and above a mere plea of guilty. Where, however, the person pleads not guilty or does not accept the statement of facts as true, from that point onwards for the rest of the proceedings the statement of facts should be completely disregarded: *Koi Konom v Nelson Watai* (1981) N297 (M).

If it is to be suggested that state witnesses are lying or mistaken or failing in accuracy of recollection, they should be questioned to that effect and given an opportunity to explain. You cannot correctly keep your own case secret until your client gives evidence and the state witness has an opportunity to respond: *The State v Stephen Isaac Awoda* (1983) N416, following *The State v Ogadi Minjipa* [1977] PNGLR 293.

No case to-answer submissions

Insofar as the "no case to answer" practice serves as a measure by which the judge controls the jury; it is for similar reasons of questionable value in our system. However, the "no case" practice serves a separate and essential purpose: it is a procedural reinforcement to the presumption of innocence in s 37(4)(a) of the *Constitution*, and to the accused's right to silence in s 37(10) of the *Constitution*. These citizen rights entail that the state must make out its case by the evidence it adduces; it cannot rely on making good any defects in its case, by cross-examining the accused or the accused's witnesses: *The State v Lasebose Kuriday* (1981) N300.

The "no case to answer" submission raises a question of law. The other submission commonly made by defence counsel at the close of the state's case is to "stop the case", and involves a question of fact. The general principle that the court should not weigh up the evidence until the whole of the evidence is in, points to this latter submission not being entertained except in what is very clearly a hopeless case. It would be the sort of case where the court itself would consider acting on its own initiative to stop what amounts to a waste of its time and public money: *The State v Lasebose Kuriday* (1981) N300.

The "no case" submission may arise in either of two broad situations First, an accused cannot lawfully be convicted if there is no evidence or no more than an iota of evidence, in proof of any one element of the offence charged. No real weighing of the evidence is involved in such a case. Second, where there is more than an iota of evidence with respect to each element of the offence, the court still has discretion whether or not to entertain the "no case" submission. However, a submission on this basis should be entertained only when the judge really has no weighing up to do. That is, it must be a very clear case, where the state evidence is so dubious, or so tainted, or so obviously lacking in weight or credibility, or has been so discredited in cross-examination, that it is clear that no reasonable tribunal could safely convict on it: *The State v Lasebose Kuriday* (1981) N300.

Regarding "no case to answer" submissions, there is a discretion in a judge in this jurisdiction to weigh the evidence and acquit the accused at the end of the prosecution case: *The State v Roka Pep* [1983] PNGLR 19, following *The State v Aige Kola* [1979] PNGLR 620, and *The State v Lasebose Kuriday* (1981) N300.

On an application for "no case to answer", it would be quite inappropriate to consider whether the court has a reasonable doubt at the close of the prosecution case. If the decision were that the court was left in reasonable doubt at this stage, the burden of proof would in effect shift to the accused who would then have to raise the doubt. That of course is in the face of clearly established principles of criminal law: *The State v Tom Morris* [1981] PNGLR 493.

On a "no case" submission, a trial judge has a discretion which may be exercised if the judge feels that the state of evidence would make a conviction unsafe. The discretion does not have to be exercised in all cases. It is not likely to be exercised unless the degree of danger involved in conviction is substantial enough to cause the trial judge to exercise the discretion. A trial judge may properly allow a case to go to a jury, even though a court of criminal appeal will upon a later review of the case decide that the state of evidence is so unsatisfactory as to require the conviction to be quashed. The quashing of the conviction in this way does not mean that the trial judge's exercise of discretion was wrong: *The State v Tom Morris* [1981] PNGLR 493.

Regarding "no case to answer" submissions, it is wrong for a judge to decide after the prosecution's case whether or not the judge is satisfied beyond reasonable doubt of the guilt of the accused before all the evidence is before the court: *The State v Delga Puri and Tapri Maip* [1982] PNGLR 395 (Kidu CJ), following *The State v Paul Kundi Rape* [1976] PNGLR 96, and *Han Tua Tau* [1981] 3 All ER 14.

It is of fundamental importance to a fair trial in our system that the judge as tribunal of fact never be required to weigh up the evidence more than once, and then only when all of the evidence is in. It follows that any weighing of the evidence by the judge or magistrate, required by a "no case to answer" submission at the close of the state case, should be kept to the absolute minimum: *The State v Lasebose Kuriday* (1981) N300.

Note the "regret" expressed by Pratt J in *The State v Lupam Lau* (1981) N309 (M), with the decision of Kearney DCJ in *The State v Lasebose Kuriday*, regarding "no case to answer submissions".

In a no case to answer submission, the test is not whether an accused ought to be committed, but whether on the evidence as it stands, the accused could lawfully be convicted. Where the prosecution fails to establish one of the elements of the crime, an accused cannot be convicted. Where, however, all the elements requiring proof have been covered by the evidence but such evidence is so unsatisfactory that the tribunal must feel considerable hesitation as to whether all or any of the essential material can be believed, an application may be made to stop the proceedings. In such circumstances, that is where there is insufficiency of evidence, an accused may, as a matter of law, be called upon to proceed with his or her defence, but there is a discretion in the judge not to call on the accused at all: *The State v Lupam Lau* (1981) N309 (M), following *The State v Paul Kundi Rape* [1976] PNGLR 96.

Where at a criminal trial it is submitted on behalf of the accused at the close of the Crown case that there is no case to answer, the trial judge should rule on the submission without requiring the defence to elect whether to call evidence or not: *Evgeniou v The Queen* (1964) 37 ALJR 508, [1964] PNGLR 45.

When there is a submission of no case to answer at the close of the case for the prosecution, the question to be asked is not whether on the evidence as it stands the defendant ought to be convicted, but whether on the evidence as it stands the accused could lawfully be convicted. This is a question of law, to be carefully distinguished from the question of fact to be asked at the close of all the evidence, namely, whether the prosecution has proved its case beyond reasonable doubt: *The State v Paul Kundi Rape* [1976] PNGLR 96.

See also *R v Kakius-Isiura* [1964] PNGLR 84.

Where there is no case to answer, an accused may not, as a matter of law, be called upon to answer it. Where there is a case of insufficiency of evidence, an accused may, as a matter of law, be called upon to answer it. However, there is a discretion in the judge either not to call on the accused at all, ie take the case away from the jury, or, at least to leave it to the jury to say whether or not they wish to hear more: *The State v Paul Kundi Rape* [1976] PNGLR 96. This statement is commonly known as the "second limb" of *Paul Kundi Rape*.

Pratt J said in *The State v Lupam Lau* (1981) N309 (M):

> "In a no prima facie case submission by the defence, matters of weight and credibility are to be ignored. As the High Court of Australia said in *May v O'Sullivan* (1955) 92 CLR 654, 658, the test is not whether an accused ought to be convicted 'but whether on the evidence as it stands he could lawfully be convicted'. When, for example, the prosecution has failed to establish one of the essential elements of the charge, then clearly an accused could not be convicted. When, however, all the elements requiring proof have been covered by the evidence but such evidence is so unsatisfactory that the tribunal must feel considerable hesitation as to whether all or any of the essential material can be believed, application to stop the proceedings may then be made under the *Benney v Dowling* [1959] VR 237, test. An analysis of these two principles is lucidly made by O'Leary AJ in *The State v Paul Kundi Rape*, in which the kernel of the entire issue appears in the following words (at 99):
>
> > 'Where there is no case to answer, an accused may not, as a matter of law, be called upon to answer it. Where there is a case of insufficiency of evidence ... an accused may as a matter of law be called upon to answer it, but there is a discretion in the judge ... not to call on him at all.'"[118]

In the test of "no case to answer", questions of the weight and creditability of the evidence are to be ignored: *R v Uno Tam* (1973) N766.

See also on no case to answer submissions, *R v Alan Edmund Montgomery* (1966) N408.

To be distinguished from the situation where there is no case to answer is the situation where the judge has a discretion to withdraw the case from the jury. The question then is not whether there is any or some evidence on which a jury could lawfully convict, but whether the evidence is so insufficient that the accused ought not to be called upon to answer it. In either case, one does not look to see whether the prosecution has proved its case beyond reasonable doubt, which is a question of fact not law: *The State v Paul Kundi Rape* [1976] PNGLR 96.

---

[118] Disagreement expressed with the decision in *The State v Lasebose Kuriday* (1981) N300.

Therefore, there are two principles laid out in *The State v Paul Kundi Rape*. In the first, where a submission of no case to answer is made, the judge examines the evidence as a question of law to determine "whether the evidence supports the essential elements of the offence": *The State v Roka Pep (No 2)* [1983] PNGLR 287.

"The second principle is where a Judge decides there is no case to answer, it has a discretion to stop a case at the close of all the evidence in appropriate circumstances: this discretion is exercisable where there is a mere scintilla of evidence and where the evidence is so lacking in weight and reliability that no reasonable tribunal could safely convict on it".

The two principles should be kept separate. The second principle is not a ruling that there is no case to answer, but a discretionary principle to withdraw the case: *The State v Roka Pep (No 2)* [1983] PNGLR 287, adopted and applied in *The State v Phillip Kamagu Mil* (1995) N1388.

It is highly undesirable for a defence witness to give evidence before the accused, and is contrary to well established rules of procedure: *Ryan v The State* (1979), following *R v Morrison* (1911) 6 Cr App R 159, and *R v Joan Smith* [1968] 2 All ER 115.

Extracts from articles and correspondence from medical journals are inadmissible: *Ryan v The State* (1979) NSC 148.

573. Speeches

(1) Before any evidence is given at the trial of an accused person the State Prosecutor is entitled to address the court for the purpose of opening the evidence intended to be adduced for the prosecution.

(2) If an accused person is defended by counsel who says that he does not intend to adduce evidence, the State Prosecutor is entitled to address the court a second time for the purpose of summing up the evidence already given against the accused person.

(3) Subject to Section 572, at the close of the evidence for the prosecution the accused person, and each of the accused persons, if more than one, may by himself or his counsel address the court for the purpose of opening the evidence (if any) intended to be adduced for the defence, and after the whole of the evidence is given may again address the court on the whole case.

(4) If evidence is adduced for an accused person, the State Prosecutor is entitled to reply.

(5) If evidence is adduced for one or more of several accused persons, but not for all of them, the State Prosecutor is entitled to reply with respect to the person or persons by whom evidence is adduced, but not with respect to the other or others of them.

(6) When an accused person who is defended by counsel is allowed by the court to make a statement to the court, the State Prosecutor is entitled to the same right of reply as if evidence had been adduced for the accused person.

Section 573(3) does not impose an obligation on defence counsel to open his or her case. However, if defence counsel does not open, difficulties are prone to arise: prosecuting counsel cannot cross-examine a current witness on matters in which further witnesses may be called, and witnesses will have to be kept in the court precincts in case further evidence or rebuttal evidence is required: Greville-Smith J said in *The State v Herman Kagl Diawo* (1980) N255:

"Such a practice would not promote the interests of justice or trust between the court and counsel, or between counsel".

It is a matter for the tribunal of fact whether it desires to take a view. Counsel or parties may suggest that a view would be desirable, but if the tribunal decides that it would not be helped by a view, that is the end of the matter. The tribunal need not go out of its way to ask an unrepresented party whether a view should be taken: *Peter Roy Wieden v Bogunu Di'i* [1976] PNGLR 101.

A view of the scene of an alleged offence by the court is part of the evidence; it is in substitution for or supplemental to plans, photographs and the like. The rule is that a view is for the purpose of enabling the tribunal to understand the questions that are being raised, to follow the evidence and to apply it, but not to put the result of the view in place of evidence: *R v Elly* [1965] No 357.

In *Kristeff v R* [1967-1968] PNGLR 415 at 418-419, the court held that the trial judge had overstepped the limits of the use that may be made of a view, by substituting for sworn evidence inferences which he had formed of the locus. Also, the defence had been given no opportunity of dealing by evidence or argument with the suggestion that there had been tampering with physical evidence at the scene for the purpose of advancing the case for the defence. The judge's belief as to tampering by the defence caused him to unfavourably assess the evidence of defence witnesses, and constituted reversible error.

Viewing the scene of an offence (here, dangerous driving causing death under s 328) is a matter of discretion for the trial judge. If a view would help, then a view of the scene should be taken. The observations from the view should not become the evidence, nor should witnesses take the liberty to invent or re-enact or even to demonstrate through the scene, what might have happened. This is particularly dangerous where a witness was not physically there at the crucial time, but seeks to reconstruct an event through tyre marks or alleged skid marks: *The State v Kevin Marcellin Daniel* (1980) N283.

575. Special verdict.

In any case in which it appears to the court that -

(a) the question whether an accused person ought or ought not to be convicted of an offence; or

(b) the proper punishment to be awarded on conviction,

may depend on some specific fact, the court shall state whether or not it finds that specific fact to be established by the evidence.

576. Incapacity of Judge.

(1) If in the course of the trial the presiding Judge becomes incapable of proceeding, a Judge may, on application by the accused person or his counsel, or by a State Prosecutor, order that the trial be discontinued.

(2) If an order is made under Subsection (1), the accused person -

(a) shall remain in custody and may be again put on his trial on the same indictment; and

(b) has the same rights with respect to admission to bail as on an original committal for trial for the offence with which he is charged, and a Judge or magistrate may, in a proper case, admit him to bail accordingly.

(3) If after an accused person has been convicted of an offence but before sentence the presiding Judge becomes incapable of proceeding, some other Judge may, on application by the accused person or his counsel, or by a State Prosecutor, proceed to sentence as though the accused person had been convicted by him.

577. Verdict on Sunday.

The taking of a verdict or any other proceeding of the court is not invalid by reason of its happening on a Sunday.

578. Further pleas.

When the issues raised by any plea or pleas, except the plea of not guilty, have been found against an accused person who has not pleaded the plea of not guilty, he shall be called on to plead again, and the court may direct the issues raised by any fresh plea to be tried by the court constituted by the same or another Judge.

See s 560 of the Code regarding pleas.

Division 5 – Evidence: Presumptions of Fact

579. Evidence on charge of treason.

On the trial of a person charged with treason, evidence shall not be admitted of an overt act not alleged in the indictment.

See s 37 of the Code regarding treason.

580. Evidence on trials for perjury and subornation.

On the trial of a person charged with an offence of which the giving of false testimony by any person at the trial of a person charged with an offence is an element, a certificate -

(a) setting out the substance and effect only, without the formal parts, of the indictment or complaint and the proceedings at the trial; and

(b) purporting to be signed by the officer having the custody of the records of the court where the indictment or complaint was tried, or by his deputy,

is sufficient evidence of the trial, without proof of the signature or official character of the person who appears to have signed the certificate.

See s 121 of the Code regarding perjury.

581. Evidence of previous conviction.

(1) On the trial of a person charged with an offence alleged to have been committed after a previous conviction, a certificate -

(a) setting out the substance and effect only, without the formal parts, of the indictment, verdict and judgement, or of the complaint and conviction; and

(b) purporting to be signed by the officer having the custody of the records of the court where the accused person was first convicted, or by his deputy,

is, on proof of the identity of the person of the offender, sufficient evidence of the conviction, without proof of the signature or official character of the person who appears to have signed the certificate.

(2) If the previous conviction was a summary conviction, the conviction shall, until the contrary is shown, be presumed not to have been appealed against.

See s 15 of the *Evidence Act*.

582. Evidence of relationship on charge of incest.

On the trial of a person charged with an offence of which carnal knowledge, or an attempt to have carnal knowledge, of a woman or girl is an element, and of which blood relationship is also an element -

(a) it is sufficient to prove that the woman or girl on whose person or by whom the offence is alleged to have been committed is reputed to be the daughter or other lineal descendant, or sister, of the person charged, or of the person with whom the offence is alleged to have been committed, as the case may be, and it is not necessary to prove that she, or any person being her parent or ancestor and being a descendant of the person charged, or of the person with whom the offence is alleged to have been committed, as the case may be, was born in lawful wedlock; and

(b) the accused person shall, until the contrary is proved be presumed to have had knowledge at the time of the alleged offence of the relationship existing between the woman or girl on whose person or by whom the offence is alleged to have been committed and the person charged, or the person with whom the offence is alleged to have been committed, as the case may be.

See ss 223-224 of the Code regarding incest.

583. Evidence of gaming.

On the trial of a person charged with an offence of such a nature that proof that any place was kept or used or restored to for playing at any game of chance, or of mixed chance and skill, is necessary, it is not necessary to prove that any person found there playing at any game was playing for any money, wager or stake.

See s 232 of the Code regarding gaming. See also the *Gaming Act*, Ch 270.

584. Evidence of authority.

The averment in an indictment that the prosecution is instituted by the direction of the Public Prosecutor, or at the request of the government of a State, is sufficient evidence of the fact, until the contrary is shown.

585. Evidence on charges of offences against Customs laws.

On the trial of a person charged with any offence of which the fact that some person was at some particular time -

(a) an officer of Customs; or

(b) employed for the prevention of smuggling,

is an element, the averment in the indictment or complaint that any person mentioned in it was an officer of Customs, or was employed for the prevention of smuggling, at any time stated in it is sufficient evidence of the fact, until the contrary is shown.

See ss 198-200 of the Code regarding offences against customs' officers.

586. Evidence on certain charges of stealing money.

(1) On the trial of a person charged with stealing -

(a) while employed in the Public Service, money that -

(i) was the property of the State; or .

(ii) came into his possession by virtue of his employment; or

(b) while a clerk or servant, money that -

(i) was the property of his employer; or

(ii) came into his possession on account of his employer,

an entry in any book of account kept by the accused person, or kept in, under or subject to his charge or supervision, purporting to be an entry of the receipt of any money, is evidence that the money purported to have been received was so received by him.

(2) On the trial of a person charged with an offence referred to in Subsection (1) it is not necessary to prove the stealing by the accused person of any specific sum of money, if -

(a) on examination of the books of account of entries kept or made by him, or kept or made in, under or subject to his charge or supervision; or

(b) by any other evidence,

there is proof of a general deficiency, and the court is satisfied that the accused person stole the deficient money or any part of it.

The words "general deficiency" and "deficient money" refer to a general deficiency of money. Where a general deficiency of goods and money is proved, and of that general deficiency money is undoubtedly a part, whatever its quantum may be, proof of a general deficiency within the meaning of this section has been made out: *R v Eric Oakari* [1974] PNGLR 182 at 186.

See note on *R v Walsh* [1971] PNGLR 293 under s 532 above.

587. Evidence on charges relating to seals and stamps.

On the trial of a person charged with any offence relating to any seal or stamp used for the purposes of the public revenue, or of the post office, in Papua New Guinea or in any part of Her Majesty's Dominions or in a foreign State, a despatch from one of Her Majesty's Principal Secretaries of State -

(a) transmitting to the Head of State, any stamp, mark or impression; and

(b) stating it to be a genuine stamp, mark or impression of a die, plate or other instrument provided, made or used by or under the direction of the proper authority of the country in question for the purpose of expressing or denoting any stamp duty or postal charge,

is admissible as evidence of the facts stated in the despatch, and the stamp, mark or impression so transmitted may be used by the court and by witnesses for the purposes of comparison.

588. Intention to defraud.

On the trial of a person charged with an offence of which an intent -

(a) to injure, deceive or defraud; or

(b) to enable another person to deceive or defraud,

is an element, it is not necessary to prove an intent -

(c) to injure, deceive or defraud any particular person; or

(d) to enable any particular person to deceive or defraud any particular person.

It was said in *The State v Asaoka Kouji of Rabaul* [1976] PNGLR 292:

> "The sort of situations contemplated by this section are, for instance, the chain letter situation, where the accused does not know who is going to end up getting the letter, or the case of the quack doctor addressing a crowd of people and urging them to buy his fancy cancer cure. The quack does not know who is going to accept his invitation, but he does his best to persuade somebody to do so."

See also *Bovelt v Lenehan* [1973] PNGLR 454.

589. Admissions.

An accused person may admit on the trial any fact alleged against him, and the admission is sufficient proof of the fact without other evidence.

A plea of guilty does not constitute an "admission" for the purposes of s 589. Kapi DCJ said, in *The State v Jeoff Ipata* [1988] PNGLR 34 at 35:

> "Where a person pleads guilty, the law is now clear that this does not result in automatic conviction. A plea is only entered provisionally subject to supporting evidence in the depositions. Consistent with this is s 563 of the Code where counsel may enter a plea of not guilty on behalf of his client. This is also consistent with the presumption of innocence until proven guilty: s 37(4) of the *Constitution*.
>
> To interpret s 589 as applicable to a plea of guilty would also contravene s 37(10) of the *Constitution*. A person who is required to plead would provide evidence against himself. Section 589 is not applicable to a plea of guilty.
>
> Admission of facts under s 589 is entirely optional. This option arises after the accused has been called upon to plead to the charge. Whether, in a plea of guilty or not guilty, the accused may then admit any fact that is alleged against him."

Brunton AJ stated, in *The State v Misari Warun* [1988-1989] PNGLR 327 at 328:

"Where the nature of the charge in the indictment is serious, defence counsel should put the admissions his client wished to make into writing to avoid any opportunity for dispute as to what was, or was not, admitted at a later date. Although the law does allow counsel to make oral admissions under the *Criminal Code* and the *Criminal Practice Rules*, as a matter of prudence, in serious cases, they should be reduced to writing."

See s 563 of the Code, and *The State v John Mugur Poka* [1977] PNGLR 27, regarding an admission made upon arraignment, followed by the court's acceptance of a subsequent plea of not guilty. See the *Evidence Act* 1975.

Division 6 – Verdict: Judgement: Appeal from Arrest of Judgement

590. Accused person insane during trial.

(1) If on the trial of a person charged with an indictable offence it is alleged or appears that he is not of sound mind, the court shall consider the matter, and if it finds that the accused person is not of sound mind it shall -

(a) record the finding; and

(b) order the accused person to be kept in strict custody in such place and in such manner as the court thinks proper until he is dealt with under the laws relating to persons of unsound mind.

(2) A person found under Subsection (1) to be not of sound mind may be again indicted and tried for the offence.

See s 28 of the Code regarding the defence of insanity, s 27 which establishes a presumption of sanity, and s 569 regarding unfitness to plead.

The expression "not of sound mind" in s 590 bears a different meaning from that which it bears in s 592, for in the latter section the term is directed to the situation where the accused is to be freed from criminal responsibility, and it must clearly be interpreted by reference to s 28. Section 592 is not directed to such a case, but to the condition of the accused at the time of trial. A finding that an accused is fit to plead under s 569 does not preclude an inquiry as to "unsoundness of mind" under this section: *R v Koiyari-Iyeva* [1965-1966] PNGLR 284.

This section is designed in part for the protection of the community and in aid of mental health legislation: *R v Koiyari-Iyeva* [1965-1966] PNGLR 284.

591. Discharge of persons acquitted.

If the accused person is found not guilty or any other verdict is given that shows that he is not liable to punishment, he shall be discharged from the charge of which he is acquitted.

592. Acquittal on grounds of insanity.

(1) If on the trial of a person charged with an indictable offence it is alleged or appears that he was not of sound mind at the time when the act or omission alleged to constitute the offence occurred, the court shall -

(a) if it finds him not guilty, find specifically whether or not he was of unsound mind at the time when the act or omission took place; and

(b) whether he is acquitted on account of such unsoundness of mind.

(2) If in a case to which Subsection (1) applies the court -

(a) finds that the accused person was of unsound mind at the time when the act or omission took place; and

(b) says that he is acquitted on account of that unsoundness of mind,

it shall order him to be kept in strict custody in such place and in such manner as the court thinks proper pending a decision by the Head of State, acting on advice.

(3) In a case referred to in Subsection (1), the Head of State, acting on advice, may give such order for the safe custody of the person pending a decision by the Head of State, acting on advice, in such place or confinement and in such manner as the Head of State, acting on advice, thinks proper.

(4) Where a person is confined under this section, the Head of State, acting on advice, may at any time order that he be released from custody either unconditionally or on such conditions as are laid down by the National Executive Council.

See s 28 of the Code regarding the defence of insanity, and s 27 which establishes a presumption of sanity. See also s 569 on unfitness to plead, and s 590 on insanity during trial.

The expression "unsound mind" is not a term of art. However, as it is directed to the situation where the accused is to be freed from criminal responsibility, it must clearly be interpreted by reference to s 28: *R v Koiyari-Iyeva* [1965-1966] PNGLR 284.

593. Convicted person to be called on to show cause.

Where an accused person -

(a) pleads that he is guilty of an offence; or

(b) on trial, is convicted of any offence,

the proper officer shall ask him whether he has anything to say why sentence should not be passed on him, but an omission to do so does not invalidate the judgement.

Prentice J said in *Agiru Aieni v Paul T Tahian* [1978] PNGLR 37:

> "The failure to administer an allocutus or otherwise give the accused an opportunity to speak on the question of penalty, renders each sentence pronounced a nullity."

It was said in *Moses Aikaba v Tami* [1971-1972] PNGLR 155 at 157:

> "As a matter of commonsense, there should be an opportunity given to a prisoner, and/or his counsel, to be heard on sentence. The allocutus 'strictu senso' is only put in a trial, not in courts of summary jurisdiction. In the District and Local Courts, however, it is imperative that the defendant or his counsel always be invited to address on the question of sentence. Failure to do so is a denial of natural justice and renders the sentence pronounced a nullity."[119]

Where no allocutus is administered before sentence, this may be sufficient to invalidate a sentence and perhaps a hearing, for the reason that by so failing to proceed properly, the magistrate may allow himself or herself to exercise his or her

[119] Followed in *Michael Gende v The State* (1999) SC 627.

discretion upon wrong principles, and justice does not appear to be done thereby: *R v Rumints Woie* (1972) N728.

Where an accused person's allocutus raises a defence, it is the duty of the court to clarify the issue with counsel: *Anton Yani v The State* (1999) SC 615.

It is clear from the authorities that there is power in the court to change a plea after the plea is confirmed and allocutus administered but before sentence is passed. The circumstances under which a plea of guilty may be changed are where:

(a) the accused had not really pleaded guilty;

(b) there was a mistake on the part of the accused; or

(c) there is a clear defence to the charge.[120]

Similar views were expressed in *The State v Peter Sari* [1990] PNGLR 48, where the court found:

> "(a) that the court's discretionary power to change the plea of guilty to not guilty where the lawyer does not apply under section 563 of the Code to change the plea can be derived from the *Constitution* section 57 to enforce guaranteed rights and freedoms and also in the exercise of the court's inherent jurisdiction to do justice in the circumstances of a case under section 155(4) of the *Constitution* and
>
> (b) that for the court to not change the plea of guilty to one of not guilty where the depositions do not disclose any offence, do not disclose all the elements of the offence charged or disclose possible defences may amount to denial of justice according to law in the context of section 37(1) and (4)(a) of the *Constitution*."

In *The State v Bafe Quati* [1990] PNGLR 57 at 60, Doherty AJ said:

> "The provision allows a convicted person to say '*why sentence should not be passed on him* ..." (my emphasis). This expression adopts the old common law words of address to the prisoner. It makes no reference to how sentence should be assessed or what matters the court should take into account in assessing sentence. The prisoner is under no obligation to answer but frequently does and raises matters such as his lack of prior conviction, provocation or other circumstances of the offence all of which are proper matters a court can consider in sentence and which the Supreme Court and National Court have ruled in various cases should be properly considered.
>
> Strictly then, such statements are not ... an allocutus in the strict sense but are a plea in mitigation."

In the same case, Doherty AJ further stated (at 61):

> "Since the powers vested in the National Court to enforce the rights under the *Constitution* are held to be unlimited by the Supreme Court, I consider that those powers include a power to reduce a sentence that might otherwise be properly passed upon a defendant who is found guilty of an offence. Other provisions and the right to claim compensation from a Government body such as the police, do not detract from the power of the National Court to assess sentence in the light of the treatment of the defendant while in custody awaiting trial."

---

[120] *The State v Joe Ivoro and Gemora Yavura* [1980] PNGLR 1.

In the absence of any rules of practice or procedure in respect of the taking into account of allegations of breaches of constitutional rights on a statement under s 593, the following ad hoc directions issued under s 185 of the *Constitution* are to be followed:

> "[A]n allegation made by a defendant on allocutus alleging brutality or breach of his constitutional rights and which the defendant raises in order to have those rights enforced by way of a lower sentence should be open to proof and to challenge as if they were statements of fact.
>
> A convicted person seeking to have reduction of sentence for breach of a constitutional right under s 36 or s 37(17) of the *Constitution* must clearly indicate that he is seeking such a remedy, and the prosecution should be given a right to reply and rebut such an allegation. In order to consider and decide whether evidence should be addressed in rebuttal, at least 4 clear days' notice should be given to the State that a defendant will raise a breach of his constitutional rights in order to allow evidence to be adduced in rebuttal. The State should have a right to cross-examine a convicted person of the allegations made and the convicted person may call witnesses if he so chooses."[121]

See ss 36(1), 37(1), 37(17)-(20), 41(1), 42(1) and 57(3) of the *Constitution* regarding treatment of persons in custody.

See s 18 of the Code regarding the types of punishments which may be inflicted; s 19 regarding construction of terms involving punishments; s 20 regarding cumulative and consecutive sentences; and s 21 regarding the prerogative of mercy. See also ss 575-576 regarding restriction of movement and conditional suspension of sentence for first offenders, and s 623A regarding restitution orders.

See s 4(e) of the *Customs Recognition Act*, regarding taking customary law into account in sentencing.

See s 22(4) of the *Supreme Court Act* regarding appeal against sentence, and s 23 regarding appeal by the Public Prosecutor against sentence.

See Strathern, "*Crime and Correction: The Place of Prisons in Papua New Guinea*", (1976) Vol 4(1) MLJ 67.

Factors in sentencing

There are many factors which may be considered upon sentencing:[122]

(a) the degree of participation;[123]

(b) the degree of ignorance of the law;[124]

(c) the age of the offender;[125]

(d) that the offender is a first offender;[126]

(e) the offender's previous good record;[127]

(f) restitution;

---

[121] *The State v Bafe Quati* [1990] PNGLR 57 at 62 (Doherty AJ).

[122] *Supreme Court Reference No 1 of 1984: Re Minimum Penalties Legislation* [1984] PNGLR 314 (McDermott J), noted in *The State v Peter John Plesman; The State v Paul Jimmy Moaina* (1997) N1657.

[123] *Secretary of Law v Kaibug Jimbun* [1976] PNGLR 288.

[124] *Secretary for Law v Ulao Amentasi* [1975] PNGLR 134.

[125] *Passingan v Beaton* [1971-1972] PNGLR 206.

[126] *Kondan Kale v The State* (1983) SC 250.

[127] *Kondan Kale v The State* (1983) SC 250.

(g) the offender's physical and mental condition;[128]

(h) remorse;

(i) the assistance given to police;[129]

(j) the plea of guilty by the offender;[130]

(k) aggravation offered by the victim or provocation not amounting to an offence;[131]

(l) the effect of the jail term on the offender's family;

(m) the effect of a jail term on the offender's job, education or income;[132]

(n) the technical nature of the offence;

(o) the customary punishment received or compensation paid to the victim;[133] and

(p) the prevalence of the offence.

Background to punishment: rehabilitation and deterrence

Kapi J expressed the view in *Acting Public Prosecutor v Uname Aumane* [1980] PNGLR 510 that "[w]e are far behind in developing our institutions and programmes to effectively carry out any rehabilitation of offenders, which is a proper purpose of sentencing."

In *John Aubuku v The State* [1987] PNGLR 267, the court adopted the tariff of sentences for rape in England. This was criticised in *Rex Lialu v The State* [1990] PNGLR 487, where Kapi DCJ noted that the tariff of sentences should reflect the values, the aspirations and the circumstances in Papua New Guinea.

Kidu CJ stated in *John Elipa Kalabus v The State* [1988] PNGLR 193 at 197:

> "[R]ehabilitation of the criminal must not be allowed to obscure the consideration of deterrence and protection of the public from the commission of crimes."

Kapi J said, in *Acting Public Prosecutor v Uname Aumane* [1980] PNGLR 510:

> "Retribution as a proper purpose of punishment is not foreign to the cultures of the people of this country. This is what is normally referred to as 'payback'. This notion grew out of many years of tradition in the village – a person who broke the rules or customs of the village deserved punishment."

The correct principles are as stated by the Court of Appeal in New Zealand in *R v Radich* [1954] NZLR 86 at 87 – that is, in sentencing, the court must take into account the notion of general deterrence on the one hand, and on the other, it must weigh the particular facts of the individual case before it: *The State v Keputong Nagong* (1980) N225.

The offence of stealing as a servant (s 372(5)) is a very serious crime. This is because there is a breach of trust which is entrusted to the offender. The prevalence

---

[128] *R v Kocan* [1966] NSWR 565.
[129] *R v McGrath* [1971] PNGLR 247.
[130] *R v McGrath* [1971] PNGLR 247.
[131] *Ure Hane v The State* [1984] PNGLR 105.
[132] *Agiru Aieni v Paul T Tahain* [1978] PNGLR 37.
[133] *Acting Public Prosecutor v Nitak Mangilonde Taganis* [1982] PNGLR 299.

of the offence is a significant consideration on sentence, and it has been held by the Supreme Court (*Paulus Mandatitip*) that where an offence is prevalent the courts must be severe in their punishment. While there is a need to maintain uniformity of sentence for the purpose of deterrence, the court should not hesitate to depart from this uniformity where the particular facts of an individual case demand it. In this case, the facts militate in favour of leniency and against the imposition of a custodial sentence: *The State v Keputong Nagong* (1980) N225.

The effectiveness and desirability of custodial sentences, driving disqualifications, fines and good behaviour bonds, respectively, for the offence of dangerous driving causing death, may differ widely between the societies of other countries and those existing in Papua New Guinea. Sentences of detention appear to be the only really effective personal and public deterrent available, and appear to be in tune with what public conscience and community feeling would demand in most cases of dangerous driving causing death: *Public Prosecutor v Willy Moke Soki* [1977] PNGLR 165.

Only in the most exceptional of cases may the necessity for public deterrence against the offence of dangerous driving be overridden by the circumstances of a particular case. As the problems of the offence of dangerous driving have reached staggering proportions in Papua New Guinea, and are often a cause of tribal fights, this calls for a stern view of the crime. Even where the accused did not want to drive and lost his wife and child, there is no reason against the imposition of a deterrent sentence. *Whittal v Kirby* [1942] KB 194, approved, in which Lord Goddard said (at 203):

> "character, antecedents, age, health or mental condition really have nothing to do with such an offence as driving to the danger of public, and it must be seldom indeed that extenuating circumstances can be found for it".

He also approved *Sheldrick v The Queen* [1960] Tas SR (NC), where Burbury CJ said (at 3):

> "that in the case of a serious case of dangerous driving I think that it is the duty of the trial judge to enforce a term of imprisonment as a deterrent to others ... those who drive in a manner dangerous to the public must, in my view, expect to go to gaol for this offence, however irreproachable their characters may be ... It is a type of case where the reformatory aspect of punishment has I think little relevance. That is to say, the individual circumstances of the offender are subordinate to the necessity in the public interest of imposing a gaol sentence to deter dangerous drivers".[134]

Wilson J said in *R v Kaupa* (1973) N765:

> "In criminal courts generally it is appropriate to take into account the punitive effect of such matters as apprehension, arrest, appearing in Court, the length of time in custody before sentence, the shame associated with disclosure to family and kinsmen, publicity, loss of employment and the like."

It was stated in *R v Iki Lida* (1973) N764:

> "In considering sentence, the Court must balance the need for public protection with the protection of the rights and liberties of the individual. Adoption of an unreserved 'retribution theory' of punishment would encourage the notion of pay-

[134] *Public Prosecutor v Sima Kone* [1979] PNGLR 294, also approving *R v Thompson* (1975) 11 SASR 17; *Public Prosecutor v Willy Moke Soki* [1977] PNGLR 165; and *The State v Alphonse Raphael* [1979] PNGLR 47.

back and on many occasions punish the offender out of all proportion to his culpability and moral blameworthiness. Harsh sentences imposed for general deterrence have limited application in a jurisdiction where there is little or no likelihood of court decisions being publicised amongst potential offenders."

In *John Elipa Kalabus v The State* [1988] PNGLR 193 at 196-197 Kidu CJ said:

"Rehabilitation or reformation is a factor to be considered in assessing a sentence. But in serious cases ... it is something to be aimed at only in so far as it is compatible with the main function of the Court of protecting the public: see *Acting Public Prosecutor v Andrew Lalaiva of Honi and Angelo Ume* [1981] PNGLR 148."

In the case of *R v Kaupa* (1973) N765 the following view was expressed:

"The tendency over recent years has been for there to be a growing recognition by the Courts of the principle of individualisation ... a distinction must be drawn between uniformity of sentence and uniformity of approach to sentencing. There is no need for the former, there is a great need for the latter."

In *Wilkeson v Grant* [1967-1968] PNGLR 112 at 117 and 118 it was stated that:

"The Court may, in sentencing, take into account the prevalence of the offence for which the accused is being punished, and impose a sentence which might act as a deterrent to those who commit that class of crime. That is a proper consideration so long as it does not result in a convicted man being made the scapegoat of other people who have committed similar crimes but have not been caught and convicted."

To do so constitutes an unsound exercise of discretion.

Concurrent and consecutive sentences: the totality principle

The totality principle requires that when consecutive sentences are imposed, a final review of the sentence be made by the court to ensure that the total is not excessive: *Public Prosecutor v Terrence Kaveku* [1977] PNGLR 110. See s 20 of the Code.

It was said in *Mase v The State* [1991] PNGLR 88 at 92:

"It is clearly laid down by this Court in the cases referred to that there are three stages to go through in coming to a total sentence. The first step is to consider the appropriate sentence for each offence charged and then consideration be given as to whether they should be concurrent sentences or cumulative sentences. Where the decision is made to make two or more sentences cumulative, the sentencer is then required to look at the total sentence and see if it is just and appropriate. If it is not, he must vary one or more of the sentences to get a just total. This principle must be observed because a straightforward addition of sentences usually leads to a total sentence that is excessive in the whole circumstances".

It was stated further in that case (at 92-93):

"How does a sentencing judge (a magistrate) arrive at a total sentence which is just and proportionate to the totality of the criminal behaviour involved in all the offences concerned? We do not consider that there is any hard and fast rule to be followed although it would be permissible for a sentencer to take into account the maximum penalties provided by law for each offence and whether or not each offence committed falls into the worst, most serious or less serious of its kind. Also the sentencer should ensure that the total sentence imposed is not substantially above the normal sentence for the more serious (not the worst type) of the offences. The rationale behind this is, we consider, common sense. Apart from the 'worst type' of cases, where the maximum sentences are justified, in cases of 'more serious type' an aggregate sentence might be too crushing, especially on young people like the appellants, or manifestly excessive."

It was also stated (at 93-94):

> "It is not wrong in principle to have regard to the prevailing community perception of the relative seriousness of the different serious offences. Indeed, it is in our view most appropriate to so have regard to the community perception of the relative seriousness of the different offences and to have it reflected in the level of sentences ... We believe that there must be some relativity between all the offences, their seriousness and criminal culpability and the sentences imposed must reflect, in principle, the relative seriousness of the offences and their consequences ... We do not mean by this that such relative regard and reference to sentences for other types of offences is to be used to determine the actual sentence for another offence."

Although it is neither desirable nor possible to lay down any all-embracing rule as to when sentences for two or more convictions should be made concurrent, sentences should, generally speaking, be made concurrent where a congeries of offences is committed in the prosecution of a single purpose or the offences arise out of the same or closely related facts: *Tremellan v The Queen* [1973] PNGLR 116.

It has been held that where there is an instance of break and enter or burglary followed by rape offences, this does not form a single transaction, and as such the prisoner is to be punished effectively for both instances of offences by way of a cumulative sentence: *The State v Michael Amuna Koupa* (1987) N595(s).

The only offence for which a person is liable to punishment, after a plea of guilty, is the precise offence with which he or she was charged. Thus, where the accused was charged with and pleaded guilty to the simple offence of unlawful striking, it was an error for the sentencing magistrate to consider the alleged fact that the accused's act was part of a larger riotous outbreak. It was improper for the accused to be punished for the totality of acts done by the "mob" in concert, which was different and more serious than the individual offence to which he had pleaded guilty: *Toiona v Bryant* [1969-1970] PNGLR 201.

The practice of imposing a multiplicity of short sentences which add up to a substantial sentence, in respect of a number of similar offences forming a series of convictions, is disapproved: *Secretary for Law v Suares* [1974] PNGLR 288. Principles of sentencing are discussed in *Kore v Alan Carling* (1972) N722.

See also *Kondon Kale v The State* (1983) SC 250 and *Ando Kenene v Gabriel Simon, Alois Gabour and George Tapu* [1983] PNGLR 179.

Considerations of custom

Under the legal system adopted in Papua New Guinea, a person may not be punished until he or she is found guilty of an offence according to law. Under s 37(2) of the *Constitution*, "nobody may be convicted of an offence that is not defined by, and the penalty for which is not prescribed by, a written law". A "written law" refers to an Act of Parliament (including any law made under the

Act), organic laws and the *Constitution*. The term has been used to distinguish it from what may be called the unwritten laws, custom as adopted under Sch 2.1 of the *Constitution*, common law as adopted under Sch 2.2, and the underlying law as developed under Schs 2.3 and 2.4: *Acting Public Prosecutor v Uname Aumane* [1980] PNGLR 510.

A sentence could be mitigated with the payment of customary compensation. However, "those who rely on customary compensation payment as a mitigating factor have the duty to prove as a matter of fact, the existence of such custom in a proper manner": Kidu CJ. The mitigation is not axiomatic and will depend on the facts of each case. It is generally considered inappropriate to deduct a specific period from a sentence: *Acting Public Prosecutor v Nitak Mangilonde Taganis* [1982] PNGLR 299.

Kapi DCJ said, in *Acting Public Prosecutor v Nitak Mangilonde Taganis* [1982] PNGLR 299:

> "The question of customary compensation to be taken into account on sentence must be clearly identified in each case. The general statement in mitigation that compensation was paid is not necessarily of any assistance in a particular case. The concept of customary payment must be clearly proven and its relationship to the concept of penalty. In the Highlands, the concept of compensation is connected with the fear of payback killing. Is that connected with the concept of customary penalty? There must be a proper evidentiary basis upon which the courts can develop the law. This is significant in this country where there are many different customs. General statements by counsel can no longer be considered sufficient."

The payment of customary compensation is an honourable exercise and exchange to restore peace and harmony between the relatives of the parties involved. An award of compensation is a "punishment" within the meaning of the Code: *The State v Philip Susuve Raipa* [1994] PNGLR 458.

In *The State v Rex Lialu* [1988-1989] PNGLR 449 at 452-453 Amet J stated:

> "I should stress categorically that compensation, however large or small, cannot exonerate the offender from criminal liability. Nor do I think that sentence will or should be reduced relative to the size of the compensation, such that it can be thought that the larger the compensation the greater the reduction in sentence should be. This cannot be the effect of compensation. If it is a genuine method of restoring peace and harmony by custom or tradition and whatever form and size it takes, it should not now be extended to obtain total exculpation of the offender. The natural flow-on effect of the acceptance of such a belief is obvious and would lead to the rich believing they can buy their way out of criminal responsibility, and the less rich feeling aggrieved if they do not receive the same treatment."

In *The State v Paulus Non Pabale* (1999) N1873 four girls were included in a payment of customary compensation. Injia J held that:

> "I will not take into account the inclusion of 4 girls as part of the compensation package because it is a custom which is repugnant to the general principles of humanity ...: see *In re Miriam Willingal* (1997) N1506. I should also say that whilst I appreciate substantial compensation in pigs and money has been paid, the value of human life cannot be adequately compensated in money and pigs which can do nothing to restore life lost. Therefore the accused still remains to be punished by this Court: see *Rex Lialu v The State* [1990] PNGLR 487."

Kapi J, with Kearney DCJ agreeing, stated in *Acting Public Prosecutor v Uname Aumane* [1980] PNGLR 510:

> "As a matter of law, a court can only impose the penalty provided by statute (in this case the *Criminal Code*, ss 19 and 299). This court has no power to impose any customary punishment. The adoption, application and enforcement of customary law, under Sch 2.1 of the *Constitution* is subject to, amongst other things, an Act of Parliament which regulates the use of customary law (Sch 2.1(3)(b)), such as the *Customs (Recognition) Act* (Chap 19). Under s 4(e) of this Act, custom *may be taken into account* in punishment, to mitigate or aggravate the sentence to be imposed. However, ultimately, the penalty to be imposed is as provided for under the Code (in this case of wilful murder) and there is no power in the court to impose customary punishment. Further, there is no room for developing the underlying law in this case. The development of an underlying law under Sch 2.3 arises only when there appears to be no rule of law that is applicable. In this case the *Criminal Code* is applicable. As to what the role of customary law *should be* in such cases, these are matters not for the court but for the legislature. Such proposals for amendment of the Code have been put forward by the Law Reform Commission but so far the Parliament has not enacted them."

Kapi J, with Kearney DCJ agreeing, further stated in *Acting Public Prosecutor v Uname Aumane*:

> "Under s 19 of the Code, a judge may impose any of the lesser punishments prescribed (upon a conviction for wilful murder under s 299 where there is a maximum sentence of life imprisonment). The crime of wilful murder is a statutory offence and the only punishment that can be imposed is set out under the Code. A judge has no power to impose any other punishment. Under s 4(e) of the *Customs Recognition Act*, custom shall be taken into account in determining the penalty (if any) to be imposed on a guilty party. This means that a particular custom (defined by Sch 1.2(1) of the *Constitution*, and recognized and enforced under s 3 of that Act and Sch 2.1 of the *Constitution*) may be taken into account to explain his behaviour; for example, he may have committed the offence under customary pressure. Custom used in this sense becomes a mitigating factor (see Clarkson J in *R v Asis and Bitimur* (1970) N559, and *R v Iu Ketapi* [1971-72] PNGLR 44; see also *R v Lakalyo Neak* (1971) N632), providing a cultural justification of the offenders' behaviour which reduces their culpability or blameworthiness. In some instances the custom may increase the seriousness of the offenders' behaviour. For instance, in incest cases, custom may regard it as immoral and may call for severe punishment. A court may also take into account customary punishment in the same way, eg whether the offender is liable to pay compensation whatever the court's decision might be. (See *R v Kaupa* (1973) N765.) All of this means that a judge may increase or decrease the sentence depending on whether custom mitigates or aggravates the offence and may impose the appropriate sentence within the range given by law. Section 4(e) of the *Native Customs Recognition Act* does not enlarge the power of the court under ss 19 and 299 of the Code; it may only operate within the range provided by those sections."

Where the accused were unsophisticated and ignorant of the introduced law which seeks to outlaw cannibalism, the extent of the accused's culpability was considerably less that that if the more sophisticated urbanised person were to commit such an offence – an effective sentence of 15 months was passed: *The State v Aubafu Feama, Nama Auri, Kafidiri Kududebe Hagima* [1978] PNGLR 301.

However, lack of sophistication can no longer be an excuse for reduction of sentence, subject to exceptional circumstances. The courts have deemed that there are now few people living in Papua New Guinea that would fall into the category of "remote area", that is, a person who does not know that there is a government with courts and police available to redress wrongs: *Public Prosecutor v Avapa Keru; Public Prosecutor Moroi* [1985] PNGLR 78, followed in *The State v Miriam Kakun* (1997) N1673.

In *Public Prosecutor v Keru Moro*, a case of payback killing according to the custom of the Goilala people, the Supreme Court held:

"(1) An offender's lack of sophistication is no longer a mitigating factor on sentence unless he comes from an area so remote that he does not know that there is a government with courts and police available to redress wrongs.

(2) The custom of payback is contrary to the 'general principles of humanity' under the *Constitution*, Sch 2.1 and is contrary to the right of life guaranteed by the *Constitution*, s 35. A person who commits a payback murder in accordance with his custom is entitled to no reduction of sentence because of that custom.

(3) A person who commits a payback murder in accordance with his custom may be entitled to some reduction in sentence for de facto provocation.

(4) Old age is not generally a mitigating factor on sentence for murder.

The first respondent should be sentenced to fifteen years imprisonment and the second respondent to life imprisonment."[135]

Extenuating circumstances and mitigating factors were discussed by Prentice J in *R v Peter Ivoro* [1971-1972] PNGLR 374 at 387:

(a) primitiveness, absence from village, ignorance of government, upbringing, tribal custom demanding killing;[136]

(b) lack of formal education, primitiveness, family situation, tribal setting;[137]

(c) immediate circumstances, state of sophistication, development of community, knowledge of Government, accessibility to and protection by Government, force of custom, ignorance, upbringing, obedience to tribe;[138]

(d) lack of sophistication, remoteness, lack of contact, commerce, ignorance of Government law, little Government influence;[139] and

(e) some doubt of degree of knowledge of illegality under administration law, youthfulness of most accused who were not from normal decision-making age group, tribal excitement, first contact out-side Highlands, some doubt as to degree of ritual association.[140]

That case was cited with approval in *The State v Yakoto Imbuni* (1997) N1558.

In *R v Lakalyo Neak* (1971) N632 it was held that although the crime of wilful murder (involving a pay-back killing) for which the prisoners were convicted occurred in an urban area:

---

[135] Quoted from headnotes.
[136] *R v Lakalyo Neak* (1971) N632.
[137] *R v Dogwaingikata Miakawo* (1971) N630.
[138] *R v Iu Ketapi* [1971-1972] PNGLR 44.
[139] Harape's case.
[140] *R v Hame Manga* (1970) N596.

"the prisoners are all primitive men who have spent only a few months on a plantation away from their villages. Their ignorance of the ways of government, their upbringing and the strong tribal traditions which have until now controlled their life and which require this killing are all circumstances which ... are proper to taken into account in determining the question of sentence."

Injia AJ stated in *The State v Billy Kauwa* [1994] PNGLR 503 at 507-508:

"The notion of payback killings is still practised throughout the Highlands ... For a person coming from the Highlands, he ought to know that if he involves himself in a night-long drinking spree with people who are not his very close friends or relatives and kills someone, a tribal conflict or warfare in his village will follow. He ought to know that he is thereby exposing the innocent members of his tribe or clan in his village, his own family, his parents or brothers and sisters to the risk of tribal warfare ... the loss of his brother and father were the direct consequences of the tribal fight which followed the killing of the deceased. Therefore, their death is not a mitigating factor."

Kapi DCJ, Woods and Los JJ held in *Mako Ranjigi v The State* [1994] PNGLR 44 at 46:

"It has been clearly stated by the Supreme Court that the fact of a tribal fight killing does not reduce the seriousness of the offence. In *Public Prosecutor v Keru* [1985] PNGLR 78, the Court held that the custom of payback is contrary to the general principle of humanity, and a person who commits a payback murder in accordance with his custom is entitled to no reduction of sentence because of that custom."

In a case involving wilful murder in the course of tribal conflict, it is not a mitigating factor that people are forced by traditional pressure to be involved in tribal fights. In *The State v Kungus Kot* (1989) N764 the accused was not from a remote area which had no understanding of the modern system and the accused showed no remorse for the killing, only pride that it was done by his line.

In the case of *Luingi Yandasingi v The State* [1995] PNGLR 268 the Supreme Court confirmed a life sentence for wilful murder with an axe. The accused attacked from behind without a warning in front of a church one Sunday morning at about 8 o'clock as worshippers gathered.

Kapi DCJ expressed the view in *Kesino Apo v The State* [1988] PNGLR 182 at 183:

"Whether a person killed is a relative or an enemy has special significance in Papua New Guinea. The notion of payback is still practised in many parts of the Highlands. The significance is that where a person other than a relative is killed, the victim's relatives would pay back by seeking to kill a member of the offender's family. This brings upon the killer and his line the risk of tribal war, death or destruction of property. There are also high compensation demands which would involve the whole clan ... Compared to this the killing of a relative can rarely result in such tribal warfare and animosity. In a sense, a killing of a relative is self-inflicting in that, a killer may lose a warrior, worker or contributor to bride price of even a helper. This may be regarded as a punitive aspect of the killing which he has brought upon himself. It should not be taken into account as a factor against him but in his favour. The trial judge was wrong in holding this against the appellant."

In the same case, Woods J said (at 184):

"It is quite clear that judges have given consideration to the fact that a killing within the family will usually mean that the perpetrator will suffer shame and the other burdens for the rest of his life for the killing of a relative and therefore a long-term of imprisonment is not really necessary or appropriate as a punishment."

The crime of breaking and entering, for which severe penalties are prescribed by Parliament, seems to be on the increase throughout the country. It is an offence which is an anathema in village society without interposition of the introduced law. In this case there were no special circumstances which called for leniency: *Paulus Mandatitip v The State* [1978] PNGLR 128.

It has also been held that "where customary landowners permit invitees to remain on their land, and one of the invitees harms a landowner, custom clearly calls for compensation from the offending clan which harbours the offender": *The State v Philip Susuve Raipa* [1994] N1268 at 5 (Brown J). In this case the court considered that the nature of the injuries caused to the victim, coupled with the offenders line "squatting" on the land of the victim, called for a maximum award of compensation.

Woods J held in *The State v Emp Mek* [1993] PNGLR 330 at 332-333:

"In recent years, there have been more and more statements that the courts should be giving more consideration to customary solutions, that gaols are inappropriate and alien to PNG society, that alternatives to punishment should be considered. If one was really able to analyse the many sentences that are handed down every year by the National Court, there is no doubt that the courts have been considering the above matters, including the relevance of customary compensation. Whilst with respect to property crimes, these matters should be considered, yet be within the range or provision under the *Criminal Code*, when one deals with unlawful killings there are wider considerations. In popular theory in the customary situation, one death may often lead to another 'payback' death, although perhaps at the end of the day there may then be a customary settlement or peacemaking by compensation. So where can the modern courts start in considering the appropriate punishment for a killing. In a murder or manslaughter, there is no victim who can forgive or who can concur with any customary settlement. The killing in itself evidences an attitude or a likelihood to violence, even where the surrounding facts suggest an accident. No society can tolerate any likelihood or possibility of violence, and anyone who shows any such inclination must be removed from the society or secured in the society for the safety of that society.

Therefore, no matter how far the lines of the relatives have agreed that everything has been settled, the courts must – and the country as a whole must be able to rely on the courts to – apply the law, as propounded by the Parliament, that a person who is responsible for a death must be imprisoned."

Sentencing policies in Papua, and later in Papua New Guinea, were built up along the lines described by Sir Hubert Murray in *Papua Today* (1924), p 85, and by Gore J in the *Annual Report for Papua*, (1930) (judgment No 213). See also *R v Peter Ivoro* [1971-1972] PNGLR 374. There are degrees of primitiveness which would cause punishment to be lightened to a greater or lesser extent. It is not the law that substantial jail sentences are called for in all cases of wilful murder despite the primitiveness of the murders. In this case, where the accused were plainly of the most primitive type possible to imagine with barest contact with other races and minimal knowledge of the government, then pre-eminently a consideration for survival and education of the group was that which should prevail over all other objects of punishment. The sentence of one year was not disturbed on appeal: *Secretary for Law v Ulao Amantasi* [1975] PNGLR 134.

Standards and beliefs of the inhabitants who are found from time to time still living amid their native customs and their native environments, could and should be taken into consideration by the judges upon the question of the proper punishment in each case: *R v Womeni-Nanagawo* [1963] PNGLR 72.

For observations on the social responsibilities of clansmen in areas such as the New Guinea Highlands, including the response of a man who has just seen his father killed (required as a matter of honour to retaliate immediately), see *R v Kauba-Paruwa* [1963] PNGLR 18.

While the court must enforce the law, it must recognise that when the prisoners are primitive people who have acted in accordance with their own customs, who have only vague knowledge of the significance of a law imposed from outside their own immediate community, and who for all practical purposes do not enjoy its day to day protection, the sentence imposed should be educative and corrective rather than one calculated only to deter or to bring retribution: *R v Asis and Bitimur* (1970) N559.

It was said in *Acting Public Prosecutor v Tumu Waria* [1977] PNGLR 170:

> "In practice, this Court has always regarded the degree of sophistication of the offender and the traditional ways of the community from which he comes as important in arriving at an appropriate sentence. But to over-emphasise considerations of this kind is to ignore what we consider to be an important role of the court in upholding the law as laid down by Parliament. The Parliament has seen fit to provide substantial penalties for crimes of violence, clearly to ensure that the people will come to learn that violence cannot be tolerated in any organised society and that those who offend will be dealt with sternly."

Compensation is not a way of buying one's liberty. In the Melanesian context it is accepting moral and legal responsibility. Here, compensation paid for an unlawful killing (manslaughter based in provocation) was taken into full account by the trial judge in imposing sentence: *The State v Tendi Kalio Ulo of Ladulam* [1980] PNGLR 350.

Andrew J said, in *Acting Public Prosecutor v Uname Aumane* [1980] PNGLR 510:

> "There is a need in circumstances such as this (the killing of an alleged sorceress by a group of men from a remote area of the Highlands) for the sentence to reflect the educative process, as well as giving weight to the nature of the offence, the element of pre-intention, the degree of sophistication of the accused, and the need for the public deterrence."

In that case, Kidu CJ stated:

> "The trial judge properly took into account the background of the respondents. For instance he found that the respondents came from a remote part of the country with minimal contact with the outside world; that they encountered 'modern life style' after they were taken into custody; that their area was sparsely populated and that what they did was out of fear of sorcery. In many communities in Papua New Guinea, belief in sorcery and its powers is very strong and we cannot brush it aside. My own people believe it and great fear is caused by such belief. That the cultural setting of the respondents must be taken into account is not disputed. This has always been done by the National Court and the Supreme Court. *Secretary for Law v Ulao Amantasi and Ors* is a case in point. However, it should not override the clear dictates of the Parliament that those who commit the crime of wilful murder attract to themselves the possible penalty of imprisonment with hard

labour for life. If Parliament represents the people of Papua New Guinea and the laws it makes reflects the attitude of the people, then courts must take heed. (Sentences of six years imprisonment substituted for sentences of three months.)"

Kapi J stated, in that same case:

"The purpose of criminal law, like the purpose of customary law in the village, is for the protection of society. In achieving the purpose of the criminal law, regard must be given to the protection of the individual. The individual has constitutional rights which must be protected. However, we should not be so pre-occupied with the right of the accused or prisoner that we forget the rights of the innocent members of our villages, tribes, cities and the country who are entitled to protection against criminal behaviour; all these considerations must be carefully balanced."

Shame is an important component of punishment in Melanesian societies and may be taken into account in assessing the appropriate penalty: *The State v Minambkali Asu, Lakap Erape and John Koipiu* (1980) N236.

The question of shame associated with disclosure to the family and relatives, and publicity to friends, are matters to be taken into account as a form of punishment: *The State v Keputong Nagong* (1980) N225.

Kapi J said, in *The State v Keputong Nagong* (1980) N225:

"Imposition of fines in this jurisdiction has been criticised by some of the judges. One of the criticisms of the fine is that in the traditional society of Papua New Guinea the offender does not himself contribute towards the fine, but all the relatives contribute towards this fine. They argue that by doing this, there is no deterrent effect on the accused personally as he does not carry the burden of providing the fine. With respect to those who hold this view, very little recognition is given to the deterrent effect of relatives contributing towards a fine in the traditional or customary sense. That is to say, where an offender contributes his own money towards the penalty, he himself bears the weight, and the real weight is only in relation to the money he loses. However, in my understanding of the traditional effect of deterrence where relatives contribute towards raising money for a penalty, this has a more deterrent effect in the sense that the accused brings upon the relatives the weight of his wrong-doing. With respect, this kind of fine-paying has a greater deterrent effect in that the accused will be deterred from repeating the type of offence which would bring upon his own relatives the same burden of contributing towards the fine, and he will ensure that he will not bring upon himself and his relatives this type of thing again."

In *Kwayawako v The State* [1990] PNGLR 6, six people were convicted on their pleas of guilty to a charge of wilful murder of a person believed to be a sorcerer responsible for an unspecified number of deaths, and were sentenced to terms of imprisonment ranging from 12 to 15 years. They claimed the killing was a payback and was done to prevent further deaths in the village in the future. The trial judge did not permit the court to take into account belief in the power of sorcery as a mitigating factor in sentence, as to do so would be contrary to s 5 of the *Sorcery Act* (Ch No 274). Section 5 of the *Sorcery Act* provides that:

"Even though this Act may speak as if powers of sorcery really exist (which is necessary if the law is to deal adequately with all the legal problems of sorcery and the traditional belief in the power of sorcerers), nothing in this Act recognizes the existence or effectiveness of powers of sorcery in any factual sense except only for the purpose of, and of proceedings under or by virtue of this Act, or denies the existence of effectiveness of such powers ..."

On appeal, Amet, Los and Hinchcliffe JJ held that s 5:

"quite clearly does not have any relevance to the question of the customary belief in the power of sorcery. It relates to the 'existence and effectiveness of powers of sorcery'. It says that even though the Act may speak as if powers of sorcery really exist, nevertheless the Act does not recognise the existence or effectiveness of powers of sorcery in any factual sense. But it does not deny the existence of the widespread belief throughout the country in the power of sorcery. They are quite different matters altogether ... Because s 5 states that the Act does not recognise the existence or effectiveness of powers of sorcery in any factual sense, it does not follow therefore that there cannot be the genuine belief in the existence of powers of sorcery. It is the fact of the genuine belief in the power of sorcery which is the issue and not the existence and/or the effectiveness of such powers."[141]

It was further said in *Kwayawako v The State* [1990] PNGLR 6 at 10:

"We do not consider that belief in a practice, which is recognised almost universally in Papua New Guinea as existing, can so simply be declared to be non-existent by the Act. It is totally unrealistic to suggest that by a mere stroke of a pen such a widespread belief in the existence and effectiveness of the powers of sorcery can be done away with or declared non-existent."

In *The State v Joseph Kule* [1991] PNGLR 404 the defendant pleaded guilty and was convicted of unlawful killing. In mitigation of sentence it was submitted that he had complied with custom and would have to comply with a further custom of giving one of his daughters to the relative of his deceased victim. It was held by Doherty J that:

"Customary compliance is a matter that can be considered in mitigation: see *Acting Public Prosecutor v Nitak Mangilonde Taganis of Tampitanis* [1982] PNGLR 299 at 301, 305 but it is not sufficient to say 'this is a custom and we are going to comply with it'. As stated in *Henry Aisi v Malaita Hoala* [1981] PNGLR 199 at 203: 'customs must be proved as a fact, that is by sworn evidence or affidavit evidence.' The court went on to say that the provisions of the *Customs Recognition Act* (Ch No 19) (as it now is) gave the court wide powers in hearing evidence to ascertain what a custom was. This included calling witnesses itself, hearing hearsay and opinion evidence, referring to books and asking question of complainants and defendants and their witnesses and ruled that failure to hear such evidence before ascertaining and ruling on the custom is an error in law ... [W]here a submission by counsel only is put forward it is insufficient evidence that a custom exists, what the custom exactly is and whether the defendant has complied with it.' Her honour refused to recognise the custom in accordance with s 2 of the *Customs Recognition Act* (Ch 19) and enforce it under s 3 as the custom was contrary to the welfare of a child under 16 years. Further, her honour held that the practice of handing over a child was similar to slavery and therefore prohibited by s 253 of the *Constitution*. The custom, therefore, could not be considered in mitigation of punishment."[142]

See s 4 of the *Customs (Recognition) Act* regarding the circumstances in which customary law may be taken into account in a criminal case.

[141] *Kwayawako v The State* [1990] PNGLR 6 at 8.
[142] *The State v Joseph Kule* [1991] PNGLR 404 at 405-407 (Doherty J).

General considerations

A person must be charged and given a chance to defend himself or herself against that charge before being punished for it. It is wrong for the court, where the accused has been charged with a comparatively minor offence, to impose sentence on the basis that the circumstances would seem to disclose a more serious offence. The law on the subject is set out succinctly and clearly by Frost J in *Toiona v Bryant* [1969-1970] PNGLR 201, and is a fundamental part of the underlying law of this country: *Paia Lifi v Phillip Dege* (1981) N291 (M).

Sentencing is not an exact science but a subjective art. It is based on an instinctive feeling for justice, a knowledge of current trends in society and among other sentencing bodies, and a breadth of experience of life itself: *Public Prosecutor v Panikuiaka Nopi* [1979] PNGLR 536.

It was said in *Henry Rakatani v The State* [1979] PNGLR 556 at 557:

> "Undoubtedly, on sentence, a trial judge is entitled to consider surrounding circumstances in deciding upon appropriate punishment. This section allows the trial judge to receive on that issue 'such evidence as he sees fit'".

See also *Tom Amaiu v The State* [1979] PNGLR 559 at 581.

As to considerations on sentence for stealing where the sum was large and was neither recovered nor repaid, and where the accused was a Member of Parliament who tricked his own people and stole their money, see *Tom Amaiu v The State* [1979] PNGLR 576 at 581.

In *The State v Frank Kagai* [1987] PNGLR 320, a suspended sentence was appropriate in a case of robbery with actual violence, where the accused had completely reformed in the three years between the crime and sentencing, and had joined the Ex-Criminal Self-Help Task Force to help prevent crime. Hinchliffe J considered that it would be quite unproductive to send the accused to prison, which would undo his good work.

Hinchliffe J stated in *The State v Frank Kagai* [1987] PNGLR 320 (citing *William Davey* [1980] A Crim R 254 (Muirhead J)):

> "The suspension of a sentence of imprisonment is not an exercise in leniency, but an order made in the community interest designed to prevent re-offending which a prison sentence standing alone seldom does."

In *The State v Evelyn Rapola* [1988-1989] PNGLR 487, where the offender, a fully trained computer operator and mother of seven, pleaded guilty to misappropriating funds from her employer, a suspended sentence upon conditions was deemed appropriate, as the community interest would best be served by ordering her to perform work free of charge in a charitable organisation that would benefit greatly from her expertise in the computer industry.

In *Rex Lialu v The State* [1990] PNGLR 487 at 489 Kapi DCJ said:

> "The exercise of the sentencing discretion must be guided by proper principles. These include the characteristics of the offence or the offender which may aggravate or mitigate the seriousness of the crime taken together with all other relevant considerations. In this regard, it is desirable that the courts must be consistent in the application of these principles. These principles of sentence do not necessarily resolve the difficult task of fixing a particular term of sentence for any one particular case. The reason is clear and it has been pointed out in previous cases that there is not mathematical or scientific formula for arriving at a particular specific sentence from the general principles."

It was further stated:

> "[T]he fact that a different judge may impose a different sentence in the same circumstances is not a proper basis for the court of appeal to interfere with a sentence imposed by the trial judge ... However, it has been established in this jurisdiction that where there is a need to increase sentences for a particular class of offences, there are well-established principles under which this may be done. It has been held that if there is an increase or there is prevalence of this type of offence, the court would increase the sentence in this class of offences, but not without a warning."

In respect of crimes of violence, see *Public Prosecutor v Kwalimu Goina* (1982) SC 230.

It has also been established that, where such an increase in sentence is justified, the increase should not be by leaps, but by a gradual increase: see *Kondan Kale v The State* (1983) SC 250 (Andrew J).

Kapi DCJ also said in *Rex Lialu v The State* [1990] PNGLR 487 at 495-496:

> "With respect, I would not encourage the Supreme Court or any other court to prescribe term of sentences for other categories of the same offence. First of all, the court does not have all the facts or considerations in order to come to the final sentence. Such an approach would enable the Supreme Court to prescribe a term of sentence on some considerations only and without all the other relevant considerations. This is likely to lead to error ... A sentence in a particular case which is reviewed by the Supreme Court would provide guidance for determining terms of punishment for other categories of the same offence. The Supreme Court would be entitled to set guidelines in respect of different categories of the same offence without having to prescribe the actual sentence. In this regard I prefer the approach by the majority decision in *Belawa v The State* [1988-89] PNGLR 496."

Kapi DCJ further held at 495:

> "No tariff of sentences should be adopted from any other jurisdiction without enquiring into the applicability of the tariff to the circumstances of Papua New Guinea."

Kearney DCJ stated in *Supreme Court Reference No 2 of 1981* [1982] PNGLR 150 at 158-159:

> "As to the criminal law, it is considered of the essence of the legislative function of Parliament in a democracy to provide both for the type of behaviour which is to be subject to criminal sanction, and the punishment which conviction is to attract. It is of the essence of judicial power, as regards the criminal law, to decide whether an accused has contravened the law; and if so, to assess the proper disposition within whatever range and type of disposition Parliament permits. The *Criminal Code Act* 1974 is an adopted Act of the Parliament, under *Constitution*, Sch 2.6. It provides exhaustively for the punishment of Code offences (see s 2 of Act, ss 18 and 19 above, and many provisions of the Code.) It does not provide anywhere for a disposition along the lines of s 20 of the *Local Courts Act* 1963 or s 657A of the Queensland Code. The principle of separation of powers permeates the *Constitution*."

In *The State v Paul Pokolou* (1983) N404, the trial judge released the prisoner on a good behaviour bond (under s 19 of the *Criminal Code*) rather than sentencing him to jail for theft "primarily on the basis that the matter had been settled according to custom in the village". In imposing sentence, the court has three interests to balance. The first is the interest of the state. Collective living within a nation state demands that individuals and villages, tribes and communities have to give up a little of their territorial and personal sovereignty. However, the nation and its arms of the law must also recognise the interests of the community to which the offenders belong. This second consideration – the impact of the penalty on the community to which the offender belongs – must be a foremost consideration. The third consideration is the question of the prisoners themselves: *Acting Public Prosecutor v Uname Aumane* [1980] PNGLR 510.

The degree of moral guilt of an offender being considered for punishment is very important and it ought not to be treated as irrelevant. In *The State v Panikuiaka Nope* (1979) N195, the accused woman, after a long history of domestic violence, attempted to commit suicide and to take her infant child with her by means of setting fire to her house. She was rescued but the child died, and the accused pleaded guilty to wilful murder. There was nothing sinister in the fact that the accused decided to take her child with her to an intended death. By custom the child was very close to her, and it was natural to her that where she went so she would take him. Here the accused had an almost total absence of moral guilt, and had suffered from the knowledge that her actions were a substantial cause of the child's death. After three month's pre-trial detention the accused was sentenced to the rising of the court. See also the Supreme Court's decision in this case, at [1979] PNGLR 536.

In *The State v Kaupa Ungi* [1980] PNGLR 199 the court considered *R v Batchelor* (1952) 36 Cr App R 64, in which it was held that a sentence can be altered after conviction so long as the court was still in session, and held that a judge of the National Court may recall a sentence and reconsider or alter such sentence at any time before the circuit is formally closed.

Where a sentence is vacated, the prisoner ought to be invited afresh to address on the allocutus and defence counsel may put fresh matters: *The State v Kaupa Ungi* [1980] PNGLR 199.

Where the sentencing judge used the same factors in suspending a portion of the sentence under s 19(f) as he had in imposing a lenient sentence, this led in effect to an impermissible double discount in the defendant's favour: *Public Prosecutor v Thomas Vola* [1981] PNGLR 412.

The review by an appellate court of a sentencing judge's discretion to suspend sentence, involves the same principles as a review of the judicial discretion to impose the head sentence itself: Andrew J.

A sentence of 12 months imprisonment, with three months to serve and the remaining nine months suspended under s 19(f), is to be viewed as a 12 months sentence and not a three months sentence with a provisional and additional cumulative sentence of nine months as a punishment for future misbehaviour should it occur: *Acting Public Prosecutor v Clement Maki and Tom Kasen* (1981) SC 205 (Miles J).

It was said in *Secretary for Law v Amuna Kaniel Peter and Kanior Iamur Beilum* [1974] PNGLR 99:

> "The police have a very important duty to perform in the preservation of law and order in the community and, whilst acting in a proper manner in the discharge of their functions, are entitled to expect and should receive the protection of the

law from unwarranted actions, such as unlawful wounding with intent to disable and attempted murder."

There is always a great deal of effort put by benches of magistrates into the attempt to attain a proper consistency as to penalties and a deterrent suitable to local circumstances. The framing of punishment policies may indeed be considered imperative in a country where the education of magistrates and their experience is in many cases far less privileged than in other countries. General policies as to sentences may be set, but not by way of fixing a rigid scale of minimum penalties. Only the Parliament may do that by way of legislation; to attempt to do that is for magistrates, in advance, to abdicate their statutory duty to exercise their discretion in each case in accordance with the facts therein disclosed: *Guje Beng v Kombel* [1975] PNGLR 49 at 50.

It is perfectly proper for a magistrates' conference to agree upon a pattern of punishments from time to time – provided the pattern is not adopted rigidly and without the exercise of discretion necessary to be brought to the consideration of each offender's circumstances, and to the facts of each particular case: *Takovong v Tarera* (1975) N837.

In *Vagi Gau v Ken Kone Eava* [1976] PNGLR 485 an appeal from the sentence of the District Court was allowed under s 236 of the *District Courts Act*, where the magistrate stated that as a matter of policy all persons convicted on stealing charges would get a three months sentence, and not a fine, and that all repeat offenders would receive the maximum sentence. The court ruled that it is impermissible for magistrates to lay down other than general rules of guidance and policy as to sentence. The court stated:

"Each case, if justice is to be done, must be considered on its own background. Every convicted person is a separate individual."

Escape from lawful custody before sentence has been imposed can be taken in different ways. It can be regarded as symptomatic of a criminal character. Equally, it can be regarded as indicating that repeated incarceration in the circumstances of some prisoners may not be likely to assist the offender: *The State v Minambkali Asu* (1980) N236.

Kearney J stated, in *William Norris v The State* [1979] PNGLR 605:

"Information as to the antecedents of a prisoner may be taken into account on sentence, without formal proof, provided it is not challenged by the prisoner. If it is challenged, it must either be properly proved, or completely ignored by the sentencing judge. This approach has been consistently applied in England by the authorities since *R v Campbell* (1911) 6 Cr App R 131. This approach accurately marks the proper limits of the degree of relaxation of the ordinary rules of evidence on sentence, and also the limits of the proper exercise of discretion under this section. Upon this approach, the concluding paragraph of the section is in effect construed in the same way as the far more explicit provisions in s 386 of the Tasmanian *Criminal Code*, as amended in 1973, except insofar as s 386(10) appears to leave to the trial judge a discretion as to the means of proof of challenged material."

Barnett J stated, in *Wellington Belawa v The State* [1988-1989] PNGLR 496 at 504:

"Clearly, restitution will usually be a mitigating factor but that effect will be lessened or even nullified if the method of repayment is itself tainted by further evidence of dishonesty. When considering sentence, the trial judge 'may receive such evidence as he sees fit' (*Criminal Code*, s 596(4)) and evidence of associated matters such as these [evidence was received that the accused used an illegally obtained loan from the Disaster Relief Fund to part-fund his restitution of the misappropriated money that was the subject of the charge] are properly taken into account as part of the general circumstances of the case (see *Tom Amaiu v The State* [1979] PNGLR 576) where the Supreme Court found that it was proper for the trial judge to refer to associated matters of obtaining by false pretences and forger. (The accused, a Member of Parliament, had been charged only with stealing.)

In this case, the appellant's conduct with regard to restitution contained aggravating factors which worked against the mitigating effect. The trial judge was entitled to take this into account 'as part of the general circumstances of the case' when considering sentence."

The breach of a position of trust may warrant a heavier sentence. Positions of trust are not limited and may extend to such de facto situations as a vehicle operator and passengers: *Meaoa v The State* (1996) SC 504. Where a lawyer misappropriated funds entrusted to him from a client, a heavier sentence was warranted: *The State v Paulus Takesi* (1996) N1468.

Wilson J said in *William Norris v The State* [1979] PNGLR 605:

"The fundamental rules of evidence regarding the reception of hearsay evidence (if it is challenged) apply, in the absence of a statutory provision to the contrary, all through the criminal law and to matters of penalty as well as to matters of guilt or innocence. After all, that principle is consistent with the historical and philosophical development of the criminal law in which, generally speaking, nothing is assumed against a person unless there is proof on admissible evidence beyond reasonable doubt."

In the same case Raine DCJ said:

"It is wrong to admit hearsay evidence during the proceedings on sentence where that evidence is objected to and/or not conceded. Of course, as a matter of practice, in the vast majority of cases neither counsel for the prosecution nor the accused are concerned about the admission of what is often hearsay. Many antecedent reports and many statements made in evidence by police officers as to background are hearsay and there is nothing wrong with this being received if no objection is taken. Often it is helpful to accused persons. Great inconvenience would be caused and much public money wasted if people had to be flown from all over the country to give evidence about uncontested matters. But if the background material as offered is objected to and/or contested then under our system of criminal law the matter must be properly proved and the situation is no different from the proceedings going to the guilt or innocence of an accused person."

Kapi J said in *Acting Pubic Prosecutor v Uname Aumane* [1980] PNGLR 510:

"On a plea of guilty, the law as to how a judge should make findings of fact for the purposes of penalty are well stated by Wilson J in the case of *Koniel Alar and Hosea Biu v The State* [1979] PNGLR 300, and need not be restated. However, in the instant case, a further point arises, namely the principle that should guide a judge in making findings of fact which are put up by the defence counsel from the bar table and not contested by the prosecution. In this regard the Federal Court of

Australia stated in *R v Tait and Bartley* (1979) 24 ALR 473 at 483:

> 'When a plea of guilty avoids the necessity for a trial, it is no doubt convenient for the facts relevant to sentence to be stated from the bar table to the extent to which those facts are agreed on or, not being reasonably open to challenge, are unchallenged. But if one of the parties invites the court to act upon an alleged fact or circumstance, whether favourable or unfavourable to the defendant, which is not common ground between the Crown and the defendant, that fact or circumstance should be proved by the calling of evidence by the party on whom the evidentiary onus rests. The strict rules of evidence can be waived if the proof tendered is sufficiently cogent, but a finding on the relevant matter cannot be sought in reliance merely upon an unsupported assertion from the bar table if the truth of that assertion is not accepted by the other party.'"

For other overseas cases on the inadmissibility of contested hearsay evidence on sentence, cited by the Supreme Court of Papua New Guinea, see *Morse v The Queen* [1977] WAR 151; *Weaver v Samuels* [1971] SASR 116; *R v Lucky* (1974) 12 SASR 136; *Nash v Haas* [1972] Tas SR 1; *R v Sargeant* (1974) 64 Cr App R 74.

Depositions dealing with the facts of the case may be used on sentence on a plea of guilty, provided the facts are not challenged and are within the bounds of reasonable possibility: *The State v Sabarina Yakal* [1988-1989] PNGLR 129 (Brunton AJ).

Kapi J stated in *Acting Public Prosecutor v Uname Aumane* [1980] PNGLR 510:

"As to the issue of the proper function of counsel for the State in sentencing, in this jurisdiction the practice has developed where counsel for the State rarely makes submissions on sentence leaving the matter up to the defence counsel and the judge. This practice by the Public Prosecutor needs to be reviewed in view of the right of appeal given to him by the *Supreme Court Act*. The functions of the prosecutor are well stated in *R v Tait and Bartley* (1979) 24 ALR 473 at 477:

> 'The Crown has been said not to be concerned with sentence, but when a statutory right of appeal is conferred upon the Crown, that proposition must be more precisely defined. It remains true that the Crown is required to make its submissions as to sentence fairly and in an even-handed manner, and that the Crown does not, as an adversary, press the sentencing court for a heavy sentence. The Crown has a duty to the court to assist it in the task of passing sentence by an adequate presentation of the facts, by an appropriate reference to any special principles of sentencing which might reasonably be thought to be relevant to the case in hand, and by a fair testing of the defendant's case so far as it appears to require it the Crown is under a duty to assist the court to avoid appealable error. A failure by the Crown to discharge that duty may not only contribute to appealable error affecting the sentence but may tend to deprive the defendant of a fair opportunity of meeting a case which might ultimately be made on appeal. It would be unjust to a defendant, whose freedom is in jeopardy for the second time, to consider on appeal a case made against him on a new basis – a basis which he might have successfully challenged had the case against him been fully presented before the sentencing court.'

I agree with these observations and I would adopt them."

In an appeal against inadequacy of sentence, delay both in the lodging of the appeal by the state and the hearing of the appeal by the court (through no fault of the respondent) must always be a relevant factor: *Acting Public Prosecutor v Joe Kovea Mailai* [1981] PNGLR 258 (Andrew and Pratt JJ).

Bredmeyer J said in *Acting Public Prosecutor v Joe Kovea Mailai*:

"When the Public Prosecutor appeals against a non-custodial sentence he must prosecute that appeal speedily. If he delays, the offender, although free, suffers the anguish and worry that if the appeal succeeds he will be sent to gaol. The longer the delay the greater the anguish and worry, which is itself a punishment. Where delay occurs, the Supreme Court may think that the suffering, together with any pre-trial period spent in custody, is sufficient punishment and decline to impose a substitute sentence; or it may reduce the sentence which it would otherwise have imposed, on account of the delay".

See also *R v Pia-Afu* [1971-1972] PNGLR 393; *R v Harley* [1971-1972] PNGLR 399; *R v Willy Moke Soki* [1977] PNGLR 165; and *Public Prosecutor v Wiwi Gok* [1977] PNGLR 161.

Refusal to make admissions to the police is not an aggravating circumstance for the purposes of sentencing. It amounts to no more than an accused standing on his or her constitutional rights (see the *Constitution* ss 37(4)(a) and 37(10)): *The State v Minambkali Asu, Lakap Erapae and John Koipui* (1980) N236.

It was said in *Hen Kuru v Wass Kombra* (1981) N292 (L):

"Despite the glib tongues of some members of the community, the inmates of our gaols do not regard imprisonment as a holiday or a joke. The court's observations are to that contrary. Putting a man in gaol is a serious business. It can cause him loss of work. Some may have cash crop gardens or small businesses to run, and families to support."

Maximum penalties

It is trite law, but nonetheless binding on all members of the judiciary, that in Papua New Guinea the principle is that only in the worst cases is a maximum penalty imposed: see *Taiba Maima v Sma* [1971-1972] PNGLR 49. The worst type of case may be, for example, one where the accused is consistently in breach of the law and constantly coming back before the courts on a particular charge. Another example may be where the circumstances surrounding the particular offence charged are very aggravating: *Paia Lifi v Phillip Dege* (1981) N291 (M).

The principle of not imposing the maximum sentence or near the maximum sentence in the case of first offenders and/or in cases other than the most serious or worst of cases, is well established in this jurisdiction and elsewhere: *Hen Kuru v Wass Kombra* (1981) N292 (L).

The most serious offences would normally attract the most severe sentences. Each case must be assessed on its on facts. In each murder case, "a person who is shown to be unlikely to offend again should merit consideration more favourably than one thought to be likely to offend again". This may not necessarily apply in murder cases committed against persons in the custody of the court. Kidu CJ said, in *Avia Aihi v The State (No 3)* [1982] PNGLR 92:

"Any person who kills another in the custody of the court deserves the maximum penalty save those who are mentally unbalanced or who are provoked, legally speaking."

Kearney J stated in *Goli Golu v The State* [1979] PNGLR 653:

"It is a general principle of sentencing that the maximum penalty should be reserved for the most serious instances of an offence, the worst possible cases normally encountered in practice. This is an application of an even more basic principle, that there must be proportion between offence and sentence. In England it appears that the indeterminate sentence is usually imposed upon mentally disordered and dangerous persons found guilty of serious crime (see *R v Hodgson* (1967) 52 Cr App R 113), not necessarily of a 'worst case' type. This is explicable against a background of a social system ensuring proper hospital treatment and monitoring under secure conditions. There is no such social 'back-up' in this community and accordingly no warrant to depart, as in England, when considering whether a life sentence should be imposed, from the basic principle of proportion that a man be given the sentence appropriate to his offence and no more. That conclusion appears to accord with the view of the majority of the High Court of Australia in *Veen v R* (1979) 53 ALJR 305, when considering whether the English approach to life sentences should apply in Australia; it was emphasised that the sentence should be strictly proportionate to the gravity of the offence."

The maximum punishment prescribed by a law should usually be preserved only for the worst cases: followed *Tabimaima v Ben Hambakon Sma* [1967-1968] PNGLR 12; *R v Harrison* [1967-1968] PNGLR 420; *Passingan v Beaton* [1971-1972] PNGLR 206; *Agiru Aieni v Paul Tohian* [1978] PNGLR 37. This principle applies to cases of adultery: *Benjol Tol v Ken Lao* (1972) N684.

Kidu CJ said in *John Elipa Kalabus v The State* [1988] PNGLR 193 at 195:

"[T]he fact that a case falls into the worst type category does not mean that the maximum sentence automatically applies. For instance, in any murder case of the worst type where the accused person is 14 years old it would not be, in my opinion, appropriate to impose the maximum sentence of life imprisonment ... It is ... a question of fact as to whether a case is the worst kind of the type of offence in question".

Kidu CJ further stated (at 195):

"[W]hen a case is a serious one such as wilful murder, murder, violent rape or violent armed robbery, a plea of guilty by itself deserves no credit".

In *Pius Embari v Wangiwa* (1973) N751, where the magistrate imposed the maximum punishment allowable in four cases of stealing, he was entitled to entertain the view that these offences came within the worst category of stealing – involving stealing from primitive persons, deliberately, after warnings of illegality, and with no monies being recovered.

Where the accused represent only a proportion of those involved in the crime, it would not be just to exact from them the extreme penalty: *R v Abia Tambule* [1974] PNGLR 250.

It is not a requirement of law in Papua New Guinea that life imprisonment be reserved only for "dangerous" offenders: *Avia Aihi v The State (No 3)* [1982] PNGLR 92 (*Goli Golu v The State* [1979] PNGLR 653 explained).

It is important to find out just what life imprisonment means. Does it mean for the term of a person's natural life? The matter is governed by the *Corrective Institutions Regulations* 1959. Sections 141-143 set up a reviewing committee structure to determine whether the prisoner appears to have been rehabilitated and other relevant matters. The least that the prisoner will serve will be 15 years. If after the 15 years has elapsed, the committee has made no recommendation that the prisoner be released (under s 143), then it could be as long as 20 years before the prisoner's case could be reviewed for the second time: *Goli Golu v The State* [1979] PNGLR 653.

Imprisonment for life is a penalty appropriate to serious wilful murder when it is attended by the additional factors of taking account of the offender's record, the offender's propensity to commit violent crime, the need to protect the community and the very serious offence of which the offender stands convicted (cited by Mason J in *Veen v The Queen* (1979) 53 ALJR 305 at 309), but not otherwise: *Goli Golu v The State* [1979] PNGLR 653.

As to the difference between a sentence of life imprisonment and a sentence of a long fixed term of years, in the case of wilful murder, see *Goli Golu v The State*, discussed under s 299 of the Code.

Where a judicial officer has misappropriated public funds which that officer has caused to come into his or her hands, and if the requisite standard of probity is to be maintained, punishment of appropriate severity is called for. Where another judicial officer was involved and a fine imposed on him or her, it would be inequitable to send the accused to jail despite the inadequacy of a fine: *R v Alphonse Sema* (1976) N105, followed *Winugini Urugitaru v R* [1974] PNGLR 283.

In *R v Ilett* (1974) FC 69 it was stated:

> "The crime of receiving has always been regarded as a very serious offence. The legislature has marked out the crime of receiving because the receiver is the carefully concealed instrument which makes theft on a wholesale scale possible".

In sentencing for dangerous driving causing death, the extent of the injury caused cannot be entirely ignored. An analogy may correctly be found in the attitudes of progressive sternness required in sentencing for thefts of say K10, K500 and K2,500. Just as the extensiveness of calamity to numerous passengers or pedestrians may highlight the degree of care which was required of the driver concerned in the circumstances, so may the seriousness of the outcome (the number of deaths resulting) be looked at as one of the relevant features in assessing what sentence is required to act as public and private deterrent, and to assure public conscience that the law in the prevailing state of this community will demonstrate an element of retribution: *Public Prosecutor v Willy Moke Soki* [1977] PNGLR 165.

It was held in *Public Prosecutor v Arape Etape* [1977] PNGLR 416:

> "Rape is a crime of violence and like other offences of violence the offence calls for a deterrent sentence. In practice this Court has always regarded the degree of sophistication of the offender and the traditional ways of the community from which he comes as important at arriving at an appropriate sentence. But to over-emphasise considerations of this kind is to ignore what we consider to be an important role of the Court in upholding the law as laid down by Parliament. The Parliament has seen fit to provide substantial penalties for crimes of violence clearly to ensure that the people will come to learn that violence cannot be tolerated in any organised society and that those who offend will be dealt with sternly. Only in this way will the incidence of violence be reduced."

For guidelines on sentences to be imposed for rape see *The State v Peter Kaudik* (1987) N597.

In offences of carnal knowledge against the order of nature and unlawful and indecent dealing with a boy under the age of 14 and with other offences of this nature, there is a strong concern, which should be reflected in the sentence, of the people of Papua New Guinea not only for the general care of children, but that young children should not be exposed to sexual treatment such as in the case, which is regarded throughout the country as a matter of gravity: *Secretary for Law v Kabua Dewake* [1975] PNGLR 100.

When assessing a minimum penalty, the court must not use the minimum prescribed by law as a base figure, but must, if it decides a custodial sentence appropriate, consider what sentence it would impose if there was no minimum provided, and if this is the same or less than the minimum then it imposes the minimum sentence. If it is higher than the minimum then it is appropriate to impose the sentence: *Boas Kuna v Police* (1994) N1296.

Sentencing co-accused; disparities

The application of the principle that the sentencing judge should take into account the sentence of one co-offender in fixing the sentence of the other, is confined to those cases where there is a true comparison of like, and where the same offence is proved against both offenders (see *Wurramarbra v The Queen* (1979-80) 28 ALR 176). In an appeal against a sentence, no aggravating matter ought to be taken into consideration in assessing a sentence, unless it is admitted or has been property proved, either in the course of the trial or in the past conviction sentence hearing (see *R v Kennedy* (1979) 25 ALR 367): *Imiyo Wamela v The State* [1982] PNGLR 269.

It was said in *Secretary for Law v Witrasep Binengim* [1975] PNGLR 172 at 175:

> "The situation often arises where Mr Justice A deals with one of a group of co-offenders one month, and Mr Justice B deals with the remainder subsequently. The second judge might feel that the first judge was lenient, but the principle is that the second judge, albeit rather unwillingly (and absent distinguishing factors of aggravation), ought to award much the same sentence as awarded earlier."

The situation can arise where a co-offender is dealt with before his or her comrade or comrades, and the latter, when dealt with later, receive far less punishment, such as might reasonably leave the first person dealt with a sense of grievance. *R v Pitson* (1972) 56 Cr App R 391 is an example of this. Such a case would be open to argument on appeal against sentence: *Goli Golu v The State* [1979] PNGLR 653.

In an appeal against sentence of life imprisonment, where one co-accused had not acted with any greater degree of participation in the crime than others, but received a higher sentence of life imprisonment due to a prior conviction for wilful murder, the court is justified in differentiating in the treatment of persons for the same crime if, in considering the public interest, it has regard to the differences in the characters and antecedents of the convicted persons, and discriminates between them because of these differences: followed *R v Ball* (1951) 35 Cr App R 164. The court may also have regard to factors connected with the actual commission of the crime, but the fact that one of several prisoners jointly indicted has received too short a sentence is not a ground to lead a court necessarily to interfere with a longer sentence passed on the others. What generally has to be shown is that the applicant on appeal has received too long a sentence: *R v Richards* (1955) 39 Cr App R 191. The Court of Appeal has on many occasions reduced a sentence to bring it more in line to the sentence imposed on a co-accused upon the basis "that only thereby can a sense of grievance be averted": see also *R v Coe* (1969) Cr App R 66; *R v Pitson* (1972) 56 Cr App R 391; *R v D'Ortenzio and Burns* [1961] VR 432; *R v Goldberb* [1959] VR 311; *R v Kite* [1969] 2 SASR 94; *R v Rameka* [1973] 2 NZLR 592; *R v Coyle* [1969] 2 NSWR 83. Although the sentence in *Winugini Urugitaru v R* [1974] PNGLR 283 taken alone could not be said to be too long upon a second conviction for murder, the disparity of sentence between the appellant and his co-accused was of such an order that, unless adjusted, a justifiable feeling of dissatisfaction and sense of injustice will occur.

Where sentences of four months were imposed on the appellants and others were only admonished, such sentences were reduced on the ground of disparity: *Tagola Baki v Meuro* (1975) N842.

The disparity of sentence principle does not operate in reverse such that a co-accused's sentence should be increased. There is no obligation on a judge to make any remarks on sentence at all, and it may constitute an error to look microscopically at any remarks made on sentence, for it is notorious that to give reasons is to invite attack: *Secretary for Law v Witrasep Binengim* [1975] PNGLR 172.

On sentencing of co-accused see *Secretary for Law v Kaibug Jimbun* [1976] PNGLR 288.

Bredmeyer J said in *Acting Public Prosecutor v Joe Kovea Mailai* [1981] PNGLR 258:

> "One of the roles of the Supreme Court in hearing sentencing appeals is to standardise sentences so far as is possible so that similar offenders who commit similar offences but appear before different judges will receive similar punishments. Trial judges should therefore follow such decisions."

Youthful offenders

See s 63 of the *Evidence Act* regarding proof of age. See s 601 of the Code regarding discharge of first offenders.

Andrew J said, in *Acting Public Prosecutor v Clement Maki and Tom Kasen* (1981) SC 205:

> "Section 37(19) *Constitution* indicates that the framers of our *Constitution* recognised that young people incarcerated should not be put in the same prison cells or part of a prison as adults and they must be treated differently from adults. In Papua New Guinea, however, prisons are not constructed in such a way that separation can be meaningfully applied. Should we then send young people to jail simply because they have committed a prevalent offence and therefore must receive the wrath of the public as well as the courts? Young people are in the main not too sophisticated in the ways of adults. They are easily led astray. Not too many are hardened criminals or have set on a determined path of life of crime. Where the courts are able, they have a responsibility to ensure that young people do not offend again. One way to do this is not to incarcerate them but to give them a chance to mend their ways and become responsible citizens, unless it becomes apparent that the young person will not change no matter how many

chances he or she is given. In *Paulus Mandatititip and Anor v The State* [1978] PNGLR 128, much reliance is placed on the statement by Herron CJ in *R v Cuthbert* [1967] 2 NSWR 329, 332, that "a plea of youth is no longer a satisfactory answer to crime". However, an examination of Cuthbert shows first an exceptional set of facts, and secondly that Herron CJ has been misquoted. He in fact said "a plea of youth is no longer *entirely* a satisfactory answer to crime" (emphasis supplied). The quote as presented in *Mandatititip* is misconceived and is inappropriate to the circumstances of the country. Youth has always been one of the most effective mitigating factors, especially in the case of a first offender. Of course other considerations must also play a part, such as in a more serious type of crime or where a particular offence has become especially prevalent and experience has shown that it is invariably committed by youthful offenders. In such cases, a plea of youth may itself be mitigated by such factors – this is what the court in *Mandatititip* was saying."

For considerations on sentence in the case of a youthful, urban offender convicted of breaking, entering and stealing, see *The State v Joe Kovea Mailai* [1980] PNGLR 148.

For considerations on sentence in a break, enter and steal (from business premises, contra s 398) involving a youthful offender, see *Bakiri Pena v The State* (1980) SC 183.

For considerations on sentence in the case of youthful offender with prior convictions convicted of unlawful killing, see *The State v John Airi* (1980) N275.

Youth has always been one of the most effective mitigating factors, especially in the case of a first offender, and this principle is elementary. However, where an offence is more serious, is prevalent and is invariably committed by young persons (as in the case of breaking and entering), then they may not receive special treatment unless there are exceptional circumstances which call for leniency: *Paulus Mandatititip v The State* [1978] PNGLR 128. See also *Acting Public Prosecutor v Joe Kovea Mailai* [1981] PNGLR 258.

Miles J, in *Acting Public Prosecutor v Clement Maki and Tom Kasen* (1981) SC 205, stated:

"In Papua New Guinea consideration must be given to the policy implicit in the *Child Welfare Act* 1961 that young offenders under the age of 16 should be dealt with under the Act. The National and Supreme Courts exercise the judicial power of the people (*Constitution*, s 158(1)) and have therefore a constitutional responsibility for the welfare of minors (*Monomb Yamba v Maits Geru* [1975] PNGLR 322). The nation's long term interest lies in the reformation if at all possible of young offenders, and reformation is more likely to be effected by assistance and supervision in the community rather than by incarceration in a prison, even though such assistance and supervision may be scarce."

In *Passingan v Beaton* [1971-1972] PNGLR 206 at 209 the following view was expressed:

"To the extent that is possible, young first offenders should not be sent to gaol. It is clear that where a court deems it proper to imprison a young first offender that it should not impose a crushing sentence. It should be remembered that there are no reformatories in Papua New Guinea and that in many cases young people share what is provided in the corrective institutions with adults."

On the issue of imposing a prison sentence on young offenders, Kirriwom J has stated:

> "I appreciate the remark made in *R v Taggart* (1923) 17 Cr App R 132 which was cited often times in many decisions of this Court and the Supreme Court which says that 'a Judge or Magistrate who sends a young man to prison for the first time takes on a grave responsibility'. Such sentiment is not out of place even today but we must also face the reality that most of the violent crimes against persons and property involving use of offensive weapons are orchestrated by juvenile offenders within the age group 13 – 25 years. They must be made to realise that peace-loving and innocent citizens are fed-up and tired of living in fear ... The prisoner in this case appears to have little regard or respect for the law. I think a deterrent sentence is called for here. I agree in principle that imprisonment should be used as a last resort when sentencing youthful offenders, but that can only bear weight if he is a first offender."[143]

For discussion on the need for punishment of young offenders to be rehabilitative, see comments on passing sentence in *The State v Justin Vincent Nyama* [1991] PNGLR 127.

The position of youthful first offenders has been recently re-examined by the Queensland Court of Criminal Appeal in *R v Casey, R v Smyth* [1977] Qd R 132, and *R v Price* [1978] Qd R 68. The thrust of these and other authorities establishes that where a youthful first offender is before the courts on a relatively minor charge, there must be quite compelling reasons in existence to warrant the imposition of a jail sentence. In *R v Price*, the court specifically adopted the views of the Chief Justice of Tasmania in *Lahey v Sanderson* [1959] Tas SR 17 at 21, where His Honour stated:

> "The courts have recognised that imprisonment is likely to expose a youth to corrupting influences and to confirm him in criminal ways, thus defeating the very purpose of the punishment imposed. There has accordingly been a universal acceptance by the courts in England, Australia and elsewhere of the view that in the case of a youthful offender his reformation is always an important consideration and in the ordinary run of crime the dominant consideration in determining the appropriate punishment to be imposed."

These statements of principle do not contain any matter which makes them inappropriate to the circumstances of Papua New Guinea. Indeed, the overcrowded conditions in many of the jails in Papua New Guinea lend special relevance to these comments. It should be noted that these matters must not be taken out of context, and that other considerations must play their part where a more serious type of crime is being dealt with: *Paia Lifi v Phillip Dege* (1981) N291 (M).

Where youthful first offenders are concerned, courts should treat imprisonment as a last resort. It may well be that in the end imprisonment is appropriate, but all the alternatives should be investigated before taking that final step: *Kuri Willie v The State* [1987] PNGLR 298. In that case, an appeal was upheld on the basis that a sentence of three years imposed on a youth for break and enter was manifestly excessive. The magistrate should have considered probation, especially given the numerous mitigating factors in the case: the youth was a first offender who came from a good home and was well educated, he was under the influence of alcohol at the time, he was associated in the robbery with people several years older than he, and his participation in such anti-social behaviour was totally out of character: *Kuri Willie v The State* [1987] PNGLR 298 (Hinchliffe J).

---

[143] *The State v Willie Paul Songul* (1997) N1757.

It was stated in *Luneme Meuso v Maiak Nagy* (1978) N139:

> "There are offences where the notion or deterrence must take priority and where sentences of imprisonment may properly be imposed, even on young first offenders, to mark the disapproval by the law of the conduct in question and in the hope that other people will be deterred from like behaviour."

Where the appellants, aged 20 and 22, were in possession of unregistered firearms in circumstances of aggravation (inter alia "sawn-off" shotguns), the appellants could not be said to have been youthful offenders. The principle regarding the avoidance, where possible, of prison sentences for youthful offenders, as enunciated by Raine J in *Passingan v Beaton* [1971-1972] PNGLR 206, has little application to a case such as this where the appellants are both in their twenties: *Baru Saka v Aloysius Sombolok; Raymond Lamon v Aloysius Sombolok* (1978) N172.

In *Public Prosecutor v Don Hale* (1998) SC 564, in a case of robbery with violence committed by a 19 year old, the court held that it was necessary to consider what type of 19 year old the respondent was:

> "19 years of age is not necessarily a young offender in PNG society, at that age a person is a full adult with the right to vote and marry. There is no clear report whether this 19 years was a young 19 years still living with his parents or whether he was living as a full responsible adult. It appears from his antecedent report that he had left his home area and therefore left his parents home and had been living in different parts of Port Moresby and even having an adult job. So it appears that he may have been acting and behaving as a full responsible adult and not still under the care and control of his parents. If a judge is to consider some leniency on sentence because of age it is incumbent on him to obtain the relevant report such as a pre-sentence report, especially around the age of 17 to 19. Age considerations may of course be more obvious to a judge if an offender is under the age of 16 years."

In *Public Prosecutor v Tom Ake* [1978] PNGLR 469, where the accused had pursued a vicious attack with determination, without provocation, not made on the sudden but with an element of pre-intention, where great force was used to inflict the injuries which killed, and he was not an unsophisticated villager, a sentence of four years for murder was increased to eight years. The plea of guilty to a charge of murder is not a mitigating factor, except to the possible extent that it indicates remorse and contrition and the possibility of a more ready rehabilitation. In the setting of all of these facts where the accused was aged in his late twenties, no question of 'youthfulness' should have been taken into consideration at all.

In *Henry Rakatani v The State* [1979] PNGLR 556 at 557, the Supreme Court held:

> "As was pointed out in *Paulus Mandatititip v The State* [1978] PNGLR 128, by this Court, and many times by the National Court, youthfulness can no longer be considered a forceful contention towards leniency, especially in cases such as this (embezzlement) which are so prevalent."

The range for attempted murder appears usually to have been between four and 10 years. In *Peter Naibiri, Kutoi Soti Apia v The State* (1978) SC 137, where sentences of life imprisonment were passed on the appellants aged 17 and 19, the sentences were upheld. Both appellants had attacked three unarmed policeman with knives, chasing two away and returning to stab the third. The police had not acted with provocation or other than complete propriety. It is difficult accepting pleas of youthfulness to serious crime, and this must be so particularly in regard to violent crime of the most serious categories. In Papua New Guinean society it is a fact that youths of 17 and 19 are frequently men accepting adult responsibility in society's affairs. The courts must do their duty to try to assist the preservation of orderly life and to convince police that they will be assisted and protected in carrying out their duties by the sanction that will be invoked against anyone who attacks them.

Matters affecting mitigation

It is not appropriate for the court to deduct a specific period for each mitigating factor: *Raka Iamo Api v The State* (1998) SC 582.

The plea of guilty admits only the essential ingredients of the offence and not any circumstances of aggravation. It is necessary that any such circumstances of aggravation be proved beyond reasonable doubt. The defendant must be given the benefit of any reasonable doubt on matters of penalty in the absence of any statutory provisions to the contrary: *R v Gabai Vagi* [1973] PNGLR 30.

Andrew J held, in *Acting Public Prosecutor v Clement Maki and Tom Kasen* (1981) SC 205:

> "In this case there has been a long delay in bringing this appeal against inadequacy of sentence to determination. The respondents have served their terms of imprisonment and have been released. Delay both in the lodging and hearing of the appeal must always be a relevant factor."

In *Kali Mari v The State* (1980) SC 175, when arrested, the appellant immediately co-operated with the police, and he pleaded guilty at his trial. These are matters which go to substantial mitigation of sentence in this case.

Kidu CJ said in *John Elipa Kalabus v The State* [1988] PNGLR 193 at 197:

> "Remorse and contrition are factors weighed in the matter of sentence in favour of accused persons, particularly if they are manifested in a plea of guilty. Whether remorse or contrition are shown by a plea of guilty depends upon the time and circumstances in which the plea is advanced. The earlier the expression of remorse or contrition after the commission of the offence the more favourable it will be for the accused. Remorse and contrition expressed at the trial weighs very lightly. It is easier to believe remorse expressed earlier than remorse expressed at the time of the trial, especially in serious cases".

Kidu CJ further stated (at 196):

> "The practice in this jurisdiction is that accused persons who plead guilty in ordinary and less serious cases are generally entitled to credit for their plea. But when a case is a serious one such as wilful murder, murder, violent rape or violent armed robbery, a plea of guilty by itself deserves no credit. In fact this Court has said:
>
>> 'Similarly, we consider that the pleading guilty ought not to avail in such a case, that of a charge of murder, except to the possible extent that it indicates remorse and contrition and the possibility of a more ready rehabilitation: (*Reg v de Haan* [1968] 2 QB 108); and in this connection we distinguish the leniency which courts extend where pleas of guilty are entered to less serious crimes thereby saving embarrassment to witnesses, or heavy inconvenience to the State: (*Public Prosecutor v Tom Ake* [1978] PNGLR 469 at 472)."

In cases concerning misappropriation and stealing, a plea of guilty coupled with full restitution is a significant factor in mitigation. Together they go a long way to redressing the harm done and are indicative of genuine remorse and unqualified recognition of wrong doing: *The State v William Peter Colin Welford* [1986] PNGLR 253.

That no action has been taken by apprehension or prosecution against a co-accused is not a factor in mitigation: *Public Prosecutor v Michael Wunap Ngudomp* [1982] PNGLR 357.

Although diminished responsibility short of insanity is no defence under the Code, justice requires that a defendant's diminished responsibility should be taken into account in mitigation of sentence: *The State v Eric Gordon Berry* [1977] PNGLR 128.

In *The State v Wak Mond* [1986] PNGLR 258, the offender was exposed to severe and acute emotional stress after seeing his parents killed. He acted immediately in the heat of emotion and grief and took the life of the person responsible for their death. Wilson J held that although such action can never be condoned, it can be understood. The fact of the emotional stress, a clinical but correct description of the pressure attending on the offender at the time he committed this crime, is something the court is entitled to take into account in mitigation of punishment. Wilson J cited with approval the judgement of Brennan J in *Neal* [1982] 42 ALR 609 at 624-625. See also *The State v Kundi Koi* (1986) N575(s), for an instance of payback killing where the accused killed a person he mistakenly believed to be responsible for the death of his brother. It was held that although factors such as acting in the grip of distress, anger and grief should be taken into account, equally important are the elements which require harsh penalties to be meted out when the crime is such that society demands retribution and service to the concept of public deterrence.

In *The State v Opoyua Helai* (1997) N1533 on the issue of whether temporary mental illness can go towards mitigation of sentence, Sawong J followed *The State v Eric Gordon Berry* [1977] PNGLR 128 and *The State v Justus Taimbari Kauri* (25 June 1987, Kidu CJ), which have established that a temporary mental disorder or diminished responsibility of the mind can be taken into consideration as a mitigation factor on sentence. A doctor's report, which gave his opinion as to the prisoner's mental state at the relevant time, was taken into consideration in mitigating the sentence:

1. He was fit to plead.
2. He was not suffering from a mental disease at the time of the offence within the meaning of s 28 of the Code. That is, the prisoner was not insane.
3. He suffered from a temporary mental disorder which caused serious impairment of his capacity to know what he was doing, ability to recognise the wrongness of the act and to exercise the full control of his actions.

Kapi DCJ said in *Kesino Apo v The State* [1988] PNGLR 182 at 183:

> "I hold the opinion that anyone who voluntarily gets himself drunk, must know that his capacity to control himself will be impaired and it is no reasonable explanation by him after the event that his self-control was affected ... In the end result, the influence of alcohol cannot be a significant factor in mitigation of sentence."

It was stated in *Mase v The State* [1991] PNGLR 88 at 91:

> "If people drink liquor, get drunk and commit crime they must not expect leniency from the courts unless, of course, the intoxication is shown to have the effect of diminishing responsibility."

This was followed in *The State v Patrick* [1995] PNGLR 195.

Jalina J said in *The State v John Waiyake Komane* [1992] PNGLR 524 at 547:

> "In regard to [the accuseds'] pleas for leniency on the basis that their imprisonment would adversely affect their respective families one way or another, I consider that the Courts must treat such requests on that basis with caution. It seems to me to be a popular excuse. It was raised in a lot of cases I have heard and, no doubt, in cases heard by other judges as well. The accuseds' here have planned and have then gone out to commit a serious crime, a crime which they no doubt knew may result in them being jailed for a long time. The welfare of their loved one's should have been taken into account before they embarked on their journey of crime."

For mitigating factors to be taken into account in sentencing for domestic murder, see *The State v Donald Robin* (1980) N230.

In circumstances involving disputes between co-wives over their common husband, the husband's role in the conflict should be considered a mitigating factor on sentence: *The State v Maria Pung (Yamai)* [1995] PNGLR 173.

Where the wife is the offender, the husband is obliged by custom to pay compensation for the wife's wrongdoing, whether or not the husband is at fault for causing or contributing to his wife's wrongdoing: *The State v Margaret John (No 1)* (1995) N1326, followed in *The State v Maria Pung (Yamai)* [1995] PNGLR 173.

The amount of a fine or the amount of compensation ordered to be paid must be within the appellant's capacity to pay: *Idau Gabe v Meriam Griffin* [1977] PNGLR 492, following *R v Hewitt* [1971] Cr LR 492 and *R v Churchill* [1966] 2 All ER 215.

In sentencing a large number of persons, the court should take into consideration the fact that it may be taking every able-bodied villager from a particular village or area: *Yamore Memere v Matthew Bisang* [1976] PNGLR 419.

To deprive a citizen of the right to drive (under the *Motor Traffic Act*) a motor vehicle, where that person requires that right for carrying out the daily duties of his or her occupation, is a penalty which, if wrongly imposed, amounts to a substantial miscarriage of justice: *Wilkeson, v Grant* [1967-1968] PNGLR 112 at 118.

The failure to administer an allocutus or otherwise give the accused an opportunity to speak on the question of penalty, renders each sentence pronounced a nullity. See *Moses Aikaba v Tami* [1971-1972] PNGLR 155, and *Agiru Aieni v Paul T Tahian* [1978] PNGLR 37.

For matters relating to the administering of an allocutus see s 593 of the Code.

As to the punishments which may be imposed, see ss 18, 19, 20 and 601.

In *Public Prosecutor v Panikuiaka Nopi* [1979] PNGLR 536, following a violent quarrel with her husband, the respondent set fire to her house with the intention of committing suicide. She was rescued, but her infant son died in the fire. The court found that a sentence of two years' imprisonment for wilful murder of her son would have been appropriate (Andrew J dissenting). However, the circumstances since sentencing – release from custody pending appeal, forgiveness by her husband, and re-establishment in the family – demonstrate advantages to both the community and the respondent which outweigh whatever merit there would be in returning her to custody. Consequently, the Supreme Court upheld the original sentence of rising of the court.

An application to adduce fresh evidence on appeal against severity of sentence was not granted where it had not been shown that the evidence sought to be given was not available at the trial, nor that it was undiscoverable by use of ordinary diligence – the usual basic prerequisites: *John Rumet Kaputin v The State* [1979] PNGLR 559 at 560, distinguishing *R v Peter Ivoro* [1971-1972] PNGLR 374.

See Auki, "*Three Approaches to Sentencing*" 2(2) MLJ 263-269; Barnett, "*Crime, Kin and Compensation: The Law as Accessory to Payback*" 1(3) MLJ 33; Bayne, "*Legal Development in Papua New Guinea: The Place of the Common Law*" 3(1) MLJ 19-20; Strathern, "*Legality or Legitimacy: Hageners' Perception of the Judicial System*" 4(1) MLJ 67-93; Weisbrot, *Note: Law Reform Commission Working Paper No 6 – "Criminal Responsibility: Taking Customs, Perceptions and Beliefs into Account*" 5(1) MLJ 164-169; Weisbrot, "*Integration of Laws in Papua New Guinea: Custom and the Crirninal Law in Conflict*" in Weisbrot et al, *Law and Social Change in Papua New Guinea* (1982), pp 59, 76-78 and 87-89.

As to sentencing for sexual offences, see Strathern, *Report on Questionnaire Relating to Sexual Offences as Defined in the Criminal Code* (Department of Law, 1975), for a comparison of the Code provisions relating to sexual offences and Papua New Guinean attitudes towards those acts; Johnson, "*Criminal Law and Punishment*" in Brown, (ed), *Fashion of Law in New Guinea* (1969), p 83.

597. Sentence of death.

Subject to Section 598, the sentence to be pronounced on a person who is convicted of a crime punishable with death is that he be returned to his former custody, and that at a time and place to be appointed by the Head of State, acting on advice, he be hanged by the neck until he is dead.

See s 37 of the Code regarding treason, ss 81-82 regarding piracy, and s 299 regarding wilful murder - the only offences for which capital punishment has been retained. The death sentence for wilful murder was removed by the *Criminal Code (Amendment) Act* 1976 (No 2 of 1976), and reintroduced by the *Criminal Code (Amendment) Act* 1991 (No 25 of 1991), s 2.

Section 35 of the *Constitution* guarantees the "right to life", subject to certain qualifications, including s 35(1)(a) which states:

> "in execution of a sentence of a court following his conviction of an offence for which the penalty of death is prescribed by law."

See also s 36 of the *Constitution* regarding freedom from inhuman treatment.

See ss 598-599 of the Code.

See Griffin, "*The Death Sentence in Papua New Guinea*" (1972) 1(3) MLJ 91-92, for the pre-amendment.

598. Recording sentence of death.

(1) When a person is convicted of any crime punishable with death, except treason and wilful murder, if the court is of opinion that, under the circumstances of the case, it is proper that the offender should be recommended for mercy, the court may, if it thinks fit, direct the proper officer, instead of asking the offender whether he has anything to say why sentence of death should not be passed on him, to ask the offender, and that officer shall ask the offender, whether he has anything to say why

judgement of death should not be recorded against him.

(2) In a case referred to in Subsection (1) the court may abstain from pronouncing sentence of death, and may, instead, order judgement of death to be entered on record.

(3) On an order under Subsection (2) the proper officer is to enter judgement of death on record against the offender in the usual form, as if sentence of death had actually been pronounced by the court against the offender in open court.

(4) A record of a judgement of death entered under this section has the same effect as if sentence of death had been pronounced in open court.

See s 597 of the Code regarding the death sentence.

599. Pregnant women.

(1) When sentence of death is passed on a woman, she may apply for an order to stay execution on the ground that she is pregnant.

(2) If an application is made under Subsection (1), the court shall direct one or more medical practitioners to be sworn to examine the woman in some private place either together or successively, and to ascertain whether or not she is pregnant.

(3) If on the report of an examination conducted in pursuance of a direction under Subsection (2), verified on oath, it appears that the woman is pregnant, the court shall order that execution of the sentence be postponed until -

(a) she is delivered of a child; or

(b) it is no longer possible in the course of nature that she should be so delivered.

See s 597 of the Code regarding the death sentence.

600. Restriction of movement.

(1) For the purposes of this section -

"home", in relation to a person, means -

(a) the place (if any) where he has resided continuously during the period of five years immediately preceding the date of the offence giving rise to the conviction in respect of which a punishment under this section is being imposed;

(b) an area of customary land on which he may by custom build or occupy a house or garden, whether in his own right or in right of his spouse or some other relation; or

(c) an area of customary land owned by a linguistic or cultural group with which he or his spouse has customary affiliations involving usage rights in land; or

(d) an area of land leased for a term of not less than 12 months or held in freehold by him or his spouse under a Law in force in the country; or

(e) in a particular case where the provisions of Paragraph (a), (b), (c) or (d) are inapplicable – any other place with which he or his spouse has connections such that it should, in the opinion of the court, be reasonably regarded as his home;

"Probation Officer" means a probation officer appointed under the *Probation Act* (Chapter 381).

(2) Where a person is convicted of an offence, the court that convicts him may, in addition to or instead of any other punishment that may be imposed, order him –

(a) not to come or be within such part of the country as the court specifies; or

(b) to be returned to his home, as specified by the court,

during such period, not exceeding five years, as is specified by the court.

(3) An order under Subsection (2) -

(a) may be made subject to such exceptions and conditions as to the court seem proper, including a condition requiring the person to report his presence at regular intervals to a District Officer or Probation Officer or member of the Police Force; and

(b) remains in force for such period as is specified.

(4) An order made under Subsection (2)(b) does not operate so as to hinder or prevent a person from leaving the country.

(5) A person who, without reasonable excuse (proof of which is on him), contravenes or fails to comply with an order made under Subsection (2) is guilty of an offence.

Penalty: Imprisonment for a term not exceeding six months.

(6) A person who is convicted of an offence against Subsection (5) is liable to be again removed from the part of the country specified in the order, or to be removed to the part of the country specified by the court, as the case may be, or a new order under this section may be made against him.

See ss 42 and 52 of the *Constitution*.

601. Conditional suspension of punishment on first conviction.

(1) When a person who has not been previously convicted in Papua New Guinea or elsewhere of an offence of such a nature that, on conviction, a sentence may be imposed restricting the liberty of the offender for a period of six months or upwards, is convicted of any offence of such a nature that he may be sentenced on the conviction, to imprisonment for a period not exceeding three years, then, if in the opinion of the court that convicts him a sentence of imprisonment for a period not exceeding three years is an adequate punishment, the court -

(a) shall proceed to pass sentence on the offender in the usual form; and

(b) may, if it thinks fit, suspend the execution of the sentence on the offender entering into a recognizance in accordance with Subsection (2), in such amount as the court directs.

[Subs (1) am Act No 29, 1983 (*Criminal Code (Amendment) Act* 1983), s 12; am Act No 17, 1986 (*Criminal Code (Amendment No 2) Act* 1986), s 39]

(2) A recognizance under Subsection (l)(b) shall be conditioned that the offender shall -

(a) be of good behaviour; and

(b) comply with such other conditions as the court, in its discretion, imposes,

for -

(c) a period from the date of the sentence equal to the term of the sentence; or

(d) if the term of the sentence is less than 12 months – for the period of 12 months,

and will not during that period do or omit to do any act by which the recognizance would become liable to be forfeited under this section.

(3) The court may, if it thinks fit, instead of proceeding in accordance with Subsection (1)(b) direct that -

(a) the offender be imprisoned for such portion of the term of sentence as it thinks proper; and

(b) execution of the remaining portion of the sentence be suspended on the offender entering into a recognizance in accordance with Subsection (4) in such amount as the court directs.

(4) A recognizance under Subsection (3)(b) shall be conditioned that the offender shall -

(a) be of good behaviour; and

(b) comply with such other conditions as the court in its discretion imposes,

for -

(c) a period from the termination of his imprisonment equal to the term of the remaining portion of his sentence; or

(d) if the remaining portion is less than 12 months – for the period of 12 months,

and shall not during that period do or omit to do any act by which the recognizance would become liable to be forfeited under this section.

(5) When a recognizance is entered into under Subsection (1) or (3), the offender shall be discharged from custody, but is liable to be committed to prison to undergo his sentence, if, during the period specified in the recognizance, any of the conditions specified in the subsequent provisions of this section happens with respect to him.

(6) A written notice shall be given to the offender on his discharge specifying the conditions under which he will become liable to be committed to prison in accordance with Subsection (5).

(7) When an offender is committed to prison in accordance with Subsection (5), the term of the sentence begins to run from the commencement of his custody on the commitment, but the term of the imprisonment does not extend beyond the period specified in the recognizance, and at the expiration of that period the offender shall be released.

(8) If the offence -

(a) has relation to property; or

(b) is an offence against the person,

the court may, on suspending the execution of the sentence under Subsection (1)(b) or (3)(b) order the offender -

(c) to make restitution of the property in respect of which the offence was committed; or

(d) to pay compensation for -

(i) the injury done to the property; or

(ii) the injury done to the person injured,

as the case may be,

and may -

(e) assess the amount to be paid by the offender in any such case; and

(f) direct when, to whom and in what instalments the amount is to be paid.

(9) An order under Subsection (8) may be enforced in the same manner as orders made by magistrates on summary convictions.

(10) The court may -

(a) require the offender to give security for the performance of an order under Subsection (8); and

(b) make the discharge of the offender from custody conditional on such security being given.

(11) An offender discharged under this section must, once at least in every three months during the period specified in the recognizance, report his address and occupation to the member of the Police Force in charge at the place where he was convicted, or at such other place as the Commissioner of Police appoints.

(12) A report referred to in Subsection (11) may be made either by the offender -

(a) personally attending; or

(b) by letter signed by him and addressed to the member of the Police Force referred to in that subsection

unless in any case the Head of State, acting on advice, directs that the report be made by the offender personally, in which case it must be made in that manner only.

(13) If, during the period specified in the recognizance -

(a) it is proved to a magistrate in a court of summary jurisdiction that an offender discharged under this section has failed to report his address and occupation to the person, at the times and in the manner prescribed by Subsections (11) and (12); and

(b) an offender discharged under this section is charged by a member of the Police Force with getting his livelihood by dishonest means, and, on his being brought before a magistrate in a court of summary jurisdiction, it appears to the magistrate that there are reasonable grounds for believing that he is getting his livelihood by dishonest means; or

(c) an offender discharged under this section is charged with an offence punishable on indictment or summary conviction, and, on his being required by the magistrate before whom he is charged to give his name and address, he refuses to do so, or gives a false name or a false address; or

(d) an offender discharged under this section is convicted of -

(i) an indictable offence, whether on indictment or summarily; or

(ii) an offence punishable on summary conviction for which imprisonment for a period exceeding one month may be imposed,

the court or magistrate before whom the offender is charged or convicted may -

(e) forfeit the recognizance; and

(f) commit him to prison to undergo his original sentence, or so much of it (if any) as remains to be undergone under the provisions of this section; and

(g) grant any necessary warrant for his committal.

(14) If during the period specified in the recognizance none of the events referred to in Subsection (13) happens -

(a) the offender is discharged from the original sentence; and

(b) the conviction on which the sentence was imposed is not, on any subsequent conviction against him, to be treated as a previous conviction for the purposes of any law under which a greater punishment may be inflicted on a person who has been previously convicted.

(15) ...

[Subs (15) insrt Act No 29, 1983 (*Criminal Code (Amendment) Act* 1983), s 12; rep Act No 17, 1986 (*Criminal Code (Amendment No 2) Act* 1986), s 39]

See s 19 of the Code regarding the sentencing powers of the courts.

When a sentence is imposed and suspended under s 601(1)(b), the sentence does not commence to run until there is a breach of the bond: see s 601(7). An accused cannot complain about the sentence because it is deferred. If no breach of the bond takes place during the period given, the convicted person is discharged from that sentence and the conviction is not to be taken into account as a previous conviction on a subsequent conviction: s 601(7). When a court considers the question of forfeiture of a recognisance under s 601(7), the court is only exercising one discretion and that is whether or not it should forfeit the recognisance and commit the person to prison. It is not exercising discretion on sentence as to the original conviction, and must impose the suspended sentence given under s 601(1)(b) or so much thereof that remains to be served under s 601(2). Compare with s 19(1)(f) of the Code, where the court is given discretion either to impose the suspended sentence, or part thereof. The committal in suspended sentence under s 601(7) is not a sentence on the breach of recognisance but a sentence on the original conviction. Once the sentence is imposed under s 601(7), the time in which to appeal begins to run and the appellant may appeal against the sentence: *Albert Nawara v Robert Karo* [1981] PNGLR 125.

602. Discharge of offender in certain cases.

(1) When a person is summarily convicted of an offence relating to property, the court that convicts him may discharge the offender, without inflicting any punishment, on his making such satisfaction to the person aggrieved for damages, with or without costs, as may be approved by the court.

[Subs (1) am Act No 29, 1983 (*Criminal Code (Amendment) Act* 1983), s 13; am Act No 17, 1986 (*Criminal Code (Amendment No 2) Act* 1986), s 40]

(2) When satisfaction in accordance with Subsection (1) has been made the offender is not liable to any civil proceedings for the same cause at the suit of the person aggrieved.

(3) ...

[Subs (3) insrt Act No 29, 1983 (*Criminal Code (Amendment) Act* 1983), s 13; rep Act No 17, 1986 (*Criminal Code (Amendment No 2) Act* 1986), s 40]

603. Taking outstanding charges into account.

(1) Where the court before which a person is convicted on indictment of an offence not punishable with death or imprisonment for life is satisfied that -

- (a) there has been filed in court a document, in or to the effect of the prescribed form, signed by a member of the Police Force and by the person so convicted, showing on the back of it a list of other indictable offences not punishable with death or imprisonment for life with which he has been charged (whether or not he has been committed for trial in respect of those other offences); and
- (b) a copy of that document has been furnished to the person so convicted; and
- (c) in all the circumstances of the case it is proper to do so,

the court may, with the consent of the State Prosecutor and before passing sentence on the person for the offence of which he has been convicted, ask the person whether he admits his guilt in respect of all or any of the offences specified in the list and wishes them to be taken into account in passing sentence on him.

(2) If the convicted person admits his guilt in respect of all or any of the offences specified in the list filed under Subsection (1) and wishes them to be taken into account by the court in passing sentence for the offence of which he has been convicted, the court may, if it thinks fit, take all or any of the offences in respect of which he has so admitted guilt into account.

(3) In a case to which Subsection (2) applies, the sentence passed on the convicted person shall not exceed the maximum sentence that may be passed in respect of the offence of which he has been convicted.

(4) The court shall certify on the document filed under Subsection (1) the offences specified in the list on the back of it that have, in respect of the conviction of the person concerned, been taken into account in passing sentence on that conviction, and afterwards proceedings or further proceedings on those offences shall not be taken against the person unless the conviction is quashed or set aside.

(5) An admission of guilt under and for the purposes of this section in respect of an offence is not admissible in evidence-

(a) in any proceedings or further proceedings taken under the exception to Subsection (4); or

(b) in any proceedings or further proceedings in respect of the offence if the offence was not taken into account under this section in passing sentence.

(6) An offence taken into account under this section in passing sentence on a person for another offence of which he has been convicted shall not, by reason of its being so taken into account, be regarded for any purpose as an offence of which he has been convicted.

(7) Where the court before which a person was convicted of an indictable offence took into account in accordance with this section, in passing sentence for the offence, any other offence or offences, then whenever in or in relation to any criminal proceedings -

(a) reference may lawfully be made to the fact that the person was convicted of the indictable offence, reference may also be made to the fact that that other offence or those other offences was or were so taken into account; and

(b) evidence may lawfully be given of the fact that that person was convicted of the indictable offence, evidence may also be given of the fact that that other offence or those other offences was or were so taken into account.

(8) The fact that that other offence or the other offences was or were so taken into account may be proved in the same manner as the conviction for the indictable offence may be proved.

(9) Subsections (7) and (8) do not affect the operation of Subsection (6).

Andrew and Pratt JJ said, in *Acting Public Prosecutor v Andrew Amona Yongga* [1981] PNGLR 314:

> "This section was introduced to give statutory basis to practice which had become established under the common law in England over a period of years. In the application of the section the common law authorities are still invaluable. Some aspects are not stipulated in the section but in our view it is clear, for example, that explicit enquiry as to whether or not the prisoner admits his guilt and does so without any pressure must be made."

There was no equivalent section under the former Queensland *Criminal Code (Adopted)*. It was previously possible under s 561 of the Queensland *Criminal Code (Adopted)* to take other offences into account though the presentation of ex officio indictments by a Crown law officer.

Before the enactment of s 603 no actual convictions were recorded so that consequential orders in relation to cancellation of licences, disqualification, re-vesting of property, etc could not be pronounced. It was difficult for the accused to raise the plea of *autrefois convict*. This section now removes such difficulties.

In *R v Kana Seiliga* (1973) N750, Prentice J said:

> "Where many charges are pending against an accused, the sensible convenient and usual approach is for the Crown to present an indictment or indictments, and to consent that the other offences may be taken into account. I consider that this should normally be done. However, if there is any good reason why it is desirable that multiple convictions be actually recorded, I can see no warrant for preventing the Crown's proceeding [in the fashion it has done here]."

Where the accused does not wish other matters to be taken into account, the Crown should be prepared to present multiple indictments at the one sitting. Prentice J further stated:

> "Where the accused is prepared to plead guilty to one or more charges and to ask that the (possibly numerous) remainder be taken into account – I would regard it as proper that the Crown should follow that course."

The practice of "taking account" of offences other than that for which an indictment is presented, is established by legislation in New South Wales, and by practice in England as well as in the Code State of Western Australia, and in Victoria and South Australia. It is the sensible, convenient and usual approach for the Crown to present an indictment or indictments, and thereon to consent that the other offences which are alleged and may wish to be admitted by the accused (if multiple), may be "taken into account". The practice enables a person to be released with a clean sheet, and it avoids a multiplicity of proceedings: *R v Nelson Timothy* (1973) N759.

Andrew and Pratt JJ, in *Acting Public Prosecutor v Andrew Amona Yongga* [1981] PNGLR 314, stated:

> "All pending charges of a similar nature ought, so far as possible, to be taken into account by the court in sentencing so that one comprehensive term of imprisonment may be imposed, thereby giving a clean sheet to the prisoner and avoiding the undesirable spectacle of a prisoner being arrested at the prison gates after concluding his original period of sentence. As in the common law, whether or not the trial judge does take into account other outstanding charges is purely discretionary and can only be done with the consent of the State Prosecutor. We would agree with the view in *Smith* 15 Cr App R 172, that it would not be proper to ask a trial judge to exercise his discretion in favour of an accused unless the offences are all of the same or closely allied class."

Where a series of similar offences is admitted by the accused, it may be appropriate for the state to employ the "sample charge" technique, whereby the indictment contains, say, only the earliest and latest counts, or only the latest count, or a typical count. The offence or offences charged is or are treated by all concerned as representative and dealt with accordingly while the offences outside the indictment are taken into account. *Acting Public Prosecutor v Andrew Amona Yongga* [1981] PNGLR 314.

Kapi J stated in *Acting Public Prosecutor v Andrew Amona Yongga*:

"The very purpose of the practice of taking other offences into account, as developed in England, was to do away with the process of a trial and conviction and not to do away with the punishment for those offences to which the accused person admits. Subsection (2) of this section is a significant provision when interpreting the practical effect of taking into account other offences. It is clear from this provision that offences which are taken into account may not be proceeded with. Having regard to this provision, I do not consider that the legislature intended that the accused should not be punished for the offences which he had agreed to take into account in sentence, or that he should receive some less punishment than he would have received otherwise had he been properly indicted."

In that same case, Andrew and Pratt JJ said:

"It was long before decided under the common law that the sentence given by the trial judge must not be greater than the maximum permissible for the offence on which the prisoner has come before the court. This restriction is provided for specifically in this section. However, the question remains whether or not the taking of other offences into account will increase the penalty which would normally have been imposed on the prisoner had he not asked for such matters to be taken into consideration. It seems clear to us that if the result of taking other offences into account meant no increase in sentence could take place, the whole procedure would rather defeat the purpose and would tend to bring the practice into contempt. The procedure of course is not only for the benefit of the accused but also for the State. One of those benefits is that a prisoner may receive an adequate sentence for all matters to which he has confessed. To have the spectacle of the court saying that in the circumstances of this particular case it imposes a particular penalty that it will not increase despite 18 other similar offences committed over many months, but that it will not reduce the penalty by any amount despite other mitigating factors because such other offences must be taken into account, to our minds has a certain air of illogicality."[144]

The accused should make the fullest and fairest disclosure possible regarding offences to be taken into account to avoid the possibility of subsequently being charged in relation to one of those offences only generally described earlier. This is now achieved by s 603(1) which allows for a list of offences to be accurately endorsed on the Court records: *R v Emere Gabau* (1960) N156.

Another case in which other offences may be taken into account arises in the circumstances where a whole series of separate offences are committed over a period of time and all of these offences form a course of conduct. The proper procedure is to charge the last of the offences committed and to give evidence upon the trial of the whole course of conduct including the earlier offences: *R v Emere Gabau* (1960) N156.

It is essential that the prisoner should admit the truth of the other charge and should expressly consent that it should be taken into consideration: *R v Heroma Poia* [1964] PNGLR 187 at 188.

The judge has a discretion as to the use of this procedure: *R v Heroma Poia* [1964] PNGLR 187.

---

[144] *R v Emere Gabua* (1960) N156 not followed.

604. Assessment of value of property: Appropriation of fines dependent on value.

(1) Subject to Subsection (2), on a summary conviction by which a penalty is imposed on the basis of -

(a) the value of any property taken, killed or destroyed; or

(b) the amount of any injury done to any property,

the value or amount shall be assessed by the convicting court and the amount, when recovered, shall be paid to the person aggrieved, unless he is unknown, or unless the property taken or injured is of a public nature, when it is to be applied in the same manner as other fines imposed by the court.

(2) When several persons join in the commission of the same offence and on conviction a penalty is imposed on each of them on the basis of the value of the property or of the amount of the injury, no sum further than the value or amount shall be paid to the person aggrieved, and the remainder shall be applied in the same manner as other fines imposed by the court.

605. Effect of summary conviction for indictable offences.

When a person has been summarily convicted of an indictable offence, the conviction shall be deemed to be a conviction of a simple offence only and not of an indictable offence.

For a list of indictable offences triable summarily, see Sch 2 of the Code.

Division 7 – Habitual Criminals

606. Declaration of convicted persons as habitual criminals.

(1) Where a person -

(a) is convicted on indictment of an offence against any provision of Division IV.2; and

(b) has been previously so convicted on indictment on at least two occasions of any of those offences (whether of the same description of offence or not),

the Judge may, in his discretion, declare as part of the sentence of the person that he is an habitual criminal.

(2) Where a person -

(a) is convicted on indictment of an offence against any provision of Division III.7, Division V.4, Subdivision VI.I.A, B, C, D, E or F, Division VI.2.A, Subdivision VI.3.A, or Subdivision VI.3.C; and

(b) has been previously convicted on indictment on at least three occasions of an offence against any provision of Division III.7 or IV.2 or any provision referred to in Paragraph (a) (whether of the same description of offence or not),

the Judge may, in his discretion, declare as part of the sentence of the person that he is an habitual criminal.

(3) Where any person -

(a) has been previously convicted on indictment on at least two occasions of an offence referred to in Subsection (2)(b) (whether of the same description of offence or not); and

(b) has been previously convicted summarily on at least two occasions of an offence punishable by imprisonment for not less than three months; and

(c) is convicted summarily of an offence punishable by imprisonment for not less than three months,

the court that convicts him may, in addition to sentencing him to a term of imprisonment, order that he be brought before the National Court or a Judge to be dealt with as an habitual criminal.

(4) Where a person -

(a) is convicted of any offence against any provision of the *Summary Offences Act* (Chapter 264) or the *Vagrancy Act* (Chapter 268); and

(b) has been previously convicted on at least four occasions of an offence against any provision of any of those Acts (whether of the same description of offence or not),

the court that convicts him may, in addition to sentencing him to a term of imprisonment, order that he be brought before the National Court or a Judge to be dealt with as an habitual criminal.

(5) Where a person is brought before the National Court or a Judge under Subsection (3) or (4), the Court or the Judge may -

(a) declare the person to be an habitual criminal; and

(b) direct that on the expiration of his sentence he shall be detained in a reformatory prison under this Code.

(6) This section applies whether the previous convictions took place within Papua New Guinea or for similar offences under similar laws of places outside Papua New Guinea.

(7) For the purposes of this section, a committal for sentence under the *District Courts Act* (Chapter 40), shall be deemed to be a previous conviction on indictment.

See ss 609-610 of the Code.

While the state should, in most cases, allow for the practice of "taking into account" offences other than that for which an indictment is presented, under s 603, the state may justifiably proceed otherwise in some cases, particularly where it may have in mind the desirability or likelihood of applying for a declaration of criminal habit under this section: *R v Nelson Timothy* (1973) SC 759.

607. Reformatory prisons.

(1) The Head of State, acting on advice, may, by notice in the National Gazette, set apart a corrective institution or other suitable place to be a reformatory prison for the detention of habitual criminals.

(2) The Head of State, acting on advice, may appoint for each reformatory prison a manager, a matron, and such other officers and attendants as the National Executive Council thinks necessary.

608. Application of Code and *Correctional Service Act* 1995.

Every reformatory prison shall be deemed to be a corrective institution and a prison, and every person detained in it shall be deemed to be a detainee and a prisoner, within the meaning of the *Correctional Services Act* 1995 and this Code.

In *Kemai v Symonds* [1975] PNGLR 81 at 82 and 83, Raine J said (in dicta):

> "Police officers must treat prisoners with respect, ie the prisoner must be treated as a human being, that he must not be bullied, and that, in the physical sense, he must get more or less reasonable treatment, eg blankets, food, water, lavatory facilities, etc. The moment that the police, or other government authorities of a like nature start to treat detainees in a brutal and indifferent way, respect for the police and authority will inevitably be lessened. This is not to say that I deplore firm, even stern, treatment of offenders. But stern treatment of offenders does not involve their abuse. Abuse of authority is extremely serious. It must be discouraged; if it is not then the rot will set in."

See also *Yamore Memera v Matthew Bisang* [1976] PNGLR 419 at 421 (Frost CJ); *Heni Pauta and Kenneth Susuve v Commissioner for Corrective Institutions and his Servants and Agents* [1982] PNGLR 7; and *Tom Amaiu v Commissioner of Corrective Services and the State* (1983) N417, regarding the constitutional (ss 36(1), 37(1), 37(17), 41(1) and 57(3)) protection against abuse of persons in custody.

609. Detention of habitual criminals.

At the expiration of his sentence, an habitual criminal shall be detained until discharged at the direction of the Minister under this Code.

See s 606 of the Code regarding declaration of an habitual criminal.

610. Discharge.

(1) A person detained as an habitual criminal may apply to the National Court or a Judge for a recommendation that he be discharged on the ground of his having sufficiently reformed or for other sufficient reason.

(2) The case of each person detained as an habitual criminal shall be submitted by the Minister to the National Court or a Judge for review at six-monthly intervals, or as near to six-monthly intervals as circumstances permit.

(3) On receipt of an application under Subsection (1) or a case submitted for review under Subsection (2), the National Court or Judge -

- (a) may make inquiry in such manner as the Court or Judge thinks proper; and
- (b) shall furnish to the Minister a report on the case of the person concerned; and
- (c) may -
  - (i) if satisfied that the person is sufficiently reformed or that there is some other sufficient reason to warrant his discharge, recommend to the Minister that the person be discharged; or
  - (ii) recommend that he be not discharged.

(4) On receipt of a report and recommendation under Subsection (3), the Minister may direct the discharge of the person concerned or otherwise as he thinks proper.

(5) If the Minister directs the discharge of a person, he may also order that, if the person remains in the country, he shall, either personally or by a letter sent by post, for a period not exceeding two years and at such intervals as are specified in the order, report his address and occupation to the member of the Police Force in charge at the place where he was convicted or at such other place as the Commissioner of Police appoints.

See ss 606 and 609 of the Code.

611. Conditions under which offender may be arrested.

(1) If during the period specified in an order under Section 610(5) the person discharged -

(a) is proved to any court of summary jurisdiction to have failed without reasonable excuse (proof of which is on him) to report his address and occupation to the proper person at the times and in the manner prescribed by the order; or

(b) is charged by a member of the Police Force with getting his livelihood by dishonest means, and on his being brought before any court of summary jurisdiction it appears to the court that there are reasonable grounds for believing that he is getting livelihood by dishonest means; or

(c) on being charged with an offence punishable on indictment or summary conviction, and on being required by the court before which he is charged to give his name and address, refuses to do so, or gives a false name or a false address; or

(d) is convicted of any offence against the *Summary Offences Act* (Chapter 264) or the *Vagrancy Act* (Chapter 268) or of an indictable offence, or of any offence punishable on summary conviction by imprisonment for not less than three months,

the court before which such proof is given, or before which the offender is so charged or convicted, may direct him, in addition to any penalty or on the completion of any term of imprisonment then imposed on him, to be recommitted to a reformatory prison, and he shall be so recommitted accordingly and the court may grant any necessary warrant for his recommittal.

(2) If during the period specified in an order under Section 610(5) none of the events specified in Subsection (1) happens, the person discharged ceases to be an habitual criminal.

See the *Arrest Act*.

Division 8 – Costs

612. Costs of prosecution in certain cases.

(1) When a person is convicted on indictment of an indictable offence relating to the person of any person, the court, on the application of the person aggrieved by the offence, may, in addition to any sentence that is passed on the offender, order

him to pay to the person aggrieved -

(a) his costs of prosecution; and

(b) a sum by way of compensation for any loss of time suffered by him by reason of the offence of which the offender is convicted.

(2) An order under Subsection (1) for the payment of costs, or of any sum awarded by way of compensation may be enforced in the same manner as a judgement of the court given in civil proceedings.

(3) If any money was found on the person of the offender on his arrest, the court may order it to be applied towards the payment of any money ordered under Subsection (1) to be paid by him.

(4) When an order is made under this section for the payment of money by way of compensation to an aggrieved person, the offender is not liable to any civil proceedings for the same cause at the suit of that person.

See ss 617-618 of the Code regarding private prosecutions.

613. Taxation.

(1) In this section -

"costs of defence" includes costs incurred by the accused person both before and after his committal;

"costs of prosecution" includes costs incurred by the person aggrieved in order to the committal of the offender, and costs incurred by him with the consent of the State Prosecutor for the purposes of the trial.

(2) Costs of a prosecution or defence shall be taxed by the proper officer of the court in which the indictment is presented.

See *Tolom Abai v The State* (2000) SC 632 for a discussion of the principles of a taxing officer's discretion in issues of taxation of costs and the court's review of the taxing discretion.

See ss 617-618 of the Code regarding private prosecutions.

Division 9 – Execution of Sentence

614. Execution of sentence of death.

(1) The punishment of death shall be carried out by hanging the offender by his neck until he is dead.

(2) The time and place of execution shall be appointed by the Head of State, acting on advice.

(3) The Sheriff, or a Sheriff's officer appointed by the Sheriff, shall be present at the execution.

(4) The officer-in-charge and the proper officers of the corrective institution (including the visiting medical officer), all justices who wish to be present, and such members of the Police Force as the Sheriff or Sheriff's officer allow may also be present.

(5) All the persons attending the execution shall remain in the enclosure until the execution has been carried out according to law, and until the visiting medical officer has signed a certificate in the following form -

> "I, ... , the visiting medical officer of the Corrective Institution, certify that I have today witnessed the execution of ... , lately, as I am informed, convicted and duly sentenced to death by the National Court and I further certify that he was, in pursuance of the sentence, hanged by the neck; until he was dead.
>
> Dated ... 1 9
>
> Visiting Medical Officer."

(6) The Sheriff or Sheriff's officer, the officer-in-charge and officers of the corrective institution, and the members of the Police Force who are present shall sign, before leaving the corrective institution, a declaration in the following form adding their description -

> "We declare and testify that we were this day present when the extreme penalty of the law was executed on ... , lately, as we are informed, convicted by the National Court, and duly sentenced to death on ... 19 , and that he was, in pursuance of the sentence, hanged by the neck until he was dead.
>
> (Signatures of Witnesses.)"

(7) Every certificate and declaration under this section shall be transmitted by the Sheriff, Sheriff's officer, or deputy of the sheriff, whichever of them is present at the execution, to the Registrar of the National Court and shall be entered and kept in his office as a record of the Court, and a copy of it is to be twice published in the National Gazette.

(8) The body of the offender shall be buried at such place as the Head of State, acting on advice, directs.

See ss 597-599 of the Code regarding the death sentence. See ss 35-36 of the *Constitution*.

Division 10 – Release of Prisoners on Licence

615. Release of prisoners on licence.

(1) In this section –

> "licence" means a licence to be at large granted under Subsection (2);
>
> "prescribed authority" means a Magistrate Grade III, or IV, or a Reserve Magistrate under the *District Courts Act* (Chapter 40);
>
> "the prescribed period", in relation to a licence, means the period commencing on the day on which the licence was granted and ending on the day that, if no remissions of sentence were granted, would be the last day of the term of imprisonment being served by the person to whom the licence was granted.

(2) Where a person is serving a term of imprisonment for an offence against a law, the Minister may, if he thinks proper to do so in the circumstances, grant to him by writing under his hand, a licence to be at large.

(3) A licence is sufficient authority for the release from prison of the person to whom it is granted.

(4) A licence is subject to such conditions (if any) as are specified in the licence

(5) The Minister may, at any time before the expiration of the prescribed period, by writing under his hand -

(a) vary or revoke a condition of a licence or impose additional conditions; or

(b) revoke a licence.

(6) The varying of a condition or the imposing of an additional condition under Subsection (5) does not have effect until notice of it has been given to the person to whom the licence was granted, being notice given before the expiration of the prescribed period.

(7) Where -

(a) a licence granted to a person is revoked; or

(b) the person to whom a licence has been granted has, during the prescribed period, failed to comply with a condition of the licence; or

(c) there are reasonable grounds for suspecting that he has, during that period, failed to comply with a condition of the licence,

then -

(d) a member of the Police Force may, without warrant arrest him; and

(e) a Magistrate Grade III or IV may, after receiving evidence on oath, issue a warrant for his arrest.

(8) Where a member of the Police Force arrests a person under Subsection (7) on a ground specified in Subsection (7)(b) or (c), the member shall, as soon as practicable, take him before a prescribed authority.

(9) If the prescribed authority is satisfied that a person brought before him under Subsection (8) failed without lawful excuse to comply with a condition of the licence, the prescribed authority shall cancel the licence.

(10) A person brought before a prescribed authority under Subsection (8) shall, unless the prescribed authority otherwise directs, be kept in custody until the prescribed authority has determined the matter.

(11) Where a licence granted to a person is revoked or cancelled -

(a) the person may, subject to Subsection (12), be detained in prison to undergo imprisonment for a period equal to the part of his term of imprisonment that he had not served at the time when he was released from prison under the licence; and

(b) a prescribed authority may give a warrant under his hand for the detention of a person under Paragraph (a).

(12) Where a prescribed authority cancels a licence under Subsection (9), the person to whom the licence was granted may appeal to the National Court against the cancellation.

(13) On an appeal under Subsection (12), the National Court may -

(a) if it is satisfied that the ground on which the licence was cancelled has been established – confirm the cancellation; or

(b) if it not so satisfied – order that the cancellation cease to have effect.

(14) An appeal under Subsection (12) shall be by way of re-hearing, but the National Court may have regard to any evidence given before the prescribed authority.

See s 19 of the Code regarding punishment.

See the power of mercy provisions in the *Constitution*, ss 151-152.

Division 11 – Information by Private Persons for Indictable Offences: Ex Officio Indictments

616. Information by leave of the Court by private prosecutors.

(1) Any person may by leave of the National Court present any information against any other person for an indictable offence not punishable with death that is alleged to have been committed by the other person.

(2) An information presented under Subsection (1) shall be -

(a) signed by the person on whose application the leave is granted or some other person appointed by the National Court for the purpose; and

(b) filed in the National Court.

(3) The person who signs the information is called the prosecutor.

(4) The information is to be intituled "The Independent State of Papua New Guinea on the prosecution of the prosecutor (naming him) against the accused person (naming him)", and must state that the prosecutor informs the National Court by leave of the Court.

(5) Except as otherwise provided, the information and the proceedings on it are subject to the same rules and incidents as an indictment presented by the Public Prosecutor and the proceedings on such an indictment as set out in the preceding provisions of this Code.

Note that this section applies to indictable offences only and not to summary offences.

Pratt J stated, in *Arthur Gilbert Smedley v The State* [1980] PNGLR 379 at 406-407:

> "The wording of this section is exactly the same as s 686 of the pre-1974 Code and was always referred to by the shorthand description 'private prosecution'. There appears to be no doubt in the minds of the court which delivered judgment in *Gouldham v Sharrett* [1966] WAR 129, that such section dealt with private prosecutions only. There is likewise no real doubt in my mind. I am not prepared to say that this section may be utilised by the Public Prosecutor or one of his deputies in connection with a matter in which the Public Prosecutor has already presented an indictment and entered a nolle prosequi. It would appear incongruous to me that in such circumstances the prosecutor is 'required to give security' in order to cover the costs of the defence, and even more incongruous that under r 26 of the *Criminal Practice Rules* (assuming they are still in operation) a stipulation should be provided for the prosecutor to be under a duty to furnish certain material to the Public Prosecutor when he is in fact already under a duty to comply with directions issued by his senior."

See ss 524-537 of the Code regarding indictments. See *Arthur Gilbert Smedley v The State* [1980] PNGLR 379 (Wilson J), discussed under s 526, regarding the failure of the prosecution in that case to obtain leave in accordance with the provisions of this section.

Pratt J further stated, in *Arthur Gilbert Smedley v State*, at 407:

> "There is an apparent conflict between the mandatory terms appearing in s 524(1), and this section. The answer may well be that the earlier section is impliedly referring to prosecutions by the State only does not intend to oust 'private prosecutions' covered by this later provision in the Code."

In *Public Prosecutor v Lindsay Kivia, Robert N'Draku and Peter Seski* [1988] PNGLR 256, the Public Prosecutor applied for leave to present informations pursuant to s 616 against three persons who had been committed for trial but discharged under s 554(4) by reason of failure to present indictments. Amet J (at 258) held that:

> "I do not believe that this section can be utilised by the Public Prosecutor purporting to prosecute in his private capacity. He has no interest in this matter as a private victim or complainant. This section quite clearly, in its terms, deals with private prosecutions only. [It cannot] be utilised, in my view, following a discharge under s 552(4)."

See ss 612-613 of the Code.

618. Cost of defence.

Subject to Section 618A, if in a case to which this Division applies -

(a) the Public Prosecutor informs the National Court that he will not further proceed on the information; or

(b) the accused person is acquitted on trial,

the Court or the Judge before whom the trial (if any) is had, may award costs to the accused person.

[S 618 am Act No 7, 1986 (*Criminal Code (Costs) Act* 1986), s 1]

See ss 612-613 of the Code.

618A. Costs of successful defendant.

(1) Notwithstanding the provisions of Section 618, the Court or the Judge shall, before making an order for costs under that section, consider all relevant circumstances and, in particular, where appropriate, shall consider –

(a) whether the prosecution acted in good faith in bringing and in continuing the proceedings; and

(b) whether at the commencement of the proceedings the prosecution had sufficient evidence to support the conviction of the defendant; and

(c) whether the prosecution took reasonable steps to investigate any matter that -

(i) came to its attention; and

(ii) suggested that the defendant might not be guilty; and

(d) whether the prosecution conducted the investigation into the offence in a reasonable manner; and

(e) whether the evidence was sufficient to support the conviction of the defendant but the information was dismissed on a technical point; and

(f) whether the information was dismissed because the defendant established that he was not guilty; and

(g) whether the conduct of the defendant in relation to -

(i) the act or omission on which the charge was based; and

(ii) the investigation and proceedings,

was such, that a sum should be paid towards the cost of his defence.

(2) There shall be no presumption for or against an award of costs.

(3) A defendant shall not be awarded costs under Section 618 or under any provision in any other Act by reason only of the fact that -

(a) he has been acquitted or discharged; or

(b) an information charging him with an offence has been dismissed or withdrawn.

[S 618A insrt Act No 7, 1986 (*Criminal Code (Costs) Act* 1986), s 2]

Part IX – Miscellaneous

619. Certain errors not to avoid conviction.

(1) A conviction shall be set aside -

(a) on the ground of the improper admission of evidence, if it appears to the court that the evidence was merely of a formal character and not material; or

(b) on the ground of the improper admission of evidence adduced for the defence.

(2) A conviction cannot be set aside for any informality in swearing or affirming any witness or interpreter.

620. Women detained for immoral purposes.

(1) If it appears to a magistrate on complaint made on oath -

(a) by a parent, relative or guardian of a woman or girl; or

(b) by any other person who, in the opinion of the magistrate, is acting in good faith in the interest of a woman or girl,

that there is reasonable cause to suspect that the woman or girl is unlawfully detained for immoral purposes by any person in any place within his jurisdiction, he may issue a warrant directed to a member of the Police Force, authorizing him to search for the woman or girl, and, when found, to take her to and detain her in a place of safety until she can be brought before a magistrate.

(2) The magistrate before whom a woman or girl is brought under Subsection (1) may cause her to be delivered up to her parents or guardians or otherwise dealt with as the circumstances permit and require.

(3) The magistrate issuing the warrant may, by the same or another warrant, direct any person accused of unlawfully detaining the woman or girl to be arrested and brought before a magistrate, and may direct proceedings to be taken for punishing him according to law.

(4) A woman or girl shall be deemed to be unlawfully detained for immoral purposes if she -

(a) is under the age of 16 years; or

(b) being of or over the age of 16 years and under the age of 18 years, is detained against her will, or against the will of her father or mother or of any other person who has the lawful care or charge of her; or

(c) being of or above the age of 18 years, is detained against her will,

and is detained by any person for the purpose of her being unlawfully carnally known by any man, whether a particular man or not.

(5) A person authorized by warrant under this section to search for a woman or girl may enter, if need be by force, any house or other place specified in the warrant, and may remove the woman or girl from it.

(6) A warrant under this section shall be executed by the member of the Police Force mentioned in it, who must, unless the magistrate otherwise directs, be accompanied by the parent, relative, guardian or other person by whom the complaint is made, if the person so desires.

See generally Pt IV, Div 2 of the Code, on offences against sexual morality.

621. Custody of girls under 18.

(1) When on the trial of a person charged with an offence against any provision of Division IV.2 relating to women or girls, it is proved to the satisfaction of the court that the seduction, prostitution or incest of a girl under the age of 18 years has been caused, encouraged or favoured by her father, mother, guardian, master or mistress, the court may -

(a) make an order divesting the father, mother, guardian, master or mistress of all authority over her; and

(b) appoint any person or persons who is or are willing to take charge of the girl to be her guardian or guardians until she has attained the age of 18 years, or any age under 18 years that the court directs.

(2) The National Court or a Judge may rescind or vary any order under Subsection (1) by the appointment of any other person or persons as guardian or guardians, or in any other respect.

622. Certificate of dismissal by magistrates.

(1) When a magistrate dismisses a complaint of an offence, whether an indictable offence or not, punishable on summary conviction he may, if required and if he thinks fit, give the accused person a certificate of dismissal.

(2) A certificate of dismissal given under Subsection (1) is a bar to any further prosecution of the accused person for the same cause.

See s 17 of the Code regarding double jeopardy, and s 560 regarding pleas.

623. Saving of civil remedies.

Except when expressly provided, the prosecution or conviction of a person for an offence does not affect any civil remedy that any person aggrieved by the offence has against the offender.

623A. Restitution of property.

(1) When a person is prosecuted, on the complaint of the owner of property or any person on whom the right to property has devolved by operation of law, on a charge of an indictable offence of which the unlawful acquisition of the property by him is an element, and is convicted of the offence on indictment, the Court may order the property to be restored to the owner.

(2) An order made under Subsection (1) has the effect of a judgement, and is binding on the offender and any person claiming through him as determining the ownership of the property, but as regards any other person has the effect only of changing the possession of the property, and does not affect any right of property or right of action.

(3) In any case referred to in Subsection (1), the Court before which the offender is convicted may order that any personal property which is found in his possession, and which appears to the Court to have been derived, directly or indirectly, from such unlawful acquisition of property, shall be delivered to any person who appears to the Court to be entitled to the property so unlawfully acquired.

(4) This section does not apply to a valuable security, if it appears that the security has been paid or discharged in good faith by some person liable to the payment thereof, or, being a negotiable instrument, has been taken or received by transfer or delivery in good faith by some person for a valuable consideration without any notice and without any reasonable cause to suspect that the same had been so unlawfully acquired.

[S 623A insrt Act No 13, 1977 (*Criminal Code (Arrest) Act* 1977), s 33]

See Criminal Law (*Compensation*) Act 1991 at Chapter 5.

624. Limitation of proceedings.

(1) An action or prosecution against any person for any thing done in pursuance of any of the provisions of this Code with respect to the arrest of offenders or the seizure of goods must be commenced within six months after the fact committed.

(2) Written notice of the action and of the cause of action must be given to the defendant one month at least before the commencement of the action.

(3) The plaintiff is not entitled to recover in an action referred to in Subsection (1) if -

(a) tender of sufficient amends is made before action brought; or

(b) a sufficient sum of money is paid into court by the defendant after action.

(4) If -

(a) a verdict is given for the defendant; or

(b) the plaintiff is non-suited or discontinues the action; or

(c) judgement, on demurrer or otherwise is given against the plaintiff,

the defendant is entitled to full costs of action as between solicitor and client.

625. Court fees in criminal cases.

No fees can be taken in any court of criminal jurisdiction or before any magistrate from any person who is charged with an indictable offence for any proceeding had or taken in the court or before the magistrate with respect to the charge.

626. Copies of depositions to be allowed to persons committed for trial.

(1) Subject to Subsection (2), a person who is committed for trial or held to bail for an indictable offence is entitled to have on demand from the person who has the lawful custody of the copies of the depositions of the witnesses on whose depositions he has been committed or is held to bail.

(2) If a demand under Subsection (1) is not made before the day appointed for the commencement of the sittings of the court at which the trial of the person on whose behalf the demand is made is to take place, he is not entitled to have a copy of any deposition unless the Judge is of opinion that the copy may be made and delivered without delay or inconvenience to the trial.

(3) The court may postpone a trial on account of the accused person not having previously had a copy of the depositions.

627. Inspection of depositions at trial.

A person who is tried for an offence is entitled at the time of his trial to inspect without fee all depositions or copies of depositions, that have been taken against him and returned into the court before which the trial is had.

628. Exhibits.

Where an exhibit is tendered in a court and it appears to the court that in the public interest the exhibit should not be returned to its owner, the court may order that the exhibit be forfeited, destroyed or otherwise dealt with.

Schedule 2

Indictable Offences Triable Summarily

[Sch 2 insrt Act No 28, 1980 (*Criminal Code (Indictable Offences) Act* 1980), s 6; am Act No 29, 1983 (*Criminal Code (Amendment) Act* 1983), s 14; am Act No 18, 1991 (*Criminal Code (Amendment No 2) Act* 1991), s 2]

Section 420.

Code Section No	*Brief description of offence*
64	Unlawful assembly
138	Aiding prisoners to escape
140	Permitting escape

141	Harbouring escaped prisoners
143	Removing, etc, property under lawful seizure
170	Intercepting things sent by post or telegraph
171	Tampering with things sent by post or telegraph
172	Wilful misdelivery of things sent by post or telegraph
173	Obtaining letters by false pretences
174	Secreting letters
175	Fraudulent issue of money orders and postal notes
176	Fraudulent messages respecting money orders
177	Sending dangerous or obscene things by post
207	Offering violence to officiating ministers of religion
216	Defilement of girls under 16 and of idiots
217	Indecent treatment of girls under 16 if girl under 12
227	Indecent acts
228	Obscene publications and exhibitions
230	Common nuisances
231	Bawdy houses
232	Gaming houses
233	Betting houses
234	Lotteries
237	False information as to health of foreign ships
238	Exposing for sale things unfit for food
239	Dealing in diseased meat
240	Adulterating liquor
322	Wounding and similar acts
328(5)	Dangerous driving of a motor vehicle causing death
335	Common assault
337	Indecent assault on males
340	Assault occasioning bodily harm
341	Serious assaults
349	Indecent assaults on females
359	Threats

362	Desertion of children
372(1)	Punishment of stealing
	Punishment in special cases:
372(2)	Stealing wills
372(3)	Stealing things sent by post
372(4)	Stealing an aircraft
372(5)	Stealing from the person
372(5)	Stealing goods in transit
372(6)	Stealing by persons in the Public Service
372(7)	Stealing by clerks and servants
372(8)	Stealing by directors and officers of companies
372(9)	Stealing by agents, etc
372(10)	Stealing property of value of K1,000.00
372(11)	Stealing by tenants and lodgers
372(12)	Stealing after previous conviction
376	Killing with intent to steal skin or carcass of animal
377	Making anything movable with intent to steal
383	Unlawfully using motor vehicles
390A	Demands for compensation or other payment
395	House-breaking; burglary
396	Unlawful breaking and entering
397	Entering dwelling-house with intent to commit crime
398	Breaking into buildings and committing crime
399	Breaking into buildings with intent to commit crime
400	Breaking into place of worship and committing crime
401	Breaking into place of worship with intent to commit crime
404(1)	Obtaining or procuring anything by false pretence -Chattel, money or valuable security
404(3)	Obtaining or procuring anything by false pretence – Credit
406	Obtaining anything by fraudulent trick
409	Pretending to exercise witchcraft or tell fortunes
410	Receiving stolen property, etc, means by which obtained:
	if a crime

	in other cases
438	Setting fire to crops and growing plants
439	Attempting to set fire to crops, etc
443	Injuring animals
444(1)	Malicious injuries in general; punishment in special cases
451	Travelling with infected animals
467	Obliterating crossing on cheques
468	Making documents without authority
472	Falsifying warrants for money payable under public authority
473	Falsification of registers
474	Sending false certificate of marriage to Registrar
475	False statement for purposes of Registers of Births, Deaths and Marriages
476	Attempts to procure an unauthorized status

Chapter 4

CRIMINAL PROCEDURE

This chapter will deal with the principal criminal procedure legislation excluding those matters of trial procedure in the *Criminal Code* which are dealt with in the following chapter. The principal pieces of legislation annotated are the *Arrest Act*, *Search Act* and the *Bail Act*.

Any discussion of criminal procedure must depart from the provisions of s 37 of the *Constitution*, which contains a number of detailed requirements guaranteeing the rights of every person in Papua New Guinea to the full protection of the law. This section is annotated in the previous chapter but it bears repetition that the principle of innocence until proof of guilt is enshrined in s 37(4)(a) of the *Constitution*, which provides that:

"A person charged with an offence -

(a) shall be presumed innocent until proved guilty according to law, ..."

Search and entry - police investigation

In carrying out investigations and searches, the Royal Papua New Guinea Constabulary does not have any general power to enter premises to search for people or property. This is constitutionally recognised in the rights to privacy (s 49 of the *Constitution*) and to the right to freedom from arbitrary search and entry under s 44:

"No person shall be subject to the search of his person or property or to entry of his premises, except to the extent that the exercise of that right is regulated or restricted by a law -

that makes reasonable provision for a search or entry in certain circumstances, or

that complies with Section 38 *Constitution*."

Against this constitutional background, the *Search Act* 1977 was passed. Under the Act, a policeman may search a person where he has reasonable grounds for believing the person has stolen goods or anything for the commission of an indictable offence: s 3(1). Also, the police may search when a person is arrested or in lawful custody: s 3 (2) and (3). However, all searches must be carried out only with decency and reasonable force: s 4. In developing standards of decency and reasonable force in searches, the courts must start afresh as all duties and responsibilities imposed by the common law in relation to searches are abolished by the Act: s 20.

Generally, all searches must be with a warrant (*Search Act*, s 6 and *Constitution*, s 44(a)(i) and (ii)) which issues from a court if the court is satisfied that there are reasonable grounds for believing that any building, craft, vehicle or place concerns a committed, or about to be committed, offence. If anything is found in pursuance of the search warrant and is seized by the police, a record of the things seized must be kept: *Search Act*, s 12.

Failure to comply with the provisions of the *Search Act* may be remediable as breaches of the rights in ss 44 and 49 of the *Constitution*, with compensation actions under ss 57 and 58. There is, however, a specific civil action under s 17 of the *Search Act* 1977 against a person who wrongfully exercises the powers conferred by the Act. Such an action may be brought in the National or District Court (within its civil jurisdictional ceiling).

The great difficulty with the Act is that the vast majority of the people are unaware of their rights, constitutional or statutory, irrespective of the remedies for compensation.

Summons and arrest

Summons

The accused (the defendant in summary offences) may be brought before a court by means of either a summons or an arrest. A summons is the usual method for attendance for summary offences before the District Courts. This is done by drawing up an information for the offence: see ss 36 and 37 of the *District Courts Act*. The magistrate then issues a summons ordering the defendant to appear at the court on a particular day. Also, it should be noted that a private citizen may lay an information and commence a prosecution in the lower courts – charges need not necessarily be preferred by the police. Indictable offences, on the other hand, may not be the subject of private prosecutions, and must be dealt with according to the provisions of the *Criminal Code*.

Arrest

A magistrate may issue a warrant to the police for a suspect's arrest if there is any likelihood that the suspect will not obey the summons: *District Courts Act*, s 100. A warrant of arrest issues if the suspect disobeys the summons. The *Arrest Act* has consolidated much of the law in arrest, and abolished common law powers, duties and responsibilities of arrest (*Arrest Act*, s 31) except in relation to contempt of Parliament. Importantly, s 8 of the *Arrest Act* provides the circumstances where the court may issue a warrant of arrest where it is impractical or undesirable to proceed by summons.

In some circumstances, a suspect may be arrested without a warrant. The police may arrest without a warrant under s 3 of the *Arrest Act*, which essentially provides that no warrant is needed where a police officer believes on reasonable grounds that a person is about to commit, is committing or has committed an offence. A member of the general public may make an arrest, but only when he or she believes, on reasonable grounds, that an offence is being or has been committed: s 5.

When a police officer makes an arrest, with or without a warrant, and the person does not resist the arrest, the officer is required to inform the person of the following matters:

(a) that he or she is under arrest;

(b) the reason for the arrest; and

(c) ask him or her to go to the police station.

If the person resists, however, the police may use such force as is reasonable in the circumstances: s 14. Again, it is open to the courts to develop standards of reasonable force in the circumstances.

After the arrest with or without a warrant, the police officer must take the arrested person without delay to a police station: s 17.

At the police station

When a person is arrested, with or without a warrant, that person must be extended his or her rights under the *Constitution*. Specifically, s 42(2) of the *Constitution* requires that an arrested person must be:

(a) told the reason for the arrest and the nature of the offence with which he or she is charged in a language he or she understands;

(b) allowed to communicate with family whenever practicable;

(c) allowed reasonable time for the preparation of his or her defence; and

(d) given adequate opportunity for legal representation and time to give instructions to his or her lawyer.

Section 18 of the *Arrest Act* gives practical effect to these provisions by requiring the officer-in-charge at the police station, when an arrested person is brought in:

(a) to release the person if he or she did not commit the offence, should not be proceeded against or can be easily summonsed before the court;

(b) to detain the person, enter the name in the arrests register, and promptly inform the person of:

    (i) the reason for his or her arrest;

    (ii) details of the charges against him or her; and

    (iii) the person's right to communicate immediately and in private with a member of his or her family or a personal friend and given instructions to a lawyer of his or her choice (including the Public Solicitor if the person is entitled to legal aid); or

(c) if the person is detained, to grant or refuse bail, and if not, take the person before a court without delay (see also s 42(3) of the *Constitution* on the requirement of bringing a person arrested before a court without delay).

In the clearest possible terms therefore, police officers cannot, under the *Constitution* and the *Arrest Act*, detain a person arrested without granting bail or taking the person before a court. However, the difficulty again is communicating this right to the vast majority of the population.

A breach of these constitutional provisions is remediable by a compensation action under ss 57 and 58 of the *Constitution*. Although there are common law tort actions for false arrest, false imprisonment and assault, there is a civil remedy provided for any wrongful exercise of powers under s 26 of the *Arrest Act*. This may prove procedurally more straightforward to those that are fortunate to know their rights and how to enforce them.

At the police station, the police may question an arrested person. The police may also question a suspect who has willingly agreed to accompany an officer to the police station. Such an interview will be reduced to notes of a record of interview. However, the necessity or desirability of interrogating the person is not a good ground for not taking the person without delay before a court: *Constitution*, s 42(4). A person arrested or a suspect has no obligation to answer police questions. Unfortunately, the police and arrested persons are still not familiar with their rights. Moreover, the police are often content to use records of interview rather than pursue full investigation. Confessional evidence is all too frequently relied upon.

Before any questioning commences, the police officer conducting the interview ought to caution the suspect (with words such as "you are not obliged to say anything but anything you do say may be put in writing and may be used in evidence against you"). Secondly, the police must not use improper methods of force, threats or inducements to extract statements or confessions. There is a requirement of voluntariness of statements or confessions. If confessions, statements or records of interview are not voluntarily given, they are inadmissible in evidence at the trial under s 28 of the *Evidence Act*. The question of admissibility is tested by proceedings upon a voire dire.

Bail

There is a right to bail under s 42(6) of the *Constitution*. The *Bail Act* was passed in 1977 to give detailed effect to this right. Under bail, a person is released from custody to attend court on a particular day and on an agreement subject to certain other conditions. In the case of serious offences, a usual condition of bail is the payment into court of money by the accused or a surety: s 19. Non-attendance results in forfeiture of the money. For less serious summary offences, bail is usually granted automatically.

In the case of wilful murder or murder, only the National or Supreme Courts may grant bail: s 4. In all other cases, any court may grant bail. The police are also empowered to grant bail (s 5) when it is not practicable to take the person before a court within a reasonable time. Bail applications can be made at any time after arrest and at any stage in proceedings: s 6. Bail is generally to be granted except where:

(a) the person in custody is unlikely to appear at his or her trial;

(b) the offence was committed while the person was on bail;

(c) the offence in respect of which the person is in custody consists of a serious assault, a threat of violence to another person, or possessing a firearm, imitation firearm, other offensive weapon or explosive;

(d) the person is likely to commit an indictable offence;

(e) it is necessary for the person's own protection to be in custody;

(f) the person is likely to interfere with witnesses or the person who instituted the proceedings; or

(g) the alleged offence involves the property of substantial value which has not been recovered and the person, if released, would make efforts to conceal or otherwise deal with the property: s 9(1).

If the bail is refused, written reasons are to be given to the person or his or her lawyer (s 16), and this does not prevent further applications being made for bail to another magistrate or judge as the case may be: s 13. As can be seen from the annotations, there have already been several judicial pronouncements on this Act.

SEARCH ACT

Chapter No 341

Being an Act-

(a) to regulate or restrict certain rights or freedoms referred to in Subdivision 111.3.C of the *Constitution*, namely-

(i) the freedom from arbitrary search and entry conferred by Section 44 of the *Constitution*; and

(ii) the right to privacy conferred by Section 49 of the *Constitution*, so as to-

(iii) provide for searches of individuals, premises and property in certain cases; and

(iv) confer on persons making searches certain powers and duties; and

(b) to abolish certain rules of common law, and for related purposes.

Part I - Preliminary

1. Interpretation.

(1) In this Act, unless the contrary intention appears -

"court" means any court, other than a Village Court, and includes a Judge or Magistrate of any court, other than a Village Court;

"craft" means-

(a) an aircraft or part of an aircraft; or

(b) a vessel or part of a vessel;

"information" includes a complaint for an offence;

"place of confinement" means a corrective institution, rural lock-up or police lock-up;

"policeman" means a member of the Police Force;

"vehicle" means any description of vehicle on wheels or runners;

"warrant" means a warrant issued under any law for the search of any place including premises, a vehicle, aircraft, vessel, luggage or freight.

(2) For the purposes of this Act, a person believes something on reasonable grounds if-

(a) he personally has that belief; and

(b) there are reasonable grounds for that belief.

2. Application.

(1) Subject to subsection (2), this Act applies, notwithstanding the provisions of any other law, to and in relation to any search whether by or under this Act or any other law.

(2) This Act does not apply to a search carried out under a warrant issued under the *National Intelligence Organization Act*.

[S 2 subst Act No 25, 1984 (*Search (Amendment) Act* 1984), s 2]

See s 44 of the *Constitution*, which guarantees freedom from arbitrary search and seizure, and s 49 which guarantees the right to privacy.

Part II – Searches of the Person

3. Circumstances where persons may be searched.

(1) Where a policeman believes on reasonable grounds that a person has in his possession

(a) anything that has been stolen or otherwise unlawfully obtained; or

(b) anything used or intended to be used in the commission of an indictable offence, he may stop and search that person in accordance with Section 4 and, where applicable, exercise the power of seizure under Section 10(1).

(2) Subject to Section 4, where a policeman believes on reasonable grounds that it is necessary to do so, he may, at the time of arresting a person, search his person, the clothing he is wearing and any property under his immediate control-

(a) for the purpose of ascertaining whether he is concealing a firearm or other offensive weapon; or

(b) for the purpose of preventing the loss or destruction of evidence relating to the offence for which he was arrested, and, where applicable, may exercise the power of seizure under Section 10(2).

(3) Where a person in lawful custody is to be detained in a place of confinement he may, immediately before he is so detained, be searched at that place of confinement by a policeman or a member of the Correctional Service, as the case requires in accordance with Section 4, who may, where applicable, exercise the power of seizure under Section 10(3).

(4) The owner of a craft or a person in command of a craft or a person authorised by either of them or a policeman may in accordance with Section 4, search a person intending to board the craft and, where applicable, may exercise the power of seizure under Section 10(3).

(5) Where a person in command of a craft suspects that a person on board the craft constitutes a danger to the safety of the craft he may, or persons authorised by him may, search that person in accordance with Section 4 and, where applicable, may exercise the power of seizure under Section 10(4).

Doherty AJ said in *The State v Benny Buen Iga* [1990] PNGLR 146 at 149-150:

> "The powers provided in s 3(4) are very wide and give an owner or a policeman or a person in command of a craft a wide and unfettered power of search. There is no suggestion in s 3(4) that the power must follow a reasonable

suspicion or grounds or be with authority in the form of a warrant from a court. There is no explanation in the preamble to the *Search Act* why these wide powers should be given in relation to a craft in contrast to any other form of search. Section 3(5) also empowers a person in command of a craft to search a person on board the craft but only if there is a suspicion that that person constitutes a danger to safety. This is in contrast to s 3(4), as I have said there is no requirement for any suspicion or grounds. It may be that Parliament had in mind the authorisation of searches commonly carried out prior to boarding of aircrafts at airports which, if not legally authorised, would be unconstitutional. However, there is no indication in the *Search Act* to this effect and the provisions of s 3(4) must be given their clear meaning. The provision applies to a person 'intending to board the craft'. Since the power is so wide I consider that it must be strictly interpreted in accordance with the clear meaning of the section and I find that the expression 'intending to board the craft' limits it to persons who are about to go on board a craft and does not extend to persons who are already aboard the craft or have not reached the stage of intending or showing an intention to go aboard.

Once aboard the craft the powers of search vested in the owner, captain or policeman by s 3(4) come to an end and the power to search a person on board the craft can only be exercised if s 3(5) applies."

4. Powers and duties relating to searches of persons.

(1) Subject to this section, a person conducting a search of a person may touch the body and clothing of the person being searched.

(2) Searches of the person shall be conducted with due regard to decency.

(3) A person conducting a search of another person shall not use any greater force than is reasonable in the circumstances.

(4) Subject to Subsection (5), a search of a female shall only be carried out by or in the presence of an adult female.

(5) Where a policeman has reasonable grounds to believe that a female he has arrested is carrying a firearm or other offensive weapon he may, with due regard to decency, seize the weapon.

(6) Subsection (5) does not justify the use of greater force than is reasonable in the circumstances.

Part III – Searches of Premises, Aircraft, etc

Division 1 – Searches without Warrant

5. Circumstances where search may be made.

(1) Where a policeman has reasonable grounds to believe that a vehicle or anything in a vehicle-

(a) has been stolen or otherwise unlawfully obtained; or

(b) has been used or is intended to be used in the commission of an indictable offence, he may stop and search that vehicle and, where applicable, exercise the power of seizure under Section 10(1).

(2) Where a policeman believes on reasonable grounds that a person has in a vehicle that he is using at the time, a firearm or other offensive weapon, he may search the vehicle for the firearm or offensive weapon and, where applicable, exercise the power of seizure under Section 10(2).

(3) Where a policeman believes on reasonable grounds that it is necessary to do so, he may, at the time of arresting a person, search any vehicle the arrested person was using at the time of his arrest, for the purpose of preventing the loss or destruction of evidence relating to the offence for which he was arrested and, where applicable, may exercise the power of seizure under Section 10(2).

(4) Where the owner or the person in command of a craft or a policeman has reasonable grounds to suspect that a situation has arisen or is likely to arise involving the safety of the craft he may or persons authorised by him may search-

(a) the craft; and

(b) any luggage and freight on board or about to be placed on board the craft, and where applicable, may exercise the power of seizure under Section 10(4).

(5) Where a policeman is in immediate pursuit of a person whom he believes on reasonable grounds to have committed an indictable offence, he may, or persons authorised him may, search any building or place in which he believes on reasonable grounds that the person being pursued-

(a) is concealed; or

(b) has, in the course of his pursuit, concealed or deposited anything.

Amet J held in *The State v Popo* [1987] PNGLR 286:

"For the purposes of s 5(5) of the *Search Act*, the words 'immediate pursuit' are to be taken as meaning immediate, physical pursuit, analogous to the notion of 'hot pursuit', where there is no opportunity or time to take any other course of action otherwise the opportunity for apprehension, seizure of property, prevention of concealment of property or prevention of escape will be lost. If investigation, follow-up or pursuit of a suspect, however notorious, is not 'immediate' then a search warrant is required under s 6(1). Where a search is carried out without first obtaining a search warrant where such a search is not in 'immediate pursuit', the search is unlawful and any evidence obtained thereby is unlawfully obtained and may be rejected."

Division 2 – Search Warrants

6. Issue of warrants.

(1) If a court, other than a Local Court, is satisfied by information on oath that there are reasonable grounds for suspecting that there is in any building, craft, vehicle or place-

(a) any thing with respect to which any offence has been or is believed on reasonable grounds to have been committed; or

(b) any thing as to which there are reasonable grounds for believing it is likely to afford evidence of the commission of any such offence; or

(c) any thing as to which there are reasonable grounds for believing is intended to be used to commit any such offence,

it may issue a warrant to search that building, craft, vehicle or place.

(2) If a court other than a Local Court is satisfied by information on oath by a commissioned officer of the Police Force that there are reasonable grounds for suspecting that there is in any building or buildings in a village or in any part of a village or village garden any thing specified in Subsection (1)(a), (b) or (c), it may issue a warrant to search the building, buildings, village, part of the village or village garden.

(3) Where a warrant has been issued under Subsection (2) the person, policeman or policemen to whom the warrant is directed shall, where it is practicable to do so, before executing the warrant, endeavour to obtain the co-operation of those persons who, by custom, are regarded as the leaders of the village in respect of which the warrant has been issued.

(4) Subsection (1) or (2) does not justify the use of greater force than is reasonable in the circumstances.

Local Courts have been abolished by the *Local Courts (Amendment) Act* 2000.

Woods J said in *Acting Public Prosecutor v Richard Saronduo* [1988-1989] PNGLR 17 at 19:

> "Section 6 ... appears to allow for two separate situations for the issue of search warrants. Subsection (1) generally provides for the issuing of a warrant to search any building, craft, vehicle or place and the only requirement is that the court be satisfied by information on oath that there are reasonable grounds. There is no restriction in subs (1) that the information be laid by a commissioned officer. Subsection (2) is clearly laying down very careful requirements where a search warrant is sought for a village or a building in a village, and the reference in subs (3) to the police officer having to endeavour to obtain the co-operation of the village leaders in the subs (2) situation only emphasises that subs (1) and subs (2) are to be looked at as dealing with two different situations and thus the requirement for a commissioned officer in the subs (2) situation is separate from the subs (1) situation. The Parliament clearly wanted searches in a village situation to be carefully dealt with by senior police officers: see *The State v James Bero Popo* [1987] PNGLR 286."

7. Direction of warrant.

A warrant may be directed to all or any of the following:-

(a) to a named person; or

(b) to the officer for the time being in charge of police in a particular province or place; or

(c) to all members of the Police Force.

8. Form of warrant.

A warrant shall-

(a) describe the place to be searched; and

(b) state briefly the offence or matter of the information on which it is founded; and

(c) order the person to whom it is directed to search the place and seize any thing he may find in that place which relates-

(i) to the offence or the matter of the information on which the warrant is founded; or

(ii) to any other offence.

Division 3 – Powers in Aid of Manner of Search

9. Powers and duties relating to searches of premises, containers, etc.

(1) A person conducting a search under Section 5 and 6 in any place (other than in a baggage or freight container) and his assistants (if any) -

(a) have power-

(i) to enter and be in that place for the duration of the search and for that purpose to use such force as is reasonably necessary; and

(ii) to the least extent necessary with the least amount of damage-to interfere with the structure of the place for the purpose of search; and

(iii) to touch any article in that place; and

(iv) to stop and search any person found in that place in accordance with Section 4; and

(b) shall, within a reasonable period after the conclusion of the search, restore the place or cause the place to be restored as nearly as possible to the same state of cleanliness and neatness that existed immediately before the commencement of the search.

(2) A person conducting a search under Section 5 and 6 in any baggage or freight container and his assistants (if any)-

(a) have power-

(i) to enter and be in the place where the baggage or freight container is situated and for that purpose to use such force as is reasonably necessary; and

(ii) to the least extent necessary and with the least amount of damage-to interfere with the structure of the place for the purpose of search; and

(iii) touch any article in the container; and

(b) shall, within a reasonable period after the conclusion of the search, restore the container and any article in the container as nearly as possible to the same state of cleanliness and neatness that existed immediately before the commencement of the search.

(3) Where a search of a container under Subsection (2) cannot otherwise be made, a person conducting a search referred to in that subsection and his assistants may destroy the container for the purpose of search.

(4) This section does not require the restoration of the structure of any place or container interfered with by virtue of the powers conferred by this section.

Division 4 – Property Located During Search

10. Certain property may be seized.

(1) Where, during the course of a search that is authorised by this Act, a policeman finds any thing that he believes on reasonable grounds-

(a) has been stolen or otherwise unlawfully obtained; or

(b) has been used or is intended to be used in the commission of any indictable offence; or

(c) will provide evidence of an offence, he may seize that thing.

(2) For the purposes of Sections 3(2), 5(2) and 5(3), where the person searching finds a firearm or offensive weapon he may seize it.

(3) For the purposes of Sections 3(3) and 3(4), where the person searching finds any thing which in his opinion may be dangerous or inexpedient to leave in the possession of the person searched he may seize that thing.

(4) For the purposes of Sections 3(5) and 5(4), where the person searching finds any thing that in his opinion-

(a) constitutes a danger or is capable of constituting a danger to the safety of the craft; or

(b) is capable of being used to threaten a person on the craft, he may seize that thing.

11. Things seized may he handed to police, etc.

(1) Where a person seizes any thing under this Act and in his opinion that thing may be evidence relating to an offence he may hand that thing to a policeman.

(2) Where the person in command of a craft is of the opinion that property seized under this Act, on board the craft during the journey may be evidence relating to an offence committed during that journey on the craft he may on behalf of the owner of the craft give possession of that property to the person he believes on reasonable grounds is a representative of the authority responsible for law enforcement in the country where the offence will be tried.

12. Police to maintain record of things seized, etc.

Where any thing is seized by a policeman under this Act or is handed to a policeman, he shall enter in a permanent register of property-

(a) a full description of the thing including where appropriate, a note of any identification marks; and

(b) the time and date the thing was seized or received by him and in the case of things received by him the name and address of the person who handed the thing to him; and

(c) the place and the person from whom the thing was seized; and

(d) other details as are prescribed.

13. Possession of certain property.

(1) Where any thing is seized under this Act by a policeman or is handed to a policeman, the thing shall be deemed to be in the possession of the State.

(2) Where any thing is seized under Section 10(4) by a person, other than a policeman, the thing shall be deemed to be in the possession of the owner of the craft.

(3) Where any thing is seized under this Act, other than under Section 10(4), by a person other than a policeman

(a) in the course of his employment – the thing shall be deemed to be in the possession of his employer; or

(b) in any other case – the thing shall be deemed to be in the possession of that person.

(4) Anything referred to in Subsection (1), (2) or (3) may be retained in possession in accordance with that subsection for the purpose of examination and investigation and in the event that a person is charged with an offence in relation to that thing or in relation to which that thing is evidence the thing may, subject to any order to the contrary of a court, be retained in that possession until the charge and any subsequent proceedings on that charge have been determined.

14. Disposal of things seized under court order.

(1) In this section -

"forgery equipment" means -

(a) any forged bank note, or any special paper, revenue paper, frame, mould, instrument, plate, wood, stone, material or other thing, of which the possession without lawful excuse is an offence; or

(b) any counterfeit coin, or any instrument, machine, tool, or other thing used or intended to be used for the purpose of coining, of which the possession with knowledge of its nature and without lawful excuse is an offence;

"seized property" means any thing, other than forgery equipment, that is seized by virtue of a power conferred by this Act.

(2) A court may order, on an application made to it by any person, that forgery equipment seized by virtue of a power conferred by this Act, be forfeited, defaced or destroyed.

(3) Subject to Subsection (4), where any proceedings for an offence relating to seized property or in which seized property is used as evidence have been determined a court may order -

(a) that the seized property be delivered to the person appearing to the court to be entitled to it; or

(b) that the seized property be otherwise disposed of in such manner as the court thinks fit.

(4) Where a person is convicted on an offence relating to seized property and an order has been made under Subsection (3), the operation of that order is suspended until the determination of any appeal.

(5) On the hearing of any appeal the court may annul or vary an order made under Subsection (3).

15. Disposal of things seized in certain cases.

(1) Where a policeman seizes any thing in a Corrective Institution under Section 10(3) he may hand that thing to a correctional officer at the institution.

(2) Where a person seizes any thing on board a craft under Section 10(4), he may throw away, destroy or otherwise deal with that thing so that the craft and persons on board the craft are no longer endangered.

Part IV – Miscellaneous

16. Powers of search conferred by other laws.

The provisions of this Act that specify the circumstances in which a person may be searched are in addition to and not in derogation of a provision of any other Act or subordinate enactment that confers a power of search.

17. Civil remedy for wrongful exercise of powers conferred by this Act.

(1) A person who-

(a) exercises a power to make a search in breach of this Act; or

(b) exercises a power conferred by this Act, other than a power of search, in breach of this Act; or

(c) performs a duty imposed by this Act in breach of this Act; or

(d) fails or refuses to perform a duty imposed by this Act, may be liable in damages to the person aggrieved by that breach.

(2) An action under Subsection (1) may be brought-

(a) in the National Court; or

(b) in a District Court,

and in the case of a District Court the court has jurisdiction within the limits prescribed by Section 21 of the *District Courts Act*.

(3) In an action under Subsection (1) a court may award exemplary damages.

(4) The provisions of this section are in addition to and not in derogation of the provisions of the *Constitution* or any other law dealing with the enforcement of any constitutional right, power, duty, restriction or prohibition.

18. Certain acts deemed to be within course of employment.

For the purposes of any civil proceeding, where the making of a search would otherwise be within the scope of a person's employment, the mere non-compliance by an employee with a provision of this Act does not, of itself, take any act of the employee, committed during the course of the search, outside the scope of his employment.

19. Abolition of certain common law powers and duties.

(1) All powers at common law to issue search warrants are abolished.

(2) All duties and responsibilities imposed by the common law in relation to searches and search warrants are abolished.

20. Regulations.

The Head of State, acting on advice, may make regulations not inconsistent with this Act, prescribing all matters that by this Act are required or permitted to be prescribed or that are necessary or convenient to be prescribed for carrying out or giving effect to this Act.

ARREST ACT

Chapter No 339

Being an Act-

(a) to specify the circumstances in which persons may be arrested; and

(b) to confer certain powers and duties on persons making arrests; and

(c) to abolish certain rules of common law,

and for related purposes.

Part 1 – Preliminary

1. Interpretation.

(1) In this Act, unless the contrary intention appears -

"authorized person" means a person empowered to make an arrest under this Act or any other law or by a warrant;

"the commencement date" means 3 November 1977, being the date on which the *Arrest Act* 1977 came into force;

"court" means any court, other than a Village Court, and includes a judge or magistrate of any court, other than a Village Court;

"craft" means an aircraft or vessel;

"information" includes a complaint for an offence;

"officer-in-charge" in relation to a police station at a particular time, means the policeman who is in charge of the police station at that time;

"place of confinement" means a corrective institution, rural lock-up or police lock-up;

"policeman" means a member of the Police Force;

"warrant" means a warrant issued under this Act or any other law for the arrest of a person.

(2) A reference in this Act to an offence for which a penalty is imprisonment does not include an offence in respect of which a sentence of imprisonment may only be imposed in default of payment of a fine.

(3) For the purposes of this Act a person believes something on reasonable grounds if-

(a) he personally has that belief; and

(b) there are reasonable grounds for that belief.

2. Application.

Notwithstanding any other law but subject to Section 24, this Act applies to and in relation to an arrest for any offence whether made by or under this Act or by or under any other law.

See generally ss 37, 42 and 76 of the *Constitution*.

See also Pt V, Div 1 of the *Criminal Code*, especially ss 245-262. The arrest sections of the earlier versions of the Code were, in large part, repealed by the *Criminal Code (Arrest) Act* 1977 (No 13 of 1977) in anticipation of the *Arrest Act*.

Part II – Circumstances Justifying Arrest Without Warrant

3. Arrest without warrant by a policeman.

A policeman may, without warrant, arrest a person whom he believes on reasonable grounds -

(a) is about to commit; or

(b) is committing; or

(c) has committed,

an offence for which a penalty is imprisonment.

4. Arrest by policeman for breach of bail condition.

(1) A policeman may, without warrant, arrest a person whom he has reasonable grounds to believe and does in fact believe -

(a) has breached a condition of his bail; or

(b) is about to breach a condition of his bail.

(2) A person arrested under Subsection (1) shall not be released on bail by a policeman but shall be brought before a court as soon as reasonably possible after his arrest.

5. Arrest without warrant by member of the public.

Subject to any requirements imposed by the law creating the offence, a person, other than a policeman, may, without warrant, arrest a person whom he believes on reasonable grounds -

(a) is committing; or

(b) has committed,

an offence for which the penalty is imprisonment.

A citizen's power to arrest and detain another person under this Act is qualified by five important conditions. They are:

1. The person arrested must be found committing or must have committed a criminal offence for which the prescribed penalty is imprisonment: *Arrest Act*, s 5.
2. The force used, if any, to make the arrest or to prevent the escape of the arrested person must be reasonable in the circumstances: *Arrest Act*, s 14(2).
3. The means or method used to detain a person arrested must be appropriate or reasonable in the circumstances: *Arrest Act*, ss 14(2) and 16(2). What is reasonable depends on the given facts of each case. Relevant factors include the seriousness of the offence, resistance to arrest and the imminent risk of escape.
4. Detention must only be for the purpose of enabling the person arrested to be conveyed to a police officer, a police station, a court or a proper place of confinement.
5. The person must not be detained for any period longer than is practically and reasonably necessary for the purposes set out in item 4 above.

The detention of a woman, suspected of stealing "hubba-bubba bubble gum", in a brick wall store room for eight hours was unlawful: *Ronald Alexander McKenzie v The State* (1998) SC 596.

See *Ronald Alexander McKenzie v The State* (1998) SC 596 for a discussion of a citizen's power of arrest and search and their duties upon arrest.

6. Arrest without warrant for offence on board craft.

Notwithstanding Sections 3 and 5-

(a) where a person is committing, is about to commit or has committed; or

(b) where the person in command of a craft suspects on reasonable grounds that a person is committing, is about to commit or has committed,

an offence relating to or affecting the use of the craft, the person in command or person authorised by him may arrest that person without warrant.

7. Arrest by person executing warrant of commitment.

Where a person the subject of a warrant of commitment is not in custody at the time the warrant is to be executed, the person authorised to execute the warrant may arrest that person without a warrant.

Part III – Arrest Warrants

8. Issue of warrant by a court other than a Local Court.

Where an information is laid before a court, other than a Local Court, that there are reasonable grounds for believing

(a) that a person has committed an offence within the country; and

(b) that it would not be practicable or desirable to proceed against the person by summons in that his arrest is necessary -

(i) to ensure his appearance in court to answer a charge for the offence; or

(ii) to prevent -

(A) the continuation or repetition of the offence; or

(B) the omission of a further offence; or

(iii) to preserve the safety or welfare of a member of the public or of the person,

the court may issue a warrant for the arrest of the person.

Local Courts have been abolished by the *Local Courts (Amendment) Act* 2000.

The old *Police Offences Acts* provided powers of arrest without summons where the arrest was necessary as proceedings against the person by summons would not be effective. The word "effective" meant effective to ensure the attendance of the alleged offender at court, but could not be limited to that meaning such that it would render the power of arrest without warrant ineffectual: *Gaigo Kakore v Sing* [1975] PNGLR 104.

The accused does not have to be present for a right of audience by his or her counsel on an application for a bench warrant, and an indictment may be presented against an accused in his or her absence: *R v Byrne* [1971-1972] PNGLR 1 (Kelly J).

9. Issue of warrant by a Local Court.

Where a complaint for an offence has been issued in a Local Court the Court, if it considers it necessary, may issue a warrant for the arrest of the defendant.

Local Courts have been abolished by the *Local Courts (Amendment) Act* 2000.

10. Issue of warrant for breach of bail condition.

(1) Where proceedings have been commenced before a court, other than a Local Court, and the court is satisfied that there are reasonable grounds for believing that a person is in breach of a condition of his bail granted in connection with those proceedings, the court may issue a warrant for the arrest of that person.

(2) A person arrested under a warrant issued under Subsection (1) shall not be granted bail by a policeman but shall be brought before a court without delay.

Local Courts have been abolished by the *Local Courts (Amendment) Act* 2000.

Bredmeyer J said in *The State v Gawi* [1988-1989] PNGLR 118 at 119-120:

"It is true in one sense that criminal proceedings formally commence in the National Court with the presentation of an indictment ... In another, broader sense, however, criminal proceedings ... commence when the defendant is arrested or when information is laid against him in the District Court. For the purpose of considering bail, I think that is the preferred interpretation. The proceedings start in the District Court on the laying of the information, the case then proceeds on a continuum, as it were, through the District Court and the National Court. I see the proceedings as one criminal proceeding processed by two courts rather than two proceedings in to separate courts. The committal is the preliminary stage and the National Court trial the final stage ...

I would interpret s 10 ... in the context of a man committed for trial in the National Court on a charge of, say, robbery and granted bail by the District Court, as follows:

> 'Where proceedings have been commenced before a [District] Court ... and the [National] Court is satisfied that there are reasonable grounds for believing that a person is in breach of a condition of his bail granted in connexion with those proceedings, the [National] Court may issue warrant for the arrest of that person.'"

Woods and Hinchliffe JJ stated in *The State v Gawi* [1988-1989] PNGLR 118 at 94-95:

"The words, 'Where proceedings have been commenced before a court,' in s 10 of the *Arrest Act* to our minds mean, in this case, where proceedings have been commenced in the National Court. The accused men were committed for trial to the National Court from the District Court. When do the proceedings actually commence in the National Court? ... We are of the view that the trial commences on the presentment of the indictment but that is altogether different from when the actual proceedings commence in the National Court ... We would agree that the proceedings do commence generally on the laying of an information or even at the arrest stage ... but s 10 ... is referring to when those proceedings actually commence in the National Court.

We are satisfied that the proceedings commence in the National Court on the day that the accused is due to answer his bail as ordered by the District Court. Up until then, he is still within the jurisdiction of the District Court ... the District Court still has jurisdiction up until the day nominated for the accused's first National Court appearance.

So it seems to us that after commencement of proceedings in the National Court and also any time after the indictment has been presented, an arrest warrant may issue pursuant to s 10 ... But after presentment of the indictment, if the accused fails to appear for his trial then an arrest warrant may issue pursuant to O 3 r 10(b) of the *Criminal Practice Rules*."

11. Direction of warrant.

A warrant may be directed to all or any of the following-

(a) to a named person; or

(b) to the officer for the time being in charge of police in a particular province or place; or

(c) to all members of the Police Force.

12. Form of warrant.

A warrant shall-

(a) name or otherwise describe the person against whom it is issued; and

(b) state briefly the offence or nature of the information on which it is founded; and

(c) in the case of a warrant to arrest a defendant – order the person to whom it is directed to arrest the defendant and to bring him before a court to answer to the information and to be further dealt with according to law.

13. Execution of warrants.

Where a warrant is directed to a person he may, in accordance with Part IV, and with assistants if necessary, arrest the person against whom the warrant is issued.

Part IV – Manner of Arrest, etc

14. Manner of effecting arrest.

(1) Where an authorised person intends to make an arrest and the person to be arrested -

(a) does not resist the arrest and the authorised person is aware that they speak a common language, the authorised person shall at the time of arrest -

(i) advise the person he is under arrest; and

(ii) advise the person arrested of the reason for his arrest; and

(iii) request the person arrested to accompany him to a police station, to a court or place of confinement, as the case may be; or

(b) does not resist the arrest and the authorised person is aware or ascertains -

(i) that they do not speak a common language; or

(ii) that he is unable to speak to the person arrested because the person arrested suffers from some mental or physical defect, the authorised person shall indicate by reasonable means to the person arrested that -

(iii) he is under arrest, and

(iv) he is to accompany the authorized person; or

(c) resists the arrest, whether by force or by refusing to move, or seeks to evade arrest, whether by running away or by other means, the authorized person may, subject to Subsection (2), use all reasonable means to make the arrest.

(2) Subsection (1)(c) does not justify the use of greater force than is reasonable in the circumstances.

The process of "arrest" under the *Arrest Act* ordinarily involves some deprivation of liberty of the person arrested, that is, it involves some form of physical or non-physical detention: *Ronald Alexander McKenzie v The State* (1998) SC 596. In *The State v Songke Mai and Gai Avi* [1988] PNGLR 56 at 69, Kapi DCJ stated that:

> "arrest is the initial step of depriving a person of his liberty. To put the matter differently, 'arrest' and 'detention' are two distinct procedures under the law and deprivation of liberty, which is common to both, commences upon 'arrest' and

'detention'. The moment a person is 'arrested', he is 'detained' from that point on. 'Arrest' is very closely followed in point of time by 'detention'. That is the law relating to 'arrest' and 'detention' in relation to persons who are suspected of committing a crime".

In a situation of "near-riot" it was held not practicable for police officers to have informed the accused of the grounds of arrest and, in any case, the evidence showed that the appellant knew the general nature of the alleged offence for which he was detained: *Gaigo Kakore v Alan John Sing; Gaigo Kakore v John Paul Nani* (1974) N820.

15. Warrant to be carried or produced.

Where a warrant issued under Section 8, 9 or 10 is directed to a person -

(a) in accordance with Section 11(a) or (b) – he shall, when executing the warrant, carry it with him and produce it on request; or

(b) by virtue of Section 11(c) only – he shall, on request of the arrested person, produce it is soon as practicable.

Part V – Duties to be Performed After Arrest

16. Duties of private citizen after effecting an arrest.

(1) Where a person, not being a policeman, makes an arrest, he shall-

(a) as soon as practicable but subject to Subsection (2), hand the arrested person over to a policeman or take the arrested person or cause him to be taken to a police station; and

(b) subject to Subsection (2), use all reasonable means to prevent the arrested person escaping.

(2) Subsection (1) does not justify the use of greater force than is reasonable in the circumstances.

17. Duties of a policeman after arrest.

(1) Where a policeman makes an arrest he shall -

(a) take the arrested person without delay to a police station to be dealt with under Section 18 or before a court; and

(b) subject to Subsection (2), use all reasonable means to prevent the arrested person from escaping.

(2) Subsection (1)(b) does not justify the use of greater force than is reasonable in the circumstances.

18. Duties of officer-in-charge of station.

(1) Where a person has been arrested and taken to a police station, the officer-in-charge of the police station shall -

(a) immediately release the person if he considers that-

(i) the person arrested did not commit the offence for which he was arrested or any other offence and there is no other reason to justify his detention under this Act or any other law; or

(ii) there are good reasons why the arrested person should not be proceeded against for an offence; or

(iii) proceedings can be effectively taken by way of summons against the arrested person; and

(b) if he does not release the person under Paragraph (a) – take the person into custody and enter in a permanent register of arrests the name of the person and if it appears that the person arrested-

(i) has committed an offence - the nature of that offence; or

(ii) has been arrested for some other reason - that reason; and

(c) promptly inform the person arrested or cause him to be informed in a language he understands of -

(i) the reason for his arrest; and

(ii) details of the charges against him; and

(iii) his right, immediately and in private-

(A) to communicate with a member of his family or a personal friend; and

(B) to give instructions to a lawyer of his choice including the Public Solicitor if he is entitled to legal aid; and

(d) as soon as practicable consider and accordingly grant or refuse bail in accordance with the *Bail Act*; and

(e) if bail is not granted under Paragraph (d) or if for any other reason the person arrested remains in custody at the station – take the person, or cause him to be taken, before a court without delay; and

(f) if bail is granted to the person by a court but for any reason the person remains in custody at the station after bail is granted – take the person or cause him to be taken before a court as soon as practicable after the expiration of 14 days after the bail is granted; and

(g) if bail is granted to the person but he remains in custody after being brought before a court on one or more occasions – take the person or cause him to be taken from time to time before a court as soon as practicable after the expiration of 14 days after the time he last appeared before a court.

(2) The officer-in-charge of a police station shall at all times permit persons arrested or detained at the police station -

(a) whenever practicable, without delay and in private to communicate with -

(i) a member of his family or a personal friend; and

(ii) a lawyer of his choice, including the Public Solicitor if he is entitled to legal aid; and

(b) to give instructions to a lawyer of his choice, including the Public Solicitor if he is entitled to legal aid.

19. Procedure in the case of a warrant of commitment.

(1) Notwithstanding Sections 16, 17 and 18 but subject to Subsection (2), where a warrant of commitment has been issued in respect of a person who is not in custody at the time and he is later arrested by the person or one of the persons to whom the warrant is directed, the person effecting the arrest shall convey the person arrested to a place of confinement in accordance with the warrant.

(2) Where a person making an arrest referred to Subsection (1) believes on reasonable grounds that the person arrested has committed an offence for which he has not been tried, the person making the arrest shall deal with the person arrested in accordance with Section 16 or 17, as the case may be.

20. Duties of officer where warrant of commitment issued.

(1) Notwithstanding Section 17 but subject to Subsection (2), where a person has been arrested and taken to a police station and a warrant of commitment has been issued in respect of that person, the officer-in-charge of the police station shall take or cause the person to be taken to a place of confinement in accordance with the warrant.

(2) Where the officer-in-charge believes that the person arrested committed an offence for which he has not been tried, the officer shall deal with the arrested person in accordance with Section 18.

Part VI – Powers of Police After Arrest

21. Finger-prints, etc.

(1) Where a person is in lawful custody on a charge of committing an offence, a commissioned officer of the police force or the officer-in-charge of a police station may -

(a) take or cause to be taken such particulars as he deems necessary for identification of that person, including his photograph, finger-prints and palm-prints; and

(b) subject to Subsection (2) - use or cause to be used such force as is reasonably necessary to secure those particulars.

(2) Subsection (1) does not justify the use of greater force than is reasonable in the circumstances.

(3) Where a person referred to in Subsection (1) is not convicted of the charge in respect of which he is in custody, or an appeal against his conviction is upheld-

(a) all records of particulars for identification of that person and all copies of those records taken under that subsection shall be destroyed within a period of one month after the proceeding is concluded; and

(b) if he so requests before they have been destroyed – he is entitled to be present, at his own expense, at a police station nominated by him to witness the destruction of those records and copies.

(4) A policeman may apply to a court within the period referred to in Subsection (3) for an order that the records of a person taken under Subsection (1)

not be destroyed.

(5) If the court is satisfied that the records referred to in Subsection (4), are required in respect of charges that have already been laid against the person it may order that the records not be destroyed until that charge has been dealt with.

22. Medical examination.

(1) Subject to Subsection (6) where-

(a) a person is in custody in respect of an offence; and

(b) a commissioned officer of the Police Force or the officer-in-charge of a police station believes on reasonable grounds that the nature and circumstances of the alleged offence in respect of which the person is in custody are such that a medical examination of the person in custody would provide evidence relating to the offence; and

(c) the person in custody has given his written consent or a court has ordered that the examination take place,

a medical practitioner, if requested by the commissioned officer or the officer-in-charge, as the case may be, may conduct a medical examination.

(2) An application for an order under Subsection (1) to a court by a commissioned officer of the Police Force or the officer-in-charge of the police station at which the person is being held may be made-

(a) in person; or

(b) where an application in person is not practicable - by telephone.

(3) If the court is satisfied on application being made to it under Subsection (2) that the commissioned officer of the Police Force or the officer-in-charge of the police station has reasonable grounds for his belief that a medical examination of the person in custody will provide evidence relating to the offence for which the person is in custody, it may order -

(a) in writing that the medical examination take place; or

(b) where the application has been made under Subsection (2)(b) and the circumstances of the case justifies its doing so orally, that the medical examination take place, but it shall confirm the order in writing within three days after the making of the order.

(4) Where the application for a medical examination is made under Subsection (2), the court granting the application shall cause its order to be forwarded to the applicant.

(5) A medical practitioner conducting a medical examination for which a court order has been issued under Subsection (3) may -

(a) use such force as is necessary to carry out the medical examination; and

(b) use assistants to help him with the examination.

(6) Subsection (5) does not justify the use of greater force than is reasonable in the circumstances.

It was said in *Migi Barton v The State* (1981) SC 213(M):

"In this case, it is regrettable that no blood or other test was taken of the deceased and the appellant (convicted of dangerous driving causing death under s 328 of the *Criminal Code*) after the accident, to determine the blood-alcohol levels. More use should be made of this section of the *Arrest Act* in appropriate cases."

Part VII – Miscellaneous

23. Powers of arrest conferred by other laws.

The provisions of this Act which specify the circumstances in which a person may be arrested are in addition to and not in derogation of a provision of any other Act or subordinate enactment which confers a power of arrest.

24. Powers, practice and procedure relating to contempt of the Parliament, etc.

(1) This Act does not affect any power, practice or procedure of the Parliament or of a court of record that, immediately before the commencement date, applied to and in relation to a person in contempt of the Parliament or contempt of court, as the case may be.

(2) An officer of the Parliament or of a court of record and any person assisting such an officer shall not be deemed to be acting unlawfully if he makes an arrest and deals with the person arrested in accordance with the practice and procedure for the time being of the Parliament or the court, as the case may be.

25. Protection from criminal liability where wrong person arrested.

Notwithstanding any other law, where -

(a) a warrant is issued for the arrest of a person; and

(b) the person to whom the warrant is directed makes an arrest in accordance with Part IV believing in good faith and on reasonable grounds that the person he arrests is the person against whom the warrant was issued; and

(c) the person arrested is not the person against whom the warrant was issued,

the person making the arrest, or any person assisting him, does not commit an offence.

26. Civil remedy for wrongful exercise of powers conferred by this Act.

(1) A person who -

(a) exercises a power to make an arrest to which this Act applies in breach of this Act; or

(b) exercises a power conferred by this Act, other than a power of arrest, in breach of this Act; or

(c) performs a duty imposed by this Act in breach of this Act; or

(d) fails or refuses to perform a duty imposed by this Act,

may be liable in damages to the person aggrieved by that breach.

(2) An action under Subsection (1) may be brought -

(a) in the National Court; or

(b) in a District Court,

and in the case of a District Court, the court has jurisdiction within the limits prescribed by Section 21 of the *District Courts Act*.

(3) In an action under Subsection (1) a court may award exemplary damages.

(4) The provisions of this section are in addition to and not in derogation of the provisions of the *Constitution* or any other law dealing with the enforcement of any constitutional right, power, duty, restriction or prohibition.

27. Certain acts deemed to within course of employment.

For the purpose of any civil proceeding, where the making of an arrest would otherwise be within the scope of a person's employment, the mere non-compliance by an employee with a provision of this Act does not, of itself, take any act of the employee, committed during the course of the arrest outside the scope of his employment.

28. Onus of proof in relation to certain civil proceedings.

(1) Where in any civil proceeding it appears -

(a) that one party to the proceeding had another party to that proceeding in his custody after the arrest of the other party; and

(b) that the first-mentioned party was not a policeman at the time of that custody,

the first-mentioned party bears the onus of proving -

(c) that he handed over the other party to a policeman as soon as was practicable; or

(d) that he took the other party or caused him to be taken to a police station as soon as was practicable; or

(e) that he dealt with the other party under Section 19.

(2) Where in any civil proceeding it appears -

(a) that one party to the proceeding had another party to the proceeding in his custody after the arrest of the other party; and

(b) that the first-mentioned party was a policeman at the time of that custody,

the first-mentioned party bears the onus of proving -

(c) that he took the other party without delay to a police station or before a court; or

(d) that he dealt with the other party under Section 19.

(3) Where in any civil proceeding it appears that at a particular time one party to the proceeding was the officer-in-charge of a police station and another party to that proceeding was in custody at the police station at the time, the first-mentioned party bears the onus of proving that he took the other party or caused the other party to be taken before a court without delay after being brought to that police station.

29. Indemnity of policemen.

(1) Notwithstanding any other law, a policeman against whom proceedings are brought under Section 26(1) shall –

(a) not join the State as a defendant in those proceedings; and

(b) subject to Subsection (2), be fully indemnified by the State in respect of those proceedings where -

(i) he had, at the time a bona fide belief that he was carrying out his duties under this Act; and

(ii) he was not acting maliciously or with wilful disregard to his professional duties and responsibilities; and

(iii) he was not grossly negligent in the performance of his duties.

(2) The court before whom proceedings are brought under Section 26(1) against a policeman may –

(a) in the case specified in Subsection (1) enter judgement for the plaintiff against the defendant and, at the same time, order that the whole amount awarded as judgement for the plaintiff be paid by the State to the defendant policeman as contribution; or

(b) in any case where the policeman was

(i) acting maliciously or with wilful disregard to his professional duties and responsibilities; or

(ii) grossly negligent in the performance of his duties,

enter judgement for the plaintiff against the defendant and, at the same time determine the amount of contribution to be paid by the State to the defendant policeman.

(3) An order under Subsection (2)(a) and a determination under Subsection (2)(b) shall be deemed for all purposes to be a judgement of the court in favour of the policeman against the State and is enforceable and appellable accordingly.

30. Abolition of certain common law powers and duties.

Subject to Section 24 -

(a) all powers at common law to arrest a person are abolished; and

(b) all duties and responsibilities imposed by the common law in relation to an arrest are abolished.

31. Regulations.

The Head of State, acting on advice, may make regulations not inconsistent with this Act, prescribing all matters that by this Act are required or permitted to be prescribed or that are necessary or convenient to be prescribed for carrying out or giving effect to this Act.

BAIL ACT

Chapter No 340

Being an Act -

(a) to provide for bail to be granted more readily; and

(b) to abolish certain rules of common law,

and for other related purposes.

Part 1 – Preliminary

See ss 42(6) and (7), 76 and 155(4) of the *Constitution*. Section 155(4) vests inherent power in the National Court to grant bail pending an appeal from a District Court where the circumstances are such that justice would not otherwise be done: *Paul Jerol Aisi v Malkom Bai* (1976) N52.

Section 565 of the *Criminal Code* (now s 533), repealed by s 32 of the *Criminal Code (Arrest) Act* 1977, was the original bail provision, now replaced by the *Bail Act*.

See also generally "*Bail: An Examination*" (1971) 45 ALJ 193.

See Griffin, *Criminal Procedure in Papua New Guinea* (1977), Ch 9.

1. Interpretation.

(1) In this Act, unless the contrary intention appears -

"bail" means approval, whether or not subject to conditions, for the release of a person from custody;

"bail authority" means a person or court empowered or required under this Act or any other law to grant bail;

"bail certificate" means a certificate issued under Section 15;

"bail obligations", in relation to a person granted bail, means the obligations imposed on the person under Section 17;

"court" means any court, other than a Village Court, and includes a Judge or Magistrate of any court, other than of a Village Court;

"guarantor" means a person who undertakes to see that a person granted bail complies with his bail obligations;

"officer-in-charge", in relation to a police station at a particular time, means the policeman who is in charge of the police station at that time;

"place of confinement" means a corrective institution, rural lock-up or police lock-up;

"policeman" means a member of the Police Force.

(2) For the purposes of this Act -

(a) The Supreme Court shall be deemed to have jurisdiction higher than the jurisdiction of any other court; and

(b) a Judge of the National Court shall be deemed to have jurisdiction equal to the jurisdiction of every other Judge of the National Court; and

(c) the National Court and a Judge of the National Court shall be deemed to have jurisdiction higher than the jurisdiction of a court or Magistrate referred to in Paragraphs (d), (e) and (f); and

(d) a District Court and a Magistrate of a District Court shall be deemed to have jurisdiction equal to the jurisdiction of every other District Court and Magistrate of a District Court; and

(e) a District Court and a Magistrate of a District Court shall be deemed to have jurisdiction higher than the jurisdiction of a Local Court or a Magistrate of a Local Court; and

(f) a Local Court and a Magistrate of a Local Court shall be deemed to have jurisdiction equal to the jurisdiction of every other Local Court and Magistrate of a Local Court.

(3) For the purposes of this Act a person believes something on reasonable grounds if-

(a) he personally has that belief; and

(b) there are reasonable grounds for that belief.

Local Courts have been abolished by the *Local Courts (Amendment) Act* 2000.

2. Application.

Notwithstanding any other law, this Act applies to and in relation to a person arrested or detained for an offence.

Part II – Grant of Bail Before Acquittal or Conviction

Division 1 – General

3. Object of Part II.

The object of this Part is to give effect to Section 42(6) (liberty of the person) of the *Constitution* which provides that a person arrested or detained for an offence (other than treason or wilful murder as defined by an Act of the Parliament) is entitled to bail at all times from arrest or detention and to acquittal or conviction unless the interests of justice otherwise require.

Kidu CJ and Andrew J stated, in *Re Bail Application pursuant to s 13(2) Bail Act 1977; Fred Keating v The State* [1983] PNGLR 133:

> "Whilst the *Bail Act* is a complete code dealing with the grant or refusal of bail, the bail authority must still consider the interests of justice as required by this section and the *Constitution*. This may involve considerations other than the criteria for refusing bail as established in s 9 of this Act."

See also annotations under s 9 of the *Bail Act*.

4. Bail only by National or Supreme Court in certain cases.

A person charged with wilful murder, murder or an offence punishable by death shall not be granted bail except by the National Court or the Supreme Court.

Division 2 – Circumstances when Bail to be Considered

5. Bail to be granted by police in certain cases.

Subject to Section 4, where-

(a) a person has been arrested for an offence and is held in custody at a police station or in the custody of a policeman; and

(b) in the opinion of -

(i) the officer-in-charge of that police station; or

(ii) a commissioned officer of the Police Force,

it is not practicable to bring the person before a court within a reasonable time,

the officer, at the time he forms that opinion, shall consider and accordingly grant or refuse bail to that person in accordance with Section 9.

6. Application for bail may be made at any time.

(1) An application for bail may be made to a court at any time after a person has been arrested or detained or at any stage of a proceeding.

(2) A court shall consider an application for bail at the time it is made unless it is satisfied that no steps that were reasonable in the circumstances have been taken to advise the informant that the application would be made.

(3) Subject to Section 4, the court shall grant or refuse bail in accordance with Section 9.

Doherty AJ said in *The State v Mene Mamaino* [1990] PNGLR 185 at 186:

> "[Section 6(1)] provides that an application for bail may be made to a court at any stage of a proceeding. This section follows on directly from s 42(6) of the *Constitution* which categorically states that a person arrested or detained for an offence (other that treason or wilful murder) is entitled to bail at all times to conviction or acquittal unless the interests of justice otherwise required. Hence the entitlement to apply for bail is a statutory one and is vested in a defendant at all times until his court case is finalised by way of acquittal or conviction.
>
> The obligation on a court to consider an application for bail is a mandatory one stated in s 6(2) ... imposing on a court an obligation to consider an application for bail at the time it is made."

An applicant refused bail previously by a judge of the National Court may re-apply afresh if changes in relevant circumstances have occurred since bail was last refused: *Re Thomas Markus* (1999) N1931.

In *Re Thomas Markus*, Injia J stated:

"In considering whether there has been a change in circumstances, the change or changes in circumstances must be relevant. In determining what changes are relevant circumstances, it is necessary to re-visit the judge's earlier reasons for refusing bail with reference to s 9(1) of the *Bail Act*. Any circumstances which did not form part of the reasons pertaining to the grounds upon which bail was refused under the criteria in s 9(1) is not a relevant circumstance for which the Court should re-consider its earlier decision to refuse bail. Indeed it would amount to abuse of process of the Court for a person refused bail by a judge of the National Court to re-apply for bail to the same judge or different judge of the National Court simply for the purpose of taking another bite at the same application before another judge, without providing evidence of any change in relevant circumstances or with evidence of change in irrelevant circumstances."

7. Bail on adjournment.

Subject to Section 4, where a person is in custody in connexion with any proceedings, including proceedings for committal for trial or sentence in the National Court, the court shall, on each occasion that it adjourns the proceedings before conviction, consider and accordingly grant or refuse bail to that person in accordance with section 9.

8. Bail after committal for trial or sentence.

Subject to Section 4, where a court commits a person who is in custody for trial or sentence in the National Court, the court shall consider and accordingly grant or refuse bail to that person in accordance with Section 9.

Division 3 – Considerations Affecting Decision on Bail Matters

9. Bail not to he refused except on certain grounds.

(1) Where a bail authority is considering the question of granting or refusing bail under this Part, it shall not refuse bail unless satisfied on reasonable grounds as to one or more of the following considerations:-

(a) that the person in custody is unlikely to appear at his trial if granted bail; or

(b) that the offence with which the person has been charged was committed whilst the person was on bail; or

(c) that the alleged act or any of the alleged acts constituting the offence in respect of which the person is in custody consists or consist of-

(i) a serious assault; or

(ii) a threat of violence to another person; or

(iii) having or possessing a firearm, imitation firearm, other offensive weapon or explosive; or

(d) that the person is likely to commit an indictable offence if he is not in custody; or

(e) it is necessary for the person's own protection for him to be in custody; or

(f) that the person is likely to interfere with witnesses or the person who instituted the proceedings; or

(g) that the alleged offence involves property of substantial value that has not been recovered and the person if released would make efforts to conceal or otherwise deal with the property.

(h) that there are, in process or pending, extradition proceedings made under the *Extradition Act* (chap 49) against the person in custody; and

(i) that the alleged offence involves the possession, importation or exportation of a narcotic drug other than for the personal, medical use under prescription only of the person in custody; or

(j) that the alleged offence is one of breach of parole.

[Subs 1(h) and (i) insrt Act No 11, 1982 (*Bail (Amendment) Act* 1982), s 1(a); Subs 1(j) insrt Act No 34, 1991 (*Bail (Consequential Amendment) Act* 1991)]

(2) In considering a matter under this section a court is not bound to apply the technical rules of evidence but may act on such information as is available to it.

(3) ...

(4) For the purposes of Subsection (1)(i), 'narcotic drug' has the meaning given to it in the *Customs Act* (chap 101).

[Subs (4) insrt Act No 11, 1982 (*Bail (Amendment) Act* 1982), s 1(b)].

There is no s 9(3) at present.

An applicant starts with a heavy presumption in his or her favour, as the *Constitution* and the *Bail Act* entitle an applicant to bail: *Re Application for Bail by Paul Lois Kysely* [1980] PNGLR 36.

Kearney DCJ said in *Re Herman Kagl Diawo* [1980] PNGLR 148:

"It is clear from the *Constitution*, s 42(6) that an applicant is entitled to bail during the course of his trial unless the interests of justice otherwise require. Some matters which are relevant to the interests of justice when considering bail during trial are set out in an English practice note ([1974] 2 All ER 794). Under the old law, while bail was very much in the discretion of the trial judge, in practice, bail during the course of trial was rarely granted. The State now carries the burden of justifying detention during trial. It is clear that the *Bail Act* is a complete code dealing with interim judicial release in this jurisdiction."

Kapi J expressed the following view in *Re Herman Kagl Diawo* [1980] PNGLR 148:

"The right to bail is a constitutional right (s 42(6)) and must be given readily unless the interests of justice require otherwise. The *Constitution* puts the onus on those who oppose bail to show why bail should not be granted. Section 9(1) sets out the considerations upon which the court may refuse bail."

Miles J stated in *Re Herman Kagl Diawo* [1980] PNGLR 148:

"It is clear that the constitutional right to bail set out in s 42(6) and repeated in s 3 of the *Bail Act* applies right up until the time of acquittal or conviction. There can be no question of it not applying in the case of a trial which is part heard. As bail is a matter of constitutional right, it is not surprising then that the *Bail Act* in this section provides a set of criteria not as to the granting of bail but as to its refusal."

In *Re Application for Bail pursuant to s 13(2) Bail Act 1977; Fred Keating v The State* [1983] PNGLR 133, Kidu CJ and Andrew J held:

"If one of the considerations in s 9 is present, it does not follow that bail must automatically be refused; there is always a discretion in the bail authority to grant bail."

See also *The State v Beko Job Paul* [1986] PNGLR 97.

Kidu CJ and Andrew J further stated in *Re Application for Bail pursuant to s 13(2) Bail Act 1977; Fred Keating v The State* [1983] PNGLR 133:

"In cases of wilful murder, only those considerations set out in s 9(1) apply, and no others, because the 'interests of justice' in s 3 of this Act and because s 42(6) of the *Constitution* does not apply to wilful murder and treason cases."

Kidu CJ and Andrew J also said in the same case:

"When considering the grant or refusal of bail in cases other than wilful murder or treason, the courts and other bail authorities are to be guided generally by s 9. But whilst the *Bail Act* is a complete code dealing with the grant or refusal of bail, by s 3, in matters other than wilful murder or treason, the bail authority may still have to consider the question of the interests of justice. This may involve considerations other than the criteria for refusing bail as established in this section."

In *Bernard Juale v The State* (1999) N1887 the applicant was charged with wilful murder of his wife. The applicant raised a number of grounds in relation to his application for bail, including humanitarian grounds, in that since the death of his wife the applicant had played both mother and father to his young children. Kirriwom J held that:

"In my view before I can venture into examining considerations not stipulated in section 9 (1) of the *Bail Act*, I have to first satisfy myself as to whether or not, any of the considerations in section 9(1) have been made out. If I do find that one or more grounds have been established, then I have to decide whether I should exercise my discretion to either grant or refuse bail. There is one school of thought that says that once I have found that one of the grounds in s 9 (1) has been established, I have no discretion to grant bail if the charge is that of wilful murder. I beg to differ with this view, even if this is the correct interpretation of the law in *Re Fred Keating*. If that is what the law is, in my respectful view, it needs to be corrected. I think there will be, as is always the case, exceptional circumstances such as those alluded to by Andrew J in his judgement in the same case that would warrant bail even in wilful murder cases. The question is always one of degree. Each case must be decided on its own peculiar circumstances. The *Constitution* under s 42(6) does not deny bail to a person charged with wilful murder. It avails bail to all persons at all times except those charged with wilful murder and treason. The fact that it excepts wilful murder and treason does not necessarily connote a negative proposition of law. It simply means that bail is not readily and automatically available but that the person charged must seek redress for bail through other avenues. That avenue is thus provided under ss 4 and 6 of the *Bail Act*. It is however unfortunate in my view that section 9 of the *Bail Act* is restricted only to those considerations exhaustively defined therein.

In the case before me notwithstanding the view I have expressed above, for reasons expressed hereinafter, I do not find the plea convincing for me to exercise my discretion in favour of the applicant."

See also *In the Matter of an Application for Bail Pursuant to s 6 of the Bail Act (Ch No 340); Paul Olape and The State* (1998) N1890.

In *The State v Beko Job Paul* [1986] PNGLR 97 it was held that, notwithstanding the consideration enumerated in s 9(1) of the *Bail Act*, the nature of an offence itself may have the effect of operating as a sufficient factor to refuse bail, unless the court is convinced that the continued detention is not justified: *Re Fred Keating* [1983] PNGLR 133 considered and applied. In the circumstances, the offence, involving as it did a clear intent to secure arms, negated any presumptive right under s 42(6) of the *Constitution* or under the *Bail Act*, and as the interests of justice would not be served by failing to give special significance to the nature of the offence, bail should be refused. Wilson J (at 99) was of the opinion that:

"the offence the nature of which involves the clear intent to secure arms negates that presumption and that the interests of justice are not served by failing to give special significance to this type of crime and the consequences that flow, or could flow from it. On the basis of this reasoning I refuse bail".

On application for bail pending trial or committal, the prosecution must discharge the onus under s 9(1)(a) by adducing evidence showing a tendency to abscond or a real possibility that the applicant will not appear. In this case, as the applicant had lived in Papua New Guinea for 10 years with his wife and children, had a house and had held the same job for six years, the onus was not discharged: *Re Application for Bail by Samir Taleb Abdullah Jaber Anabtawi* [1980] PNGLR 195.

Breach of a bail condition by failing to report to a police station does not necessarily show that an applicant will not appear for his or her trial (s 9(1)(a)) if the failure to report is in the nature of an oversight: *Re Application for Bail by Paul Louis Kysely* [1980] PNGLR 36.

The word "likely" in s 9(1)(f), following *Livingstone-Thomas v Assoc Newspapers Ltd* (1969) 90 WN (NSW) 223, means likely in the sense of a tendency or a real possibility, and does not mean "more likely than not", "probably" or "very likely": *Re Application for Bail by Paul Louis Kysely* [1980] PNGLR 36.

In *Re Application for Bail by Paul Louis Kysely* [1980] PNGLR 36, one attempted interference with a state witness having occurred, and having regard to the rest of the evidence, there was a real possibility of a contravention of this provision (s 9(1)(f)).

Re Application for Bail by Paul Louis Kysely [1980] PNGLR 36, was followed in *Re Application for Bail by Samir Taleb Abdullah Jaber Anabtawi* [1980] PNGLR 195.

Part III – Grant of Bail After Conviction

10. Bail after conviction and before, sentence.

Where a court convicts a person but adjourns the proceeding before passing sentence, it may, in its discretion, grant the person bail.

11. Bail after lodging appeal.

Where a person lodges an appeal against his conviction or sentence or both -

(a) the court which convicted him; or

(b) a court of equal jurisdiction; or

(c) a court of higher jurisdiction,

may, in its discretion, on application by or on behalf of the appellant, grant bail pending the hearing of the appeal.

Pratt J held, in *John Jaminan v The State* [1983] PNGLR 122:

> "For bail to be granted following conviction, there must be 'exceptional circumstances' shown, not merely 'special circumstances'. Relevant matters may include the likelihood of success of the appeal (where the outcome is a foregone conclusion and readily apparent), or where the preparation of the appeal may be assisted by the release of the appellant, or where there is a lengthy intervening vacation in the calendar of the appeal court. *R v Southgate* (1961) 78 WN (NSW) 44, followed. The fact that the appellant was a member of Parliament and that his electorate would not be represented if he were not granted bail, was not an exceptional circumstance."

In *Yaki v The State* [1990] PNGLR 513, the Supreme Court, on appeal, rejected the application by a member of Parliament for bail on the grounds of attention to political duties and accounting for government funds. These were not exceptional circumstances.

The courts are vested with a wide discretion under this section. It is to be remembered that under s 42(6) of the *Constitution*, and under the *Bail Act*, the right to bail of an ordinary person (ie, a person accused of any crime other than treason or wilful murder) is guaranteed to that person "at all times from arrest or detention to acquittal or conviction unless the interests of justice otherwise require". No such right is preserved to the person after conviction, rather suggesting that the legislature contemplated that bail would be refused at that stage unless circumstances could be shown to exist which justified the exercise of the judicial discretion. This section nowhere mentions "exceptional circumstances", and the judicial gloss has been put upon the section because of the view that "the guilt of the person accused has been established ... in what must be taken until the contrary be shown to be a trial properly conducted without effort by law": *Arthur Gilbert Smedley v The State* [1978] PNGLR 452.

Section 11 confers a wide discretion upon the court. However, applications after conviction are rare, as the authorities both in Papua New Guinea and Australia make it clear that they are viewed with very great care. The situation after conviction is different from that before conviction, when the presumption of innocence still prevails. Post-conviction the applicant must show there are "exceptional circumstances": *Rolf Schubert v The State* [1979] PNGLR 66.

After conviction, an applicant for bail must show "exceptional circumstances" exist before bail is allowed pending appeal. The fact that a vacation is imminent, which might cause the hearing of the appellant's appeal to be delayed for several months, is not in itself an "exceptional circumstance". Likewise, the fact that the grounds of appeal are prima facie arguable does not itself constitute an "exceptional circumstance": *Arthur Gilbert Smedley v The State* [1978] PNGLR 452 (*Re Ilett* [1974] PNGLR 49 not followed).

An accused person who appeals to the Supreme Court after conviction will be granted bail pending the appeal only in very exceptional circumstances: *Himson Mulas v The Queen* [1969-1970] PNGLR 82.

Where an application is made for bail pending an appeal against a short sentence, bail will generally not be granted if the appeal can be speedily heard: *Paul Jerol Aisi v Malkom Bai* (1976) N52.

Williams J said in *Pou v Kose* (1973) N746:

> "The court has the power to order that the period during which the appellant was released on bail shall be taken into account in calculating length of the sentence of imprisonment imposed upon him. This power is one to be exercised sparingly and upon it being shown that special circumstances exist."

See also *Logalio Piaro v Philip Kumbamung; Pup Tumbant v Philip Kumbamung* [1976] PNGLR 283, and *Secretary for Law v Gabriel Poleneu* [1973] PNGLR 85.

12. Bail during hearing of appeal.

Where a court hearing an appeal adjourns proceedings, it may, in its discretion, grant bail to the appellant on application by or on behalf of the appellant.

Part IV – Procedure on Grant or Refusal of Bail

13. Further application may be made after refusal.

(1) Where a person is refused bail by a Magistrate he is entitled to apply for bail, immediately if he so desires, to a judge of the National Court.

(2) Where a person is refused bail by a Judge of the National Court he is entitled to apply for bail, immediately if he so desires, to the Supreme Court.

(3) Where an application is made under Subsection (1) or (2), the applicant shall produce a copy of the reasons given under Section 16.

(4) An application may be made under Subsection (1) or (2) whether or not bail was refused –

(a) under this Act (including this section) or under any other law; or

(b) on an application.

Part V – Procedure on Grant or Refusal of Bail

14. Person granted bail need not be present.

Bail may be granted notwithstanding that the person to be granted bail is not in the presence of the bail authority.

15. Bail certificate.

(1) Subject to Subsection (3), at the time of granting bail to a person the bail authority shall issue to him a certificate -

(a) stating that he is entitled to bail; and

(b) specifying conditions (if any) of bail; and

(c) containing such other particulars as are prescribed.

(2) Unless required by his legal representative or other agent, a person granted bail shall retain in his possession at all times until his bail obligations are discharged, a copy of the bail certificate.

(3) Where a person is granted bail on his committal for trial or sentence in the National Court, the Clerk of the Court which commits him shall, as soon as possible, forward a copy of the bail certificate to -

(a) the Public Prosecutor; and

(b) the Public Solicitor.

(4) Where a person is granted bail but is committed to a place of confinement until condition is complied with, a copy of the bail certificate shall be attached to the warrant of commitment.

(5) Where a court issues a certificate under Subsection (1) in respect of a person and that person is not in the presence of the bail authority at the time, the Registrar or Clerk of the Court, as the case may be, shall, as soon as possible, forward the certificate to the person holding the person in custody who shall ensure that a copy of the certificate is handed to that person as soon as possible.

16. Reasons for refusing bail to be given and recorded.

(1) Where bail is refused the bail authority shall at that time give the reasons in writing for its decision to the person in custody or his legal representative.

(2) Where the bail authority refuses to grant bail, whether or not application has been made, the bail authority shall ensure that the reasons for its decision are recorded -

(a) if the bail authority is the officer-in-charge of a police station or a commissioned officer of the Police Force in the register of arrests at the police station where the person is held in custody; and

(b) if the bail authority is a court-in the court papers relating to the charge against the person.

Part VI – Obligations and Conditions Relating to Bail

17. Obligation of person granted bail.

A person granted bail -

(a) shall appear at the time and place specified by the bail authority and at every time and place to which, during the course of the proceeding the hearing may be from time to time adjourned; and

(b) shall comply with all conditions of bail fixed under section 18.

18. Bail may be granted subject to conditions.

(1) Subject to this section, a bail authority may grant bail to a person subject to conditions, including conditions to be complied with before release from custody, but in fixing conditions under this section the bail authority shall satisfy itself that the bail conditions -

(a) will not cause undue interference with the person's domestic life; and

(b) will not interfere with the person's legitimate means of earning a living or making himself available for work; and

(c) will not interfere with the person's rights to political freedom of action or movement except insofar as it is necessary to ensure that he appears at court when required; and

(d) will not cause the person financial hardship; and

(e) are not unreasonable in all the circumstances.

(2) Where a bail authority fixes a condition to be complied with before release from custody, it shall, in the bail certificate, stipulate the person or class of persons to verify compliance with that condition.

(3) Any person may, unless the contrary intention appears in the bail certificate, perform on behalf of the person granted bail, any condition to be complied with before release from custody.

19. Guarantors.

(1) A bail authority may require as a condition of bail that no more than two guarantors approved by it undertake to see that the person granted bail appears at the time and place set for his trial and complies with the condition (if any) of his bail.

(2) A bail authority shall not require any guarantor to give any undertaking under Subsection (1) unless it is of the opinion that the person granted bail will not appear at his trial or will not comply with the conditions (if any) of his bail unless a guarantor is approved.

(3) If the bail authority is a court it may authorise a commissioned officer of the Police Force or an officer-in-charge of a police station to approve a guarantor.

(4) A bail authority or an officer authorized under Subsection (3) may not refuse to approve a person as a guarantor unless it or he is satisfied on reasonable grounds that the proposed guarantor will not honour the undertaking required of him under Subsection (1).

(5) A bail authority may require a guarantor –

(a) to lodge an amount of money in support of his undertaking; or

(b) to undertake to pay the State an amount of money if the person granted bail fails to appear at the time and place set for his trial or comply with the conditions of his bail.

(6) In fixing the amounts of money referred to in Subsection (5) the bail authority shall take into account the financial means of the guarantor.

(7) If the person granted bail fails to appear at the time and place set for his trial or fails to comply with the conditions (if any) of his bail the court dealing with his matter may order -

(a) that the sum of money or part of it lodged by the guarantor be paid to the State; or

(b) that the guarantor pay to the State the amount or part of the amount he undertook to pay under Subsection (5).

(8) A guarantor who is affected by an order under Subsection (7) may, within 14 days after the making of the order, apply to the court making the order for variation or revocation of the order.

(9) The court after hearing an application under Subsection (8) may make any order it considers just in the circumstances.

Part VII – Variation, Revocation, Etc, of Bail

20. Variation of bail.

(1) Subject to Subsection (2), a person granted bail in relation to a proceeding or the other party to the proceeding may apply to a court at any time, after reasonable notice to the other party, for a variation of the terms and conditions of bail.

(2) An application under Subsection (1) shall be made to a court which has jurisdiction not lower than the jurisdiction of the court which granted bail.

21. Revocation of bail.

(1) Where it is alleged that there are reasonable grounds for revoking bail granted to a person and the person appears or is brought before a court, the court shall consider whether the bail should be revoked.

(2) If, after hearing all the evidence including that of the person granted bail and his witnesses (if any), the court is satisfied that the circumstances so require, it may -

(a) revoke the bail, discharge the person from his bail obligations and commit the person to a place of confinement; or

(b) subject to Subsection (3), vary the conditions of the bail.

(3) Where there is a guarantor for the person granted bail, a court shall not impose conditions of bail more onerous on the guarantor than the existing conditions of bail without first obtaining the consent of the guarantor.

22. Forfeiture of security.

(1) Where a person granted bail contravenes or fails to comply with his bail obligations, a court may make an order forfeiting the whole or part of the security given by him to secure his bail obligations.

(2) Subject to Subsection (3), where an order is made under Subsection (1), the order -

(a) in the case of money undertaken to be paid in the event of a breach or contravention of the bail obligation - shall be deemed to be a judgement of the court that the person pay to the State a sum not exceeding the sum undertaken to be paid and;

(b) in the case of a deposit - may authorize payment of the whole or part of the deposit into the Consolidated Revenue Fund.

(3) A person who is affected by an order under Subsection (1) may, within 14 days after the making of the order, apply to the court making the order for variation or revocation of the order.

(4) The court after hearing an application under Subsection (3) may make any order it considers just in the circumstances.

In *Mili Rumints v William Wulat* (1982) N369(M), the court found that a forfeiture of bail ordered under this section was unjust, as the magistrate led the defendant to believe that an adjournment would be granted.

Under s 22(1), bail may be forfeited even though the defendant is not present. If it is later learnt that the forfeiture was unfair, say because the accused was ill in hospital when he or she was due to answer bail, the accused may apply for revocation of the forfeiture under s 22(3) within 14 days, or to the Supreme Court for a review of the decision under s 155(2)(b) of the *Constitution* at any time: *The State v Junior Steven Gawi & Toliman Juki Viru* [1988-1989] PNGLR 118.

In *Special Constitutional Reference No 12 of 1984 and Supreme Court Reference No 12A of 1984* [1985] PNGLR 224 it was held that an order varying or revoking an order forfeiting bail cannot be made on an application made outside the 14 day time limit prescribed by s 22(3) of the *Bail Act*.

Part VIII – Miscellaneous

23. Permission to leave the country in certain cases.

(1) Where for urgent personal reasons or by reason of his occupation a person granted bail in relation to a proceeding wishes to leave the country for a temporary period before the commencement or conclusion of that proceeding, he may, after reasonable notice to the other party, apply to the National Court or Supreme Court for permission to do so.

(2) Permission shall not be granted under Subsection (1) unless the court is satisfied that the person will return to Papua New Guinea for the proceeding.

(3) A permission granted under this section may be subject to conditions.

(4) A person may apply for permission under this section at the same time that he applies for bail.

(5) Where permission is granted under this section, a note to that effect shall be endorsed on the copy of the bail certificate held by the person granted bail.

Permission under this section is in the discretionary power vested in the court (disapproving *Ex parte Smedley* [1978] PNGLR 156). Opposition from the Public Prosecutor is relevant but not conclusive, for the court decides upon being satisfied that the applicant will return to the country for the hearing: *Re Stephen Mark McMillan* [1980] PNGLR 1. For consideration of factors involved in the granting of permission to leave the country for urgent medical treatment, see *Francis Sia v The State* (1987) N631.

24. Grant of bail under other laws.

The provisions of this Act which specify the circumstances in which a person may be granted bail are in addition to and not in derogation of any other Act or subordinate enactment that provides for the granting of bail.

25. Civil remedy for wrongful refusal to grant bail.

(1) A policeman who -

(a) wrongfully refuses to grant bail to a person under Section 5; or

(b) imposes conditions on bail to a person under Section 18 contrary to the requirements of that section; or

(c) wrongfully refuses to approve a guarantor for a person under Section 19,

may be liable in damages to that person.

(2) An action under Subsection (1) may be brought -

(a) in the National Court; or

(b) in a District Court,

and in the case of a District Court the court has jurisdiction within the limits prescribed by Section 21 of the *District Courts Act.*

(3) In an action under Subsection (1), a court may award exemplary damages.

(4) The provisions of this section are in addition to and not in derogation of the provisions of the *Constitution* or any other law dealing with the enforcement of any constitutional right, power, duty, restriction or prohibition.

26. Abolition of certain common law powers and duties.

All powers, functions, duties and responsibilities conferred or imposed by the common law in relation to bail are abolished.

27. Regulations.

The Head of State, acting on advice, may make regulations not inconsistent with this Act, prescribing all matters that by this Act are required or permitted to be prescribed or that are necessary or convenient to be prescribed for carrying out or giving effect to this Act.

28. Offences.

A person who -

(a) is alleged to have committed an offence the penalty for which is or includes imprisonment for a period exceeding 12 months; and

(b) has been granted bail; and

(c) contravenes or fails to comply with his bail obligations,

is guilty of an offence.

Penalty: A term of imprisonment not exceeding 12 months.

[S 28 insrt Act No 11, 1982 (*Bail (Amendment) Act* 1982), s 2]

Chapter 5

OTHER CRIMINAL MATTERS

Adultery and Enticement Act 1988

Background

The *Native Regulations* in Papua were first made under the *Native Board Ordinance* 1889 (No 9 of 1889) and later under the *Native Regulation Ordinance* 1908 (No 25 of 1909). In New Guinea the regulations were called *Native Administration Regulations*, and were made under the *Native Administration Ordinance* 1921 (No 21 of 1921). See Chalmers, *Full Circle: A History of the Courts of Papua New Guinea* (LLM thesis, UPNG, 1978); and Wolfers, *Race Relations and Colonial Rule in Papua New Guinea* (1975).

These two sets of regulations were substantially repealed by the National Executive Council in March 1976, with the specific exception of the adultery provisions. The administrative and criminal regulation of adultery was explained by JHP Murray, the Lieutenant-Governor of Papua, in his monograph *Papua or British New Guinea* (1912):

> "Adultery and sorcery are the most common among the offences which are cognisable in the courts of the native magistrates. Both are forbidden by regulation and are punishable with six months imprisonment, but adultery is an offence only if the woman is married. A married man, therefore, may commit adultery with impunity so long as his paramours are unmarried; but if a man, whether married or not, misconducts himself with a married woman both man and woman are equally liable; a woman who is married to a man by native custom is looked upon as his wife for the purpose of the regulation. The reason for these somewhat elaborate provisions is that in the old days before the white man came, adultery was punished by death – that is to say, the injured husband would generally kill both his wife and her lover, and would have been considered as acting entirely within his rights in doing so. When the Government was established this mode of procedure by club and spear was much too sudden to gain approval, but at the same time it did not seem right to leave the happy home of the Papuan entirely at the mercy of any village Don Juan who happened to pass by, and a regulation was therefore made punishing adultery with imprisonment; the reason why it is punished only when a married woman is concerned is that the gravamen of the offence lies in the fact that, according to native ideas, it is really theft, for the wife is the property of the husband, and the adulterer has stolen her from him".[145]

[145] Murray, *Papua or British New Guinea* (1912), pp 201-202.

Notwithstanding the dated language, Murray's identification of "the gravamen of the offence" accorded with local feelings and was consistent with comments by Narokobi AJ in *Tabo Sipo v Mukara Meli* (1980) N240:

"Adultery, in most, if not all Melanesian societies, strikes at the root of the society ... The law of adultery is intended to protect the institution of marriage by preserving rights and privileges of sexual intimacy to the spouses, to the exclusion of others. When others encroach upon those rights, tensions emerge which may lead to eventual family break-up. The result of this can, in many instances, be quite serious. The Law Reform Commission recognised that in Papua New Guinea marriage is 'not only a matter of two willing parties entering into an exclusive life-long partnership, but also a coming together to or a cementing of the woman's group with the man's group. Because of this dual aspect of marriage, adultery can and does cause social discord and sometimes violence in our societies'."

In 1973, the Justice Department engaged the anthropologist Professor Marilyn Strathern to investigate the attitudes of Papua New Guineans towards the sexual offences, with the aim of reforming the law to be "in line with Papua New Guineans' conceptions of what is unacceptable behaviour". Professor Strathern reported, in *Report on Questionnaire Relating to Sexual Offences as defined in the Criminal Code* (1975), that the essence of adultery in Papua New Guinea was "the trespass on the sexual rights established by marriage":

"[The] offence generally has much wider social repercussions than it does in Western societies ... The act of adultery necessitates settlement not because the sexual act in these circumstances is itself offensive, but because of the social disruption it either leads to or signifies. It may be seen as disrupting the conjugal bond, as disrupting otherwise peaceable relations between neighbours or kinsmen, or as contributing to hostilities between enemies; because men's rights over women are invariably at issue, adultery may have the character of a challenge and insult to a man's standing, as well as involving direct sexual jealousy (p 56) ... Indeed of all the sexual offences considered here, adultery seems most likely to lead to violent reactions".[146]

In February 1977 the Law Reform Commission released its Report No 5, *Report on Adultery*. The commissioners noted the depth of feeling among the general public, finding that in most minds adultery was the third-ranked offence in terms of seriousness, behind only wilful murder and theft of property. Consequently, the commission's "recommendations seek to harmonise the rigours of some of our traditional cultural values and the changing moral attitudes at least among some people, regarding adultery": p 3. In the end, the commission recommended that the surviving *Native Regulations*, which were described as "discriminatory", "part of the colonial era", and "contrary to our country's independence and to the spirit of its *Constitution*" (p 2), be repealed and replaced by an Adultery and Enticement Bill 1977. See McRae, "*The Law Reform Commission's Report on Adultery*" (1977) (No 1) MLJ 115 and the comments on the regulations in *Rebeka Ambi v Mary Rabi* (1980) N279, *Asi Burunge v John Kaupa* (1983) SC 258, *Tabo Sipo v Mukara Meli* (1980) N240, and *Susan Moru v Tikeling Sakin* (1981) N362 (M).

The Law Reform Commission's recommendations were acted upon by the Parliament a decade later with the passage of the *Adultery and Enticement Act* 1988.

[146] Strathern, *Report on Questionnaire Relating to Sexual Offences as defined in the Criminal Code* (1975), p 58.

It should be noted that a special affirmative defence to adultery exists under s 15 of the *Sorcery Act*, where the accused person established on the balance of probabilities that he was induced by sorcery to have the illicit sexual intercourse in question and that this would amount to an excuse under customary law.

There are a number of cases under the previous *Native Regulations* that have some historical relevance in respect of the background to some of the terms used in this Act. See *Constitutional Reference No 1 of 1977 in the matter of Schedule 2.3 of the Constitution of the Independent State of Papua New Guinea and in the matter of Poisi Tatut complainant and Chris Cassimus defendant* [1978] PNGLR 295; *Idau Gabe v Meriam Griffin* [1977] PNGLR 492;and *Tabo Sipo v Muraka Meli* (1980) N240 (on knowledge of marriage as a constituent of adultery).

ADULTERY AND ENTICEMENT ACT 1988

No 5 of 1988

Being an Act to regulate certain aspects of disputes relating to adultery and enticement, as a matter of national interest.

Part I - Introduction

1. Interpretation.

In this Act, unless the contrary intention appears -

"compensation" means -

(a) in relation to an action arising out of an act of adultery - compensation for the act of adultery; and

(b) in relation to an action arising out of enticement - compensation for the enticement;

"Court" means a Local Court or District Court;

"spouse" includes a party to a relationship between a man and a woman which can reasonably be considered as a subsisting relationship having the status of a marriage.

In *Copland Oa and Esther Korua v Nelson Korua* (1999) N1871 Injia J considered the meaning of the term "spouse" in a customary marriage. His Honour held that:

"In a case where the complainant relies on the existence of a subsisting marriage of one form or another, and the defendant denies the existence of any such marriage relationship, the Court must be clear about the precise kind of 'marriage' relationship in issue in the proceedings. There are three kinds of 'marriage' relationships covered under the definition of 'spouse' in s 1 – a registered marriage under Part V of the *Marriage Act* (Ch No 286), a customary marriage recognised by Part II of the *Marriage Act* and, if I may use the term 'status marriage' for want of better term, described in s 1 under the definition of 'spouse.' The onus is on the complainant to prove the existence of any of these three types of 'marriages' as required by s 2 and it is for the defendant to prove the absence of any of these types of relationships as prescribed by s 9(1)(c). The proof of the existence or otherwise of a registered marriage and customary marriage should not pose any great difficulty whereas proof of a 'status marriage' does."

In *Re Wagi Non and Section 42(5) of the Constitution* [1991] PNGLR 84 the defendant had been taken to a village court on a complaint from relatives of her husband that she had committed adultery. She claimed that she had been unlawfully or unreasonably detained pursuant to s 42(5) of the *Constitution*. Woods J commented on one unusual feature of the matter, in that it was not the husband who made the complaint to the village court but the husband's relatives, and there is no suggestion that he gave permission for this or even knew of it. His Honour said that:

> "[t]he new *Adultery and Enticement Act* 1988 was an attempt by the Parliament to remove the criminal element in the old adultery legislation and the new legislation puts strong emphasis on mediation in adultery situations realising that adultery situations may have arisen out of other family problems. However, it is quite clear that the village court has paid no heed to such considerations in its dealing with this matter ... The village courts must recognise the nature of the changes in Papua New Guinea and that the enforcement of custom must not conflict with the principles and rights given in the Constitution."

In *John Gawi and Diana Apes v Mary Gawi* (1997) N1584 there had been previous proceedings between the same parties for this adulterous relationship, and these proceedings had resulted in a mediation on 23rd February 1996 and orders for the payment of compensation by the same two defendants to the plaintiff. Woods J held that:

> "all the acts of adultery committed after 23rd February are to be seen as including the acts of adultery before 23rd February and to be read as the one act of adultery. There has been action taken under Section 4 of the Act for these acts of adultery namely the mediation which resulted in the Order of 23rd February. Therefore there can be no repetition of this action."

In *Anton Webim Buka v John Lenny* [1978] PNGLR 510, the court considered the meaning of "nearest relative" under the *Native Regulations* where a complaint was brought by a nearest relative in the absence of the aggrieved party.

See also, on the meaning of "nearest relative", *Labian-Saiuwen v Yerei-Yautan* [1965-1966] PNGLR 152.

7. Time limitation for bringing action.

(1) An action under this Act shall be brought not later than six months after the day when the act of adultery or the enticement, complained of, was committed.

(2) Where by virtue of Section 4(2) acts of adultery are regarded as one act of adultery, the period of six months referred to in Subsection (1) shall commence to run on the day next following the day when the last of those acts of adultery was committed.

(3) Where in the opinion of the Court, a person has reasonable cause for not bringing an action within the period specified under Subsection (1), the Court may permit the person to bring the action after the expiry of that period but in any event not later than three months after the expiry of that period.

8. Joining of actions.

(1) Where in respect of an act of adultery, two actions are brought by the same person, one against the spouse and the other against the person with whom the spouse committed the act of adultery, the Court may, at its discretion, hear the two actions together.

(2) Where -

(a) enticement is committed; and

(b) the enticed spouse commits an act of adultery with the person who committed the enticement; and

separate actions are brought in respect of the enticement and the act of adultery by the same person,

the Court may hear the actions together.

(3) Where, in respect of an act of adultery, an action is brought against only one of the parties to the act of adultery, the party against whom the action has been brought may request the court to order that the other party to the act of adultery be joined as defendant to the action and the Court may, whether or not that other party is available or cannot be located, order accordingly.

9. Defences.

(1) A defendant to an action under this Act, may, without prejudice to any other defences which he may raise, raise any or all of the following defences:-

(a) that the person entitled to bring the action has, prior to the commission of the act of adultery or enticement, consented to the act of adultery or enticement, as the case may be; or

(b) that the person entitled to bring the action has, after learning of the act of adultery or enticement, forgiven the defendant; or

(c) that the defendant believed on reasonable grounds that the spouse with whom the act of adultery or enticement was committed, was not married.

(2) Where, on evidence, a defence is established under Subsection (1), the Court shall dismiss the action.

On the application of the defence in s 9(1)(c), see *Betty Hosea and Michael Maya v Eau Maya* [1988-1989] PNGLR 382 and *Copland Oa and Esther Korua v Nelson Korua* (1999) N1871.

Part III - Penalties, Compensation And Enforcement Of Orders

10. Mediation.

(1) Before hearing an action under this Act, a Court shall endeavour to have the action settled by mediation.

(2) Sections 31, 32 and 33 of the *Local Courts Act* (Chapter 41) applies to a mediation under Subsection (1).

In *Re Moki Nikints and section 42(5) of the Constitution* [1988-1989] PNGLR 164, on a complaint that the respondent had encouraged the complainant's wife to leave the complainant and live with someone else, a Village Court magistrate made an order for compensation and, on the same day, an order for imprisonment for failure to pay the compensation. On appeal, Woods J held that insofar as the complaint was one for the offence of enticement under the *Adultery and Enticement Act* 1988, the failure to comply with the statutory provisions thereunder rendered the order for imprisonment unlawful under s 42 of the *Constitution*. There was nothing to show that there was any attempt at mediation nor that proper matters were considered in assessing compensation. Further, the order for imprisonment was made the same day as the order for compensation was made. Thus, no time was given to the applicant to find the compensation. His Honour held that this matter was not an offence for which imprisonment was the primary penalty. The intent and purpose of the *Adultery and Enticement Act* is clearly not to create criminal offences, but rather to regulate disputes relating to adultery and enticement and to provide for compensation in appropriate cases, with criminal sanctions only as a last resort.

11. Compensation.

Where in an action under this Act -

(a) mediation in accordance with Section 10 has failed; and

(b) the Court is satisfied, on the hearing of the action, that the act of adultery or enticement, complained of, was committed; and

(c) a defence under Section 9 has not been established,

the Court may make an order for compensation to the complainant against all or any of the defendants.

12. Amount for compensation for an act of adultery.

(1) An order for compensation in an action brought in respect of an act of adultery shall be for an amount not exceeding K1,000.00.

(2) Where separate actions are brought by the same person or on behalf of the same person in respect of the same act of adultery, the total amount of compensation shall not exceed K1,000.00.

In *Betty Hosea and Michael Maya v Eau Maya* [1988-1989] PNGLR 382 the first and second appellants had been ordered by the District Court to pay the respondent K600 and K1,000 respectively. Kapi DCJ held that:

> "the principle is that whether actions are brought separately or jointly, as in the present case, the total amount awarded against both defendants is not to exceed K1,000."

On the application of these considerations see *Betty Hosea and Michael Maya v Eau Maya* [1988-1989] PNGLR 382.

17. Payment of compensation.

(1) Subject to Subsection (2), compensation may be ordered to be made -

(a) in cash; or

(b) in goods specified in the order; or

(c) partly in cash and partly in goods so specified.

(2) Alcoholic liquor of any kind shall not be regarded as goods for the purposes of Subsection (1).

(3) Compensation may be ordered to be made -

(a) at one time; or

(b) subject to such conditions (if any) as the Court thinks proper, by instalments determined by the Court.

18. Non-compliance with order for compensation.

A person, who fails to comply with an order for compensation made against him under Section 11, is guilty of an offence.

Penalty: A term of imprisonment not exceeding six months.

19. Standard of Proof.

The standard of proof to be applied in proceedings under this Act shall be that applied in civil proceedings, namely, proof on the balance of probabilities.

20. Enforcement of orders.

An order of a Court shall be enforced under the *District Courts Act* (Chapter 40) or the *Local Courts Act* (Chapter 41), as the case may be.

Part IV - Miscellaneous

21. Abolition of certain common law rights.

(1) Subject to Subsection (2), actions or claims for compensation or orders for compensation on the ground of -

(a) adultery; or

(b) enticement,

shall not be brought or made, as the case may be, except in accordance with this Act.

(2) Subsection (1) does not affect any action or claim for compensation that has commenced, or the enforcement of an order for compensation that has been made, before the commencement of this Act.

22. Repeal of certain provisions of the Native Regulations (Chapter 316) and the Native Administration Regulation (Chapter 315).

Section 2 of the *Native Regulation* (Chapter 316) and Section 2 of the *Native Administration Regulation* (Chapter 315) are repealed.

The Sorcery Act 1971

Sorcery has been the subject of statutory control in Papua New Guinea since the promulgation of the *Native Board Regulations (Sorcery)* (No 11 of 1893) in Papua. The succeeding *Native Regulations* also proscribed sorcery, in the following terms:

Reg 80 –

(1) Sorcery is only deceit, but the lies of the Sorcerer frighten many people and cause great trouble, therefore the Sorcerer must be punished.

(2) Any native who –

(a) practises or pretends to practise sorcery; or

(b) threatens any person with sorcery whether practised by himself or any other person; or

(c) procures or attempts to procure any other person to practise or pretend to practise or assist in sorcery; or

(d) is found in possession of implements or "charms" used in sorcery; or accepts payment or presents in the shape of food or otherwise when the obvious intention of making such payments or presents is to propitiate a Sorcerer,

shall on conviction be liable to a fine not exceeding three pounds or in default of payment to imprisonment for any period not exceeding six months, or to imprisonment in the first instance for any period not exceeding six months.

Given the view of the authorities that sorcery was "only deceit", but that allegations of sorcery were a precipitating factor in social unrest and tribal fighting, reg 71 was also utilised against persons who made allegations of sorcery. This regulation punished any "native who ... (b) spreads lying reports tending to give rise to trouble or to ill-feeling amongst the people as a whole, or between individuals".

The rationale behind the regulations was discussed by the Lieutenant-Governor of Papua, JHP Murray, in his monograph *Papua or British New Guinea* (1912):

> "Sorcery is another offence which comes very frequently before the native magistrates' courts, for it is, under the regulations, punishable with six months imprisonment ... The penalty imposed is perhaps sufficient to act, to a certain extent, as a deterrent, but it is quite insufficient as a substitute for private vengeance ... The difference is that the Papuan looks upon sorcery as reality, whereas the European (as a rule) does not; to the former no punishment would be sufficient short of death, or at any rate a long term of imprisonment, either of which seems to us to be out of the question in the case of what is after all, according to our view, only an imaginary offence".[147]

The *Native Regulations* relating to sorcery have since been repealed (see above, discussion of adultery), but sorcery was made an offence under the *Village Courts Act* 1973 by reg 3(b) of the *Village Court Regulations* 1974. This regulation prohibits the following:

(a) practising or pretending to practise sorcery;

(b) threatening any person with sorcery;

(c) making someone else perform an act of sorcery;

(d) possession of implements or charms used in sorcery; or

(e) payment for the performance of sorcery.

---

[147] Murray, *Papua or British New Guinea* (1912), pp 202-203.

Breach of the regulation invokes the general criminal jurisdiction of the Village Court to impose a fine or community work order where appropriate. Compensation may of course be awarded for injury or death resulting from an act of sorcery, under the Village Court's civil jurisdiction.

The most comprehensive treatment of the legal aspects of sorcery came with the enactment in 1971 of the *Sorcery Act* (No 22 of 1971, now Ch 274 of the *Revised Laws*). The Act contains an unusual preamble, which states the assumptions underpinning the legislation:

(a) that there is a widespread belief in sorcery throughout Papua New Guinea;

(b) that there is a need to distinguish between evil sorcery, which should be punished, and innocent sorcery, which should not;

(c) that irrespective of the "reality" of powers of sorcery, acts of sorcery for evil purposes should be punished "just as if sorcery and the powers of sorcerers were real, since it is just as evil to ... do evil things by sorcery as it would be to do them ... in any other way";

(d) that actions under the influence of sorcery, or under the belief that they are under the influence of sorcery, "may not be morally (and should not be legally) blameworthy"; and

(e) that baseless, spiteful or malicious accusations of sorcery should be guarded against.

Sections 6-9 and 11 of the Act define and punish offences relating to the practice of forbidden sorcery and possession of implements used in forbidden sorcery. Section 10 makes it an offence to falsely accuse, or threaten to accuse, another of being involved in acts of forbidden sorcery. Sections 12-13 provide for forfeiture of implements used in forbidden sorcery, and ss 14 and 18 provide for the awarding of reparation and compensation.

Sections 15 and 16 provide for defences to other charges which may arise out of the accused being the victim of, or believing he or she is the victim of, sorcery. Section 15 creates a special offence in relation to charges of adultery (discussed above under the *Native Regulations*) where the accused acts under the effects of sorcery. Section 16 clarifies the situation with regard to the interplay of sorcery and the defence of provocation. In some colonial courts it his been held that acts of sorcery, even sorcery killings, did not amount to lawful provocation, since belief in sorcery was not a belief which could be held by the "reasonable man".

See, for example, Seidman, "*Mens Rea and the Reasonable African: A Problem of Society Under Radical Social Change*" (1965) 28 Mod LR 46 at 59-60.

Section 16 expressly states that sorcery may amount to provocation under s 266 of the *Criminal Code*, whether or not the act of sorcery occurred in the presence of the accused, and whether or not the act of sorcery was directed at a third person. However, the accused still must effectively show, in order to succeed (that is, to reduce murder to manslaughter), that an act of sorcery has taken place (or that he or she held honest and reasonable although mistaken belief as to this) and that the other elements of provocation are present – that is, that the realisation was in the heat of passion and was proportionate to the provocation, and that the ordinary villager in similar circumstances would likewise have been provoked beyond self-control.

A common problem occurs where "unexplained" deaths are attributed to sorcery, and the accused kills the alleged sorcerer to avenge the deaths which already occurred and/or to prevent more deaths by sorcery. The accused may have acted with the approval of his or her society, or even upon its bidding, but it is unlikely that the provocation defence would even serve to reduce murder to manslaughter (under the Code, s 303) in these circumstances, where the accused did not act suddenly in the heat of passion, and where the intent to kill was premeditated. See, for example, *Acting Public Prosecutor v Uname Aumane* [1980] PNGLR 510.

It has been suggested that the introduction of a qualified defence of diminished responsibility for sorcery killings, reducing murder to manslaughter or creating another category of unlawful homicides, would be a better and more just way of dealing with these situations where the moral culpability is sufficiently mitigated so as to make conviction for wilful murder unfair. See O'Regan, "*Sorcery and Homicide in Papua New Guinea*" (1974) 48 ALJ 76. Adoption of the Law Reform Commission's proposal for the creation of a new general class of "diminished responsibility killings", where the act occurred under the colour of customary perceptions and beliefs (discussed in Ch 1, above), would accomplish this.

The Law Reform Commission also has a specific reference on sorcery, having been asked in 1977 by the former Minister for Justice, Mr Ebia Olewale, to inquire into the practice of sorcery in Papua New Guinea and the effectiveness of the present legislation. The commission released its *Occasional Paper No 4: Sorcery* in October 1977. This lays out, in basic terms, the current laws on sorcery and some of the issues and problems, and appends a questionnaire which solicits information on any attitudes towards the practice of sorcery and its regulation.

The commission observed that:

> "There is no doubt that the practice of sorcery is widespread in Papua New Guinea. Its existence causes much fear, fighting, quarrels and killing. There are some laws which deal with sorcery. At the same time people have their own way of dealing with sorcery. Most disputes about sorcery seldom come before the official courts of the country. They are dealt with by the people themselves under the traditional legal system."[148]

The commission further observed that:

> "It is possible that the amount of sorcery is increasing as a result of the uncertainties involved in modern development or 'underdevelopment' in Papua New Guinea. In a society in which differences in status and income are increasing and traditional obligations are no longer as strongly upheld as they used to be, people often act against those who get too far ahead in social status through sorcery."[149]

That the practice and fear of sorcery are still widespread, and perhaps even growing, is confirmed by the findings of the Committee Investigating Tribal Fighting in the Highlands in its 1973 Report (see below), which listed the perception of death by sorcery as one of the main triggers of tribal fighting and unrest.

The commission has also released two background papers on sorcery, being *Occasional Paper No 8: Sorcery Among the Tolai People* (April 1978), and *Occasional Paper No 10: Sorcery Among the East Sepiks* (October 1978). However, the commission has not yet reported on this topic, and judging from recent annual reports, the reference appears to have lapsed.

---

[148] Law Reform Commission, *Occasional Paper No 4: Sorcery* (October 1977), p 1.
[149] Law Reform Commission, *Occasional Paper No 4: Sorcery* (October 1977), p 7.

SORCERY ACT

Chapter No 274

Being an Act to prevent and punish evil practices of sorcery and other similar evil practices, and for other purposes relating to such practices.

Preamble

There is a widespread belief throughout the country that there is such a thing as sorcery and that sorcerers have extraordinary powers that can be used sometimes for good purposes but more often for bad ones, and because of this belief many evil things can be done and many people are frightened or do things that otherwise they might not do.

Some kinds of sorcery are practised not for evil purposes but for innocent ones and it may not be necessary for the law to interfere with them, and so it is necessary for the law to distinguish between evil sorcery and innocent sorcery.

There is no reason why a person who uses or pretends or tries to use sorcery to do, or to try to do, evil things should not be punished just as if sorcery and the powers of sorcerers were real, since it is just as evil to do or to try to do evil things by sorcery as it would be to do them, or to try to do them, in any other way.

Sometimes some people may act, or may believe that they are acting, under the influence of sorcery to such an extent that –

(a) their conduct may not be morally (and should not be legally) blameworthy; or

(b) actions that would ordinarily be regarded as customary offences may, in traditional social groups, be regarded as excusable or capable of being compensated for.

There is a danger that any law that deals fully with sorcery may encourage some evil- intentioned people to make baseless or merely spiteful or malicious accusations that their enemies are sorcerers solely to get them into trouble with other people, and this is a thing that the law should prevent.

Part I – Preliminary

1. Interpretation.

(1) In this Act, unless the contrary intention appears –

"act of sorcery" means any act (including a traditional ceremony or ritual) that is intended to bring, or that purports to be able or to be adapted to bring, powers of sorcery into action, or to make them possible or carry them into effect;

"forbidden sorcery" means sorcery other than innocent sorcery;

"harmful result" includes fear, intimidation or injury in mind, body or property;

"implement of sorcery" means any thing that –

(a) is designed or intended for use in acts of sorcery generally, or in a particular act or class of acts of sorcery; or

(b) has, by some ceremony, ritual or act (including an act of sorcery), been adapted for use in acts of sorcery generally, or in a particular act or class of acts of sorcery;

"innocent sorcery" means sorcery of a kind referred to in Schedule 1;

"social group" includes a family, an extended family, a lineage, a kinship group, a descent group and a local group or community;

"sorcerer" means a person who –

(a) claims to have powers of sorcery; or

(b) directly or indirectly pretends to have, holds himself out to have or professes to have, powers of sorcery;

"sorcery" includes (without limiting the generality of that expression) what is known, in various languages and parts of the country, as witchcraft, magic, enchantment, puri puri, mura mura dikana, vada, mea mea, sanguma or malira, whether or not connected with or related to the supernatural.

(2) A reference in this Act to custom shall be read as a reference to the relevant custom of the social group or groups concerned.

(3) A reference in this Act to proceedings brought by virtue of this Act shall be read as a reference to proceedings in which reliance is placed, for the purpose of bringing the proceedings, on any provision of this Act, to the extent that the provision or its application is in question in the proceedings.

2. References to social groups.

(1) A reference in this Act to a social group shall, in its application to any matter before a court under this Act, be read as a reference to the social group or groups that, in the opinion of the court, is or are of the most relevance.

(2) In this Act, a reference to a social group includes a reference to any settled community, or a part of that community, whether it is a traditional community or is composed of members of different traditional or other social groups.

(3) This Act does not prevent a person being regarded as a member of more than one social group or community.

Part II – Principles, Application and Effect of Act

3. Preamble as statement of objects and principles.

Notwithstanding anything in any other law or rule of statutory construction, in the interpretation and application of this Act the provisions of the Preamble shall be taken fully into account in all cases, and each provision of this Act shall be read and construed as being intended to give effect to those provisions.

4. Innocent making of certain implements of sorcery.

(1) Subsection (2) does not apply where –

(a) to the knowledge of the person relying on that subsection, the implement of sorcery concerned was made or adapted for use in a particular act of forbidden sorcery; or

(b) the implement of sorcery concerned was intended to be used in an act of forbidden sorcery.

(2) Notwithstanding this Act, the mere making of an implement of sorcery (including the adaptation of a thing so as to be an implement of sorcery) is not an act of sorcery, nor is a person who claims to have the power to make an implement of sorcery a sorcerer by virtue only of his claiming that power, if the implement is designed, intended or adapted for use both in acts of innocent sorcery and in acts of forbidden sorcery, depending on the use made of it in any given set of circumstances.

(3) The burden of proof that Subsection (2) applies in relation to an implement of sorcery is on the person relying on that subsection.

5. Existence and effectiveness of powers of sorcery.

Even though this Act may speak as if powers of sorcery really exist (which is necessary if the law is to deal adequately with all the legal problems of sorcery and the traditional belief in the powers of sorcerers), nevertheless nothing in this Act recognizes the existence or effectiveness of powers of sorcery in any factual sense except only for the purpose of, and of proceedings under or by virtue of, this Act, or denies the existence or effectiveness of such powers.

Belief in the power of sorcery is contrary to s 5 of the *Sorcery Act* (Ch 274). It is therefore not proper to take into account any belief by the accused persons that the deceased sorcerer was responsible for the death of their relatives. The *Customs Recognition Act* is to be read subject to the *Sorcery Act*: *The State v Osborn Kwayawako* [1988] PNLGR 174.

Part III – Offences, Etc, in Relation to Sorcery

Division 1 – Offences

6. Sorcery generally.

(1) This section does not apply in cases where the sorcery involved is innocent sorcery only.

(2) A person who, directly or indirectly, pretends to be, holds himself out to be, or professes to be a sorcerer is guilty of an offence.

(3) A person who influences or attempts to influence the acts of another person by the use or threatened use of the powers or services of a sorcerer as such is guilty of an offence.

Penalty: On conviction on indictment – imprisonment for a term not exceeding two years.

On summary conviction – imprisonment for a term not exceeding one year.

This section shifts the evidential burden to the accused: *Balu Mau'u v Pare* [1973] PNGLR 64.

Forbidden sorcery is evil, not only according to the Holy Scripture (Rev 22:14-15), which is now a pillar of the Papua New Guinea state, but it is also evil in Melanesian societies. Social consequences of forbidden sorcery are many and varied. In many societies such evil practices work as forces of social balance. Sorcery also works as a force of destruction. In other places, sorcery prevents enterprising individuals from progressing commercially or educationally. Fear produced by practices of evil sorcery often prevent many Papua New Guineans living in towns from returning to their villages, either to live or to establish contact with their homes of origin: *The State v Noah Magou* [1981] PNGLR 1.

7. Criminal acts of sorcery.

A person who –

(a) does any act of forbidden sorcery; or

(b) aids, abets, counsels or procures, or by act or omission is in any way knowingly concerned in or party to, the doing of any such act,

is guilty of an offence.

Penalty: On conviction on indictment – imprisonment for a term not exceeding five years.

On summary conviction – imprisonment for a term not exceeding one year.

The real difficulty with the *Sorcery Act* is that it was enacted by Australians who are not aware of the real and factual effects of sorcery. In s 5 it is imagined that sorcery really exists, but it does not recognise sorcery as a reality, or the existence or effectiveness of powers of sorcery in any factual sense. The Act itself provides for much relaxed procedure and onus of proof in Sch 2: *The State v Noah Magou* [1981] PNGLR 1.

There is no doubt that sorcery is widespread in Papua New Guinea. Forbidden sorcery is practised, or is believed to be practised, throughout Papua New Guinea. Sorcery is dealt with as a subject peculiar to Papua New Guinea under the *Sorcery Act*. There is a comprehensive preamble to the Act, which emphasises the prevalence of sorcery fear, and distinguishes innocent sorcery from evil sorcery. Innocent sorcery is described in the Sch 1 of the Act. Basically, it is protective or curative sorcery, and is generally regarded by the accused and his or her customary group as being harmless, legitimate or not offensive: *The State v Noah Magou* [1981] PNGLR 1.

The Act does not specify different punishments depending on the outcome. Thus, it is not an element of the offence under this section to consider whether the victim of forbidden sorcery had died or taken ill. Section 1 provides a definition of sorcery which envisages all possibilities, including bringing powers of sorcery into action, or making powers of sorcery possible, or carrying them into effect. The state may consider amending the *Sorcery Act* to provide for different consequences of sorcery where the victims may be ill only, where the victim has become insane, where the victim has died or where a consequence of that act of sorcery is damage to or destruction of the property to which the sorcery is intended or directed: *The State v Noah Magou* [1981] PNGLR 1.

Customary punishment for sorcery is retribution. Destructive sorcery is met with more powerful destructive sorcery and also with banishment, which is often permanent. In some ways, the custodial sentence of 15 months (imposed in *The State v Noah Magou* [1981] PNGLR 1) is a modest reflection of the banishment that would have been inflicted in some cases of sorcery in traditional societies. This punishment by the court upon the accused must be the only punishment. Should the village people impose any other form of customary punishment, whether of sorcery or otherwise, on the accused or any of the accused's relatives, they shall be dealt with according to law.

8. Attempting to commit offence by means of sorcery.

(1) If an act of sorcery is intended to produce or purports to produce any unlawful result, the person doing the act is guilty of an attempt to produce that result and is punishable accordingly.

(2) Notwithstanding anything in any other law, the fact that the unlawful result did in fact follow the act of sorcery does not prevent a charge of an attempted offence being brought under Subsection (1), but nothing in this section affects the operation of Section 20.

9. Administering sorcerous substances, etc.

(1) This section does not apply where the act of sorcery involved is an act of innocent sorcery only.

(2) A person who unlawfully administers to another person or to an animal –

(a) any substance that has been subjected to an act of sorcery; or

(b) any substance in the course of or in fulfilment of an act of sorcery,

is guilty of an offence.

Penalty: Imprisonment for a term not exceeding eight years.

10. False report of sorcery, etc.

(1) This section does not apply in cases where the sorcery involved or allegedly involved is innocent sorcery only.

(2) The *Defamation Act* does not apply to or in relation to an offence against Subsection (3) or (4).

(3) A person who (except in the course of, or for the purpose of the institution of, legal proceedings or in any other case in which such an accusation or threat is privileged or excused by law) falsely accuses, to a third person, or threatens to accuse another person of –

(a) being or of having been a sorcerer; or

(b) performing or having performed an act of sorcery; or

(c) having been concerned in or a party to an act of sorcery,

is guilty of an offence.

(4) A person who spreads a false report that another person –

(a) is a sorcerer or performs or has performed an act of sorcery; or

(b) is or has been concerned in, or a party to, an act of sorcery,

is guilty of an offence.

Penalty: Imprisonment for a term not exceeding one year.

A direct accusation is not covered and, if no third party is involved, complaint is not made out: *Karafa Uari Aero Evera v Haroharo Taurake* [1976] PNGLR 337.

11. Possession of implement of forbidden sorcery.

A person who, without lawful excuse (proof of which is on him), has in his possession an implement –

(a) made or adapted for use in a particular act of forbidden sorcery; or

(b) intended for use in an act of forbidden sorcery,

is guilty of an offence.

Penalty: Imprisonment for a term not exceeding one year.

Division 2 – Forfeiture and Reparations

12. Forfeiture of profits of sorcery.

(1) Where a person –

(a) is convicted of an offence against this Act; or

(b) is convicted, by virtue of this Act, of an offence,

the court that convicts him may order any money or other thing that has been paid or given to him in consideration of the performance of an act of forbidden sorcery to be forfeited to the State and, subject to Section 14 –

(c) the money shall be paid into the Consolidated Revenue Fund; or

(d) the other thing may be dealt with in such manner as the Head of State, acting on advice, directs,

as the case may be.

(2) If the convicted person is no longer in possession of the money or thing, the amount of the money or the value of the thing, as assessed by the court, is a debt due to the State and the court may make an order for its payment.

13. Forfeiture of implement of sorcery.

(1) Where a person –

(a) is convicted of an offence against this Act; or

(b) is convicted, by virtue of this Act, of an offence,

the court that convicts him may order any implement of sorcery owned by him or in his possession or under his control to be forfeited to the State.

(2) A court may at any time order any implement of sorcery that can be used in an act of forbidden sorcery to be forfeited to the State.

(3) An implement of sorcery forfeited to the State under this section shall be dealt with in such manner as the Head of State, acting on advice, directs.

14. Reparations.

(1) Where a person is convicted of an offence involving an act of sorcery, the court that convicts him may order him to make such compensation as the court thinks proper to –

(a) any person at whom the act of sorcery was directed; or

(b) the social group to which any person at whom the sorcery was directed belongs or belonged at the time of the act.

(2) An order under Subsection (1) may be made at the time of conviction or

sentence, or if the court thinks it proper to do so at a later date, and the court may in any event –

(a) admit further evidence, after conviction or sentence, in relation to the question of compensation; and

(b) adjourn the matter in order to enable the parties to reach agreement on the compensation to be made,

and may make such further or other order as it thinks proper.

(3) An order under this section may include an order that any money that has been or is liable to be forfeited to the State under Section 12(1), or any amount that is recovered or recoverable by the State under Section 12(2), be paid as part or all of the compensation.

This section provides for reparations where a person is convicted of an offence involving an act of sorcery, and may be applied where there is evidence pointing to whether compensation is a part of the custom or culture of the accused: *The State v Noah Magou* [1981] PNGLR 1.

Part IV – Defences Arising out of Acts of Sorcery

15. Special defence in relation to charges of adultery.

(1) In this section, "charge of adultery" means a charge of an offence against –

(a) Section 17 of the *Native Regulation* (Papua); or

(b) Section 14 of the *Native Administration Regulation* (TNG),

or against any corresponding or analogous provision of any other law.

(2) It is a defence to a charge of adultery that an act of sorcery had been performed, without the consent (express or implied) of the accused person, of such a nature as to be generally believed, in the social groups of which the husband and the wife are respectively members, to have the effect –

(a) of inducing the accused person to have the sexual intercourse in question; and

(b) by custom, to excuse the act of intercourse in all the circumstances of the case.

(3) The burden of proof of a defence under Subsection (2) is on the accused person, and that burden need not be discharged beyond reasonable doubt.

(4) Subject to Subsection (5), the circumstances referred to in Subsection (2) include any circumstance (including any customary compensatory or conciliatory arrangement) that arose before the act of adultery, or that arose, or that the court dealing with the matter is satisfied will arise, after the act.

(5) The circumstances referred to in Subsection (2) do not include any act, matter or thing that –

(a) constitutes, or is an ingredient of, an offence committed by or on behalf of the accused person against any other law; or

(b) is repugnant to the general principles of humanity or is not in the public interest; or

(c) is, in the opinion of the court dealing with the matter, improper to be taken into account.

See the discussion of the *Native Regulations* above.

16. Sorcery as provocation.

(1) An act of sorcery may amount to a wrongful act or insult within the meaning of Section 266 of the *Criminal Code*.

(2) It is immaterial that the act of sorcery –

(a) did not occur in the presence of the person allegedly provoked; or

(b) was directed at some person other than the person allegedly provoked.

(3) The likely effect of an act of sorcery relied on by virtue of this section shall be judged by reference, amongst other things, to the traditional beliefs of any social group of which the person provoked is a member.

(4) A defence provided by this section is in addition to and not in derogation of any defence that is –

(a) available by reason of any effect attributable, under any other law, to the act involved; or

(b) otherwise available to an accused person.

See ss 266-267 and 303 of the *Criminal Code* regarding provocation generally.

See *R v Ferapo Meata* (1967) N419, for a discussion of the law relating to sorcery and provocation, the principles of which are now embodied in the section.

Minogue CJ and Kelly J stated, in *R v KJ* [1973] PNGLR 93 at 102-103:

> "The relevant fact is not that the person concerned is a sorcerer (or where s 25 of the Code applies is honestly and reasonably but mistakenly believed to be a sorcerer) but that he has committed or is committing an act of sorcery (or where s 25 applies, is believed to have committed or be committing such an act). What must be looked at is the nature of the act itself and not the personality of the actor. It is not every act of sorcery which amounts to a wrongful act or insult: for example the act may be one of innocent sorcery."

See the judgment of Miles J in *Agoara Kebo and Karunai Uraki v The State* (1981) SC 198, for observation on the proper evidentiary basis to be supplied to the court on the belief and extent of belief in sorcery for the purposes of sentence. That case is annotated under s 19 of the *Supreme Court Act*.

See *The State v Yale Gesie and Buamuwe Guluwe* (1980) N254, for a discussion of this section in relation to a two day delay before a father and three accomplices killed an alleged sorcerer.

For considerations on sentence where the wilful murder has been prompted by fear of sorcery, see *Acting Public Prosecutor v Uname Aumane* [1980] PNGLR 510 (Kapi J), discussed under s 596 of the *Criminal Code*.

See *The State v Mole Manipe* (1979) N196.

Part V – Procedure, Evidence, Etc

17. Evidential effect of possession of implement of sorcery.

(1) For the purpose of any proceedings under or by virtue of this Act, evidence that a person has at any time owned or had in his possession or under his control, otherwise than in an official capacity or in a capacity not implying or suggesting the possession of powers of sorcery, an implement of sorcery is evidence that he has been at all relevant times a sorcerer.

(2) The burden of proof of a matter referred to in Subsection (1) is on the person alleging it.

(3) The provisions of Subsection (1) are in addition to and not in derogation of the other provisions of this Act.

18. Evidence, proof, etc.

Schedule 2 applies to and in relation to proceedings brought under, or by virtue of, this Act.

19. Saving of Customs Recognition Act.

Except so far as this Act expressly provides to the contrary, this Act does not affect the operation of the *Customs Recognition Act*.

The *Customs Recognition Act* is Ch 19 of the *Revised Laws*.

See also Sch 2.1 of the *Constitution* regarding the recognition, application and enforcement of customary law.

Part VI – Miscellaneous

20. Preservation of rights and liabilities under other laws, etc.

Except where the contrary intention appears, nothing in this Act takes away from any person any defence, right or liability, whether civil or criminal –

(a) that is or has been available, acquired or incurred; or

(b) that will or may be available, acquired or incurred,

to or by him under any other law, but nothing in this section shall be deemed to show a contrary intention within the meaning of the *Interpretation Act* or to affect Section 16 of the *Criminal Code*, or any other similar law.

21. Regulations.

The Head of State, acting on advice, may make regulations, not inconsistent with this Act, prescribing all matters that by this Act are required or permitted to be prescribed, or that are necessary or convenient to be prescribed for carrying out or giving effect to this Act.

Schedules

Schedule 1

Sec 1(1)

Definition of Innocent Sorcery

Sch 1.1. For the purposes of this Act, innocent sorcery is sorcery that –

(a) is protective or curative only, or is not intended to produce, and does not purport to be calculated or able or adapted to produce, any harmful or unlawful result, or to exert any harmful, unlawful or undue influence on any person; and

(b) is generally regarded in the social groups of which –

(i) the accused person; and

(ii) the person at whom the act was directed; and

(iii) the person whose conduct was intended to be influenced,

are respectively members as being, by custom, legitimate or harmless and not offensive in all the circumstances of the case.

Sch 1.2. Subject to Section Sch 1.3 the circumstances referred to in Section Sch 1.1 include any circumstance (including the courtship of an unmarried person by an unmarried person, betrothal, marriage, the fact that the act of sorcery was intended only to counteract or nullify the effect of a previous act of sorcery or any customary compensatory or conciliatory arrangement) that arose before the act of sorcery, or that arose, or that the court dealing with the matter is satisfied will arise, after the act.

Sch 1.3. The circumstances referred to Section Sch 1.1 do not include –

(a) any act, matter or thing that constitutes, or is an ingredient of, an offence committed by or on behalf of the accused person against any other law; or

(b) any act, matter or thing that is repugnant to the general principles of humanity or is not in the public interest; or

(c) any other act, matter or thing that, in the opinion of the court dealing with the matter, is improper to be taken into account.

Sch 1.4. For the purposes only of Section Sch 1.3(b) and (c), an act of sorcery shall not, simply as such be deemed to be not in the public interest or improper to be taken into account.

Sch 1.5. For the purpose of allowing any circumstance referred to in Section Sch 1.1 to arise, if the court dealing with the matter considers it proper and in the interests of justice and the amicable settlement of social or personal disputes or differences to do so the court may by order adjourn the hearing of the matter for such period and on such terms and conditions (including the entering by any person into a recognizance for any purpose connected with the matter) as the court thinks proper.

Schedule 2

Sec 18

Evidence, Proof, Etc

Sch 2.1. (1) Evidence that-

(a) an act is, in the social group to which the doer of the act belongs, believed to be an act of sorcery; and

(b) a person believed that –

(i) the act was directed at him or at some other person; or

(ii) his conduct or the conduct of some other person was intended to be influenced by or as a result of the act,

is evidence that the act is an act of sorcery within the meaning of this Act and that the doer of the act knew it to be an act of sorcery.

(2) Where in a prosecution for an offence against this Act there is evidence of a general belief in the social group to which the doer of the act belongs that an act is an act of sorcery, the doer of the act shall, in the absence of the evidence to the contrary, be presumed to have intended the act to be an act of sorcery.

Sch 2.2. If in a prosecution for an offence against or in reliance on Section 8 the accused person is proved to have done an act of sorcery then –

(a) it is immaterial that the thing done was incapable of causing, or was not adapted to the fulfilment of, the result intended, if either –

(i) the accused person; or

(ii) the person at whom the act was directed; or

(iii) any person whose conduct was intended to be influenced,

believed that it was capable of producing the intended result or some similar result, and in the case of a person referred to in Subparagraph (ii) or (iii) the belief was known to the accused person; and

(b) until the contrary is proved, both the belief and the knowledge referred to in Paragraph (a) shall be presumed on the part of the accused person.

Sch 2.3. (1) In considering for the purposes of this Act the question of the existence or effect of a traditional belief or of its being generally held in a social group, a court –

(a) is not bound to observe strict legal procedures or to apply technical rules of evidence; but

(b) shall –

(i) admit and consider such relevant information as is available (including hearsay and expressions of opinion); and

(ii) otherwise inform itself as it sees fit.

(2) For the purposes of deciding a question referred to in Subsection (1), a court –

(a) may refer to books, treaties, reports or other works of reference, or statements by Local Government Councils or committees of Local Government Councils, as to any custom (whether published or not), and may accept any matter or thing stated in them as evidence on the question; and

(b) may of its own motion call such evidence or require the opinions of such persons as it thinks fit,

but this section does not limit the discretion of the court in obtaining evidence or information for itself on the question.

Sch 2.4. The burden of proof that an act of sorcery is an act of innocent sorcery is on the person alleging it.

The Inter-Group Fighting Act 1977

Tribal fighting has been considered a major and long-time problem in Papua New Guinea, especially in the Highlands regions. For anthropological discussions of the nature of tribal fighting, see Meggitt, "*Blood Is Their Argument*" (1977), and Strathern, "*Contemporary Warfare in the Highlands*" (1977) 4 *Yagl-Ambu* 135. The Vol 5, No 2 (June 1978) edition of *Yagl-Ambu* is devoted entirely to perspectives on tribal fighting, particularly in the Enga Province.

After a particularly serious upsurge of tribal warfare in the early 1970s, the government established, in 1973, a committee of inquiry under the chairmanship of Mr Phillip Paney, a former Local Court magistrate and, at the time, the Chairman of the Liquor Licensing Commission. The committee was asked to investigate the causes of tribal fighting, police procedures used in dealing with tribal fighting, and the substantive law, legal procedures and sentencing policy relating to tribal fighting.

The committee's report, published in late 1973, identified a number of precipitators of tribal fighting, and also a number of longer-term, more entrenched or structural causes of the fighting. The precipitating factors included:

(a) disputes over land ownership and boundaries, intensifying in areas such as Simbu Province with increasing population pressures and a shortage of useable land;

(b) allegations of sorcery killings (see discussion of the *Sorcery Act*);

(c) killings which initiate or continue a chain of pay-back responses;

(d) disputes over relations with women, including divorce and brideprice conflicts and claims of adultery or rape; and

(e) disputes over pigs, still the prime source of wealth, power and prestige.[150]

The longer-term causes of the fighting are, according to the committee:[151]

(a) intense kin group loyalties which sometimes have the effect of escalating what would otherwise be minor, private disputes into major, inter-group disputes;

(b) "the need to fight" caused by anxieties over the very rapid cultural and economic changes taking place, and the feeling of relative political powerlessness;

(c) the alienation of the population from the imposed legal system, and the consequent reluctance of the people to utilise the courts for dispute settlement;

---

[150] Paney Report (1973), pp 12-18.
[151] Paney Report (1973), pp 4-11.

(d) the concentration of government resources, including police, in the urban centres, and the concomitant lack of an official presence in the rural areas; and

(e) social problems, particularly the lack of employment opportunities for school drop-outs, who have been educated to expect a certain Western lifestyle.

The committee made 60 specific recommendations aimed at eliminating or mitigating both the long and short-term causes of tribal fighting. Some of these recommendations led to, or supported existing proposals for, the enactment of several pieces of significant legislation. The *Village Courts Act* 1973 was passed in 1974, and established a system of courts with the aim of mediating disputes at the village level (discussed in more detail in Ch 3, above). The *Motor Vehicles (Third Party Insurance) (Basic Protection Compensation) Act* 1974 established a no-fault personal injury/death compensation scheme for motor vehicle accident victims, partly to forestall pay-back killings by providing "instant" compensation. The *Business Groups (Incorporation) Act* 1974 and the and *Groups (Incorporation) Act* 1974 provide a mechanism for the incorporation of customary groups, and confers on them the power to conduct business enterprises, to borrow money, and to acquire, hold, dispose of, and manage land. The *Land Disputes Settlement Act* 1975 established a system similar to the Village Courts, with jurisdiction over disputes involving customary land.

With regard to law enforcement, the committee made numerous recommendations as to the improved training, development and co-ordination of police and patrol officers, and recommended a more active involvement of magistrates in defusing potentially violent disputes.

The committee also recommended that new legislation be brought in to deal specifically with tribal fighting, creating new offences and facilitating enforcement procedures. It was the committee's view that prior experience demonstrated that the existing offences in the criminal calendar, such as assault, fighting, unlawful assembly, riotous behaviour, going armed in public so as to cause terror, affray, and so on were ineffective in tribal fighting situations for practical reasons, such as identifying a particular accused from among hundreds of massed warriors, and in sifting and sorting evidence in these circumstances, even where arrests could be effected.

Accordingly, the committee called for:

(a) the creation of new summary offences for failing to disperse from, or planning, or inciting a tribal fight;

(b) the reversal of the onus of proof in tribal fighting cases, such that a person arrested at the scene of a tribal fight, who was affiliated with one of the warring groups, would have to prove affirmatively that he was not a participant in the fighting; and

(c) the institution of group liability and group punishment for tribal fighting offences.

A 1975 Bill incorporating the recommendations of the Paney Report with regard to changes in the criminal law was drafted, but was never tabled in Parliament because of the concern of both the Secretary and Minister for Justice that the provisions on group punishment might result in the injustice of "a guilty few sharing the burden with the innocent many".

Over the next few years, however, continued and increasing tribal fighting swung public opinion round to the clear majority view that the problem was of such gravity as to warrant the imposition of tougher laws and increased police powers. On 8 September 1977, after spirited debate, the National Parliament passed the following motion put by Highlands Member of Parliament, Mr Paul Torato (later to be Minister for Justice):

> "That in view of the widespread and serious tribal fighting in the Highlands ... and that no measure taken to date seems to be an effective deterrent, this Parliament resolves that the Government introduce legislation to provide for heavier penalties for people involved in tribal fights ... and to punish groups or clans rather than just individuals on a personal guilt basis with the imposition of such gaol sentences or other measures as would effectively deter tribal fighting."

An inter-departmental committee was set up pursuant to the resolution. The committee used the 1975 Bill as its model, and made few substantial alterations in drafting the 1977 Bill, which was enacted by Parliament in November.

The *Inter-Group Fighting Act* 1977 (No 43 of 1977) represented the first fundamental statutory modification in the law of criminal responsibility in Papua New Guinea. The Act establishes in each province a Peace and Good Order Committee, consisting of the Provincial Premier (as Chairman), the premier's nominee, and the officer-in-charge of the police force in the province, the member of National Parliament representing the provincial constituency, the Head of the Department of the province, or their nominees, and a senior District Court Magistrate resident in the province nominated by the Chief Magistrate. When the Peace and Good Order Committee "is satisfied that it is desirable in the interest of the preservation of peace and public order to do so", it may declare that the provisions of the Act are in force, pursuant to s 4, in all or part of the province for up to three months. This then brings into effect Pts III and IV of the Act which, respectively, contain special offences relating to tribal fighting, and provide for the imposition of group punishment in certain prescribed circumstances.

The new offences created are:

(a) preparing to take part in an inter-group fight (s 10);

(b) taking part in an inter-group fight (s 11);

(c) organising an inter-group fight (s 12); and

(d) inciting another person to take part in an inter-group fight (s 13).

"Inter-group fight" is defined by ss 10-11 to mean a situation where any member of an unlawful assembly (referred to in s 10(1)) assaults or attempts to assault or commences to fight with a member of another group of persons.

Provisions of the *Inter-Group Fighting Act* have twice come under the scrutiny of the Supreme Court, and twice have been found to be unconstitutional and invalid. In *Supreme Court Reference No 3 of 1978* [1978] PNGLR 421, the court considered the validity of the reversal of onus provision then contained in s 11 (taking part in an inter-group fight), which was regarded by the proponents of the legislation as an essential, if controversial, feature of the Act. Section 11(3) provided that:

> "A person charged with an offence against this section is guilty of that offence unless he proves, to the satisfaction of the court, that he did not take part in the actual fighting."

By a 2-1 majority, the Supreme Court held that s 11(3) offended against the constitutionally guaranteed presumption of innocence contained in s 37(4), and was thus invalid. Section 37(4) of the *Constitution* provides that "a law may place upon a person charged with an offence the burden of proving particular facts which are, or would with the exercise of reasonable care be, peculiarly within his knowledge". The court found that (p 435):

> "the situation of taking part in the actual fighting ... is not a matter peculiarly within a defendant's knowledge ... One's partaking in the fight would in the normal course be a matter known to many people, including friend, foe and others."

In *Supreme Court Reference No 1 of 1981* [1981] PNGLR 151, the court considered the validity of the scheme established by ss 16, 17 and 20 of the Act, which deals with the imposition of punishment (penalties of up to K20,000 in cash or kind or imprisonment for non-payment of the penalty) on group leaders for the group's part in an inter-group fight. By a 4-1 majority, the Supreme Court held that the combined effect of the sections contravened several provisions of the Basic Rights division of the *Constitution*, and were thus invalid.

In particular, the court found that the group punishment scheme violated s 37(2) of the *Constitution*, which states that (except in the case of contempt of court) "nobody may be convicted of an offence that is not defined by, and the penalty for which is not prescribed by, a written law", in that the group leaders being penalised were not necessarily themselves guilty of any offence. Similarly, contrary to s 37(4)(b), the leaders are not "charged with an offence" and given the details of the nature of the offence charged. Nor are they, having been charged with an offence, afforded a fair hearing within a reasonable time by an independent and impartial court, as required by s 37(3). Nor should they be penalised for an act which "did not, at the time when it took place, constitute an offence", contrary to s 37(7). Also, perhaps most fundamentally, no person shall be deprived of his or her personal liberty except "in execution of the sentence or order of a court in respect of an offence of which he has been found guilty", according to s 42(1)(b).

The court found that ss 16, 17 and 20 of the Act were not saved by s 42(1)(c) of the *Constitution*, which permits deprivation of liberty by reason of a person's failure "to comply with the order of a court made to secure the fulfilment of an obligation ... imposed by law", since an order under s 17 was not an order made to secure the fulfilment of an obligation within the meaning of s 42(1)(c). There was no pre-existing obligation to pay the penalty; the court order itself imposes the obligation. In his separate concurring judgment, Pratt J also pointed out that the reverse-onus escape clause in s 17(3)(b) of the Act, whereby a group leader could avoid responsibility where "he satisfies the magistrate that he did everything reasonably within his power to prevent the inter-group fighting taking place", violated the constitutional prescription of innocence under s 37(4) of the *Constitution*, in the same way that s 11(3) of the *Inter-Group Fighting Act* was found to have in the earlier Supreme Court reference.

The principal Act has also been legislatively amended four times to date. The *Inter-Group Fighting (Amendment) Act* 1978 (No 37 of 1978) and the *Inter-Group Fighting (Amendment) Act* 1979 (No 25 of 1979) were primarily concerned with restructuring the composition and procedures of the Peace and Good Order Committees, to take into account, among other things, the new system of decentralisation through provincial governments. The 1978 amendment also modified the s 10 (preparing to fight) offence, and the 1979 amendment repealed and replaced s 11 to conform with the Supreme Court decision in *Constitutional Reference No 3 of 1978* [1978] PNGLR 421.

The *Inter-Group Fighting (Amendment) Act* 1981 (No 18 of 1981) altered s 4(b), to make Pt III (ss 10-13) and ss 21 and 23-25 of Pt IV of the principal Act applicable in all areas of Papua New Guinea. The amendment Act also amended ss 10-13 by adding sub-sections which provide that a son present at the scene of an inter-group fight shall be deemed to have taken part, unless he has a "reasonable excuse, the burden of proof of which rests upon him". These onus reversing provisions have presumably been drafted with the intent to avoid again running foul of the words of s 37(4)(a) of the *Constitution*, if not the spirit. Unlike the old s 11(3) which was declared unconstitutional in *Constitutional Reference No 3 of 1978*, the accused here need not disprove taking part (for that is deemed), but rather must establish a reasonable excuse, which may be said to be a fact "peculiarly within his knowledge" and therefore within the exception to s 37(4)(a).

Finally, the 1981 amendment altered ss 15-17 and repealed and replaced s 20, consequent upon the decision in *Supreme Court Reference No 1 of 1981* [1981] PNGLR 151. The new s 20 makes non-payment of the penalty imposed on group leaders under s 17 an offence in itself, punishable by up to six months imprisonment. This is clearly meant to satisfy the Supreme Court's objection to the deprivation of liberty based only on the failure to pay the court-ordered penalty, by creating a new offence which meets the requirements of ss 37 and 42 of the *Constitution*. It should be noted that while the Act authorises heavy penalties for tribal fighting, it does not provide for the ordering of compensation payments, which are generally crucial in ending hostilities.

The *Inter-Group Fighting (Amendment) Act* 1983 (No 13 of 1983) was one of the three pieces of minimum penalties legislation enacted by the Parliament as a package. The 1983 amendment modifies the penalty provisions of ss 10-13, by increasing the maximum punishment available and imposing a minimum term of imprisonment in each case.

See the discussion of the *Criminal Code (Minimum Penalties) (Amendment) Act* 1983 above.

While the Act, particularly in its strengthened form, has been praised as a factor in reducing tribal fighting, or at least facilitating the policing of inter-group fighting, it obviously does not strike at the underlying causes of conflict as identified in the Paney Report – economic under-development, culture shock, political powerlessness, and so on. With tribal fighting continuing, it may be anticipated that the Parliament will authorise the use of even greater sanctions and the further increase of police powers. Indeed, in late 1979 when tribal fighting broke out on a large scale in four Highlands provinces, the government looked past the *Inter-Group Fighting Act* and declared an unprecedented state of emergency in those provinces under the emergency powers contained in Pt X (ss 226-246) of the *Constitution*. At the time of writing, the current government was considering legislation which would authorise the imposition of strict curfews in designated trouble spots, and other similar legislation intended to preserve "law and order".

INTER-GROUP FIGHTING ACT

Chapter No 344

Being an Act to provide for –

(a) the suppression of fighting between groups; and

(b) the creation of offences in relation to inter-group fighting,

and for related purposes.

Part I – Preliminary

1. Interpretation.

In this Act unless the contrary intention appears –

"Chairman" means the Chairman of a Committee;

"Committee" means a Peace and Good Order Committee established by Section 5(1);

"group" or "group of persons" means a traditional kinship or other customary, social or community group, and includes –

(a) a family; and

(b) an extended family; and

(c) a sub-clan; and

(d) a clan; and

(e) a moiety; and

(f) a tribe; and

(g) any other group of persons recognized by custom as having a common interest in a dispute;

"inter-group fight" is an inter-group fight within the meaning of Section 11(1);

"Magistrate" means a District Court Magazine or a person appointed under Section 23(2) to be a Magistrate for the purposes of this Act;

"officer" means a District Officer, a member of the Police Force or a Village Peace Officer;

"province" includes the National Capital District;

"this Act" includes the regulation made under this Act.

2. Purpose of this Act.

The purpose of this Act is to discourage fighting between groups of Papua New Guineans by providing for –

(a) the creation of offences in relation to such fighting; and

(b) the imposition of severe penalties for such offences; and

(c) the collective punishment of the leaders of groups involved in fighting; and

(d) the imprisonment of group leaders for non-payment of penalties imposed on them as a result of their groups participation in such fighting.

3. Non-derogation of other provisions.

The provisions of this Act are in addition to, and not in derogation or amendment of, the provisions of any other law.

4. Application.

(1) Subject to Subsections (2), (5) and (6), where the Peace and Good Order Committee for a province is satisfied that it is desirable in the interest of the preservation of peace and public order to do so, it may declare that the provisions of this Act apply and have full force and effect throughout the province or in such part of the province and for such period not exceeding three months, as it considers necessary to achieve the purpose of this Act and those provisions apply and have full force and effect accordingly.

(2) A declaration under Subsection (1) may be renewed by the Committee at any time for periods each not exceeding three months.

(3) A declaration under Subsection (1) or a renewal under Subsection (2) of a declaration shall come into effect immediately it is made or renewed, but as soon as practicable after it is so made or renewed shall be published in the National Gazette and shall be given such publicity in the area to which it relates as the Committee considers is the most practicable means available in the circumstances to bring the fact of the declaration or renewal, as the case may be, to the notice of the people of that area.

(4) Failure to comply with the requirements of Subsection (3) or with those requirements within a particular time, does not make the declaration or renewal invalid.

(5) The Committee may at any time, and shall, within three days of receiving a direction to do so from the Minister, revoke a declaration under Subsection (1) or a renewal of a notice under Subsection (2) and shall, as soon as practicable after the revocation, cause a notice of the revocation to be published in the National Gazette.

(6) Parts 1, 11 and III and Sections 21, 23, 24 and 25 apply in all areas of Papua New Guinea.

[Subs (6) am Act No 18, 1981 (*Inter-Group Fighting (Amendment) Act* 1981), s 1.1]

(7) The provisions of this Act do not apply except as provided by this section.

The Act has no force or effect until a declaration of a fighting zone is made under s 4. The declaration cannot have retrospective effect. Where a declaration is not made, other laws must operate. There are ample other laws that the state can invoke, such as the *Summary Offences Act* and the *Criminal Code*. In *Kowi Nayu v Thomas Nabenduo* (1981) N291, the appellants were deprived of their liberty for over a year despite the fact that the fighting zone was declared after their arrest, and so they were entitled to compensation.

Kowi Nayu v Thomas Nabenduo (1981) N291 was approved by Woods J in *Digal David v MR Kalasim* (1986) N576(M).

Section 4(3) states that a declaration shall come into effect immediately it is made. Therefore, an oral declaration which is not signed by the Premier as Chairman or even the whole committee, but by the Police Commander as a member of the committee, so long as it is supported by the fact of a meeting of the Peace and Good Order Committee, is an effective Declaration: *Park Wemin v Henry Guawi* [1987] PNGLR 346.

Part II – Peace and Good Order Committee

5. Peace and Good Order Committee.

(1) There is established in each province a Committee to be known as the Peace and Good Order Committee.

(2) Subject to Subsection (3), each Committee consists of –

(a) the Provincial Premier, who shall be the Chairman; and

(b) a person nominated by the Provincial Premier; and

(c) the officer for the time being in charge of the Police Force in the province or his nominee; and

(d) the member of the National Parliament representing the provincial constituency or his nominee; and

(e) the Departmental Head of the Department of the Province or his nominee; and

(f) a Senior District Magistrate resident in the province nominated by the Chief Magistrate.

(3) In the case of the National Capital District, the Committee consists of –

(a) the Lord Mayor of the City of Port Moresby, who shall be Chairman; and

(b) the officer for the time being in charge of the Police Force in the National Capital District; and

(c) the District Commissioner for the National Capital District or his nominee; and

(d) the Departmental Head of the Department of the Prime Minister or his nominee.

6. Deputy Chairman.

(1) The Deputy Chairman of a Committee shall be –

(a) in the case of a Committee under Section 5(2) – the person appointed under Section 5(2)(c); and

(b) in the case of the Committee under Section 5(3) – the person appointed under Section 5(3) (b).

(2) The Deputy Chairman shall have all the powers and functions of the Chairman during the absence or inability to act of the Chairman.

7. Meetings of Committees.

(1) A Committee shall meet at such times and places, as in the opinion of the Chairman, are necessary for the efficient conduct of its affairs.

(2) At a meeting of the Committee –

(a) a quorum –

(i) under Section 5(2) – is three; and

(ii) under Section 5(3) – is two; and

(b) the Chairman, or in his absence the Deputy Chairman, shall preside; and

(c) questions arising shall be decided by a majority of the votes of the members present and voting; and

(d) the person presiding has a deliberative and, in the event of an equality of votes on a matter, also a casting vote.

(3) A Committee shall cause minutes of its meetings to be kept.

(4) The exercise or the performance of any function of a Committee shall not be invalidated by reason only of a vacancy in the office of a member of the Committee.

(5) Subject to this Act, the procedures of a Committee are as determined by the Committee.

8. Powers, functions and duties of Committee.

(1) The primary function of a Committee is to keep in constant review the need to make or continue in effect declarations under Section 4 and to make, renew or revoke such declarations as the need arises.

(2) The Committee shall, from time to time, advise the government, both National and provincial, on what it considers to be the best use that can be made of available personnel, goods and services in areas the subject of declarations under Section 4 in order to achieve the objects of this Act and to protect life and property.

(3) As soon as practicable after a declaration or renewal of a declaration under Section 4 has been made, the Committee shall give a report of its actions and the reasons for its actions to the Minister and shall give to the Minister such further reports, and at such times, as he may require.

9. Considerations to be taken into account by a Committee.

(1) A Committee, when considering whether to make a declaration under Section 4 shall consider –

(a) whether there exists a serious dispute involving a group in the province; and

(b) where a dispute does exist –

(i) whether there is a likelihood of the dispute being settled by any lawful means; or

(ii) whether the dispute has resulted in, or may, in the immediate future, result in, a serious breach of the peace or a breakdown in law and order.

(2) When considering whether to renew a declaration under Section 4, a Committee shall consider whether-

(a) there exists a serious dispute involving a group in the province, and

(b) the dispute has resulted in, or may, in the immediate future, result in a serious breach of the peace or a breakdown in law and order; and

(c) any negotiations have been commenced between the groups which may result in a settlement of the dispute.

Part III – Inter-group Fighting

10. Preparing to fight.

(1) For the purposes of this Act, a gathering of five or more persons, any one of whom is armed with an offensive weapon, which –

(a) is taking part; or

(b) appears to be about to take part; or

(c) appears to be preparing to take part,

in a fight with any other group of persons or a member of that other group of persons, is an unlawful assembly.

(2) A person who takes part in an unlawful assembly referred to in Subsection (1) is guilty of an offence.

(3) For the purposes of Subsection (2), a person who, without reasonable excuse, the burden of proof of which rests upon him, is present at an unlawful assembly referred to in Subsection (1), shall be deemed to have taken part in that unlawful assembly.

Penalty: Imprisonment for a term not less than two years and not exceeding four years.

[Subs (3) insrt Act No 18, 1981 (*Inter-Group Fighting (Amendment) Act* 1981), s 2; Penalty provision am Act No 13, 1983 (*Inter-Group Fighting (Amendment) Act* 1983), s 1]

In its normal usage, the phrase "take part" would certainly connote some degree of active participation beyond mere presence in the assembly. To succeed on a prosecution under s 10(2), the state must prove beyond reasonable doubt some active participation by the defendant which associates the defendant with the assembly. Probably the mere carrying of a spear, shield or bow and arrow or the uttering of threatening words would be prima facie sufficient. Each case of course would depend on its own facts. It should not be forgotten that in attempting to establish such participation, the prosecutor would be entitled to rely on all the areas covered by s 7 of the *Criminal Code*. The existence of s 7 of the Code side by side with this section strengthens the view that, in order to prove a "taking part" in an unlawful assembly, the prosecution must prove some activity which amounts to aiding, abetting, counselling and so forth, others at the assembly to participate in such assembly. It may be that in some circumstances even feeding those gathered, for the purpose of sustaining them during the assembly, is sufficient to warrant the conviction. Mere presence at such a gathering is not itself sufficient to warrant conviction under s 10(2): *Wui-Wapi v Ludwick Kembu* [1980] PNGLR 7.

The word "gathering" refers to a coming together of people with a common interest, although not necessarily a mutual sympathy. Some may be at the gathering merely to observe, while others may be there to criticise openly. One must therefore take some notice of the object of a gathering in order to establish whether it indeed is an unlawful gathering within the meaning of the section, and whether those who are physically present may be said to be members of that gathering: *Wui-Wapi v Ludwick Kembu* [1980] PNGLR 7.

The government and the people face an increasing problem from tribal fighting in the country. The legislature has introduced special measures in an attempt to deal with the problem. A magistrate is in a special position to appreciate the particular problems of his or her area. That is generally recognised and it is especially pertinent in relation to offences committed under the *Inter-Group Fighting Act*. There is clearly a need by the courts to increase the deterrent aspect of sentence in this area: *Hen Kuru v Wass Kombra* (1981) N292(L).

Wilson J, in *John Tolna v Paul Ari* [1980] PNGLR 23, quoted Andrew J in an unreported 1979 case:

> "If the maximum penalty is to be reserved for the worst or most serious of cases there must be some enquiry as to how seriously any particular person was involved in the offence; whether, for example, he was a fight leader or played a lesser role. Further there needs to be some enquiry into the individual antecedents of each prisoner. Considerable care must be taken with such 'mass' cases."

See also *Porewa Wani v The State* (1979) SC 170 and *Agiru Aieni v Paul T Tohain* [1978] PNGLR 37, regarding "mere presence" at the scene of a crime.

See *John Tolna v Paul Ari* [1980] PNGLR 23, regarding sentencing of persons convicted under this section.

11. Taking part in inter-group fight.

(1) For the purposes of this Act, an inter-group fight is deemed to have taken place if any member of an unlawful assembly referred to in Section 10(1) assaults or attempts to assault or commences to fight with a member of another group of persons.

(2) A person who takes part in an unlawful assembly, referred to in Section 10(1) which is involved in an inter-group fight, is guilty of an offence.

Penalty: In relation to an inter-group fight in which a person is killed – a term of imprisonment not less than four years and not exceeding six years.

In relation to an inter-group fight in which no person is killed – a term of imprisonment not less than three years and not exceeding five years.

[Subs (2) penalty provision am Act No 18, 1981 (*Inter-Group Fighting (Amendment) Act* 1981) s 3; am Act No 13, 1983 (*Inter-Group Fighting (Amendment) Act* 1983), s 2]

(3) Subsection (2) shall not be construed as restricting the penalty to which a person may be subject under any other law for an offence arising out of or connected with an inter-group fight.

(4) For the purposes of subsection (2), a person who, without reasonable excuse, the burden of proof of which rests upon him is present at an unlawful assembly referred to in Section 10(1) which is involved in an inter-group fight, shall be deemed to have taken part in that unlawful assembly.

[Subs (4) insrt Act No 18, 1981 (*Inter-Group Fighting (Amendment) Act* 1981), s 3]

Section 11(3) of the *Inter-Group Fighting Act* 1977 provided that:

> "A person charged with an offence against this section is guilty of that offence unless he proves, to the satisfaction of the court, that he did not take part in the actual fighting."

This provision was declared invalid, by a majority of the Supreme Court in *Constitutional Reference No 3 of 1978* [1978] PNGLR 421, since it was in contravention of s 37(4)(a) of the *Constitution* (the presumption of innocence).

The Supreme Court found that the various provisions in s 11 were not severable, so the whole of the section was invalidated. A new s 11 was added by s 6 of the *Inter-Group Fighting (Amendment) Act* 1979 (No 25 of 1979).

12. Organizing, etc, an inter-group fight.

A person who plans, organizes or assists in the planning or organizing of an unlawful assembly referred to in Section 10(1) is guilty of an offence.

Penalty: Imprisonment for a term not less than two years and not exceeding four years.

[Penalty provision am Act No 18, 1981 (*Inter-Group Fighting (Amendment) Act* 1981) s 4; am Act No 13, 1983 (*Inter-Group Fighting (Amendment) Act* 1983), s 3]

13. Inciting, etc, person to fight.

A person who assists, aids, incites, encourages, urges or counsels any person to take part in an inter-group fight is guilty of an offence.

Penalty: Imprisonment for a term not less than two years and not exceeding four years.

[Penalty provision am Act No 18, 1981 (*Inter-Group Fighting (Amendment) Act* 1981), s 5; am Act No 13, 1983 (*Inter-Group Fighting (Amendment) Act* 1983), s 4]

Part IV – Group Punishment

14. Non-derogation of Part III.

This part is in addition to, and does not derogate, Part III.

15. Inquiry by Magistrate.

A Magistrate may, on his own initiative, and shall if requested to do so by any other Magistrate who has presided over proceedings arising from an inter-group fight, or by the Committee or an officer, conduct an inquiry into an inter-group fight to determine –

(a) the nature and size of the groups, and where appropriate, the names of the groups, involved in the inter-group fight; and

(b) the nature and details of the dispute or disputes which caused the inter-group fight; and

(c) the names of the leaders of the groups involved in the dispute or disputes; and

(d) whether the persons taking part in the fight were doing so on behalf of, and with the knowledge and approval of, a majority of the members of the group of which they are members; and

(e) the prevalence of fighting between the groups involved in the fight or between a group involved in the fight and any other group or groups; and

(f) whether any attempts have been made by any of the groups involved in the fight to settle the dispute by mediation, arbitration or other peaceful means; and

(g) whether one or more of the groups has refused to attend mediation or arbitration proceedings or any other meeting concerned with negotiating peaceful settlement of the dispute or disputes; and

(h) whether one or more of the groups has made unreasonable demands for payment of compensation leading to delays in negotiations; and

(i) whether one or more of the groups has made threats of violence to any person or threats of damage to the property of any person in support of its claims for payment of compensation; and

(j) where a dispute has been settled subject to the payment of compensation or the making of restitution, or both – whether the group or groups responsible for the payment of compensation or the making restitution, or both, has or have refused or failed within a reasonable time, to pay that compensation or make the restitution, as the case may be.

[S 15 am Act No 18, 1981 (*Inter-Group Fighting (Amendment) Act* 1981), s 6]

16. Notice to show cause why penalty should not be imposed.

Where a Magistrate after conducting an inquiry under Section 15 is of the opinion that in all the circumstances the actions of the group may be such that a penalty should be imposed on its leaders for the group's part in the inter-group fight in respect of which the inquiry was held, the Magistrate shall by notice, either oral or written, served personally on those persons who are, in his opinion, leaders of the group, by an officer or a person appointed by the court for the purpose, call on those leaders to show cause, within the period specified in the notice, why a penalty should not be imposed on them on behalf of the group.

[S 16 am Act No 18, 1981 (*Inter-Group Fighting (Amendment) Act* 1981), s 7]

17. Imposition of penalty.

(1) Where, in the opinion of the Magistrate, the leaders of a group on whom a notice to show cause has been served, under Section 16, have failed to show cause or adequate cause why a penalty should not be imposed on them or any of them, those leaders, or such of them who have not shown cause or adequate cause, shall jointly and severally be liable, on behalf of the group, to a penalty of a fine not exceeding K20,000.00.

(2) In determining the penalty to be imposed under Subsection (1), the Magistrate shall, in addition to any other matter that he is bound to consider, take into account –

(a) whether the group has previously been involved in inter-group fighting; and

(b) the size of the group; and

(c) the wealth of the group; and

(d) the seriousness of the fight in which its members were involved; and

(e) the likelihood of a recurrence of inter-group fighting involving the group; and

(f) the apportionment of blame for the starting of the fight; and

(g) the punishment that has already been imposed on individual members of the group.

(3) A person shall not be liable to a penalty under this section if –

(a) at the time that the relevant inter-group fight took place he was not present in the area occupied by the group or where the fight took place; or

(b) he satisfies the Magistrate that he did everything reasonably within his power to prevent the inter-group fight taking place.

(4) The Magistrate referred to in Subsection (1) shall not be the same Magistrate who conducted an inquiry under Section 15 into the inter-group fight, the group's part in which is the subject of the opinion under Subsection (1).

[Subs (4) insrt Act No 18, 1981 (*Inter-Group Fighting (Amendment) Act* 1981), s 8]

18. Magistrate may order penalty to he paid in goods.

(1) Where, in the opinion of the Magistrate –

(a) the group on whose leaders he intends to impose a penalty is not able to pay the penalty in cash; or

(b) it would act as a greater deterrent to involvement by the group in future inter-group fighting,

the Magistrate may, instead of ordering the payment of a penalty in cash, order that the penalty be paid in prescribed goods.

(2) Where no goods have been prescribed under Section 19 the Magistrate may, after due inquiry, determine the goods to be paid and, at the same time, shall determine a value for each unit of the goods.

(3) A penalty payable in prescribed goods shall not exceed in value the sum of K20,000.00.

(4) Goods received by or on behalf of the State in satisfaction of a penalty under Section 17 are forfeited to the State.

19. Regulation may prescribe goods and value of goods.

(1) A regulation may prescribe goods and the value of goods, for the purposes of Section 18.

(2) The regulation referred to in Subsection (1) may be expressed to apply in respect of the whole of the country or a part of the country.

20. Non-payment of group penalty an offence.

(1) The non-payment of a penalty imposed under Section 17 within three months after the date on which it was imposed is an offence.

Penalty: Any one or more of the persons liable for the penalty may be imprisoned for a period not exceeding six months.

(2) Where at any time after a person has been imprisoned for an offence under Subsection (1) and before his release, the penalty is paid in full or in part, any person may apply to a Magistrate to have the sentence of imprisonment reviewed.

(3) Where an application for a review is made to a Magistrate under Subsection (2), the Magistrate –

(a) shall, where the penalty has been paid in full, cancel the warrant of imprisonment and direct that any person being held in custody for an offence under Subsection (1) in respect of that penalty be released; and

(b) may, in any other case, reduce the term of imprisonment imposed on any person under the sentence being reviewed by such amount as, in his opinion, is proportional to the amount of the penalty paid, and shall amend the sentence of imprisonment accordingly.

[S 20 subst Act No 18, 1981 (*Inter-Group Fighting (Amendment) Act* 1981), s 9]

Part V – Miscellaneous

21. Records of peace-making ceremonies to be kept.

(1) Where a ceremony is held by two or more groups jointly or by one group for one or more other groups for the purpose of –

(a) settling or attempting to settle a dispute; or

(b) recognizing the settlement of a dispute; or

(c) paying compensation for the death of or injury to any person or for damage to any property,

the leaders of the group or groups involved in the ceremony shall cause the details of the ceremony to be given to a District Officer within one month after the ceremony for recording in the records of the District Office for the district in which the group or groups, or any of them, reside.

(2) Where the details of a ceremony referred to in Subsection (1) are not given to a District Officer within one month after the ceremony, each of the leaders of the group or groups involved in the ceremony is guilty of an offence.

Penalty: A fine not exceeding K50.00.

22. Powers of Magistrate on inquiry.

In conducting an inquiry under Section 15 a Magistrate has all the powers of a District Court, and, in addition –

(a) is not bound by any rule of law, evidence, practice or procedure other than this Act; and

(b) may call and examine witnesses; and

(c) may otherwise inform himself on the matter before him in such manner as he thinks fit; and

(d) may appoint such number of assessors to sit with and advise him as he considers necessary.

23. Proceedings to be brought in District Court only.

(1) Proceedings under this Act shall be brought in and dealt with by a District Court and shall not be –

(a) brought in or transferred to a Local Court; or

(b) brought in a Village Court;

(2) The Judicial and Legal Services Commission may, by notice in the National Gazette, declare a person who is not a District Court Magistrate to be a Magistrate for the purposes of this Act and a person while so appointed shall be deemed to be and to have all the powers of a District Court Magistrate for and in relation to those purposes.

24. Jurisdiction of District Court.

A District Court has jurisdiction in relation to all offences and all proceedings under this Act and where but for this section, a District Court would not have jurisdiction in relation to any offence specified in this Act, whether as to penalty or otherwise, it shall be deemed to have jurisdiction.

25. Regulations.

The Head of State, acting on advice, may make Regulations, not inconsistent with this Act, prescribing all matters that by this Act are required or permitted to be prescribed, or are necessary or convenient to be prescribed, for carrying out or giving effect to this Act.

Criminal Law (Compensation) Act 1991

On 17 September, 1992, the *Criminal Law (Compensation) Act* 1991 came into force.

Kapi DCJ said in *The State v Peter Kose Wena* [1993] PNGLR 168 at 169-170:

> "In every case where the court is considering sentence, it must have regard to the terms of this Act, in addition to any other punishment that may be imposed under any other law (s 2(1)) ... Prior to this Act, customary compensation was considered to be a relevant factor in sentence (s 4(e) of the *Customs Recognition Act* Ch 19). The practical result of this is that the court may increase or decrease sentence on account of custom within the range of sentence prescribed by law ... This allowed the courts to take into account customary compensation wherever it was paid or promised to be paid. However, the law did not authorise the courts to order customary compensation as a form of punishment ... [The *Criminal Law (Compensation) Act* 1991] [authorises] the courts to make a compensation order as a form of penalty against the offender. The consideration of customary compensation is one of the factors upon which a court may make the compensation order (see s 3(1)(d)). Compensation may be ordered in the form of cash, goods, services or any other kind or method of compensation which the court considers appropriate (see s 5)."

Regarding the means assessment report, Kapi DCJ stated in *The State v Peter Kose Wena* [1993] PNGLR 168 at 171:

> "It is clear ... that a means assessment report contains relevant information applicable to what I have called the primary decision (whether or not a compensation order should be made) and the secondary decision (the actual order

as to the amount, form, nature, method of payment, the period of payment, etc). The means assessment report is relevant to both stages (s 3(1)). A single report would cover both stages of the decision."

In *The State v Philip Susuve Raipa* [1994] PNGLR 458 at 462, Brown J said:

"Where the maximum award of compensation is awarded, Courts should militate against a severe sentence otherwise appropriate in the circumstances. This is the principle underlying s 2 of the Act, which equates an award of compensation with a punishment".

Brown J said further in that case (at 460):

"I am satisfied, if damages in a civil suit were to be assessed, the extent of his injuries would call for an award in excess of the K5,000 provided for under the *Criminal Law (Compensation) Act* 1991, even before any assessment for continuing disabilities or loss of enjoyment of life was taken into account. In other words, compensation for his injuries and disabilities could be expected to far exceed the maximum available to me to award under the Act".

Consequently, in that case the maximum of K5,000 was awarded.

Where the victim of the crime is a small child, including crimes of a sexual nature, compensation under the Act is not appropriate. However, where substantial compensation is demanded by the victim child's relatives and paid by the accused prior to trial, it may be taken into account as a mitigating factor on sentence: *The State v William Muma* [1995] PNGLR 161.

CRIMINAL LAW (COMPENSATION) ACT 1991

No 26 of 1991

Being an Act to provide for the making of compensation orders in criminal cases, and for related purposes,

MADE by the National Parliament to come into operation in accordance with a notice in the National Gazette by the Head of State, acting with, and in accordance with, the advice of the Minister.

1. Interpretation.

In this Act, unless the contrary intention appears -

"Chief Probation Officer" means the person appointed as such under the *Probation Act* (Chapter 381), or his delegate for the purposes of this Act;

"compensation order" means an order for compensation made under Section 5;

"court" means the National Court or a District Court;

"means assessment report" means a report under Section 4;

"offender" means a person convicted of an offence;

"relative" means father, mother, brother or sister.

2. Compensation as punishment.

(1) Notwithstanding that payment of compensation is not specified as a punishment for an offence, a court may, in addition to any other punishments imposed, order an offender to pay compensation in accordance with this Act.

(2) When a court is considering the punishment or punishments to be imposed for an offence, it shall also consider whether in the circumstances of the case, compensation should be ordered.

The word "shall" in this section means that the court, in every criminal case, must consider whether compensation should be ordered: *The State v Peter Kose Wena* [1993] PNGLR 168.

3. Factors to be considered in making compensation orders.

(1) Where a court is deciding whether to make an order of compensation under Section 2, or is deciding upon the compensation to be ordered under Section 5, it shall take into account the following factors:-

(a) the nature and seriousness of the offence;

(b) the degree and nature of any personal injury or damage to property suffered by any person as a result of the commission of the offence;

(c) any factors regarding the commission of the offence or the offender's attitude which may be considered in mitigation or aggravation of the punishment;

(d) any relevant custom regarding compensation, including but not limited to -

(i) any custom regarding the nature, the amount, the method of payment and the appropriate person or persons to be paid the compensation; and

(ii) any custom which relates the amount of compensation to the age or life expectancy of the person suffering injury or loss;

(e) the information provided in the means assessment report, including any recommendations made by the Chief Probation Officer in the means assessment report;

(f) any other relevant matter.

(2) In considering a matter under this section, a court is not bound to apply the technical rules of evidence but may act on such information as is available to it.

The primary decision the court needs to make is "whether in the circumstances of this case, a compensation order should be ordered": *The State v Peter Kose Wena* [1993] PNGLR 168. See also *The State v Peter Barnes & Douglas Ume* (1993) N344 (Kapi DCJ).

One of the factors that should be taken into account under s 3(1) of the Act is the degree and nature of any personal injury or damage to property suffered by any person as a result of the commission of the offence. If no damage or injury is suffered as a result of the commission of the offence, a compensation order is not appropriate: *The State v Peter Barnes & Douglas Ume* (1993) N1190. See also s 623A *Criminal Code* on restitution of property.

4. Means assessment report.

(1) Where a court considers that an order for compensation should be made, it shall -

(a) request the Chief Probation Officer to furnish to the court a means assessment report in respect of the offender; and

(b) order the offender to report to the Chief Probation Officer in order to determine the person's means and financial circumstances.

(2) Upon receiving a request under Subsection (1), the Chief Probation Officer shall -

(a) interview the offender and his immediate relatives and report to the court on the means and financial circumstances of the offender; or

(b) advise the court that it is not practicable for him to furnish the report.

(3) A means assessment report may include a recommendation by the Chief Probation Officer as to the amount, nature and method of payment of the compensation to be ordered and any other matters in relation to the order which he considers relevant.

(4) Where the Chief Probation Officer advises the court that it is not practicable for him to furnish a means assessment report, the court may proceed under this Act without one.

5. Compensation orders.

(1) Upon receipt of the means assessment report or the Chief Probation Officer's advice under Section 4(2), the court may, after taking into account the factors specified in Section 3 -

(a) order the offender to pay, within such period and in such manner as the court determines, compensation to a person or group of persons specified in the order; and

(b) direct the Chief Probation Officer to supervise compliance with the compensation order.

(2) Subject to Subsection (3), compensation may be ordered in the form of cash, goods, services or any other kind or method of compensation which the court considers appropriate.

(3) No compensation ordered under this Act -

(a) shall include the use or payment of alcohol; and

(b) whether in the form of cash, goods, services or any other kind or method of compensation shall exceed in value K5,000.00,

and the value of any form of compensation other than cash shall be as determined by the court.

Where the accused have offered to pay compensation, it is a requirement of the *Criminal Law (Compensation) Act* that this be taken into account. Where co-accused have offered to make these payments as a group, the total amount is to be divided into equal amounts between the prisoners to determine if each amount falls within the maximum amount of K5,000.00 prescribed by s 5 of the Act. The maximum default penalty prescribed by the Act for value of compensation exceeding K3,000.00 is six months imprisonment: *The State v Angaun Kakas* [1994] PNGLR 20 (Injia AJ).

Injia J stated in *The State v Margaret John (No 1)* [1995] PNGLR 446:

> "Generally speaking, the welfare of a child born in prison is not a relevant consideration affecting the exercise of sentencing discretion of the mother. A compensation order cannot be made against the offender's spouse, relatives, tribal group or village. Nevertheless, where the prisoner who is the second wife of the husband, killed the deceased who is the third de facto wife of the husband and where the husband's assault on the prisoner led to the prisoner killing the deceased, it is in the interest of justice that a means assessment report under the *Criminal Law (Compensation) Act* 1991 should be done on the prisoner's husband as to his liability under local custom to pay compensation to the deceased's relatives on behalf of the prisoner and his ability to pay such compensation demanded by the victim's relatives or ordered by the court."

The *Criminal Justice (Sentences) Act* 1986 was made by the National Parliament on 21 March 1986.

Section 3(2) of the *Criminal Justice (Sentences) Act* 1986 "does not fetter the court's discretion or oblige the court to take cognisance of people who were allowed bail and those who did not exercise this right". Time spent voluntarily in custody constitutes a deprivation of liberty and accordingly may be taken into account in determining sentence: *Public Prosecutor v Posopon Salaiau* [1994] PNGLR 53 (Doherty J).

Chapter 6

EVIDENCE

General evidentiary matters

Evidence of identification

The dangers of identification evidence are well recognised in common law countries. In practice, the judge is required to give the jury a warning, the nature of which must depend upon the circumstances of the case before the court. There is no rule of law that the evidence of one witness as to identification is insufficient, nor is there any rule of law that there must be a police parade for the purposes of identification, nor is there any rule of law that in every case a warning must be given. "Where the identification of a single witness is relied upon, the jury should be informed that mistakes in the past [have] occurred in regard to identification, thereby occasioning a miscarriage of justice." Matters to be taken into account in assessing the accuracy of the witness are:

> "what opportunities the person identifying had to form a judgment of the identity of the person who committed the crime ... the position of the parties ... the lighting, the opportunities to form a judgment, and generally the circumstances in which the identifying witness formed his judgement as to identification."[152]

The Supreme Court considered *John Beng v The State* [1977] PNGLR 115 in *Biwa Geta v The State* [1988-1989] PNGLR 153. The majority held that, while it may be helpful for a trial judge in his or her reasons for judgment to advert to the legal principles involved in the dangers inherent in, for example, identification evidence, failure to do so will not of itself constitute an error of law if a critical examination of the evidence is given which demonstrates the adherence to those principles.

Where evidence of identification is relevant, the court should be mindful of all the inherent dangers and the need for caution before convicting on the correctness of identification. A mistaken witness could be a convincing one: *The State v Kobale Rau* (1997) N1509.

Where identification evidence points to two different persons, a trial judge must show clearly why he or she has accepted one and not the other. Existence of other evidence which may point to an accused's involvement in a crime does not lessen

[152] *The State v John Beng* [1976] PNGLR 481, upheld on appeal in *John Beng v The State* [1977] PNGLR 115.

the need to warn of inherent dangers of identification: *Gibson Gunure Ohizave v The State* (1998) SC 595.

Recognition may be more reliable than identification of a stranger. However, even when the witness is purporting to recognise someone whom he or she knows, the jury should be reminded that mistakes in recognition of close relatives and friends are sometimes made. All these matters go to the quality of the identification evidence. When the quality is good, the jury can be safely left to assess the value of the identifying evidence even though there is no other evidence to support. When the quality of the identifying evidence is poor, such as a fleeting glance or a longer observation made in difficult conditions, the judge should then withdraw the case from the jury and direct an acquittal unless there is other evidence which goes to support the correctness of the identification: *John Beng v The State* [1977] PNGLR 115, followed in *The State v Natuai Tibone and Thomas Some* (1982) N361(M).

The State v Yakoto Imbuni (1997) N1558 followed *John Beng v The State*. Three eyewitnesses gave evidence that they saw the incident involving the killing of three people, which lasted about 10 to 15 minutes. The attack took place in broad daylight and the attackers did not cover their faces. In the circumstances, Akuram J held that he could safely say that the witnesses' identification was good and they could be believed. It was irrelevant that the witnesses were unable to name the accused in their witness statements to the police.

On the issue of identification of suspects by community leaders, Injia J held in *The State v Buka Pepekon* (19 May 1995, unnumbered):

> "Speaking of people in the area of the three accused, it is true that there was a lot of investigation carried out by the village people to identify those responsible. It was not an easy task. But through a painstaking process which took some time, they have singled out these three accused ... Once the accused are singled out through this rigorous process in the village and reported to the police or apprehended and delivered to the police, the village people would be pretty sure of the accused's involvement in the crime. Therefore, the Court should not treat these accused lightly as some suspects brought to Court on mere conjecture. Once there is sufficient evidence before the village people implicating the suspects, their involvement in the crime is readily inferred as a matter of course. The onus then shifts to the accused to show reasonable cause why that should not be so. If the accused's defence is one of alibi, he should give evidence of a good alibi and where necessary, supported by alibi witnesses. That is the practice in the village and I see no reason why this Court should not give due weight to this method of screening the evidence against the accused."

Similarly, in *The State v Anis Noki* [1993] PNGLR 426, Woods J held at 427 that the coming forward of the leaders and people of the community to hand over the suspects must be duly recognised. Of course, it should be seen in and with the evidence. There must be other evidence. It becomes a matter of evidence which must be admissible. Again, the communal nature of Papua New Guinea society makes one realise that there can be very few secrets. When something happens everyone soon knows. There are no strangers in the night. So, if village leaders have come forward with their own knowledge and "made" people surrender, there must be some weight in that.

The State v Yakoto Imbuni (1997) N1558 followed *The State v Buka Pepekon* and *The State v Anis Noki*. Akuram J stated that:

"once a leader and villagers hand in a suspect, that in itself be regarded as a matter of course or seen as:

(a) An identification of the accused by his own clansmen;

(b) Supported by credible and admissible evidence.

And that the following factors must be considered in the light of (a & b) above that:

(i) Leaders to give evidence and reason why those suspects arrested may not be the ones responsible on balance of probabilities;

(ii) The recognition of the relevance and knowledge of leaders and community as paramount in their discharge of Criminal justice; and

That the accused then be called upon to prove his innocence on the balance of probability except on matters which are peculiarly within his own knowledge which he needs to prove beyond reasonable doubt."

Prentice J said in *Papalamnan v Nuakona* (1973) N771:

"Where evidence of identity is given by a witness whose previous knowledge has not made him familiar with the appearance of the accused and where he has been shown the accused alone as a suspect and has on that occasion first identified him, the conviction of the accused is not safe unless his identity is further proved by other evidence."

Reliance on personal identification will depend upon, inter alia:

(a) the impression left by the eyewitness as to his or her reliability and accuracy;

(b) the existence of a motive for giving false testimony as to the identity of the offender(s);

(c) the circumstances in which the person to be identified has been observed;

(d) the circumstances in which the eyewitness finds himself or herself when making the observation;

(e) the existence or otherwise of the evidence of other witnesses confirming or contradicting the evidence of the original eyewitness;

(f) the existence or otherwise of other evidence, direct or circumstantial, of facts or circumstances independently proved.[153]

Voice evidence is admissible to prove identification of the accused where:

(a) the voice is known by the witness and recognised by the witness; and

(b) the voice is not previously known to the witness but has such distinctive features that it leaves a clear mental impression in the mind of the witness enabling him or her to draw the conclusion on hearing it later that it was the same voice.[154]

Evidence of fingerprints or palm prints alone is sufficient evidence of identity to support a conviction beyond reasonable doubt: *R v Koito-Gaocatai* [1967-1968] PNGLR 217.

It is open to a judge sitting alone upon the whole of the evidence from which an inference can be drawn, beyond reasonable doubt, to act upon fingerprint evidence

---

[153] *R v Uno Tam* (1973) N766.

[154] *The State v Daniel* [1988-1989] PNGLR 580.

as connecting the accused with the crime, although such fingerprint evidence is the sole evidence: *R v Koito-Gaocatai* [1967-1968] PNGLR 217.

Kidu CJ stated in *The State v Thomas Some* (1982) N366(M):

> "An identification parade must be fair to suspects. A witness who is asked to identify suspects in such a parade should never be told that *the* suspect (or suspects) is in the parade. A witness should merely be asked to view such a parade to see if he or she recognises anybody. All those in the line-up should be of the same age, height and roughly the same physical description - it would be a farce if the suspect clearly stood out. Where it is alleged that the suspect may be identified by his voice, what he/she said to the witness should be repeated in the language he/she is alleged to have used."

Circumstantial evidence

The principle involving circumstantial evidence in *Barca v The Queen* (1976) 50 ALJR 108 at 117, and in *McGreevey v DPP* [1973] 1 WLR 276, are applicable and appropriate to the circumstances of Papua New Guinea: *John Peng v The State* [1982] PNGLR 331 (Pratt J, with Kidu CJ agreeing). See also *The State v Tom Morris* [1981] PNGLR 493, in which Miles J held *Barca v The Queen* is applicable in Papua New Guinea.

> "When the case against an accused person rests substantially upon circumstantial evidence the jury cannot return a verdict of guilty unless the circumstances are 'such as to be inconsistent with any reasonable hypothesis other than the guilt of the accused': *Peacock v The King* (1911) 13 CLR 619, 634. To enable a jury to he satisfied beyond reasonable doubt of the guilt of the accused it is necessary not only that his guilt should be a rational inference but that it should be 'the only rational inference that the circumstances would enable them to draw': *Plomp v The Queen* (1963) 110 CLR 234, 252. See also *Thomas v The Queen* (1960) 102 CLR 584, 605-606. However, 'an inference to be reasonable must rest upon something more than mere conjecture. The bare possibility of innocence should not prevent a jury from finding the prisoner guilty, if the inference of guilt is the only inference open to reasonable men upon a consideration of all the facts in evidence': *Peacock v The King,* 661. These principles are well settled in Australia."[155]

Where the evidence in a criminal case is wholly circumstantial, the court must acquit unless the facts proved in evidence are inconsistent with any reasonable hypothesis other than the guilt of the accused: *Paulus Pawa v The State* [1981] PNGLR 498 (Kearney DCJ) (followed in *The State v Jupui Kapera* (1986) N567; *The State v Marianno Wani Simon & Alan Oa Koroka* (1987) N600; *The State v Michael Gende* (1997) N1678; *Garitau Bonu and Rosanna Bonu v The State* (1997) SC 528; *The State v John Wanjil* (1997) N1516).

In *The State v Marianno Wani Simon and Alan Da Koroka* (1987) N600 the accused were charged with the murder.

> "The issue of the accused's false denials and false statements needs to be addressed. Great care must be taken in a case such as this concerning the use to be made of false statements. As a general proposition, it must be accepted that a false denial does not prove guilt. For good reason, it has been said that people

[155] *The State v Tom Morris* [1981] PNGLR 493.

confronted with allegations of wrong doing may have other reasons not to tell the truth, apart from hiding their guilt."

Documentary evidence

No doubt where it is shown in any particular case that the interests of justice require that such a statement should be produced to the defence, the court may well order its production as was done in *R v Hall* (1959) 43 Cr App R 29. See also *R v Power* [1940-1941] St R Qld 111 and *Archbold* (37th ed), para 1374. There is no practice prevailing in the criminal procedure of this court, nor is it suggested that any such practice exists in Australia or England, for general discovery to be granted to an accused person either before or at the trial. The procedure of mutual discovery has no application to criminal proceedings: *R v Vollert* [1974] PNGLR 84.

Where an accused person is shown a document and it is sufficiently identified or is acknowledged, that document becomes part of the contents of the record of interview: *Joshua Yaip Avini and Plaridel Nony Acosta v The State* (1997) SC 523.

Hearsay evidence

It was held in *The State v Willie Orki Briza* [1976] PNGLR 517, that where the spontaneity of screamed remarks discounted the possibility of concoction of fabrication, the remarks, while hearsay, were admissible as part of the *res gestae*. The words are admissible not only as to the fact of their having been said, but as to the truth of the facts they purport to describe. The case of *R v Ratten* [1972] AC 378 was applied. *The State v Willie Orki Briza* was followed in *The State v Michael Gende* (1997) N1678.

In *The State v Peter Raima* [1993] PNGLR 230 the state sought to tender the statement made to police by a principal witness in the trial. The statement was annexed to an affidavit sworn by the witness who was unwilling to give evidence in the court through fear. It was held that the witness' fear was reasonable. Following Lord Wilberforce in *R v Ratten* [1972] AC 378 at 387:

> "The mere fact that evidence of a witness includes evidence as to words spoken by another person who is not called, is no objection to its admissibility. Words spoken are facts just as much as any other action by a human being. If the speaking of the words is a relevant fact, a witness may give evidence that they were spoken. A question of hearsay only arises when the words spoken are relied on 'testimonially', ie as establishing some fact narrated by the words."

The conversation with the accused recounted in the witness' statement was relevant only to the state of mind of the accused, in relation to the possible defence of duress raised by the accused. It was not admissible as proof of the facts stated in the conversation. The court refused to follow *The State v Warum* [1988-1989] PNGLR 327.

Similar fact evidence

In the application of the general principles of relevance, it is plain that the degree of resemblance and connection between the fact in issue and the fact sought to be adduced in evidence must be closely examined. Mere general resemblance is insufficient: *Martin v Osborne* (1936) 55 CLR 367. In *R v Jamieson* (1972) N698 the evidence of similar fact went to establish a fraudulent intent as required and to rebut defences of innocent dealing, inadvertence, mistake or mishap, and were admissible. The probative value of the facts proffered was potentially high and the evidence substantial: Followed *Harris v DPP* (1952) AC 703.

In *The State v Camilus Siwi Kindagl* (1990) N846, the State Prosecutor sought to call evidence through an inmate from the Baisu Corrective Institution. Such evidence would relate the terms of a conversation prior in time to this offence of attempted murder, whereby one of the accused disclosed a grievance against the Catholic Mission in general and the Brothers in particular. One of the Brothers was injured in a subsequent attack involving three persons, one of whom was alleged to be the accused. Identification was in issue. Brown J held:

1. Evidence of a conversation had by the accused prior in time to the alleged offence was allowed on the basis of "similar facts".
2. Such evidence was admissible to rebut the accused's denials, in his record of interview, of malicious intent towards the victim.
3. Probative value of such evidence in relation to victim's testimony, and hence indirectly on the question of identification, was sufficient to justify reception.
4. Circumstances of conversation showing bad character do not of themselves prevent acceptance of such evidence where such conversation is of rational probative value.

Evidence of facts similar to a fact in issue is not, in general, admissible to prove either the occurrence of the fact in issue or the identity of its author. Such evidence must be evidence of the acts of the accused; evidence of acts of a person other than the accused does not fall within the exclusion. Accordingly, in *The State v Daniel* [1988-1989] PNGLR 580, on a charge of robbery, evidence of a witness as to a previous aborted robbery attempt was admissible as part of the continuing plan and intent.

Expert evidence

It is up to the court to decide whether or not to accept the expert evidence of a medical doctor and attach such weight as it thinks fit to the medical evidence: *The State v Paul Taupin; The State v Jim Kandamain* (1995) N1323.

No case submission

When a "no case submission" is made, the question that the court must decide is not whether on the evidence as it stands the defendant ought to be convicted, but whether on the evidence as it stands an accused could lawfully be convicted: *The State v Paul Kundi Rape* [1976] PNGLR 96. This case was adopted in *The State v Roka Pep (No 2)* [1983] PNGLR 287 and *The State v John Wanjil* (1997) N1516.

The test is whether the evidence so far adduced by the state supports essential elements of the offence. The question of proof beyond reasonable doubt does not come into play. That question is decided ultimately at the end of all the evidence both for the state and defence: *The State v John Wanjil* (1997) N1516 (Lenalia AJ), following *Zanetti v Hill* (1962) 108 CLR 438, where Kitto J said at 442:

> "The question whether there is a case to answer, arising as it does at the end of the prosecution's evidence in Chief, is simply the question of law whether the defendant could lawfully be convicted on the evidence as it stands – whether that is to say, there is with respect to every element of the offence some evidence

which, if accepted, would either prove the element directly or enable its existence to be inferred. That is a question to be carefully distinguished from the question of fact for ultimate decision, namely whether every element of the offence is established to the satisfaction of the tribunal of fact beyond a reasonable doubt."

The procedure for no case submissions does not need to be adopted in every case, and failure to adopt this procedure cannot invalidate subsequent proceedings: *Joshua Yaip Avini and Plaridel Nony Acosta v The State* (1997) SC 523.

Corroboration in sexual offence cases

On the need for corroboration in sexual offence cases, see s 347 of the *Criminal Code*.

Accused may stand trial other than from the dock

It is a matter of long-standing practice that an accused person stands trial from the dock. However, where an accused is defended by counsel and wishes to sit in court near his or her counsel, the accused is entitled to do so. It is not a matter of indulgence by the court. If it is not a matter of indulgence, then requests to sit near counsel should now be very freely granted in the interests of dispensing justice to the individual: *The State v Allan Woila* [1978] PNGLR 99.

See the *Constitution*, ss 22, 37, 57 and 158(2).

Bias

It was held in *Lemu Maribui v Croft* (1968) N496 that where the magistrate had a strong interest in assisting and advising the respondent, no matter how well intentioned and perhaps soundly based was the magistrate's advice to the respondent, it showed he was biased in her favour. The matter was remitted for hearing before another magistrate.

Wrongly admitted evidence does not necessarily mean that a conviction will be set aside if there is sufficient other evidence and it is reasonably probable that the evidence wrongly admitted did not influence the decision. In *Anide v Denehy* [1973] PNGLR 215, where the informant was the Acting District Commissioner and the magistrate was the Deputy District Commissioner, a suspicion may have been engendered that the magistrate might not bring to the resolution of the questions arising before him a fair and unprejudiced mind. Bias was therefore made out.

Alibis

The *Criminal Practice Rules* 1987, O 4, r 4, provides that an accused shall not, without leave of the court, adduce evidence of an alibi unless notice in respect of the prescribed matters is first given to the prosecution within specified time. On an application by an accused to adduce evidence of an alibi without notice and following the close of the state case on an indictment for wilful murder, it was held:

"The discretion of the court under O 4, r 4, of the *Criminal Practice Rules,* is to be exercised judicially. The mere fact that the necessary information was not given within the prescribed period does not, of itself, as a general rule, justify the court in refusing permission for the evidence to be called. *R v Sullivani* [1970] 2 All ER 681, adopted and applied.

Matters relevant to the exercise of the discretion include:

(a) whether the exercise of the discretion would accord favourably with the accused's constitutional rights under s 37(3) and s 37(4)(f) of the *Constitution,* to give evidence, to call witnesses and to a fair hearing;

(b) whether, if the discretion is exercised, the prejudice to the accused would outweigh the prejudice to the public interest in seeing offenders brought to justice.

In the circumstances, leave should be granted to the accused to adduce evidence of an alibi, subject to the service of notice out of time, and allowing the prosecution such adjournment as was appropriate in order to enable the police to investigate the alibi in accordance with O 4, r 4 to 8, of the *Criminal Practice Rules*: *The State v Robert Wer* [1989] PNGLR 444 (Brunton AJ)."

In *The State v Bernard Vargi* [1991] PNGLR 54, following charges of armed robbery and unlawful use of a motor car, a notice of alibi was provided to the State Prosecutor pursuant to the *Criminal Practice Rules* 1987, O 4, Div 2. No alibi evidence was led on trial, during which the accused made, in evidence, two obviously false statements. It was held that because a notice of alibi is a document passing between the accused's lawyer and the prosecutor and does not become evidence unless tendered, failure to lead evidence in accordance with such notice does not entitle a trial judge to ask questions thereon. In the absence of evidence in chief or cross-examination on a topic, a judge should not actively seek evidence thereon: *The State v Bernard Vargi* [1991] PNGLR 54 (Ellis J).

Interim matters of procedure

There is a statutory provision for tender of written statements by consent of counsel, but this is subject to consent of the court.

The duty of the court is to ensure that:

(a) the best evidence available is brought before it; and

(b) it hears and assesses that evidence before making a decision.

Statements may be tendered where there is no doubt or challenge to their facts.

While the court must maintain impartiality and not take upon itself the role of prosecutor or defender, it has an inherent power and a duty to ensure evidence is brought and presented before making any decision of facts: *The State v John Bill White (No 1): Ruling on an Interim Matter of Procedure* [1996] PNGLR 262.

Miscellaneous evidentiary matters

Can witnesses testify if they are present in court and hear evidence during the trial?

A trial judge should not expressly or by tacit implication prevent or hinder a witness from testifying simply because the witness was present in court and heard the evidence during the trial. The evidence the witness gives is a matter of weight to be assessed at the end of all the evidence.

In *Bakeri Pen v The State* (1997) SC 514, where the trial judge indicated to a witness, before she gave evidence, that the court would give very little weight to her evidence because she was present in the court, and where this influenced the defence counsel not to call the witness, this amounted to the court, by tacit implication, preventing or hindering the witness from giving evidence. This was a fundamental procedural error which vitiated the trial, and for which a new trial was ordered.

Rebuttal evidence and s 8 of the Supreme Court Act

The other party may call rebuttal evidence in answer to additional evidence given under s 8 of the *Supreme Court Act*: *Ted Abiari v The State (No 2)* [1990] PNGLR 432.

Child witness not told of consequences of telling lies in court

In *Beraro v The State* [1988] PNGLR 562 it was held that where the child understood that it was not good to tell lies, but was not asked about, or told, that he could be punished if he told lies it court, the trial judge should have ruled the witness incompetent to give evidence.

Confession by accused sufficient to support a conviction

In *The State v Malepo (No 2)* [1996] PNGLR 252 the confession of the accused was the only evidence available. It was held that, in the circumstances, this was sufficient to support a conviction.

EVIDENCE ACT

Chapter No 48

Part III - Evidence

Division 1 - General Rules

9. Witness interested or convicted of offence.

A person shall not be excused from giving evidence in any legal proceedings on the ground that -

(a) he has or may have an interest in the matter in question; or

(b) he has or may have an interest in the result of the proceedings; or

(c) he has previously been convicted of any offence.

10. Persons present without subpoena.

Where a person is present at any legal proceedings in which he might have been compellable to give evidence and to produce documents by virtue of a subpoena or other summons or order duly issued and served for the purpose, he is compellable to give evidence and to produce documents then in his possession and power in the same manner, and in case of refusal is subject to the same penalties and liabilities, as if he had been duly subpoenaed or summoned for the purpose.

12. Accused as witness.

A person charged with an offence is a competent but not a compellable witness for himself in any legal proceedings in connexion with the offence with which he is charged.

Kearney DCJ said in *Paulus Pawa v The State* [1981] PNGLR 498:

> "No accused person may be compelled to testify. He may choose not to do so. In that event the court may well be left with an incomplete picture. In such circumstances the court may draw inferences which properly flow from the evidence, and reach its conclusions thereon, without being deterred from so doing by the incomplete state of the evidence, or by speculation as to what the accused might have said had he testified. See *R v Sharmpal Singh* [1962] AC 188, 198 (PC). Only in that sense may an accused by not testifying 'strengthen' the State case."

In *Paulus Pawa v The State* [1981] PNGLR 498, Andrew J stated:

> "[a]n innocent man charged with a crime or with any conduct reflecting upon his reputation, can be expected to refute the allegation as soon as he can by giving his own version of what happened (see *R v Sparrow* [1973] 57 Cr App 352)".

His Honour further stated (at 504) that he agreed with the conclusions of Professor O'Regan in his article "*Adverse Inferences from Failure of an Accused Person to Testify*" [1965] Crim LR 711, that:

> "1. The failure of an accused person to testify is not an admission of guilt and no inference of guilt may be drawn from such failure to testify.
>
> 2. Failure to testify may, however, tell against an accused person in that it may strengthen the Crown case by leaving it uncontradicted or unexplained on vital matters.
>
> 3. Failure to testify only becomes a relevant consideration when the Crown has established a prima facie case.
>
> 4. The weight to be attached to failure to testify depends on the circumstances of the case. Significant circumstances include:
>
>   (a) whether the truth is not easily ascertainable by the Crown but probably well known to the accused;
>
>   (b) whether the evidence implicating the accused is direct or circumstantial;
>
>   (c) whether the accused is legally represented; and
>
>   (d) whether the accused has before trial given an explanation which the Crown has adduced in evidence."

In Papua New Guinea, a gross abuse of process is involved, warranting the quashing of an indictment, where a person, who is a participant in a joint crime and who is ignorant, unsophisticated, backward and generally primitive, is called to give evidence and incriminate himself or herself. No amount of warning against self-incrimination can possibly cure the situation: *R v Simbene Dandemb* [1969-1970] PNGLR 207.

Self-serving statements by an accused person, contained in a record of interview or in a statement made pursuant to s 103 of the *District Courts Act*, may be evidence in favour of an accused: followed *R v Sarufa* [1974] PNGLR 173.

It was said in *The State v Gaius Helex Malaia* (1978) N158:

> "Facts, including self-serving statements related by an accused in a signed statement to the police put in evidence by the Crown, and in a statement made on oath ... and subjected to cross-examination, are evidence in favour of the accused but must be considered along with all the other evidence in the trial, and the weight to be attached is a jury matter."

Kapi J expressed the following view in *Paulus Pawa v The State* [1981] PNGLR 498:

> "With respect, I do not agree with authorities that suggest that an adverse inference against the accused may be drawn from his failure to give evidence. This is against the principle that the accused has a fundamental right to remain silent. Whether an accused person is guilty or not of an offence must be determined on the evidence of the prosecution alone and no inference of guilt by the failure of the accused to call evidence should improve a prosecution case which may be unsafe. In other words, if at the close of the prosecution case it dues not measure up to a standard beyond reasonable doubt, the case cannot be improved by an inference from the failure of the accused to call evidence. All that can be said is that the court will determine the case solely on the evidence of the prosecution."

The wife of one of the co-accused in a joint indictment cannot give evidence against the other accused. The plain reading of the words "shall not be called in any proceeding in connection with that offence" is clear. Following *R v Thompson* (1872) 26 LT 667, which is the common law basis for this section, it is quite clear that where two or more persons are indicted jointly, the wife or husband of any such defendant is not an available witness against any co-defendant. In such a case, it is within the discretion of the trial judge to order a separate trial of that co-accused: *Wemp Mapa v The State* [1979] PNGLR 135.

In *The State v Tu'uo Ibru* (1999) N1940 the accused was charged with murdering her husband's sister. The husband was listed as a witness on the indictment. He was not tendered as a witness when the accused objected to him giving evidence against her. Kirriwom J held that the accused was entitled to raise that objection under s 13:

> "The only clear exception where a wife or husband can be a witness for the prosecution or defence without the consent of the person on trial is where the husband or wife is charged with bigamy. The Act does not specify other instances where the husband or wife can be compelled to give evidence against the other. Applying the law as it presently stands in the Act, the State was correct in my view in not compelling the husband to give evidence for the prosecution, although the husband was quite free to give evidence for the accused."

The common law principle that a spouse is not a compellable witness when the other spouse is charged with a serious offence involving violence to a child under the age of 16 years, who is residing under their care in the matrimonial home, is not inapplicable or inappropriate to the circumstances of Papua New Guinea at this time: *The State v Uniss Kamugaip* [1985] PNGLR 278.

14. Accused as witness for prosecution.

(1) A person charged with an offence shall not be called as a witness by the prosecution in any legal proceedings in connexion with the offence.

(2) Notwithstanding Subsection (1), where a person charged with an offence is a witness he may be asked any question in cross-examination notwithstanding that it would tend to criminate him as to the offence.

See s 37 (10) of the *Constitution* regarding the right not to be compelled to incriminate one's self.

The general rule of law is that an accused person is not a competent witness for the prosecution in any criminal case, and there is a further rule that one co-prisoner cannot be called by the prosecution to give evidence against another: *R v Simbene Dandemb* [1969-1970] PNGLR 207 at 213. See also annotations under s 12 of the *Evidence Act*.

15. Accused as witness as to prior convictions, etc.

A person charged with an offence and called as a witness by virtue of this Act shall not be asked or required to answer a question tending to show that -

(a) he has committed, or been convicted or been charged with any other offence; or

(b) he is of bad character,

unless -

(c) proof that he has committed or been convicted of the other offence admissible evidence to show that he is guilty of the offence with which he is then charged; or

(d) he has personally or by his advocate asked questions of the witnesses for the prosecution with a view to establishing his own good character, or has given evidence of his own good character; or

(e) the nature or conduct of the defence is such as to involve imputations on the character of the prosecutor or the witnesses for the prosecution; or

(f) he has given evidence against any other person charged with the same offence.

Allegations of violence, fabrication, forgery and duress in relation to a record of interview amount to "imputations on the character of the prosecution witness": *The State v Rain* [1976] PNGLR 43.

In determining whether the court should exercise its discretion in allowing cross-examination of an accused as to prior offences:

(a) the possible prejudicial effect of such an introduction should be weighed against the damage that could be considered to be effected to the prosecution's case by the imputations; and

(b) whether it might be unfair to the prosecution's case to leave the prosecution witnesses under the imputations laid, while preventing the bringing out of any record on the part of the accused through his or her answers, should also be considered.[156]

[156] *The State v Rain* [1976] PNGLR 43.

16. Giving of evidence from witness box.

A person charged with an offence and called as a witness, shall, unless otherwise ordered by the court, give his evidence from the witness box.

See s 557 of the *Criminal Code* on pleading to an indictment, and s 572 and the cases there annotated, on evidence in defence.

17. Deaf and dumb witnesses.

(1) In any legal proceedings, a witness who is unable to speak or hear is not incompetent but may give evidence in writing or by signs or in any other manner in which he can make it intelligible, and a person who is able to convey to the court what the witness requires to communicate must be sworn as an interpreter.

(2) For the purposes of Subsection (1) -

(a) evidence in writing must be written; and

(b) a sign or other kind of communication must be made,

in the presence, sight and hearing of the court and of any party to the proceedings, or any representative of a party to the proceedings, who is present at the hearing of the proceedings.

18. Communications during marriage.

(1) A husband is not compellable in any legal proceedings to disclose a communication made to him by his wife during the marriage, and a wife is not compellable in any legal proceedings to disclose a communication made to her by her husband during the marriage.

19. Communications to clergymen and medical practitioners.

(1) A clergyman of a church or religious denomination must not divulge in any legal proceedings a confession made to him in his professional capacity, except with the consent of the person who made the confession.

(2) A medical practitioner must not without the consent of his patient, divulge in any civil legal proceedings (unless the sanity of the patient is the matter in dispute) a communication made to him, in his professional capacity, by the patient, if it was necessary to enable him to prescribe or act for the patient.

(3) Nothing in this section protects a communication made for a criminal purpose, or prejudices the right to give in evidence a statement or representation made to or by a medical practitioner in or about the effecting by a person of insurance on the life of himself or any other person.

20. Dying declarations.

A statement made orally by a person before his death relating to the circumstances resulting in his death is admissible in any legal proceedings if -

(a) at the time when the person made the statement he believed, or may be reasonably supposed by the court to have believed, that his death was imminent, whether or not -

(i) he entertained at that time any hope of recovery; or

(ii) he thought that legal proceedings might eventuate; and

(b) at the time when the person made the statement he would have been a competent witness in the legal proceedings; and

(c) the person making the statement could, if he had not died, have given direct oral evidence in the proceedings of the matter in the statement.

Eyre CB said in *R v Woodcock* (1789) 168 ER 352 at 353:

> "The principle on which this species of evidence is admitted is that they are declarations made in extremity, when the party is at the point of death, and when every hope of this world is gone; when every motive to falsehood is silenced, and the mind is induced by the most powerful considerations to speak the truth; a situation so solemn and so awful is considered by law as creating an obligation equal to that which is imposed by a positive oath administered in a Court of Justice."[157]

A dying declaration may be received into evidence only where the declarant would have been a competent witness. In considering the competence of evidence from a weak-minded or incapacitated person, that person's ability to be rational must be considered, and if that person is not thought to be rational, the witness may be declared to be incompetent: *R v Nere Pundali* (1973) N767.

If the personal beliefs of a declarant are not examined in England or Australia, where it can safely be assumed that a sensible part of the community holds no religious beliefs and no belief in divine punishment, it is difficult to see on what basis such an examination should be undertaken in Papua New Guinea. The true position may well be that this court would not now embark on inquiry as to the personal religious beliefs of a declarant to determine admissibility as opposed to weight: *R v Kipali-Ikarum* [1967-1968] PNGLR 119.

It is not a condition of admissibility of a dying declaration that the declarant had a belief in Christianity or in some faith laying down stern rules of behaviour and a belief in the hereafter. Thus, before ruling on the admissibility of a dying declaration there should be no examination of the personal religious belief or degree of belief held by the declarant. Such belief, non-belief or even disbelief are not significant, except possibly as to the weight to be given to the dying declaration, where the declarant is a normal citizen of sound mind and a member of a community where people have some appreciation of what is right and what is wrong: *R v Ambimp* [1971-1972] PNGLR 258.

In *The State v Enny Bulen* [1990] PNGLR 43 Kidu CJ stated:

> "[t]here is nothing in s 20 which suggests that the religious belief of a declarant is a relevant consideration as to whether his/her dying declaration should be accepted as evidence. The legislature has laid down the conditions that must be satisfied before a dying person's statement can be admitted into evidence. These conditions do not include the religious beliefs of the person making the statement or dying declaration ... So in Papua New Guinea a dying declaration may be admitted into evidence only if such declaration comes within the ambit of s 20. Religious belief or conviction has nothing to do with s 20."

---

[157] *R v Ambimp* [1971-1972] PNGLR 258 at 264.

A dying declaration may be accepted from a deceased who was not a practising Christian or who held no belief in the hereafter, so long as "every motive to falsehood is silenced, and the mind is induced by the most powerful considerations to speak the truth": *R v Angalio Kaimagali* (1972) N725.

For an example of where a dying declaration was not admitted as part of the *res gestae* as it was not an integral part of the event between the declarant and his assailant, see *R v Madobi-Modogai* [1963] PNGLR 252.

21. Discrediting of witness.

A party producing a witness may not impeach his credit by general evidence of bad character, but may contradict him by other evidence.

22. Contradictory statements of witness.

A witness -

(a) on his examination in chief; or

(b) under cross-examination,

may be asked in any legal proceedings whether he has made a statement relative to the subject matter of the proceedings that was inconsistent with his present testimony (the circumstances of the alleged statement being referred to sufficiently to designate the particular occasion), and if he does not admit that he made the statement proof may be given that he did in fact make it.

23. Cross-examination as to previous statements.

(1) A witness may be cross-examined as to previous statements made by him in writing or reduced to writing relating to the subject matter of the proceedings without the writing being shown to him, but it is intended to contradict the witness by the writing his attention shall, before the contradictory proof is given, be called to those parts of the writing that are to be used for the purpose of contradicting him.

(2) The court may at any time during the proceedings require the writing to be produced for its inspection, and may make such use of the writing for the purposes of the proceedings as it thinks fit.

The existence of a prior inconsistent statement does not of itself make a witness' evidence unreliable. The prosecution is entitled to call other evidence to verify the correctness or truth of a hostile witness' previous written statement to prove that his or her subsequent sworn testimony is untrue: *David Kandakason v The State* (1998) SC 558.

24. Depositions as evidence for defence.

(1) Subject to Subsection (2), the deposition of any witness called and examined before a magistrate by and on behalf of any accused person who is committed for trial may, if the accused person so requires, be read as evidence in his defence at the trial where -

(a) the witness is dead or so ill as not to be able to travel; or

(b) the magistrate who committed the accused or held him to bail has certified before the committal or holding to bail that the evidence of the witness is material and that he believes that the witness is willing to attend the trial but is unable to bear the expense of attendance.

(2) No deposition may be read on the ground referred to in Subsection (1)(b) if the witness has, in due time before the trial, been subpoenaed by the prosecution.

25. Proof of previous conviction of witness.

A witness may be questioned as to whether he has been convicted of an offence, and if on being so questioned, he denies or does not admit the fact, or refuses to answer, the cross-examining party may prove the conviction.

26. Cross-examination as to credit.

(1) If a question put, on cross-examination, to a witness in any legal proceedings relates to a matter not relevant to the proceedings except so far as it affects the credit of the witness by injuring his character, the court -

(a) shall decide whether or not the witness shall be compelled to answer it; and

(b) may, if it thinks fit, warn the witness that he is not obliged to answer it.

(2) In exercising its discretion under Subsection (1), the court shall have regard to the following considerations:-

(a) such a question is proper if it is of such a nature that the truth of the imputation conveyed by it would seriously affect the opinion of the court as to the credibility of the witness on the matter to which he testifies; and

(b) such a question is improper if the imputation that it conveys relates to a matter so remote in time or of such a character that the truth of the imputation would not affect, or would affect only in a slight degree, the opinion of the court as to the credibility of the witness on the matter to which he testifies; and

(c) such a question is improper if there is a great disproportion between the importance of the imputation made against the witness's character and the importance of his evidence.

(3) This section does not make a witness compellable to give evidence on a matter that he is, by law, privileged from disclosing.

R v Pointon [1967-1968] PNGLR 395 considered an application for leave to cross-examine the accused as to his antecedents on the ground that the nature and conduct of his defence was such as to involve imputations on the character of the prosecutor or his witnesses. An accused is not to be regarded as depriving himself or herself of the protection of the section, because the proper conduct of the defence necessitates the making of injurious reflections on the prosecutor or his or her witnesses. Where the cross-examination attacks the general character of the witness, the accused throws his or her shield away. The protection deals not with the denial of the truth of the Crown case and of the evidence with which it is supported, but with the use of matter which will have a particular or specific tendency to destroy, impair or reflect upon the character of the prosecutor or witnesses for the prosecution independently of the possibility that such matter, if it were true, would in itself provide a defence.

If the truth is not easily ascertainable by the prosecution, but is probably well known to the defendant, then the fact that no explanation or answer is forthcoming is a consideration making the inference of guilt from the evidence for the prosecution less unsafe than it might possibly appear: *R v Abia Tambule* [1974] PNGLR 250.

In general, where the defence gives critical evidence, the prosecution should cross-examine the witness. Failure to do so may be held to imply acceptance of the evidence, and certainly will go to the weight of the witness' evidence. This is not a "cast-iron rule", however; where the evidence-in-chief is "quite stupid, or obviously a pack of lies, or possesses an incredible and romancing character", the prosecution need not cross-examine. This rule should also be relaxed in the lower courts, where the persons appearing often have little experience and may inadvertently fail to cross-examine on a material point: *R v Abibi Keri* (1973) N749.

In *The State v Ogadi Minjipa* [1977] PNGLR 293, Prentice DCJ (following *Browne v Dunn* (1893) 6 R 67 (HL)) criticised concealing the defence case and not putting to state witnesses the version upon which the defence relies. Conversely, if the prosecution intends to ask the tribunal to disbelieve a witness, it is right and proper that that witness be challenged by cross-examination while in the witness box and it be made plain that his or her evidence is not accepted.

In *The State v Peter Oh Piom Mo* (1998) N1703 the failure by the State Prosecutor to put the state's case to each of the defence witnesses as required by the rule in *Browne v Dunn* was not fatal so as to allow the accused to be acquitted. The failure only goes towards what weight is to be attached to the unchallenged testimony, to be considered in light of all other matters in evidence.

On the rule in *Browne v Dunn*, see *The State v Simon Ganga* [1994] PNGLR 323.

27. Indecent or scandalous questions.

A court shall not allow any question that it regards as -

(a) indecent or scandalous, even if the question may have some bearing on the case before the court, unless the question relates to -

(i) facts in issue; or

(ii) matters necessary to be known in order to determine whether or not the facts in issue existed; or

(b) intended to insult or annoy, or needlessly offensive in form, even if the question is otherwise proper in itself.

28. Confessions induced by threats.

A confession that is tendered in evidence in any criminal proceeding shall not be received in evidence if it has been induced by a threat or promise by a person in authority, and a confession made after any such threat or promise shall be deemed to have been induced by it unless the contrary is shown.

See s 42(2) of the *Constitution* regarding the rights of a person under arrest or detention.

The confessional statement

A confession is prima facie evidence of the incriminatory matters unequivocally admitted to therein. If the admission was based on hearsay, faulty inference, mere assumption, or "a wavering preference for one or two or more possible hypotheses", this would weaken or destroy the probative value of the confession: *The State v Steven Tolira and Bendedict Okole* (1980) N216.

A person can confess to his or her own acts, knowledge or intention, but cannot "confess" to the acts of other persons which he or she has not seen and of which he or she can only have knowledge by hearsay. A failure by the prosecution to prove an essential element of the offence cannot be cured by an "admission" of this nature: *Fred Eiserman v J Nanatsi* [1978] PNGLR 457.

Unless those very special circumstances exist, for example, "where an accused goes right off the rails and says quite wicked or stupid things", the trial judge:

> "should resist any effort by the State to cross-examine the accused on a record of interview not tendered by the State in the State's case-in-chief. If a conscientious and fair prosecutor harbours doubts about the confessions or admissions made, then in my view he should resolve the question during the case-in-chief."[158]

Fullagar J said in *Gaio v The Queen* (1960) 104 CLR 419 at 426-430:

> "As a general rule, while evidence by A that B has made a confession to A is admissible, evidence by A that B has narrated to A a confession made by C to B is not admissible. The concept of agency is irrelevant here; where A and B, having no common language, converse through C, who is bilingual, it is not the case that there are really two conversations taking place, the one between A and C and the other between B and C. In truth and in substance, what is taking place is a single conversation between A and B; and none the less because a means of communication has to be used which would be unnecessary if they had a common language. C is not in any real sense a party to the conversation. He contributes nothing of his own that is material. He is merely the mouthpiece alternatively of A and B. Subject to the condition that the accuracy of the means of communication employed is verified, there is no reason why A or B should not give evidence of the conversation."

Dixon CJ said in *Gaio v The Queen* (joining with Fullagar, Kitto and Menzies JJ in the majority):

> "Where the accused spoke no English, the translation word by word or sentence by sentence by the interpreter is not an ex post facto narrative statement of an event that has passed within the rule against the admissibility of hearsay, but is an integral part of one transaction consisting of communication through the interpreter."

It was stated in *R v Gabi Kopa* [1964] PNGLR 257:

> "[I]f an interpreter repeated in one language to the police officer what the accused said to him in the other language, the evidence of the police officer as to the statements of the accused would be admissible. The evidence of the police officer in these circumstances does *not* constitute hearsay evidence."

Where a record of interview has been recorded in a language different to the accused's own (for example, where the interview was conducted in Hiri Motu but

[158] *R v Medafumeye Urainumai* [1975] PNGLR 58 at 61 (Raine J).

the statement was recorded in English), and has been read back to the accused in his or her own language, then the accused's signature is more than acknowledgment of the translation, but is acknowledgment of the truth of the document, and hence such document is admissible as evidence: *Fande Balo v The Queen* [1975] PNGLR 378 and *R v Aivei Ieme* [1973] PNGLR 1.

Frost CJ expressed the obiter view that where an interpreter was used to translate an accused's statement, that statement was not precluded from evidence by the hearsay rule. Besides being impractical in Papua New Guinea with its many languages, such a rule would be unsound and unreal because "what is in the truth and in substance taking place is a single conversation": *Fande Balo v The Queen* [1975] PNGLR 378, followed in *The State v Allan Honiem* (1983) N421(M).

In *R v Wendo* [1963] PNGLR 217 at 230-231, where the original record of interview was lost, a carbon copy was the only one in existence and in the possession of defence counsel. It was held that the document was not privileged as it had been supplied to the defence in accordance with usual practice, and a document supplied to a party by or on behalf of the opposite side is not privileged.

The principles regarding confessions only apply where the confession is made to or obtained by a person in authority. Here the accused only had a telephone conversation with a witness in relation to missing money. The fact that a person may be a witness does not, of itself, make him or her a person in authority: *The State v Canute Rambio* (1983) N410. See *Commissioner of Customs and Excise v Harz* [1967] 1 All ER 177; [1967] AC 760.

In *The State v Jupui Kapera* (1986) N567, an unsigned record of interview was tendered in the prosecution's case with the agreement and consent of the defence counsel. In such an instance, however, the document does not become part of the defendant's evidence in a strict sense, as it is not evidence he gives on oath nor is it evidence on which he has been cross-examined. It is perhaps best described as material in evidence which the court is entitled to consider.

Standard of proof

There is a difference of opinion on the issue of standard of proof with regard to voluntariness of a confessional statement.

In *R v Fari Pako* (1962) N259, *R v Amo and Amuna* [1963] PNGLR 22 at 23, and *R v Wendo* [1963] PNGLR 217 at 228, it was held that the standard of proof of voluntariness of a confession is proof beyond reasonable doubt, with the onus upon the state.

In *The State v Allan Woila* [1978] PNGLR 99, Kearney J held that the standard of proof of voluntariness of confessions is that of proof beyond reasonable doubt. The only rule of law dealing with the standard of proof of voluntariness of confessions is to be found in one element of the underlying law, namely the common law adopted by Sch 2.2 of the *Constitution*. The common law rule in England at that time was that the voluntariness of a confession must be proved beyond reasonable doubt: *DPP v Ping Lin* [1975] 3 All ER 175.

The admissibility of a confession is on the balance of probabilities. See *The State v Joseph Maino* [1977] PNGLR 216. Also see *R v Loe (No 1)* [1969-1970] PNGLR 12, and *Wendo v The Queen* (1963) 109 CLR 559, [1963] PNGLR 242.

See *The State v Allan Woila* [1978] PNGLR 99 generally regarding the history of the standard of proof required to prove the voluntariness of a confession as applied in Papua New Guinea, and the split of authority that has developed.

The tests on admissibility of statements apply equally to statements made before coronial inquests subject to proof of voluntariness: *R v Akundagru* (1963) N282.

Matters to be raised on voir dire

The voir dire does not constitute a separate and special proceeding, in that in the case of a trial by a judge sitting alone any evidence necessarily and properly called and admitted during trial is in fact before the trial judge for all the purposes of the trial, and it is a judge's duty, so long as that evidence remains on the record, to give such weight to it, on questions to which it may be relevant, as is proper: *R v Amo and Anuma* [1963] PNGLR 22 at 24-26.

Where the accused alleges that his or her confession was induced by a threat or promise contrary to this section, the defence must present evidence or cross-examine the prosecution witnesses on this point. The prosecution need not specifically negative such a threat or promise unless in the course of the trial circumstances appear which suggest that the confession has been improperly induced: *R v Gelu-Gaua* (1962) N256.

Jalina J stated in *The State v Leo Aiyak* (1990) N799:

> "The necessity to call evidence from both sides on a voir dire has been widely accepted by the courts in Papua New Guinea. An accused is not only required to merely make an allegation of police impropriety and leave it at that. If, in cross examination by defence counsel, the police deny the allegation, certainly the accused has no choice but to give evidence himself and also call other evidence."

On voir dire the accused may not be asked questions as to culpability: *R v Minai* [1963] PNGLR 195.

Upon the hearing of a voir dire, the judge has a discretion whether to read the confessional statement or not: *Uda Liki Gasida v The State* [1983] PNGLR 58, following *R v Suk Ula* [1975] PNGLR 123.

The court may read a confessional statement to assist in assessing the credibility of the accused and the interviewer when its admissibility is challenged: *R v Tovarula* [1973] PNGLR 140.

In *The State v Goi Mubin* [1990] PNGLR 99, on the voluntariness of answers given in a record of interview, an objection was raised that the unsigned record of interview could not be admitted. Failure or refusal to sign did not disbar admission unless the defendant could show that he did not agree to the record.

In *The State v John Yambra Pai* (1986) N535 the cross-examination and evidence by the accused on voir dire is restricted to the issue of involuntariness or unfairness. The defence cannot lead evidence on the claim that the confession was not made – that is a question of fact for the trial proper.

Where admissions and confessions are ruled admissible on voir dire, the weight and value are still questions for the jury, and cross-examination of police witnesses again about the circumstances in which they were made is perfectly permissible: *R v Smith* (1956) N93.

Proceedings upon a voir dire cannot be regarded as constituting a separate collateral proceeding. In Papua New Guinea, where there is no jury, it is not possible to say that certain evidence is before a judge for one purpose and not another; evidence called on voir dire is before the court for all the purposes: *R v Amo and Amuna* [1963] PNGLR 22 at 26-27.

Objections as to whether the confessional statement in question reflects accurately what was said during the interrogation is a question for the jury and does not go to the question of voluntariness or admissibility: *The State v Joseph Maino* [1977] PNGLR 216.

Where the issue of admissibility of a record of interview has been decided, the state cannot reopen the issue by calling fresh evidence: *The State v Paro Wampa (No 2)* [1987] PNGLR 281. In that case, the fact that there was failure on the part of the constable and the prosecution to go over the evidence before the trial, is not a valid reason for reopening the case.

Voluntariness

There is no presumption that where a person has given evidence upon oath or affirmation before a tribunal legally constituted and empowered to take such evidence, that this evidence was given voluntarily: *R v Wendo* [1963] PNGLR 217.

An inducement may take many forms, including fear of prejudice or hope of advantage exercised by or held out by the person in authority. Untrue representations made to an accused person, as well as threats and promises held out to him or her by persons in authority, are well within the principle and rules of the common law and are applicable and appropriate to the circumstances of Papua New Guinea at this time: *The State v August Toiamia* (1978) N145.

The defence does not have to show that the inducement actually induced the confession in a causative sense; all that is necessary for the defence to show is that the inducement preceded the confession and that the inducement had not been removed: *The State v August Toiamia* (1978) N145.

It was said in *Commissioners of Customs, Excise v Harz* [1967] AC 760 (quoted in *R v Kom* [1967-1968] PNGLR 265):

> "Whilst a so-called inducement may be so vague that no reasonable man would be influenced by them one must remember that not all accused are reasonable men or women and may be very ignorant and terrified by the predicament in which they find themselves".

Where a confession has been admitted in evidence, and fresh evidence later shows that the confession has been extorted by threats and assaults, the confession may be disregarded by the court: *R v Mumford* (1953) N48.

A confessional statement can be admitted only if it shown to be voluntary. This does not mean that it was volunteered, but rather was made in the exercise of a free choice to speak or remain silent. It was said in *McDermott v The King* (1948) 76 CLR 501 at 511:

> "If [the accused] speaks because he is overborne his confessional statement cannot be received in evidence and it does not matter by what means he has been overborne. If his statement is the result of duress, intimidation, persistent importunity, or sustained or undue insistence or pressure, it cannot be

voluntary".[159]

Despite improprieties or illegalities, despite the lack of caution, confessional evidence may be admitted if it is established to have been given voluntarily: *R v Suk Ula* [1975] PNGLR 123.

Failure of an accused to complain, when given the opportunity, that a confession has been obtained by force, threats, intimidation, etc, does not necessarily outweigh other factors suggesting the confession was so obtained: *R v Kar Moro* [1975] PNGLR 14.

Part of a confessional statement may be excluded and the rest admitted where the accused does not fully appreciate his or her right to remain silent: *R v Tovarula* [1973] PNGLR 140.

If a statement is deemed to be voluntary, it is not a ground for rejection (by the court in its discretion) that there is uncertainty of disagreement about what was said: *R v Amo and Amuna* [1963] PNGLR 22 at 31-33.

A confession is not inadmissible merely because no, or no adequate, caution was given to the accused, nor that the accused was in custody at the time. The warning that the accused has the right to remain silent need not be made in precise terms; regard may be had to the surrounding circumstances to ascertain whether the accused spoke because of some importuning or threat or whether it was because he or she chose to do *so: The State v Kwambol Embogol* (1977) N91.

Where an accused is interrogated by police officers upon arrest, beginning with the words "We will now interview you. I shall ask the questions, you will answer them, and Constable S will type the answers on the typewriter", those are words of compulsion and imply a threat of prejudice if the questions are not answered. Unless there is a clear caution, the resulting confessional statement is inadmissible: *The State v Peter Joseph Hayden (No 2)* [1976] PNGLR 509.

It was stated in *R v Ato-Mumu* (1967) N447:

> "The police should be very, very careful to make it clear to the accused that it really is a matter of indifference to them whether he speaks or not; it is up to him."

A confession may be voluntary although the confessor has not been told either expressly or impliedly that he or she has a right to remain silent. It is compulsion or pressure that offends against the common law, not the absence of a caution: *R v Ginitu Ileandi* [1967-1968] PNGLR 496.

The police must fully explain that a suspect who is not formally charged is not under arrest, or it is difficult to show that a statement is voluntary: *R v Aingo* [1983] PNGLR 271.

There is great danger in extracting confessions without witnesses. The proper course is to charge the accused and then inform him or her of the nature of the charge, administer the customary caution, and that he or she may make a statement. Once an accused is charged, a "close season" should be observed as to questioning unless to clear up some obvious ambiguity: *R v Haua-Kekedo* (1958) N119.

---

[159] *The State v Kwambol Embogol* (1977) N91.

It is necessary for every interviewing officer to use enough words, emphasis and explanation, and even in some cases to get an accused to express in his or her own words the accused's understanding of the right not to speak, so that it is clear that the person understands his or her rights: *R v Fari Pako* (1962) N259.

With regard to voluntariness of a confession, the accused must understand his or her position, and more particularly his or her right to refuse to answer any questions put to him or her by the police interrogator: *R v Emanuel Patrick-Domara* (1953) N43.

In *R v Dubik Ien* (1965) N346, where the interrogator did nothing to make the accused frightened, but the accused was nevertheless frightened and confessed because he realised that his previous admissions to others had put him into a difficult predicament, the confession is voluntary and admissible but the accused's state of mind may go to the weight of the confession.

A confession may not be admissible when obtained because of persistent questioning by persons in authority (a village police officer and a councillor): *R v Bia-Uneme* (1959) N145.

A person, summoned to a police station and who believes he or she is a witness and not an accused, is not necessarily in custody: *R v Ginitu Ileandi* [1967-1968] PNGLR 496.

Cases decided elsewhere draw a distinction between a person who is merely suspect and a person charged and arrested, for the purposes of interrogation. The practice apparently persists of bringing witnesses, suspects and others, for the convenience of investigating officers, to headquarters and interrogating them until a confession is obtained. These people are undoubtedly in police custody, albeit illegally, and it does not alter the position if the police officer has not as yet sufficient evidence to lay a charge, or decided to make a formal arrest: *R v Banji* (1962) N254.

See generally *R v Toronone-Tombarbui* (1962) N234; *R v Loe* [1969-1970] PNGLR 12; and *R v Tovarula* [1973] PNGLR 140.

Where an accused has been improperly induced to confess, and further assistance is rendered to police as a consequence of the original inducement, evidence obtained as a result of that assistance is also inadmissible: *R v Loe* [1969-1970] PNGLR 17.

It is important that confessions be corroborated so as to negative the assumption that persons may volunteer to accept the blame for the misdeeds of others: *R v Hame Manga* (1970) N596.

A court, taking proper safeguards, may, even on a charge of wilful murder, act on a confession which is uncorroborated, but it will do so only after the closest scrutiny and testing of the confession, and only after an examination of "the considerations, if any, supplying hypotheses by which the making of a confession may be explained more or less reasonably consistently with innocence": *McKay v The King* (1935-1936) 54 CLR 1 at 9 (Dixon J); *R v Namiropa Koinbondi* [1969-1970] PNGLR 194 at 197.

Where a confession is not admissible, a subsequent confession is equally not admissible unless it can be shown that the circumstances under which the first confession were rendered inadmissible have dissipated: *R v Kar Moro* [1975] PNGLR 14.

See also *R v Mon and Debong* [1965-1966] PNGLR 42 and *R v Smith* (1956) N93.

Fairness: discretion to exclude

The court has a broad discretion to exclude statements if it considers that they were unfairly or improperly obtained, that it would be unfair to the accused to admit them, or possibly, if it considers that they should be rejected as a measure of judicial control of the investigation of crime: *R v Wendo* [1963] PNGLR 217 at 232.

It is well established that the question of discretion is separate from the test of strict admissibility. This is important where primitive persons have no real understanding of their legal rights and have a very common notion that they must, or at least a traditional desire that they should, try to comply with the apparent expectations of anybody in authority: *R v Amo and Amuna* [1963] PNGLR 22 at 32.

The court may reject a confession made voluntarily on the basis that it was unfairly obtained. The onus of proving unfairness lies on the accused. In exercising its discretion, the court must weigh its disapproval of improper police conduct against the public interest in seeing that all relevant evidence for and against the accused is before the court. Failure to comply with the provisions of s 42(2) of the *Constitution,* for that reason alone, do not render subsequent admissions by an accused person necessarily inadmissible. However, the court may, upon its own initiative or upon the application of the accused, determine whether a protective order should be made under s 57 of the *Constitution* to exclude the admission. Upon the facts of a case, the court may very well feel bound, as the only way to protect the accused's rights, to reject an admission obtained in consequence of the breach: *Constitutional Reference No 1 of 1977* [1977] PNGLR 295.

Section 42(2) of the *Constitution* confers rights only on persons arrested or detained: *Constitutional Reference No 1 of 1977* [1977] PNGLR 295.

If a confession is not voluntary it is not, as a matter of law, admissible. However, though voluntary, if it were obtained by improper or unfair means, its admission is a matter to be determined by the exercise of the discretion of the trial judge, considering such factors as the age, education, sophistication, intelligence and background of the accused: *The State v Kwambol Embogol* (1977) N91.

A person charged, in addition to being told of the right to see a lawyer, should be given a proper chance to decide whether to exercise that right and a real opportunity to exercise it in practice. If such an opportunity is not extended, the confessional material may be regarded as unfairly obtained, and may be excluded: *Maxwell Arthur Schliebs v Singh* [1981] PNGLR 364.

In *The State v Albert Monja* [1987] PNGLR 447, the accused raised the question of whether the time and the unavailability of legal advice amounted to a denial of his rights. King AJ held that s 42 only requires that a person be told of his or her rights. From that it follows that the person must be given an opportunity to exercise these rights.

> "It may well be that most people would want to do so immediately, but in order to find out, I do not think it unfair to ask whether the lawyer is to be seen 'now or later' or for a person not tired or drunk or otherwise at a disadvantage to say 'later', even selecting some days off. None of the grounds relied on individually or in combination, render the record of interview unfair, and it is therefore admissible."

The court may survey the demeanour of witnesses and the evidence as it is available, and decide whether it would be fair to the accused to admit certain so-called confessional statements: *The State v Lakio Tambai* (1980) N235.

In *The State v Kiki Hapea* [1985] PNGLR 6, McDermott J did not consider that the narrow interpretation of the English Courts was appropriate in view of the rights provisions in the *Constitution* and in view of the other interpretations of voluntariness. He rejected the confession on this ground as a matter of law. McDermott J held that the confession followed a proper caution but was tainted with threats prior to the interview, and hence was inadmissible on that ground.

In considering an objection taken in reliance upon the discretionary rule, it is better to adhere to the question of fairness to the accused as the ultimate test rather than to rely upon the question of improper conduct: *R v Ginitu lleandi* [1967-1968] PNGLR 496 at 506 and 507.

See *The State v August Toiamia* (1978) N145, generally for a lengthy discussion on the exercise of judicial discretion in rejecting confessions.

Discretion as to whether the court should admit or reject a confession is, of course, to be exercised judicially, and it is a question of forming "a judgment upon the proprietary of the means by which the statement was obtained by reviewing all the circumstances and considering the fairness of the use made by the police of their position in relation to the accused": *McDermott v The King* (1948) 76 CLR 501 at 514 (Dixon J); *R v Skelly* [1965-1966] PNGLR 105 at 107.

The court has very wide discretion regarding the admissibility of statements made by the accused to police officers under questioning. It was stated in *R v Bernard* (1960) N166 that, particularly in Papua New Guinea, many persons:

> "have little or no idea of the ingredients of particular offences, and no idea of the difference that an admission will stake in a case ... which requires corroboration. It would be wrong to lay down rules to limit the effect of an unlimited discretion which has long been recognised as essential to justice, and I will not attempt to do so."

A judge at trial should exclude confessional statements if in all circumstances the judge thinks that they have been improperly procured by officers of the police force, even though the judge does not consider that the strict rules of law, common law and statutory, require the rejection of the evidence: *R v Gelu-Gaua* (1962) N256.

The reason why special care needs to be taken when police are interrogating persons in custody is that it is manifest to everyone's experience that, from the moment a person feels himself or herself in custody on a charge, that person naturally becomes much more accessible to every influence that addresses itself to his or her hopes or fears: *The State v August Toiamia* (1978) N145.

Where an accused was tricked into making a confession by way of a false representation made to him that a co-accused had confessed and implicated him, the confession was excluded by the court in the exercise of its discretion. The common law has always opposed accused persons being misled to their own prejudice by false statements being put to them in order to trap them into an admission: *The State v August Toiamia* (1978) N145.

Section 42(2) of the *Constitution* envisages something more practical and useful than a mere mechanical caution being administered to give effect to this section: *The State v Joseph Maino* [1977] PNGLR 216.

In the case of an unsophisticated and uneducated person, particular care should be exercised to make that person fully aware of his or her right to remain silent: *R v Gelu-Gaua* (1962) N256.

Where the failure to warn was a minor omission not of any consequence in the circumstances, and there was no prolonged interrogation, and the accused's response was apparently freely made, the admission may be admitted into evidence: *R v Demana-Harina* [1965-1966] PNGLR 144 at 145-146.

A promise to pay cash by an agent provocateur to attempt to influence a customs officer in the discharge of his or her duty is not necessarily to be excluded as having been obtained by unfair means if the evidence is relevant: *The State v Malala Hore* [1981] PNGLR 536.

Where a prisoner had been asked questions while in custody, the character of the questions, the absence of any insistence or pressure in putting them, the fact that no questions were put directed to breaking down or destroying the prisoner's answers or statements, and the fact that there was no attempt to entrap, mislead or persuade the prisoner into answering any questions, still less in answering them in any particular way, are all matters which negative such degree of impropriety as to require the exclusion of the testimony: *R v Kom* [1967-1968] PNGLR 265.

Regard must be had to the conduct of the police and all the circumstances to decide whether it would be unfair to use a statement of the accused against him or her. In *R v Fum Boto (No 1)* [1967-1968] PNGLR 435 a statement was rejected after the police had questioned the accused in such a way as to suggest that they had evidence of the involvement of the accused in a killing.

In *The State v Anton A mes Turik and Wickie Jack Peltham* [1986] PNGLR 138 the accused was questioned at length and a record of interview was made some 18 hours after he made a full confessional statement. Pratt J rejected the record of interview:

> "I do not think the system which seems to have been developing of late of taking a detailed confessional statement followed up with a record of interview is one which should be encouraged by the courts. Either the police must be satisfied if they get a long confessional statement and leave it at that or they must avoid anything except perhaps the barest admission if they wish to pursue the matter by way of record of interview."

Similarly in *The State v Mana Turi* [1986] PNGLR 221, McDermott J stated that:

> "five days detention, the giving of two full confessional statements by the accused, his continued detention without charge or judicial remand and then subjecting him to a full question and answer Record of Interview amounts to impropriety. It is a mistake to approach the matter by asking as separate questions, first, whether the police officer concerned has acted improperly, and if he has, then whether it would be unfair to reject the accused's statement. It is better to ask whether, having regard to the conduct of the police and all the circumstances of the case, it would be unfair to use his own statement against the accused."[160]

The State v Simon Tanuma (1999) N1872 followed *The State v Anton Turik* [1986] PNGLR 138 and *The State v Mana Turi* [1986] PNGLR 221.

---

[160] See *R v Jefferies* [1946] 47 SR (NSW) 284.

While it is not desirable for police to interview one suspect in the presence of another, such a practice is not unfair and may even be desirable where the two suspects appear to have acted in concert throughout. In these circumstances, the exercise of the court's discretion to reject confessions unfairly obtained may not involve the rejection of a confession made by an accused after hearing a confession from an accused which implicates him or her: *R v Ginitu Ileandi* [1967-1968] PNGLR 496.

There is no authority which condemns *generally* the reading to an accused of statements obtained from fellow prisoners or from the complainant, although there may be circumstances in which such a reading could be part of unfair or improper conduct: *R v Skelly* [1965-1966] PNGLR 105 at 108.

The Judges' Rules

Although the emphasis of the Judges' Rules is on the conduct of the police, it is clear that the discretion to reject a statement may arise from circumstances not attributable to any conscious action of the police, but to factors such as tiredness and lack of capacity in the accused to do justice to himself or herself: *R v Amo and Amuna* [1963] PNGLR 22.

Although the Judges' Rules do not form part of the law of Papua New Guinea, they may be taken into account by the trial judge in the exercise of his or her discretion whether or not to admit confessional evidence: *R v Gelu-Gaua* (1962) N256.

The Judges' Rules have been used as a means of enabling the court to indicate to the police the kind of standard of practice and behaviour which the judges think appropriate. It is only a guide, and the judge's discretion extends beyond the contents of the rules. The rules represent a pattern of conduct which has the general approval of the Courts of England and Papua New Guinea, and breach of these rules should be a matter to be closely investigated and considered, but not regarded as a matter conclusive on the question of admission or rejection: *R v Demana-Harina* [1965-1966] PNGLR 144 at 145.

See also *R v Kom* [1967-1968] PNGLR 265 and *R v Kanoa Les* (1973) N776.

Continued reference to the Judges' Rules is confusing and unnecessary. The Judges' Rules are a statement about police conduct: conduct to be investigated and considered for signs of impropriety and unfairness, and if so found, to be considered in the exercise of the judicial discretion to admit or reject evidence of admission so obtained. It is doubtful whether they are part of the underlying law as such, and therefore they are a relevant consideration only: *The State v Turi* [1986] PNGLR 221.

Where an accused, under questioning by the police, made an offer to pay compensation to the family of the alleged victim, there was a breach of the Judges' Rules in that a caution was not administered. However, the court refused to exercise its discretion in favour of the accused and exclude the admission because, in the opinion of the court, it was not shown in any way that the statements of the accused were extracted from him under conditions which would render it unjust to allow his own words to be given in evidence against him: *The State v Peter Joseph Hayden* [1976] PNGLR 509.

In *The State v Win Kwainfelin* [1986] PNGLR 106 Pratt J held that:

1. "In exercising the judicial discretion to exclude evidence of confessions

and admissions on the ground of unfairness regard may be had to the Judges' Rules 1912 as part of the underlying law of Papua New Guinea.

2. Rule 3 of the Judges' Rules 1912 which states that 'persons in custody should not be questioned without the usual caution being first administered' is not to be interpreted as encouraging or authorising the questioning or cross-examination of a person who has been taken into custody and charged.
3. In the circumstances the lengthy questioning of the accused 28 days after being charged with the offence amounted to harassment of a person placed under the protection of the judicial system and to cross-examination of a person in custody, contrary to the Judges' Rules, r 3."

It is a breach of r 8 of the Judges' Rules, adapted to local circumstances in dealing with illiterate accuseds, for the police to give one co-defendant the substance of a statement by the other co-defendant, in circumstances which would undoubtedly be understood by the former as calling upon him or her to reply, or perhaps to supply information for the police: *R v Amo and Amuna* [1963] PNGLR 22.

Any statement made by a person should, wherever possible, be taken down in writing and signed by the person making it after it has been read to the person and he or she has been invited to make any corrections he or she may wish: Judges' Rules, r 9.

A person making a voluntary statement must not be cross-examined, and no questions should be put to him or her about it except for the purpose of removing ambiguity in what was actually said: Judges' Rules, r 7.

See O'Reagan, "*Admissibility of Confessions - The Standard of Proof*" [1964] Crim LR 287-291; O'Reagan, "*Procedural Problems in Challenging Confessions*" (1975) 3(2) MLJ 314-325.

31. Comparison of disputed hand-writings.

A comparison of a disputed hand-writing with a sample of hand-writing proved, to the satisfaction of the Court, to be genuine may be made by witnesses, and the hand-writings and the testimony of the witnesses respecting them may be submitted in the Court as evidence of the genuineness or otherwise of the hand-writing in dispute.

In *The State v Andrew Baine* [1991] PNGLR 1 Brunton AJ stated:

"The law is that although expert evidence is not essential for a tribunal of fact to come to a conclusion about comparative handwritings, there is danger involved when a tribunal of fact proceeds without expert testimony (see *O'Sullivan v The Queen* (1969) 53 Cr App R 274 at 284, per Winn LJ: 'The fact remains that there is a very real danger where the jury make such comparisons, but as a matter of practical reality all that can be done is to ask then not to make the comparisons themselves and to have vividly in mind the fact they are not qualified to make comparisons. It is terribly risky for jurors to attempt comparisons of writing unless they have very special training in this particular Science') ... In my view, the rule in *O'Sullivan v The Queen* (1969) ... is both applicable and appropriate to the circumstances of Papua New Guinea and is part of the Underlying Law."

See also *R v Magalu* [1974] PNGLR 188, in which Frost ACJ held that the precursor to s 31 did not prevent the court from reaching its own conclusions as to the genuineness or otherwise of writing in dispute by reason of the absence of any expert witness called to make a comparison of the writings. Nevertheless, his Honour reminded himself that a judge sitting alone should bear in mind the danger of reaching a conclusion upon a comparison of the handwriting when unassisted by expert evidence.

BPT (PNG) Pty Ltd v Sam Torobon (1995) N1383 followed *The State v Andrew Baine* [1991] PNGLR 1. Sawong J said:

> "I am not a handwriting expert. The Court can only make comparison, and should not come to any conclusion without any expert testimony about comparative handwriting. I am mindful that it is dangerous to do so".

The court has a discretionary power to accept evidence on affidavit. However, s 34(2) of *Evidence Act* is mandatory – it has three pre-conditions which fetter the courts discretion:

(a) that the witness is bona fide required (bona fide means genuine and not a spurious request where the facts cannot be validly challenged);

(b) that the witness is reasonably required; and

(c) that the witness can be produced.

All these requirements must be satisfied: *The State v Maraleu and Wat* [1994] PNGLR 579.

44. Judicial proceedings.

Evidence of—

(a) a judgement, decree, rule, order or other judicial proceeding of -

(i) a court of Papua New Guinea, the High Court or a Federal Court of Australia or a court of a State or Territory of Australia; or

(ii) a Judge, justice or magistrate of any such court; or

(b) an affidavit, pleading or legal document filed or deposited in any such court,

may be given in a court by the production of a document purporting to be a copy of it, and -

(c) proved to be an examined copy of it; or

(d) purporting to be sealed with the seal of the court; or

(e) purporting to be certified as a true copy by a registrar or chief officer of the court.

In *Oscar Tuguine v Michael Gotaha* [1984] PNGLR 137 Bredmeyer J held that:

> "section 44 of the *Evidence Act* has no application to an admission made in evidence in another court. That admission was contained in a statement given on oath in another court, ie a deposition. That deposition is not a 'judgement, decree, rule, order or other judicial proceeding' so s 44 has no application."

See s 1 of the *Customs Recognition Act* and see the definition of "native" in s 2 of the *Native Regulations*.

63. Age.

In any legal proceedings, if the court does not consider that there is evidence or sufficient evidence to determine the age of a person the court, having seen the person, may itself determine the question.

See s 30 of the *Criminal Code* regarding immature age and criminal responsibility; ss 211, 213-217 and 220 regarding sexual offences involving minors; and s 596 regarding the sentencing of youthful offenders. See generally the *Child Welfare Act* (Ch 276).

On evidence generally, see Minogue, "*The Law of Evidence*" in Brown (ed), *Fashion of Law in New Guinea* (1969), p 105.

Chapter 7

CUSTOM

The Role of Custom

The *Constitution* of the Independent State of Papua New Guinea contains important provisions relating to the development of the legal system in general and custom in particular.

Section 20 *Constitution* provides that an Act of Parliament shall declare and provide for the development of the underlying law of Papua New Guinea. This was done with the promulgation of the *Underlying Law Act* 2000. Schedule 2.1 provides that: "custom is adopted, and shall be applied and enforced, as part of the underlying law" except:

> "in respect of any custom that is, and to the extent that it is, inconsistent with a Constitutional Law or a statute, or repugnant to the general principles of humanity."

Schedule 2.1(3) also provides that an Act of Parliament may:

"(a) provide for the proof and pleading of any custom; and

(b) regulate the manner in which, or the purpose of which, custom may be recognized, applied or enforced; and

(c) provide for the resolution of conflicts of custom."

An affirmative duty is placed on the National Judicial System, particularly on the Supreme and National Courts, to formulate an appropriate rule as part of the underlying law where neither custom nor the common law are applicable. In formulating such a rule of underlying law, under Sch. 2.3 the court must have regard to:

"(a) in particular, to the National Goals and Directive Principles and the Basic Social Obligations; and

(b) to Division 111.3 (Basic Rights); and

(c) to analogies to be drawn from relevant statutes and custom; and

(d) to the legislation of, and to relevant decisions of the courts of any country that in the opinion of the court has a legal system similar to that in Papua New Guinea; and

(e) to relevant decisions of courts exercising jurisdictions in or in respect of all or any part of the country at any time, and to the circumstances of the country from time to time."

The role of the judiciary and the profession

Schedule 2 places upon the judiciary the responsibility for the development of the underlying law. Sch. 2.3 requires the bench to formulate new rules of underlying law where necessary. Schedule 2.4 provides that:

> "In all cases, it is the duty of the National Judicial System, and especially of the Supreme Court and the National Court, to ensure that, with due regard to the need for consistency, the underlying law develops as a coherent system in a manner that is appropriate to the circumstances of the country from time to time, except insofar as it would not be proper to do so by judicial act."

Schedule 2.5 provides that in their annual report to Parliament, under s 187, the judges shall:

> "if in their opinion it is desirable to do so ... comment on the state, suitability and development of the underlying law, with any recommendations as to improvement that they think it proper to make."

In *Sangumu Wauta v The State* [1978] PNGLR 326, the Supreme Court considered whether an accused could be convicted of incest under s 226 of the *Criminal Code* (now s 223) for having carnal knowledge of a girl alleged to be his adopted daughter under custom (in accordance with the *Adoption of Children (Customary Adoption) Act* 1969, s 5(1)). Prentice CJ held that the section did not apply as between adoptive parent and child.

In *Acting Public Prosecutor v Uname Aumane* [1980] PNGLR 510, five accused including a son of the deceased, were charged with the wilful murder of an old woman who was allegedly known in the community as a sorceress, responsible for a large number of deaths. Four accused pleaded guilty (the other was acquitted at a subsequent trial) and each were sentenced by the trial judge to three months imprisonment with hard labour, and each was ordered to pay compensation of five mature pigs to the deceased's other son. The Public Prosecutor appealed to the Supreme Court against the inadequacy of this sentence. The five judges unanimously upheld the appeal, quashing the order for compensation and imposing a six year sentence on the four accused (less seven months time already served in custody). On the question of sentence, all judges expressly agreed with the Chief Justice that the penalty imposed by the trial court was "grossly inadequate for the crime of wilful murder". Kidu CJ wrote that while it was quite proper to consider cultural factors in sentencing, they:

> "should not override the clear dictates of the Parliament that those who commit the crime of wilful murder attract to themselves the possible penalty of imprisonment with hard labour for life. If Parliament represents the people of Papua New Guinea and the laws it makes reflect the attitude of the people, then courts must take heed." (at 513)

The courts have on a number of occasions remarked on the lack of proper evidence of custom being adduced by counsel, and the lack of room to manoeuvre in the development of the underlying law.

In *The State v Paul Pokolou* (1983) N404, Andrew J. commented that:

> "There are basically two reasons why custom is not recognised by the courts and the underlying law has not been developed. First, in almost every case before the courts lawyers have not made any attempts either to produce evidence or

material necessary for the judges to use to recognise custom or to develop the underlying law. Judges have not the time and resources to undertake their own research in most cases ... Secondly, the Parliament of Papua New Guinea has failed to perform its duties as given to it by the Constitution [to enact legislation providing for development of the underlying law, under s 20]. Until that time ... Sch 2 does not permit the court to ignore the statutory law and the decisions of the Supreme Court and pronounce a new law based on custom."

Customs and the underlying law

In a case where the underlying law under the *Constitution* and the *Underlying Law Act* 2000 are in question or is an issue, the inquiry should always begin with the examination of custom. Formulation of new law under *Constitution* and the *Underlying Law Act* does not arise until it is established that custom under Sch 2.1 and common law under Sch 2.2 are inapplicable (see Kapi J in *Re Petition of MT Somare: SCR No 4 of 1980* [1981] PNGLR 265 at 285).

On the question of whether there was a custom that "big-men" could speak in any forum, Kidu CJ with whom Kapi J agreed (at 288), held that for a custom to be applicable in Papua New Guinea under this provision evidence that at least the majority of the 19 provinces have the custom would be required. Evidence of a similar custom in a few provinces or areas is not sufficient: *Re Petition of MT Somare: SCR No 4 of 1980* [1981] PNGLR 265.

The *Constitution* has given a more important role to customary law than it hitherto enjoyed. Prior to Independence, there were a number of statutory provisions dealing with customary law, the chief of which was the *Native Customs (Recognition) Act* 1963. That Act remains in force, but under the hierarchy of laws carefully established by the Constitution, custom now occupies a premier place in the underlying law. By Sch 2 of the *Constitution*, custom is applied first to a problem and, only if it is inapplicable, due to one of the circumstances specified in Sch 2.1, is the court to turn to the common law and equity: per Bredmeyer J in *Henry Aisi v Malaita Hoala* [1981] PNGLR 199 at 202.

Under the legal system we have adopted, a person may not be punished until he is found guilty of an offence according to law. Under s 37(2) of the *Constitution*:

"nobody may be convicted of an offence that is not defined by, and the penalty for which is not prescribed by, a written law."

A "written law" refers to an Act of Parliament (including any law made under the Act), organic laws and the *Constitution*. The term has been used to distinguish it from what may be called the unwritten laws, custom as adopted under Sch 2.1 of the Constitution, common law as adopted under Sch 2.2 and the underlying law as developed under Sch 2.3 and 2.4: *Acting Public Prosecutor v Uname Aumane* [1980] PNGLR 510.

"As a matter of law, a court can only impose the penalty provided by statute (in this case the *Criminal Code*). This court has no power to impose any customary punishment. The adoption, application and enforcement of customary law, under Sch 2.1 of the *Constitution* is subject to, amongst other things, an Act of Parliament (such as the *Customs Recognition Act*), which regulates the use of customary law (Sch 2.1(3)(b)). Under s 4(e) of this Act, custom may be taken into account in punishment, to mitigate or aggravate the sentence to be imposed. However, ultimately, the penalty to be imposed is as provided for under the *Code* (in this case of wilful murder) and there is no power in the court to impose Customary punishment. Further, there is no room for developing the underlying law in this case. The development of an underlying law under Sch 2.3 arises only when there appears to be no rule of law that is applicable. In this case the *Criminal Code* is applicable." Per Kapi J, with Kearney DCJ agreeing, in *Acting Public Prosecutor v Uname Aumane* [1980] PNGLR 510.

Where the accused was charged with stealing, it was submitted that the trial should not proceed as the accused had alleged!y been pardoned by his people, and that custom should be incorporated into the underlying law of Papua New Guinea through Sch 2.1 of the *Constitution*. The court, however, held that the relevant custom had not been established, and in any event Sch 2 of the *Constitution* does not operate so as to displace existing applicable statute law: *The State v Paul Pokolou* (1983) N404.

Judicial development of the recognition of custom

Subsection (1) [of s 2 of the *Customs Recognition Act*] means that customs must be proved as a fact, that is by sworn evidence or affidavit evidence. The following subsections widen the court's powers somewhat. The court's basic duty under s 5(1) is to hear evidence of custom. This is necessary even though the magistrate may feel that he or she knows the customs very well. If he or she does not do so, the magistrate has erred at law. Unrepresented parties in the District Court are unlikely to lead evidence of custom so the best way for the magistrate to get evidence of it is to put questions to the parties and their witnesses designed to ascertain the principles of customary law. Having obtained evidence on the customary law applicable the magistrate should weigh up the evidence on custom stating which witness he or believes or does not believe and resolving any conflicts of custom. The magistrate should state the customary law which he or she intends to apply. The magistrate's reasons for decision should state findings of fact, the law he or she considers applicable, and he or she should then apply the law to the facts to get the result. Per Bredmeyer J in *Henry Aisi v Malaita Hoala* [1981] PNGLR 199 at 203.

See *Constitutional Reference No 1 of 1977: Poisi Tatut v Chris Cassimus* [1978] PNGLR 295, in which Prentice CJ (at 298) held that in order for a custom to be adopted as part of the underlying law under Sch 2.1 of the *Constitution*, it must be shown to obtain throughout the whole country.

One of the difficulties with arguments about custom is that a court has to decide how far it can take custom into account as a matter of judicial knowledge and how far it should rely on evidence from witnesses as to what constitutes the custom relied upon. In this case, counsel for each side offered their opinions on the existence of a particular custom and were in disagreement. Assistance from the bar table on matters of this nature are welcome, especially when counsel are Melanesians. In the absence of evidence, however, it is very difficult to decide who is correct. Per Miles J in *Siwi Kurondo v Lindsay Dabiri* (1980) N258.

"Some judges have taken into account compensation payments in considering appropriate penalties for homicide cases ... A word of caution is, however, required. Those who rely on compensation payment as a mitigating factor have the duty to prove, as a matter of fact, the existence of such custom in a proper manner. Evidence from the bar table is not the proper manner..., it is not every society in Papua New Guinea that requires payment of compensation in cases of homicide or death." Per Kidu CJ in *Acting Public Prosecutor v Nitak Mangilonde Tanganis of Tampitanis* [1982] PNGLR 299 at 302 (on questions of sentencing and custom see cases annotated at s 596 *Criminal Code*).

In *Michael Madaku v Patrick Wau* [1973] PNGLR 124 at 130, Minogue CJ said regarding s 6 [*Customs Recognition Act*]:

"the section is mandatory in its terms and directs all courts to recognize and enforce native custom... The section has a dual function – to provide for both recognition and enforcement of native custom. The command for recognition I think is intended to enable a court to take native custom into account in a number of situations not necessarily involving direct enforcement; for example, concluding as to a state of mind or as to the reasonableness of conduct. Enforcement on the other hand relates to the imposition of sanction either civil or criminal in respect of conduct which ..... breaches the customary norm. Section 4 ... restricts the ambit of both recognition and enforcement in criminal cases, and s 5 in civil cases ... I am of the view that each of these sections is attempting compendiously to say in what circumstances native custom shall be either recognized or enforced."

Where the accused was charged with stealing, it was submitted that the trial should not proceed as the accused had allegedly been pardoned by his people, and that custom should be incorporated into the underlying law of Papua New Guinea through Sch 2.1 of the *Constitution*. The court, however, held that the relevant custom had not been established, and in any event Sch 2 of the Constitution does not operate so as to displace existing applicable statute law: *The State v Paul Pokolou* (1983) N404.

Where it was submitted on sentence that the prosecutrix was raped by the prisoner as dictated by custom (as payback – here the prosecutrix's brother had allegedly raped the prisoner's sister), the court held that even if this was a custom, it was repugnant to the dictates of Papua New Guinea's *Constitution*: *The State v Wasale Nerius & Ramilang Tingas* (1982) N397.

Custom may be relevant in determining whether language is insulting, under this section. However, in this case sufficient evidence was not led on this point. Moreover, there are places where custom may not be as important as say in a village. Melanesian magistrates do not allow litigants to work out their differences by shouting at each other in the court room. Customary ways of this nature may not be wholly applicable in a police station (per Miles J in *Siwi Kurondo v Lindsay Dabiri* (1980) N258).

"This section [s 4 *Customs Recognition Act*] is attempting compendiously to say in what circumstances native custom shall either be recognised or enforced. Where the custom raised is not within any of the specific subject matters set out in the section, a court can only assume jurisdiction if it considers that by not taking the custom into account, injustice will or may be done to a person. This is a consideration which must be given to each custom and set of circumstances as they come before a court. It is conceivable that there are many ways in which injustice could be done to a person or persons in the community concerned if a custom which is designed to preserve the social fabric of the community is not enforced – that is a matter for a tribunal of first instance to investigate. Here, a Local Court ordered the defendant to pay K100 in damages for having had sexual intercourse with a first cousin, in breach of the local custom on incest. In the

National Court, Minogue CJ reversed, finding that in this case the record did not disclose the scope or ambit of the custom nor how injustice would arise if it were not enforced": *Michael Madaku v Patrick Wau* [1973] PNGLR 124 at 130.

A person cannot be convicted of a customary offence which is not an offence under the written criminal law: *Rebeka Ambi v Mary Rabi* (1980) N279.

Under s 19 of the *Code*, a judge may impose any of the lesser punishments prescribed (upon a conviction for wilful murder under s 299 where there is a maximum sentence of life imprisonment). The crime of wilful murder is a statutory offence and the only punishment that can be imposed is set out under the Code. A judge has no power to impose any other punishment. Under s 4(e) of the *Customs Recognition Act*, custom shall be taken into account in determining the penalty (if any) to be imposed on a guilty party. This means that a particular custom (defined by s 4 of that Act, and recognized and enforced under s 6 of that Act and Sch 2.1 of the *Constitution*) may be taken into account to explain his behaviour; for example, he may have committed the offence under customary pressure. Custom used in this sense becomes a mitigating factor (see C!arkson J in *R v Asis & Bitimur* (1970) No559; *R v Iu Ketapi* [1971-72] PNGLR 44; and *R v Lakalyo Neak* (1971) No632), providing a cultural justification of the offenders' behaviour which reduces their culpability or blameworthiness. In some instances, the custom may increase the seriousness of the offenders' behaviour. For instance, in incest cases, custom may regard it as immoral and may call for severe punishment. A court may also take into account customary punishment in the same way, eg, whether the offender is liable to pay compensation whatever the court's decision might be (see *R v Jim Kaupa* (1973) No765). All of this means that a judge may increase or decrease the sentence depending on whether custom mitigates or aggravates the offence and may impose the appropriate sentence within the range given by law. Section 4(e) of the *Customs Recognition Act* does not enlarge the power of the court under ss 19 and 209 of the *Code*; it may only operate within the range provided by those sections. Per Kapi J, with Kearney DCJ agreeing, in *Acting Public Prosecutor v Uname Aumane* [1980] PNGLR 510.

For remarks on the relationship between the *Criminal Code* and local custom, see *Sangumu Wauta v The State* [1978] PNGLR 326 at 332-333 per Prentice CJ.

On reviewing the sentence of a person convicted of disobeying a lawful order of the court, Prentice CJ stated that:

> "I cannot see the relevance of the evidence sought to be called as to the structure and sanctions in Tolai society. What was in question here was the breach of an order of this Court, not a breach of any customary law, and the National Court was concerned with the question of whether a sanction provided for in the *Criminal Code* should be applied. This Court is concerned as to whether the sanction was or was not appropriate. What customary society might have done to ensure compliance with the order of this Court, but apparently did not do, seems beside the point. And it would be open to customary society to mould its sanctions to a particular case the light of what sanction has been imposed in the National Court." *Kaputin v The State* [1979] PNGLR 559 at 561, 566.

In *The State v Paul Pokolou* (1983) N404, the trial judge released the prisoner on a good behaviour bond (per s 19 of the *Criminal Code*) rather than sentencing him to gaol for theft "primarily on the basis that the matter had been settled according to custom in the village".

> "In this jurisdiction, some judges have taken into account compensation payments in considering appropriate penalties for homicide cases... A word of caution is, however, required. Those who rely on compensation payment as a mitigating factor have the duty to prove, as a matter of fact, the existence of such custom in a proper manner. Evidence from the bar table is not the proper manner ... It is not every society in Papua New Guinea that requires payment of compensation in cases of homicide or death": per Kidu CJ in *Acting Public Prosecutor v Nitak Mangilonde Tanganis of Tampitanis* [1982] PNGLR 299 at 301.

"Compensation payment has always been taken into account ... on the basis that compensation has a punitive effect on the accused. In principle, this is no different from taking into account the punitive effect of such matters as apprehension, arrest, appearance in court, time spent in custody, loss of employment and the like": per Kapi Dep CJ in *Acting Public Prosecutor v Nitak Mangilonde Taganis of Tarnpitanis* [1982] PNGLR 299 at 302.

Index

[References are to page numbers]

www.ingramcontent.com/pod-product-compliance
Lightning Source LLC
LaVergne TN
LVHW061633090926
847533LV00005B/26